THE TWO AMERICAN PRESIDENTS

Other Books by Bruce Chadwick

Brother Against Brother

THE TWO AMERICAN PRESIDENTS

A Dual Biography of Abraham Lincoln and Jefferson Davis

Bruce Chadwick

A BIRCH LANE PRESS BOOK
PUBLISHED BY CAROL PUBLISHING GROUP

For Margie and Rory

A Birch Lane Press Book
Published by Carol Publishing Group
Birch Lane Press is a registered trademark of Carol Communications, Inc.

Editorial, sales and distribution, rights and permissions inquiries should be addressed to Carol Publishing Group, 120 Enterprise Avenue, Secaucus, N.J. 07094.

In Canada: Canadian Manda Group, One Atlantic Avenue, Suite 105, Toronto, Ontario, M6K 3E7

Carol Publishing Group books may be purchased in bulk at special discounts for sales promotion, fundraising, or educational purposes. Special editions can be created to specifications. For details, contact Special Sales Department, Carol Publishing Group, 120 Enterprise Avenue, Secaucus, N.J. 07094.

Manufactured in the United States of America
10 9 8 7 6 5 4 3 2 1

Library of Congress Cataloging-in-Publication Data

Chadwick, Bruce.
    The two American Presidents : a dual biography of Abraham Lincoln and Jefferson Davis / Bruce Chadwick.
        p.   cm.
    Includes index.
    ISBN 1–55972–462–5 (hc)
    1. Lincoln, Abraham, 1809–1865.   2. Davis, Jefferson, 1808–1889.
    3. United States—Politics and government—1861–1865.
    4. Presidents—United States—Biography.   5. Presidents—Confederate States of America—Biography.   I. Title.
    E457.C44   1998
    973.7'0922—dc21
    [B]   97–51193
                                                          CIP

CONTENTS

Part V: A Time of Hope and Desperation

Part VI: Mortal Conflict Without End

Part VII: The Last Years

ACKNOWLEDGMENTS

TELLING THE STORIES of Abraham Lincoln and Jefferson Davis was not an easy task. The presidents were two titanic figures on the American landscape. This book compares their work as legislators, commanders-in-chief, politicians, husbands and fathers. Research into all these varied aspects of their lives carried me down dozens of intriguing avenues.

I had valued help along the way. Larry Bartels and Fred Greenstein, professors at Princeton University, were helpful in discussing my research and theories and in helping me to see the ways in which Lincoln and Davis acted as politicians—through campaigns and personal, legislative and cabinet action. Jackson Lears, of Rutgers University, helped me to see Lincoln as a cultural fixture and to understand why Americans, then and now, have attached such great importance to him and seen so much of themselves in him. Ansley LaMar and Alene Graham, at Jersey City State College, were extremely helpful in guiding my research into personality development and its implications for Civil War era figures.

John Coski, head librarian at the Museum of the Confederacy, in Richmond, Virginia, and his wife Ruth Ann offered considerable help in my research on Jefferson Davis, suggesting documents and material to study, particularly on the home life of the Confederate president and his family. The staff of the microforms division of Alderman Library, at the University of Virginia, offered considerable assistance in locating Civil War era newspapers for me; the special collections division there helped with the papers of different associates of Davis.

Of particular help were the people who run the microforms room at Princeton University's Firestone Library, where one set of the papers of Abraham Lincoln is stored. Their patience with me as I requested box after box of materials is appreciated. The reference staff at Jersey City State College, in Jersey City, N.J., and at Rutgers University, in New Brunswick, N.J., provided considerable assistance in tracking down early books on history and politics. Jersey City State computer expert Elvis Emmanuel organized my electronic files.

For the photos which appear in this book, I am indebted to Terri Hudgins, of the photo archives at the Museum of the Confederacy; Kevin Ray, director of the photo archives at the University of Alabama; Cindy Van Horn, director of photo services at the Abraham Lincoln Museum in Fort Wayne, Indiana; and the staffs at the Library of Congress and the National Archives. Many thanks, too, to my wife Marjorie and my son Rory for putting up with me for over a year while I spent some time with Mr. Lincoln and Mr. Davis.

I am particularly indebted to Hillel Black, the editor of this book, who helped me to see the story of these two men as riveting drama, and not just an historical record, and who used his extensive expertise in finetuning the manuscript. I am grateful, too, to my agent, Carolyn Krupp, of the IMG Literary, who understands why the past is so useful in understanding the present.

AUTHOR TO READER

THERE HAVE BEEN more books written about the Civil War than any other American conflict and more books written about Abraham Lincoln than any other American. There has been a number of works about Jefferson Davis and studies of the Confederacy's cabinet members and top generals. Historians and strategists have authored thousands of volumes on the war, its soldiers and its battles. Yet there has never been a comprehensive book comparing the two presidents, Lincoln and Davis, to examine how the differences in their characters and styles of leadership affected the outcome of the war.

Every world leader has considerable influence on the conduct and outcome of each war he or she wages. People with distinct and forceful personalities, and men with the rare gift to convince different factions in the military and government to work together for a common cause, win wars. Perhaps the best example of dynamic presidential leadership was Franklin Roosevelt, who accomplished a small miracle in mobilizing America for World War II and then in working with personalities as diverse as Winston Churchill and Joseph Stalin to build an alliance for victory in a war fought on two fronts.

Abraham Lincoln and Jefferson Davis were born within twelve months and a hundred miles of one another in Kentucky, and yet they grew into adults as different as any two men could be. Davis, who went to the leading prep schools and graduated from West Point, was one of the best-educated men in America; Lincoln had less than a year of formal schooling. Davis was one of the richest men in the country; Lincoln grew up in poverty. Davis was a hero in two wars; Lincoln was a militia captain who saw no action. Lincoln was healthy and an exceptionally strong man; Davis was sickly all of his life. Lincoln had a charming personality that made even his staunchest enemies enjoy his company; Davis had a disdainful, neurotic personality that frequently led even his closest friends to shun him. Lincoln was able to work with everyone, and continually put together coalitions of diverse legislators and cabinet officials to pass legislation and fight the war; Davis could not work with nearly anyone, and was never able to form coalitions to help him. Lincoln was an innovator who would try as many programs as necessary in order to find one that worked; Davis was set in his ways and insisted on continuing programs even when they were clearly failing. Lincoln was a man who, as an adult, grew constantly as an individual and a statesman; Davis remained static throughout his life, unable to grow.

This is a book about the Civil War, but it is primarily a book about the two men who came to lead the North and South. Individuals often make the difference between the success and failure of nations. Could England have survived the early days of World War II with someone other than Winston Churchill as prime minister? Could someone other than Gandhi have secured independence for India? Could someone other than George Washington have won the American revolution? No one can say that events simply happen, that the tide of history is not changed by individuals; events happen the way they do because key people shape them decisively.

Politics, too, changes history. What if Franklin Roosevelt had been unable, after three long ballots at the 1932 Democratic convention, to win his party's presidential nomination? Whom would the Democrats have selected and how would he have fared in the depression and World War II? What if Abraham Lincoln's managers at the Republican convention in 1860 had not promised cabinet posts to his chief opponents to secure the presidential nomination for Lincoln? What if that election had wound up, as well it might have, in the House of Representatives, where the Democrats held the majority of votes? What would have happened if Harry Truman had believed the polls that showed Thomas Dewey far ahead in the 1948 presidential race, and decided not to embark on his breakneck whistlestop train tour, which brought him victory at the last moment? What if a few thousand people in several states had voted the other way in 1960 and denied John F. Kennedy the presidency?

The two-party political system was a constant force in Abraham Lincoln's presidency. He and his party had to face elections every two years. Lincoln's policies, war and domestic, were constantly influenced by his need to be reelected and, just as important, to have Republican governors, senators, congressmen, and state legislators elected each fall. He used all his political skills, including the crucial timing of the announcement of the Emancipation

Proclamation and the siege of Atlanta, to stay in office and keep his party in power.

Jefferson Davis never had to run for president. He was selected, not elected to a single, six-year term. He never faced reelection and completely ignored politics, refusing to aid any candidates in yearly county, state, and congressional elections. Thus Davis wound up an isolated leader, surrounded by angry dissidents in Congress and in the state houses, lacking the support of a network of influential men to help him.

What made Abraham Lincoln succeed and Jefferson Davis fail? Lincoln faced harsh criticism in the press, just as Davis did. There were well-organized peace movements to end the war in the North, just as there were in the South. Strong factions in Congress opposed many of Lincoln's programs, just as quarrelsome congressional groups opposed Davis's. Lincoln's generals routinely failed him, just as Davis's generals frustrated him. Hundreds of thousands of men died in the North, just as they did in the South.

Some historians have argued that the Northern economy was so strong that it could have fueled the Union war machine for many years and that the U.S. Army, which often outnumbered the Confederate Army two to one, and had five times as many men to draw upon from the civilian population, could never have lost. Yet on several occasions it appeared that the South would win the war. Other historians have written that the South had the advantage because it could fight defensively, forcing the Union to continually invade its vast territories. It's leaders thought that if they could just hold out long enough, public opinion in the North would turn against the war, which would thus end in victory and nationhood for the South. Yet the South lost.

Was the outcome of the war, and the transformation of the country, then, determined by the two presidents and the way they interacted with other politicians, the press, their generals, and the people? And if it was, how did the wildly different personalities and political skills of Abraham Lincoln and Jefferson Davis contribute to their success and failure?

The Civil War changed the United States forever. It was transformed from a slave empire to a country in which all men were free, regardless of color; a very nationalistic country which rode the crest of the industrial revolution to economic strength and, a generation later, took steps to become a world power. The Civil War changed the role of the president from the manager of a small federal administration to the leader of a much larger national government, a symbolic figure for the hopes and dreams of all

Americans, and the voice of the people. The war greatly expanded the president's authority, too, making him more powerful than Congress or the courts.

All of these changes were determined by the awful war that consumed the United States from 1861 to 1865, a war which left hundreds of thousands of men dead and maimed, dozens of cities and towns ruined, families divided, and the moral framework of America changed forever.

INTRODUCTION
NOVEMBER 1860

Springfield, Illinois

AT 11:30 P.M. on November 6, 1860—presidential election day—Mary Todd Lincoln pulled the bedcovers up over her shoulders, turned on her side, and went to sleep. She had just learned that Stephen A. Douglas, the Democratic candidate, had swept New York City, carrying it by more than 30,000 votes. It seemed impossible that her husband, Abraham Lincoln, could get enough votes outside the city to overcome such a staggering plurality and win the Empire State. She knew, too, from a note her husband had shown her—and her alone—two days earlier, that New York's political boss was almost certain that his state would be lost to the Republicans. Her husband was hopeful he could carry enough Northern states to gain the presidency, but winning New York's thirty-five electoral votes was critical to his election. If he couldn't carry the Empire State, he would fall five votes short of the 152 needed to win the election, which would then be thrown into the House of Representatives, where the Democrats had enough votes to elect one of their three candidates president. Douglas's sweep of the city was enough to send Mary, who had been frustrated so often by her husband's defeats, to sleep.

Down at the Springfield telegraph office, on the second floor of a wood frame building, Abe Lincoln lay morosely on a small sofa, his seemingly endless legs and size fourteen shoes stretched out over the end of it. He did not share the doomsday New York note with anyone and nodded gloomily when one of his campaign team leaders tried to encourage him by reminding him of the Republicans' superhuman voter registration drive in upstate New York. He was certain he had lost yet another election.

Then, slowly, returns started to trickle in from New York's upstate cities and counties. The Republicans had taken Oswego, Schenectady, and Saratoga. They swept to victory in the western counties of the state and in those bordering Lake Erie. Lincoln had pulled from behind to win in Syracuse, Buffalo, and other large cities upstate. Slowly, but surely, with landslide margins of 15 to 20 percent in city after city and county after county in the northern and western regions of the state, Lincoln was eroding Douglas's New York City plurality.

In Springfield, hundreds of residents gathered around the building where Lincoln sat, while others continued parties started earlier that night in streets festooned with banners and enormous, oversized illustrations of Abe Lincoln and his running mate, Hannibal Hamlin. Inside the telegraph office, some of Lincoln's closest advisers—Jesse Dubois, Leonard Swett, Norman Judd—as well as his longtime law partner and friend, Billy Herndon, paced back and forth, casting long, forlorn looks at the telegraph. They had worked so hard since the beginning of May, had come close, so very close, to putting their friend in the White House, and now, at the final moment, defeat hung in the air like stale smoke.

Finally, at 2 A.M., as the nominee sat, tired and drained, and hundreds of his longtime friends crowded around the building on the street, murmurs about the New York vote began to be heard, like the sound of a far-off train approaching, as the final tallies came in from the east. With loud clacks and thuds on the telegraph pad, the news came in and the final tally was posted. Abe Lincoln had carried New York State with 53.7 percent of the vote, earning him its thirty-five electoral votes and surely making him the sixteenth president of the United States.

Lincoln's campaign headquarters became a bedlam. Men and women danced, bands played as loud as they could, rockets went off, the women who manned the food tables hugged each other. Lawyers whom he had worked with—and against—lifted glasses to his good fortune. Those men and women whom he had helped without regard to circumstance cheered lustily. Banners were hauled down and carried through the streets, torches twirled in the night air, and cheers sounded for the Railsplitter every few seconds. Jesse Dubois, ecstatic, spun around the telegraph office breaking into a chorus of Lincoln's campaign song, "Ain't You Glad You Joined the Republicans." Most of the others in the office joined in, and the tune was picked up down below in the street and became the anthem of the political party founded in 1856.

As the festivities grew, Lincoln quietly slipped down the stairs and headed home, his gray eyes downcast. There was much to cheer about, but there was also much to worry about. The editors of several important Southern newspapers had called for secession if Lincoln was elected. Dozens of powerful politicians had stated repeatedly that Lincoln's election would mean that at least five Southern states, possibly the entire South, would secede and form their own country. They did not believe that Lincoln intended to leave slavery untouched in the Southern states, as he had promised in the campaign, and they had many of his speeches to prove it, such as one he delivered in the late 1850s, when he said: "Either the opponents of slavery will arrest the further spread of it, and place it where the public mind shall rest in the belief that it is in course of ultimate extinction, or its advocates will push it forward, till it shall become alike lawful in all the states, old as well as new, North as well as South."[1]

Lincoln kept in his desk drawer highly confidential letters from U.S. army generals warning him that they expected Southerners, led by army officers from Southern states, to seize federal arsenals within days. An officer at Fort Sumter, in Charleston Harbor, South Carolina, warned him that South Carolinians planned to shell the fort if the Republicans won the election. General Winfield Scott told him he had heard from authoritative Southern sources that within months the United States would be cut by secession, not just in two, but that four different countries would be carved out of the existing United States. One Midwest governor had become convinced that secession was merely a front and that when the United States was divided into two countries, it would be invaded by Great Britain. Lincoln had notes from friends who had learned firsthand of complicated plans to murder him. It was the best, yet most worrisome, night of Abe Lincoln's life.

Brierfield Plantation, Mississippi

Jefferson Davis, the six foot, one inch tall, thinly built, handsome United States senator from Mississippi, a former soldier who carried himself with ramrod stiffness, heard the news of the election early the next morning, November 7. He was at his sprawling plantation, Brierfield, in Mississippi, where he oversaw the work of over one hundred slaves in his cotton fields. The outcome did not surprise him. He did not believe, as had the three Democrats who ran for president, that splitting the vote would enable them to stop Lincoln from winning and force the election into the House. Republican victories in different state races in October had convinced Jeff Davis not only that Lincoln would win, but that the brand-new, five-year-old Republican party would sweep most of its congressional and senatorial candidates into office as well, giving Lincoln's radical antislavery party solid majorities in both legislative houses and control of the White House.

Davis was one of the leaders Southerners turned to immediately after the election. As a former congressman and secretary of war, and a current U.S. senator, he had enormous prestige in the North as well as the South. He had spoken out in Congress against abolition, and, should it become necessary, for secession. Yet, in his heart, Davis hoped the slavery issue would be settled without secession or war. He had gone on record for secession as early as 1850. Soon afterward, Davis had referred to himself as "a pretty good secessionist," and had been a leader in the movement ever since. When asked in 1851 whether Mississippi should secede if another state did, he roared: "I answer yes!" And if the U.S. Army tried to suppress it? Davis answered just as vehemently: "I will meet force with force!"[2]

In this fateful election year of 1860, though still hopeful of a peaceful settlement on slavery, Davis told an audience that if the Republicans won the White House, the Union would have to be dissolved. "I love and venerate the Union of these states," he said, "but I love liberty and Mississippi more."[3] Yet Davis, a champion of secession in front of crowds and at parties filled with Southern politicians, continued to work feverishly in the Senate to pass compromise bills to save the Union.

A day after he learned the results of the presidential election via telegraph from nearby Vicksburg, Davis received an urgent letter from Robert Rhett, a Democratic leader in South Carolina, which had threatened to secede immediately if Lincoln was elected. Rhett sought Davis's advice, certain that the Mississippi senator would urge him to take his state out of the Union. Instead, Davis, perhaps a little frightened by the pace of events, told Rhett to do nothing. South Carolina could accomplish little by seceding on its own, he said. Its leaders should wait to see what the other Southern states, particularly Georgia, would do. If all the Deep South states decided to quit the Union, Davis told Rhett, he was certain all the rest of the Southern states would flee in a mad rush, particularly if the federal government acted to bring any of them back by force. He declared, "The planting states have a union of such magnitude that their union, sooner or later [will prevail] for the protection of that interest is certain."[4] Davis was cautious, though, and told Rhett that nothing could be accomplished until all the Southern states had left, and that would be some time away, if at all.[5] He said he believed Mississippi would wait to see what everyone else did.

Davis was wrong. Mississippi was ready to secede. He and other political leaders were summoned to the office of governor John Pettus shortly after the election to discuss secession. Davis, unsure of what his state should do, found himself a lonely voice of wait-and-see moderation among men howling for secession. He pleaded with them to delay: to follow events, not make them. "Mississippi had better move slowly," he said. No one listened. A few days later, Governor Pettus called for a secession convention to take place in early January.

Even as Davis was meeting with the incensed Mississippians, pleading with them to wait until after Lincoln's inauguration to see what his policies would be, he received a telegram from a Mississippi congressman urging him to return to Washington at once, for all was chaos there. He had read the same news in a letter from his wife, Varina, who acted as his personal political barometer. She wrote: "There is a settled gloom hanging over everyone here. Everyone is scared."[6] Jefferson Davis, faced with events he had often talked of but never truly expected, rode back to Brierfield, and then hurried north to Washington.

Within weeks of Lincoln's election, a group of Southern states issued a call for all the states of the South to take part in a convention for the purpose of forming a new government independent of the United States. By the end of December, most Southern newspapers, even those which had been pro-Union during the election, were urging all the slave states at least to hold statewide conventions to discuss secession[7] and to resist any troops the North might send to put down a secession movement. In the North, panic swept Wall Street and the stock market plunged, while hundreds of Southerners living in New York left the city and returned home to await the outcome of the turmoil, whatever it might be. Southerners who were generals and colonels in the U.S. Army met to discuss what to do if the Southern states seceded and war came. Men throughout the South joined existing militias or formed new ones. Presidents of Southern colleges put extra guards on campus buildings in which guns and ammunition were stored.

From the cotton fields near Savannah to the docks of Boston, from the mining camps outside San Francisco to the Pittsburgh ironworks, Americans turned to Springfield, most urging the president-elect to make some kind of conciliatory statement to forestall secession. Lincoln, though, made no public statement, irritated that everyone seemed to think that now that he was president-elect he would change views he had formed over a lifetime. While Lincoln waited, refusing to respond, chaos erupted in the North and the South.

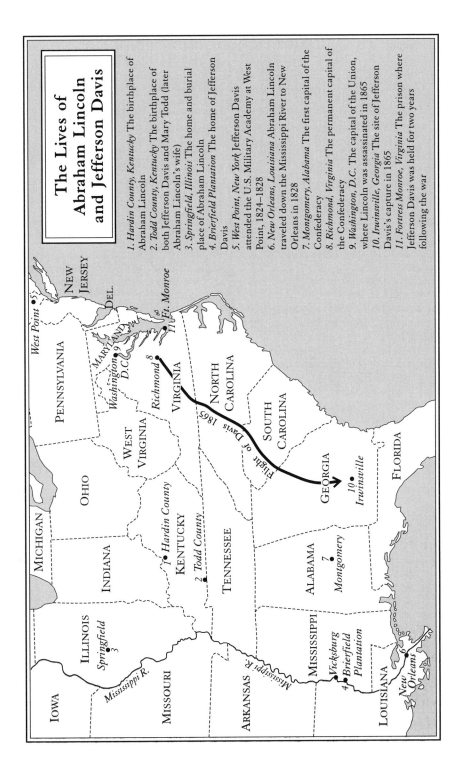

The Lives of
Abraham Lincoln
and Jefferson Davis

1. *Hardin County, Kentucky* The birthplace of Abraham Lincoln

2. *Todd County, Kentucky* The birthplace of both Jefferson Davis and Mary Todd (later Abraham Lincoln's wife)

3. *Springfield, Illinois* The home and burial place of Abraham Lincoln

4. *Brierfield Plantation* The home of Jefferson Davis

5. *West Point, New York* Jefferson Davis attended the U.S. Military Academy at West Point, 1824–1828

6. *New Orleans, Louisiana* Abraham Lincoln traveled down the Mississippi River to New Orleans in 1828

7. *Montgomery, Alabama* The first capital of the Confederacy

8. *Richmond, Virginia* The permanent capital of the Confederacy

9. *Washington, D.C.* The capital of the Union, where Lincoln was assassinated in 1865

10. *Irwinsville, Georgia* The site of Jefferson Davis's capture in 1865

11. *Fortress Monroe, Virginia* The prison where Jefferson Davis was held for two years following the war

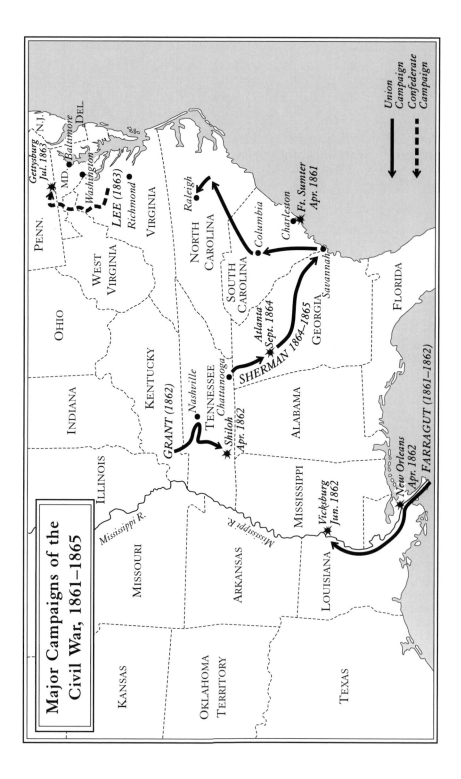

Major Campaigns of the Civil War, 1861–1865

Union Campaign
Confederate Campaign

Gettysburg Jul. 1863
N.J.
MD.
Baltimore
DEL.
Washington
PENN.
LEE (1863)
Richmond
WEST VIRGINIA
VIRGINIA
OHIO
Raleigh
NORTH CAROLINA
Ft. Sumter Apr. 1861
Columbia
Charleston
SOUTH CAROLINA
Savannah
INDIANA
KENTUCKY
Nashville
TENNESSEE
Chattanooga
Atlanta Sept. 1864
SHERMAN 1864–1865
GEORGIA
FLORIDA
GRANT (1862)
Shiloh Apr. 1862
ALABAMA
ILLINOIS
Mississippi R.
Mississippi R.
MISSISSIPPI
Vicksburg Jun. 1862
New Orleans Apr. 1862
FARRAGUT (1861–1862)
MISSOURI
ARKANSAS
LOUISIANA
KANSAS
OKLAHOMA TERRITORY
TEXAS

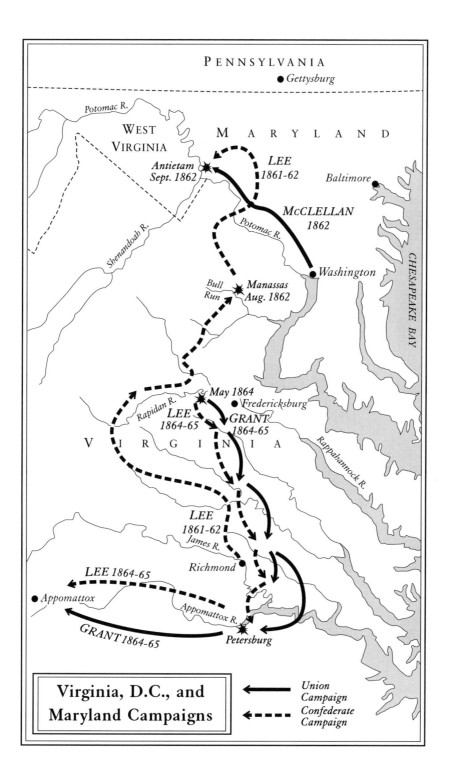

PENNSYLVANIA

● Gettysburg

Potomac R.

WEST
VIRGINIA

MARYLAND

Antietam
Sept. 1862

LEE
1861-62

● Baltimore

Potomac R.

McCLELLAN
1862

Shenandoah R.

Bull
Run

Manassas
Aug. 1862

● Washington

CHESAPEAKE BAY

Rapidan R.

May 1864

● Fredericksburg

LEE
1864-65

GRANT
1864-65

VIRGINIA

Rappahannock R.

LEE
1861-62

James R.

Richmond ●

LEE 1864-65

● Appomattox

Appomattox R.

GRANT 1864-65

Petersburg

Virginia, D.C., and
Maryland Campaigns

⟵ Union
Campaign

⟵ Confederate
Campaign

PART I

THE EARLY YEARS

1

THE GENTLEMAN FROM
BRIERFIELD PLANTATION

THIRTEEN-YEAR-OLD JEFFERSON DAVIS was tired of school. The bright, well-read boy returned from Wilkinson Academy, a few miles from his cotton plantation in Mississippi, put his books down on the table firmly, and told his father, whom he feared, that he would not return. His father eyed him carefully, shrugged, and told him he agreed with his decision. He could not be idle, though, Samuel Davis said, and if his youngest son was not going to live a life in which he worked with his intellect, then he had to live a life in which he worked with his hands.

The next morning, Samuel Davis awakened his son just after dawn. Giving him one of the large, thin cloth bags their slaves used for picking cotton, Sam Davis took young Jeff out to the cotton fields. There he put him in a long line of slaves, all of whom knew the boy and were surprised to see him, and told him he was going to pick cotton to support the family. The boy glowered back at him, and then Sam Davis rode off. Dust filled the early morning air as Sam Davis disappeared down the road toward the house.

The sun was hot that day, but Jefferson did not complain of it at dinner. The next day was even hotter. Each time Sam rode by to see his son toiling in the field with the slaves, he smiled a bit to himself. The boy's hands hurt from the picking and sweat stuck to his shirt. Picking cotton is monotonous, repetitive, and, for novices, painful to the fingers and wrists. The boy and the slaves performed the same actions all day long, under a scorching sun, a few miles from the Mississippi River. The planter's son worked just like a slave, was treated like a slave, and, among the crew of black laborers, felt like a slave. He did not like it. The morning of the third day, he was no longer in the line in the cotton field. Instead, he was back sitting in a classroom at Wilkinson Academy, his books open, taking notes.[1]

THE end of the American Revolution and the formation of a new nation began a trek across the Appalachian mountains and over the green saddle of the Cumberland Gap for thousands of American families in search of broader freedom on the frontier and opportunities they felt to be lacking in the new states. They pressed on, over creeks and through thick woods, battling the elements and trying to live peacefully among Indians as they moved.

Samuel Davis was among the first to leave the East in pursuit of a better life. The son of a Philadelphia merchant who fought in the revolution, Sam Davis had the reputation of a fine horseman, a productive farmer, and a community leader in Georgia. In 1793 he packed up his growing family and two slaves and headed first to Kentucky, where he farmed for nearly a decade and where Jefferson, his tenth child, was born in 1808, and then moved on to Mississippi.

It was there, amid the cotton fields, magnolia trees, and the sweet smells of the poplar groves, that Jefferson Davis spent his boyhood. The Davis plantation grew into a marginally profitable farm during Jefferson's early years. Surrounded by four loving brothers and five sisters, he talked easily with the slaves on his plantation and the free men who labored there as well, often wrestling with the slaves for sport. Jefferson learned to hunt and fish from his brother Isaac, a dozen years older, and all in all enjoyed a childhood typical of a boy growing up on a small slave plantation in the South.

His relations with his mother were good ("There was so much for me to admire and nothing to remember save good," he said of Jane Davis[2]), but his relations with his father were stormy. Sam Davis worked hard on the plantation and spent most of his days in the fields or in the nearby towns. The only time Jefferson saw his father was in the evening, at the dinner table or afterward in the living room. He remembered Sam as a cold, aloof man who disciplined his children harshly.

At the root of the problems between Samuel Davis and his tenth and youngest child, Jefferson, was age. At fifty-two, he was too old to bring up Jeff as he had his other children: the gap between the young boy and his father was enormous. Jeff, like his brothers and sisters, fell victim to Sam Davis's strict rules and quick punishments. Orphaned on the early death of his own father, Evan, Sam Davis had no real experience at fathering to give any of his children, especially his last. He made up his own rules of deportment, rules devised to fit his sour personality and busy life. Two of the greatest crimes in the Davis household were refusal to eat whatever meal was served and refusal to go to bed whenever Sam decided it was bedtime. Punishment was long confinement to one's bedroom. These are hard rules for young boys, particularly for young Jefferson, who was headstrong and stubborn almost from birth. He railed against his father's attempts at discipline: apparently he was ordered to his room so many times that the punishment was etched forever in his memory. He frequently complained about it as an adult, charging that confinement to a room was "incomprehensible cruelty" to children.[3]

It was the punishments, and the walls of his room, that Jefferson remembered, and never any praise that came from his father. Jeff was shut out by his father, and from his earliest years his self-esteem eroded from lack of paternal praise or nurturing. Sam insisted, as well, that whatever he said was correct and that his children had to abide by his decisions. There was no discussion and certainly no argument. "My father was a silent, undemonstrative man," wrote Jefferson. "He was usually of a grave and stoical character and of such sound judgment that his opinions were a law to his children."[4] Later in life, the only praiseworthy thing he could say about his father was that he knew how to ride horses well. Like many children, however, Jeff would grow up to be just like his father, a cold, aloof man who had difficulty getting along with people who did not agree with him.

When Jefferson turned nine, his parents decided to send him away to boarding school, hopeful that the boy, who everyone said was unusually intelligent, could receive a fine education that would prepare him for life as a planter or in a profession. He was sent off to St. Thomas, Kentucky, for two years and then spent five years at a local school. During that time, as Jeff mastered Latin and literature, his beloved brother Joseph, twenty-four years older than he, moved to Natchez to pursue business opportunities and became one of the wealthiest men in the state. Joseph, outgoing and loving, soon replaced Sam as the father figure in young Jeff's life.

Jefferson, who always studied hard, did well at his different schools. Most of them were run by harsh headmasters, whose strict rules further cemented his own view that men had to be tough, rigid, and inflexible in order to succeed. Along with his father and tough military figures, his headmasters were Jefferson's role models.

St. Thomas was run by strict brothers from the Dominican order of the Catholic church. The headmaster, Brother Richard Miles, ran his school, which owned slaves, in military fashion. Rules were enforced, classes demanding, and teacher-student relations very formal. Jeff spent two long years there, and the headmaster, who whipped students,[5] became a harsh role model for him. Sam wanted him closer to home, so he enrolled him in Jefferson College, in Mississippi, where instructors also hit students.[6] He soon left the college. Jefferson, memories of boys being hit clear in his mind, returned home to attend the newly opened Wilkinson Academy. Students there told family and friends that Davis seemed to have a deep need to be liked by others. At sixteen, he was a master at Latin and Greek and well read in history and literature. An outstanding student, Jefferson Davis was ready for a university.

He went to Transylvania College, in Lexington, Kentucky, a school with tight rules and iron discipline at which the headmaster and teachers still disciplined students with wooden paddles.[7] The program of study was extremely difficult: Students had to pass demanding courses in Latin, Greek, surveying, ancient history, philosophy, astronomy, chemistry, writing, and speaking.

Jeff Davis began to show the same authoritarian tendencies as his father and his headmasters. Students who knew him at Transylvania later said that by the age of sixteen or seventeen he had become taciturn, tough, and unbending. He was often frustrated by his own lack of perfection and by all the imperfection and laziness he saw in others. He seemed much older than his age, with the personality of a man of thirty, and always seemed, despite a certain buoyancy at social events, unable to relax in the company of others. He was always tight, formal, distant.[8] Those traits would be permanently instilled in him when he attended the U.S. Military Academy at West Point.

Davis originally wanted to study law at the University of Virginia. His decision to go to West Point was greatly influenced by his brother Joseph, who secured an appointment for him at the end of his junior year at Transylvania, the same year his father died. Joseph urged him to accept the appointment immediately and forgo his final year at the Lexington college. Jefferson waffled, but then decided his brother, whom he so much admired, probably knew what was best for him. Joe promised him that if he did not like West Point after a year, he could transfer somewhere else.

Run by Sylvanus Thayer, a tough disciplinarian, West Point combined rigorous studies with a disciplinary code in which almost every irregular act counted as an infraction to be marked against a student's record. Just living at the academy was difficult. Students were not permitted to sleep in standard beds. They had to sleep on mattresses on the hard floors of the dormitories. Talking was not permitted at meals. Students were not allowed to play cards, to smoke or chew tobacco, to drink any alcohol, or even to read novels or magazines in their rooms.

Even the taciturn and distant Davis, used to hard rules at his boarding schools, found West Point difficult. From time to time the stubborn student tried to bend the rules of the military academy, but invariably wound up being punished. Thayer had ruled that any student who piled up two hundred infraction points had to be dismissed. Davis came close, accumulating 137 demerits. Davis was also almost dismissed for drinking, barely surviving a court martial.

He had little admiration for cadets from the Northern states ("You cannot know how pitiful they generally are," he wrote his brother[9]). Students who knew him well at West Point admired his diligence and intellect but wondered about his ability to function in any arena, such as the army, politics, or business, where social and political relations were important—relations instructors at West Point tried hard to teach the army's future officers. Said one fellow student: "His [Davis's] four years at West Point...instead of inculcating in him the pliancy and assumed cordiality of the politician, was to develop a personality of the reverse order."[10]

Jefferson Davis, who never did get to study law in Virginia, finally graduated in 1828, ranking an unimpressive twenty-third in a class of thirty-three, and immediately went into the army. He was twenty.

He was a fine-looking soldier. He walked almost regally, with his chin tilted slightly into the air, looking like a knight from a Sir Walter Scott novel in a U.S. Army uniform. If anyone perfectly fit the description of the Southern cavalier, the wealthy, aristocratic, brave, and bold warrior in uniform, which began to appear in so much literature at that time, it was Jeff Davis. He was sent by the army to the Iowa area to start his seven-year enlistment. His army life was not much different from that of other brand-new second lieutenants just out of the academy. He went on routine patrols, helped engineers build sawmills and warehouses, and kept track of various storehouse inventories at military installations. Since he was in a western state, he took part in sporadic Indian fighting, like many other soldiers. Once again Davis came under the authoritarian leadership of a gruff, tough disciplinarian who would be another disciplinarian father figure and model for him—Colonel Zachary Taylor. The rugged Taylor, who would gain fame as "Old Rough and Ready" in the Mexican War and afterward become president, was already a grizzled veteran when Davis was assigned to his command. Taylor, forty-eight years old in the summer of 1828, had been in the army since 1808. Thinking Davis had a future in the army, Zachary Taylor took him under his wing.

The highlight of Davis's early military career came in the Black Hawk War. While he took part in no battles, in a bizarre stroke of fate Davis wound up capturing Chief Black Hawk himself. The army had learned that Black Hawk was hiding on an island in the middle of the Mississippi River. Zachary Taylor, seeking publicity for his protégé, sent Davis's regiment to look for him. As they rode up the riverbank near the island, the Sauk and Fox chief emerged from a wood on the eastern bank of the river and, spotting the soldiers in their camp, immediately surrendered. With the fabled chief his prisoner, Davis then served as Black Hawk's jailer on a riverboat for more than a week.[11] The Indian and the West Pointer earned each other's respect during hours of long talks on the boat as it drifted down the Mississippi, and Black Hawk later referred to the young lieutenant as "a good and brave young chief." The capture of the chief, a stroke of great good fortune for a young lieutenant, gained Davis considerable publicity and fostered the legend that he was a military genius.

From 1832 to 1834, Davis spent much of his time keeping peace between the Indian tribes and the settlers in the area. He tried his best to prevent skirmishes between mine workers and Indians and built a solid reputation as a soldier. He tolerated the army, but did not love it, and often toyed with the idea of resigning. He had personal difficulties, too. He never seemed happy about his lot in the army. He once became so angry that several officers junior to him at West Point had been promoted over him that he fired off a nasty letter of complaint to the War Department. Davis's hotheadedness, and fear of what always amounted to nonexistent threats, resulted in a second court martial in 1835 when he acted disrespectfully to an officer he did not like.

He also had to deal with Zachary Taylor. The gruff commander had taken a liking to the young West Pointer. His daughter Sarah took an even greater liking, and the two began a secret affair, right under her father's roof. Taylor, while he approved of Davis, did not want Sarah to marry a soldier. He knew all too well what a difficult life the army was for a young married couple.

The growing hostility between Taylor and Davis was sharpened further after the 1835 court martial. Taylor ordered his daughter to break off with Davis, but she refused. She was in love with the dashing young lieutenant, and he was completely smitten with her, sending her long and romantic letters. "Sarah, whatever I may be hereafter, neglected by you I should have been worse than nothing. Shall we not soon meet, to part no more? Often I long to lay my head upon that breast which beats in unison with my own, to turn from the sickening sights of worldly duplicity and look into those eyes, so eloquent, of pity and love," he wrote the girl.[12]

The temperamental Davis, angered at Taylor's attitude and obsessed with his daughter, rode home and sought advice from Joseph. Like everyone else, his older brother was captivated by the charms of Sarah Taylor.

Joe urged his young brother to leave the army and told the star-crossed young lovers to get married right away. They did, on June 17, 1835. Then, in a burst of magnanimity, Joe gave him as a wedding gift nearly 2,000 acres of land right next to his own plantation, Hurricane, and let him use a cabin which had been on it for several years as an office in the fields. Jeff and Sarah lived at Hurricane while Jeff worked the plantation. Knowing he needed good labor to make the plantation successful, Joseph took his younger brother by riverboat to New Orleans where they bought ten slaves. Joined by some of Joseph's slaves, they cleared Jeff's plantation, which he named Brierfield, after its many brier bushes.

Everyone who met the slender, attractive Sarah, from wealthy planters to the slaves of Brierfield, said she was a perfect match for Jeff. Their acquaintances foresaw decades of happiness for the couple, and a deep friendship between the two brothers. Sarah was a bright and witty girl, a perfect mate for Jeff Davis, but she was also a pleasant and cheerful woman who loved children and would be a wonderful mother.

Then, as it did for so many in the South in the hot, close, sticky lazy summer months, tragedy struck. Jeff Davis and his twenty-one-year-old bride came down with malaria. A deadly disease then, since there was no cure, malaria was carried by the hundreds of millions of mosquitoes that inhabited the Deep South in the hottest weeks of the summer, most abundantly near rivers and in the lowlands. Jeff Davis and his wife were bitten at the same time, probably as they slept together. Within days they were passing in and out of delirium as they battled for their lives in separate bedrooms. Meanwhile Joseph, his wife Eliza, and the slaves of Hurricane rushed in and out of their rooms with doctors, nurses, and all the help and medicine money could afford. Jefferson Davis, drenched in sweat by a fever that climbed ever higher, tossed and turned in his bedroom. Yet his strong young body, toughened by years in the army, was able to fight off the disease. Sarah, thin and frail and not used to Southern summers, was not. Her fever never broke; Sarah died on September 15, with her barely conscious young husband at her side, desperately holding her hand as she slipped away.[13]

Crushed by the loss of his beautiful young bride, Jeff Davis took months to recover physically from his own malaria (he recuperated that winter in Cuba, with its soft tropical breezes and warm weather, longtime slave James Pemberton at his side). When he was healed, doctors discovered that he had an eye affliction, which they blamed on either the malaria or pneumonia in the army.[14] Davis would never admit that he had made a fatal mistake in bringing Sarah to Mississippi in the hot summer, which he knew was a risk.[15]

Back and well, finally, in the spring of 1836, Davis, twenty-eight years old, realized that his young bride's death had taken away all his interest in the outside world and made him a prisoner of grief. He had no desire to return to the army nor any interest in another profession. Shutting the gates of Brierfield against the world, he began years of isolation. Davis never disguised, and never explained, the isolation and melancholy or the years of unconquerable grief. All he could say was: "Thereafter I lived in great seclusion on the plantation in the swamps of Mississippi."[16]

As a means of recovering from his broken heart, Davis plunged into the work of turning Brierfield into a profitable cotton plantation. The harder he worked, the less he felt his sadness. Aided by James Pemberton, who had raised him from childhood and had probably saved his life when he was wracked with pneumonia while in the army, Davis occupied himself with the development and management of Brierfield.

Brierfield comprised nine hundred acres of reasonably good land on the eastern bank of the Mississippi River about thirty miles south of Vicksburg. The 1850 census valued it at $25,000. About 450 acres were eventually planted;

the other 450 served as a wooded area, a site for a home Jeff Davis later built, long rows of cabins for the growing slave community (Brierfield was home to seventy-two slaves in 1850 and 106 in 1860), and a variety of storehouses for corn and other crops, plus the small shops, such as a blacksmith's, which dotted most of the larger Southern plantations.[17] He continued to live in Joseph's house at Hurricane, a devastated bachelor incapable of seeing women socially or rejoining the social world of Mississippi.

Neither Brierfield nor Hurricane was a plantation typical of Mississippi or most of the Southern states. The large majority of Mississippians were not successful planters, but small farmers with no slaves (only twenty percent owned slaves).[18] The average Southern small farmer lived very much like the subsistence farmers north of the Ohio River and in the Middle Atlantic states.[19]

The most unusual aspect of Brierfield Plantation was not its land but its slaves. Jefferson, at the suggestion of his brother Joseph, was exceedingly good to his slaves. Joseph had pioneered master-slave relations at Hurricane with innovative tactics that left many of his neighbors aghast. The Davis brothers never whipped their slaves or meted out other physical punishment. Instead, they set up a slave-run courthouse, the Hall of Justice, on the plantation. There a jury of slaves decided the guilt or innocence of slaves accused of transgressions. Slaves were not given nicknames, as they were at most plantations, but selected their own names. Many were given permission to travel throughout the area alone, and some were even encouraged to read. Slaves with skills in reading and math were given key jobs in running the plantation, which usually went to whites, such as supervision of livestock, cotton inventory, and the purchase of foods and supplies. Slaves did not live on rations, but were permitted to grow their own food and, if that was not enough food, to take some from the plantation's sales quotas. Creative slaves were urged to spend time on arts and crafts and permitted to sell their work to other slaves and even to nearby planters. Jeff Davis became so close to his slaves, particularly James Pemberton, that he often dined with them as an equal, bestowing on his favorites, such as Pemberton, cigars.[20] His wife, brother, and business associates said that the wealthy planter and his favorite slave were "devoted friends."[21]

The liberal policies of the Davis brothers worked. Hurricane was enormously profitable, and so, too, after a few years, was Brierfield. The well-treated slaves worked hard for their masters, who were probably the most liberal in the state, perhaps in the entire South. Records in the 1850s show that when the popular Davis was at Brierfield, monthly profits were much higher than when he was away and white overseers ran the plantation.[22]

Most planters refused to let their slaves step beyond the boundaries of the plantation, but Davis sent his on errands all over Mississippi, confident they would return. On a given day, he might send a slave to Vicksburg to retrieve a horse and buggy and another to deliver business papers to Natchez. He often left work orders on his library table for slaves to pick up, read, and carry out just as any middle manager would. Slaves were asked to go into town, unescorted, on errands. None ever tried to escape. Some remained with him for years, and many stayed with the family long after the Civil War. Sam Charlton was purchased by Jeff Davis in the mid-1830s and remained with him, as a slave and freedman, until 1880.[23]

Jeff Davis was very concerned about the happiness and welfare of the slaves at Brierfield. He had a particular hatred of harsh overseers whom he caught beating any slave or heard had punished a slave severely. Overseers did not last very long at Brierfield: Davis, at the first evidence of violence, fired them. Davis's wrath was not directed only at violence, but at negligence as well. He returned to Brierfield on a Sunday morning in 1857 to discover that a slave girl's child was dying because the overseer and his wife, in a hurry to dismiss them, had given the child an overdose of quinine and calomel. He fired the overseer within an hour.[24]

The Davises cared for slaves like their own children.[25] He spent hours walking and riding around his plantation to chat with slaves and their families, always inquiring about their health and welfare, addressing them by their first names and always showing special concern for the children. He made certain that good clothing was available to them, bought wedding dresses for slave women about to marry, and paid for lavish parties at his slaves' weddings. Davis engaged a dentist from Vicksburg to visit Brierfield periodically to care for the slaves' as well as his own family's dental problems. He paid a local Methodist minister to visit Brierfield weekly to lead prayer services for the slaves. He spent considerable time supervising the personnel at the hospital he ran for slaves at the plantation, which employed a full-time nurse, and kept track of medicines to be given to all slaves seasonally. If a slave was sick and the nurse could not help, he brought in other nurses or women in the area who had medical skills. If they failed to cure him, he had other slaves take the ailing slave to a doctor in Vicksburg.

When all else failed, Davis sent the slaves to Dr. Samuel Cartwright, his personal physician in New Orleans. In 1859, when Julia Ann Allen, the tiny daughter of Hagar Allen, one of his most trusted slaves, came down with rheumatism, he was unsure that his physician was in town and, to make certain she received proper care, sent the little girl to the home of his brother-in-law, who cared for her until the doctor returned. Family and friends in New Orleans often cared for any sickly slaves Davis sent to the city for expert care and would nurse them back to health there after the visits to Cartwright. When Julia Ann Allen arrived, the little girl mistakenly thought that her trunk had been put on the steamer from Vicksburg (it had not). Friends then insisted, to an irritated captain, that workers search the entire boat for the trunk.[26]

Davis often described the slaves as "the people" when discussing them with outsiders and, with others or within the gates of Brierfield, almost always referred to them by their first names. He referred to the slave children as his own, in 1857 writing about illnesses that "the children have suffered throughout the summer."[27] The slaves, in turn, enjoyed the personal affection of Davis and returned it, always gathering about him whenever he arrived and constantly inquiring about his wife and children, his brother Joe, and other relatives,[28] sometimes grabbing at Davis's knees and threatening to pull him down.

White friends in Mississippi scoffed at the treatment of the Davis slaves and referred to them as the "Davises' free Negroes" and joked, when hoop skirts for wealthy women became popular, that Jeff Davis and his brother Joe would have to plant their cotton rows wider so that the women slaves wearing the latest fashions they bought for them would have room to walk. Whites who knew Jefferson Davis in Washington derided his habit of bowing to any blacks, freed or slave, who bowed to him first.[29]

Jefferson Davis liked and respected his slaves as much as he did nearby planters and friends and appreciated their admiration of him and members of his family. This underlined his feeling that there was nothing morally wrong with slavery in the Southern states. How bad could slavery be, he wondered, if his own slaves, the slaves he saw and talked to every day, were so content with their lives and had such an attachment to him and his family?

Spending most of his time at Brierfield, he traveled little in the South. The barbaric conditions slaves faced on other plantations escaped him. For example, to earn money in lean years, some planters sold husbands to one planter and wives to another. Children were sometimes sold off to traveling slave traders and carried hundreds of miles away, where they were sold to someone else. Slave women begged nearby masters to buy their children so they could visit them. One woman who lost her son in a sale wrote: "I don't want a trader to get me. Albert [her son] is gone and I don't know where. I am heartsick."[30]

Slaves worked long hours and were vulnerable to diseases because their diets consisted of low levels of protein and nutrients. Thousands died from pneumonia, diptheria, malaria, cholera, and smallpox. Many unfree women suffered from menstrual illnesses because of unsanitary plantation conditions. Slave women forced to work in the cotton and tobacco fields while pregnant had an inordinately high number of miscarriages. Black women were sometimes molested by their white owners or the owners' sons.[31]

Many slaves complained of cruel physical treatment. Some were beaten by drunken owners and some murdered. Many were whipped as punishment and to maintain discipline on the plantation. Most had few clothes to wear, regardless of the weather.

No other issue, of course, was to figure so prominently in Jeff Davis's life and in the life of the nation in the coming years as slavery. The man who at one time would own over one hundred slaves certainly believed in the system. Davis felt that slavery "is a common law right to property in the service of man; its origin was Divine decree—the curse upon the graceless sons of Noah."[32]

From 1836 until 1843, Jefferson Davis was content to rummage through the vast library in his brother Joseph's home, where books were jammed into bookshelf spaces and seemed ready to tumble out onto the floor, and spend almost all his time away from the plantation reading works of philosophy, history, and politics. After dinner, the two brothers would sit opposite each other in the large library at Hurricane and define and redefine what their views were on national, state, and local politics. Years of reading had convinced both men that the strengths of the nation were the principles of Thomas Jefferson and the concepts of states' rights and national expansion, whether through purchase (the Louisiana Territory); annexation (Texas); or in war (New Mexico and Arizona). Joseph was a firm believer in the slave system and easily convinced his younger brother of its merits. (Joseph once wrote Jefferson that he approved wholeheartedly of a politician's warning to Kentuckians uncertain about slavery that if the slaves were freed, "330,000 half starved, ragged, dirty thieving niggers" would flood Kentucky and take away the jobs of all the white men there.[33])

Jeff Davis did not develop any thirst for the political arena in those years and seemed content to live as a gentleman farmer. Tucked away in his library nook at Brierfield, he seemed content, except for constant sickness, which made his mood increasingly sour. As late as 1840, five years after Sarah's death, he considered himself a wealthy planter without ambition. He wrote a friend that "I am living as retired as a man on the great thoroughfare of the Mississippi can be, and just now the little society which exists hereabout has been driven away by the presence of the summer's heat...."[34]

His life was changed forever by two events in 1843. The first was a letter from a leader of the Mississippi Democratic Party, who begged him to run for Congress after its candidate quit the race. The second occurred at his brother's annual plantation Christmas party when, for the first time, Jefferson Davis, thirty-five, met Varina Howell, of Natchez, only seventeen. She was a bright and perceptive young woman who was taught by her own tutor. Varina was well read and a very political young woman, another oddity among the belles of Natchez. She read the *National Intelligencer*, a political newspaper, every day.[35] Her glossy, thick black hair, long, smooth face, large dark eyes, large mouth, gave her an exotic, sultry look. She liked Jefferson right away.[36] "[He] is most agreeable and has a peculiarly sweet voice and a winning manner of asserting himself," she said in a letter to her mother, and was astonished that he "was refined and cultivated....and yet he is a Democrat!"

After just one meeting, Varina noticed something unusual about Davis. "He impresses me as a remarkable kind of man, but of uncertain temper, and has a way of taking for granted that everybody agrees with him when he expresses an opinion," she wrote, and joked: "He is the kind of person I should expect to rescue me from a mad dog at any risk, but to insist upon a stoical indifference to the fright afterward."

Varina Howell was a complex woman. She was five feet ten inches tall and attractive, with a graceful walk and an olive complexion. She was a very intelligent woman who cared deeply for those she loved. Her greatest strengths were an iron will, a tough exterior which deflected most criticism, and a fiercely independent nature. She was a woman who believed in her man, stood by him, and encouraged him to go as far as he could go in his career. She had no intention of permitting her man to dominate her, though. She was her own woman, an individualist who firmly believed that a woman could be right on an issue just as often as a man, and that marriage was not based on love alone, but on a negotiated relationship between a man and a woman in which neither dominated. She also believed that a much older husband should not view his much younger bride as a daughter or schoolgirl. Varina's attitude was radically different from that of most well-bred young women in the South, the belles held in such high esteem that they were permitted to do little. Varina was not going to let her husband run their relationship or their home; that fierce independence would create great problems in her marriage.

Jeff Davis fell deeply in love with Varina Howell, feeling like a schoolboy again as he carefully weighed everything she did or said. Varina, uncertain of her feelings at first, may have worried that he would become a father figure, not a husband. She came to love him. She wrote him often, putting pressed flowers or locks of her hair in the pages of her letters. Davis hid them in a secret spot at Hurricane where no one could find them and, late at night, when everyone was asleep, would read and reread them.

He wrote passionate love letters to the young Varina. He once told her that her letter "came to dispel my gloomy apprehensions, to answer the longings of love," and that "I have to be with you every day and all day," and that she should never read by candle at night because it would "punish your angel eyes."[37]

Eight long years after Sarah's death, Jeff Davis seemed to love Varina Howell with the passion he had had for Sarah. "Your spirit is with me. I feel its presence. My heart is yours. My dreams are of our union. They are not dreams, for I will not wake from them," he wrote her during their courtship.[38]

Varina would become extremely attached to Jefferson, worrying constantly about his precarious health and his obsessive need to work himself into exhaustion. She accompanied him nearly everywhere. She went with him on trips to different Southern cities. When he was sent to Congress, she traveled to Washington, arriving after an incredibly uncomfortable three-week trip which included a stagecoach ride so bumpy that one passenger had his ribs broken by the jostling on the roads. She would miss Jefferson when he was gone, even though she complained often about the forays into politics or the army which took him away from her. She wrote: "[Politics] meant long absences, illness from exposure, misconceptions, defamation of character, everything which darkens the sunlight and contracts the happy sphere of home."[39]

On his trips to New Orleans and other cities, Jefferson would make friends with influential men in the Democratic Party. They saw him as another member of the club—a wealthy slaveowner like themselves. He had reached middle age, shared the concerns of most cotton planters, had an attractive wife, and a wealthy brother who could fund campaigns, and was a hero of the Black Hawk War. At the urging of Joseph, now fifty-nine, Jefferson attended the Mississippi Democratic State Convention in 1843. People got to know him there, and when the party's congressional candidate withdrew with less than two weeks left in the race, Davis was asked to run. He had done nothing to get the nomination except let people know he was available.

Davis jumped into the short campaign and managed, in just ten days, to debate former congressman Seargent Prentiss, one of the Whigs' top public speakers, twice. Prentiss won the debates, but Davis did well. The brand new politician could not speak as eloquently as Prentiss, and certainly not as long (Prentiss spoke for over three hours at their first meeting and Davis for just thirty minutes), but Davis impressed those who were there.

"Mr. Davis's friends anticipate for him a proud and honorable career, should a sphere for the display of his talents once be presented," said James Ryan, the editor of the *Vicksburg Daily Sentinel,* who heard him speak at a rally in front of the two-story Vicksburg Court House. [40] Later, in 1844, when Davis was a presidential elector, Ryan told readers that although he lacked passion, Jeff Davis was "highly intellectual."[41]

He lost the race, as everyone expected he would but he did much better than projected, capturing 43 percent of the vote, winning one of the five counties in the district and coming within just eleven votes of taking the largest. He also impressed Democratic Party officials, who were pleased that the planter from Brierfield had agreed to be their candidate in their time of need.

The newspapermen he privately despised seemed to like him. "He is dignified, with a bold and noble countenance, commanding great attention, using chaste and beautiful language, giving no just ground for offense, even to his opponents who are, at the same time, withering under his sarcasm at every sentence," wrote the editor of the Macon (Mississippi) *Jeffersonian.* [42]

One year later, he was asked by local Democrats to be their congressional candidate at the state convention. Davis, again not seeking office but graciously accepting a draft, won the nomination after intense balloting, and then embarked on his first complete political campaign.

That campaign (Mississippi did not choose its congressmen by district, but statewide as at-large representatives) showed the many sides of Jefferson Davis. In just a year, he had become an accomplished public speaker, if not a great one, who could hold the attention of a crowd. He relied on logic and reasoned arguments, backed up with piles of statistics, and not emotion. He pleaded for fair tariffs, more independence for Southern planters, river improvements, and the annexation of Texas to strengthen the South politically ("daily we are becoming weaker," he said of the North-South power struggle in Congress[43]). He complained bitterly that the North had all the military power and all the navy "whilst there stand the cape and keys of Florida unprotected, through which flows the whole commerce of the South and West...."[44]

Editors of Democratic papers were impressed by him. "[He] left behind him fame as an orator and statesman," wrote one.[45] Although at first he appeared wooden, as he had in 1843, he rapidly warmed up to a crowd, even when he had to follow a long-winded Whig orator. Davis, the sophisticated planter, stumped as well as any candidate that fall, making several dozen speeches up and down the state. He campaigned for a tariff to help American workers, advocated expansion of American territories, and expressed the fervent wish that Texas, Oregon, and California would join the Union as states. He favored a national bank and an independent treasury system that would safeguard moneys in federal institutions instead of in state and local banks.

That first campaign showed other things, too, dark things. Davis did not accept press criticism well. He did not shrug off the arrows of the opposition newspapers as part of the political game, as did so many others. He took critical editorials, even in Whig papers, as insulting personal attacks. Instead of plunging ahead with his campaign, Jeff Davis spent hours defending himself in public against attacks which no one else took seriously.

He became sick again, as well. The campaign carried him through much of Mississippi. Many of his speeches were made at outdoor rallies, and his stumping carried him to numerous open-air receptions and barbecues. The exposure irritated his sensitive eye, which soon became red and inflamed and ached constantly. "He looks very badly," Varina wrote during early September. Davis and his doctors blamed his condition on a combination of recurring malaria and the pneumonia which had made him so ill in the army. The symptoms, however, indicate a viral herpes, some scholars suggested, perhaps contracted before his marriage. It would impair him throughout his life.[46]

Herpes simplex of the eye, the disease that afflicted Davis, is usually contracted by men between the ages of sixteen and twenty-five through sexual relations. It causes hundreds of tiny black growths to appear all around the eye and severely inflames and infects the eyelids and cornea. The disease produces a film which covers the cornea and causes blindness. A harmful side effect is the general weakening of the entire muscular system, usually forcing victims to stay in bed. The disease usually persists for between four and six weeks and then goes away. It is reactivated by stress, exposure to sunlight or wind, or a high fever.

Davis would contract it whenever he was outside working in Brierfield's cotton fields or on the campaign trail or when he was under stress. It recurred several times a year. There was no cure for it, and men had it all their lives. Doctors could only scrape the cornea, to restore some eyesight until the inflammation went down, and bathe the entire area with a solution of mercury chloride and iodine ointment.[47]

Davis won the election easily. He spent the following weeks wrapping up his business as a planter and packing for the move to the nation's capitol. Davis moved gracefully into the political and social world of Washington, D.C. He cut an impressive figure in Washington, quickly defining the gentlemen planter from the South, and, in his case, a very well-read one, too, a man as knowledgeable on his Plato as his cotton bales. He began to impress everyone.[48]

Jeff Davis was not only refined, but appeared so. He was one of the best-dressed congressmen in Washington, sporting dark frock coats and suits and favoring bright white shirts. His custom-made suits looked splendid on his tall, thin frame. The new congressman plunged into his job, working himself into exhaustion most days. He continued to suffer from the eye inflammation and, in winter, earaches. Varina fretted over his often fragile condition. "He has not been well since we arrived here," she wrote her mother. "He sits up until 2 or 3 at night, until his eyes lose their beauty even to me. They look so red and painful."[49]

He was assertive. Freshman congressmen rarely spoke in the House, but Davis delivered a major address denouncing nativist Americans who opposed immigration. His attack on the nativists, a growing political force whom few openly criticized, was hailed by congressmen, North and South. He said: "We must either make naturalization easy or we must withhold it entirely. For if we admitted foreigners, yet denied them the enjoyment of all political rights, we did but create enemies to our government and fill our country with discontented men."[50]

Davis was careful. A month later he delivered another major speech calling for the expansion of the Union to the shores of the Pacific, including Oregon, but, in a long, drawn-out, and very logical speech, urged Congress not to go to war with England, which also claimed Oregon. He had studied the nation's military and found it sadly wanting and unlikely to do well in an international conflict. He favored negotiations rather than war. He felt strongly that the year 1845 was not a time for war. "My constituents need no such excitements [war] to prepare their hearts for all that patriotism demands," he said.[51]

He was soon viewed as a bright, informed political leader who, with the backing of the Mississippi Democrats, would probably be in the House for many years and perhaps become its speaker. He seemed to have an unlimited future in Congress. Many began to see in Jeff Davis the kind of intellectual that moderate people could follow as North and South continued to argue over slavery and sectionalism. He seemed a potential national figure, like Henry Clay, who could serve as an ameliorating sectional bridge. His time in Congress would not be long, however: there was Mexico.

In late April, 1846, Mexican troops, angered by the U.S. occupation of Texas, its former territory, crossed the Rio Grande and attacked an American force commanded by Davis's former father-in-law, Colonel Zachary Taylor. Numerous U.S. troops were killed and, within days, the United States declared war on Mexico. Congressmen spent the months of May and June hailing the war, but Jefferson Davis was not among them. Incensed that foreign forces had attacked the U.S. Army, and eager, perhaps, to get back into what appeared to be a good fight, he quit Congress and enlisted in a Mississippi volunteer company and was off to the war.

"I felt my services were due to the country and believed my experience might be available in promoting the comfort the safety and efficiency of the Mississippi Regiment...I could not delay until the close of the Congressional session," he told Mississippians in an open letter to the state.[52]

The 913 men of the First Mississippi Volunteers, who knew him as a popular congressman, a former army lieutenant from West Point, and a hero of the Black Hawk War, elected him colonel of the regiment. He soon angered most of them by hard, relentless drills which he thought were needed to whip them into shape for combat. That came soon enough. On September 21, Davis led the Mississippi Volunteers, with a group of Tennesseans moving at the same time, in a charge on the fort of La Tenera, one of the forts protecting the town of Monterrey. Davis and his men took the fort as the Mexicans fled, and Davis, hot in pursuit, singlehandedly captured twenty Mexican soldiers. His regiment suffered ten killed and forty-four wounded in the battle. The next day Davis and his men occupied a second fort and cleared Monterrey of snipers in house-to-house fighting, the thin Mississippi congressman bravely leading the mop-up. The Mexicans surrendered the following day, and Taylor, impressed with Davis's courage, named him one of the commissioners to work out a surrender agreement.

Back on furlough, in Mississippi, Davis was promptly hailed a hero, even though many in his regiment grumbled that they found him overbearing. After two months at home, he caught up with the army in February at Buena Vista, where he encountered General Santa Anna, who had become infamous in the United States for massacring Davy Crockett and 186 freedom fighters at the Alamo, in San Antonio, Texas, eleven years before.

At a critical juncture in the battle of Buena Vista, when the Mexicans seemed likely to overwhelm Taylor's forces, Davis spotted a group of Mexican soldiers heading toward a plateau which would give them decisive field position. He rode back to his regiment and ordered it to charge, then led 370 Mississippi volunteers against a force of nearly four thousand trained Mexican soldiers. "The moment seemed to me critical," he said, "and the occasion to require whatever sacrifice it might cost to check the enemy."[53]

Halfway across the field toward the plateau Davis was shot in the foot. Ignoring the blood and pain (he used a handkerchief to wrap it while he stayed in the saddle), he continued to lead his men.

Later that day, Davis was caught by surprise when over two thousand Mexican cavalry charged his position. Standing in the open with untrained men and unable to muster a large enough force for an adequate defense, the quick-thinking Davis, still bleeding badly from his shattered foot and nearly immobile on his horse, organized his men and a nearby regiment into a right angle, from which they fired a withering, crosscutting volley at the Mexicans as they readied to charge. Several dozen of the enemy were killed and wounded as the entire Mexican cavalry, surprised by the ad hoc maneuver, fled across the plateau.[54]

Jeff Davis was cited for "highly conspicuous bravery" by General Taylor.[55]

A soldier who followed him, watching his foot bleed badly in the charge, said that "he could infuse courage into the bosom of a coward, and self-respect and pride into the breast of the most abandoned. He could lead them into hell."[56] Even the enemy had high praise for him, one Mexican general noting "the flashing sword of Davis" at Buena Vista.[57] As a final touch, Davis played the humble soldier, content merely to serve his country, and turned down a promotion to general by a gushing President James Polk.

Jefferson Davis, his foot still mending, returned home to Mississippi a much-publicized war hero, hailed for his courage under fire and for his ability to lead men in battle by newspapers throughout the country, North and South. Only Zachary Taylor and Winfield Scott received more publicity than Davis. The two generals' notoriety pushed Scott to the top of the military and enabled Taylor to become president two years later. Because he was a congressman turned patriot-soldier, Jeff Davis probably was mentioned in the newspapers more than an unknown but talented young army colonel named Robert E. Lee, whose exploits in the Mexican War had also been impressive. The dashing West Pointer Davis, the captor of Black Hawk in 1832, had done it again, helping Old Rough and Ready rout the Mexicans in 1846. He was a congressman who performed brave deeds—offering his life for his country— while other politicians merely gave speeches.

Davis's bravery at Buena Vista and Monterrey had cemented forever in the minds of Southerners the image of Jefferson Davis as a military legend, even though his heroism there was, in reality, that of a minor battlefield commander and not a strategist. He returned home in triumph. The governor of Mississippi showed his appreciation for his battlefield heroism by appointing him to fill an unexpired term in the U.S. Senate. Davis returned to Washington as a national hero who, better than anyone else, truly represented the South and its people, a man who, people whispered, might be president someday.

But Jeff Davis was troubled. The war, and his role in it, had further convinced him that his decisions were always the right ones and that his view was always correct. His role as the commander of a regiment stiffened the truculence of his personality and strengthened in him the notion that he was without question the best person to lead whatever group he belonged to, whether it was a regiment, a plantation, or a political body.

His strong-willed wife, Varina, resented the very close relationship her husband had with his older brother and married sisters. Joseph often argued with her and was highly critical of her father and brothers. Then Jeff told her he was going to redesign the main house at Brierfield so that his sister Amanda, a widow, could move in with her children. Shortly thereafter, Jeff Davis rewrote his will, leaving Varina only one-third of his estate and giving the other two-thirds to his sisters Amanda and Anna, a scheme Varina believed involved the hidden hand of his brother Joseph.

Varina exploded. Unfortunately, she said, women in the South, no matter how independent or educated, were wholly dependent on their husbands for their lifestyle, finances and, in the event of their husbands' deaths, an estate. They had no other source of livelihood. For Jefferson to give away two-thirds of his estate to his sisters and move his sister and her family into Varina's home was too much to bear. Davis shouted at her that she had no right to be so critical of him and wondered why he ever tolerated the independent thinking of such a young girl in the first place. Why didn't she know her place like all the other women who lived on plantations?

The two argued back and forth for two months, without any resolution. They were cold and aloof toward each other. Varina's resentment of Joseph and the sisters grew daily. Davis hoped that she would restrain herself, but she would not. He told his wife he didn't need that kind of turmoil on the eve of his departure for Washington to take his seat in the Senate. He would go alone. Varina stayed home, and the marriage headed toward divorce.

Davis arrived in Washington in early December, alone, and took a room in Gadsby's Hotel. Publicly, he was seen as a genuine war hero. As he hobbled about Washington on a single crutch, people gratefully held the door for him.

Privately, he was a steaming cauldron. His wrath toward Varina grew within. Finally, on edge about his wife and wondering how she could disobey him so frequently, he got into an argument at the hotel with his fellow senator from Mississippi, Henry Foote. The argument over slavery grew more intense, and suddenly Davis, unable to stand Foote's refusal to agree with him, lurched across the room and punched the senator. Before anyone realized what was happening, Jeff Davis beat up Foote. Others in the room, most of them congressmen, managed to pull him off before he injured Foote critically, but Davis broke free and threatened to kill him. Another senator grabbed Davis and punched him, and Davis punched him back, pushed him to the floor, and beat him repeatedly with his fists.[58]

Neither senator pressed charges against Davis, and neither insisted on a duel, as they might have. Others who had been present dismissed the encounter as a holiday affray probably brought on by too much spiked punch. They had to have known, from that night on, regardless of the reason Davis snapped, whether it was the argument or his deep anger at Varina, that Jefferson Davis had a dark and sinister side. Yet they ignored it then, and they would ignore it later.

2

A HUMBLE MAN

I believe slavery is morally and politically wrong.

ABRAHAM LINCOLN, SEPTEMBER 17, 1859

WHEN HE WAS A YOUNG MAN, Abraham Lincoln and a friend boarded a steamboat that slowly sailed down the Ohio River to St. Louis. On the first day of the trip Lincoln, walking the decks of the ship, encountered a slave trader from Kentucky who had purchased twelve slaves in different parts of his state and was taking them to a cotton plantation in the South. The slaves were chained together, with less than a foot of chain between each man. The sight of the men sickened young Lincoln. Later he recalled: "The Negroes were strung together precisely like so many fish upon a trot-line. In this condition they were being separated forever from the scenes of their childhood, their friends, their fathers and mothers, and brothers and sisters, and many of them from their wives and children and going into perpetual slavery."[1]

ABRAHAM Lincoln was born in Kentucky on February 12, 1809, in a small log cabin on a farm in the middle of a forest. Jefferson Davis was born in another Kentucky log cabin just one hundred miles away, one year earlier. Their families had moved to Kentucky as part of a wave of men and women determined to carve out better lives for themselves in the American wilderness. Abraham Lincoln's grandfather, Abraham, left Virginia in 1782, just a year before the end of the Revolution, and traveled through the

25

Cumberland Gap to settle along the slow, rolling Greene River in Kentucky. There he laid claim to a two-thousand-acre farm where, he thought, with great pleasure, he would spend the rest of his days.

He did not have much time to work his farm; he was killed by Indians in 1784. His son Tom worked the land and soon bought another farm, a 238-acre spread near Mill Creek. Tom bought a third property, three hundred acres, on a nearby creek and built a log cabin on it. In 1806, he married Nancy Hanks. One of their children, Thomas Jr., died in infancy, but a daughter, Sarah, grew up to be a healthy little girl. Abraham Lincoln was born there in 1809. When he was old enough, he helped his father with simple farming chores, such as planting corn on a seven-acre plot.

Thomas Lincoln was not happy in Kentucky. Crops were not good and he had trouble keeping all of his properties because of confusing land titles in the state. What he hated most about Kentucky was slavery, which was growing in the Bluegrass State. Kentucky had been admitted to the Union in 1792 as a slave state, and by 1811 there were as many slaves as white workers. Thomas Lincoln was opposed to slavery, the only person in his family who felt that way. His uncle Isaac and brother Mordecai both owned slaves. Nancy Hanks's guardian owned three slaves.

A devout Baptist, Thomas hated slavery because he felt that it was morally wrong for one man to enslave another. He despised slavery, too, because it created two systems of labor. He feared that slaves working without pay on large plantations would ruin his ability to profit from his small farm. The larger, slaveowning farmers would always be able to underprice him in the marketplace. These problems drove him into Spencer County, in southern Indiana, in 1816, where land could be bought free and clear directly from the federal government. There, in a state free of slavery, he started a new farm, along Pigeon Creek.[2]

The family struggled there. Abe, now seven, helped his father plant and harvest crops, clean stables, and groom animals. Nancy Lincoln's sister Elizabeth and her brother-in-law Thomas Sparrow came to the farm to help with the work, but then a wave of milk sickness, acquired from cows, struck the Pigeon Creek settlement. The area, lacking in medical care, was ravaged by the illness. First Tom Sparrow, then Elizabeth died, after which Nancy Lincoln fell ill and passed away.

His wife's death not only saddened Thomas Lincoln, but left him emotionally rudderless. He was a hardworking farmer, but not a very successful one. He was not a practical man, nor were his domestic or business affairs well organized. Like many frontiersmen of the era, he needed a wife who was loving, and, even more important, hardworking and able to raise a family. He remarried, bringing his bride Sarah Johnston and her three children back from Elizabethtown. Sarah was a wizard at domestic organization. When she arrived sitting on the front seat of their cluttered wagon, which looked like an old overstuffed dresser, she had a pile of furniture behind her. There were tables and chairs, knives, forks, spoons, bedding, a dresser, and a spinning wheel. The children watched with wonder as she supervised her husband and the boys in building and installing their first wooden floor, patching up the roof, and cutting a new covered window into one of the walls. She insisted on cleanliness, too. Within weeks, she had taken the Lincoln children under her wing, turning them from scruffy, ill-clad youngsters into reasonably dressed and presentable children. In just a few months, Sarah Lincoln restored order to the household and became a mother to the Lincoln children as well as her own.

Most of all, Sarah Lincoln gave the Lincoln children love. Young Abe liked Sarah immediately, and the two became very close. She loved him like his own mother had, and he soon began to call her mama. Their relationship flourished. He adored her for her caring and kindness, and Sarah loved the boy for the many qualities she saw in him. "Abe was the best boy I ever saw or expect to see," she said years later.[3]

His boyhood in Indiana was a happy time for Abe Lincoln. His stepmother Sarah provided the love he needed and he enjoyed the company of his sister, Sarah. Abe and Sarah got along well with their stepbrothers and stepsisters, even though the five children and two parents had to live in a single room in a crude log cabin. The physical closeness seemed to bring them together. The Lincolns and Johnstons became one family, despite typical children's squabbles.

None of the children received much of an education. They went to organized schools for less than a year. Later, when Lincoln went to Congress and was asked to fill out a member's form, Lincoln wrote "defective" in the education category.[4] On his own, Abe became a voracious reader, devouring Shakespeare and books on American history and George Washington. He pored over books, most borrowed from neighbors or brought home from school, by the light of the fire in the log cabin or, in good weather, sat down on the ground under a tree near the house, leaned back against the trunk, and read for hours. His mother and sister encouraged his reading. As a boy, he showed enormous intellectual curiosity, even though he had to generate it himself.

He also had a way about him which dazzled classmates during the few months each year he did attend school. He told one-line jokes, regaled students with long and amusing stories, and got along well with his teachers. He starred in the few athletic activities available at school and at community gatherings, because he was so tall and much stronger than most of his boyhood friends. Everyone who knew him saw in him the makings of a young leader.

He was an odd-looking leader, hopelessly thin and remarkably tall, a foot taller than most of his classmates. He often wore a coonskin cap tilted dangerously askew on his head. His pants, never the right size while he was growing, had cuffs that were always halfway up his legs. His voice was higher than that of most children and he had a very homely face, highlighted by high and prominent cheekbones, oversized ears, and soft gray eyes. His jet-black hair was never cut or combed just right, and it stuck out from under his cap. His hands were enormous and bony.

He seemed all wrong as a leader of schoolchildren, as the center of everyone's attention wherever he went—and yet in many ways he seemed right. He was a very different boy, one nobody could ignore, and no one would forget.

By the time he was seventeen, Abe Lincoln had grown into one of the strongest boys in southern Indiana. He had reached his full height of six feet, four inches, but weighed just 162 pounds. He had developed a hard body, his muscles finely sculpted and his arms and huge hands powerful from farm work. Abe cleared fields for planting, pushed plows, chopped hundreds of cords of wood, carried rocks, dug up ground, and planted seeds. He did not care much for his father, who pushed him to work hard and even hired Abe out, at a price, to work for neighbors. The boy resented laboring for others and often thought he was working as hard as the slaves in Kentucky, who were also hired out for money.

On his own, Abe went to barn raisings and helped dozens of neighbors build houses and clear their fields. He learned to split rails, too, in order to make fences for people, and was considered, at seventeen and eighteen, the best railsplitter in the county. It was a skill he thought nothing about at the time. Sometimes he asked for money and sometimes he did not. Wherever he went, he lighted up the farm with his vibrant personality and endless storytelling, sometimes regaling dozens of grown men with his well-plotted, meandering, and always humorous tales. He liked to frequent the general store in the area, and sat for hours with other men, listening to tall tales and spinning his own.[5]

It was there, too, at general stores throughout the frontier states, that men talked endlessly about individualism and their brand-new democratic political system, less than forty years old. That entire system, young Abe came to believe, was built on the lives of farmers and men who worked the land with their hands or worked as blacksmiths or carpenters to make a town and make a nation. The ideas of democracy embraced by the Declaration of Independence had deep roots in the western states, particularly after the ascension to national prominence of Andrew Jackson, from Tennessee. On the frontier pioneers struggled to earn a living while abiding by the tenets of this revolutionary political system while at the same time maintaining a strident and fierce sense of individualism.

Young Lincoln became well known in the area through his work on farms, but he did not want to continue working on farms all his life. Eager to meet more people and see more of the Indiana countryside, he began to row people across the Ohio River for fun. One day he was startled when someone paid him for his efforts. "I could scarcely believe my eyes as I picked up the money," he said. "I could scarcely credit that I, a poor boy, had earned a dollar in less than a day.... The world seemed wider and fairer before me."[6] A neighbor, James Gentry, who was looking for a hardworking man to take a cargo of produce down the Mississippi to New Orleans with his son, Allen, hired Lincoln to build a flatboat and serve as assistant captain for the trip. Lincoln, eager to see New Orleans, jumped at the chance.[7] So did Tom Lincoln when he learned Abe would be paid $8 a month for the trip. It was the boy's first trip outside the region.

The trip downriver took Gentry and Lincoln and their tiny flatboat past the large slave plantations along the Mississippi and then to New Orleans, a bustling and colorful seaport city in 1829, loaded with riverboats, paddlewheelers, steamboats, and docks smothered with cargo piled higher than the rooftops. Men caroused through the streets until late at night, fought over women, and stuffed expensive imported cigars into the corners of their mouths as they played cards in saloons. People dressed in fine clothes of a kind Lincoln and Gentry had never seen before. White women and creole women cruised the streets. Slaves straggled by, chained to one another. Businessmen haggled over prices. Sea captains looked for work. It was a splendid journey for the two young men and was the first window on the larger world through which Abe Lincoln had ever peered.

When Abe returned, he learned that in his absence the milk sickness had almost taken the lives of several neighbors. Tom Lincoln thought death was closing in around him. In 1828 his daughter Sarah, Abe's sister, who had married Aaron Grigsby died in childbirth. Tom Lincoln had lost a wife, an infant son, and a daughter, and he did not want to take any more chances with his remaining child, Abe, and Sarah's three children. Besides, he had heard from his cousin, John Hanks, who lived in central Illinois, that there was rich but cheap farmland available there. If Tom Lincoln could pack his family into wagons and get there, Hanks would help him find land and clear it. Tom Lincoln, as fed up with Indiana as he had been years earlier with Kentucky, moved again.[8]

The Lincolns left Pigeon Creek in 1830, when Abe was twenty-one. Abe took his books. Everyone would smile at Abe and his books, which he carried so often that they seemed like a natural part of him, like his arms and legs. Dennis Hanks remembered later that young Lincoln was always reading a book of some kind, whether on the farm or in a town. Some called him lazy because he found it so easy to drop his lanky frame down on any piece of furniture or patch of grass he could find and read. Abe would pick up newspapers wherever he went and read every word of every column. None of this impressed his father, who became even more rigid over the years, creating a wide emotional gap with his son. Thomas Lincoln often accused Abe of laziness because he wasted time reading books. Abe never disputed such charges from his father or anyone else. He would just smile and keep reading. His father was illiterate; Abe Lincoln did not want to be like him.[9]

The Lincolns met John Hanks in Macon County, Illinois, at a place he had bought for them on the banks of the Sangamon River, which ran through the middle of the state, ten miles southwest of Decatur. They built a strong home for the Lincoln family there, with a separate smokehouse. Hanks had cut the logs for their farmhouse, and Abe and Tom helped him clear out fifteen acres for planting. When the farm was finished, Abe and John Hanks traveled to neighboring farms, also just starting, and split three thousand rails for fences.

While taking a cargo of produce down the Sangamon on a flatboat a year later, in 1831, Abe Lincoln came upon the riverfront village of New Salem, Illinois. It would change his life forever. New Salem sat next to a mill dam.

Lincoln, although he was familiar with the river, did not see the dam in time as he and two friends guided the flatboat down the Sangamon. The flatboat got stuck on the dam, and the trio's frenzied activity to free it drew most of the townspeople as spectators. When Lincoln cut a hole in the boat to permit the water in the bow to run out and force the boat upright and over the dam, they gave him a rousing cheer. Denton Offutt, the Sangamon area entrepreneur who had sent them on the journey, offered the enterprising Lincoln a job running a general store he planned to build in New Salem. Lincoln, after his gaze had drifted around the small, quaint village, accepted. When he returned from the cargo run to New Orleans, he began working on the construction and opening of the store with Offutt.

New Salem sat on a bluff overlooking the Sangamon and supplied the neighboring farm communities as well as serving as their social hub. The town had a blacksmith's shop, a cooper's shop, a wool shop, a hatmaker, several general stores, a tavern, and dozens of small, nicely built homes for its several hundred residents. Like many western towns, it fed off the river and its traffic. It was the American frontier in microcosm, with its horses and wagons, visiting preachers, God-fearing families, one-room school, brawls, taverns, and, always lurking in the distance, Indians.

Residents found it easy to like Abe Lincoln, who, at twenty-two, decided New Salem was the place he was going to make the break from his family and his youth and get away from his father forever. He became a fixture in local stores and porches, where he would sit for hours spinning his yarns and anecdotes, causing men and women to quake with whoops of laughter. Visits to Offutt's general store became welcome trips for men and women, who used the occasion to listen to young Lincoln's stories and get to know the personable clerk better. The stories not only changed their moods, but his as well. Lincoln, who suffered from bouts of depression, used his storytelling powers to lift himself as well as his listeners. Said a friend: "His countenance would brighten up, the expression would light up not in a flash but rapidly, from the inner corners of his eyes, and extend down and diagonally across his nose, his eyes would sparkle, all terminating in an unrestrained laugh in which every one present willing or unwilling were compelled to take part."[10]

He was a hardworking and diligent man who toiled long hours for Offutt, keeping updated inventories, making certain the store was heated in winter and kept cool in summer, and constantly sweeping the floor. He was honest, too. Once he overcharged someone and walked several miles to his home to repay the difference. Farmers with little money found they could establish rather easy credit with Lincoln (often never fully paid), because he was once a poor farmer himself. Little children quickly learned that the tall stranger with the homely face and warm smile often looked the other way when they were near the candy jars.

He made two quick impressions in New Salem which would last throughout his years there. The first was physical. Lincoln was a big man. By the time he arrived in New Salem he had grown to his full height, a bit over six foot four (several men who were six feet tall remarked that they had to bend their necks to look up at his face, indicating he might have been even taller) and weighed 185 to 190 pounds. He had exceptionally long arms and large hands. Farm work and rail splitting had made him muscular. He rather handily defeated Jack Armstrong, the local tough and, for that day, a very large and bulky man, in a wrestling match witnessed by the entire town. Armstrong was the strongboy of the Clary's Grove gang, farmboys from a nearby village who were supposed to be the roughest men in the state. Armstrong, losing, acknowledged Lincoln's enormous strength. The gang threatened to attack Lincoln in retaliation for the manhandling of their leader. Lincoln responded by offering to fight them all—one at a time. Armstrong interceded, becoming Lincoln's instant and close friend. (Lincoln sometimes compared the art of wrestling to the art of debating—knowing when to attack, when to dodge, when to grab, when to back off, when to throw a man, when to become defensive.[11])

People who knew him as a young man remembered his physical strength as much as his engaging personality. R. G. Rutledge, a New Salem friend, said he once saw Lincoln lift a large whisky barrel weighing several hundred pounds to eye level to entertain his audience. Another friend swore Lincoln could chop three to four times as much firewood as any man alive. All who knew him, regardless of their yardsticks, marveled at his strength. "He was the strongest I have ever took hold of," said Rowan Herndon, a neighbor.[12]

His intellectual curiosity also made a lasting impression. A half dozen residents were college educated. They found Lincoln an eager learner and spent much time helping him in his self-education. One man told Lincoln he needed a grammar book for his studies but said that the only one available in the county was owned by a friend who lived six miles away. Lincoln shrugged, put on his coat, and walked the six miles to borrow it. The townspeople were also impressed by his deep interest in the Bible and his frequent quoting of scriptures, even though no one seemed to remember seeing him in church. One of the New Salem residents even talked him into joining a local debating society, where he was able to polish his speaking skills and spend long evenings talking about politics.[13]

Everyone wanted Abe Lincoln around, whether it was the roughhouse crowd at Clary's Grove, the debating society, or the farmers who spent hours at his store, enamored with his stories. He gained a quick reputation as an honest and trustworthy store clerk who treated all customers fairly, whether they were the town's most prosperous businessmen or its poorest laborers. Even the local judge asked him to sit in on court cases so he could lighten up the drudgery of long evenings at court with funny stories that came to mind as he listened to the cases.[14] In less than a year he had become the most popular man in New Salem. People liked his sense of humor, his eagerness to help them, whether in purchasing goods or splitting their fence rails, his honesty and integrity, and the easy manner he had with people, particularly small children. He was able to get along with people, too, even those who disagreed with him or, at first, did not like him. He turned Jack Armstrong from a foe to a friend while beating him up. He easily made friends, in his debating society, of people who strongly disagreed with his politics.

Several men in town urged Lincoln to get into politics and run for the state legislature, even though he was only twenty-three years old. He eagerly accepted. He had less than a year of formal education, yet on his own and under the tutelage of college-educated men and women in New Salem he had become well read. He had devoured newspapers all of his life and talked endlessly about news and politics to many of the people he met. He had come to feel he knew as much about government as any town councilman. He was convinced that he was as good as any other man.

What people did not understand about Abraham Lincoln was that even at twenty-three he had a relentless ambition to succeed in politics. He once noted about himself, "Every man is said to have his peculiar ambition. Whether it is true or not, I can say that I have none other so great as that of being truly esteemed of my fellow men by rendering myself worthy of their esteem."[15]

He was clever, though, about his ambition. As early as 1832 he was writing very careful letters for local newspapers describing himself as a "humble man," a man simply looking for some small recognition from his fellow man.[16] He would wrap that cloak of humility around him all his life, as ambition flourished beneath it. Time after time, in speech after speech, he reminded people that he was not personally ambitious, but that he needed to be in public life to pursue causes which were important. Yet privately he told friends that if he lost his first election he would run again and again until he won. He told Lynn Greene, a neighbor who helped him with English grammar, that some people were born to do great things and that he felt he was one of them.[17] He told a local schoolteacher that he was certain that he would succeed in politics eventually.[18] Later, his law partner and lifelong friend Billy Herndon said that Lincoln always thought of success, even when he failed, and he often failed. "He was...always planning ahead. His ambition was a little engine that knew no rest."[19]

He decided to run for a seat in the Illinois state assembly in 1832, and pledged to solve the problems of the common man. He was a man, he told people, who worked with his hands, just like most people did, and could understand their problems. He never abandoned this image of the well-intentioned, hardworking, plain man of the people, which would propel him far down the political road.

Though still unpolished, Lincoln gave several speeches during the election campaign, promising to make advances in religious freedom and education and to work hard for internal improvements—railroads, canals, roads—but he lost the election, even though he won 277 of the 300 votes cast in New Salem, which greatly pleased him. The defeat did not worry him; he would campaign again in 1834.

The year 1832 was the year of the Black Hawk War, an Indian war which for Abraham Lincoln would be nothing more than a way to earn a paycheck and work up a few funny stories about his bungling in it. Lincoln was penniless. The militia was a chance for him, as it was for many, to earn some money. The local militia, mostly Clary's Grove men, promptly elected Lincoln their captain, an honor which years later he said was the greatest ever bestowed on him, more important to him than any election he had won.

Captain Lincoln, who knew nothing about military science, and did not care to learn anything about it, either, led them on endless marches up and down the state for several months, never seeing action. Lincoln himself found nothing but trouble. He got into a wrestling match with the head of another company and lost. He was ordered to carry a wooden sword for two days as punishment for permitting his men to get drunk. On another occasion he was punished for firing off a pistol in camp.

He once joked with someone who also fought in the war that "if he saw any live, fighting Indians, it was more than I did," and added that "I had a good many bloody struggles with the mosquitoes…and never fainted from the loss of blood."[20]

His militia unit was finally disbanded and the men sent home, but Lincoln, out of patriotism and financial need, reenlisted twice and eventually served eighty days (and was paid $95). He returned to New Salem with the other ad hoc soldiers in the middle of August after suffering a final military indignity—their horses were stolen. He and the men walked and hitched rides on wagons down the state and stumbled into New Salem on foot, woeful-looking conquering heroes.[21]

The Black Hawk War marked a turn in Lincoln's life. On his return to New Salem he closed Offutt's sinking store and went to work for another general store, constantly striving to make ends meet. The likable Lincoln was helped by the people of New Salem, who wanted him to succeed. One group of friends lobbied to get him a part-time job as the postmaster for New Salem, a post which enabled him to make money and to read all the newspapers which were mailed to the post office. Another group landed him a part-time job as a surveyor, which gave him a chance to ride about the county and do some fruitful politicking. During the slow winter of 1832–33 he read every newspaper that came in and plunged into dozens of books about history. He had seen much of Illinois and heard stories of dozens of other towns and cities where men lived. He knew he had a good home in New Salem, however, and decided to stay there, get back into politics, and become a lawyer.

Unable to afford the study of law at a college, Lincoln, twenty-three, borrowed dozens of books about the law, reading them over and over again in an effort to make himself into a lawyer, just as he had made himself into a store clerk and small businessman. Unable to afford new books, he frequented local auctions, where he could buy them cheaply. He spent several years studying law books, convinced that he could combine what he considered his above-average intelligence and his engaging personality into a profitable career in law. He befriended every lawyer he knew.

John Stuart, of Springfield, was the most helpful. Lincoln met Stuart when both served in the Black Hawk War. Lincoln admired Stuart's legal expertise and intellect, while Stuart admired Lincoln's easy manner with people and his determination to become a lawyer and get into politics. Stuart advised him to run for the legislature again, but this time as a non-partisan candidate, appealing to both Democrats and voters from the brand-new Whig

Party. To do this, Stuart advised, Lincoln had to campaign on a platform of generalities so as to offend neither Democrats nor Whigs. Stuart, a political man himself, told Lincoln to avoid the appearance of a man too connected to any radical view, to run as a moderate in an effort to capture the votes of the growing middle-class farmer and village population of the county. Lincoln followed his advice. Staying vague on the issues, he stumped throughout his district and won his first race, finishing second in a field of thirteen candidates (the top four were elected).[22]

In the legislature, which then met at Vandalia, Lincoln, who roomed with Stuart, supported programs aimed at improvements for the state of Illinois, including bills to promote new railroads and dig new canals, and legislation to ease the problems of the poor and debtors. He became an associate party leader, working under Stuart's tutelage, and was soon writing bills and steering them through committee to legislative approval. He quickly learned the gentle art of persuasion and the skill of winning over votes on one bill in exchange for support on another. He could be outrageous, too, as on the day he and two other Whigs leaped out of a first-floor window on the House floor in order to avoid having to cast their votes. He could be very funny, too. After the legislature had accidentally named someone to a job to replace a man who had died, it was learned that the dead man was quite alive, and still in office. Lincoln rose to his full height, cocked an eye at his embarrassed colleagues, and solemnly told them that he could not take the man's job away if he persisted in not dying.[23] He very rapidly grew into an effective, and quite popular, legislator.

Now twenty-five, Lincoln had lived in New Salem for three years. He was pleased with himself. His rough life on the farm had made him a self-driven, resourceful, hard worker who had succeeded in the harshness of the rugged frontier. He had become an independent man, served in a war in which men elected him their commander, won a seat in the state legislature, run two different businesses, had been appointed postmaster and surveyor, and decided on a career in law.

And he had fallen in love.

The women in the town constantly tried to play matchmaker for Lincoln, whom they thought would make any young girl a fine husband. He was homely in appearance, but a bright and witty man who worked very hard. He exhibited all the traits of a successful husband in a small river town in 1830s Illinois. Their problem was their subject. Lincoln, so outgoing among men, was very shy among women. Most of the teenage girls or young women the local matchmakers tried to introduce to Lincoln frightened him. Not Ann Rutledge.

Lincoln liked to spend time at a local tavern, where he met Ann, the tavernkeeper's daughter. She was, villagers said, a pretty girl who was five feet, three inches tall, weighed about 120 pounds and had fair skin, blue eyes, and auburn hair. Lincoln enjoyed her company, and could speak openly and easily with her because she was already engaged to another man, the rather mysterious John McNeil. He turned out to be John McNamar, and disappeared one day, after telling Ann he had to return to his family in upstate New York but would come back soon. He never did.

Lincoln began to get serious about Ann when she realized her relationship with McNamar was over. Their close friendship developed into a romance, and in the spring of 1835 they were unofficially engaged, each content to wait at least a year until marriage so that Abe could pass the bar exam, become a lawyer, and earn enough money to support a wife and family. Lincoln was thrilled by the engagement. An ungainly man with women, he had finally found a girl whom he could talk to, joke with, and, most important, who seemed just like him. They had many common interests, common friends, and a yearning for a good and prosperous future in New Salem.

The summer of 1835 was one of the hottest in Illinois history, and it rained every day. Stagnant water in hot areas was often accompanied by the dreaded typhoid fever. Wellwater would become contaminated, and those who drank it would contract the fever. The death rate was high. The Rutledge well became contaminated that summer, and Ann grew very ill, spinning in and out of consciousness with "brain fever." Her condition worsened day by day. Lincoln, scraping together all the money he had, paid for doctors, but there was no cure. She finally succumbed to the fever, on August 25, her last request a visit by Abe Lincoln, who held her hand tightly as she slipped away. A few days later, after family, friends, and just about everyone in New Salem had paid their respects at her funeral, Abe buried her, just as he had buried a mother, a brother, and a sister.[24]

Lincoln was crushed by Ann's death. All his dreams seemed to die with her, and he plunged into a long depression. He disappeared from the taverns and general stores for almost a month, grieving privately, trying to determine how to go on with his life. Finally, certain that hard work would drive away his depression, he began to read his law books again. A month after her death, he returned to his job as a surveyor, riding his horse slowly through Sangamon County to finish his jobs.

As he got over Ann's death, his old buoyant personality returned, and he began to be seen at his former haunts, telling stories. His vast array of stories included numerous parables presenting, in very humorous ways, serious ideas Lincoln wanted to convey. (These chestnuts could be simple, such as "Don't change horses in the middle of a stream" and "You can fool all of the people some of the time and some of the people all of the time, but you can't fool all of the people all of the time," or they could be complicated, layered stories).

He understood that while the rich could be appointed or selected to office, the poor, including Lincoln, had to work through the political system. To succeed in politics, Lincoln became a consummate political operative, whether running, campaigning for others, organizing campaigns, or conducting polls. He built extended networks of politicians whom he helped and whom he wanted to help him one day. He had to compromise on bills to enable their passage, support others' bills in return for their support of his. He had to travel to different states to campaign for other Whig candidates, raise money to finance his campaigns and those of others, cajole support from reluctant newspaper editors, and enlist other politicians as go-betweens to the state organization or even to members of his own clique. He had to write hundreds of letters cultivating politicians in Illinois to stay viable as a political figure.

Winning office at the bottom rungs of the political system required that Lincoln be a very practical, pragmatic politician. Canvassing, organizing, almost begging, was just the start of what it took. Having begun public life with no education, position, money, or friends in high places to offer a helping hand, he had to work harder than anyone else to win a small toehold there. Most important, he had to get along with different kinds of men, many of whom did not share his views. He was able to adopt a flexible enough political persona to do so. It was perhaps his strongest asset when he was president. It was something others in politics, particularly the rich, never had to worry about.

Joshua Speed was probably the first man to speak to Abe Lincoln when he rode into Springfield on April 15, 1837, all his belongings in the saddlebags slung over the back of his horse. Speed ran A. Y. Ellis & Company, the general store on the town square, and lived upstairs. He recognized Lincoln as soon as the tall young lawyer walked through the door. Speed had heard Lincoln give a speech once, had been impressed, and had read about his fledgling political career. Lincoln didn't even have the $17 needed to purchase a mattress and sheets he would need—provided he could find a room he could afford. Speed told him that he could room with him, upstairs, until he earned enough money to establish himself. Lincoln thanked him profusely. When Speed asked him why he had moved to Springfield, he told him that he was there to "experiment as a lawyer."[25]

His future prospects were better than those of that morning. He had a job in the legislature, where he was serving his second term, the promise of work in Stuart's small law office, a coterie of friends from the statehouse, as many law books as one could squeeze on to the back of a horse, and boundless ambition.[26]

Springfield, in 1837, was a small town of 1,500 people, but it seemed like a large city to Lincoln, arriving from tiny New Salem. It had a dozen stores, residences built of clapboard and brick, a large courthouse, and four hotels. He soon made friends, as he did wherever he went. He moved into a room with Joshua Speed, who would become a lifelong friend, and even shared a double bed with him, a common practice at the time. Speed introduced him to many businessmen and residents of Springfield, as did Stuart. Lincoln, with his unique and appealing personality, was soon a fixture in the social whirl.

People who met him for the first time were struck both by his vibrancy and his odd physical appearance. His clothes could never seem to contain his long limbs. No barber could rein in his bushy black hair. His hair was rarely combed properly and always gave him a rough edge, no matter how expensive the suits he wore later. All noted that he had an odd gait. He had gray, reflective eyes which, by themselves, seemed sorrowful, but his amiable and animated face made his eyes light up whenever he was telling a funny story.[27] Physically, years of splitting rails and farm work had given him a hard, muscular, healthy body. He never visibly suffered from any sickness.

Lincoln was a good lawyer. His self-taught lawyering, and the hundreds of hours it took, turned out to be just as effective as law learned at college. He and Stuart took on small cases, with fees ranging from $5 to $10. They filed hundreds of deeds and certificates with county offices on behalf of clients and handled hundreds of bankruptcy cases. To Lincoln, the law was rather simple. He put his long legs up on to his desk, listened to a prospective client's story, and then made a snap decision. He either told the client he would represent him on what Lincoln thought was a winnable case, or he told him the case was not winnable and that he would work toward a settlement. Sometimes he told the client to go home.

Lincoln, who read all the law books he could find in Stuart's office or at the county courthouse, rarely had problems with actual cases. When he did, Stuart was there to help. Lincoln soon joined other lawyers in town in riding the circuit through the state. Setting up shop on coffee tables in hotel restaurants, he made himself available to handle legal problems for people in small villages without lawyers. He would represent these clients in front of Judge David Davis, a corpulent, three-hundred-pound circuit court judge who became a friend and admirer of Lincoln and would remain so throughout his life. On the circuit, Lincoln made additional money and learned more about the law. Most important, he met hundreds of other lawyers and thousands of plain citizens, all of whom seemed to like him, for they saw qualities in Abe Lincoln they rarely saw in other men.

They certainly thought he was a capable lawyer. Everyone who ever saw him in a courtroom marveled at how good he was at summing up cases and pleading them to a jury, as ardently as a politician on the stump. Folks thought he was a lawyer of integrity. Some remarked that he never seemed to work as hard for clients who seemed guilty as he did for those who seemed innocent. Most of all, like everyone else, they loved his stories.

Herndon recalled, "Judges, jurors, witnesses, merchants...have laughed at these jokes...till every muscle—nerve and cell of the body in the morning was sore at the whooping and hurrahing exercise."[28]

These people, from large cities and small towns, from the north and the south and the east and west of the circuit, would be there years later when he needed them, and they would be there for him again and again.

Lincoln worked with Stuart for several years, then moved to the law offices of Stephen Logan. In 1844 he set up his own law office with Billy Herndon. They would be partners until the day Lincoln left Springfield for Washington to become president. While he worked and lived in Springfield, he met several Illinois politicians who would go on to become congressmen, U.S. senators, federal judges, and newspaper editors. The most brilliant was the dynamic young Stephen Douglas, a portly man barely five feet tall with a large, leonine head that was hopelessly oversized for his tiny body. Douglas, nicknamed the Little Giant for his short frame and soaring oratory in political debates, was twenty-one when Lincoln first moved to Springfield. The short,

Democratic Douglas and the tall Whig, later Republican, Lincoln, were personal friends but political rivals all of their lives.

As a legislator, Lincoln's bills and programs all aimed at the growth and industrialization of Illinois. He was born in a one-room log cabin, was raised on small farms, and split rails on large farms, but Abe Lincoln was convinced that the future in Illinois was in the industrialization of America. He pushed hard for railroads, canals, and roads; programs to help newly arrived citizens find land and jobs; and, most of all, high tariffs on foreign imports to protect the jobs of hardworking citizens of Illinois. He learned hardscrabble politics in the state legislature, too, especially in working on a bill to get the state capital moved from tiny Vandalia, where he started out as a lawmaker, to his new hometown of Springfield.

The drive to make Springfield the capital was typical, legislative give-and-take. Lincoln, one of the sponsors of the bill, sent a team of political operatives out the night before the vote, in a snowstorm, to talk legislators into changing their votes, dangling the prospect of state jobs for friends in front of some, the prospect of railroad lines in their districts before others. It worked, and was a good example of how well Lincoln could twist arms and earn votes.[29]

During his legislative years, Lincoln began to play a bigger role in Whig Party activities. The Whigs were a relatively new party, founded in 1828 in opposition to Democrat Andrew Jackson. The Democrats, under the flamboyant Jackson, championed individual rights and a limited federal government which did not interfere with state and local authority. Jackson staunchly opposed federally operated national banks in favor of smaller, localized state banks, for example. The Whigs favored a large, strong federal government, a national bank, high tariffs to protect American manufacturing, and humanitarian causes. Lincoln believed in a large federal government that could support the industrial revolution just beginning to take shape in America and was convinced that the future of Illinois, then a frontier, agrarian state, was with industrialization, not farming.

He traveled around the state campaigning for other Whigs and making friends with the editors of newspapers. In 1840 he began the first scientific voter polls in Illinois, keeping tabs on every race in every district for the party, and keeping records on the election results. His skills at politics earned him the admiration of others in the Whig Party and the respect of the Democrats. The politicians liked him for jokes, stories, and good company, but they liked him, too, because he was a good party man and a good politician who got things done.

It was in Springfield that Abe Lincoln met Mary Todd. Mary had arrived there in 1839 to live with her sister, Elizabeth, and brother-in-law, the wealthy Ninian Edwards, after she left the Kentucky home of her slaveholding family following a heated dispute. Elizabeth, who enjoyed playing matchmaker, had just succeeded in marrying off one of their sisters to a successful Springfield doctor, and Mary decided she might as well be next.

Mary loved to attend the Edwardses' parties. They knew all the wealthy and powerful men in Illinois, such as the charismatic Stephen Douglas and other politicians. It was at one of these parties that she first spotted Abe Lincoln crossing the crowded living room to meet her. She could not miss the lawyer, who stood a head above almost everyone else there. He walked up to her, with his body rambling a little from his height, the way it always did, and told her that he wanted to dance with her in the worst way. They had one dance together, then Mary suggested they sit and talk, whereupon she told him, his oafish steps fresh in mind, that he did, indeed, dance with her in the worst way.

Everyone was convinced that Mary, a social climber back in Kentucky, wanted to marry a rich man, but she didn't. She was looking for a man who was going to become famous and powerful. She saw those qualities in Abe Lincoln, who was in his third term in the legislature when they met. She saw in him a man with a good future, who needed an aggressive woman like her to push him along a bit.

Lincoln did not need any pushing. He was already the most ambitious man in Illinois, but he did need a wife who understood his own drive for political office and, most of all, who understood the labyrinth of state politics and was willing to put up with its demands. Mary Todd was not only a political woman who understood politics, but was a fire-breathing Whig herself.

She was a bit plump, but Lincoln liked plump women. She had a very pretty face, moved gracefully, was exceedingly well groomed and well dressed, and presented herself in a very acceptable fashion. She had all the social graces of a woman who drifted in the higher ranks of the social world of Illinois, enjoyed cultural connections through her sister and brother-in-law, and was well read and well educated, a finishing school graduate.

Abe and Mary began to see each other often, going for walks, riding horses, and lunching and dining together. He was enchanted by her rich conversation and felt very comfortable around her, as he did not with most women. Mary was different from Ann Rutledge, his first love. Ann was a small-town girl, while Mary was a sophisticated woman who moved easily in city circles. Within weeks, the couple felt they were in love with each other.

Mary's sister and brother-in-law were critical of Lincoln's frontier ways but did not object to the marriage. Others tried to talk Mary out of the marriage, arguing that if she wanted a man who was going far she was picking the wrong one in the homely-looking, gangling, awkward Abe Lincoln, whom they believed was going nowhere. They urged her to marry Stephen Douglas, the promising young politician who might one day hold high office, but Mary was convinced that her future was with Abe Lincoln. They urged Douglas on her because, they always reminded her, she had vowed as a teenager that the man she married would one day be president of the United States.

Abe and Mary had their share of arguments and carried on a difficult courtship. After they became engaged, they suddenly broke off under murky circumstances. They kept apart, then began seeing each other again. At length, they were engaged a second time, finally marrying in 1842, only after Lincoln endured such a depression[30] over his relationship with Mary that he tried to get Stuart to pull strings to get him a job in South America away from her.[31] Lincoln was thirty-three when he married.

The Lincolns began married life in a hotel room in Springfield, where they lived until Lincoln, working harder than ever as a lawyer, earned enough money to buy a modest two-story home. The windows looked out over a quiet neighborhood. Their worries about one another during their turbulent courtship faded quickly as they settled into married life.

Mary gave birth to their first son, Robert, in 1843. Lincoln, the proud father, would show off their son to anyone he encountered in the streets of Springfield. Three years later, Edward was born. His death at age four shook the Lincolns. Abe sank into another of his melancholy moods. Mary, extremely upset, grieved over the little boy for months, at times distraught and unable to control her weeping and anguish. A third son, Willie, was born in 1850, and his birth helped the Lincolns heal the loss of Edward. Their last child, Tad, was born in 1853. Lincoln's relationship with Robert, even though he was the first born, was always distant and stiff. It was Willie and Tad, the younger boys, whom Lincoln loved the most.

Everyone loved Willie. He was amusing and well behaved. No matter what his childhood antics, they were taken with good humor by friends and family. He was a delight to all who knew him. Tad was different. Today, he would be described as a child with attention-deficit disorder and emotional problems. He acted out all his feelings and frustrations, knocking tables over to get attention, shouting at parents and friends and fighting with everyone. Tad also had a severe speech impediment which caused him to slur his words badly.

The Lincolns had a tangled marriage. Mary Lincoln was enigmatic and tempestuous. High strung, she possessed a hair-trigger temper. No one and nothing in Springfield seemed to please her. She quarreled with her sister and her friends. She often acted impulsively, with no regard for the consequences of her actions or remarks. She could be crude and abusive and frequently said things about others, in tones of biting sarcasm, which most people would keep to themselves. In one instance she ripped into Lincoln's friend and law partner, Billy Herndon, after he danced with her at a party and made some innocuous remark she took the wrong way.

Mary would often lose her temper inside the Lincoln home, particularly since Lincoln was as casual about life as Mary was demanding. She feuded with neighbors and friends, argued with merchants, and on several occasions kicked Lincoln out of the house for the night, forcing him to sleep in his law office, the homes of friends, or on the back porches of neighbor's houses.

During the early 1840s Lincoln admitted to his friend Joshua Speed, himself a new husband, that he had suffered from deep melancholy for years, and feared that he had a sensitive personality which would continually bring on depression over the slightest setbacks. He was often depressed during the day and then, at night, while he slept, he was the victim of endless nightmares which either woke him or at least caused him to toss in his sleep. In many of them he died, and in some he found himself running a country that was involved in a bloody war.[32] In later years, he would wake up from a nightmare in which he was a guest at his own wake. His taste in literature was somber. While others read light novels, Lincoln spent hours reading and rereading *Richard III* and *Macbeth*. His depression tormented Mary, but it also drove him to think deeply about life, making him more reflective than most men, and to hard work, to put things that bothered him out of his mind.

His depressions were sometimes brought on by life with Mary, but they were often the cause of his troubles with Mary, who was struggling with her own temper tantrums and worry. Lincoln was little help in the house, forever tossing his coat somewhere that it did not belong, frequently being late for meals, and never cleaning up. He loved to sit in front of the fire and read when he returned from his law office and did not understand why Mary, her hands full with the activities of their children all day, insisted that he engage her in conversation. He was often lost in thought while he read or pondered things and paid no attention to her. Once she asked him three times to put a log on the fire. He paid no attention. After the third time, exasperated, she picked up the log and hit him over the head with it.[33]

Lincoln was also gone for months each winter, on the circuit. He needed to bring in money to pay for his house and the needs of his growing family. While Mary accepted his absence, she did not like it. She complained bitterly to other wives that while he was off riding about the countryside, eating in hotels and regaling the multitudes with his funny stories, she was stuck at home raising children and taking care of a large household. She told a friend "if [her] husband [had] stayed at home as he ought to [that she] could love him better."[34]

Lincoln, a lifelong politician, knew that every political candidate lost races. The trick, as he saw it, was to survive a loss, learn from it, and win the next time. That was how he looked at his own career, which was sprinkled with losses. Mary, however, could not bear defeat. She would stay angry for months, unable accept the loss and bearing grudges against whoever had defeated her husband. She stopped speaking to Mrs. Lyman Trumbull, a close friend for years, after her husband defeated Abe in a race for the U.S. Senate. Lincoln, who never took Mary's view, remained close friends with Trumbull and his wife. Whenever he wrote them, he always invented a line at the end to the effect that Mary sent her best regards to Mrs. Trumbull.[35] Mary was also insanely jealous of any woman Lincoln spoke to at a party, at his office, or on the street, and howled at him that these women were trying to steal him away from her.

Despite their fights, Edward's early death, and Tad's troubles, the Lincolns thrived and prospered in Springfield. Like all married couples, they fought and made up, forgave and forgot, and tried their best to compromise in order to continue a marriage they wanted. They put up with their children and often were exceedingly lenient with them in order to let them have the fun they seemed to yearn for and could not find. Abe worked harder than ever as a lawyer, traveling the circuit often. In the 1850s, the Lincolns expanded their home on several occasions to nearly double its original size.

Lincoln left the state legislature after his fourth term, in 1842, and was elected to Congress in 1846. His single term was unimpressive. He spent some of it stumping for Zachary Taylor in the presidential campaign of 1848, traveling to New England to round up votes for Taylor and to make an impression there for himself, where no one had heard of him. Much of the time he was lonely and missed Mary and the children. He returned to Springfield after living in a single room in the capital and, at times, brought them to Washington.

Lincoln attracted attention only on two issues. He became an antiwar congressman opposed to the Mexican War of 1846. The war was quite popular with Congress and the people, and few opposed it. The war's supporters, and they were vocal, were stunned that anyone, especially a veteran of the Black Hawk War like Lincoln, would oppose the war against Mexico, which ultimately gained vast territories for the United States.

Lincoln charged that only Congress had the right to declare and wage war and that President James Polk had started the war by himself and, in doing so, had made himself a king in a country that had staged a revolution to break away from the powers of a king.[36] In his criticism of Polk, Lincoln said, "Allow the President to invade a neighboring nation whenever he shall deem it necessary to repel an invasion and you allow him to do so whenever he may choose to say he deems it necessary for such purpose, and you allow him to make war at pleasure...."[37]

He argued that the war started because the army was where it was not supposed to be. "It is a fact that the U.S. army in marching to the Rio Grande marched into a peaceful Mexican settlement and frightened the inhabitants away from their homes," he said.[38] He predicted that the land gained from the war would become a battleground between slavers and abolitionists, "leading to a new war."[39]

The only other issue he worked on was slavery. He had opposed slavery bitterly all of his life. "Slavery is founded on both injustice and bad policy," he said in 1837.[40] Knowing that in the cold winter of 1847–48 the nation was not ready for the emancipation of all the slaves, however, Lincoln cautiously took a half step by drafting a bill to ban slavery in Washington, D.C. He and many other congressmen were sickened by the open-air slave markets they passed on their way to and from the Capitol. Lincoln's bill was simple: The slaves should be freed and their owners compensated by the government for their value so that owners did not suffer. The bill gained some support, but it was opposed by many Southerners because it seemed like a first step toward the total abolition of slavery and by Northerners because paying slaveholders gave the entire institution legitimacy. Lincoln never introduced the bill, explaining, "I dropped the matter knowing it was useless to prosecute the business at that time."[41] The slavery-hating Lincoln also voted for the Wilmot Proviso, which sought to prohibit slavery in any territories acquired from Mexico after the war, on five separate occasions.

Ever the politician, Lincoln used his congressional office to keep up with Whig Party matters back home[42] and to dispense patronage to office seekers in Illinois,[43] who now besieged him with requests for federal as well as state jobs.[44] Lincoln, a firm believer in the patronage system, did what he could to find employment for those who contacted him. They were a varied group. One man promised eternal political support in return for any position.[45] Another did not need a job, but had a son who was living in Oregon, so he asked Lincoln to land him a job.[46] Abe Lincoln tried to help them all. His loyalty to the patronage system was so complete that he lobbied the Illinois secretary of state to get a job for one man whose name he forgot.[47]

Lincoln served only one term and then returned to private life. The Whigs in his state rotated their congressmen. He was out of Congress and, with the Whigs the minority party in Illinois, had no prospects for a run for the U.S. Senate. He had no interest in lowering himself from the level of Congress and returning to the state legislature. His complaints about slavery fell on deaf ears as politicians in Washington worked hard to hammer out what would become the Compromise of 1850, aimed at deflating the slavery issue by allowing slavery in some areas and prohibiting it in others. Abraham Lincoln was a politician without an issue and a man without an office. At the age of thirty-nine, he had retired from public life, with no prospects for a political future.

PART II

RISE TO POWER

3

JEFFERSON DAVIS: WAR HERO AND RISING POLITICAL STAR

JEFFERSON DAVIS'S ARRIVAL in Washington in the winter of 1847 as a U.S. senator seemed like a coronation. The famous war hero, at thirty-six, was recognized wherever he went on his return to the nation's capital, and was greeted warmly by everyone, even those who had not known him during the few months he was in the House of Representatives before giving up his seat and enlisting in the army. There were warm embraces for the hero of Monterrey and Buena Vista from Northern as well as Southern senators. Jeff Davis was the first genuine war hero in the Senate in its fifty-eight years, a hero to the people of Washington, Mississippi, and the country.

Just a single month in Mexico allowed Davis to leap from the House to the Senate. His rise to prominence occurred as one generation of leaders died or retired—Henry Clay, John C. Calhoun, John Q. Adams, Daniel Webster, Thomas Hart Benton—and a younger one, led by men such as Davis (39), Stephen Douglas (35), Andrew Johnson (39), Alexander Stephens (35), Salmon Chase (39), and William Seward (46). Davis began to give important speeches to the Senate and to make a name for himself as a force on the Washington scene. Everyone sensed he had a real future in politics.

His glorious return was cause for discussion everywhere, even though he was soon crippled by one of his worst bouts of neuralgia.[1] Jeff Davis found the Senate very comfortable. A more prestigious body than the House, it seemed to offer him a chance to show what he could do legislatively and to become a leader in a much smaller group. He waded into Senate work with great enthusiasm, spending hours at his office and even more hours in his hotel, attending to paperwork until midnight and sometimes beyond. He made friends with a number of Southern senators, wrote letters, took care of constituents' complaints, and met with dozens of middle- and lower-level officials in various federal departments. He spent many evenings on the Washington social circuit, without Varina, who, still squabbling with her husband, remained home with her family in Mississippi. He impressed people wherever he went as a well-read, well-educated, and highly capable man, although rigid in his views and a bit hotheaded.

Early in 1848, Davis outlined his position on the slavery issue, just starting to simmer that presidential election year. His position was that slavery was appropriate anywhere south of 36° 30', the line established in the Missouri Compromise to divide slave and free states. That split the West in two, with most of the land won in the Mexican War falling below that line. His commitment was further deepened the following year, when he signed the "Southern Address," a stern and strident proclamation written by John C. Calhoun, which called for all Southern senators and congressmen to band together, regardless of party, to work together to ward off any attack on the slave system by Northerners. Those men were convinced, like so many other Southern slaveholders, that there was nothing wrong with slavery and that their "freedom" as Americans was the freedom to own slaves if they chose, just as it was Northerners' freedom not to own slaves. Any problems with slavery, they were convinced, were not problems with the idea of slavery, but problems with an individual owner who mistreated slaves. There was nothing wrong with the system. It had been in place for two hundred years and they wanted to keep it.[2]

Davis declared: "It is enough for me to know...that it was established by decree of Almighty God, that it is sanctioned in the Bible, in both testaments...that it has existed in all ages; has been found among the people of the highest civilization, and in nations of the highest proficiency in the arts."[3]

Later that year, Davis, in yet another effort to convince people that slavery could flourish anywhere, and not just in cotton and tobacco fields, talked of colonizing part of the territories won from Mexico with a cadre of a hundred

Mississippi planters and several hundred of their slaves, who would begin vast copper- and silver-mining operations. He later said the same thing about the feasibility of bringing slaves to work in the gold fields of California, where he suggested their adaptability to hot weather would increase profits. He wrote that "the production of rice, sugar and cotton is no better adapted to slave labor than the digging, washing and quarrying of the gold mines."[4] Their success, he said, would show all Americans that slave labor could succeed anywhere, in any industry, and that Southerners could successfully colonize a new territory for the country. He promised that the planters who would become miners, and their slaves, would make a fine fighting force and ward off any attack by either the Mexican army or the Apaches.[5] In 1850 he strongly advocated a conference of Southern states that would declare for secession if Northern abuses continued, a conference which would show the North that the South meant business. Two meetings were initially held in Nashville, but the delegates did little more than reaffirm their faith in the Missouri Compromise.

Davis gained much support in public from other Southern senators and in private from many citizens. He even had the support of his former father-in-law, Zachary Taylor, now president, who wrote to him in 1847 that the South needed to consider secession and should have "arms in their hands" if it ever happened.[6]

The slave issue festered, from Maine to Mississippi to California. By the time the controversial Compromise of 1850 was proposed, Davis had become one of the most vocal public officials in the South in his opposition to any efforts to curb slavery. He was one of the influential Southerners who saw antislavery laws as not merely assaults on the Southern labor system but as an effort by the North to demonstrate supremacy over Southerners on all political matters.

He declared, "Can anyone believe, does anyone hope, that the southern states in this Confederacy will continue…to support the Union, to bear its burdens, in peace and in war, in a degree disproportioned to their numbers, if that very government is to be arrayed in hostility against an institution so interwoven with its interests, its domestic peace and all its social relations?"[7]

There were many components to the Compromise of 1850: abolition of the slave trade in the District of Columbia, statehood for California as a free state; a set boundary between Texas and New Mexico; the admission of New Mexico and Utah as territories, with slavery there unresolved; and a fugitive slave law to force Northerners to return runaway slaves.

Davis immediately became a leader of the opposition to the Compromise, telling senators that for him the only issue was slavery. He did not want any free territories below the free-slave line established by the Missouri Compromise of 1820, would not vote in California as a free state, and did not want the borders of Texas, a slave state, shrunk by New Mexico, which might now be a free territory. A radical on slavery, Davis even startled others by opposing the Fugitive Slave Law, which, he said with great sarcasm, was useless because Northerners would never return runaway slaves, no matter how many laws were passed.

In the Compromise debates, Davis again and again tried to make the Southern position a national legal issue, charging that the Compromise would erode all Southern states' rights. "What do we have to gain by having a written Constitution if sectional pride or sectional hate [Northerners] can bend it, as passion, or interest, or caprice may dictate. What do we gain by having a government, based upon this written constitution, if, in truth, the rights of the minority are held in abeyance to the will of the majority?" Once again, he positioned the South as a victim of a callous Northern political cabal,[8] carefully framing the Southerners' argument of minority vs. majority within the same majority vs. minority arguments advanced so brilliantly by James Madison in the original debates over the U.S. Constitution.

He also spoke at length on the movement of Southerners and slaves into new territories, including any land won from the Mexican War and any territory west of the Mississippi River. The Compromise, he said, should include a clause that permits the transportation of any property into those territories and said that the Senate had to consider slaves as a man's property.[9]

Passage of the compromise would further tear asunder an already divided country. "A moral crevasse has occurred; fanaticism and ignorance—political rivalry, sectional hate, strife for sectional dominion—have accumulated into a mighty flood, and pour their turgid waters through the broken constitution," he said.[10]

Davis was emerging as a strident and influential proslavery voice at the exact same time that the leader of the Southern cause, the venerable John C. Calhoun, was dying. The mantle of Southern leadership which Calhoun wore with such élan for so many years was passing to the shoulders of Jefferson Davis, and the first-term senator pulled it tight. The Compromise of 1850 debates were making him the leader of the entire Southern rights–states' rights movement. Secessionists considered Davis a hero. "You are still my leader...and I look to your prudence and courage to mark out the course of our struggle," wrote South Carolina's Robert Barnwell.[11]

The debates over the Compromise of 1850 were heated. No one was more visibly upset by the series of bills than Jeff Davis. He could not understand why so many people wanted to eliminate slavery. What was so bad about the system? Wasn't his own personal slave, James Pemberton, a close friend? Didn't the slaves at Brierfield and Hurricane live under their own democratic system of rules? Didn't the Brierfield slaves welcome him with embraces when he visited them in the cotton fields?

He rose to speak fifty-four times, more than any other senator, and lobbied extensively off the floor of the Senate to kill the series of bills he found so repulsive and such a threat to the slave system. He blamed the abolitionists for the bills and harped in one speech: "I see nothing short of conquest on one side or submission on the other."

Davis became the staunchest of the South's senators on slavery during the debates. His speeches showed him a strong proslavery advocate who saw the slave system as necessary for the survival of the Southern states. The secession of some kind by any number of Southern states, though, was not treason, he argued, if the Northern states voided the promises of the Constitution. The Founding Fathers, he asserted, created a new country, separating from England, because of British abuses. Again and again, he carefully outlined the history of slavery within the framework of the history of the United States, reminding his listeners that in the 1700s many Northerners owned slaves, that Northern ships carried the slaves from Africa to the southern colonies, and that the leaders of the new nation, Washington and Jefferson, were slaveowners. Time after time, he pointed out, the federal government not only recognized the right of Southerners to keep slaves, but supported their efforts to retrieve runaway slaves, even when they fled to territories owned by foreign nations, such as Florida.[12]

The Constitution's vague definition of states' rights, and the right of states to determine what was property, Southerners believed, would enable the Southern states to secede if there were abuses of the slave system by Northerners. "They are the true friends of the union who resist by all means every invasion on the constitution and seek to strengthen every barrier which is found insufficient for the use to which it was appropriated. In the struggle for right against aggressive power, the South will not be alone if she meets the conflict as becomes her cause," he said in 1851, framing the legal and

philosophical argument which he and others would repeat until 1861.[13] He
further warned, ominously, that "if civil discord is to be thrown from this
chamber upon the land—if the fire is to be kindled here with which to burn
the temple of our Union—if this is to be made the center from which civil
war is to radiate, here let the conflict begin."[14]

Privately, he wrote friends that he fully believed secession was a possibility if
Northern political attacks continued and if Southern strength in Congress
eroded, as seemed likely after the Compromise of 1850. He told them that
feelings would become so emotional that nothing could hold them in check. In
the spring of 1851 he predicted: "The bitter waters [North-South arguments]
have spread far and wide and as the torrent rolls on, it will acquire volume and
velocity, from inexhaustible sources of supply. When it becomes palpable to
every man's sense, that from the free states we have nothing to expect but eternal
war upon the institution of slavery (and the coming of the time is certain as
death), I believe the southern people will awake and unite, not to preserve the
constitution, or the union, but to organize a government for themselves."[15]

Davis defended slavery with every argument he could find throughout the
1850s as the issue came to a boil, starting with the hundred-year-old mantra
that slavery was good for illiterate, childish Africans. He said, "It benefits
them, in removing them from the bigotry and the heathen darkness which
hangs like a cloud over the country in the interior of Africa to the enjoyment
of all the blessings of civilization and Christianity."

He argued in those years, and continued to do so through the Civil War,
that slave labor made the Southern economy work and that the South's exports
benefited not only the Northern states, but, through cotton and textiles, the
whole world.

He insisted that slaves were happy with their present state and offered
other arguments twisted to suit his needs (that slavery was started and
continued for the benefit of Northern businessmen, who he said began the
slave trade in the seventeenth century) and some which were completely
ludicrous, such as his contention that the more slaves a planter owned, the
better off the slaves were. A master who had many slaves could treat them
well, offer medical assistance and good housing and food, "but a man who
only owned a few had no vested interest in their well being and was not
prosperous enough to care for them."[16]

He rooted his defense of slavery, and the South's need to defend it, in four
basic claims: (1) Northerners had no business telling Southerners what to do

with their property, and slaves were property; (2) all Northern agitation over slavery was just a smokescreen for the crippling of the South economically so that the North could grind it down under its political heel; (3) freed slaves would overrun the country, taking jobs from whites, rob stores, and marry white women; (4) slaves were too simple and childish to emancipate and could not survive on their own.

By 1851, Davis had added still another argument. He began to see the slavery question not merely as a political issue in itself but one by which Northern states could take away the rights of Southern states. Davis, not known for long speeches when on the stump, delivered a two-hour-long, well-reasoned, highly organized speech in Fayette, Mississippi, in July 1851, in which he very carefully arranged his new argument. Davis charged that the Northern states were not merely outlawing slavery—they were outlawing any rights Southerners had to any political positions which the North opposed. He said it opened the door for the growing Northern domination of the country, which would enable the North to demand not only curbs on Southerners' right to take slaves west but their rights to own them at all.[17] The summer of 1851 was also a summer in which Davis began to refer liberally to Northern politicians or Northern states as "our Northern aggressors," which he had not done before.[18]

Jeff Davis did not view slavery within any moral or religious terms, which allowed him to see it merely as an issue of labor and economics, making it impossible for him to understand the intense feelings many Northerners had against it. He almost never quoted the Bible, except when he wanted to use passages from it about slave ownership, and never attended churches of any kind. He declared himself an Episcopalian at West Point, probably because his favorite professor was also an Episcopalian minister; he was a nominal Christian all of his life, but Christianity did not breed within him a sense of religious morality concerning his fellow man.[19] For Jefferson Davis, there were bonds between white men because of color, but no bonds between whites and blacks. He never grasped the moral idea that all men, regardless of color, were equal, and often dismissed the notion that they were as "a moral blot" on the United States.[20]

Northerners, he insisted, who began the Atantic slave trade, were against slavery because it was no longer as profitable in the North as it was in the South. If it were profitable in the Northern states, there would be slavery in Massachusetts, Ohio, and even Illinois. He repeatedly told audiences that slavery existed in all thirteen colonies on the eve of the Revolution but that circumstances, not morality, had eliminated it later in most Northern states. "Subsequently, for climatic, industrial and economical—not moral or sentimental—reasons, it was abolished in the northern, while it continued to exist in the southern states."[21]

He charged that Northerners were duplicitous and greedy. "Those states which now insist upon restricting slavery were the same that extended the period to which slaves were introduced into the United States.... Those who grew rich in the traffic [in the North] have been ever since making public demonstration of their horror of the crime...."[22] That great difference about the morality of slavery was the foundation of the views on the slavery issue of both North and South, two diametrically opposed beliefs which would never change until Appomattox.

In the South Davis did not have to resort to philosophy to defend slavery. All he had to do is what politicians and planters had been doing for generations: Convince all the whites, even those who owned no slaves, that slavery was good for them. He did that in his speeches and correspondence. He went on the stump in the summer and fall of 1850, using endorsements of different Democratic candidates as an excuse, to promote his views on slavery. In city halls and on courthouse lawns he preached the same religion about slavery that had long held Southerners together: white people had to stick together to keep slavery intact or the state would be overrun with freed blacks who would ruin the economy, sexually assault white women, and annihilate all political systems. Freed blacks were equal blacks, Davis told his audiences, and that scare about the destruction of racial superiority always worked. It was such a quick and handy emotional framing of the issue that Davis used it again and again throughout the 1850s, and it anchored his famous speech in front of the Mississippi legislature that year.

"You too know that among us white men have an equality resulting from a presence of the lower caste, which can not exist where white men fill the position here occupied by the servile race. The mechanic who comes among us, employing the less intellectual labor of the African, takes the position which only a master workman occupies where all the mechanics are white, and therefore it is that our mechanics hold their positions of absolute equality among us," he told the legislators, adding that slavery was needed not just for the economy but also for the preservation of the white race itself. It was a powerful sermon, and it worked.[23]

The ties between the rich planters and poor white farmers of Mississippi and other Southern states did not make sense on either an economic or political level. The planters were far richer than the poor farmers due to their slaves, and because they were rich, they were influential, controlling the state and local political machines. They were rich because of their slaves. Less than twenty-five percent of the white men in the Southern states owned slaves, but those who did dominated politics. The other seventy-five percent, who lived modestly or in poverty, should have resented that, but they did not.

There were peculiar, but strong, racial and cultural bonds between the two classes. These ties stretched back to the 1720s, when the poor white farmers would do whatever the rich white, slaveowning planters suggested, because they saw the rich planters as educated, successful, influential men who therefore knew what was right. The poor farmers also felt that if they could attach themselves to the rich planters, they could elevate themselves. They, too, believed in white domination.[24] Rich and poor whites, despite their differences, were the same color and could only maintain the world they enjoyed by holding down people of a different color. Money, influence, and station in life did not make them equal, but color did. White supremacy, then, made them "equal" and bound them together.[25]

In the end, Davis said, the sectional differences over slavery might only be resolved by conflict. "We should part peaceably, and avoid staining the battle-fields of the Revolution with the blood of civil war," he argued,[26] and told audiences that if Northerners wanted a fight, "I will meet force with force!"[27]

Davis repeated his defense of slavery, and threat to secede, in many speeches in Washington and back home in Mississippi, where banners with THE HERO OF BUENA VISTA emblazoned on them hung behind the speaker's platform.[28] By the mid-1850s, however, Jeff Davis, in his heart was really no secessionist. He did not truly believe the Southern states should secede from the Union, and he did not want them to secede. In 1853 he wrote former Indiana congressman William Brown that newspapers had distorted his feelings on secession. Davis reminded Brown that members of the Davis family had fought in the Revolution, the War of 1812, and various Indian wars and that he himself had fought in the Mexican War to save the United States, not to destroy it.[29] He was convinced, however, that constant sword-rattling over secession would force the Northerners to leave the Southerners alone. It was a daring game of bluff that Davis and many other Southerners played with the North, a game which would soon become dangerous.

The five acts that comprised the Compromise of 1850 passed, with many

Southern congressmen voting for them to buy themselves time. Jeff Davis, convinced he was right, as always, could not see that other Southerners wanted a safe compromise now in order to maintain the balance of power for a while longer. Unable to tolerate opposing views, defeated in the Senate, he looked for some way to vindicate himself. What the country needed, he believed, was a prominent public figure who would campaign against the Compromise in a major, highly visible, well-covered effort and then win election in a landslide to prove that the Compromise of 1850 was wrong. Davis, with three years of his Senate term remaining, was in no electoral jeopardy in 1851, but he felt so strongly about slavery and detested the Compromise so much that when asked to run for governor of Mississippi on an anti-Compromise platform in 1851, he jumped at the chance and resigned his Senate seat. He was certain that he was right in opposing the Compromise of 1850, and certain of his personal popularity as well. He may also have been eager to run because his opponent was his archenemy, Henry Foote. If Davis won, he would be able to add the governorship to his growing list of titles and at the same time send a message on slavery to Northerners and any wavering Southerners.

Davis replaced another Democratic nominee and ran a spirited contest. Foote, originally a slavery stalwart, now supported the Compromise. Davis viewed the offer to run for governor as just another in the long line of invitations extended to him throughout his career, invitations he never had to pursue, and at first thought he would merely remain at Brierfield until elected. "Being assured that I was not expected to take any active part, and that the party asked only the use of my name, I consented to be announced," he said haughtily.[30] He soon realized, however, that he was in a close race, and he campaigned hard.

Despite making numerous speeches during the seven-week campaign and expending a considerable sum of money on it, and despite twisting as many arms for support as he could, Davis lost by just over 1,000 votes. Once again, as always happened when he campaigned outdoors, he became very ill. His campaigning was cut short by another eye inflammation, which forced him to stay at home for weeks. His doctor had him bathe his bad eye with chloroform sponges and take doses of quinine and opium, plus several teaspoons of castor oil each day. The medicine did little good. Davis tried to continue the campaign, wearing dark green goggles and a bandage over his eye, but it did not work.[31] (Davis never tried to conceal his eye problems and often discussed them with friends in letters and at public meetings, where his eye inflammations engendered much sympathy.) By the fall of 1851 the problem had become severe, and he admitted that for periods of time he was blind in his left eye.[32] Mississippi loved Jeff Davis, but in the autumn of 1851 they loved harmony even more. Mississippians were so eager for peace and unity with the North, despite their differences, that they cast aside their favorite war hero.

Sick, defeated, and out of the Senate, his marriage still rocky, Davis returned to Brierfield. Sunlight irritated his eye so much that for many weeks he slept all day and stayed up all night, pacing the floor and reading by a single candle while his wife and the others were asleep. He was still sick in early 1852, once again losing all sight in his left eye, as well as much weight. He resumed his strange hours, sleeping all day, pacing the floors, reading by candlelight in his shadowy world at night. Friends who saw him at the 1852 Democratic state convention thought he was about to die.[33] He was believed to be so near death that former army officer Franklin Pierce wrote him a relieved letter when he heard that Davis had, in fact, survived. (Davis's war hero status was still strong enough that Pierce mistakenly referred to him as General Davis.)[34]

Davis recovered, as he always did, and regained his health. Varina became closer to him than ever, washing his diseased eye and tending to him as she always had. At Brierfield, he and Varina came to an understanding about their marriage. Varina vowed to be less independent, and Davis apparently agreed to spend more time at home and treat her as a wife rather than as a daughter. The compromises they made at this time lasted throughout their lives. Although Varina would never have the independence she yearned for; like so many women in the South at that time, she carefully made herself her husband's political adviser, confidant, and close friend. The love between Jeff and Varina grew again as they planned and built a home at Brierfield, a handsome, sprawling one-and-a-half-story house with lots of open, airy rooms and a kitchen, surrounded by wide verandas. The slave quarters, consisting of two separate rows of slave cabins housing nearly one hundred people, was close by. Varina was happy, and the couple soon learned they would become parents.

The strength of their marriage consisted of a genuine liking for each other, a loving and robust family, anchored by children they adored, and a marriage cemented by politics as much as romance. Varina read political newspapers every day of her life, devoured books, and talked politics wherever she went. She became a very successful Washington hostess, a favorite with senators and congressmen because she knew so much about government and the politics that went into it.

Mrs. Roger Pryor, a capital socialite, said Varina was "one of the most cultivated women of her time...greatly sought by cultivated men and women."[35] She fully understood all her husband's problems. That made Varina an integral, and invaluable, part of Jefferson Davis's life, and he knew it. Later, when he really needed a loving consort and treasured friend, he never had to look further than the other side of the breakfast table.

The Davises also managed, despite his illnesses, absences, and the uncertain world of politics and government, to retain a giddy puppy love for each other. Jefferson lovingly referred to her as Waafe (for loving wife) and Winnie. She called him Banny. Their letters to each other exuded the romantic feelings of teenagers.

In 1849, worried about his health, Varina, twenty-four, wrote her forty-one-year-old husband every day, sometimes twice a day, telling him that "much as I have loved and valued you, it seems to me I never knew the vastness of my treasure until now. If you have no fear for yourself, have it for your Winnie, your thoughtless, dependent wife....Sweetest, best husband, don't go out at night, don't drink wine, don't eat any fruit....You were never selfish, so then be yourself now and think of your wife."[36]

In another letter sent that same day, she exclaimed: "My own bright love, farewell. Kiss wife and say goodnight. Winnie is her husband's baby and baby is your devoted wife."[37]

Her attitude and tone never changed. A decade later she was sending him the same romantic letters, often bringing up fond memories of their first years together. "I have experienced that queer annihilation of responsibility and of time and gone back fourteen years to the anxious, loving girl, so little of use, yet so devoted to you," she wrote.[38]

Jeff's letters to her had a similar romantic tone. If she was in the least danger, he was apprehensive for her safety. Once, after she had been ill, he wrote her father that "my anxiety for Varina was uncontrollable."[39]

Varina's letters to Jeff always reminded him how much she and the children loved him. "Little Jeff is constant to a degree I have never seen in a little dear baby before. He shouts fifty times a day, 'I love my daddy!'...He and Maggie ran away the other day and were discovered across the street taking a stroll, hand in hand, 'like the babes in the woods,' Maggie said....Jeff is burnt quite red, his cheeks look so red they would do honor to a winter apple...." she wrote him in 1859, signing her letter "love, Waafe."[40]

Davis did not remain on his plantation long. In 1852 president-elect

Franklin Pierce asked him to return to Washington to be his secretary of war. Davis's supporters in Mississippi—and throughout the nation, North and South—were thrilled with the selection. Who better to run the War Department than the hero of two wars? Davis was eager to return to Washington to join Pierce's cabinet, but his arrival was considerably dampened by tragedy. His boy Sam, who had just celebrated his second birthday, fell ill with a bad case of measles and, despite constant doctor's care, died in their Washington home. He was two years old. Davis and his wife were inconsolable. Little Sam, whom Davis proudly referred to as "Le Man," had a close relationship with his father. Varina proudly told friends that she always knew when her husband would be home because little Sam would begin to sit next to the front door waiting for him exactly fifteen minutes before he returned. One of the grief-stricken mourners was President Pierce, whose own young boy had recently been killed in a train wreck.

Jefferson Davis was an outstanding secretary of war. The former second lieutenant, put in charge of the store, relished his work. He authorized new model rifles for soldiers, approved the use of the new Minié ball for ammunition, made the army larger in size while streamlining its burdensome organization, won pay raises for officers and enlisted men, supported new infantry tactics, and founded the army medical corps. He failed in his efforts to make promotions strictly by merit and not by seniority, but succeeded in working with Robert E. Lee, the commandant of West Point, to improve education and training there. He even tried to expand the program of study from four to five years in order to turn out better educated graduates and better soldiers. In an exotic move, he conducted an experiment in which U.S. soldiers used camels, instead of horses, in desert maneuvers.

Davis was a visionary who used military resources in expanded fashion. He became directly involved, via the army corps of engineers, in the construction of two new wings of the Capitol. He urged the Gadsden Purchase to acquire additional land along the northern edge of Mexico, in order to develop railroad lines from Southern states through the newly acquired territories to California. He also ordered army personnel to map out that entire area of the country for the military (Later, the maps would serve the developers of the railroads).

Southerners applauded and Northerners grumbled about War Department favoritism towards Mississippi and other Southern states. The army supervised improvements along the lower Mississippi River, where it bordered Davis's home state. The proposed Southern Pacific Railroad would aid Southern planters. Many of the army forts Secretary Davis used as large weapons arsenals were in the South. The secretary of war paid no attention to his critics, arguing, with Pierce's support, that what was good for the South was good for the nation. The United States was in the early stages of the industrial revolution, and water routes and railroads would be needed to transport the billions of dollars worth of goods already in production in factories, north and south, east and west.

Privately, away from the public eye, Davis was still unable to restrain either his temper or his penchant for denigrating anyone who disagreed with him. He feuded with many generals and wrote caustic, scathing letters denouncing them. In a disagreement over expenses with General Winfield Scott, the hero of the Mexican War, Davis called Scott a liar and said the general was trying to undermine Davis. "Nor am I to be deterred from a full exposure of the groundlessness of your charges by the threats you make of rendering my part in this correspondence a memorable example to be shunned by my successors. This is the merest bravado in one who himself affords the most memorable example on the records of this department of a vain controversialist, defeated, and a false accuser exposed."[41]

His days as secretary of war reaffirmed the belief of all Southerners unaware of his private outbursts, from the heights of the U.S. Senate to the levees along the Mississippi River and the cotton warehouses of Savannah, that Jefferson Davis was a military genius. He had been a hero of two wars and a member of the Senate military affairs committee and was now secretary of war. He knew more about the army than any other American. The people forgot that Jefferson Davis was in charge of a War Department without a war.

THE 1854 Kansas-Nebraska Act, which gave citizens in the two new territories the right to decide whether the two areas should be free or slave, divided the country in half. This was the first rolling stone of a political landslide—the Supreme Court's Dred Scott decision, warfare in Kansas, John Brown's raid on Harper's Ferry—that brought about the Civil War. The Kansas-Nebraska debate set Northern Democrats against Southern Democrats, caused the creation of the Republican Party, tripped up the presidential hopes of Stephen Douglas, and buried the Whig Party. It was also the bill that pulled Jeff Davis toward the presidency for the first time.

Southerners wanted to introduce the Kansas-Nebraska bill, but the

Missouri Compromise restrictions prohibited it. They lobbied to get President Pierce to rule in their favor, citing the new Compromise of 1850, but he had little interest. Needing someone who had Pierce's confidence, a group of senators led by Stephen Douglas persuaded Davis to get them an audience with the president. Davis, who shared their view, talked the president into meeting with them. After two hours Pierce went along with the legislation and did what they wanted, opening the door to the introduction of the Kansas-Nebraska bill by Douglas and the political fireworks which followed.

It was the first step in a long journey for Jefferson Davis. Now, after four long years of proslavery and Southern rights speeches, he started referring to himself to friends as "a pretty good secessionist."[42] Feeling useless in the sectional crisis in his War Department office and unable to speak publicly, he resigned at the end of Pierce's term and sought his old Senate seat.

Davis's efforts to win back his seat reflected his weak intraparty political skills. He had spent considerable time working with senators, congressmen, cabinet members, and army generals as secretary of war but precious little with middle- and lower-level politicians back home in Mississippi, a necessity for any man seeking office in the Senate or House. Why should he have? After all, his first congressional nominations had been handed to him, and he had been elected to the Senate the first time, and then for a full term, by acclaim. He was a famous man, a war hero, and a rich planter. Why should he involve himself with politics on the local level, polling cotton overseers, making small talk with Vicksburg barbers, asking small-town mayors to support him, when there were White House parties to attend and national committees to address. He was no local hack compelled to spend much of his time working for the party, taking polls in the rain, attending small-town teas, and writing endless letters offering and seeking support from the little people, whom Jefferson Davis never needed.

There is little indication that he thought he needed grassroots local support, but much evidence to suggest that he hated the kind of campaigning that local politics required. Most public speaking and political rallies took place outdoors then, and campaigning, involving exposure to the weather and sunlight and the attendant stress, continued to cause Jeff Davis's herpes-based neuralgia to flare up, indeed nearly blind him. His wife probably thought extended politics might even kill him. Davis was a politician who hated politics.

Davis's disdain for local politics became a huge problem for him when he became president of the Confederacy, but in 1857 it was already troublesome. He had few real allies in Mississippi. He should have known this and spent more time working on party matters. The state legislature elected U.S. senators then, and Davis ignored the very men who would vote for or against him. He won election, but by a single vote, a surprising embarrassment for a national figure.

On his return to the Senate, Davis resumed where he had left off six years earlier, in 1851. He quickly resumed leadership of the Southern cause and, as always, impressed people with his logical and philosophical, if not emotional, speeches and his ability to persuade others to support his bills because, in a competitive two-party Senate, he had to. He worked hard with President Buchanan to get Congress to support a proslavery constitution for Kansas, but his health continued to fail. He had campaigned for others after his own Senate nomination, but had had to quit and go home when his eye ailment flared up again. Later, after a cold spell in Washington, Davis became so ill that once again it was feared he was going to die. He was now nearly blind in his left eye, frail and sickly. Davis soon lost all power of speech. He was in the dark and without his voice for nearly a month.[43] He insisted on going to the Senate for votes on the Kansas issues on his return to Washington but was so ill he had to be carried into the Senate chamber. He came back the next day, leaning on his doctor for support. He looked awful. One man said Davis, forty-six, was a "pale, ghastly looking person, his eye bandaged with strips of white linen, his whole aspect denoting feebleness."[44]

Jeff Davis never tried to hide his illness, as politicians tend to, and talked about it to anyone who visited him or mentioned it. When he was ill, he was often visited by Senator William Seward of New York, the fiery abolitionist, whom he loathed politically but liked personally. No one cared as much for him, or hoped he would find some kind of a cure for his eye problems, as Seward. In 1858, just months before critical congressional and senatorial elections, Senator Davis described in grisly detail just how sick he was in a letter to former President Franklin Pierce: "[I am] suffering under a painful illness which has closely confined me for more than seven weeks and leaves me at this time quite unable to read or write."[45]

Davis, ill or not, became even more belligerent as the 1850s progressed. He constantly argued with senators, Democrats or Republicans. He was involved in at least four different disputes which nearly resulted in duels. His brother-in-law got into a duel and shot a man twice, an ungentlemanly act which reflected very badly on Senator Davis. Davis, apologetic for his own near duels, later told his wife that his debilitating illness sometimes caused him to lose control of his passions and his temper. She and others knew that he was hotheaded even when his eye was not bothering him, and they worried that he would kill someone or be killed himself. Jeff Davis could not control his temper in a heated arena, the U.S. Senate, where control meant everything.

What he needed, Jeff Davis thought, and his family agreed, was a long vacation. So, in the summer of 1858, Davis and his family, which now included two sons, traveled to Maine. On the way home, Davis agreed to speak at a number of New England towns, including Boston, where he lectured at historic Fanueil Hall. He must have been amused at his reception in New England. The people there were not as harsh as their senators, he told friends, and his speeches about conciliation between North and South, even though he endorsed slavery in all of them, were applauded by large throngs and by New England newspapers.

The New Englanders who heard him speak, even the abolitionists, were as astonished at his appearance as he was at their response. To the surprise of many, Jefferson Davis did not have two heads, did not walk with Satan, and did not emit five-foot long spears of fire from his mouth when he spoke. He was traveling with his wife, whom everyone found pleasant, and his children, whom New Englanders found adorable, and he seemed to smile a lot.

Davis was invited to several militia encampments, where soldiers welcomed the chance to shake hands with one of the country's greatest war heroes. They cheered his praise of them and all the Americans who fought in the nation's wars.[46] In several speeches he suggested that the situation of the South was comparable to the colonies during the revolution. "We...are in a minority; and if legislation is to be directed by geographical tests, if the constitution is to be trampled in the dust, and the unbridled will of the majority in Congress is to be supreme over the states, we should have the problem which was presented to our fathers when the colonies declined to be content with a mere representation in parliament."[47]

He suggested to Maine Democrats that they should look at Southern states as if they were Maine. Would they permit the federal government to tell Maine what to do? In frustration, he told audiences that all arguments over slaves in territories were moot because there would never be a need for slaves in most of them.

Everywhere he went, the states' rights champion preached conciliation. He was never better than in a brief speech at a state fair in Augusta, Maine, where he told audiences: "If shadows float over our disc and threaten an eclipse; if there be those who would not avert, but desire to precipitate catastrophe to the Union, these are not the sentiments of the American heart; they are rather the exceptions and should not disturb our confidence in that deep seated sentiment of nationality which aided our fathers when they entered into the compact of Union and which has preserved it to us."[48]

People were impressed with Jefferson Davis wherever he went. The wealthy planter mingled easily with poor rural farmers at the state fair just as easily as he did with the politicians who ran the state at private dinners (legislators in Mississippi sneered that he mingled graciously with everyone—unless they opposed his bills). His wife and children quickly became the first family of Maine. Some newspapers even suggested that Jeff Davis might quickly become a national figure if he continued to serve as such an agreeable bridge between the slaveowners and the abolitionists.

Senator Davis had clearly become the leader of the Southern cause by that summer through his tireless work for Southern state rights in the Senate, on the stump in New England, in columns in newspapers, correspondence, and general discussion. He had so cemented his position of leadership that Republican leaders began to refer to him as the states' rights champion. In an 1858 speech, one Republican quoted what Davis had said about slavery in his New England swing, his standard litany of slaves as property and portable anywhere, then turned it his way to tell audiences that since slaves were men and women, and not property, they could not be moved into the territories as property. He added that, therefore, "Jefferson Davis took the same view of the subject that I did."[49] The comment was made by former congressman Abraham Lincoln.

Many Mississippians were appalled by his moderate speeches in New England, however. Numerous Southern newspapers criticized Davis, charging that the secessionist had sold out to Northerners after a few outdoor barbecues. Davis, determined to regain his position as leader of the states' rights cause, thereupon delivered several tough proslavery speeches in Mississippi in which he hinted at secession more strongly than at any time in his life. Finally, in Jackson, Mississippi, he told a crowd that if the Republicans captured the Senate, House of Representatives, and White House in the 1860 election, Mississippi should leave the Union and prepare to defend herself. A few weeks later, to make certain everyone knew what he meant, he told another crowd that if a Republican were elected in 1860, he should not be permitted to take office "even if blood should flow," and that he, Davis, would rather "appeal to the God of Battles at once than attempt to live longer in such a Union."[50]

Forewarned that newspapers would oppose him, Davis lashed out at editors who charged him with selling out to Northerners. "Was it expected that to public and private manifestations of kindness by the people of Maine I should repel their generous approach with epithets of abuse?"[51]

Despite the arrival of a third son, Joseph, in 1859, Davis's personal problems grew. Brierfield and Hurricane were nearly ruined by torrential rains which flooded thousands of acres. Varina became ill, and Jeff had to rush to Washington to be at her side. Finally, in June 1859, Davis's eye was operated on. A surgeon cut a slender line in the cornea to relieve the buildup of fluid. The operation gave him temporary relief, but nothing more. His eye was permanently damaged, and he would suffer from it for the rest of his life.

Davis traveled to Mississippi in the summer of 1859 to recover from his operations. Back in his home state, he delivered one of his most rousing speeches, one that stunned observers allowed even had some passion in it. At the very end of his speech, perhaps calculatingly, perhaps not, Senator Davis again bellowed that if the Republicans won the White House the following year, the Union must be dissolved and the Southern states had to secede to form a new nation. "I love and venerate the Union of these states," he said. "But I love liberty and Mississippi more!"[52]

Was Jefferson Davis again posturing, as most Southern newspapers suggested, trying to get Northerners to leave the South and its slaves alone? Or did he really mean it? In the winter of 1860, he introduced a group of resolutions, the "Davis Resolutions," intended to stake out the hardline Southern states' position on slavery, to thwart all Northern attempts to curb slavery, and to serve as a forerunner of the Democratic Party's 1860 platform, a platform that he thought would become a major document. In speech after speech, Davis kept rattling the secession saber, threatening the North with the wholesale departure of the South. As always, however, he never actually took steps to lead Mississippi anywhere. He was, in reality, a sword-rattler whose blade was securely sheathed.

Davis did not want the Southern states to secede, but he hurled secession at the North as a man brandishes a torch to ward off a dangerous animal. He was not alone. Dozens of Southern senators and congressmen, and hundreds of newspaper editors, beat the secession drum. Davis and others beat it so loudly that they began to make people believe. Secession had become tinder in need only of a match.

The presidential election of 1860 was that match.

THE election was the culmination of four years of sectional battling and political maneuvering. Between 1856 and 1860 local war had broken out between the pro and antislavery forces in Kansas, where dozens of people were killed. The territory, quickly nicknamed Bleeding Kansas by the press, steeled itself for intrastate warfare just about every week through 1858, when its proslavery constitution was delayed by Congress, averting further strife. Kansas came to symbolize the future of the slavery question, unless that question was settled once and for all by whatever government was installed in 1861.

Later, in 1856, Southern congressman Preston Brooks, insulted by remarks concerning a plantation owner friend of his, used his cane to badly beat Senator Charles Sumner, of Massachusetts, an abolitionist, on the floor of the Senate. In 1857, the U.S. Supreme Court handed down its Dred Scott decision, which classified slaves as property, upheld the fugitive slave law, and gave slavers the right to retrieve slaves from territories as well as states. The election year of 1858 saw the so-called Black Republicans gain control of the House of Representatives and make plans for the capture of the Senate as well as the White House in 1860. John Brown's raid on the U.S. arsenal at Harper's Ferry in 1859 convinced Southerners that Brown was just the first of thousands of abolitionists headed their way with muskets and knives.

Brown's raid stunned Davis, as it did most Southerners. It was the armed attack they had dreaded for years. Davis was seething in his condemnation of it. "[It was] an invasion of a state by a murderous gang of abolitionists....the crime connects with all that is most [horrible] to humanity, the violation of every obligation to social compact, the law, the constitution, the requirement of public virtue and personal honor," he said.[53]

The Democrats were divided over their frontrunner in 1860, Stephen Douglas. He had been a solid Democrat all of his life, always tolerating the Southern Democrats' view on slavery, and had bolstered the Southern cause by introducing the proslavery Kansas-Nebraska Act in 1854, but in his 1858 Senate contest he had betrayed the South. Pressed hard by Abraham Lincoln, Stephen Douglas told the world that he expected the voters in Kansas and Nebraska to approve slavery there, but that it was fine with him if they voted to bar slavery from their territories. Southerners could not believe it. They saw Douglas as not only a man who had become an opponent of slavery, but an old friend who had betrayed the cause.

Senator Davis, who had no interest in the presidency, stayed home and watched in shock, like hundreds of thousands of Democrats, as the convention in Charleston collapsed, dozens of Southerners marching out to protest Douglas. The party failed to nominate anyone (Davis received fifty-seven votes). The Democrats, badly bruised, held a second convention a few weeks later in Baltimore, where even more delegates walked out, but Douglas was finally nominated.

Chaos followed. A third party, the Constitutional Unionists, made up of moderate Democrats who wanted to run a campaign without mentioning slavery as an issue, emerged in mid-May and nominated sixty-three-year old former House speaker John Bell as a middle-of-the-road candidate for president right after the debacle in Charleston. Then a fourth party, the Southern Democrats, was formed the week after Douglas won the splintered party nod at Baltimore, and chose Vice President John Breckinridge, of Kentucky, thirty-nine, as its nominee. Many Democrats, particularly Southerners, felt that at least one of them could stop the Republicans. Somehow, some way, Breckinridge, Bell, or Douglas would win enough Northern states to hold off the radical Republicans.

Jefferson Davis, however, realized that such an outcome was not possible. He was certain that the three Democrats would split the vote, opening the door for Abe Lincoln's victory. He knew, too, that the single worst thing that could happen to the South was Lincoln's election. Desperate to stop the Republicans from winning the White House, Davis, showing more political acumen than at any other time in his life, hosted a dinner party at his Washington home that was attended by Breckinridge and by friends of both Bell and Douglas during the last week of June. His proposal was unprecedented in American politics: scrap the Democratic convention, eliminate its nominee, forget the two new parties, and start anew with a different, acceptable compromise candidate who would appeal to voters North and South.

Davis had a popular, strong, compromise, moderate choice, too—former New York Governor Horatio Seymour. Everyone at the dinner party liked Seymour. He was a moderate, had publicly supported the right of Southerners to maintain slaves over the years, had numerous business interests in the

South, many friends in Southern businesses, and close ties to both Northern and Southern politicians. He could carry all the Southern states and win the moderate vote in many Northern states. Most importantly, he could carry New York easily. The Republicans had to take New York to win the election; they could not with Seymour as the nominee. Davis thought his plan was perfect. Seymour would be a one- or two-term caretaker president. His election would end the career of the upstart Lincoln. Finally, as he might have shrugged that night as dessert was being served, the time that would be gained might even give both sides a chance to come up with some kind of acceptable solution to the slavery issue.

Everyone at the table thought Davis's idea made perfect sense. Bell agreed to drop out of the race and so did Breckinridge, whose heart was never really in it. Davis was convinced that he could talk Douglas out of it, even though Davis had denounced the Little Giant to his face in a scathing speech in the Senate on May 17. Douglas was not at the dinner party, but Davis saw him either the next day or the day after that and outlined the proposal. Their meeting was abrupt. Davis's great compromise ended at the doorway of Stephen Douglas's office. Douglas, intent on becoming president, and still angry at Davis's strong words about him, refused to drop out, insisting that he could beat Lincoln. When they learned that Douglas would not drop out, Breckinridge and Bell told Davis they would continue their campaigns. Davis's noble idea, which might have worked just as he had planned, died stillborn.

A demoralized Davis had little to do with the national campaign of 1860. No one asked him for advice. He had stumped as an elector in 1844, but in the intervening sixteen years he had not ventured beyond the gate of Brierfield to canvass for national candidates. He did not have to campaign for any of them, or for state or local candidates, as most politicians did. In the fatal autumn of 1860, Jefferson Davis sat on the sidelines, along with millions of others, to wait and see what happened next. He wondered, as they did, what the next step would be. He had foretold what he saw as the Gothic horror that would descend upon the South if a radical Republican were elected president. He had told a hundred audiences in a hundred towns that a Republican victory would plunge America into its worst hour.

Now that hour was at hand.

4

ABE LINCOLN:
MASTER POLITICIAN

ABRAHAM LINCOLN WAS THE FINAL SPEAKER at the convention to organize Illinois's Republican Party on May 29, 1856. Nearly three hundred delegates were jammed into Major's Hall, in Bloomington, to hear him. After receiving a warm round of applause, Lincoln walked with his awkward gait across the stage to the small wooden podium. He had left the Whigs and his old life behind to embrace the Republicans. Lincoln had decided, conclusively, that slavery had to be stopped. In what friends said was his greatest speech, he exhorted the crowd to use the party to change America forever, telling the men that slavery and slavery alone was the nation's greatest problem and would remain so until it was stamped out.

He pounced on every argument the slaveowners used, telling cheering listeners that he would join anyone willing to fight slavery and that "the Union must be preserved in the purity of its principles as in the integrity of its territorial parts...."[1] Within minutes, he had gripped the crowd. His speech brought interruptions of loud applause every few moments. At times he had to stop because the cheering became so loud and lasted for so long. "[People] rose to their feet and stood on chairs and benches," said John Moses, who was there. "They were hushed and breathless, with tears filling the eyes."[2]

Lincoln continued to criticize slavery and, walking across the stage, bellowed that "as sure as God reigns and school children read, that black, foul lie can never be consecrated with God's hallowed truth!"[3] He ended by quoting Daniel Webster: "Liberty and Union, now and forever, one and inseparable."[4]

Much of what he said they had heard before. What surprised the radical Republicans gathered in the hall for the speech was the way in which Lincoln's speech was delivered. This was a new and different Abe Lincoln. The storytelling was gone, the jokes were missing, the self-deprecating humor had vanished. There was a fire in Lincoln that had not been there before, as there was a fire in the country that had not been there before. Abraham Lincoln had galvanized and mesmerized the crowd as no speaker had ever done before.

"His speech was full of...energy and force," said Billy Herndon, who stood and cheered with the others when Lincoln finished. "It was logic; it was pathos; it was enthusiasm; it was justice, equity, truth and right set ablaze by the divine fires of a soul maddened by the wrong, it was hard, heavy, knotty, gnarly, black with wrath."[5]

John Nicolay, a newspaper reporter present at the speech, and later Lincoln's personal secretary, never saw a crowd react with such enthusiasm. "Its effect lives vividly in the memory of all who heard it," he said.[6]

The Kansas-Nebraska Act, introduced by his personal friend and political nemesis Stephen Douglas, enraged Abraham Lincoln for nearly two years. It pulled him out of his law office to decry the latest effort of Southerners to extend slavery throughout the territories. It was a national issue which united all of the divergent antislavery politicians and brought them—Democrats, Whigs, Liberty men, and Free-Soilers—into the brand-new Republican Party. The country was seething. Lincoln's unimpressive term in Congress and his retirement from politics did not matter anymore. He no longer needed a set of issues to allow him to judiciously reenter the political arena. He got all of that and more from the battle over Kansas-Nebraska.

The legislation, which would have permitted residents of the two territories, equal in area to about one fifth of the existing United States, to make up their own minds on slavery, overturned the Missouri Compromise's prohibition of slavery in the territories and Compromise of 1850's restriction on slave states and territories.[7] It was the first epic struggle between North and South over slavery in the 1850s. It was accompanied by the Dred Scott decision; the publication of two bestselling antislavery books, *The Impending*

Crisis by Hinton Helper, a Southerner, and *Uncle Tom's Cabin* by Harriet Beecher Stowe; and the seizure of the federal arsenal at Harper's Ferry by abolitionist John Brown. Kansas-Nebraska also arrived at the same time that millions of Northerners, energized by the evangelical religious movements of the era, were channeling their passions into the antislavery movement.

The Republican Party, born in the flames of the uproar over Kansas-Nebraska, quickly replaced the dying Whig Party, torn in half when its Northern wing pulled away from its Southern wing on slavery, the Northern faction disintegrating when its members continued to squabble over the issue. Republicans won hundreds of local, county, state, and federal elections in 1854 and 1855 and put many new politicians into office. The new party opened the door for both political neophytes and discarded politicians such as Abraham Lincoln.

Lincoln, sure that the political tides had given him new life, did not actually join the Republicans for nearly eighteen months after its formation, in 1856, because he did not want to offend people in the anti-Catholic, anti-immigrant Know-Nothing Party, still strong in 1854 and 1855, risking their future support.[8] As always, he was extremely careful to gain the support of the widest possible majority and to avoid the opposition of any sizable minority.

Lincoln's reentry into politics would soon change the direction of his life. He was no longer a lone politician trying to win elections, but a man riding the back of a huge social, cultural, and political movement which promised to change the face of his country. His dynamic speech at Bloomington, which energized all the formerly divergent politicians in the hall who were now Republicans, made him one of the founders and leaders of the Illinois Republicans, a vibrant voice in the antislavery cause, and a man on the move again.

To ABRAHAM Lincoln, slavery was wrong, "a moral, social and political evil"[9] that was born of politics, subsisted in politics, and now had to die. "Do they really think the right ought to yield to the wrong? Are they afraid to stand by the right? Do they really think that by right surrendering to wrong, the hopes of our Constitution, our Union and our liberties can possibly be bettered?" he asked in 1856.[10]

Most public speakers and politicians of the era delivered long and complicated speeches at public rallies. It seemed better to be long-winded: to dazzle audiences with circuitous logic filled with attacks on opponents and spirited defenses of oneself. Most political speeches were hard to follow, and so inflated with bluster that audiences paid little attention to the orators.

Abe Lincoln was different. He was direct and simple, yet there was power and eloquence in his words and phrasing. He had a rare ability to see a problem and define it, not only for himself, but for thousands of people, in a powerful, yet easily understandable, way. This ability enabled Lincoln to see slavery the way most Northerners saw it, but to argue against it better than anyone else. He could also humanize it and make people see how wrong he thought it was by describing it in terms of ordinary humanity.

He believed slaves were human beings, not mere pieces of property, like stoves or cattle, and therefore could not legally be property, as Southerners had insisted for over one hundred years. Since slaves were people, Lincoln argued, they had to be seen as protected by the Declaration of Independence and Bill of Rights' guarantees of equality no less than whites. And they could not remain slaves. Once Lincoln developed that view, he never changed it.

He first attacked the Kansas-Nebraska Act in 1854, two years before he joined the Republicans. He returned to the political arena in the fall of 1854. On October 16, in Peoria, he sounded a ringing denouncement of slavery, framed guardedly within the Declaration of Independence, in attacking Stephen Douglas's neutral stand:

> I hate it because of the monstrous injustice of slavery itself. I hate it because it deprives our republican example of its just influence in the world—enables the enemies of free institutions, with plausibility, to taunt us as hypocrites—causes the real friends of freedom to doubt our sincerity, and especially because it forces so many really good men amongst ourselves into an open war with the very fundamental principles of civil liberty—criticising the Declaration of Independence, and insisting that there is no right principle of action but *self-interest*.[11]

Just a week before, he had impressed an audience in the Illinois House of Representatives with another stirring speech, in response to Douglas, in which he said slaves were humans and described the United States as a moral nation. He told his audience that the whole issue of slavery really came down to "whether a Negro is *not* or is a man," charging that Douglas did not see blacks as men, as Lincoln did. "No man," Lincoln then said, "is good enough to govern another man, *without that other's consent*. I say this is the leading principle—sheet anchor of Republicanism." He went on to shred slavery and his arguments resounded through the hall as he became more and more passionate, declaring, "There can be no moral right in connection with one man's making a slave of another."

Finally, by permitting the expansion of slavery, he told his enraptured audience, "We were proclaiming ourselves political hypocrites before the world...by thus fostering human slavery and proclaiming ourselves, at the same time, the sole friends of human freedom."[12]

He delivered several speeches against the Kansas-Nebraska Act, often in front of largely Republican audiences, even before he joined the party, both because he wanted to and because local political leaders asked him. Nobody was as powerful in front of an audience as Abe Lincoln.[13] Many political leaders congratulated him for his "victory" over Douglas in the Peoria exchange.[14] He replied to all that his feelings on slavery had never changed and that, as he moved toward his new party, "my opposition to slavery is as strong as that of any member of the Republican Party."[15] In an undelivered 1854 speech, he wrote sarcastically that "although volume after volume is written to prove slavery a very good thing, we never hear of the man who wishes to take the good of it, *by being a slave himself.*"[16]

One of Lincoln's most telling statements came in 1855, in a rare criticism of the ultraconservative, anti-Catholic and anti-immigrant Know-Nothing Party, explaining what would happen to everyone if slavery persisted. "Our ·progress in degeneracy appears to be pretty rapid," he declared. "As a nation, we began by declaring that *'all men are created equal.'* We now practically read it 'all men are created equal *except Negroes.*' When the Know Nothings get control, it will read 'all men are created equal, except Negroes, *and foreigners and Catholics.*' When it comes to this I should prefer emigrating to some country where they make no pretense of loving liberty—to Russia, for instance, where despotism can be taken pure, and without the base alloy of hypocrisy."

There was no doubt where he stood in the 1850s. In an 1859 speech in Chicago, Lincoln brought an audience to its feet when he concluded that: "I think slavery is wrong, morally and politically. I desire that it should be no further spread in these United States and I should not object if it should gradually terminate in the whole Union."[17]

Abe Lincoln was always careful, however, except at those times when his passions got the better of him, to remind audiences, whether at dinner in his home or at a huge outdoor rally, that while he hated slavery and wanted its expansion stopped, and fervently prayed for its ultimate extinction, he was content to let it thrive where it existed in Southern states for the time being, hopeful that it would simply die out and that the slaveowners' religion and conscience would speed the end. "They are accountable to God and their posterity, and not to us. It is for them to decide, therefore, the moral and religious right of the slavery questions for themselves...let each state mind its own business and let its neighbors alone and there will be no trouble on this question."[18]

Lincoln, ever the politician, and not merely the moral radical, had read all the speeches of Southern politicians warning white Southerners that freed slaves would steal their jobs and rape their women. Due to such fears among the white population, North as well as South, Lincoln could never advocate as his definite policy the immediate elimination of slavery. That would have been moral redemption but political suicide.

He was also careful to explain to his audiences that while he thought slavery was wrong, he did not think that there was much equality between blacks and whites, who constantly kept a distance from blacks, slave or free. Most white Northerners were opposed to slavery, but they were in no hurry to socialize with freed blacks or open the doors of their homes or schools to them. Lincoln needed the support of these people and always steered clear of overly close associations with slaves, as opposed to the abolitionists, whose dealings with blacks kept their numbers small and their political influence negligible. Abe Lincoln was a good politician, and knew where his votes were. He said in 1858:

> I will say...that I am not, nor ever have been, in favor of bringing about in any way the social and political equality of the white and black races—that I am not nor ever have been in favor of making voters or jurors of Negroes, nor of qualifying them to hold office, nor to intermarry with white people. There is a physical difference between the white and black race which I believe will forever forbid the two races living together on terms of social and political equality. And inasmuch as they cannot so live, while they do remain together there must be the position of superior and inferior, and I as much as any other man am in favor of having the superior position assigned to the white race.[19]

Later, in the Lincoln-Douglas debates, in 1858, sick of the arguments in defense of slavery, he managed to leap into the minds of his listeners, barking out at Stephen Douglas, and to any and all slave owners or those who supported them: "You say it must not be opposed in the free states, because slavery is not here; it must not be opposed in the slave states, because it is there; it must not be opposed in politics, because that will make a fuss; it must not be opposed in the pulpit, because it is not religion. Then where is the place to oppose it?"[20]

It was in the debates with Douglas, too, in town after town and on platform after platform, that Lincoln hammered home his feelings on blacks and white equality. "He [the Negro] is not my equal in many respects....But in the right to eat the bread, without the leave of anybody else, which his own hand earns, he is my equal, and the equal of Judge Douglas and every living man," he said.[21]

LINCOLN was glad to be back on the political stage. Ambition burned in him like an incandescent candle. It drove him to work harder, politick better and do everything he could to simultaneously fight slavery, build a better America, and advance his fortunes.[22]

From his home in Springfield, he helped to run the Republican Party, and the state committee, just as he helped run the Whig Party years before. He interviewed candidates for office, raised money for campaigns, conducted polls in different congressional districts, sent out letters, supervised the printing of broadsides and flyers, worked with Republican editors to produce the best pro-Republican newspapers. He even owned a newspaper himself for a year.

The respected and popular Lincoln was also given the tricky duties of settling feuds between rival politicians within the party and recruiting supporters from outside the party. He often played the role of Solomon, as in the spat between two men who argued over who should get the Republican nod for a state assembly seat. The man who lost the nomination initially agreed to back the winner, then changed his mind. He was a man of great influence who had to be praised and made to feel loved after a shattering defeat. Lincoln settled the argument.[23] On another occasion he had to untie a succession of knots in a feud between one of his best friends, Norman Judd, and one of his strongest political supporters, Chicago Mayor John Wentworth, both of whom wanted to run for governor. He needed Judd to help run his

campaigns and Wentworth for the critical support of Chicago and Cook
County. His solution was to find a credible third candidate whom neither man
disliked; he persuaded both to campaign for the new man.[24]

On a personal level, Lincoln felt the Republicans could put him back into
national politics, in Washington, where his antislavery feelings now matched
the fervor of large parts of the nation. It was yet another chance to redesign
himself, this time in the image of the new Republicans, just as he had done so,
in the image of the old Whigs, before. It was a golden opportunity to revive
his defunct political career, to become a political Lazarus.

Abe Lincoln had close ties not only to the people of Illinois, but to all
America in the course of his workday. From the moment he left his house and
encountered residents of Springfield on the way to his law office in the
morning, to the early hours of the evening, when he patched up local
differences at political meetings, to late at night, thanks to his voluminous
correspondence, he learned what newspaper editors, politicians, and plain
citizens all over his city, state, and country were thinking. Perhaps no
politician in American history, including contemporary leaders with access to
the Internet and daily polls, has kept his finger on the pulse of the nation as
well as Lincoln did.

His skill as a born orator, and his position of power in the party, gave him
the launching pad for another effort to win high office in 1855, when he
sought to become a U.S. senator from Illinois, an election determined by the
state legislature. He campaigned hard, supervising men around the state[25] who
lobbied on his behalf and assured him the seat was his.[26] He was eminently
qualified, would do a good job, and, after years of work, certainly deserved it.[27]
He lost. He and another candidate, Joel Matteson, received an almost equal
number of votes from the state legislators, while a third man, Lyman B.
Trumbull, got only a few. Lincoln could not get enough to win and in the end
had to support the man with minimal support in order to stop his opponent.
None of his friends were in a position to break the logjam and help him. He
stood by, helpless.

A lesser man would have quit politics or sought vengeance on the men
who had denied him the prize. Instead of fuming, Lincoln shrugged off the
defeat. He immediately supported the winner, Lyman B. Trumbull, in hopes
that everyone in the legislature and in the Republican Party, including
Trumbull himself, would remember that he accepted defeat gracefully,
continuing to back the party and its leaders.

Many of the men who had opposed him, voted against him, or helped to defeat him for some office or other would soon be approached by Lincoln as a friend and political ally who was willing to forget past differences. He was able to turn these men from enemies to friends by letting them get to know him. It was Lincoln's belief that any politician who understood him would support him.

The enemies who befriended Lincoln could fill a legislative chamber. One of the first was Norman Judd, a legislator who voted against Lincoln in his unsuccessful 1855 Senate bid but later became one of the three men who ran his campaign for president. Another was Leonard Swett, a lawyer who worked against him in several court cases yet later became one of his most trusted advisers. Still another was Trumbull, the man who won the 1855 Senate seat over Lincoln. Five years later, Trumbull would convince the splintered Illinois delegation to give Lincoln its unconditional and unanimous support before it went to the 1860 Republican convention, helping him win the presidential nomination.

The loss of the Senate seat in 1855 did not diminish Lincoln's ambition. The way he responded to defeat won him many friends, such as Julian Sturtevant, the president of Illinois College, who, impressed with his politics and his resiliency, urged him to run for Congress again.[28] Lincoln plunged back into party work, campaigning for local candidates in 1856 and 1857, writing hundreds of letters to win support for them, making even stronger bonds with newspaper editors. He gave more than fifty speeches for the Republican presidential nominee in 1856, John C. Frémont. He argued as forcefully as he could that voters should ignore the third-party candidacy of former president Millard Fillmore (the American Party's nominee) and give their votes to the new Republican Party.

Lincoln stumped for himself just as assiduously as he did for Frémont. He would deliver the party line on the major issues and then usually launch into his own beliefs. He spoke up for the rights of workers, particularly blue-collar workers, for high tariffs to protect American manufacturers, and for better working conditions in factories. He wrapped many of his speeches in support of workers into speeches about slavery, carefully tying the two together to let voters know that whites were just as important to him as slaves. "It is well known that I deplore the oppressed condition of the blacks; and it would, therefore, be very inconsistent for me to look with approval upon any measures that infringe upon the inalienable rights of white men...." he declared.[29]

In 1856 Lincoln thus was laying a wide and firm foundation for a future campaign of his own for national office: getting his face and name in front of the voters, endorsing local Republicans throughout Illinois, and even traveling to other states to stump for local men (and Frémont) there.

Lincoln reveled in lengthy, one to three hour speeches. Despite his reedy voice, after ten or fifteen minutes of spirited speaking his audience adjusted to their unusual orator with ease. Lincoln could be crusading and he could be bold. He gauged his tone of voice to run up and down the octaves of sound and emotion, creating a highly charged emotional environment that excited his crowds, which ranged from a few hundred at picnics to over twenty thousand at outdoor rallies.

He also enjoyed entertaining people. Abe Lincoln was, by 1858, when he was forty-nine years old, one of the country's best storytellers. His folksy humor, and complicated stories, all with a funny twist at the end, captivated his listeners. Homilies and sayings seemed to tumble out of his stovepipe hat or to leap from the large pockets of his frock coat: "You can fool some of the people all of the time and all of the people some of the time, but you can't fool all of the people all of the time," "Don't change horses in the middle of a stream," and "Cross a bridge when you come to it." His audiences grew and grew as his fame as a speaker spread. They came wide-eyed, mouths curved in smiles, expecting an evening of fire and brimstone, laughter and merriment, from the homely and enchanting man from Springfield.

Newspaper reporters who heard him were amazed at the public reaction to Lincoln. "We have never seen an audience held for so long a time in the open air to listen to an argumentative speech," wrote one journalist in 1856 after listening to Lincoln in Chicago's Dearborn Park.[30]

"He spoke in a clear and cool, and very eloquent manner for an hour and a half, carrying the audience with him in his able arguments and brilliant illustrations, interrupted by warm and frequent applause," wrote a reporter who heard him speak in New England in 1848.[31]

No COUNTY fair in Illinois had as much carnival atmosphere as the June 16, 1858, Republican convention, held in the statehouse in Springfield. The Republicans arrived from every village, city, and county throughout Illinois, determined to nominate Abe Lincoln for the U.S. Senate. At that time, state legislators elected U.S. senators, but the candidates ran against each other in a nonbinding fall election which was supposed to influence legislators. They had to do it with flourish and style, however, because Stephen Douglas, the state's leading Democrat and presidential hopeful, had become, over the past few years, one of the strongest politicians in the nation. Seared by criticism after his introduction of the Kansas-Nebraska Act, he later led the crusade to stop Kansas from adopting a proslavery constitution in 1858, and was hailed for it throughout the North. Douglas had become so popular by the summer of 1858 that Horace Greeley and other Republican newspaper editors were urging Illinois Republicans to support him. Lincoln and the Republicans knew that only a united front, and unanimous support for the Republican candidate, could defeat Douglas. Lincoln stirred up politicians throughout the state by writing private letters suggesting that the Democratic Party was weak and its leaders had "an abundance of trouble."[32]

Anyone who felt that way would have been thrilled by the convention. The first roar to shake the old statehouse came when the Cook County delegation arrived, some of its members carrying a large, colorful banner that read COOK COUNTY IS FOR ABRAHAM LINCOLN. A moment later, one of Lincoln's friends leaped to his feet and asked that the Chicagoans change their motto to: ILLINOIS IS FOR ABRAHAM LINCOLN. Wild cheering followed.[33] It was a day filled with enthusiastic speeches and intense politicking; the Republicans were determined to defeat Douglas. The all-day session ended in the evening, when the newly nominated Republican candidate for U.S. senator, Abe Lincoln, walked to the front of the crowd. He held his head up high, his back as straight as a barn board, his long legs giving him a very long stride. He wore his traditional frock coat and white shirt. His hair was unkempt, as always, and his large gray eyes twinkled a bit when he spotted a friend in the audience. He put his hands behind his back as always, looked about for a moment, and began to speak.

After a short preamble which suggested the slavery crisis created by the Kansas-Nebraska Act was more critical than ever, and that the efforts of many to end it during the last five years had failed, Lincoln plunged into his speech, a speech he thought so sensitive and so important that he had refused to show it to either friends or political colleagues while he was writing it. After a well-constructed opening, he jolted the convention:

"A house divided against itself cannot stand." he said, and continued:

> I believe this government cannot endure permanently half *slave* and half *free*....It will become *all* one thing or *all* the other. Either the *opponents* of slavery will arrest the further spread of it, and place it

where the public mind shall rest in the belief that it is in course of ultimate extinction; or its *advocates* will push it forward, till it shall become alike lawful in *all* the states, *old* as well as *new*—*North* as well as *South*.[34]

This speech, which thrilled abolitionists and radicals, alarmed the South and infuriated Lincoln's close advisers, who thought he had gone too far and might lose his moderate base.[35] Lincoln disregarded their complaints but, remembering their objections, did not deliver the "house divided" speech again during the campaign. He had delivered the speech because, even though it was a risk in the Illinois race of 1858, the attention it received would help him later.

The legendary speech began the Senate race against Douglas. The Little Giant was the favorite. Lincoln followed behind his campaign with his own, speaking where Douglas had spoken a day or a week earlier, lagging behind in public opinion, but was finally able to talk Douglas into meeting him in a series of debates. Douglas was considered the finest public speaker in the nation, the best debater in the Senate, a man who could easily defeat any opponent, above all in outdoor debates held on rough-hewn wooden platforms in his native Illinois in front of large crowds of the people who so often had sent him to Washington. His aides pushed him to debate Lincoln, confident Douglas would annihilate him on any public platform. Douglas agreed reluctantly. He had known Abe Lincoln since they were young men. He had heard him debate, listened to him speak, seen him in court, and himself laughed at Lincoln's stories. Lincoln, in any kind of verbal exchange, Douglas ruefully told his campaign managers, was "the most dangerous man in America."

Douglas not only had to campaign against his old friend Lincoln but had to take on Lincoln's brand-new image: "the Railsplitter." Someone had decided that Lincoln's profession as a young man, splitting thousands of rails, was a perfect way to sell him as a blue-collar, hardworking man of the people. Lincoln, in reality his own campaign manager; close friend Judge David Davis, Lincoln's official campaign manager; and others covered Illinois with broadsides and newspaper advertisements showing Lincoln, a rather well-to-do, successful, upper-middle-class lawyer at this point, as a rough-and-tumble, axe-swinging railsplitter. The image created an instant connection between Lincoln and every man who put up fences on his own farm, trudged through work, sooty and soiled, in any of Illinois's hundreds of factories, or ever worked with his hands.

Certain of the Lincoln-Douglas debates were attended by as many as twenty-thousand people, but it was the unprecedented newspaper coverage of them that made Abe Lincoln a national figure. Some people in the North knew him because of his 1848 trip to New England and his ill-fated opposition to the Mexican War while in Congress. But to most he was a complete unknown, an oversized and odd-looking frontier lawyer. The widespread press coverage of the debates, which showed Lincoln to be on an even footing with the famous Douglas, helped make him a recognized personality throughout the country.

Lincoln was certain he would win the debates, but he had other objectives beyond the dominating wooden platforms of Freeport and the other small towns in which he met the Little Giant. Lincoln believed he could trip Douglas, whom he always accused of talking before thinking, into giving a conclusive answer on whether or not he thought slaves could be barred from Kansas and Nebraska if voters there authorized it. His advisers begged him not to push the question. If Douglas answered yes he would win the support of every abolitionist and antislavery voter in Illinois, giving him the election.

"But I am killing larger game," Lincoln said with a glint in his eye in a hotel room just before the Freeport debate. The next day he lured Douglas into telling his audience, with great enthusiasm, that if Kansans and Nebraskans wanted to keep out slaves, that was fine with him. Lincoln knew it might cost him the Senate, but he also knew that the South would now abandon Douglas, and it would cost the Little Giant the presidency.

Abe Lincoln lost his bid for a Senate seat yet again that fall. He did, in fact, win slightly more popular votes than Douglas in the general election, used then only as a barometer, but the state legislature was once again Democratic and reelected Douglas. Mary Lincoln was enraged that he could win the popular vote but lose the election because of what she felt was an unfair legislative voting system. It was yet another defeat. Her husband had now lost two races for the Senate and two attempts to be speaker of the Illinois legislature.

It is difficult to determine when Abraham Lincoln first thought he could capture the 1860 Republican nomination for president. Everyone had assumed it would go to New York Senator and antislavery firebrand William Seward, but in 1859 Lincoln began to campaign for Republican candidates outside Illinois and made considerable efforts to increase his visibility and allies in other states, hoping that candidates he helped that year might help him later.

A trip to Dayton, Ohio, in the fall of 1859 was typical of Lincoln's campaigning beyond his state's borders. In Dayton, he spoke on behalf of several men running for the state legislature, making a good impression on a large crowd and the local press, just a day after Stephen Douglas, his nemesis, had stumped there for the Democrats.[36] Lincoln was so impressive that one of the men for whom he campaigned, Edwin Parrott grasped his hand, shook it vigorously, and told Lincoln he should be president. Later, Parrott, who won the election, and another man Lincoln had stumped for in Ohio sent him letters of thanks and urged him to run for president in 1860. Lincoln sent back his usual vague reply, downplaying any desire on his part to be president, but told each that whatever they did for him at any future date would be appreciated.[37] The following year both men were named delegates to the Republican national convention and, on critical ballots, helped swing the Ohio delegation to Abe Lincoln.

The years 1858 through 1860 were productive ones for Lincoln. His enormous self-confidence continued to work for him. The evidence of that self-confidence, and the success it bred, although not in elections—yet—was everywhere. It enabled him to become one of the leaders of his party in Illinois and to introduce new ideas.

He expanded the comprehensive polling techniques which he had developed as a young man in the Whig Party. Lincoln had party members continually poll voters in every county throughout Illinois to determine who was favored as a candidate and which issues were most important to the people. His data permitted Republicans to concentrate their funds and workers on districts with tight races and to ignore districts in which they would win easily. The polling results allowed the party to restructure campaign platforms based on the popular opinion on the issues. Lincoln also persuaded the Republicans to secure ownership of newspapers needed to support their political campaigns and causes. It was Lincoln's self-confidence that permitted him to fearlessly run against and debate the best speaker in the entire country, Douglas. His self-confidence was evident in his continued and intensified letter-writing campaigns aimed at politicians throughout the Midwest and Northeast. It could be seen in his increasingly successful law practice, in which he won a majority of cases he argued before the Illinois

Supreme Court. And it enabled Abe Lincoln, who finally had some of the visibility he craved, if not yet through elected office, to plan moves which might make him president of the United States.

Those moves began on February 27, 1860, with a speech at the Cooper Union, a college established by manufacturer and educational reformer Peter Cooper in New York City. Lincoln saw the speech as a turning point in his political life, because it was an opportunity to address a large crowd in New York, which would include some of the most influential politicians and newspaper editors in America, including Horace Greeley, editor of the *New York Tribune*. It was, at long last, a chance for the little-known lawyer from Illinois to present himself to the American people. That night, February 27, 1860, in one of the best speeches Lincoln ever delivered, a carefully crafted and soaring oration, he brought the crowd to its feet with one of his most stinging denunciations of slavery.

"Thinking it wrong, as we do, can we yield to them?...Neither let us be slandered from our duty by false accusations against us, nor frightened from it by menaces of destruction to the government nor of dungeons to ourselves. Let us have faith that right makes might, and in that faith let us, to the end, dare to do our duty as we understand it," he said to thunderous applause.[38]

ABRAHAM Lincoln received national attention from his debates with Stephen Douglas, his speech at Cooper Union, and his campaigning for Republicans in Ohio and New England, but despite all of these Herculean and physically draining efforts, he was still a relative unknown when the Republican convention opened in Chicago in May 1860. So unknown was he that an 1859 newspaper poll of the top twenty contenders for the Republican nomination did not even list his name, and the several newspapers which did spelled it wrong.[39]

The likely nominee, William Seward, the longtime U.S. senator and former governor of New York, was the most widely known political figure in the country, President James Buchanan included. He had become the champion of the antislavery crusade in 1850, when, in one of his best speeches, he said that there was a "higher law" than the Constitution, and that higher law overrode any legislation or court decisions on slavery.[40] Then, in 1858, at the same time Abe Lincoln was debating Douglas, Seward, with his memorable "irrepressible conflict" speech in Rochester, New York, affirmed his leadership in the antislavery cause.

Seward had a national reputation, controlled New York's thirty-five electoral votes, and possessed unlimited funds. He had the best campaign manager in America in Thurlow Weed, hundreds of due bills owed him by politicians from coast to coast, and the support of the abolitionists, the old Whigs, the Free-Soilers, Liberty Men, and all the anti-Nebraska voters. Even Abe Lincoln was behind him, telling friends as early as 1858 that he did not see how Seward could lose.[41]

If Seward were not the candidate, it would be Salmon Chase, the abolitionist governor of Ohio, or Simon Cameron, the independently wealthy governor of Pennsylvania, or Rep. Edward Bates of Missouri, all very well known, longtime figures on the American political landscape. It certainly was not going to be the untested Abe Lincoln.

Lincoln had a brilliant campaign team, however, and that made all the difference. They convinced the national committee to hold the nominating convention in Chicago, Lincoln's backyard, where they were confident they could deliver substantial press and public support for their friend. They methodically contacted the delegates of every swing state, in meetings and in groups, and presented their argument: William Seward was well known all right, but he was too well known. Although he might win all the abolitionist votes, he would lose the moderate votes of people who were against slavery but did not want a war over it.

Lincoln was an honest man, free of scandal, and as such could be critical of the corruption-riddled Democratic administration of James Buchanan and do well in an era when most Americans were convinced that politics was dishonest.[42] Seward, involved with Weed in a corruption scandal in New York, could not. The American blue-collar and middle-class work force was growing as the industrial revolution grew. To the millions of farmers, ironworkers, blacksmiths, ditchdiggers, carpenters, and laborers, Abe Lincoln was the "railsplitter," a commoner just like them who could command their votes, unlike the wealthy, patrician Seward. Lincoln, who rarely uttered a critical word against the rowdy Know-Nothing (American) Party, which captured 20 percent of the vote in 1856, could win its support. Seward, on record in favor of state aid to Catholic schools, could not.[43]

Most important, Lincoln's greatest weakness was also his greatest strength—he was an outsider. He had been out of government for so long that he would have no old enemies firing barbs at him during the campaign. He would not fall victim to old feuds, as Seward and the others would. Of course, he had delivered fiery speeches on slavery, and was as radical on the issue as Seward, but the famous Seward's speeches were printed in hundreds of newspapers. Nobody outside of Illinois read much about Abe Lincoln's speeches. Besides, his backers argued, voters were fed up with the government and wanted fresh faces.

After they presented their case in concise fashion, Lincoln's operatives, led by Judge David Davis, promised cabinet posts to all of the other contenders if they would step down in favor of Lincoln.[44] Lincoln's carefully worded and quickly forgotten note to Davis not to make any ties that bound him has been repeatedly quoted by historians as proof that Lincoln was too principled to make such pledges. It is, in fact, proof that he could send the note in a precise way in order to insinuate that the ties would bind Judge Davis, not the nominee, and *appear* to put him above politics, when it fact it did not.[45] That done, they arranged for Chicago newspapers to run stories advancing Lincoln's cause every morning of the convention and made sure all the delegates received copies. Finally, they managed to get copies of tickets to the convention and counterfeited thousands of them, handing them out to Lincoln supporters who jammed the convention site, the Wigwam, a large, two-story wooden auditorium. They cheered wildly for Abe Lincoln as police kept out thousands of supporters of Seward, Chase, and others who had legitimate tickets.[46]

The delegates had their doubts, as Lincoln knew they would, and although Seward took a large lead on the first ballot, he could not win the nomination. Votes began to shift to Lincoln, led by the men promised cabinet jobs, and on the third ballot, in one of the most stunning upsets in political history, the relatively unknown lawyer from Springfield, Illinois, was nominated for president.

The delegates went home satisfied. They had rejected Seward, a fiery abolitionist, who might lose, and nominated Lincoln, a successful moderate whom they believed would not drive away the South and win. What they did not realize was that Abraham Lincoln was at heart no moderate at all.

In Ohio, in 1859, he told a large crowd that the expansion of slavery into the territories would mean "the revival of the slave trade...a territorial slave code and the new Dred Scott decision that is to carry slavery into the free states."[47] Earlier in that same stump swing, he told an audience that if slavery was permitted to exist Americans should "muzzle the cannon which thundered its annual joyous return on the Fourth of July...blow out the moral lights around us...eradicate the love of liberty...." He said that slavery in the territories was just "another turn" in a screw and that, next, people would "support the slave trade, revived with all its horrors, a slave code enforced in our territories and slavery up into the very heart of the free North."[48]

Lincoln framed his argument historically and contemporarily in speeches delivered within the eighteen months preceding the 1860 Republican convention. He explained carefully that, as far back as 1787, the Northwest Territory, which later became five Midwest states, forbade slavery, and that the feeling had not changed and would not change until slavery was gone everywhere. "The whole country [from 1787 on] looked forward to the ultimate extinction of the institution [slavery]," he said, and then noted that "at the time the constitution of the United States was adopted it was expected that the slave trade would be abolished."[49] He often asked audiences, who cherished the Constitution, "Would they have not done this if they had not thought slavery wrong?"[50] Then he told audiences that the feeling had not changed. "We shall probably not have perfect peace in this country with it until it either masters the free principle in our government, or is so far mastered by the free principle as for the public mind to rest in the belief that it is going to end."[51]

Even more illustrative of Lincoln's fear of the slave crusade was an 1859 speech. "When this is done [slavery in the territories], the miners and sappers will have formed public opinion for the slave trade. They will be ready for Jeff Davis and [Alexander] Stephens and other leaders of that company, to sound the bugle for the revival of the slave trade, for the second Dred Scott decision, for the flood of slavery to be poured over the free states, while we shall be here tied down and helpless and run over like sheep."[52]

People in the North may not have read these speeches or paid attention to them, but people in the South, via Southern newspapers in Kentucky and other states close to Illinois, did.

A LOOK at the papers of Abraham Lincoln shows that from May until November he carefully mapped out a shrewd electoral strategy which brought victory despite not winning the election outright, thanks to the three Democratic nominees splitting their party's vote. The Republicans targeted must-win states. They funneled their money, speakers, and resources into these states, giving others that appeared safe just enough to insure victory. They hammered out a campaign platform that was antislavery, but in a moderate way, less strident than their fiery 1856 slavery plank. They favored a high tariff and pushed that issue hard in Pennsylvania, where many jobs were held by ironworkers whose livelihoods would be jeopardized by foreign competition. They hit hard on the issue of federal corruption, which angered most Northerners, marching down streets with enormous banners emblazoned with huge letters: HONEST ABE. The Republicans pushed internal improvements, including better harbors for port cities, and promised a Homestead Act in order to win Western and farmer votes. It was a very well balanced platform, anchored by a moderate stand on slavery, designed to win over the swing states and moderate voters, no matter where they were.

His papers show that Lincoln clearly ran his own campaign and did a magnificent job of it. First, he decided not to give any speeches, to the relief of his advisers, who feared that his speeches, taken the wrong way, or given at the wrong time, might ruin his campaign, as had happened with other candidates. ("Write nothing for publication!" urged a friend, John Fry. "[That] killed Clay. For God's sake, don't let it kill you.") His advisers were afraid that Lincoln would become overly passionate and deliver a second House Divided speech that might wreck his chance to win the moderate vote. Even though Lincoln did not think that would happen, he remembered vividly how he himself had lured Douglas into wrecking his presidential chances in their 1858 debates.

Lincoln did not waste time in Springfield. He took charge of the campaign as soon as the convention was over, making peace with all his Republican enemies and cajoling people in every state, whether they supported him initially or not, to work for his election. He moved quickly to invite powerbrokers such as New York's Thurlow Weed, Seward's garrulous and strapping campaign manager, to his home in Springfield and cemented alliances. He sent his campaign aides to troubled states to straighten out problems, end feuds, and patch up party differences. He worked with the Republican money men to send money to states where it was needed; he knew, personally, county by county, where it would prove most helpful. He maintained a brisk correspondence with political operatives throughout the country in order to determine what public opinion was and how he could work to shift it. He arranged for German speakers, such as Midwest German-American community leader Carl Schurz, to make long speaking tours in German communities, and for Know-Nothing speakers to stump cities and counties where Know-Nothing support was still strong.

There was enormous work done on the Lincoln campaign. All of it was supervised, directly or indirectly, by the Republican nominee. He did not do so with apprehension or trepidation. He never fretted over whether one effort would work, whether another would fail. He had the self-confidence to run his campaign with single-minded determination, to gain the support of powerful enemies, to solicit large amounts of money from contributors, and to earn the backing of local, state, and congressional candidates. He had, by the fall of 1860, the peak of his political life, spent a lifetime as a hard-nosed politician, whether by walking down dirt roads to knock on people's doors in tiny New Salem, by twisting arms in the Illinois statehouse, or running for president of the United States. He had learned how to be a master politician and to do it for what he believed in—the noble cause of fighting slavery and improving the lot of his fellow Americans. Abraham Lincoln had, in his political wars, whether he won them or lost them, developed political and people skills which, combined with his self-confidence, made him a man capable of enormous success as a president, particularly a president who would have to deal with diverse personalities, critical newspapers, a sometimes angry and frightened public, warring political factions, and a divided body politic in the tragic years ahead.

PART III

INTO THE EYE
OF THE STORM

5

JEFFERSON DAVIS: SECESSION

I trust there is to be no collision.

JEFFERSON DAVIS, DECEMBER 20, 1860, FORTY-SIX DAYS
AFTER LINCOLN WAS ELECTED PRESIDENT

CHARLESTON, SOUTH CAROLINA, is a city laced with palmetto trees and tall oaks dripping with spanish moss. On December 20, 1860, the 169 delegates to the state's secession convention gathered there in a festive mood. Every prominent official in the state was at the convention, including four former governors and three future governors, four presidents of South Carolina colleges, four former U.S. senators and five former U.S. congressmen. Half of the delegates were farmers or planters, including some of the wealthiest men in America. There were twelve doctors, six judges, four ministers, three teachers, the state's attorney general, and the presidents of the state's largest insurance company and the state's largest railroad. More than 90 ninety percent of them were slaveowners, most owning more than fifty slaves. They were there to take South Carolina out of the Union, in order to safeguard what they saw as their rights as South Carolinians, as Southerners, and as men and to protect slavery.[1]

Following strident speeches, the delegates approved secession unanimously, 169–0, in the chamber of the South Carolina Institute, which was jammed with every member of the South Carolina legislature and three thousand spectators. Each delegate signed the secession bill in an elaborate ceremony that began at 7 P.M. and lasted past 9 P.M. as thousands gathered in the streets outside. A thunderous roar erupted when the final signer scribbled his name. "The roar [of the crowd] shook the very building, reverberating, long continued, and rose to heaven," wrote a reporter for the *Charleston Mercury*.[2] Outside, all Charleston joined in one of the largest and loudest celebrations in the history of the South. Ad hoc parades marched from one neighborhood to another. The Palmetto flag flew from countless buildings, and was draped from the second-story windows of innumerable homes. Hundreds of fireworks exploded. Bands played from one end of the city to the other. Mothers let their children stay up late and go into the streets with them to join in the cheering. Taverns were jammed with celebrators. Cadets at the Citadel fired off cannons. Dozens of churches scattered throughout the city began pealing their bells at 7 P.M. and kept it up for hours. Men from the various volunteer militias donned their uniforms and rushed into the streets. Within five minutes of the passage of the secession bill, hawkers were on the streets selling six thousand copies of it, printed by the *Charleston Mercury*. The telegraph offices were packed with people sending the good news to friends and relatives throughout the South. It was a party to rival any New Year's Eve celebration, and it would change the history of the American people forever.[3]

That same day, Jefferson Davis stood in the well of the U.S. Senate to make yet another appeal to citizens of North and South to avert secession. He had met with Mississippi's governor and other officials right after Lincoln's election and urged them to maintain a calm, middle course until Southerners knew what the Lincoln administration would do. He kept silent as Southern newspapers urged secession on Mississippi and other states. As the South Carolina convention began, he worked in the Senate to keep the political peace.

In a discussion about the army's plans to stay in forts in Charleston, he urged his fellow senators to pursue peace, not war. After a long speech about the military, he looked up at his colleagues. Clearly speaking about secession, he told them to be careful, that Southerners were finished with mere threats, and ready for action. "It is not by crimination and recrimination that the sense of the people is likely to be changed.... The occasion for such arguments has passed by. We have to deal with events which are now transpiring and about to be consummated," he warned. He concluded hopefully, "I trust there is to be no collision."[4]

The idea of secession ignited a festival in Charleston, but evoked a feeling of anguish in Jefferson Davis. He knew that South Carolina was not alone. Politicians in Texas, Alabama, Mississippi, and other states had called for secession since the late 1840s, but it had never happened, because the Democratic Party had controlled the country and the South had always controlled much of the Democratic Party. As long as the antislavery forces were kept out of power, all was well. That changed in 1856, when the new Republican Party began to win large numbers of seats in Congress. The party's electoral sweep of Congress, the Senate, and the White House in 1860 put the antislavery forces on notice. The South believed that a sectional, antislavery party would control the country, and eventually eliminate slavery.[5] How could Lincoln, without 51 percent of the vote, have the right even to take office?[6]

Although Davis called publicly for theoretical secession in a July 1860 speech, he never believed that it would occur. The movement was never well organized, even though the Deep South states, the core of the movement, were united, and their agents went to leaders in each of the other Southern states to convince them to secede. The agents themselves had little effect.[7] Each state's legislature or secession convention decided its own fate. There was no region-wide Southern referendum on secession, and elections concerning secession conventions and delegates varied from state to state. There was considerable opposition to secession in several key Southern states, such as Alabama, where it only carried by nine votes at the Convention, and in Georgia, where it passed only after heated arguments between prosecession forces, led by Robert Toombs, and antisecession groups, led by Alexander Stephens.[8] A special referendum in Georgia polled 50,243 votes for secession and 37,127 against. Many charged vote fraud, claiming that the actual count had been a dead heat.[9]

Only seven states—Texas, Alabama, Louisiana, Georgia, Mississippi, Florida, and South Carolina—seceded during the winter of 1860–1861. Upper South and border states—Virginia, North Carolina, Tennessee, Arkansas, Missouri, Maryland, Kentucky, and Delaware—did not leave the Union then, insisting on waiting until Lincoln took office to see what he would do on the slavery issue.

Residents in those states were just as opposed to secession in the winter of 1860 as residents of the Deep South states were in favor of it. The Arkansas secession convention voted it down, 39–35. Voters in Tennessee did not hold a secession convention; they turned down the idea of one by 67,675 to 57,798. Pro-Union delegates who would have attended if there had been one defeated secessionists by a stunning 91,803 votes to just 24,749. The citizens of North

Carolina turned down the convention idea in a referendum: The pro-Union delegates on the ballots defeated secessionist delegates by a three-to-two margin. Missouri's secession convention voted down secession 89–1 and its voters gave pro-Union delegates 110,000 votes to just 30,000 for secessionist delegates. The Kentucky legislature spurned a convention throughout 1860 and early 1861, eventually voting, in May 1861, to keep the state neutral by a 69–29 margin.[10]

Davis's friends in the House and Senate from the border states constantly reminded him that no coalition of Deep South states would pull them out of the Union just yet, and hinted that without them there could be no real Confederacy. John Pendleton Kennedy, a leading Maryland politician, declared: "Is it not very obvious that Virginia, Kentucky, Tennessee, Missouri, North Carolina, and Maryland cannot, with any respect for their own dignity, without any regard for their own welfare, or with any security for their own peace, suffer themselves to be dragged into that track of revolution and civil war, of wild experiment and visionary project into which Carolina is endeavoring to force them?"[11]

Now, after the election of Lincoln, Jeff Davis finally began to fully understand the deep-seated fears of most Southerners. He wrote in his autobiography, "It was not the passage of 'personal liberty' laws, it was not the circulation of incendiary documents, it was not the raid of John Brown, it was not the operation of unjust tariff laws, nor all combined, that constituted the intolerable grievance, but it was the systematic and persistent struggle to deprive the Southern States of equality in the Union."[12]

The fever was able to spread quickly, too, because the leading political figures of the secessionist movements were governors, senators, and congressmen who had great influence. More important, the key secessionists in the South had control of the Democratic Party, by then the only party in the Southern states, and that gave them access to the party newspapers, printing presses, polls, voting stations, and party political machinery. It made secession easier.[13]

As the secession tide grew, it began to carry Davis with it. From November 1860 through January 1861 he spoke out in favor of the states' right to leave the United States. He had modified many of his arguments. On December 20, 1860, Davis blamed the North for trying to inflict its political will on the South.[14] He sided with the anti-Lincoln forces, but on the basis of a broad defense of secession occasioned by the election. He said that no Southern state had seceded because of Lincoln's election. Rather they left the Union because "they recognized in him the representative of a party professing principles destructive to their peace, their prosperity, and their domestic tranquillity" and that secession "was generally regarded as the remedy of last resort to be applied only when ruin or dishonor was the alternative."[15]

A senator well versed in history and law, Davis frequently discussed the North-South relationship as a long time-line dating back to 1776 and offered dozens of examples of states' rights separate from federal intervention, always returning to slavery and the South. "It is evident, therefore, that the people of the South...had no lack either of precept or of precedent for their instruction and guidance in teaching and the example of our brethren in the North and East. The only practical difference was that the North threatened and the South acted."[16]

Davis feared what everyone feared, that secession would become a runaway train. Even visitors to the South who knew little about the secession movement had seen the storm brewing for years. "The whole South is like one of its cotton steamers...filled from the hold to the topmost deck with the most inflammable matter, everything heated up to the burning point," wrote Englishman James Stirling on a visit in 1859.[17]

THROUGHOUT the secession crisis—from the raid of John Brown and his followers on the arsenal at Harper's Ferry in 1859 through the election of Abraham Lincoln and the subsequent Southern state secession conventions— Jefferson Davis labored tirelessly to hold the country together amid the hotheads of the North and the firebrands of the South. He was a calm and reasoning politician, working through all the proper channels to prevent civil strife. He stood in the Senate well again and again in those troubled days, reminding senators that it was their job to save the Union.[18]

Jeff Davis had spoken out for years on the rights of the state and its people to live as they wanted, holding slaves, without interference from the federal government. Since 1850 he had agreed with slaveholders that they had the right to bring their slaves into the territories if they chose; that they should be allowed to populate the new western lands obtained from Mexico, taking their slaves with them; that they could welcome new states as slave states. He believed that no Mississippian could be deprived of his rights by the Black Republican Party. He believed that if it became necessary, the Southern states including Mississippi, had the right to secede.

Still, few Americans were as loyal to the United States during that period as Jeff Davis. A moderate through much of that winter, he was instrumental in each effort to keep the peace and hold the Union together. As a devoted public official who worked hard to salvage the country while his fellow Southern senators and congressmen did little more than bellow and fume during those volatile months, Jefferson Davis tried to erase the rhetoric of secession he himself helped to build over a decade.

One of the first things Davis did after the election was meet with President James Buchanan. Davis told the president bluntly that he could not be harsh on the South because of the views of its people and could not threaten any of the secessionists or their states with force. Davis, with easy access to power, returned to his Washington home confident that Buchanan would take his advice so that he could leave office with the country still intact.

Davis's advice was ignored. Buchanan stood firm against secession. He told the public that the Union not only would never recognize secession, but had the right to use military force to hold any of its Southern forts threatened by Southern military groups. Buchanan's speech, to Congress on December 3, 1860, was a fervent plea for the salvation of the Union.

Buchanan called the United States "the grandest temple which has ever been dedicated to human freedom." Determined to avert secession or civil war, the president acquiesced to some Southern demands, calling for constitutional amendments to protect slavery in the South and supported the fugitive slave law, but he also forbade secession and threatened to use force to stop it.[19]

Looking haggard and worn out, Buchanan declared, "By such a dreadful catastrophe [secession], the hopes of the friends of freedom throughout the world would be destroyed, and a long night of leaden despotism would enshroud the nations. Our example for more than eighty years would not only be lost, but it would be quoted as conclusive proof that man is unfit for self-government."[20]

Immediately after Buchanan's speech, Davis and a long parade of Southern politicians asked the president to reconsider. If he would not do so, they would then ask the Senate and House of Representatives to ignore him and to pass laws protecting Southern slavery and its right to move into the territories, in order to avert the certain trouble that was now at hand.

Some Congressmen worked behind the scenes, such as Herschel Johnson of Georgia, who warned Northerners that "the emergency is great." He went on: "The peril to the government is imminent. The interests at stake are incalculable."[21]

Some pleaded in public, such as Georgia representative Thomas Cobb, who said the country was out of time. "My prayer is that something may be done by which that state may remain in this Union. I am not a secessionist. I desire peace. But sir, I desire that my state may be awarded her rights under the Constitution."[22]

The country was collapsing quickly as Davis tried to work with others to keep it together. The Buchanan cabinet fell apart in mid-December. Howell Cobb, secretary of the treasury and Buchanan's most trusted adviser, and three other cabinet members resigned over secession. Vice President John Breckinridge, Buchanan's choice to succeed him in the Oval Office before the elections, went home to Kentucky to work with officials there to keep Kentucky, a slave state, neutral if secession threatened or if war came.

In December, Buchanan decided to appoint two bipartisan committees to solve the problem, one in the House and one in the Senate. The House committee had thirty-three members, one for each state, and the Senate committee had thirteen. The president was convinced that Democrats and Republicans, and Northerners and Southerners, working together at the final hour, could save the nation. The influential Jeff Davis was one of the first people Buchanan named to the Senate committee.

Almost immediately, the Committee of Thirteen received proposals for a solution to the crisis from Senator John Crittenden of Kentucky. His proposals were proslavery. They guaranteed slavery in the South; permitted its extension to the territories, but only in the southern half of the territories; and upheld the Fugitive Slave Law. But Buchanan and many others hoped that the immediate threat of secession might make the senators approve them, if only as a temporary measure to buy the country more time.

Jeff Davis and Georgia's Robert Toombs wanted to hold the Union together, even if it meant abandoning some of their most cherished beliefs about slavery. After various amendments and counterproposals found their way to the committee table, Davis told the Northern Republicans that he was even willing to agree to give up the extension of slavery into most territories if the Southerners could just maintain it in New Mexico, where, he pointed out, the climate would probably prohibit slavery anyway.

Unable to win any concessions from Northern senators or congressmen,

Davis became fed up and talked more and more of secession. "The remedy for these evils is to be found in the patriotism and the affection of the people, if it exists; and, if it does not exist, it is far better, instead of attempting to preserve a forced and therefore fruitless Union, that we should peacefully part and each pursue his separate course," he had said in December, 1860, even before the committee was appointed, and warned senators they were running out of opportunities. "The time has passed when appeals might profitably be made to sentiment. The time has come when men must of necessity reason, assemble facts, and deal with current events."[23]

The conciliatory gesture by Davis and Toombs on the Committee of Thirteen was not only turned down by the Republicans on the committee, but met with a belligerence which angered Davis. He soon became convinced that the Republicans were apparently under orders of some kind, from some quarter, not to yield on any issue involving slavery. They stonewalled all Southern offers or compromises. Even Douglas admitted that it was the Southerner Davis, and not any Northerner, who pushed for conciliation.[24]

The senators on the committee often ended sessions by shouting at each other. Douglas said the debate itself would inflame the passions of Southerners, "driving them into revolution and disunion."[25] Tom Pugh, of Ohio, a hot-tempered abolitionist, shouted at one Southerner that the demands on the Committee of Thirteen in the Senate and the Committee of Thirty-three in the House of Representatives would produce trouble. "You know, and I know, that it means war; and that war will follow it," he said.[26]

Davis saw the South losing everywhere. It had lost in its efforts to gain concessions from Buchanan in his speech. The Southerners had no more success on the Committee of Thirty-three in the House than they did on the Senate committee.

Davis suspected the Committee of Thirteen would accomplish nothing. He lamented what he saw as Buchanan's betrayal of the South and was certain, from talking to Republicans, that the new Lincoln administration would be harsh on the South. He tried with great fortitude to continue the fight to prevent secession, even as different states announced secession conventions, but finally, after a particularly argumentative day during deliberations by the Committee of Thirty-three in the House on December 13, Davis gave up. On December 14 he, and others, signed a statement proposing secession. "The honor, safety and independence of the Southern people require the organization of a southern confederacy," the statement said.

"The primary objective of each slaveholding state ought to be its speedy and absolute separation from a Union with hostile states."[27]

Jefferson Davis, who jokingly had called himself a "pretty good secessionist" in 1851, had, a decade later, finally become one.

SOUTHERN politicians like Jeff Davis, no less the ordinary Southerners, were swayed by their newspapers, which, more than any other factor, convinced most Southerners to secede. American newspapers, North and South, were highly partisan at the time. Almost all were owned or controlled by political parties or individual politicians and their stories were absurdly one sided. Just as abolitionist newspapers whipped up public fervor in the North, highly biased prosecession newspapers stoked fires in the South. After Lincoln's election, almost all of them began howling for secession.

The Richmond *Whig* suggested that any move by Lincoln to bring South Carolina back into the Union would force general rebellion. "He would at once unite the whole southern people in resistance and produce a universal conflagration," its editor wrote.[28] The West Baton Rouge (La.) *Sugar Planter's* editor agreed, declaring, "if the administration of Mr. Lincoln in any manner interferes with those states [which secede] can the others, who may not agree with them, stand idly by and witness the outrage? Certainly not. Every Southern sword will leap from its scabbard to avenge an insult to a southern state, be she in the right or wrong."[29] The editors at the *Memphis Daily Appeal* joined the chorus: "We will shake from the soles of our feet the dust of the federal government and dissolve our political ties with it, having at home the undivided cooperation of a united South."[30]

These journals, like hundreds of Southern newspapers, switched from pro-Union to secessionist right after the election. The reversal was so quick that by Christmas, there were fewer than a half dozen pro-Union papers in any single Deep South state.[31]

The Southern press also printed as fact many wild rumors emanating out of Washington. Two of the most bizarre rumors involved Lincoln and Davis. One was that Abe Lincoln had promised a Virginia politician in the winter of 1860–61 that if Virginia refused to secede and stayed in the Union, Lincoln would turn over Fort Sumter to the state of South Carolina, defusing what was a tense situation there in order to prevent a war.[32] Another was that any congressmen or senators who openly espoused secession or resigned from Congress would be arrested and put in jail.[33] A third was that Jefferson Davis had once again lost his temper in an argument with Senator Andrew Johnson, from Tennessee, and been shot by him in a duel. That rumor was printed in so many papers in Mississippi that when Davis returned home in January, 1861, people asked to see his wounds.[34]

Secessionists had little reason to believe the North would make an attempt to stop them from forming their own country or that a civil war would eventually erupt. Southerners joked at parties that secession would bring about no more blood than would fill a thimble. The silent Abe Lincoln, they assumed, would simply rule over his half of the "house divided" and let someone else rule over the other half.

James Grayson of South Carolina wrote two years later, in 1863, "To reduce the simple people into the volcanic fires of revolution and war, they were told the act of dissolution would produce no opposition of a serious nature, that not a drop of blood would be spilled, that no man's flocks, or herds or negroes or houses or land would be plundered or destroyed."[35]

At the time, however, no one expected war, especially not Jefferson Davis, who, as a former secretary of war, knew that none of the Southern states had been stockpiling weapons. He said later, "This fact is a clear proof of the absence of any desire or expectation of war. If the purpose of the northern states to make war upon us because of secession had been foreseen, preparation to meet the consequences would have been contemporaneous with the adoption of a resort to that remedy."[36]

ACTUAL secession began with South Carolina in December. Mississippi seceded on January 9, Florida on January 10, Alabama on January 11, Georgia on January 19, Louisiana on January 26, and Texas on February 1. Although some held back, many believed that more states would secede in the spring, especially if Lincoln, after his inauguration, made any moves to get the prodigal states back.[37] Northerners wondered how a small group of radicals in each state could convince a much larger group of moderates to take so revolutionary a step as to secede from the Union. All of the outward evidence which Lincoln, the Republicans, and the Northerners saw indicated that the majority of Southerners wanted to remain in the Union. The two Southern Democratic presidential candidates in 1860, John Breckinridge and John Bell, had not run on secessionist platforms, but on pro-Union platforms. Southern Democratic leaders, such as Jeff Davis, Alexander Stephens, and even the oratorical firebrand William Yancey, had pledged to preserve the Union in recent speaking tours of the North.

Nonslaveholders faced an equally perplexing dilemma. Only about twenty-five percent of Southerners owned slaves, and of them about eighty percent owned fewer than ten. Numerically, prosperous slaveholders were a small group. They were the richest group of men in the South, so their domination of the various states' political machines was no secret, but their cultural and social control over the nonslaveholding masses was a deeper matter, and one which Northerners, including Lincoln, never fully understood. They had somehow convinced the other seventy-five percent of the people, who had little money or influence, that it was to their advantage to perpetuate a slave economy that did not in any way benefit them.

They did so in 1861 as they had always done before, by convincing middle- and lower-class white men and women that they needed to band together with rich slaveholders and politicians to maintain white supremacy and to empower a system which elevated all whites, regardless of class, by keeping all black slaves under their collective heel. This was a wide-ranging and deep-rooted white supremacy, which also enabled the middle and poor classes to feel that their racial identity enabled them to bond with the rich slaveholders, elevating them in the fringes of the upper classes. Slaveholders and politicians reached out to the poor farmer again and again, particularly at election time, whether at barbecues or rallies, and embraced him. They permitted the poor farmer to firmly believe that by supporting the slave system they could mingle with the rich. That could happen because they were both white, but they could only do it by keeping the blacks down.[38]

It was a compact in which the slaveholding politicians also convinced the poor farmers, craftsmen, dockworkers, clerks, cotton factors, and laborers that freed blacks would take their jobs and rape their white women. The tapestry woven by slaveholders was not one of simple economic and sexual fear, however. They were also careful, in speech after speech, year after year, to show the white lower classes that blacks would appropriate their entire culture. They would become leaders and members of the white churches, hold office in white city councils, belong to white social clubs, and run white newspapers. They would turn the entire Southern white culture into a Southern black culture.[39]

The prospect of four million freed blacks, fifty percent of the total

Southern population, and in some communities ninety percent, co-opting Southern culture and taking white jobs was numbing. The idea that millions of black men would be free to molest their women and produce a new race of mulattoes was unthinkable. In 1861, in speeches and letters, again and again, Southerners expressed real fear of it. Indeed, this racial alliance of rich and poor would continue for generations after Appomattox.[40]

Jefferson Davis was a longtime proponent of this racist mantra which held rich and poor whites together. Labor and the mingling of the races was waved like a red flag throughout the South by Davis and others. He had spoken about white supremacy at length in several public speeches. A speech Davis gave in Aberdeen, Mississippi, in 1851, provides an example of the way in which he framed white supremacy and the cultural ties between poor and rich whites as necessary to preserve the power of all whites over all blacks.

He told a large crowd of poor and middle-class whites that "now they stand upon the broad level of equality with the rich white man" because they were all white. He explained that many rich whites were once middle-class or poor themselves and that all of the poor whites in the South had that same opportunity if only all the whites together held down the blacks. He reminded them that no matter how poor whites were, they were of a superior class because the black slaves, of necessity, were the inferior class. The poor whites would be even poorer, and the middle-class whites ruined, if all of the millions of black slaves were free to steal their jobs. The poor whites in that situation, out of work, would be as low as the black class, indeed assimilated into it, becoming black themselves. He added that color divided classes, that even though all white men were not equal in land and money, they were equal in class, culture, dignity, and honor, and that had to be maintained at the expense of the slaves. A white man, rich, poor, or middle class, always had opportunity so long as the blacks were kept in bondage.

A reporter for the *Monroe Democrat*, at Davis's May 29, 1851, speech in Aberdeen reported, "Col. Davis said that he always thought and sincerely believed that the institution of slavery, as it now exists among us, is necessary to the equality of the white race. Distinctions between classes have always existed, everywhere, and in every country...destroy them today and they will spring up tomorrow. Menial services have to be performed by someone and everywhere the world over those persons [slaves] by whom menial services have been performed as a class have been looked upon, as occupying, and are reduced to a state of inferiority."

Addressing all whites, and connecting them, Davis declared, "The rich, by siding with the party in power…will always be safe. Not so with the poor. Their all is suspended upon their superiority to the blacks…the social equality of their wives, daughters and sons are all suspended upon and involved in this question."[41]

Finally, after making logical appeals to the poor whites of his audience, he turned to their women and children, the social cog necessary to complete his grisly picture of a white South tainted forever by freed blacks. He would tell the crowd that the social equality of their wives and children rested solely on their whiteness and their desire to consolidate with all the other white women and children in the South to keep their class, their family, and its heritage untainted by any mingling with black slaves.[42]

Davis was not alone in his feelings. Many influential Southern writers agreed. Writer James Debow summed it up in an 1860 pamphlet widely distributed throughout the South: "Low as would this class of people [blacks] sink by emancipation in idleness, superstition and vice, the white man compelled to live among them, would by the power exerted over him, sink even lower, unless as is to be supposed he would prefer to suffer death instead."[43]

Even to those white Southerners who did not directly tie freed slaves to assaults and race tainting, the race problem seemed unsolvable outside of slavery. South Carolina's U.S. senator James Hammond wrote a friend in 1861 that "we have here two races—white and black—now both equally American, holding each other in the closest embrace and utterly unable to extricate ourselves from it. A problem so difficult, so complicated, and so momentous never was placed in charge of any portion of mankind."[44] Some Southerners even suggested that every nonslaveholder should be given, free, by wealthy planters, one slave apiece so that all Southerners could be slaveholders and unite in a common cause.[45]

Finally, Southern extremists swore by the long-term association between rich and poor as exemplified by the "cavalier" myth. In that myth, the great masses of middle-class and poor whites saw the rich planters and politicians as the "cavaliers" of a feudal society. They looked up to the cavaliers because of their achievements but never resented their success, convinced, primarily from speeches by cavaliers, that they, too, would one day be wealthy and influential. They also saw the cavaliers as polished, cultured, and well educated, men who could and should be relied upon for leadership. Poor whites did not resent the rich planter cavaliers because they had many slaves, but instead admired them for it. The ownership of slaves was seen as a barometer of success and symbol of power.

That admiration and attachment was carried over to the politicians whom the wealthy cavaliers put in office (the cavalier attachment was so strong in Alabama that secession fever was hottest in counties with small farms, not in those with large plantations). The cavalier also represented the honor of the South. It was the cavalier who held Southern women in such high esteem and fought for the rights of his family, city, county, and state.[46] The symbol of the cavalier was very important to poor white Southerners, whose importance Lincoln never understood. Extremists used that symbol to bring reluctant farmers and workers into the secession fold.

No one represented the cavalier myth better than the senator from Mississippi. Jeff Davis possessed all of its ingredients. He was well educated and, unlike the majority of "well-educated" Southern men, who had been to local schools for just a few years, he had attended two different colleges and then graduated from the U.S. Military Academy at West Point. Most Mississippians owned ten or fewer slaves, as did most Southerners, but Jeff Davis at one point owned over a hundred. He was well dressed, carried himself as an aristocrat should, was married to a prototypical Southern belle, and maintained extraordinarily good relations with his slaves, proving the Southern point that if a master is good to his slaves there can be no problem with slavery. Most of all, though, Jeff Davis was no mythical cavalier, no novelist's idea of a Southern gentlemen who went off to defend hearth, home, and culture against its enemies. He *did* leave everything he had to risk his life in the Black Hawk War, and again in the Mexican War. No fictional cavalier could match Jeff Davis.

The politicians' ability to convince Southern whites of all classes that a new confederacy of slave states was necessary, plus the enormous effect of the southern press, gave secession its popularity and its incredible power. Northerners complained bitterly that a few firebrands had brought about the break-up of the Union, but Southerners knew better; regardless of the reasons, almost everyone in the Deep South was for secession by the end of December 1860 and, if need be, would fight for it. By late winter 1860, the secessionist feelings of many Southerners were clear finally to Davis and others when states voted for secession. Texas held a referendum on secession, and voters backed it by an overwhelming three-to-one margin. In Virginia the secession referendum (held after Fort Sumter) carried by an overwhelming majority, 125,350 to 20, 373.⁴⁷ "The act of secession from the United States was done by the people and by them alone," declared the editor of the *Sandersville* (Georgia) *Central Georgian*.⁴⁸

Still, Northerners were convinced both that seceded states would return and that no other states would leave the Union. Southerners could not understand them. "Nobody in the North believes we are in earnest," wrote Mrs. Mary Chesnut, wife of South Carolina's U.S. senator James Chesnut.⁴⁹

JEFFERSON Davis decided to resign his seat in the U.S. Senate when Mississippi seceded and went to the Senate for the very last time on January 21. He was one of a long parade of southern senators and congressmen who were leaving the government of the United States as their states seceded. It was a time of anguish for many as they ended long and distinguished careers and parted from men who had been their close friends for years. Their feelings were hardened by secession, though, and thus their farewell speeches were mixed stories of warm personal memories and bitter political feelings.

When Jeff Davis made up his mind to leave the Senate, he sent a warm letter to his old friend and boss, former president Franklin Pierce, telling him sadly that "the hour is at hand which closes my connection with the United States, for the independence and Union of which my father bled and in the service of which I have sought to emulate the example he set for my guidance," adding that he was certain that the Republicans would start a civil war against the South.⁵⁰

Jefferson Davis's own farewell to the United States, delivered the following morning, was a mixture of political and personal heroism. The stress of the Davis Resolutions, introduced to stall conflict; his work on the Committee of Thirteen; Senate speeches; trips back and forth to Mississippi; daily politics; endless rumors; and the never-ending parade of seceding states had once again crippled Jeff Davis. His eye neuralgia flared up in early January, and he was forced to remain in his darkened bedroom, unable to see, losing weight, growing weaker and weaker. He was determined to deliver his farewell speech in person in the Senate on January 21, regardless of his illness, and he ignored his physician's warning that making the speech might kill him.⁵¹

The Senate chamber was filled to capacity that morning. The galleries, hallways, even the cloakroom, were jammed with people who had arrived at 9

A.M., long before Davis's address, to claim a place. Davis rose slowly and looked up at his wife, Varina, in the gallery, dressed all in black for the occasion. He stood silently as he drank in his last moments in the Senate. He started to speak, in a quaking whisper, obviously sick, but his strength picked up as he spoke, and his voice grew healthier.[52]

Acknowledging his illness, and that stress would make it worse, he started by telling the senators that at last he had become a firm secessionist. "Secession belongs to a different class of remedies. It is to be justified upon the basis that the states are sovereign. There was a time when none denied it. I hope the time may come again," he said, looking up at the people in the galleys and at his fellow senators. "Secession is necessary and proper...."[53]

Then he reminded them that he was there not for a final argument which might make him ill, but for a goodbye to old and dear friends and to his country. He explained why Mississippi had seceded, defended the departure of the other states, and warned the Senate that legally the U.S. government could not war on any seceded state.[54] Then, leaning on his desk for support, his voice growing stronger and stronger, he looked at each senator and finished in a touching goodbye.

"In the course of my service here, associated at different times with a great variety of Senators, I see now around me some with whom I have served long. There have been points of collision; but whatever offense there has been to me, I leave here, I carry with me no hostile remembrance. Whatever offense I have given which has not been redressed, or for which satisfaction has not been demanded, I have, senators, in this hour of our parting, to offer you my apology for any pain which, in heat of discussion, I have inflicted....it only remains to me to bid you a final adieu.[55]

His speech was interrupted many times by applause from the senators and citizens in the gallery. When he finished, spent, the elegant final adieu over, the old Senate chamber shook with the thunder of the applause as people shot to their feet and cheered. Dozens of senators, North and South, surrounded Davis to shake his hand and wish him well.[56]

Just days after his farewell speech, as hundreds of Southerners working in Washington began an exodus to their home states, Davis became ill again, so ill this time that he spent more than a week in bed, unable to work and unable to move, before he finally began the long journey home to Brierfield plantation, exhausted, to await history.

6

LINCOLN: SECESSION

I will suffer death before I will consent to any compromise [on slavery].

ABRAHAM LINCOLN

THE SECOND YOUNGEST MAN ever elected president (the youngest at that time was Franklin Pierce, 48) stretched his long legs and bounded up the stairs of the Illinois state house two or three steps at a time, his strong hands sometimes grasping the railing as he made his way to his office, smiling at friends, nodding good morning to porters, and waving to the people who yelled up at him from below. Lincoln was one of the healthiest men in Illinois, his body strong from years of rail splitting, wrestling, farming, riding the circuit, and fording innumerable streams on his horse to wherever his law cases took him. In the days which followed his election he was full of energy and enthusiasm for his new job. A minority president, with just 39 percent of the vote, he had nevertheless won an electoral majority and the job. Lincoln's northern coalition of abolitionists, immigrants, and workers had brought him a solid victory, even though he had earned no electoral votes, and few popular votes, in the South. His minority status did not occasion any worry. His election had not even wound up in the House of Representatives, as had the contest between Thomas Jefferson and Aaron Burr in 1800 and the election between Andrew Jackson, Henry Clay, W. H. Crawford, and John Quincy Adams in 1824.

The large, two-story white clapboard house in Springfield was so busy during the first few days following the election that Lincoln, at Mary's rather

111

insistent urging, decided to move his postelection office from the friendly
confines of his living room to an office the governor offered him in the state
house. Lincoln walked through the streets of Springfield each morning to his
office to read the day's mail, talk to advisers, and, probably more often that he
wished, greet people from all over America, singly, in families, or in groups,
who were passing through Springfield and wanted to shake hands with the
new president-elect.

His office was not large, just twelve feet square, and he shared it with one
secretary, John Nicolay, and later a second, John Hay, two brilliant young men
whom he would take to Washington with him. Like any office that Abe
Lincoln sat in, it became cluttered instantly as papers were tossed haphazardly
on top of chairs and desks. The president-elect, when not greeting people,
read the newspapers while comfortably resting his feet on top of a desk.

His time was usually taken up with deciding on the appointment of
cabinet secretaries, which became complicated, and the formation of a brand-
new Republican government, but the rush of events precluded that. Lincoln
quickly discovered that just about everyone in America wanted him to make
some kind of statement to mollify the Southerners about his views on slavery
and to end all the harsh talk about secession that unnerved people, North and
South. He needed to do that, they urged, because too much time would pass
before his inauguration, on March 4, 1861. Four months in the uncertain,
heated political climate of the winter 1860–61, with so many factions jousting
with each other, seemed like a lifetime. States threatened to secede on an
almost daily basis. United States army generals told Lincoln there were plots
to assassinate him. Captain Abner Doubleday garrisoned at Fort Sumter wrote
him a long and extremely intelligent letter warning that South Carolina
militia might fire upon the fort at any moment, killing dozens of soldiers,
leveling the structure. Wall Street lawyers and stockbrokers, who had survived
a postelection plunge in the stock market, were fearful that if Lincoln did not
end the secession crisis immediately the nation's economy might collapse.

Even though President James Buchanan had delivered a tough state of the
Union speech on December 3, the people, North and South, did not look to
Washington for help. Buchanan would be out of office in four months.
Although he still had a Democratic Congress, there were so many Republicans
in it already that the chances of any effective curb on secession from the White
House were severely limited. The people looked to Springfield.

Northerners and Republicans once again wanted the president-elect to assure Southerners that he would not do anything to jeopardize slavery where it was then entrenched. Southerners wanted an assurance that, now newly elected, he would change his mind and permit the extension of slavery into the territories and, despite Republican majorities in Congress in his administration, guarantee that Northern politicians would not curb any other states' rights, beyond the slavery question.

Lincoln was exasperated by Northerners and Southerners alike. What his critics wanted to do, he fumed, was hold the election all over again. The people had spoken. The Republican Party, and Lincoln, had been as clear as it could be on its slavery policy: they would continue to permit slavery where it existed but prevent it anywhere else. Lincoln had argued that policy for seven long years in a hundred public places, and had been quoted on his grudging support for slavery where it was entrenched and on his opposition to it in the territories in a thousand newspaper stories. Yet Southerners still insisted that he acquiesce to their demands in order to prevent secession. Northerners, too, pushed him to make concessions, charging that a divided Union would be social, political, and financial ruin.

He would not do it. He explained to friends that he understood people's worries and the apprehensions of Wall Street bankers but did not feel it was necessary to outline his views again. They had not changed since 1837.[1] Lincoln told a Missouri newspaper editor, Nathaniel Paschall, that he "could say nothing which I have not already said."[2]

He knew Southerners would again press him on the extension of slavery, but he did not expect that from Northerners, especially from Republicans and most especially from members of his own campaign team. Yet as soon as Lincoln was elected, Thurlow Weed, so instrumental in raising money for his election, asked him to do just that. Weed had organized an emergency meeting of governors to discuss the impending financial crisis and implored Lincoln to let the South bring slaves into the territories in order to keep the country and its financial market together. Weed was sure he could convince Lincoln to change his mind, but Lincoln was firm with Weed: "I will be inflexible on the territorial question and I probably think that the Missouri line extended [which would permit slavery in southern territories but not northern]...would lose us everything we gained by the elections...,"[3] he said, destroying Weed's efforts.

If he was irritated by Northerners, Lincoln was just baffled by the South. He had been careful, in years of speeches, to reassure Southerners that he would not free any slaves where slavery was legal, yet he received letter after letter telling him that everyone in the South was afraid that, now elected, he would renege on his promise and free all of the slaves in the southern states. Lincoln completely misunderstood this fear and angrily dismissed it. That was an extraordinary miscalculation, but he made it again and again. In one letter to his friend Alexander Stephens, a former Georgia congressman whom he met during his one term in the House, he underscored his lack of understanding.

"Do the people of the South really entertain fears that a Republican Administration would, *directly or indirectly,* interfere with their slaves? If they do, I wish to assure you, as once a friend, and still, I hope, not an enemy, that there is no cause for such fears."[4]

He misjudged the South for two reasons: He saw their postelection demands as bargaining chips to elicit some kind of compromise on slavery from him before he actually took office, and since Southerners had threatened to secede for so long, since 1832 in South Carolina alone, he did not take such threats seriously. He saw the threats as one huge bluff. "We are told in advance the government shall be broken up unless we surrender to those we have beaten. In this they are either attempting to play upon us or they are in dead earnest. Either way, if we surrender, it is the end of us, and of the government," he wrote to Rep. James Hale, who wanted to introduce a constitutional amendment guaranteeing slavery in states where it already existed. He added that concessions in 1860 would only be the beginning of a long string of them.[5]

Although many Southerners begged Lincoln to reconsider, insisting that this time secession was a real possibility, other Southerners assured him that it was not, that this was just one more case of a few radical Southern firebrands, like William Yancey in Alabama and Robert Toombs in Georgia, blowing off more steam. Several Southern politicians told him that canvasses they had undertaken in their own counties showed that the great mass of Southerners were not in favor of secession. Lincoln believed these reports, because he wanted to.

Technically and constitutionally, Lincoln was powerless until his inauguration, four long months away, but he knew, as did others, that as president-elect and leader of the Republican Party, he could influence national events with "hidden hand" diplomacy. Previous presidents, who had taken office in peacetime, did not exercise this obvious prerogative, but Lincoln saw its vast potential. He could, and did, attempt to control events by influencing those who exercised actual constitutional power—senators and congressmen—throughout that winter. Any party leader and president-elect who has not yet taken office has a certain influence over sitting representatives, but Lincoln had considerably more, because the Republican Party had been born as an antislavery party, and many sitting congressmen and senators had been elected on its antislavery planks. Their new leader, a strong antislavery advocate, was to them more than simply the man elected at the head of the party ticket. He was the moral and political leader of the Republican crusade. Lincoln was thus able, despite squabbles between factions in the party, to control sitting representatives from November 1860 to March 4, 1861, and that power enabled him to shape events even more than the congressmen.

Lincoln's two most important interventions were in the Senate's Committee of Thirteen and the House of Representative's Committee of Thirty-Three. The Republicans could control each if they achieved complete solidarity because there were wavering Democrats on both committees. Lincoln issued strict instructions to the leading Republicans on each committee, ordering them to hold the party line in any and all dealings with the Democrats. He had never wavered from his position against the extension of slavery into the territories, and he expressed his opposition to that idea fervently and directly to people who visited him, telling one that "I will suffer death before I will consent or will advise my friends to consent to any concession or compromise [on slavery]," adding that "I should regard any concession in the face of menace the destruction of the government itself."[6]

He sent William Seward, a leading member of the Committee of Thirteen, a terse and unequivocal note on February 1, 1861, ordering party solidarity on the slavery issue: "I am for no compromise which assists or permits the extension of the institution on soil owned by the nation. And any trick by which the nation is to acquire territory, and then allow some local authority to spread slavery over it, is as obnoxious as any other. I take it that to effect some such result as this, and to put us again on the high road to slave empire is the object of all these proposed compromises. I am against it."[7]

The hidden hand reached deep into the House chamber, too. He told Rep. William Kellogg to "entertain no proposition for a compromise in regard to the *extension* of slavery"[8] and was even tougher with his longtime friend, Rep. Elihu Washburne, whom he told to hold "firm, as with a chain of steel," on the prohibition of slavery in the territories."[9]

Lincoln also had to put up with the wild rumors that swept through the North, always winding their way to Springfield. Most of the rumors seemed to be believed by Lincoln's trusted advisers or appointees, such as the false report that Southerners planned to attack Washington, D.C., some time in January, seize the government, and prevent the Electoral College from meeting to vote Lincoln in as president. This rumor was believed by every important person in the Republican Party, including William Seward, who told Lincoln he had to sneak into the capital sometime in January, set up an office, and then appear suddenly in public so that Southerners, seeing him already in charge, would not attack.[10]

The president-elect had a large network of information he tapped every day of his life. He had spent a lifetime in the Midwest getting to know thousands of people whom he considered barometers of information. These were not just politicians and editors, but also small businessmen, farmers, mechanics, factory workers, and their families. He talked to these people when they came to his office or when he saw them on the street, polling them on the issues of the day. It was their conviction that he had to oppose slavery and that, no matter how tough his stand, there would be no war.

Lincoln, who read several newspapers a day, felt comfortable taking this position, in part because it was fully supported by editors throughout the North. Throughout the winter of 1860–61, Northern newspapers became as fervently pro-Union as Southern papers became pro-secessionist, but most, like Lincoln, dismissed Southern threats to secede. Most Northern editors portrayed Southern politicians and newspaper editors as little children throwing temper tantrums and told them to keep quiet and remain in the Union. Since most businesses were doing well because of the spreading industrialization, the Northern newspapermen saw no reason why anyone would jeopardize a booming economy with talk of dividing the country.

To some Northern editors, the economy was so good, and labor so cheap (because of the flood of European immigrants), that it made little difference whether the South seceded. An editor of the *Cincinnati Commercial* wrote: "We are not in favor of retaking by force the property of the U.S. now in possession of the seceders. We would recognize the existence of a government formed of all the slaveholding states and attempt to cultivate amicable relations with it."[11]

Some Northern papers seemed glad to see the Southerners go. "If the Cotton States shall become satisfied that they can do better out of the Union than in it, we insist on letting them go in peace," wrote Horace Greeley in the *New York Tribune*. "The right to secede may be a revolutionary one, but it exists nevertheless."

Most papers begged the Southern states which had seceded to reconsider, and implored the states which had not, and the border states, to remain within the Union. These journals called for cool heads in hot times; nearly all sought a peaceful solution. Some had a dark vision of the future and promised civil war over secession. The editor of the *Pittsburgh Gazette,* a Republican paper, said that the speeches of Jefferson Davis, Robert Toombs, and others were mere bluster and should be ignored but, if these men actually did take their states out of the Union, "it will be time to string them up." If any states actually did secede, "the time may come when the whole country will have to interfere." The editor of the *Indiana American,* too, wrote that Northerners would "settle the question by the sword if need be." Even more ominous was an editorial in the December 20, 1860, edition of the *Daily Illinois State Journal,* in Springfield, Illinois, considered a house organ for Abe Lincoln's views. In a scathing editorial, the editor wrote that "disunion, by armed force, is *treason,* and treason must and will be put down at all costs."[12]

Others said later that even though he misjudged the South's anger and intentions, Abraham Lincoln could have prevented secession and civil war if he had just made a public statement assuring Southerners that the North would not trample their rights. Yet the Southerners further insisted on his agreement to slavery in the territories in any such statement. Lincoln knew he could not do that. If he agreed to give Southerners equal political power in 1861 and subsequently, he would be undercutting the foundation of a proportionate democratic government in which the people elect represent-atives and presidents who agree to carry out policies they favor. If Lincoln had agreed to permit slavery in any territory, he would have been denouncing his own party platform; he would be not only a minority president, but a president who would have lost most of the support of the paltry 39 percent of the public who did vote for him.

If it conceded with him on the slavery extension question, the party would have been badly beaten in the 1862 elections and lost both the Senate and House to the Democrats and risked ruin. And in conceding to prevent secession, Lincoln would have denied the reason he reentered politics, to halt the extension of slavery, turned his back on all the antislavery senators, governors, and congressmen elected with him, and, worst of all, betrayed his own deep and unshakable beliefs that slavery was morally wrong. Abraham Lincoln did nothing to prevent secession because he could not.

THE Lincolns began preparations to leave Springfield and move to Washington in January. Mary Lincoln took their eldest son Robert to New York, where, luxuriating in her husband's coming $25,000 salary (five times his current income), went on a spending spree which annoyed him. He missed his wife desperately while she was gone. Anticipating her return but uncertain of the night, he trudged through the snow, alone, to the Springfield train station three nights in a row in hopes of meeting her train.

Lincoln began to make his goodbyes to the people of his hometown. He was feted by friends at parties, lunches, and dinners. He himself hosted a huge reception in Springfield. He told his usual yarns and stories to the amusement of the crowds. He brought roars of laughter at a farewell dinner at which a strident Unionist vowed to the president-elect that he would shed his last drop of blood for the United States. Lincoln said it reminded him of the energetic man going off to war whose sisters made him a belt on which was stitched the motto "Victory or death." The soldier nervously asked them to reword it to read "Victory or hurt pretty bad."[13]

He visited the law office of Lincoln & Herndon to tell Billy Herndon, his bombastic young law partner, to keep the sign over the door, that when he finished his years as president he would return and resume practice.[14] On January 30 he traveled to visit his stepmother, Sarah Lincoln, whom he had not seen in years, and to pay respects at his father's grave. A sad Sarah told him to be careful. She later told friends she knew it would be their last meeting, that she knew "something would happen...and that I should see him no more."[15]

Finally, on February 11, with Mary gone to St. Louis to do yet more shopping, Lincoln prepared to leave Springfield. He had rented his house to a retired railroad executive and packed all his trunks on his own, identifying himself on luggage tags for the railroad simply as *A. Lincoln*. Early on the morning of the eleventh, he walked to the train station with friends, his beard now full grown and, at 7:55 A.M., stood on the platform of the rear car and turned to say goodbye.

"My friends," he started, with emotion. "No one, not in my situation, can appreciate my feeling of sadness at this parting. To this place, and the kindness of these people, I owe everything. Here I have lived a quarter of a century, and have passed from a young to an old man. Here my children have been born, and one is buried. I now leave, not knowing when, or whether ever, I may return, with a task before me greater than that which rested upon Washington. Without the assistance of that Divine Being, who ever attended him, I cannot succeed. With that assistance, I cannot fail....let us confidently hope that all will yet be well. To His care commending you, as I hope in your prayers you will commend me, I bid you an affectionate farewell...."

The train jostled as it started to pull out of the station and the people stepped forward a bit to wave goodbye. Lincoln waved back, his hand coming up halfway, at waist level, and then he turned and disappeared through the door of the railroad car.

7

JEFFERSON DAVIS
TAKES OFFICE

They will soon feel southern steel....

JEFFERSON DAVIS

JEFFERSON DAVIS left Brierfield plantation early in the morning on February 9 after hugging Varina and bidding his slaves, gathered around him, an emotional farewell. He had received word of his selection as the first president of the new Confederate States of America by the Confederacy's convention in Montgomery, Alabama, the day before, and had to leave his longtime home immediately.[1] He took some bundled-up clothes, stuffed into a satchel, and climbed into a long rowboat manned by several slaves, who rowed him out into the middle of the Mississippi River and headed north, past the plantations of the Davis brothers. He was headed for a nearby upriver landing where he would catch a packet for Vicksburg. As the oars of his slaves dipped into the waters of the river, Jeff Davis looked back over his shoulder at Brierfield. The next time he saw the beautiful plantation on the banks of the river it would be in ruins...and so would he.

Davis did not want to be president of the Confederacy. If anything, he wanted to be the general of any Mississippi regiment which might be formed if civil war came, but he had no desire to run a government. Now that he was president, though, he was determined to rally Southerners to the Confederate cause. It was not necessary. He learned that as soon as his steamer arrived in

120

Vicksburg. There he was greeted with one of the largest receptions he had ever witnessed, larger than those which greeted the armies returning from the Mexican War.[2] A parade had been organized as soon as word arrived that Jeff Davis was on his way, and bands led militia companies through the town, one of them proudly carrying an old flag from Davis's own regiment in the Mexican War. Davis, deeply moved by the thunderous reception, made a short but stirring speech to the crowd. He told them that he did not want war, but if it came he would be with them "by shedding every drop of my blood in your cause."[3]

The Vicksburg celebration was the first of many which greeted president-elect Jefferson Davis on a triumphal six-day trip to Montgomery to be sworn in. The nation, North and South, had never seen anything like it. At a stop on his way to Jackson, a local military academy turned out several regiments of its proud young cadets, immaculately dressed in their stiffly pressed uniforms, to salute him. He was feted in Jackson on February 12, and, in a speech before a huge crowd, said once again that if there was war, he would be with them, taking the war into the enemy's territory.[4]

On February 14, after a telegram from the secession convention told him to hurry to Montgomery, he departed in another parade, this time surrounded by the First Mississippi, his old regiment, carrying their flag.

Davis's reception was the same at every stop on the circuitous train route (the Southern states had notoriously poor train service) which took him through Tennessee, Georgia, and then into Alabama. He was greeted as a hero in Tennessee, which had not seceded, and saluted like royalty in Atlanta, where he again promised victory if war came and told enthusiastic crowds that the Confederacy might annex the West Indies and parts of Mexico.[5] He delivered twenty-five speeches in two days before cheering crowds gathered at train depots and city squares at every any major town on the train's route.

During his journey, the new president of the Confederacy missed his wife and children deeply. "I miss you and the children even more than usual," he wrote Varina, "and when the military came on route, including a company of boys, I wished the children could have seen it, to be remembered in after years....Kiss my children and tell them to be good and love one another. Farewell, dear wife. May God have you in his holy keeping...."[6]

The train finally chugged into Montgomery, six days after Davis left Brierfield, arriving at 10 P.M. Despite the late hour, several delegations from the Confederate convention, along with hundreds of townspeople, were at the depot to greet him. As he got off the train, he was greeted by booming cannons and a lusty roar of approval from the milling crowd, which surged toward him.[7] Davis told the crowd that Northerners might soon "smell southern powder" and "feel southern steel."[8] The Confederacy, and its new president, were off to a fine start.

The new president, though cheered by the public, had not been the darling of the convention. Jeff Davis was a compromise choice, a man who satisfied everyone but entirely pleased no one. The two best presidential candidates, each having the support of millions of Southerners, were John Breckinridge and John Bell, who had run for president against Lincoln. Either would have received the unanimous support of the convention and the people, but neither was available because Kentucky and Tennessee had not yet seceded.

The people of Kentucky, Breckinridge's home state, were torn over the issue and in the end decided to remain neutral. In many towns of Kentucky, residents flew both the Confederate and American flags in front of the same buildings.[9] Breckinridge was still vice president of the United States. Secession, he said, had wrecked the Union, that there was no Union, and that he and his state would stay out of the squabble.[10] Breckinridge was pro-Union until long after the war started.[11]

Bell, too, was in an impossible position. A strong Unionist, he had run on a conservative, but pro-Union platform, and saw himself as a pillar of the Union in his state. He was a former speaker of the House of Representatives.

The secessionist convention delegates did not pick anyone from South Carolina, such as Robert Rhett or Robert Barnwell, because they wanted a separate nation, not a war, and they feared that any firebreathing radical from South Carolina would unnecessarily anger the North. Most believed the three best candidates were Robert Toombs, Alexander Stephens, and Howell Cobb, all from Georgia. Toombs, the favorite, was a U.S. senator. Stephens was a former congressman. Cobb, forty-five, the boy-wonder of southern politics, was the recently resigned secretary of the treasury and former congressman and governor who, many thought, had there been no secession, would one day have become president of the United States.[12]

Stephens had little real support because he was not a true secessionist. The diminutive Stephens had led the faction that opposed a confederacy in the secession debates in the Georgia legislature, snapping at one man that he would never fire the first shot in any civil war. In the lobby of the Exchange

House in Montgomery on the night before the vote for president, he told a South Carolina delegate that he did not want the job and assumed it would go to the popular Toombs. "Mr. Toombs [has] superior qualifications for the Presidency...[to] any man connected with the...secession movement," he said.[13]

Delegates did not worry about the dedication of the bombastic Toombs to the cause, but they worried about his drinking. An alcoholic, he became hopelessly drunk on the night of February 6, "higher than ever," according to observers.[14] That all-night drunk probably ruined his chances for election. Delegates worried, too, about Cobb's tactics. His brother Thomas, determined to thwart both Stephens and Toombs, spent the night of February 8 going from room to room, lying to the delegates, falsely informing them that the Georgia delegation was solidly behind his brother, and, in rather haughty fashion, that the election was locked up. The Georgians, discovering the plot in the morning, turned against the Cobbs. The Georgia delegation let it be known that they were divided among the three men and had no choice at all. The rest of the delegates, furious with Cobb's duplicity and attitude, decided they would not support any of the Georgians and looked for a compromise candidate.

That was Jeff Davis. While no one supported him enthusiastically, no one was opposed to his election. Davis's Mississippi friends had a strong argument for their weak candidate: In Davis, the Confederacy had two leaders in one. He was not only a widely known senator but also the hero of two wars and a former secretary of war who could, if conflict came, serve as commander in chief as well as president.[15] He had other qualities. He was from Mississippi, a Deep South state, and had the support of the Deep South at a time when the Confederacy was uncertain whether the Upper South would secede. He was a moderate, not a radical, and would earn the respect of moderates in the South. Just as important, as a moderate he would be able to negotiate with the Northerners.[16] Although a politician, Davis was renowned as an intellectual who would have the respect of educated Southerners, whose support and money was needed. As a war hero, he would have the support of middle- and lower-class whites who owned no slaves but respected him for his wartime service. And as former secretary of war, he had substantial administrative experience that no other candidate had.[17]

"Possessing a combination of these high and needful qualities, he was regarded by the whole South as the fittest man for the position," said South

Carolina delegate James Chesnut.[18] Virginia's W. Porcher Miles added that his long and varied experience in public life, experience most others did not have, also figured in his selection.[19]

Davis, at home at Brierfield during the process, played no part in his election and never ran for any office beyond a military commission before the convention met. He wrote a friend, Alexander Clayton: "The post of President of the provisional government is one of great responsibility and difficulty. I have no confidence in my capacity to meet its requirements. I think I should perform the functions of general if the executive did not cripple me in my operations. I would prefer not to have either place, but in this hour of my country's severest trial will accept any place to which my fellow citizens may assign me."[20]

Now, suddenly, he had to form a government, lead a country, and consider the possibilities of a civil war. He did not hesitate. On February 18 Davis looked out over a crowd of about five thousand people gathered in front of the handsome portico of the white state house in Montgomery and delivered his inaugural address. Some of his supporters found his address compelling, while most politicians and reporters felt it was lackluster, a routine, long, and tepid Jeff Davis speech aimed at explanation rather than inspiration. "Personally, he is the last man who would be selected as a 'fire eater,'" wrote one reporter.[21]

Davis was cautious. He spoke to the northern as well as the southern states and went over, again, the reasons for secession. He told the well-dressed and enthusiastic crowd that the Declaration of Independence gave Southerners the right to secede and that the future of the Americas was clearly one of two nations. "I mistake not the judgment and will of the people. A reunion with the States from which we have separated is neither practicable nor desirable."

He said that the South now just wanted to go about the difficult work of starting a brand-new government, but, ominously, he announced that his first order of business would be the establishment of an army and navy. He warned that any military or economic action by the North, such as halting the flow of cotton exports, would be answered, and that if the North intervened in the South at all "a terrible responsibility would rest upon it, and the suffering of millions will bear testimony to the folly and wickedness of our aggressors."[22]

He assured them the people would make the cause succeed. "Obstacles may retard, but they cannot long prevent the progress of a movement sanctified by its justice and sustained by a virtuous people," he said. Then he looked out, past the edges of the crowd and the streets of Montgomery, and seemed to speak directly to Abraham Lincoln—issuing a warning that if the United States took any action against the Confederate States "a terrible responsibility will rest upon it, and the suffering of millions will bear testimony to the folly and wickedness of our aggressors."[23]

His address was greeted with joyous shouts from the thousands gathered in front of the Alabama state house. Bands struck up martial music, and the president, Vice President Alexander Stephens (selected to appease Georgia), and others were driven through the streets of the city in a procession of carriages as children jumped up and down to see them. The new president smiled at everyone, but he knew this was no ordinary presidency and no ordinary time. He wrote to his wife: "Upon my weary heart were showered smiles, plaudits and flowers; but, beyond them, I saw troubles and thorns innumerable. We are without machinery, without means and threatened by a powerful opposition."[24]

Davis would not have been able to deliver his inaugural address if the convention had met just a month earlier. They would have sent their telegram to a man desperately ill, again confined to his bed, debilitated and unable to move, the shutters tightly drawn to keep out any daylight, his wife and slaves washing him, feeding him, and caring for him as he struggled through another one of his herpes bouts, unable to see, read, or sleep.

THE Confederate cabinet was, like any other cabinet, a patchwork of politics, friendship, and expediency. From the start, however, there were problems within the first cabinet of the Confederacy, troubles which would constantly undermine the stability of the new country.

Davis's plan to form a representative and effective cabinet was simple: give someone from each state in the Confederacy a post so that every state would be happy and support the new government—sometimes regardless of skill. His efforts were quickly mired in small-minded politics and explosive personalities.

Davis's very first cabinet effort was to recruit his longtime friend Robert Barnwell, of South Carolina, to be secretary of state. In Barnwell he would have not only a trusted confidant and a man who understood him, but someone from South Carolina to constantly ward off any criticism of the Davis government by hotheaded radicals. Barnwell stunned him by turning down the offer. South Carolinians insisted that Davis must have one of their own, and they offered Christopher Memminger, whom Davis did not know, but he did not want state—he wanted treasury. A successful banker in South Carolina, Memminger understood national and world markets, espoused sound money as the basis of Southern finances, and was a champion of public schools. Davis did not know that most people who dealt with Memminger could not stand him and that, as one put it in a single sentence, he was "rude, dogmatic, narrow-minded, and slow" and, others said, paranoid and extremely defensive.

In need of a secretary of state who was well known, Davis then turned reluctantly to Toombs, who had never liked him and felt that he, not Davis, should be president. Toombs was a big, bulky man with a pale complexion and jet-black, stringy hair. Some said that he had the face and demeanor of an intellectual, but that when he opened his mouth he became a bold and forceful politician, one of the best speakers in the nation. Critics said that he was incapable of listening to opinions besides his own, and that he bristled at cabinet meetings whenever anyone disagreed with him.[25]

Davis deliberately sidestepped Alabama's most famous leader, William Yancey, as secretary of war, fearful that the famed Yancey would be more popular than he. Losing Yancey didn't worry Davis, because he was certain his longtime friend Clement Clay would take the job, but Clay refused. Davis then unwisely turned to Leroy Walker, whom he had never met. The Alabamian, who was not well, quickly gained fame as a procrastinator. He privately accused Davis of trying to run the War Department for him.[26] He also offended all the women, and most men, he met in Montgomery with his incessant tobacco chewing and spitting.[27]

Davis initially had less luck filling the position of postmaster general, receiving brisk turndowns from the two men he approached in Montgomery. It wasn't until Texas finally joined the Confederacy that he talked John Reagan into taking it. Reagan accepted, but told Davis at their final meeting that he was accepting only reluctantly and really had no real interest in the cabinet post. Then, to further anger an already upset Davis, Reagan told him bluntly that he would never have voted for Davis if he had been at the convention and that Davis had no business being president of any country.

The only two members of his cabinet with whom Davis was comfortable were Stephen Mallory and Judah Benjamin, and even they turned out to be minor problems. Mallory, a U.S. senator from Florida who had just resigned, was named secretary of the navy and wanted the job. He was the chairman of the Senate Committee on Naval Affairs, had numerous contacts in the navy, and was extremely knowledgeable about the latest naval and maritime technology. Davis wanted Mallory and supported Mallory; even as he chose him, the new president was pressured to dump Mallory by men from his own state, who claimed he was not as vocal a secessionist as they were. Davis named him anyway.

Judah Benjamin had no critics. The former U.S. senator from Louisiana, was a brilliant man and one of the country's best public speakers. He quickly picked up the nickname "the brains of the South." He joined the cabinet as attorney general but might have been better suited, many thought, for secretary of state.

Later, when the cabinet was finally complete, Jeff Davis walked into a crowded room in Montgomery's Exchange House for its first meeting. His appointees sat around a large table and murmured to each other as the new president entered. He looked around the room, conscious that history was being made. The diverse group of men stared back at him as he sat down. He carefully took stock of his first cabinet, the cabinet on which he had to rely to get the government going and, perhaps, fight a war. As he surveyed the room with his one good eye, his bad eye once again inflamed, he saw Toombs, who hated him; Reagan, who told him he would make a poor president; Memminger, whom people were already calling an autocratic despot, and whom Davis wanted somewhere else; Walker, who did not like him either, and who spat tobacco into a corner spittoon throughout the meeting; and Benjamin, who (correctly) thought he was running the wrong department. And then, of course, there was the waifish-looking, tiny, sickly Alexander Stephens, his vice president, whom everyone in Montgomery began to despise after it was learned that Abraham Lincoln, in a conciliatory gesture, was seriously considering asking him to be in *his* cabinet.

The cabinet secretaries stared back at a changed man. Davis still walked like the young army lieutenant he once was, with a regal air and military bearing, his back ramrod straight and his head high in the air. He was still a fine-looking man who favored slate-colored suits and wore a neatly fixed black silk handkerchief around his neck. His hair was always neatly trimmed and his boots clean and polished.

His numerous bouts with neuralgia and herpes had taken their toll, however, and by the winter of 1861 he had begun to look old and haggard. The lines in his high, square forehead were deeper, his cheeks sallow, and his deep-set eyes sad-looking. His bad eye, now practically blind, was inflamed every day, and the neuralgia caused noticeable ticks in it that annoyed him and those in his presence. People who worked at his home said he was very sick with his eye condition just about every day. The illness, which never seemed to abate, made him constantly edgy and irritable. What made him most different to those meeting him again was a new beard, narrow and sparse, which grew under his chin.[28]

President Jefferson Davis, back behind a desk again, resumed his life as a workaholic. Just as he had as secretary of war, he took on all the work of the new government himself, delegating few responsibilities to others. The paperwork alone was mountainous. Davis was inundated with letters from people looking for jobs, and seeking commissions in the army and navy (at least seventy a week), as well as requests for government contracts and from people trying to convince Davis to push one bill or another, usually for their profit. He waded through piles of letters containing wild suggestions from his new constituents, ranging from pleas for money to long, detailed plans for military attacks. One suggested a full-scale invasion by an army of twenty-thousand Confederates in February of 1861 to seize Washington and kidnap Abraham Lincoln, who, of course, was far away in Springfield, Illinois. One innovative man wrote Davis that he had designed an airplane which could take off from any field in the Confederacy, fly over Washington, D.C., and drop bombs on the White House and Capitol.

Davis would arrive at his office around 8 A.M. He was often the first person in the Exchange House restaurant, where he had a quick breakfast, usually interrupted by government workers and locals who sat down with him and stayed until dinner. He made repeated efforts to socialize with cabinet officers and politicians in the capital, often dining with the Cobbs, who outwardly seemed to enjoy his company but privately despised him ("not a great man" Thomas Cobb noted in a letter home). Often his efforts to finish work were interrupted by well-wishers, old friends, and people from Montgomery and other Alabama towns who just wanted to shake his hand. Work was constantly interrupted by meetings with cabinet officials (at first, Davis met with cabinet secretaries almost daily) and others working in the brand-new government.

Davis's accomplishments in the winter of 1861 were impressive. He quickly signed the new constitution, which was a remarkable document. On the advice of Davis and Alexander Stephens, the convention used the U.S. Constitution as a model for its own, except for additional language about slavery that declared that it could not be eliminated for any reason and that slaves were property which could be taken to any new territories the new Confederacy might annex in the future. The new constitution called for a radical new executive branch in which the president would only serve a single, six-year term, gave him line-item veto power over any proposed legislation and permitted him to dismiss any member of his cabinet. It also mandated that no bill in Congress could have a "rider," or special legislative clause, attached to it, and that a two-thirds vote in the new, five hundred member Congress was necessary for any tax legislation to pass. Immigrants were forbidden to vote and the post office was ordered to operate as a self-sufficient company.[29]

Davis worked with others to construct an executive branch of government, speedily appointing undersecretaries to the different cabinet departments. He moved quickly, with determined steps, to prepare the new Confederate States of America for a civil war, should it come. He asked farmers to restrict cotton production and, instead, to plant some cereal and other food to fill Southern granaries for the soldiers. He met with the presidents of all the Southern railroads and won a pledge from them to charge half fare for soldiers, in peace or war, and to accept Confederate bonds for ticket payment. Federal forts in the Deep South taken over by Confederate states were reorganized and renovated. Warehouses for medicine and soldiers' clothing were established. Davis managed to get wealthy planters to agree to donate a percentage of their food crops to the army, and he talked bankers into making large loans to the new government.

He expected attacks on his warlike posture, which he hoped would dissuade any military action by the North. He declared, "I am prepared for the criticism which the truth often bestows upon necessary caution but if success follows and the blood of the brave be thus saved, I will be more than content to have the censure which in the meantime may be encountered."[30]

Davis paid special attention not only to raising an army but to guaranteeing that the best generals in the United States Army, many of whom were Southerners, turned in their swords and joined the Confederate Army, just in case war came. As early as March 1, less than two weeks after his inauguration, he began seeking out and appointing generals, giving field commands to men such as Joseph Johnston and Robert E. Lee,[31] and made preliminary plans to begin building ships for the Confederate Navy. He also took time to order that no teenagers under the age of eighteen could be mustered into the army.[32]

He moved to establish relations with European nations, particularly England and France, whose help he deemed critical if civil war came. A student of history, Jeff Davis knew how important France had been as an ally in the American Revolution. He knew, too, from his years of studying economics and politics, that European nations depended on the South for all of their cotton for textiles. He assumed they would be willing to lend diplomatic and even military assistance to the Confederate states in any civil war in order to secure their cotton shipments. Davis wasted no time in attempting to win over England and France as allies. On March 16 he sent a three-man commission to Europe to reach accords with governments there.[33]

Davis usually worked from his offices at the Exchange House. He also set up an office in the handsome new Montgomery mansion which the government leased for him at an exorbitant $5,000 a year (Davis earned $25,000 a year, the same as President Lincoln.) The two-story white wood frame mansion was a classic federal home building with ample sleeping quarters upstairs and a large room for entertaining on the first floor.

Varina, who arrived in late February, immediately became a much-admired first lady, hosting dozens of parties at the president's mansion. She was a gracious hostess who knew how to organize parties, whom to seat together and what kinds of fine foods and drink to serve, but people did not come to her parties just for entertainment. They came to see her. President Davis missed many parties, but few party-goers missed him. His wife was always the center of any group of women discussing families or education, but she was also frequently the center of a group of men discussing economics and politics.[34] Varina, one of the best-educated and shrewdest women of the South, helped make Davis's important early days a success.

The work and stress crippled his health, though, and within a few weeks of his inauguration his bad eye went almost completely blind, forcing him to move about the rooms of the mansion carefully while navigating with his one good eye. The relentless stress made his eye so bad that just about every reporter who interviewed him in February and March of 1861 commented on the debilitating condition of the left eye and Davis's generally tired, gaunt appearance.[35]

The hard work of the new Southern president and the immediate popularity of his wife were applauded throughout the South. The celebrations for Davis began at the February 18, 1861, inaugural, when a booming cannon salute honored his swearing in, followed by mad cheers from a crowd of some five thousand people and a small parade. A reception the following night drew thousands of people. Many Southern cities set aside February 22 as a day of national celebration for their new government and president.[36] Davis was congratulated wherever he went in Montgomery and, later, Richmond, and regiments of soldiers drilling as he passed cheered him lustily.

His arrival in Richmond, which later became the South's capital, was greeted by a roaring throng of well-wishers.[37] An equally large crowd greeted Varina when she arrived there several days later. Varina's greeters let out a roar heard through Richmond when a door to one of the train's baggage cars slid open and someone brought out Jefferson Davis's horse, saddled up for battle. The citizens were sure, now that his horse was in town, that the hero of Monterey and Buena Vista would head up the army himself and lead their boys to victory.

A New Orleans newspaper suggested that Montgomery be renamed the District of Davis, after the North's District of Columbia. The owner of a new commercial vessel built in Charleston named her the *Lady Davis* after Varina. Society women who met the first family had nothing but good things to say about Davis and his wife. Editors of leading Southern newspapers, so long critical of Davis, joined the chorus of well-wishers. One editor even applauded Davis for turning an ad hoc revolutionary convention into a "model government." Jeff Davis had done such a good job, and won so much acclaim, that Bowdoin College, in Maine, the North's northernmost state, even bestowed an honorary degree on him.[38]

Beneath the surface, however, many began to complain about Montgomery, the president, and the new government. Montgomery, people said, was not a proper capital for a state, much less a new nation. It was a quiet Southern city of eight thousand people, the population of which nearly doubled when the Confederate government was formed. It had a tiny business district and offered spotty entertainment, and the residents were parochial. A reporter in town to cover Davis's inaugural compared it to a sleepy small town deep in the middle of Russia.

The city was bursting at its seams now, and could not expand quickly enough to handle all the new residents, who complained bitterly about it. There were only two full-service hotels in town. Government employees, from cabinet members to clerks, had to live there, often four men to a room in hotels whose rooms were dirty, prices high, and service invisible.[39] Office space for the new government was minimal, and entire cabinet departments, identified by handwritten cardboard signs nailed to old doors,[40] were shoe-horned into one or two rooms in inadequate office buildings.

The city was also infested with bugs that winter. One bitter British reporter in town to cover the inauguration joked that "had it not been for the flies, the fleas would have been intolerable."[41] Wealthy planters and their families who had traveled to Montgomery for the inaugural and to help form the new government, left quickly instead, complaining about the dirt, bugs, and heat.[42] Lower government officials, packed into small, dreary, flea-infested rooms, began to wonder aloud why Jeff Davis needed such a large mansion while they suffered.

People began to complain quietly that while Davis was being feted in the mansions of Montgomery, and would be the target of Richmond social queens when the capital was moved there, as it soon was, he was once again exhibiting the personality traits that had annoyed people for decades. He was starting to snap at secretaries, cut meetings short, ignore solicited advice, and upstage lower-ranking officials. He was once again, as he had as secretary of war, taking on too much work from too many departments and refusing to delegate responsibility.

There was subsurface dissension among Davis's cabinet members and leading Southern politicians, too. The chancy composition of the cabinet, in which region counted more than talent, was not as responsible for that as were the personalities of its members. Toombs never liked Davis. The relationship between the two men had been fragile ever since an altercation in 1853, when Davis, as secretary of war, called Toombs a liar and Toombs called him a "swaggering braggert."[43] Toombs's job as secretary of state did nothing to soothe his massive ego. He was belligerent from the outset, and within weeks of the inauguration was critical of nearly everything Davis did. He assumed a comical stance to make his derision seem innocent, for instance, accusing Davis of acting like a European king. Davis, Toombs said, was only the leader of six states and joked that he was "President of six nations and Texas."[44]

Howell Cobb and his younger brother, Thomas, still seethed over Georgia's failure to unite behind them to win Howell the presidency and were intensely jealous that Jeff Davis lived in the mansion which rightly should have been the Cobbs'. They were even angrier that Stephens, who had denounced the Cobbs in the testy Georgia secession debates, wound up as vice president. Thomas Cobb felt his selection as vice president was "a bitter pill to us, but we have swallowed it with as good a grace as we could. The man who has fought against our rights and liberties is selected to wear the laurels of our victory."[45]

Stephens, skeptical of the entire Confederate adventure from the beginning, tried to remain on good terms with Davis and did everything he could to support the new government. On his own, from February to April, he went on the stump through the South and gave forty-two prosecession speeches. He did it for the cause, though, not for the president. Even though he was eager to speak whenever and wherever just about anyone wanted, he refused Davis's requests to make important speeches on behalf of the government to the secession convention in Arkansas and to a Mississippi group. He reluctantly honored a Davis request to go to Virginia to coordinate the merger of the Virginia military forces with those of the new national government, but only because friends talked him into it.[46]

Nor would Stephens follow Davis's guidelines on speeches, either. The president wanted Stephens, and all his cabinet officers, to frame secession in terms of states' rights and not slavery. Davis and Stephens split within a month when Davis criticized him for a speech he gave in Savannah that strongly supported slavery but failed to support states' rights, essentially defining the Confederacy as a white man's country. Stephens's speech in early March, reported widely in the North, earned the wrath of abolitionists and radical Republicans, who saw it as further proof that it was slavery, and not states' rights, that drove the seceding states out of the Union. Davis had worked hard to maneuver secession through political shoals in order to prevent a war over slavery, and now Stephens, in a single hour, had ruined his carefully worked out plans. It was the first serious split between them; it would soon grow into a war between these two determined leaders of the South, almost wrecking the new government before it got started.[47]

Others in the cabinet, while not directly critical of Davis, objected to his constant meddling in their departments, particularly Leroy Walker. Walker had taken the War Department job fearful that Davis, a former secretary of war, wanted to run the department himself. Davis allowed Walker no independence, never trusting the judgment of his assistants, abhorring teamwork, and constantly arguing with Walker and his subordinates.[48] War

Department officials complained that the spats between Walker and Davis prohibited the hurriedly forming Confederate army from being as well equipped as it should have been.

Others complained that Davis's personality was not suited to so high an office, that while he was accomplishing much publicly in starting the new government, he was having considerable difficulty, first in Montgomery and later in Richmond, in getting along with people in private. Men throughout the government complained that he was a perfectionist. He drove secretaries crazy with paperwork that had to be rewritten numerous times. It was said that he was stubborn, that he insisted he was always right, and that, if ever wrong, he blamed someone else. They said that his ego, large enough in the Senate, was now overinflated. One politician, discussing the proposed cabinet, said that it would appoint "for secretary of State—Hon. Jeff Davis; War and Navy—Hon. Jeff Davis; Interior—Ex-Senator Davis; Treasury—Col. Davis; Attorney General—Mr. Davis."

He was a perfectionist, aides said, and no one could ever meet his standards. He always felt that he was doing his best but that the entire country was letting him down. This attitude was expressed best in a note to General Joe Johnston during the subsequent war: "Everybody disappoints me in their answers to my requisitions for troops and the last hope of a large force of militia coming to your aid seems doomed to add another to past disappointments."[49]

Even Varina did not believe her husband was the most capable man for the job. Years later she said, "I thought his genius was military, but that as a party manager, he would not succeed. He did not know the arts of the politician and would not practice them if understood."[50]

The feuds in the cabinet, the bills being introduced almost daily in the new Confederate Congress, the reorganizations of the state governments, the price of cotton, relations with Europe, the thousands of office seekers, and the hundreds of appointments he was making to the army all concerned President Davis, but none concerned him as much as Fort Sumter.

8

LINCOLN TAKES OFFICE

We are not enemies, but friends...

ABRAHAM LINCOLN

THE TALL MAN EMERGED cautiously from a side entrance of the hotel in Harrisburg, Pennsylvania, a soft felt hat pulled down over his head to conceal his face, his body covered with a long overcoat, the darkness of the winter night concealing his identity, and, with two other men walking on each side of him, hurried toward a carriage which took them to the train station. No one noticed the odd trio moving stealthily through the streets. Nobody noticed that an extra train had suddenly and quietly appeared at the Harrisburg train station. Few were aware, or cared, that all telegraphic communication in and out of the city had been cut off without explanation just before the three left the hotel.

At the train station, the tall man and the others moved quickly to their railway car and entered it. As soon as they were on board, the special train pulled slowly out of the station, its engineers and conductors aware only that very important persons were on the train and that secrecy was imperative. The train glided down the tracks, scarcely noticed by the railroad workers milling in the area. The tall man's companions, both armed, kept watch for strangers. An hour later, the special train pulled into Philadelphia, where the trio switched to another train. The armed men escorted the man in the felt hat and overcoat into a sleeping compartment they told the conductor they needed

135

for their friend, whom they said was an invalid. The porters shrugged, found them a compartment, and walked away as the men locked the compartment door and pulled curtains across the windows.

The "invalid," president-elect Abraham Lincoln, tried to sleep but could not. He spent most of the next few hours watching the moonlit landscape move past the train as it chugged toward Baltimore, where he was again whisked through the train depot unnoticed, then hustled aboard a third train by the two men, bodyguard Ward Lamon, a personal friend who would do anything for the president-elect, and Allan Pinkerton, founder and head of the Pinkerton National Detective Agency.[1]

Pinkerton, who worked for the Wilmington and Baltimore Railroad, had been told by his agents in Baltimore that prosecessionist men there planned to assassinate Lincoln when he switched trains during a much-publicized stop en route to his inauguration. Pinkerton went to Leonard Swett, traveling with Lincoln, and then to the president-elect himself, who at first discounted the threats. Later that night Lincoln remembered that during the campaign he had received dozens of letters in Springfield about assassination plots against him, and that even after the election he had been mailed a letter which begged him to stay out of Washington until his inauguration, because there were plans to kill him.[2] General Winfield Scott, who saved all the letters, told him later that there had been 130 different assassination letters from fifteen states.[3]

The day after the latest rumor from Baltimore arrived in Harrisburg, Fred Seward, William Seward's son, rushed to Harrisburg to tell Lincoln that his father had heard the same reports in Washington, checked them out, and believed they were true. He, too, urged Lincoln to slip into Washington late at night. No one at Willard's Hotel, where Lincoln was scheduled to arrive the following day, could figure out why Seward was pacing back and forth in its lobby at 5 A.M. as the sun rose.

Slip in is exactly what the president-elect did. He left the train in Washington with Lamon and Pinkerton close beside him, holding the coat and hat tight to disguise his identity as he sneaked through the railroad station at 6 A.M. to a waiting carriage. Lamon and Pinkerton almost shot longtime Lincoln friend Elihu Washburne, who, tipped off, was waiting for Lincoln at the train station and shouted to him as he recognized him. Lincoln's dawn, backdoor entry into Washington in disguise became front-page news a day later after a reporter wrote, erroneously, that the president-elect had worn a Scottish tam and kilt as a disguise. Cartoonists used this image to make

Lincoln look ridiculous. It was a less than majestic start for the nation's sixteenth president.

Lincoln realized that his cloak-and-dagger arrival in the capital would not endear him to government workers or politicians, even in his own party: it had been a mistake. Presidents who arrive in Washington for the first time gain much political leverage by appearing to be completely in command of themselves and their party, prepared, thanks to the people's electoral mandate ,to carry out campaign promises[4] and to make sweeping changes.[5] They do not sneak up the back stairs.

Lincoln *did* feel he had a mandate from the people, despite his winning only 39 percent of the vote, because his party had swept both houses of Congress and he had easily won the election with a large margin of votes in the Electoral College. He had been victorious in every single Northern and Western state, carrying many of them in landslides. He had fallen well short of a popular majority because he had not been on the ballot in most Southern states, and had received few votes in those where he was. He was also a man of enormous self-confidence, who was certain that his natural skills with people could quickly win over any skeptical residents of the capital.

Wrong about the late-night, side-door entry into Washington and eager to rectify his mistake, Lincoln began a campaign that morning to be seen in as many public places as possible to assure everyone that he feared neither assassins nor anyone else. After a few hours' sleep in his five-room suite at Willard's, he had breakfast with Seward and cheerfully greeted astonished diners. Lincoln and Seward then made a surprise visit to the White House, where they interrupted a meeting between President Buchanan and his cabinet. The president and the others were surprised to see Lincoln a day early, but nonetheless delighted. Lincoln shook hands firmly with each of them and seemed in buoyant spirits.

As word swept through the capital that Lincoln was a day early, the most important men in the army and government interrupted their plans to meet him. General Winfield Scott arrived at Willard's shortly after 3 P.M. for a genial meeting. The happiest man to see him was his presidential rival, Senator Stephen Douglas, who arrived effervescent with joy at seeing his longtime friend, bringing the entire Illinois congressional delegation with him, to Lincoln's great satisfaction.[6]

Over the next few days, Lincoln met with senators for breakfasts in public hotels, had lunch with congressmen, and attended every reception and party he could, particularly those in public arenas. He even went with friends on public carriage tours of Washington, shaking hands and waving to residents as he met or passed them in the streets. He was quick to project the image of a family man, bringing Mary and his children, who had arrived by train a day after him, to many of the festivities.

Lincoln charmed everyone in Washington, as he had for a generation in Springfield. He took great care to mention his surprise at how intelligent the men of Washington were, and how lovely the ladies (he did this when Mary was not around), taking great pains to compliment the woman who played host at whatever party he attended. He remembered, by face or name, many people he had met years before, recalling some from as long ago as an 1848 campaign swing through New England.

Lincoln used that two-week preinaugural round of parties to feel out many Republican senators, soliciting their advice on whom he should appoint to his cabinet and in what post. This enabled him to get expert advice while at the same time building bonds with legislators who now saw themselves as not only the president's acquaintance, but his personal confidant. It was a trick Abe Lincoln had learned long ago, and it always worked for him. He even kept an informal poll on whether Republicans wanted him to appoint Chase or Cameron secretary of the treasury. Chase won easily, so Lincoln blithely switched Cameron, for whom he had little regard, to the War Department, which he thought was rather unimportant since there was not going to be a war.

Away from the reception lines and the punch bowls, Lincoln put together his cabinet, deferring some appointments until the last minute in an effort to achieve a politically strong, representative group that would please everyone, hold party factions together, and help him settle the secession storm.

Lincoln was pleasantly saddled with his cabinet. Aides operating on his behalf at the Republican convention had promised several cabinet posts to prospective opponents in order to win the nomination. A direct promise was made at the convention to Governor Simon Cameron, of Pennsylvania, even though many Pennsylvanians, and many in his own party, told Lincoln that Cameron was corrupt. Another explicit promise was made on the convention floor to Governor Samuel Chase of Ohio at the last moment, as the critical third and final ballot ended. Veiled promises appear to have been made to the Montgomery Blair family of Maryland, and to Schuyler Colfax and Caleb

This striking photograph of Davis was taken in the early 1850s, probably during his first term in the U.S. Senate. (Courtesy of the Museum of the Confederacy)

(*Right*) Davis's first love was Sarah Knox Taylor, the daughter of General Zachary Taylor, who opposed the romance. Sarah died of malaria a year after the couple married. Davis was devastated. The same month Sarah died, Anne Rutledge, Abraham Lincoln's first love, died in New Salem, Illinois. (Courtesy of the University of Alabama Hoole Collection)

(*Opposite*) Davis's older brother Joseph, one of the South's wealthiest businessmen, gave him Brierfield Plantation, next door to his own home on the Mississippi River. Davis, who owned 107 slaves, was one of the South's most benevolent slaveowners. James Pemberton, one of the slaves closest to Davis, was probably his best friend. (Courtesy of the Museum of the Confederacy)

When he was thirty six, Davis married Varina Howell, a vivacious, intelligent, very political and headstrong eighteen. She was his confidant through his years as a planter on the Mississippi and his stormy political career. (Courtesy of the Museum of the Confederacy)

The Davises had five children. This postwar photo shows, from left to right, Jeff Jr., Maggie, Varina Anne, and William. Joe (inset) died at the Confederate White House in 1864. All three Davis boys died before the age of 22. (Courtesy of the Museum of the Confederacy)

A crowd estimated at over five thousand gathered in front of the statehouse in Montgomery, Alabama, on February 18, 1861, to see Jefferson Davis inaugurated as the president of the Confederacy. The ceremony was followed by a triumphant parade through the city led by bands playing "Dixie." (Courtesy of the University of Alabama Hoole Collection)

This mansion, known as the "Confederate White House," was home to Davis and his family throughout the war. It had its own stable for horses. (Courtesy of the Library of Congress, Museum of the Confederacy)

Like Abraham Lincoln, Jefferson Davis grew a beard soon after he became president. (Courtesy of the University of Alabama Hoole Collection)

Varina Davis as she appeared when she became the first lady of the South. The highly opinionated Mrs. Davis was scorned by Richmond high society when she arrived and became, like her husband, a constant target of criticism for anyone unhappy with the progress of the war. (Courtesy of the University of Alabama Hoole Collection)

The participants in this inventive painting of President Davis and his cabinet never actually posed. The artist aligned them as they would have looked in Davis's dining room and then added General Lee, who rarely met with the cabinet. They are, from left to right: Seated: Navy Secretary Stephen Mallory, Attorney General Judah Benjamin, and Davis. Standing: Leroy Walker, the first of six secretaries of war. Lee is in the middle. Then, seated: Postmaster John Regan and Treasury Secretary Christopher Memminger. Standing: Vice President Alexander Stephens and Secretary of State Robert Toombs. (Courtesy of the Museum of the Confederacy)

(*Above*) Alexander Stephens, the Confederacy's vice president, broke with Davis early in the war and remained a constant political enemy. He led a mid-war peace movement which failed. (Courtesy of the National Archives, Museum of the Confederacy)

(*Left*) Joe Johnston began the war as one of Davis's trusted generals but quickly fell from favor as soon as he began to disagree with the President's military decisions. Davis's hatred of Johnston was so great that he refused to attend any postwar parades or ceremonies if he knew Johnston would be there. (Courtesy of the National Archives, Museum of the Confederacy)

Robert E. Lee, in charge of the Army of Northern Virginia, was Davis's chief military advisor and a close personal friend. When Davis went on trial for treason after the war and all others had abandoned him Lee rode to the courthouse and volunteered to appear as a character witness for him. (Courtesy of the Museum of the Confederacy)

(*Below*) Davis spent two years in prison at Fortress Monroe, outside of Washington, D.C. on treason charges. While in jail, he earned the respect of Dr. John Craven, depicted here at his bedside, and the guards. He was finally released in 1867. (Photo courtesy of the University of Alabama Hoole Collection)

By the time he was eighty, he was often invited as an honored guest to Confederate reunion celebrations, parades, and rallies. His funeral in New Orleans in 1889 was one of the largest in U.S. history. (Courtesy of the Museum of the Confederacy)

Smith, both of Indiana, who had swung their states into Lincoln's column at the convention.

Just after the convention, in an effort to win the financial and political support of the New York Republican machine, Lincoln's men promised the State Department to William Seward, who, pleased, then campaigned for Lincoln throughout the country. Always worried about Seward, Lincoln sent friend Lyman Trumbull to New York after the election to see if Seward was connected to a recent governmental corruption scandal there. He was not.[7]

Lincoln promised his vice president, Hannibal Hamlin of Maine, that he would name someone from New England to give the cabinet regional balance. He was certain that Hamlin would, as he did, select Gideon Welles, a Connecticut newspaper editor and a key Lincoln supporter at the convention. Lincoln was unable to extricate himself from the promises his aides had made on his behalf. Although he was sorely tempted to do so in the case of Cameron, he was reminded by Judge Davis and Leonard Swett that they had made a firm commitment and could not go back on it.[8] Other Lincoln advisers said that Cameron would make the party stronger in Pennsylvania.[9]

He very much wanted to appoint a Southerner. Many Southerners, in confidential letters, urged it,[10] several suggesting that he even divide his cabinet in half, with four secretaries from free states and four from slave states[11] (while others insisted that no abolitionists of any kind be considered[12]).

Lincoln approached Rep. John Gilmer, of North Carolina, who turned him down, and toyed with the idea of naming Alexander Stephens of Georgia (several people urged naming John Bell, whose nomination would quiet the South[13]). He eventually contented himself with two men from border states, Edward Bates (Missouri), as attorney general, and Montgomery Blair (Maryland), as postmaster general. He named Caleb Smith of Indiana, a tireless Republican worker who gave 125 speeches for Lincoln in 1860, secretary of the interior to fill a western slot.

Looking for broad-based support from Congress, the partisan press, and the public, Lincoln sought Republicans who were formerly Whigs, Free Soilers, and Democrats, too. Finally, the crafty Lincoln, knowing that even if there were no permanent secession there would surely be political trouble ahead, wanted to put the men who might be the loudest critics of his administration into his cabinet in order to mute them. He did that with Chase and, above all, Seward.

In his efforts to meet party and regional needs and to keep his promises, Lincoln left no room for personal friends and political aides, the men every president puts in his cabinet first. Presidents need longtime friends and aides who understand their needs and support them regardless of how brutal the storms ahead. Lincoln was unable to name Judge David Davis (although he later appointed him a justice of the U.S. Supreme Court), Leonard Swett, or Norman Judd (who became minister to Prussia), his three closest advisers, to cabinet posts.

The cabinet wound up including not only some of his political opponents—it was no secret that Seward's supporters wanted him to replace Lincoln on the 1864 ticket—but several former Democrats and Whigs who had converted to Republicanism, and men from slave states, whom the cabinet members from the free states did not trust. In fulfilling his promises and satisfying his several criteria, Lincoln put together a cabinet of politicians, not statesmen, of men who had been at each other's throats for years. The cabinet secretaries, particularly Chase, Bates, Cameron, and Seward, were experienced and strong-willed men who were not intimidated by their new boss, whom they saw as an untested political novice.

One nervous Lincoln aide told the president-elect that the cabinet was full of men determined to use their new posts to further their own agenda at his expense. He told Lincoln that it would be difficult to achieve any unity. "They'll eat you up," he said. The confident Lincoln shook his head. "They'll eat each other up," he answered.

Lincoln knew he had a cabinet full of aggressive, ambitious and opinionated men, but he also knew they were among the best and brightest politicians in the nation, men who had built up impressive credentials through decades of service to their cities, states, and country. They were leaders who could help him guide successfully a nation at peace and, more important, they had the administrative skills and wisdom to help him lead a nation at war. Lincoln knew, and they did not, that he had the self-confidence to harness their energy and not let them trample him.

William Seward was a born politician. The short, thin, dapper secretary of state had graduated from college at nineteen, become a lawyer, and been first elected to the New York State Senate at the age of twenty-nine, as a candidate of the struggling Anti-Masonic Party. He joined the newly formed Whigs in 1834 and in 1838 was elected and then reelected governor of New York. A staunch reformer as governor, he instituted numerous prison and educational reforms and refused to turn over any fugitive slaves to their southern owners. Seward retired from politics after his two terms and became a wealthy lawyer, dividing his practice between lucrative corporate law and minimal income cases defending runaway slaves and antislavery organizations.

The growing slavery movement drew him back into politics in 1849, when he was elected as a Whig candidate to the U.S. Senate. Within months, Seward became the leading antislavery politician in America, delivering a speech in which he told Americans that although the United States had laws supporting slavery, there was a "higher law" than the Constitution: God. Seward was not only a fiery orator, a forceful, popular politician, perhaps the best-known man in America in 1861, but a man who had led three different parties in his career, twice served as governor of the nation's largest state, and worked in the Senate for twelve years.

By the mid-1830s, Salmon Chase was one of the leaders of the antislavery movement. At no charge he served as lawyer to dozens of escaped slaves looking for safety in Ohio, and arguing a case against slavery before the U.S. Supreme Court. Critics called him "the attorney general of fugitive slaves." In 1849 a coalition of unhappy Democrats and Free Soilers in the Ohio legislature elected Chase, head of Ohio's upstart Liberty Party, to the United States Senate, where he led the antislavery forces against the Compromise of 1850 and the Kansas-Nebraska Act. Fed up with the Democrats, whose southern wing clung to slavery, Chase quit them and helped form the Republican Party in Ohio. He was elected governor in 1855 and reelected in 1859.

Edward Bates, the oldest man in the cabinet, had spent a lifetime in the rough-and-tumble world of Missouri politics. He was a long-term state legislator and U.S. Congressman. An energetic leader, Bates helped form the Whig Party in Missouri, and after it collapsed in the early 1850s, helped organize the Republican Party there. He was not only a veteran political leader from a state with divided pro- and antislavery loyalties, but a man with considerable administrative experience.

Postmaster General Montgomery Blair, a graduate of the U.S. Military Academy, and a former Democrat, had represented slave Dred Scott in his case before the U.S. Supreme Court.

Gideon Welles, who sported a thick white beard and wore a gray wig, was not only a longtime political leader in Connecticut and a man who had held important administrative posts, but a former newspaper editor (*Hartford Times*). Like all editors, he had an innate sense of how the American people felt about key issues, something Lincoln believed invaluable. His political career began in 1827 when, at age twenty-five, he was elected to the Connecticut state legislature as a Democrat. Welles served four terms in the legislature and then spent a year as the state's comptroller, in charge of Connecticut's finances. After three years in the naval department in Washington, he returned to Connecticut and, in 1855, helped found the Republican Party there. He was the party's nominee for governor in 1856. Welles spent the years 1856 to 1861 solidifying the Republican Party, running it as if it were a company. In 1860 he led his state's delegation to the Republican National Convention and, at a crucial juncture, swung the Connecticut vote to Lincoln.

Even though he was the cabinet's weakest link, Simon Cameron, too, had extensive political and administrative experience. He built a well-oiled and smoothly functioning political machine which, by the early 1850s, totally controlled Pennsylvania politics, enabling him to be elected to the U.S. Senate. He was an efficient, well-organized party leader who had developed intricate networks throughout the state. Lincoln believed he could run the War Department with efficiency. He had promised Cameron a cabinet spot, and he delivered—despite howls of protest from Pennsylvanians that Cameron was corrupt and that, as one wag said, "the only thing he would not steal was a hot stove."

The one man Lincoln's aides were afraid would eat him up, of course, was Seward. The secretary of state decided, while Lincoln was finalizing the cabinet, that he was more of a prime minister than head of a department. Seward began to make his own decisions on government goals, to lobby for his own choices in the cabinet, and even to conduct his own foreign policy. A political cyclone blowing throughout Washington, Seward quickly became a problem for Lincoln, who had to rein him in, control him, but still allow him enough independence to bolster Lincoln's administration. He also knew that the publicly popular, politically influential, and very opinionated Seward was far more dangerous outside the cabinet than he was in it.

Seward was renowned for quiet discussions with members of opposing political parties, midnight legislative deals, wild schemes, and secret meetings. A Republican joke was that the nation had yet to find a congressmen from whom Seward had not stolen an idea. For years he carried on clandestine meetings with Edwin Stanton, Buchanan's attorney general, in order to spy on the president.[14]

Seward's fireworks began right away. He went to Lincoln, full of bluster and bravado, and demanded that the president-elect keep Samuel Chase, as big a political lion as Seward, out of the cabinet: There wasn't room enough for both of them in Washington, and if Chase was coming, Seward was going.

Lincoln knew he had to cut off Seward immediately, and he did so. Lincoln told friends who he knew would report to him within an hour that if Seward wanted to resign there were plenty of others who wanted to be secretary of state. He also reminded him, abruptly, that it was the president, not the secretary of state, who made policy; that, indeed, Lincoln did have a policy; and that Seward, if he was paying any attention at all to anyone besides himself, would know that.[15] Then, at the last minute, when Seward had agreed to join the cabinet and moderate his views, Lincoln, as was his custom, made Seward an extraordinary gesture and asked him to review and suggest changes in his inaugural address.[16] That gesture, from one nationally recognized orator to another, helped bring William Seward into line as secretary of state.

On the personal level, Lincoln did everything he possibly could to befriend Seward, and to let everyone know, in a very public way, that the men were allies. The first man he had breakfast with, the morning after he slipped into Washington, was Seward; the first man with whom he rode through the streets of Washington was Seward. These were the gestures, like so many others, stretching back to the wrestling matches in New Salem and the political clubhouses in Springfield, that turned hostile enemies into ardent admirers of Abraham Lincoln.

The president-elect worked on his inaugural address, as he did on most of his speeches, for weeks. He was sure of his speech and sure of his goal, but uncertain that the address, the most important of his life thus far, struck the right tone. Lincoln needed to cajole the Southern states back into the Union, not to scare them away, and he believed some of his language might do that. Eager to solidify the Union, he asked several people, including Chase and Seward, to help him edit the speech. They did, softening some sentences, deleting certain paragraphs, and adding sentences and thoughts they thought appropriate. Much of the moving finale was suggested by Seward.

The speech was crucial to Lincoln and the new administration. Millions North and South waited to hear what he would say about the secession crisis and the future of the divided nation. Would he meet all of the concessions the South required, or at least compromise on some of them, in order to lure them back into the Union? Would he advocate, as James Buchanan had, a national convention of some kind for Northerners and Southerners to iron out their differences? Would he threaten the South if they did not extinguish their secession fires and come back to the United States, which was ready to embrace them?

It was an eerie inauguration. General Winfield Scott, who warned Lincoln of assassination plots, ordered two artillery batteries set up at the Capitol, where the oath of office was to be administered, in case there was trouble. Further protection came from dozens of U.S. Army sharpshooters ordered to watch windows and to patrol the rooftops of buildings along the inaugural parade route. Hundreds of uniformed, armed troops cordoned off the major streets to permit Lincoln's carriage to pass down Pennsylvania Avenue as safely as possible.[17] Although the day began as a crisp, overcast morning, by noon soft winds had blown most of the clouds away, the temperature had risen to fifty degrees, and the sky was a fine cobalt blue.[18]

Lincoln woke at 8 A.M. and had eggs for breakfast with his wife in his hotel suite. He wanted to spend the morning with his family, wrestling with his sons, and Seward was the only outsider allowed to visit. Outside, the last few drops of rain stopped falling and the Lincolns could see hundreds of people walking toward the Capitol for the inauguration. People continued to arrive for the next four hours, lining the parade route eight and ten deep and covering acres of land around the Capitol. The Lincolns could hear the sounds of fife and drum corps playing martial music in the distance. Soon they saw thousands from the Wide Awakes, the men's clubs that had worked so hard to make him president, marching in regimental formation in their traditional oilskin coats.

At about 11 A.M., President Buchanan, in his carriage, picked up Lincoln in front of his hotel. Their small procession, accompanied by more soldiers, made its way through city streets to the Capitol as thousands applauded as they went by. Once at the Capitol itself, Lincoln walked past more troops and entered through passageways in the building which soldiers had secured to prevent assassination attempts. Lincoln and Buchanan attended the swearing in of Hannibal Hamlin as vice president in the Senate. Finally, with Buchanan at his side and the others behind him, Lincoln emerged on to the east portico of the Capitol just before 1 P.M. As he strode confidently across the wooden platform erected for the inauguration, he was greeted by a burst of mighty applause from a crowd of about thirty thousand people.

Onlookers, held back by police lines, stretched for blocks. Men sat on the rails of fences erected for the inaugural; small boys climbed trees and perched themselves on limbs. A drunk fell from a tree onto a group of men below, to the laughter of onlookers.[19] Congressmen unable to get seats on the platform sat wherever they could. One legislator, Lewis Wigfall of Texas, unable to find a seat, climbed up on a statue of Columbus and an Indian girl, wrapped his arms around it, and listened to the address while hanging on for an hour.[20]

When it was time, Lincoln, seated, went over his speech again, then stuck his spectacles in the pocket of the new, black suit he had purchased for the occasion. He did not know where to put his stovepipe hat, however. He turned left, then right, but there were no empty seats or places on which to rest it. Suddenly, reaching out to take it and care for it, was the small, pudgy hand of Stephen Douglas.[21]

The new president seemed full of self-confidence and poise as he looked out over the vast throng. During his twelve-day trip from Springfield (before the secrecy of the leg from Harrisburg to Washington) he had given short speeches in a number of cities, and the response of the people had been overwhelming. His train had been so mobbed by people in one city that it had to pull out inch by inch as police tried to keep the people away. His speech in Pittsburgh, where he told the crowd that "there is no crisis excepting such a one as may be gotten up at any time by turbulent men, aided by designing politicians" was interrupted by applause and cheers seven times in one minute.[22] His speech to the New Jersey legislature had to be stopped at one point because the legislators and audience, rising to their feet, cheered so loudly that the president-elect could not continue. His speech in Philadelphia took twice as long as planned because of constant cheering from the crowd.

The inaugural was a well-delivered address which, in dignified fashion, implored the seceded Southern states to rejoin the Union, but it was a disjointed speech. At times, Lincoln seemed belligerent, restating his long-held belief that secession was wrong, and refusing to give in on any Southern demands concerning slavery. He absolutely forbade secession, which he said was prohibited by the Constitution. A first draft which ordered the federal government to seize, with force, all installations captured by secessionists was changed at the insistence of Chase and Seward.[23] At other times Lincoln was conciliatory, reminding the crowd that while he was against the extension of slavery, he was not against its existence where it was established, and that the federal government would not do anything, by force, on the slavery question. He appealed to the faithful, telling the crowd that God considered America his favorite land. And he reminded his listeners that the nation was nearly one hundred years old and had successfully weathered many storms before this one.

It was a new, stronger Abraham Lincoln who delivered the inaugural address. Writers who had covered him for years were surprised that his high, reedy voice was gone: He gave the address in a deeper, richer, melodious voice that rang out loud, clear, and deliberate.[24] The crowd couldn't wait to cheer their new president. As soon as he began to speak, getting out only the phrase "Fellow citizens of the United States...," the crowd roared its approval.[25] The people interrupted the speech dozens of times with loud applause and cheers, particularly when Lincoln said that, speaking of secession, "physically speaking, we cannot separate. We cannot remove our respective sections from each other, nor build an impassable wall between them. A husband and a wife may be divorced...but the different parts of our country cannot do this."[26]

Finally, Lincoln looked past the crowd to speak directly to the South. He begged for patience and for time. "In *your* hands, not in *mine,* is the momentous issue of civil war....*You* have no oath registered in Heaven to destroy the government, while *I* shall have the most solemn one to 'preserve, protect and defend it,'" he said. Then, in lilting and touching oratory, he added: "We are not enemies, but friends....The mystic chords of memory, stretching from every battlefield, and patriot grave, to every living heart and hearthstone, all over this broad land, will yet swell the chorus of the Union, when again touched, as surely they will be, by the better angels of our nature."[27]

Throughout the speech William Seward kept smiling and muttering "Yes, yes" as Lincoln touched on all the points they discussed. Douglas, the opposition leader, was just as impressed with his old friend's speech, shouting, "Good! Good!" repeatedly as Lincoln begged for peace. Northerners thought it was the best political speech they had heard in years; later, after the speech ended, a number of Southerners went over to Seward and told him how highly they thought of the president's inaugural address.[28]

New technology permitted telegraph wires to carry the speech as it was delivered to New York, where it was set in type and published in special editions by dozens of newspapers by four o'clock that same afternoon, a journalistic first. Every paper in the country carried the speech either that day or next morning, often with editorial comments on it. Many just published it as is, on a separate sheet, and distributed it by nightfall.[29]

While Lincoln's address was well received in the North, it was largely ignored in the South. The Deep South states, now in their own Confederacy, vowed to remain a separate new nation. Lincoln and his wife went to the White House after the speech, under extraordinarily heavy military guard, and that night attended the inaugural ball. Despite the day's solemnity, Lincoln enjoyed himself, particularly when he spotted Douglas across the ballroom. The two men, and Mary Lincoln, swapped stories about politics and friends back in Springfield. Mary and Douglas even led the procession. It was a long and happy night for Lincoln, who had achieved his lifelong dream at a perilous time.

It was, perhaps, his last night of happiness. The next morning, while crews were still cleaning up after the parties, carpenters were tearing down the inaugural stand, soldiers were returning to their barracks, and James Buchanan was heading home to Pennsylvania, a secretary dropped a carefully written report from a Major Robert Anderson on Lincoln's large wooden desk. Anderson informed the president that supplies at his post would run out in six weeks and that, if not resupplied, he would have to surrender Fort Sumter.

PART IV

THE EARLY WAR YEARS

9

FORT SUMTER: WAR

FORT SUMTER was an unfinished, eerie-looking brick fort anchored on an island in the middle of the harbor at Charleston, South Carolina. The 300 by 350 foot pentagonal U.S. Army bastion, which only had 48 of its 140 guns operational, was occupied by the nervous Major Robert Anderson, who took command of it in December 1860. Anderson, from Kentucky, was a former army comrade of Jefferson Davis. Fearing an attack on the federal garrison at Fort Moultrie, their previous home in Charleston Harbor, he had moved his 128 troops to what he believed was the safety of Fort Sumter. The move was taken as a sign by the Southern states that the Federals would not surrender the fort, as they had surrendered other forts in seceded states, and might try to use it to bombard Charleston.

Since South Carolina was the first state to secede, Sumter became the symbolic lightning rod of the North–South crisis.[1] Across the waters of the harbor, South Carolina commanders, and later Confederate Army generals, stationed artillery batteries.

Lincoln's advisers in the capital told him he had only two options. He could either evacuate the fort and turn it over to the Confederacy, or he could resupply it. The second option ran the risk that the South would take it as a sign of aggression and open fire on the supply ships or the fort itself, initiating civil war.

Jefferson Davis's advisers, in Montgomery, were just as edgy as Lincoln's. They told him that any resupply of Fort Sumter meant that the North wanted to hold it and thus coerce South Carolina, and then the other seceded states, back into the Union, that this would be diplomacy at the mouth of a cannon. They advised Davis that he had to either accept the resupply and coercion or attack the fort before supply ships could arrive, initiating civil war.

March 9, Day One

WASHINGTON   Abraham Lincoln, who knew so little about the fort that he continually referred to it as "Fort Sumphter," slumped back in his chair at the first full cabinet meeting on the crisis and listened as army and navy officers offered opinions on the feasibility of resupplying or the advisibility of surrendering Sumter. General Winfield Scott, the head of the army, told Lincoln to surrender the fort, that it was not possible to resupply it. Naval leaders disagreed. By the end of the meeting, which dragged on all afternoon, most cabinet members, except for Postmaster General Montgomery Blair, sided with Scott. So did Lincoln.[2]

MONTGOMERY   Jefferson Davis, who had dispatched a three-man "peace commission," Martin Crawford, Andre Roman, and John Forsyth, to Washington to amicably settle the Fort Sumter problem, learned that Lincoln would not see them, nor would Secretary of State William Seward.[3]

March 12, Day Four

WASHINGTON   Eager to supply Sumter, Montgomery Blair summoned Navy Department aide G. V. Fox, his brother-in-law, who agreed with him, and the two met with Scott and Lincoln. Scott continued to argue for evacuation, but Lincoln told Fox to visit Sumter to see if it was practical to send in supplies.[4] The president, caught in the Sumter muddle, still did not believe that the Charleston installation could lead to any real trouble. Sometime on March 11 or 12, he met with Ohio Senator John Sherman, who introduced him to his brother, William Tecumseh Sherman, then the president of a college in Louisiana. When Sherman told Lincoln that everyone in Louisiana was ready for war, Lincoln laughed at him. "Oh well!" he chuckled. "I guess we'll manage to keep house."[5]

March 15–16, Days Seven–Eight

WASHINGTON   Lincoln walked quickly into his packed cabinet room for another critical session on Fort Sumter. This time he was accompanied by Fox, his naval aide, who outlined what appeared to be a reasonable plan to resupply the fort with men and food by a naval armada. If necessary, the navy would shoot its way into Charleston. The plan met with considerable opposition. Five of the seven cabinet secretaries were completely against it, warning Lincoln that it would lead to war and that, even if successful, it would merely keep intact a fort the United States did not need anyway.

The majority was led by the persuasive Seward, who argued that the seceding states, if left alone, would be unable to attract any more secessionist sisters and, within months, would come crawling back to the United States Seward had been entertaining postinaugural parties with this same assurance, going so far as to invite editors of Virginia newspapers—who wanted Virginia to secede—to Washington, where he flatly promised them that Sumter would be evacuated.[6] Seward had even enlisted the editor of the *National Intelligencer* as an emissary, sending him to the hotel room of George Summers, head of the secession convention in Virginia, to assure him of Sumter's evacuation.[7] (Seward then stunned Lincoln by telling him that the deal could be wrapped up if Lincoln would nominate Summers to the U.S. Supreme Court.[8])

Most cabinet members agreed with him.[9] Only two supported holding Sumter. Salmon Chase, who liked the idea of resupplying the fort, nonetheless had considerable misgivings. Montgomery Blair argued heatedly that surrendering the fort to the Confederates would only strengthen their coalition, and they would just keep asking for more. Blair argued that saving the fort would demonstrate an overall U.S. resolve which would, shortly, crush the Confederacy.[10]

Lincoln faced a delicate problem. He did not really mind leaving Fort Sumter alone and waiting for the South to make the next move. He even permitted General Scott to draw up an order for Lincoln to sign ordering the evacuation. He did not want to fire the first shot, start a war, and allow the Confederates to cast themselves on the defensive, as violated victims. Marshaling public opinion for a war over Fort Sumter would be difficult. What he had to do was somehow resupply Sumter, while leaving the door open for Jefferson Davis to take a rash step. On March 15, Lincoln did not know, and would not learn until much later, that on that very day William Seward had guaranteed the evacuation of Sumter to the peace commissioners sent by Jeff Davis.

MONTGOMERY   On the same day that Lincoln met his cabinet, Davis learned that his peace commissioners, unable to see Lincoln or Seward, had approached two Supreme Court justices, John Campbell of Alabama and

Samuel Nelson of New York, who agreed to act as intermediaries. Nelson was a longtime personal friend of Seward. On the fifteenth, Nelson went to Seward, and Seward assured him that within five days Fort Sumter would be evacuated.[11]

Asked how soon he could do something officially, Seward said he would send a letter to Davis that afternoon, and a telegram shortly afterward.[12] Davis was relieved to be "assured on the highest authority."[13] Justice Campbell told Davis that he was certain Seward was speaking for Lincoln.[14]

Davis seemed relieved, too, that Seward, and not the inexperienced Lincoln, was directing the government. Friends in Washington had told him and other Southern leaders that Lincoln had foolishly put the strongest men in the North in his cabinet and that they, not Lincoln, would run the country. The minority president would be nothing more than a caretaker until his term expired in 1864. Now that Seward seemed intent on peace, Davis was delighted, although in the back of his mind he worried about a frank telegram which he received the day after Lincoln's inauguration from Congressman Lewis Wigfall, warning Davis that Lincoln was far tougher than he let on publicly, a self-confident man who would not be bullied by anyone.[15]

Jefferson Davis was ready for war. Publicly, he preached peace, but privately, and often, he told friends that he fully expected war. He had talked of war even before his inauguration. He told William Sharkey, chief justice of Mississippi, whom he met at a train station on his way to his inauguration, that war seemed inevitable and that it would be "long and bloody."[16] Just two days after he was sworn in as president of the Confederacy, he wrote South Carolina governor Francis Pickens that "my mind has been for sometime satisfied that a peaceful solution of our difficulties was not to be anticipated and therefore my thoughts have been directed to the manner of rendering force effective."[17] Friends told him as soon as he became president that there would be war, and he agreed.[18]

Davis also agreed with secret resolutions passed by the Confederate Congress on February 15 that if peace could not be reached over Fort Sumter, Confederate forces should attack the installation. On March 1, Confederate secretary of war Walker, acting on Davis's orders, told Pickens that "the President shares the feelings expressed by you that Fort Sumter should be in our possession at the earliest possible moment."[19]

A few days later Davis wired General Beauregard in Charleston to ignore the peace talks and prepare for war. Davis instructed forces in Alabama to prepare an assault on another federal installation, Fort Pickens, outside Pensacola, Florida.[20] He wired Florida's governor that peace talks should not interfere with his state's efforts to ready their defenses. Davis named General Braxton Bragg, one of his first appointees, commander of an army and ordered it from Mobile, Alabama, to surround Fort Pickens and prepare for an attack, if need be, on April 3. His orders contained detailed instructions on how Bragg should position mortars around all sides of Pickens, which he described as a fort "to be battered."[21] Davis's orders to Bragg also included a promise to send him more troops.[22] That same day the president who spoke publicly of peace wrote: "I am still very confident we shall have a collision."[23]

As he talked of peace, Davis issued dozens of orders to procure uniforms and provisions for soldiers. He sent men North to buy guns, ammunition, and machinery and emissaries to Europe to purchase weapons and ammunition and to negotiate for additional supplies in the future. On April 4 Davis met with James Rogers of Texas to negotiate the transfer of a state cavalry unit to the new Confederate Army.[24] Finally, on the morning of April 8, Davis sent letters to the governors of seven Southern states and asked them to raise twenty thousand troops for the Confederate Army.[25]

Davis sent a team of representatives (William Yancey, Dudley Mann, and Pierre Rost) to London to secure an alliance with Great Britain should war be threatened. He was certain that the support of England, the principal trading partner of the United States, would dissuade Lincoln from warring against the South. The British would support the South, Davis knew, because they depended on the South for cotton. His representatives would issue a veiled threat that Jeff Davis would cut off all of England's cotton if the British did not support the new government.[26]

March 17, Day Nine

WASHINGTON   The Northern press started a campaign to hold Fort Sumter as soon as reporters heard of Anderson's shortages. Dozens of big city newspapers, Republican and Democratic, urged Lincoln to send all the food and clothing the soldiers required and as many troops as necessary to hold the fort, without delay. "Have We a Government?" asked one newspaper.[27] The *New York Times* urged immediate activity of some kind. "The Administration *must have a policy of action,*" wrote its editor.[28] The *Boston Journal* declared that "secession is treason" and that if another state seceded, Lincoln should commence a war on all of the South.[29] Strangely, the crosstown *Boston Daily Evening Traveler* did not care what happened to Fort Sumter, but upbraided the Lincoln administration for not pledging a fight to the finish for Fort Pickens, editorializing that Lincoln's silence on both showed "weakness, imbecility, cowardice and flunkeyism."[30]

The editors of the *Daily Courier* of Lafayette, Indiana, were so eager for war that they criticized Lincoln for his "peace policy."[31] The *New York Herald* boldly told the president that if the U.S. Army did not have enough troops to hold Fort Sumter, twenty thousand of its readers were ready to do it in their place.[32] The *New York Post* was no less giddy than others in its patriotism. Its editor wrote: "If the rebels fire at an unarmed supply ship, and make a perfectly proper act the pretext for shedding the blood of loyal citizens, on their heads be the responsibility."[33]

Lincoln was also put under considerable pressure from his own party. Republicans took turns giving speeches demanding that Lincoln support Fort Sumter and not capitulate to the Confederates. On March 28, Lyman Trumbull, his longtime friend and senator from Illinois, introduced a resolution in the Senate insisting that the president use all the means in his power to "hold and protect public property [Sumter]."[34] A frustrated Carl Schurz, who had helped deliver the German vote in the 1860 election, asked Lincoln: "What is the policy of the administration?"[35] Cabinet officers, too, were criticized by constituents. "The *do nothing* policy of our government is disastrous," wrote Peter Deyo of New York to Seward.[36] Despite his early personal ambivalence about the issue, Lincoln now ran the risk of his own party abandoning him if he evacuated Fort Sumter.

MONTGOMERY   Davis learned that Seward had again promised Judge Nelson that Sumter would be evacuated. Davis, like Lincoln, was slowly becoming a target for newspapers. He, too, was sent editorials and stories from various newspapers all over the South urging the new Confederate government to *do something* to show that the U.S. could not push it around. After all, editors demanded, the United States had given up every fort and arsenal throughout the South, so why not Sumter?[37] Some papers, such as the *Mobile Mercury,* even suggested that the new Southern nation was gripped with "fatal apathy," and that the government had to revive the citizens with some kind of move on Fort Sumter.[38]

March 20–21, Days Twelve–Thirteen

MONTGOMERY   Davis learned that Seward had once again assured him the fort would be evacuated, and that Seward was more determined than ever to prevent a confrontation. Seward had received letters telling him that a show of force might drive Virginia out of the Union[39] and a sharp letter from former vice president John Breckinridge that warned of fiery tempers in the South. "Better to try to quell it now by peaceable means...than to wait until the people are run mad with delight at their brand new government."[40]

WASHINGTON   Fox telegraphed Lincoln that he had arrived at Fort Sumter for an inspection. At some point in late March, Lincoln decided to send longtime friend Ward Lamon to Sumter, too, for a second opinion.

March 25, Day Seventeen

WASHINGTON   Ward Lamon completed his inspection of Sumter but then, for no apparent reason, met with South Carolina Governor Pickens to tell him that the troops might be evacuated and to suggest that he might relay that information to Jefferson Davis. The Confederate president was relieved. He knew that Lamon was not only a security adviser to Lincoln, but one of his old Illinois political cronies.[41]

While Lamon was in Charleston, Lincoln, unannounced, knocked on the door of a house in Washington at which Mary Doubleday, the wife of Colonel Abner Doubleday, was staying. Doubleday, second in command at Fort Sumter, had sent long, perceptive letters to Lincoln during the presidential campaign, never acknowledged, warning him of an attack on Sumter. The president asked a startled Mrs. Doubleday if he could read any and all letters she had received from Fort Sumter. She went to another part of the home and returned with a thick sheaf of personal letters from her husband. Mrs. Doubleday sat quietly in the corner while the president, hunched over a table in the sunlit room, his long legs occasionally causing his knees to bang against the underside of the table, carefully went through the stack of lengthy letters.[42] One that shook him was a short note telling Mary that food was running out and that fuel was so low that the men planned to burn doors, floorboards, and carriages to keep from freezing in the fort.[43]

Rumors flew throughout Washington and Montgomery: Major Anderson had mined Fort Sumter with hundreds of pounds of explosives and would, if not resupplied or attacked, blow up the fort, and himself, and all the soldiers in it[44]; if Sumter was attacked, all the western states would secede and form their own, third, country; if civil war came, New York City would secede from the United States and form its own country or over five thousand armed men, in secret militias, would riot and seize the city and declare its independence; more than fifteen thousand Virginians, awaiting a signal, were about to attack Washington and seize the entire government[45]; and, finally, that, under the cover of darkness and using only a rowboat, a disguised Jefferson Davis had sneaked into Fort Sumter and arranged an evacuation with his old friend Anderson.[46]

March 28–29, Days Twenty–Twenty-One

WASHINGTON   As an enjoyable reception in the White House was breaking up, President Lincoln, as casually as possible to avoid alarm among guests, had an aide ask each of the cabinet members present to meet him in a midnight session to discuss the latest developments at Fort Sumter. He told them, showing great emotion for the first time since Sumter had become a potential fuse, that General Winfield Scott, after an investigation, was now not only insisting that the government abandon Fort Sumter, but abandon Fort Pickens as well. Lincoln asked them for their opinion, eager to gain a sense of how the cabinet as a whole was leaning on the critical issue.

The hot-tempered Montgomery Blair, glowering at Seward, whom by then he suspected of unofficial dealings with Southerners, angrily denounced Scott, whom he called a politician and not a soldier. Blair urged Lincoln to supply Sumter and to defend it at all costs.[47] Some of the cabinet chiefs were for standing by Sumter and some were against. Lincoln, tired and gaunt after the long night, asked them to come back the next day, Good Friday, for a final, decisive meeting. After walking the group to the door, he returned to the high -ceilinged halls of the White House, where he wandered most of the night, rubbing his eyes, going from room to empty room, unable to sleep, thinking about some way to support Fort Sumter and yet not provoke a war.

The president drifted off to sleep toward dawn, but only slept a few hours. Exhausted, he got up for a late breakfast and told staffers that he was extremely depressed.[48] By the time the cabinet met again, at noon, Lincoln was certain he had to resupply Fort Sumter. It had been several days since the last cabinet meeting on Sumter and the president, and cabinet, had come under enormous pressure to save Sumter from both political leaders and newspapers. Lincoln polled his cabinet secretaries in search of support, and this time it was there. Four of them—Blair, Chase, Welles, and Cameron—were strongly in favor of resupplying the fort. Welles feared the effort might start a war, but shrewdly noted that if the fort was attacked it would justify war against the South.[49] Two secretaries, Smith and Bates, were mildly in favor. Bates never made up his mind, telling Lincoln just to do something, anything, but at once.[50] Only one cabinet member, Seward, was against, arguing that any resupply "would provoke an attack...war at that point."[51]

Lincoln did not waver, as many had expected. He was decisive, bold, and quick. He told his cabinet he felt that sentiment had decidedly shifted[52] and that he would resupply the fort. He would only resupply it with provisions, however, not arms and men, and Southerners would not open fire on a food ship. He ordered the navy to send a supply expedition from New York to Sumter, and asked Scott for a comprehensive report on Sumter and U.S. military strength, which the aging general put on the president's desk the very next morning[53].

That cabinet meeting changed the opinion of some men in the cabinet about Lincoln, who, they realized that Good Friday, was not the fumbling prairie lawyer they had read about. Lincoln, his decision made, relaxed a bit, believing, as he had believed for months, that despite everything told him and everything he read in newspapers, north and south, that the Southerners would not start a war.

Deep inside, however, Lincoln the politician knew that he could not afford to ignite an armed conflict by shooting his way into Fort Sumter or shelling Charleston. The national and international fallout would have been unacceptable.[54] If war was to start, it had to be by Confederate guns. Lincoln's friend Orville Browning explained the folly of an attack in a detailed advisory he offered in mid-February, when he predicted that any expedition to Sumter would be attacked and that "then the government will stand justified, before the entire country, in repelling that aggression."[55]

April 1–2, Days Twenty-Four–Twenty-Five

WASHINGTON Lincoln, beset on all sides over the never-ending Fort Sumter controversy, walked through the halls of the White House to his office. There he was startled to find a fantastical memo from Seward advising him to declare war on Spain and France. Disbelieving this incredible plan, he read Seward's memo a second time. Seward argued that Spain and France had illegally meddled in Mexico and had to be taught a lesson. He told a bewildered Lincoln that not only would this provocative move be good for foreign policy, but that it would revive the patriotism of the Confederacy, which would come to the United States' side and battle the foreign powers as a single army. Then, when the war was over, the Confederate states would rejoin the Union. At the conclusion, Seward said that if Lincoln did not want to lead the war, he, Seward, would be glad to do it himself.

Lincoln was staggered. He did not know, of course, that the idea was a wild, desperate effort by Seward to cover up his secret promises to the South over Fort Sumter. He worried that Seward was trying to take over the government, just as Lincoln's friends warned. This, he knew, was the time to show the New Yorker who, indeed, was president. Lincoln sternly rebuked Seward for the memo, which he rejected out of hand, and reminded him that he, Lincoln, was president, and not Seward.[56] Lincoln added, sharply, that if something needed to be done in foreign policy, "*I* must do it."[57]

MONTGOMERY   Davis's belief that Fort Sumter would be evacuated was bolstered by a telegram from Commissioner Martin Crawford, who assured Davis that no one in Lincoln's cabinet was in favor of resupplying Sumter and that reliable sources now reported that Lincoln, whom Crawford felt had no spine for confrontation, would simply wait until Anderson ran out of food and then, troops starving, let Anderson evacuate the fort on his own.[58]

Yet, Davis was also receiving reports of frenetic activity in the Brooklyn Navy Yard, in New York, where hundreds of workers toiled on a secret, breakneck project. Southerners fed him reports of U.S. army troops being withdrawn from frontier posts for possible reassignment to Florida. Reports reached Davis from Washington that U.S. army officers were talking of an attempt to save Sumter and, when the fort was secure, of bombarding Charleston with its cannons.[59]

April 4, Day Twenty-Seven

WASHINGTON   Lincoln made yet another, circuitous effort to avoid trouble at Fort Sumter by seeing a representative of the Virginia secession convention, which was meeting to decide whether or not to join the Confederacy. The president had met with Virginians several times since arriving in Washington for the inaugural.[60] He had sounded out several on a deal in which Lincoln would evacuate Fort Sumter if the Virginians could guarantee that their state would not join the Confederacy. Lincoln was certain, as were many, including Southerners, that without prosperous and politically powerful Virginia, the Confederacy, until then only a collection of Deep South states, would soon collapse. Now, as preparations were being made to send warships to South Carolina, Abraham Lincoln made another effort to avert a possible war, this time promising the Virginia delegate, John Baldwin, the same deal.[61] Nothing came of the meeting.

April 6, Day Twenty-Nine

MONTGOMERY   Reports continued to arrive in Davis's cramped office in Government House that a fleet of some kind was preparing to sail from New York City. His aides told him it was a fleet of warships intent on attacking Charleston or resupplying Fort Sumter with men and guns.

It was one of the worst weeks in Jeff Davis's life. Bad news followed bad news. All conversations in Montgomery were about Sumter and war. Because Davis continued to insist on issuing nearly every order of the war department and on taking on most of the responsibilities of the executive branch personally, rather than delegating jobs to others, the Confederate president was already physically exhausted. He slept badly; neighbors reported the lamps of his office in the executive mansion were lit on most nights. He ate little, exercised not at all, attended no social events and, friends said, had begun to lose weight and look pale. The increasing stress Davis was under made his health worse. His disposition turned sour and his eye, once again, flared up. This time, the left eye became so bad that a thick filmy layer covered it completely. So great was the pain that Davis, in meetings and conversations, often kept both eyes closed tight, opening the good one to shoot glances of approval or disapproval.

Worst of all, Varina was gone. Convinced that Sumter would be evacuated by Seward and conflict averted, Davis had sent Varina and the children back to Brierfield for some rest. She was not there to prepare his favorite food, host parties, invite friends over for dinner, or have the children ready for him when he trudged back from the office. Nor was she there to give him the political advice he had yearned for and depended on for much of his adult life. In his most important hour, he missed her desperately.[62]

162THE EARLY WAR YEARS

April 7, Day Thirty

WASHINGTON   Extremely nervous about Sumter and the rumored resupply by sea, the Southern intermediaries in Washington went back to Seward to seek a final agreement. Once more, Seward assured them the fort would be evacuated. "Faith as to Sumter fully kept. Wait and see," he wrote them in a quick note.

It rained hard in Washington that night, so hard that in some streets there were puddles a foot deep. The city's just greening lawns soaked up the water like sponges. The rain pounded hard on the roof of the White House, where Abe Lincoln made a last desperate plea to a Virginian to make a deal to avert war. This time he talked to an old friend from his congressional days, John Minor Botts, a heavyset, longtime political power broker and Unionist. Botts had Lincoln's complete trust, even when his judgment was unsound.

Botts told the president that the evacuation of Sumter would avert a war, but that any fighting there would start one. Lincoln again offered to abandon the fort in exchange for Virginia's promise to stay in the Union, and Botts said he would try to make a deal. Lincoln, frustrated, flung his arms up and down. "It is too late," he said, knowing the ships were on their way, and then told Botts that he did not want war. "I am not a war man....I want peace more than any man in this country..."[63]

April 8, Day Thirty-One

WASHINGTON   Robert Chew, Lincoln's representative, arrived in Charleston, which by now was an armed fortress, and read a telegram to Governor Pickens and General P. G. T. Beauregard announcing the attempt to resupply Fort Sumter, but with provisions, not guns or men.[64] He told them Lincoln had given him the telegram on April 6, the day before Seward once again promised Southern intermediaries Fort Sumter would be evacuated.

MONTGOMERY   Jefferson Davis, well dressed as always, his body ramrod straight, strode angrily into an emergency cabinet meeting. He felt he had been deceived by Ward Lamon, whom he now believed was in Charleston not to prepare an evacuation, as he said, but to assess the strength of both Sumter and the Confederate artillery and to buy time for Lincoln while he prepared to attack. He believed he had been lied to by Seward, and that Seward had been lying for nearly a month to keep the South at bay while Lincoln secretly prepared to resupply Sumter and organized an expedition of warships to do it.

Now, with armed ships and men on the way, Lincoln was trying to coerce the South into submission.

Jeff Davis had been ready for war for nearly two months, and he conveyed his attitude to his cabinet. Unlike Lincoln, who did not make up his mind until after holding numerous meetings and weighing numerous options, Jeff Davis never flinched from his early decision to go to war. He never looked at the crisis through the eyes of Northerners, and never considered what consequences rash steps might bring. He knew what to do. His cabinet secretaries, as agitated as Davis, needed little coaxing to go along with his desire to shell Fort Sumter if it was not evacuated immediately, and to open fire before the Northern ships could arrive to reenforce it. Surprisingly, the radical Robert Toombs, his new secretary of state, was opposed, arguing that an attack now would start a long war. Vice president Alexander Stephens, too, would have opposed the attack on Sumter, but he was traveling.[65]

The Confederate president waited until the next day to send any orders. Then, convinced he was right after one last night of deliberation, Jefferson Davis, the hero of Buena Vista and Monterey, ordered Beauregard to bombard Sumter if Anderson would not evacuate it.

April 9, Day Thirty-Two

WASHINGTON   Lincoln had his aides secretly leak a statement to Washington reporters which insisted the federals were merely sending food to starving soldiers, not challenging Confederate forces. In a line which must have been Lincoln's own, it ended with the assertion that "the administration will not be the aggressor."[66]

MONTGOMERY   Davis thought Lincoln was behind Seward's stonewalling, that he had been lulled into thinking Sumter would be evacuated merely as a cover so that Lincoln could equip and sail a fleet of warships down the Atlantic coast to Charleston. He refused to believe Seward was acting on his own. He said, "The absurdity of any such attempt to disassociate the action of the President from that of his Secretary, and to relieve the former of responsibility from the conduct of the latter, is too evident to require argument."[67]

Davis slept little during the next few nights. He told clerks to wake him if any telegrams arrived, adding that any war would be Lincoln's responsibility, not his:

The forbearance of the Confederate government is perhaps unexampled in history. It was carried to the extreme verge, short of a disregard of the safety of the people who had entrusted to that government the duty of their defense...The attempt to represent us as the *aggressors* in the conflict which ensued is as unfounded as the complaint made by the wolf against the lamb in the familiar fable. He added that the aggressor is not the man who fires the first shot, but the man who is the first to aim his pistol.[68]

April 12–13, Days Thirty-Five–Thirty-Six

WASHINGTON   At 3:20 A.M., just as Lincoln's fleet of supply ships approached the coast of South Carolina, U.S. Army Major Robert Anderson was ordered to surrender Fort Sumter within the hour by Beauregard, acting on instructions from Jefferson Davis. Anderson refused. At 4:30 A.M., the forty-seven howitzers and mortars under Beauregard's command began shelling the fort.

The attack on Sumter was grand theater for the residents of Charleston. Thousands of Charlestonians, in their finest suits and dresses, with their small children beside them, watched. As the sun pushed through the clouds over the Atlantic the firing continued. Fort Sumter, enveloped in exploding shells and thick gray smoke, resembled a Fourth of July celebration gone mad.

Reporters jammed telegraph offices to file stories and residents began letters of jubilation to friends. Officers and local officials made certain to keep telegraph lines open to inform Jefferson Davis and his cabinet. The shelling lasted for two entire days until, finally, Anderson surrendered the fort. As Confederate soldiers and Charleston citizens watched silently, Major Anderson clutched Sumter's tattered American flag in his arms.[69] Then he and his men boarded a steamer and sailed out of the harbor.

10

ABRAHAM LINCOLN AT WAR: 1861

STEPHEN DOUGLAS walked with slow steps through the dimly lit corridors of the White House. There was nothing gigantic about the Little Giant anymore. In the 1860 campaign he had become the first presidential candidate to stump the nation in person, and it had drained him. By September, he was a shell of his old bombastic self, losing his voice, coughing endlessly, and, friends said, drinking again. He put on weight, his hair thinned even more, his jowls drooped, and dark circles formed under his eyes.

The White House was lonely that night. Its only occupants were two doormen and the president, waiting in his second-floor office for Douglas. Abraham Lincoln was glad to see his old neighbor. The president's eyes softened, and a slow smile grew on his lips as Douglas walked into his office. Lincoln, as always, had his size fourteen feet resting on his desk. The two men had courted the same women, shared the same friends, gone to the same picnics, argued cases before the same judges, dined together countless times, and laughed long and hard at each other's stories. For nearly thirty years, their lives had been intertwined. Douglas always seemed to be the Democrat that Abe Lincoln, first as a Whig and later as a Republican, had to oppose in debates, and the judge had always been the man Lincoln had to beat to realize his dreams, first for the U.S. Senate and then the presidency.

Now, on the eve of a civil war that threatened to rip the nation apart, they were meeting once again, in a far grimmer atmosphere. Lincoln had invited Douglas to the White House because he was the leader of the Democratic Party, the opposition, and he felt obligated to tell him that in the morning he would call for 75,000 volunteers to put down the rebellion. Politically, Lincoln wanted Douglas's support in the oncoming war. The Republican Party could not fight the war alone: Lincoln needed the opposition party's complete support. He also wanted to see Douglas because Douglas had been his friend for so many years, and on this particular night Abraham Lincoln, in a new home in a new city surrounded by strangers and trouble, needed an old friend.[1]

The last six weeks had been the worst in Lincoln's life. He later told a friend, "Of all the trials I have had since I came here, none begins to compare with those I had between the inauguration and the fall of Sumter. They were so great that could I have anticipated them I could not believe it possible to survive them."[2]

Lincoln slid his order for the callup of 75,000 volunteer troops out of one of his desk drawers as he talked, and asked his old friend to support him in the crisis. Douglas, ever the patriot, the man who had pleaded with Southerners to stay in the Union no matter who was elected president, no matter which party was swept into office, no matter what speeches were given or what threats were made, promised that he would. He told Lincoln emphatically that 75,000 men would not be enough, that he should call up 200,000.[3] The two men talked about old times and old friends for more than two hours, and then, the hour late, they shook hands. Douglas turned and left, walking slowly out of the White House he had coveted so much all of his life. The two would never see each other again.[6] To Lincoln's delight, Douglas would announce his total support of Lincoln in a statement to the press the next day.[4] (Lincoln shrewdly floated a rumor that he might ask Douglas to become a Union general, as well, to increase Democratic support.[5])

The state of the U.S. Army, its unreadiness for war, and the bungling of its leadership, was revealed during the Fort Sumter crisis. Lincoln, unnerved, decided he needed to take fast and bold steps as both president and commander in chief to put down the rebellion, as he always called the war, and to preserve the Union.

In the spring of 1861 the United States Army could have been given a tough fight by any well-trained city militia. The army which had fought so magnificently in Mexico had been reduced to less than seventeen thousand men scattered among dozens of remote posts throughout the country, many of them in the far west, thousands of miles from Washington. Most of its commanders were old, and General in Chief Winfield Scott, seventy-four, suffered from numerous ailments, could no longer ride a horse, and often fell asleep at meetings. Few of the army's generals had ever been in combat. Many of the bright young men who were captains and colonels in the army in the 1850s, unhappy with army pettiness and a frozen promotion chain, had left and gone into private business. The army was so woefully equipped that as late as 1862 Union generals serving in the West had to buy maps from local bookstores.[7]

Many of the army's officers were headed for Southern regiments. The cavalier culture of the South had always held the military in high esteem. The sons of wealthy planters often gravitated to it, their rank admired by the South's men and their uniforms adored by its ladies. The South had cultivated its military tradition from the days of George Washington, and large numbers of Southerners served in the army. Seven of the eight military schools in the nation were in the South, and their students and alumni flocked to the Confederate Army. One-third of the officers in Virginia field regiments were from the Virginia Military Academy alone, and 1,781 of the 1,902 graduates of V.M.I. fought for the South.[8] More than one-third (313) of the U.S. Army's officers had already or were about to quit and join the Confederacy. The country's last four secretaries of war, including Jefferson Davis, had been Southerners.

The U.S. Army had no draft and no mechanism, beyond the enlistment of state militias, to fight any kind of a war. The enrollment of soldiers was often chaotic as individual towns raised their own volunteers; for example the recruitment of six free-standing Ohio regiments, which wound up in their own army, were not commissioned by Ohio, the federal government, the governor of Ohio, or the president.[9]

The army and navy were filled with confusion. Lincoln was angry that on the night the supply ships left New York for Fort Sumter one sailed to Florida instead, and the ships were delayed for hours because their orders were badly mixed up. Fort Sumter itself was yet another example of the disorder in the army. Official reports to Lincoln had glossed over all of the fort's problems, and he had had to rely on the private letters Capt. Abner Doubleday had written to his wife for his only accurate portrait of conditions there.

As the shells were bursting over Fort Sumter, President Lincoln found himself adrift legally and politically. The House and Senate were not in session and could not immediately be requested either to approve the call-up of volunteer troops or to appropriate millions of dollars in immediate emergency expenditures needed to pay for the army, the size of which had to be more than quadrupled overnight. Legally, only Congress could declare war, and only Congress could pay for it.

The president was determined not to let the inefficiency, weakness, and bungling of the army permit the rebels to slash the United States in half, and unwilling to let the absence of Congress handcuff him. In extraordinary steps, Lincoln moved, within twenty-four hours of the bombardment of Sumter, to take control of the army as its commander in chief. He called for volunteers from the state militias and from the civilian ranks and authorized emergency federal payment of soldiers' salaries as well as expenditures to buy cannons, rifles, and ammunition and to build ships for the navy.

In other extraordinary moves, Lincoln ordered the navy to blockade as many Southern ports as it could. He suspended the writ of habeas corpus to permit the army and the attorney general to arrest and jail—without trial—civilians they deemed to be traitors under broad guidelines. This brought swift and severe criticism from judges, lawyers, and newspaper editors, especially, later, after he had the mayor of Baltimore and members of the Maryland legislature arrested. ("For God's sake, don't put your trust in the Union men of Maryland," a local had warned him.[10]) Lincoln had, in just days, seized complete control of not only the military, but the entire government, suspended some of its most precious civil rights, and become perhaps the most powerful president in the history of the United States—in order, he firmly believed, to save the country.

Assuming unprecedented war powers, an act that bordered on dictatorship, did not worry Lincoln. The Fort Sumter crisis reaffirmed his desire to remake the presidency in his own style and to interpret the powers and responsibilities of the presidency his own way, a way by which the office would become the most powerful in history and give the president, and all the presidents who followed him, much more power than the Constitution had intended. The president had powers, he believed, that were independent of those of Congress, and he had to use those broad powers to run the country and save it.[11]

The president, Lincoln was convinced, could act alone, and properly, without regard to the Congress. He needed to interpret the powers of his office generously to do so, and he did. His view of the attack on Fort Sumter and the formation of a one hundred thousand man Confederate Army was not that the United States was at war, as many maintained, but that a rebellion had begun which had to be put down by his government. Since it was not war, he felt he did not need congressional approval to call up troops or to order them into battle to end the rebellion. He carefully married the "commander in chief" responsibilities of his office under the Constitution to its language that the president had to "take care that the laws be faithfully executed" in order to buttress his feeling that the nation was in a war emergency, and since Congress was not in session, the president *had* to assume vast war powers.[12]

Lincoln also knew that if a good lawyer could not find a precedent for a case on one shelf of books, he could always find it on another. He dug through U.S. lawbooks and unearthed an old act of Congress, the 1795 Militia Act, which permitted the president to call up state militias to protect the nation if existing forces were insufficient. It was under that act, and not the executive powers enumerated in the Constitution, that Lincoln called up the 75,000 volunteers.[13]

He also decided that the habeas corpus precedent, which forbids holding people in jail without trial, was vague and needed interpretation. Lincoln's primary concern was to prevent the Union from collapsing. He wanted to put people he considered traitors or dangerous to the preservation of the Union behind bars, without bail, for the several months it would take to bring them to trial. While he may have seemed a bit radical in arresting politicians and public speakers, he felt he was right to arrest, and jail, dozens of known Southern sympathizers. Local observers estimated that a full one-third of the residents in border states such as Maryland, Missouri and Kentucky were either Confederate sympathizers or working covertly for the South. Maryland, in particular, was home to many spies and guerrillas who opened fire on federal troops,[14] burned bridges, and cut telegraph lines.[15] Many, particularly in Missouri, were members of guerrilla bands which were at war with the Union.[16]

Criticism was swift. Several congressmen and senators, such as Republican Thaddeus Stevens, a radical Republican from Pennsylvania, told him he had completely overstepped his boundaries as president and was breaking the law. Lincoln adopted one of his best political disguises—the hayseed country lawyer. He shrugged off Stevens's barbs, telling him that he was just a country lawyer, that out west they did not practice the law of nations, but that Seward said what he had done was all right and a New York city slicker like Seward ought to know. Stevens pressed him on it, but Lincoln evaded him with a nice feint, saying, "but it's done now and can't be helped...so we must get along as well as we can."[17]

Lincoln's suspension of the habeas corpus writ also enabled him, through the army, to suspend or shut down newspapers he considered guilty of treason because of their criticism of the government's handling of the war. This was not a problem for editors and publishers in the spring of 1861, when the country was united in its support of the new administration after the smoke cleared over the ramparts of Fort Sumter, but it would explode into enormous controversy in the fall of 1862 and again in 1863. Lincoln's curbs on press freedom were so severe that by 1865 the government would shut down several dozen critical newspapers, one way or another.

Lincoln said little in public about criticism from legislators, citizens, or reporters, but in private he bristled, especially on the question of habeas corpus writs. He always believed their suspension was necessary for the preservation of the Union. "Are all the laws *but one* to go unexecuted and the government itself go to pieces lest it be violated?" he asked in a July 4, 1861, message to Congress.[18]

The president knew that Congress and the courts could overrule him, but he also knew that the two-party political system made that unlikely. The Congress, which was not yet in session, was overwhelmingly Republican. Lincoln's party held thirty-three of the forty-eight seats in the Senate and 106 of 176 in the House of Representatives. Most of them were as determined to use the army to end the rebellion as he was ("We cannot...negotiate with traitors," said New York senator Preston King[19]). Lincoln's party had the votes to pass any legislation it desired, and it held all the committee chairmanships in the House and Senate. Lincoln had personally campaigned for many of the newly elected Republican leaders over the years, and his workers and fundraisers had helped them to victory. They owed allegiance to him.

The Republican Party would control all legislative action and decide which bills became law. Lincoln's party would not repudiate his actions because it would be repudiating itself. The elections of 1860 gave the Republicans a mandate and the elected president in the White House was their national leader. In their eyes, Lincoln, despite his 39 percent of the vote, was no minority leader, because the Republican Party was not a minority party. The Republicans, and the Republican president, ran the country. The people, through the elections, had put their faith in them. To succeed, Lincoln had to rely on the Republicans in Congress, and he had their complete support. He also knew that if his policies failed, Congress and the party, as well as the president, would be blamed by the people. The party and its supporters knew, too, particularly after all the preinaugural assassination rumors, that if anything happened to Lincoln, his vice president would continue his policies. Lincoln joked that since Hamlin was far more radical on slavery than he, the vice president was his "assassination insurance."

Lincoln knew that there would be opposition from the Democrats, but it would not be overwhelming. The Democrats, he felt from numerous conversations, would support him to save the Union. That much was evident when their leader, Douglas, was asked the morning after his meeting with Lincoln what he would do about Southern sympathizers. "I'd hang them all within forty-eight hours!"[20]

The president, working quickly as the crisis mushroomed, was a sharp judge of popular moods. He could detect every tiny shift of public opinion and predict the public's next heartbeat. He was certain that the bombardment of Fort Sumter would create an uproar for revenge in the North that would howl from the busy streets of New York to the gold fields of California. The war fever would run so high that Lincoln's extraordinary assumptions of powers would not be faulted by the people, by Congress, or by the press. That tidal wave of public support would next make it impossible for the courts to undermine his questionable moves to call up the troops and to suspend civil liberties. Three decades in the courts, riding the circuit in Illinois, had taught him that judges, whether appointed or elected, are as aware of the will of the people as everyone else.[21]

He defended his bold steps to Congress after it reconvened on July 4, pointing the finger of blame for starting the war directly at the South. "They assailed, and reduced, the Fort [Sumter]…to drive out the visible authority of the Federal Union and thus force it to immediate dissolution," he said, adding that that was a direct repudiation of his inaugural appeal for conciliation.

In an address read for him, on July 5, he told Congress: "So, viewing the issue, no choice was left but to call out the war power of the government and so to resist force, employed for its destruction, by force, for its preservation."

He added that "what men cannot take by an election, neither can they take by a war," and that if he had used illegal measures in calling up troops or suspending the habeas corpus writ, he had no apologies, that his actions had been taken by popular demand and were "a public necessity."

Lincoln told the legislators that he would not step back from the war, that the time had come to define the nation. "This is essentially a People's contest. On the side of the Union, it is a struggle for maintaining in the world that form and substance of government, whose leading object is to elevate the condition of men—to lift artificial weights from all shoulders—to clear the paths of laudable pursuit for all—to afford all, an unfettered start, and a fair chance, in the race of life."[22]

In private, he was even tougher. One of his biggest problems concerned the people of Maryland, which was full of Southern sympathizers. In April a mob had opened fire on U.S. troops on their way through Baltimore. Later that month a group of fifty men from the Baltimore Young Men's Christian Association met with Lincoln at the White House to convince him to sue for peace. After listening to their pleas for a few minutes, he cut off their speaker and lashed into them:

"You express great horror of bloodshed, and yet would not lay a straw in the way of those who are organizing in Virginia and elsewhere to capture this city. The rebels attack Fort Sumter and your citizens attack troops sent to the defense of the government, and the lives and property in Washington, and yet you would have me break my oath and surrender the government without a blow. There is...no manhood nor honor in that."[23]

Lincoln was also convinced that the presidency had to be remade to fit the emergency, that the powers of the president had to contract and expand depending on changing conditions. The president could not be like George Washington, a man above politics and turmoil; he had to be a self-confident leader[24] and man of strong character[25] intricately involved in governing the nation and fighting the war on a daily basis.

Americans North and South would also soon see that Lincoln was a resilient man who could bounce back from political and military defeats, often stronger than ever. He had learned from a lifetime of setbacks that small losses do not necessarily mean ultimate defeat and that many men and women, like himself, had to lose in order to win later. This resilience led him to accept the bombardment of Fort Sumter, then move past it toward raising troops to end the rebellion once and for all.[26]

The president was also in remarkably good health. He rarely missed a day of work. He was a strong man, thanks to his years of farming and railsplitting. Hard work had given him a body able to fight off most diseases and infections. Lincoln had never been seriously ill in his life—not even a lingering cold—and throughout his presidency he would never miss work because of illness, except for a short period in 1863, when he was still able to work from his bedroom. He slept soundly, despite nightmares which occasionally woke him. During the times of crisis throughout his presidency, Lincoln's good health, despite his frequent weariness, served him and the Union well.

Ending the insurrection, as he called it, was troublesome. Virginia had seceded on April 17 and was followed shortly after by Tennessee, Arkansas, and North Carolina. Now the enemy stared back at him every time he walked over to one of the tall windows in the White House and looked across the Potomac River. Friends told him he was fixated on the Virginia shore, that he should not worry because the rebellion would soon end. "If Virginia strikes us, are we not to strike back, and as effectively as we can?" he asked them.[27]

He did manage, through hard politicking, to keep Kentucky and Maryland in the Union. During late April 1861, that was not yet certain, however, and Lincoln faced the distinct possibility of being surrounded by the Confederacy and forced to abandon the capital. The Virginians had already captured the federal arsenal at Harper's Ferry and a navy yard at Norfolk. U.S. troops had been fired upon in Baltimore; four had been killed. Maryland secessionists had burned several bridges in the state and cut telegraph lines. Defending the capital, and the president, were a few untrained regiments.

Panic spread throughout Washington, from the White House to the homes of the capital's residents. Rumors flew. One of the strongest concerned a secret army of Southerners, in civilian clothes, who were training in Maryland and Virginia and would attack Washington within days, holding it until the Confederate Army could occupy the capital. General Scott believed the rumor and urged Lincoln to authorize several navy steamships to patrol the Potomac in front of the Capitol and White House.[28] Influential congressmen, fearful of soldiers assaulting the House chamber, begged Scott to station men there.[29] A friend of Lincoln told him that a man who knew all the members of the Davis cabinet assured him that a team of Confederate guerrillas was planning to seize Washington and drive Lincoln out of town.[30]

A Rhode Island man told Lincoln that he had heard that an assault across the Potomac was imminent, and was raising a regiment to repel it.[31] German-American leader Carl Schurz heard the same rumor and told Lincoln he would have a regiment ready to fight in forty-eight hours.[32] A Kansas man offered to train one thousand men and rush them to Washington.[33] The women in Washington were just as frightened as the men by the invasion rumors, particularly after one woman returning from Montgomery told her society friends that Varina Davis told her to tell her old Washington friends that "I'll see them in the White House in June."[34]

Later that month, Lincoln stood on the White House balcony with Mary and his two boys and watched with pleasure as the first volunteers, after arriving in the capital, paraded up Pennsylvania Avenue. "Thank God!" he told Mary. The seventy-five thousand volunteers had been raised quickly and were eager to fight. They went off to war after rallies, bonfires, and serenades. The streets of Boston, home to the Sons of Liberty eighty-five years before, teemed with regiments marching off to battle, tens of thousands of residents packing the route, waving flags. In New York, more than one hundred thousand people gathered in Union Square to protest the bombardment of Fort Sumter. A few days later the city streets were clogged with newly formed regiments going off to fight. New Yorkers joked that one regiment, from the Bowery, was filled with so many men of questionable character that you had to have been in jail to enlist in it. Some regiments from tiny villages included nearly all able-bodied men.

Women sewed flags for local companies. Young girls kissed their sweethearts goodbye, Mexican War vets reenlisted, and preachers of all denominations wished the boys Godspeed. Bands on every village green and city corner struck up the popular tunes of the day. Soldiers wrote poems about Lincoln.[35] Newspapers put out war editions as their editors, some using biblical passages to justify the action, urged the sacking of Richmond.[36] The spirit of the people was well reflected in the sharp letter Lincoln received from a young New Yorker who enlisted as soon as he heard of the call-up: "Give those South Carolinians hell!"[37]

Throughout these tense early months, while he tried to scrape together an army, Lincoln was still besieged by job seekers as he exercised his right as president to fill federal jobs with political appointees. He was inundated with letters from people looking for jobs, often party hacks, and people recommending people looking for jobs, usually other party hacks. Some job seekers had letters signed by a party leader, others had long petitions signed by over one hundred party leaders.[38] Some party men recommended one friend for a job, and others recommended six to eight at a time.[39] Everybody wanted something. Many wanted the same job—Robert Gould wanted to be the U.S.

naval agent for New York,[40] but so did Henry Bennet, who, local party leaders assured the president, was "resolute, energetic and faithful."[41]

Lincoln did all he could to get party men jobs. He had been in politics since he was twenty-three years old and knew how important patronage was to the party machinery. The winners procured jobs for the party faithful—it was the politician's eleventh commandment, whether he was a local ward boss or president of the United States. The thousands of people in those jobs owed their allegiance to the party and the man who put them there. It was especially important for Lincoln to place party men in jobs because he was the first president of the six-year-old Republican party. If the party was to become as strong as the Democrats or the Whigs had been, it needed thousands of party faithful running the government. Lincoln knew this and so did the Republicans, who were aware of how strongly Lincoln believed in patronage.

Lincoln was so determined to reward friends and workers—and install the party machinery in every level of the U.S. government—that by the time he finished doling out political appointments he had set a new record, getting rid of 1,195 Democrats out of 1,520 officeholders from the old administration and replacing them with Republicans, giving his party control of the federal government at every level.[42]

The sea of job seekers constantly reminded him that jobs were rewards and that a position not given to a Republican might wind up in the hands of a Democrat. A Pennsylvania man wrote that "the true [party] men of East Pennsylvania" needed government jobs so they "would not be in danger."[43] A man in Virginia wrote that the Republican Party, weak as it was in that Southern state, might collapse completely without government jobs handed out by the president. Republicans asked for every conceivable job, from a local Ohio librarian, a man "of personal character and literary culture" who wanted to work in the Library of Congress,[44] to the wealthy and influential Don Antonio Maria Peco, who wanted to be tax collector in Monterey, California.[45]

If Lincoln could not get a party loyalist or old friend a job in one department, he would ask government workers to find one in another, as they did for his crony Nathan Sargent, who could not be placed in the postal department but was able to be squeezed into a Treasury job in Connecticut.[46] Lincoln never forgot the help various religious groups gave him in the campaign, and after he was elected told the Methodist Church of Illinois he would name whomever they wanted as governor of the Washington territory.[47]

Lincoln and his men dealt out so many jobs that results were sometimes comic. Senator Preston King wound up with two men named Smith trying to land the same patronage job. In a series of letters back and forth with Chase and Lincoln, the two Smiths got mixed up. The second Mr. Smith was appointed to a job in the auditor's office after the first Smith gave up his quest.[48]

Lincoln helped his friends whenever he could. Mrs. Charles Corneau, from Springfield, had lost her husband and was struggling financially, so Lincoln gave her brother a job in the Treasury Department.[49] It was one of his many appointments to friends of friends, especially those who were in economic difficulty, particularly from Springfield and Illinois.

He took care of his in-laws and the in-laws of friends. When the Speaker of the House, Galusha Grow, asked him to find a job somewhere, anywhere, for his brother-in-law, Joseph Street, Lincoln landed him a post as a judge in Nebraska.[50] He opened several governmental doors for his brother-in-law, Ninian Edwards, of Springfield, after his business floundered.[51] His old friend John Hardin, of Illinois, needed a job for his brother-in-law, Alexander McKee, a Kentucky county court clerk, but could not find one and turned to the president. Recommending McKee as "an out and out Republican," Lincoln told Seward to find him something: McKee wound up in the consul's office in Panama.[52] Several friendly newspaper editors landed jobs in the foreign service.

Lincoln solved a sticky problem for Secretary of the Interior Caleb Smith in October 1861. Smith had a perfectly reliable chief clerk in Moses Kelly, a longtime voter and party worker, but wanted to give his son that job. Lincoln let him do it and found Kelly another job.[53] Some in-law pleas he could not answer, such as one from longtime friend and campaign strategist Jesse DuBois, who wanted him to name DuBois's son-in-law an Indian agent in Minnesota because his desperately ill daughter needed the bracing climate of Minnesota for her health. Lincoln's hands were tied; those jobs had to go to party men in that state.[54]

Sometimes the requests became ludicrous. Lincoln himself acknowledged as much in the case of Mary's cousin Elizabeth Todd Grimsley, who wanted him to give her the Springfield post office job. Lincoln threw up his hands, reminding her that he had appointed too many in-laws and friends in Springfield to jobs already and asked, "[W]ill it do for me…to divide out all the offices among relatives?"[55]

The job crusade never seemed to end, but it was important to Lincoln, so important that at the very height of the Fort Sumter crisis, on April 5, as the final decision was being made to supply the fort and risk war, Lincoln took time to write a personal note to secure a judgeship for a longtime friend and Pennsylvania politician, Ethelbert Oliphant.[56]

A major criterion was that job seekers had supported the Republicans and the president in the election. Sometimes Lincoln had to wait to fulfill a campaign promise of a job. The one man he wanted to reward was his longtime friend Judge David Davis, who had managed his successful presidential campaign. Lincoln wanted an important post for Davis. There was nothing worthwhile for him in the cabinet or in any undersecretary's office, and Lincoln did not wish to give him one of the many judgeships now under his control. So Lincoln bided his time until the right job came along and, finally, after nearly two long years it did—in 1862 the president named his old friend an associate justice of the Supreme Court.

Oddly, Lincoln's very public patronage in the halls of the White House seemed to instill a good feeling in the people about him, a feeling that he was not an aloof or unreachable politician, like most, but a man you could talk to, a common man with uncommon skills.

The job seekers usually formed lines early in the morning on the first and second floors of the White House, dozens sitting on the steps leading from the first to the second floor. They had to be early for any chance to get a glimpse of the president or a minute of his time. Lincoln rose at six o'clock, just after daybreak, and was usually in the second-floor office by seven or eight o'clock. He worked until at least 8 P.M. most days and, Mary complained, often did not return to their apartment until ten or eleven o'clock at night.

He spent hours each day on patronage, seeing as many job seekers as he could, to the dismay of his two secretaries. Most he entertained with jokes or stories of some kind, his legs on top of his desk and his head tilted back against the rear of his chair. He somehow seemed to have a mutual acquaintance in common with every job seeker, and the two would swap stories. The president also used these endless interviews to pick the brains of everyone he met, from congressman to custodian, to see what they thought about the government and the war, continuing his uncanny ability, honed through taking polls as a young man, to know what everybody in the country was thinking. No president until Franklin Roosevelt would understand how the people thought, from day to day, as well as Abraham Lincoln. The ritual never let up, and with his reelection in 1864 it started all over again. The job seekers, who brought him peaches and pears and bags of candy and were always made to feel at home, began to call him "Father Abraham" that first spring. The name was picked up by the papers, and it stuck.

A large black walnut table in the middle of the large office was used for meetings. The president worked at a smaller desk near the windows, a sofa and two chairs and another, weather-beaten desk with cubbyholes for letters.[57] There were small rooms adjacent to his office for his three secretaries, John Hay, John Nicolay, and William Stoddard, who helped him with correspondence and served as aides. They were highly organized, unlike the president, who was totally disorganized but somehow, some way, always knew what was going on and who was doing what in the White House and on Capitol Hill.

The president worked on the war, and on his hundreds of job meetings, but he also was the leader of his party in drafting and proposing hundreds of bills on non-war subjects, from riverfront funding to the Homestead Act. He spent considerable time working with Republican congressmen on bills they each agreed upon and even more time with Democrats to get them to vote for his legislation. Then, in late afternoon, he would attend meetings on diplomatic issues and tax plans and write letters to a variety of foreign heads of state. Lincoln was a man who brought considerable skills to the office and developed more while he was there.

Those skills were tested early.

LINCOLN relied on General Winfield Scott for advice because the aging general, still a hero long after the Mexican War, was all he had. Scott turned in lengthy two- and three-page reports each day detailing his own efforts to build the army.[58] On Scott's advice, the president called up a half million troops, with three-year commitments, during the spring. Scott knew he had seen his last campaign, though, and after months of hard work without much resolution regarding the war, and conflicts with rising stars in the ranks, he resigned in November.[59] Irvin McDowell, a voracious eater and teetotaler who wore a French-style beard and sported a funny looking European-style hat, replaced him as Lincoln's number one general in the field that summer.

A new general named, Lincoln then decided to give himself a crash course in military science. He turned to the Library of Congress for books on army strategy and tactics, talked to military people about campaigns, and learned as much about the army as he could.

Lincoln began naming generals as soon as the first fresh troops began arriving in Washington. He named them carefully. The army was full of volunteers who had been prominent Republican and Democratic politicians back home. State governors like Nathaniel Banks of Massachusetts, U.S. senators, congressmen, and mayors filled the ranks. Lincoln took great pains to promote as many Democrats as he could to the rank of general and colonel in order to achieve political peace. He encouraged the idea of regiments electing their own colonels, who were often the town's mayor, regardless of party. He never held the party of any regular army general against him, happily bestowing generalships on longtime Democrats such as George McClellan. Building a nonpartisan army looked good to the people in the various states, and Lincoln believed he was better off with his leading opponents in the army giving orders for him instead of back home at rallies giving speeches against him.

The president had named hundreds of officers by July 4, when Congress finally convened. It met Lincoln's defense of the troop call-up and habeas corpus writ suspensions with approval, something he was certain Congress would do, and issued a call-up for 43,000 more troops, telling the public that "existing exigencies demand immediate and adequate measures for the ...preservation of the National Union."[60] The approval of Congress rejuvenated Lincoln, who was sometimes weighed down by bouts of depression.

"If to be head of hell is as hard as what I have to undergo here, I could find it in my heart to pity Satan himself," he said of the pressures of office.[61]

He wanted to start the war in earnest. Lincoln did not want to wait for a major battle any longer. He had Congress's complete support and the people's backing, and he was under considerable pressure from newspapers to strike a blow of some kind at the Confederates. He understood quickly, and never forgot, that he needed public opinion on his side to fight the war and that politics and public opinion would often be as important as military strategy in winning it.

Confident the hastily expanded U.S. Army could win one decisive battle and crush the rebellion, on July 9 he ordered McDowell to march the largest Union army, the Army of the Potomac, with more than thirty thousand men, toward Richmond and quiet numerous editorial writers who had adopted the "Forward to Richmond!" battle cry of Horace Greeley and others.[62] Scott, who did not want to attack anyone yet, argued that the commanders were not ready and the troops were too green. Lincoln insisted the country needed to end the rebellion immediately. McDowell waited a week before he moved, giving spies in Washington enough time to find out that he was headed toward Manassas, Virginia, near Bull Run Creek, and the Confederate government time to move a huge army there.

The forces clashed on July 21, 1861. Lincoln's hopes for a one-day war crashed down around him late that night after the battle, which seemed winnable most of the day, turned into a rout. He had assumed, like many, that the Union was winning the battle—smoke from the battle could be seen from the White House[63]—and even the final dispatch to the War Department from the field was encouraging: "...our troops here at least stood their ground." Reports from the press, too, were wrong, including the final despatch filed by the New York Herald at 5:30 P.M.: "We have carried the day."[64] Most Northern newspapers erroneously reported a great Union victory in the next morning's editions. Hundreds of Washingtonians took carriages to Manassas to watch the battle and some even planned celebratory dinners in nearby restaurants. All fled along with the soldiers as the Confederates swept the Union army from the field."[65]

Up until 6 P.M. there were conflicting reports. The president went to see General Scott and found the old commander sound asleep in his chair. Lincoln, frustrated, awakened him, and the general assured him victory was imminent. The president, a bit relieved, walked to the White House stables, saddled up a horse, and went for an hour-long ride. While he was gone, Seward arrived at his office, out of breath, and, not finding Lincoln there, told his secretaries that the battle was lost and that Lincoln had to join him at his office as soon as he returned.

The president returned from his ride at 8 P.M., stabled his horse, dusted himself off, and, with long strides, went to his office expecting to hear news of a great victory. John Nicolay informed him of the defeat and of Seward's message to meet him. Lincoln was at first stone-faced, then angry. He said nothing, but turned abruptly and left.[66]

Lincoln, so hopeful of victory, was irate. The Union army should have won the battle. The South, tottering through the day, was strengthened by the arrival of new troops by train in the afternoon and the bravery of forces under Thomas Jackson, who held their ground and repelled a Union attack. (Confederate soldiers watching said Jackson stood "like a stone wall," and the nickname stuck.)

Rumors flew again in Washington. A nurse with Confederate sympathies told people that her army would be in Washington within days,[67] and a New York businessman said he heard Confederate agents in New York City planned to blow up several buildings.[68] Lincoln, who was depressed by the defeat and convinced now that the war would be a long one, was also encouraged by Northern reaction. The army might have lost a battle, but the people were eager to continue the war. They rallied and pledged as many troops as the president needed to beat the rebels. From Illinois came a telegram alerting the White House to the emergency muster of extra regiments there.[69] From the governor of New York came a note pledging several more.[70] Governor William Curtin promised three regiments within the day from Pennsylvania.[71] Indiana's Governor Oliver Morton promised ten thousand men.[72] And from everywhere came cheers from the common people, who assured Lincoln they would respond "splendidly."[73]

The defeat at Bull Run taught Lincoln several lessons. He was not altogether wrong in thinking that an amateur like himself knew more about strategy than the military. The war would last a long time. He needed another commanding general. Single battles like Bull Run would decide little; to win the war, the Union must pressure the South at as many points as possible.

On July 26, he went to his office and hastily jotted down a military plan of his own which, scrawled on just two eight-by-ten-inch sheets, served as a strategic blueprint for the entire war. It was a remarkable example of Lincoln's clear thinking on military matters, despite no other military training than his few months in the Black Hawk War.

Among his strategic goals were: a strong naval blockade of most Southern ports, to use nearby Fortress Monroe as a jumping-off point for all invasions of the South, to keep Maryland in the Union, to send an army into the western part of Virginia, to secure Missouri, to use McDowell's army to protect the capital, to send the new, three-month volunteers into action as quickly as possible, to seize a northern Virginia town as a base of operations in that state, and to send two western armies into the South in hopes of a breakthrough which might force the Confederates to quit.[74]

The president also felt that the government had to begin the largest military mobilization in its history—in weapons and supplies as well as men—and that he had to delegate extraordinary powers to the secretary of war, Cameron, to do that. He knew, too, that the war had to be won before the South could persuade France or England to jump in on its side. The United States could not fight Europe and the South at the same time. To fend off the

European powers he would have to rely on the diplomatic skills of Seward and his undersecretaries. He needed to raise unheard of amounts of money to fight the war. For the United States, the cost came to $1 million a day, or $40 million a day in contemporary currency. He needed Treasury's Salmon Chase for that. Lincoln would oversee his cabinet secretaries, work with them, and support them, but he needed to have their support with a minimum of exertion on his part.

The president never believed that he was much of a military man, but did think he had enough common sense to see that the Union could only win by pressing the Confederacy wherever it could—and starving it out via blockade. He also realized, from the beginning of the conflict, that the Union had an enormous numerical advantage over the South in potential battle-ready soldiers because it enjoyed a nearly five-to-two advantage in population over the South. The Union also had a booming economy, a well-entrenched federal administration whose tentacles reached to every state, county, and village, and a long-established army system.

Lincoln's July 1861 military plan was a substantial departure from the accepted military strategy of the era. Most strategists followed the teaching of the Swiss strategist Antoine Jomini, who had served with Napoleon. Jomini believed that wars were won by armies targeting and capturing towns and cities. The enemy, having lost enough towns, or their capital, would then surrender. This strategy was reinforced in the textbook *Outpost,* by Dennis Hart Mahan, a veteran instructor at West Point. His book was required reading for all cadets, who to a man adopted that strategy when the Civil War began. The civilian Lincoln had never learned these theories. Ignoring Jomini's sacred strategy, which he thought was too time consuming, he ordered his generals to engage the enemy armies instead. It was a radical departure that only a civilian could make, and for a long time his own generals resisted it.[75]

The new president also believed that the best strategy was not to rush to Richmond, or any other Southern city, and capture it as a trophy. The way to win the war, he felt from the beginning, was to find the enemy and constantly attack him until his armies were destroyed. When the army was defeated, the South would be beaten. He tried to instill the desire to crush the enemy's armies in every general he met. He wrote Joseph Hooker in 1863 that his ideas about getting to Richmond via the Rappahannock or James River were misguided, that they were "a contest about nothing," and that "our prime object is the enemies' army in front of us."[76]

President Lincoln saw himself as a man elected by the people to hold the nation together. He had to operate as a civilian, with the good of all the people, not just the army, as his goal. He tried to combine the best traits of an administrator and a politician to make himself the most capable armchair general he could be. Lincoln may not have been a military genius, but as Karl von Clausewitz said of successful civilian wartime leaders, he was a man with a "superior mind and strength of character."[77]

Lincoln, the amateur soldier, became a determined commander in chief and worked with whoever was his general in chief in Washington on a daily basis. He not only took part in all strategic sessions but led them, learned how to write military orders, directed military policy, kept an eye on supplies, had agents shop for the newest equipment and rifles, and encouraged the sanitary commission to send its hundreds of volunteers into army camps for health and morale. He kept long lists of brigades and corps and made certain that he had homegrown troops fighting in their own state rather than men from other states, who might have less spirit. This was particularly true in divided Missouri.[78]

Lincoln was intricately involved in the promotion of just about every officer in the army, from generals all the way down to captains. He sent promotion lists of twenty to thirty officers at a time to his generals and often changed his mind about who should go where, crossing out one regiment and penciling in another. He was eager to promote men who had already demonstrated bravery, such as Colonel Robert Anderson of Fort Sumter (to general) or who had given him useful advice, such as Abner Doubleday, who was promoted to colonel. He also promoted friends of friends and their in-laws, such as James Cutts Jr., the brother-in-law of Stephen Douglas.[79] He would name brigade commanders and then tell them he was appointing their regimental commanders for them.[80] He became so involved in personnel that he even intervened to note who was and was not appointed to commissary posts in army units halfway across the country.[81]

Lincoln's initial orders for attacks and campaigns were rather simplistic, but within six months he was issuing orders as detailed and comprehensive as any by his top generals.[82] His orders were not only specific about offensive action, but included instructions concerning different possible options, even what action to take if the enemy was too strong.[83] Lincoln knew the strength of each army and its divisions, corps, and regiments on a day-to-day basis, often when his commanders did not. He issued orders to move particular armies which included precise numbers of Union troops, and told his generals how many rebel troops they could expect to encounter, down to the hundreds. When he sent General George Thomas toward the Cumberland Gap in October of 1861, he told him he had six thousand men and would meet a Confederate force of eight thousand rebels.[84] He wrote directly to generals to tell them what he thought they were doing right and wrong. He intervened to keep feuding generals and admirals apart and, to make his point, provided very specific orders for each.[85] He had become, within a few short months, one of the best generals in the Union army.

Yet Lincoln's greatest skill as commander in chief, besides his close watch on the war, was in supporting his generals as much as he could and in giving them the freedom to plan their own movements and battles within his overall campaign plan. He set policy and planned campaigns, but did not intervene in day-to-day operations, and left all the mobilization and supply operations to the War Department. He made infrequent visits to the war zone to consult generals; when he did, he listened carefully to everything they had to say and talked long into the night about their battle plans. He was rarely critical, and always took a moment to thank them for their hard work and to assure them that the people supported them. He treated his generals respectfully and never held personal grudges, even against those who constantly ignored or insulted him. He did not permit arguments over military rank. He never refused to work with or promote generals whom he did not like or knew did not like him. Once he even told Hooker, when it was rumored the general felt he was popular enough to become dictator, that he would rather let Hooker be dictator and take his job than lose the war.[86]

Even when he was critical, Lincoln would add a line in his note letting the general know that Lincoln genuinely liked him and approved of his overall work, despite this single barb. Most of all, Lincoln gave encouragement, lauding each victory and doing all he could to let his generals know, whether they won or lost, that he, and the people, were proud of them. After a particularly hard fight in November 1861, in Missouri, he wrote General John McClernand that "you and all with you have done honor to yourselves and the flag and service to the country."[87]

In the hot and humid summer of 1861, however, Lincoln needed a good general, certainly a better one than McDowell. The disaster at Bull Run energized the Union for a few weeks, but when autumn arrived, there were no victories, and public support of the war began to sag. Lincoln was on a swaying tightrope, trying to rally public support for the war, to keep both Democrats and Republicans behind him, to appease the press, and to bolster the morale of the shocked troops. The president needed a new general, one who could at once inspire the admiration and confidence of the entire nation—and win the war.

11

JEFFERSON DAVIS AT WAR: 1861

THE TRAIN RUMBLED toward Manassas Junction. As it came to a slow stop, its wheels screeching on the rails, Jefferson Davis shouted to the Confederate soldiers he saw milling nearby. Covered in dust, they seemed uncertain which way they were walking. He asked them for news of the battle, the first engagement of the war, which had been going on since early morning, a battle to which he had been sending every regiment he could find in the army. The battle had been lost, they shouted back, and the president, regal in his black suit, ordered the conductor to drive the train on to the site of the skirmish, three miles ahead. The conductor said it would be too dangerous for the passengers, so Davis told him to uncouple the locomotive and get him there. The workers on the train separated the cars, and Davis, accompanied by his aide and nephew, Joe Davis, stood in the cab of the locomotive as it moved slowly toward the scene of the battle near Bull Run Creek, the sound of booming cannon and incessant musket fire surrounding them.

At the field, Davis and his nephew found horses and raced off toward the fighting. They rode through long lines of stragglers who did not know the battle was finally being won. "Go back! Go back!" shouted Davis; few did.[1] They found General Joe Johnston, who told them that late that afternoon, after the arrival of reinforcements and a heroic stand by General Thomas Jackson and his men, the tide of the battle had turned in the South's favor.

Davis rode off to the battlefield, scoffing at warnings that he might be shot. He visited a field hospital full of wounded and bloodied soldiers, where he encountered General Jackson, whom he had never met. Jackson, recognizing him from photos, shouted to the wounded, "Three cheers for President Davis!" and the men yelled loudly.

Davis rode on, following a Southern cavalry unit as it chased Federals back toward Washington, the sound of musketry all around him. Word spread quickly that the president was there, ramrod straight on his horse, racing through the Manassas fields better than any rider in either army. "The president! The president!" men cheered as he passed them,[2] and one young boy doffed his cap and bowed when he saw him, a wide smile on his face, which buoyed Davis.

The president and his nephew rode on for nearly seven miles, stopping wherever they found small bands of troops gathered under the drifting smoke of the battle. Davis leaned over the saddle of his horse and delivered short pep talks to the men, thanking them for their service and hard work and congratulating them on their victory. Finally, as dusk fell, he and his nephew turned their mounts and rode back to field headquarters to meet with Generals Joe Johnston and P. G. T. Beauregard,[3] who led his armies.

Beauregard and Johnston had beaten the Federals with panache at Bull Run, driving them back toward Washington in chaos. They won because President Davis had furiously ordered regiment after regiment to join both their armies and had commandeered railroad cars for Johnston's men so his army could speed to Bull Run when the first shots were fired. The commander in chief had supplied them with soldiers and cannon, sent them explicit orders, and organized the campaign. He had ridden among the troops, rallying stragglers and cheering on the victors. The next morning he even turned reporter, sending his own dispatch about the battle, "a glorious victory," to an adjutant in the War Department, who read it to the Confederate congress and made sure it appeared in the Richmond newspapers under Davis's byline.[4] That night there was a nagging apprehension that the commander in chief was not merely advising the army, but leading it.

Bull Run was a great victory for the Confederate Army. It had met McDowell's army and crushed it, sending it and Union hopes for a quick victory reeling back to Washington. The South's casualties were 1,981, the North's 2,645.[5] The Southern army had shown the South, and the world, that it could win. The question that night, when the commanders met, was what their armies should do next. The immediate temptation was to chase McDowell over the Potomac and seize the capital, perhaps capturing Lincoln and winning the war in a single day. Beauregard, Johnston, and Davis decided against it.

Davis said it was "impossible" because the Southern army was weakened by heavy casualties, the men were tired and hungry, and the officers inexperienced. The president said, "It could not be expected that any success on the battlefield could enable our forces to carry the fortifications on the Potomac," defended by McDowell's large army.[6]

The next day, as Davis and his nephew sat in the passenger car of a train back to Richmond, Davis was convinced that the South could not lose the war. They had the best generals. They had nearly three hundred thousand men in the army already, and the War Department was turning away recruits. The Southern press ran tables explaining to its readers that although the North had 2.3 million available men and the South only 611,000, the number of Northern men fit for fighting was just 261,000, while the number in the South was 281,000.[7] The Confederacy did not have to attack, merely fight a defensive war, winning enough battles to keep the Union from occupying any Southern cities until it was forced to simply give up. Actually, the South didn't even have to do that; all it really had to do was hold on until the Northern public tired of the war. The Federals had to attack to win the war. That meant erecting the largest army in history in order to invade a country which had a perimeter of over three thousand miles. That would not work, either. The victory at Bull Run would surely convince European powers, particularly England, to recognize the Confederacy as an independent nation, which would mean the United States would have to abandon the war or risk trade conflict, even war, with England and France.

President Davis was greeted by a large, cheering crowd on his return to Richmond. After offering condolences for the dead and wounded, he assured the residents of Richmond that the war would soon be over. "Your little army—derided for its want of numbers, derided for its want of arms, derided for its lack of all the essential materials of war—has met the grand army of the enemy and routed it. We have taught them a lesson in their invasion of the sacred soil of Virginia," he said to the thunderous roar of the crowd.[8]

Davis was delighted to be back in Richmond. Since his tumultuous arrival in early June, when all of the city turned out to greet him in a wild celebration, it had become a happy second home to him. He told the people then that "to the remotest limits [of the Confederacy] every proud heart beats high and with indignation at the thought that the foot of the invader has been set upon the soil of old Virginia. There is not one true son of the South who is not ready to shoulder his musket to bleed, to die or to conquer in the cause of liberty here...."[9]

Once again, as in Montgomery and on his arrival in Richmond, his personal popularity seemed at an all-time high. Local editors said that he was a good leader and a brilliant man.[10] "The confidence manifested in our President...shows that the mantle of Washington falls gracefully upon his shoulders. Never were a people more enraptured with their chief magistrate," wrote one.[11] A traveler who met him said he was a distinguished executive who spoke slowly, persuasively, and eloquently.[12]

The president told Congress, "[The people's] attitude of calm and sublime devotion to their country...will be renewed from year to year with unfaltering purpose."[13]

Yet despite his early popularity and the rout of the Federals at Bull Run, within months Jefferson Davis faced a barrage of criticism which continued unabated through the summer and fall. Everybody—press, politicians, and public—wanted to know why Davis did not order the army to chase McDowell back to Washington and take the Yankee capital. The war could have been won, and Davis, critics said, had let the chance slip away.

One South Carolinian wrote, in a widely published letter, "Our generals were...either unaware of their advantages and, therefore, incompetent to fill the positions which they held or they were unwisely restrained by the miserable political jugglery of President Davis."[14]

Throughout the summer and fall of 1861, complaints continued that the Confederacy had lost its chance for victory and should strike a blow at Washington immediately while the Federals were occupied training their armies. Morale in the army sank, too, and soldiers wrote home that military life was boring and pointless. Generals in the west told Davis that it was becoming impossible to recruit troops because the army did not fight.[15] Residents began to complain that in the rush to start a war, the army had allowed too many civilians, many of them public officials, to enlist, crippling the administration of town halls, schools, and civic groups on the home front. They feared that the army had attracted all the good public officials, leaving the administration on the homefront in tatters, a situation that later would hamper the collection of taxes and the growth of the army.[16] Some complained that the soldiers had bad food and poor supplies and that the commissary department was corrupt.[17]

The criticism stung him, but, as always, Davis ignored it and told aides that all criticism hurt the cause. Jefferson Davis knew what was right and he was not about to let anyone tell him he was wrong. He declared, "Though these unjust criticisms weakened the power of the government...I must bear them in silence, lest to vindicate myself should injure the public service by turning the public censure to the generals on whom the hopes of the country rest."[18]

He was determined, that last week of July, to reorganize the army so it could meet any Union threat and take the offensive to secure northern Virginia to mute criticism at home, and to work on the new finances of the government. None of that was possible, however, because, again, he fell sick.

Unable to speak at the dinner table, his eye inflamed, weak, feverish, and debilitated, Davis was bedridden for weeks. Blinds drawn, his wife and family attended him. These were critical weeks. In the wake of Bull Run, the Northern army was in tatters, its general dismissed. The army was trying to reorganize just outside Washington, while Northern leaders feared an attack. Without orders and guidance from the bedridden commander in chief, the Southern armies floundered. The chaotic Confederate cabinet, which had been already fractured by two resignations, drifted. The Confederate Congress, without bills from Davis, did nothing. Efforts to draw England into the war on the Southern side were stalled.

It was the first of the many illnesses, all stemming from herpes and neuralgia, which would profoundly hinder Davis throughout the war. The bouts of neuralgia would become progressively more serious and by 1864 new bouts of herpes would paralyze his arm and parts of his face. The sickness that prostrated him from July through the end of August of 1861 was one of the worst. His bad eye became inflamed and turned red, and a sickly looking film grew across it. He could not see out of his left eye and feared permanent blindness. The eye was the most infected Varina had seen it in thirteen years.[19] Their friend Mary Chesnut, who saw him that summer, said he was "in wretched health."[20] He was so sick that J. B. Jones, his clerk in the War Department, who saw him regularly, was certain he was going to die. Several Northern newspapers even ran obituaries.[21] Vice President Alexander Stephens was told to prepare to take over the presidency. Friends said Davis would never see 1862.

Davis's health remained poor throughout the war. His herpes flared up under stress. Nearly every time the Confederate armies lost a major battle, or whenever he feuded with his cabinet or generals, the stress would cause Davis's left eye to become inflamed, his body to weaken, and he would become irritable. He never tried to hide his ailments when he was in the U.S. Senate, but as president he did not want the public to think their leader was an invalid. He began wearing a large woolen cap in the winter of 1861–62 which he would pull down to hide his infected eye. His family covered up his sickness the best they could. Except for rumors, little news of it reached the newspapers beyond a line or two to announce that the president was sick again. The Southern newspapers never reported the extent of his illnesses unless it appeared he was going to die. At times, his immediate family and two secretaries did such a good job of concealing his problems that family members living in different states assumed his health was fine. Davis's mother-in-law believed he had recovered completely in the summer of 1862, according to what she read, but her husband, staying with the Davises in Richmond, wrote her that "[his] health is not so good as reported."[22]

After the summer of 1862, most Northerners, including members of the Lincoln administration, knew of Davis's ailments because his slave carriage driver, William Jackson, had run away and been interviewed by a reporter for the *New York Tribune,* who chronicled the constant sicknesses of the Confederate president.[23]

Davis recovered from the summer illness of 1861, but a year later, in July 1862, immediately following the Peninsular Campaign and the Seven Days battle, which had threatened Richmond, he was bedridden again, too weak to walk or ride to his downtown office. He had to run the country from his home, while severely curtailing his work time to stay in bed and recover. He traveled nearly three thousand miles in December of 1862 and January of 1863 to visit his generals and cheer up the troops. On his return he was so stressed and exhausted that the herpes flared up, sending him to bed for nearly a week. A few months later, in late April, as he fretted about Hooker's army moving toward Chancellorsville, he became so ill that he not only lost sight in his eye again but lost all power of speech for a week. Later that year, in July, following Lee's defeat at Gettysburg and the fall of Vicksburg, Davis became ill again. He was incapacitated for weeks, and his longtime physician, who was usually an optimist about his condition, said he was going to die. Davis fell badly ill again in October 1863 after a stressful trip through the South to confer with military leaders and encourage the demoralized public. In November of 1864, while the Union army laid siege to Petersburg, he came perilously close to death once more, lying bedridden for weeks. During these illnesses, his cabinet meetings would be canceled, and little was accomplished throughout the administration. That December, Northern newspapers were again reporting his death.[24] Davis's physical incapacity, triggered by the stress of critical moments in the war, jeopardized his administration and left the Confederacy without its governmental and military leader when it most needed him. Wrote a reporter for the *Richmond Dispatch,* "Many times when the weight of responsibility of the Confederate cause rested heavily upon him he was racked in pain."[25]

An example was the peace mission of Vice President Stephens in 1863. Stephens, who hated Davis, put aside their differences and convinced the president that he might be able to arrange a top-secret meeting with Abraham Lincoln, an old friend of the vice president, and reach a settlement to end the war. On June 12, Stephens earned approval from Davis and the cabinet to sneak across the Potomac and try to meet the Union leader. The following morning, as Stephens was preparing to depart for the White House, he learned that President Davis was again bedridden.

Stephens was able to meet with Davis on June 13 and June 14 and was ready to go, but the ailing Davis was unable to authorize all the details of Stephens's mission for several weeks, work that he could have done in a morning had he been healthy. By the time Stephens reached the Potomac, on July 1, Lincoln had learned from Grant that Vicksburg might fall within weeks and from couriers that Lee had invaded Maryland and Meade's army was after him. The Union's chances of victory had improved dramatically in one week, and Lincoln canceled the proposed meeting. If Stephens had been able to get to Washington on June 12, he might have met with Lincoln and perhaps reached a settlement to end the war.[26] Another mishap occurred in September and October of 1861 when the irritability always brought on by his sicknesses resulted in scathing letters to Joe Johnston he might not have written when well.[27]

Davis's illnesses, which put him in bed, unable to work in nearly any capacity for a total of several months during the war—usually at key moments in the conflict—crippled his effectiveness as president. That ineffectiveness at crucial junctures in the war caused the Confederate government to be ineffective and kept the Confederacy in constant jeopardy.

Davis's herpes, an infection he picked up as a young man, was not his only medical problem. He suffered from chronic insomnia most nights and was up until one or two in the morning. He would then sleep until 9 A.M. or later and not get to his office until 10 or 11 A.M. Davis normally went home at 4:30 or 5 P.M., putting in a short day (he rarely did much work at night). He walked the six blocks back and forth to his downtown office but tried to sit as much as he could because his foot, which had been shattered by a musket ball in the Mexican War, had never healed properly; it hurt whenever he took a step. Davis was in constant pain from one or another of his many ailments.

His sickness in the summer of 1861 could not have come at a worse time. His cabinet was in chaos. Robert Toombs, the secretary of state, accused Davis of running the State Department: handpicking diplomats, engineering the mission to England and France, and repeatedly overruling him, giving Toombs little to do. He resigned right after Bull Run and demanded a commission as a general. Davis, glad to be rid of him, agreed. Two months later Secretary of War Leroy Walker quit, inundated by paperwork created by the president and powerless as Davis ran the War Department by himself, ignoring Walker. Walker obtained a generalship.

The Davis cabinet, chosen to represent the different states of the new country and for few other reasons, tottered from the beginning. Davis convened it every day of the week before the bombardment of Fort Sumter and kept his cabinet secretaries working past midnight. A workaholic himself, he made everyone around him work hard. Little changed after the government moved to Richmond. The president convened full cabinet meetings three times a week, sometimes more often, and met with individual cabinet secretaries on a near daily basis. The six hours he was at the office he worked nonstop and demanded the same of everyone else.

If Davis was unable to get to his office because of illness, he invited his aides and colleagues to the Confederate White House for early morning breakfasts or post-dinner rendezvous. Cabinet members reported that the meetings were long and boring. Davis would digress into long and tedious discussions about unimportant matters. He would talk endlessly about the Mexican War, his role in it, and the need for the Confederate Army to win battles as he had at Monterrey and Buena Vista. Davis spent enormous time going over trivial matters with each different secretary, creating mountains of paperwork over minutiae for all of them.

Most of his cabinet officers complained that he meddled in their departments and personally ran the entire country. Secretary of State Toombs was extremely critical of Davis to other cabinet secretaries, congressmen, and anyone who would listen. Toombs, who firmly believed that he, and not Davis, should have been president, complained that Davis's meetings were too long, that they accomplished nothing, and that Davis bogged himself down with so much work that no major decisions were made. "Davis works slowly, too slowly for the crisis," he said.[28] Toombs, who had thirsted for war in the Senate just before secession, charged that no one in the cabinet, not even the secretary of war, had anything to do with running the war. Davis ran the war himself.

Walker, the secretary of war, agreed. The president communicated directly with his generals, sending out anywhere between six and twelve orders per day, often over Walker's head. He also appointed friends to key War Department positions without consulting Walker, then had them report directly to him. Once, when Walker rode to the Orange County courthouse to visit a wounded friend, Davis went so far as to appoint an acting secretary of war without Walker's knowledge.[29] The president thought nothing of countermanding Walker's official orders without telling him,[30] and the generals soon began to pay little attention to what Walker said, awaiting word from Davis.

Davis ran Walker ragged with demands, and endless accounting of railroad cars, men, and supplies. Walker once snapped at his clerk that "no *gentleman* can be fit for office."[31] The president had so little faith in him— only he, Jefferson Davis could really run the War Department—that when friends suggested Davis take a vacation in September 1861, he refused, letting everybody, including Walker, know that the War Department could not be run without the president. Davis finally drove Walker to resign, as he intended.[32]

The cabinet, whose members bickered among themselves, as well, was a revolving door, as men were fired, forced to resign, or quit. From 1861 to 1865, the Confederate cabinet had three different secretaries of state, six secretaries of war, two treasury secretaries, and four attorney generals. The only men who remained throughout the war were John Reagan, postmaster general; Stephen Mallory, navy; and Judah Benjamin, the president's only true confidant, who at different times served as attorney general, secretary of war, and secretary of state. The Confederate Congress considered the cabinet so disorganized and ineffective that in 1863 it tried, unsuccessfully, to limit cabinet terms to just two years.[33] Many attacked the principle by which cabinet members were selected from different states instead of from those considered to be best qualified—regardless of state.[34]

Some saw the ineptness of the cabinet as representative of the ineptness of the entire administration.[35] In 1864, members of the Virginia delegation in the House asked Davis to fire most of his cabinet and let Congress name the replacements. Davis shot back that it mattered not who was in the cabinet—he ran it.[36] No one disputed him. The editor of the *Richmond Examiner* underlined Davis's feelings when he wrote that the cabinet members were nothing more than "mere clerks" who did his bidding. "They are fit for nothing else.... None of them is a statesman of a caliber equal to these or any other times."[37]

Cabinet members complained that Davis never discussed the war with them. "The president does not consult of cabinet as to plans...of campaigns or the appointment of military men in office and I think he errs in not doing so," said the navy secretary, Mallory, who added that Davis constantly meddled in the War Department.[38] He may not have discussed the war out of concern for the constant leaks from the cabinet. General Joe Johnston once went directly from a top-secret cabinet meeting to a friend's dinner party, and by the time he arrived everyone at the party knew what was said in the meeting.[39]

Others claimed that Davis ruined any real impact the War Department might have with his tyrannical takeover, his continual reorganizing, and nonstop hirings and firings. He issued hundreds of orders without consulting the secretary of war, planned entire campaigns without consulting anyone in the department, and made promotions without anyone else's approval or knowledge. Davis further insisted that the secretary of war, his undersecretaries, and clerks have long conferences with him on every single appointment on which he did seek advice—entailing hundreds of hours wasted in unneeded meetings—and then would ask the clerks to spend countless more hours preparing unnecessary paperwork. The president himself would then plunge into the paperwork he had ordained, and it would consume further days of his valuable time each month.

On one day, a clerk in the department noted that there were fifteen hundred letters, orders, and notes on the president's desk, all of them work any dozen undersecretaries should have handled through their staffs, yet President Davis sat down and handled each and every one of the documents.

"No one can administer the War Office, or the government, on the terms laid down by the president," wrote Robert Kean, head of the War Bureau, a management division of the War Department.[40]

Because the president could not get along with any of its members, the cabinet was always in confusion. The only two people in the entire administration who worked genuinely well with Davis were Benjamin and General Robert E. Lee. They had to constantly hold their tongues to do so. Davis had no respect for individual talents or the experience or opinion of others. He would not let the cabinet help him run the government or the army. He treated them as he treated house servants. His coldness and temper annoyed nearly everyone, and he would not tolerate any disagreement with his views. "The President is the most difficult man to get along with," said one of his war secretaries, James Seddon.

Davis had chosen his original cabinet from men for whom he had no regard, but who represented the different seceding states. He had also avoided choosing strong personalities who might dominate the cabinet, which he planned to rule.[41] Davis did not believe there was any reason for him to befriend his cabinet secretaries. Since his was a one-party government, he did not appoint cabinet secretaries with their ability to represent this or that party faction in mind. In a one-party system Davis did not need a secretary who controlled campaign war chests for different races in different states, or who had powerful newspapers in his pocket which could support the administration. Davis never understood that bad relations with a cabinet member meant bad relations with all the undersecretaries in his department, and a general reluctance to work hard for the administration.

Few in the Confederate government could put up with Davis and his truculent personality. "He is inveterately obstinate to a serious fault," said Congressman W. B. Machen. James Hammond, a veteran politician, called the president "the most irascible man I ever knew...quick tempered, arbitrary, overbearing...." William Porcher Miles, head of Congress's military affairs committee, a man the commander in chief should have worked hard to befriend, said that "he cannot brook opposition or criticism and those who do not bow down before him have no chance of success with him."[42]

The Confederate Army's ordnance head, General Josiah Gorgas, agreed. "The President seems to respect the opinions of no one; and has, I fear, little appreciation of services rendered...he seems to be an indifferent judge of men and is guided more by prejudice than by sound, discriminating judgment."[43]

Perhaps Stephen Mallory, his longsuffering and loyal navy secretary, summed it up best when he described Davis's relationship to the cabinet, Congress, and people in government. "In his manner and language there was just an indescribable something which offended their self esteem and left their judgments room to find with feelings bordering closely upon anger...and with a determination hastily formed, of calling no more upon him...and were alienated from this cause...."[44]

A chief asset of any president is the power of persuasion, the ability to use his personality to get members of his cabinet and Congress to do what he wants because it is in their best interest as well as his. To do this, he needs to bargain with them, trading off some of his policy initiatives to enable support for others. He has to form cordial associations with them outside the cabinet room and the government offices—visiting their homes, befriending their wives and children, inflating their importance in the newspapers, and letting them know how important they are to him.[45] It is also important for a chief executive to play cabinet members off against each other, to make them vie for the president's favor through productive endeavor, thus producing success for the administration. Jefferson Davis was never able to do any of these things with his cabinet or, later, with his Congress, and it helped cripple his effectiveness as chief executive.

JEFFERSON Davis and the army were one and inseparable. Even though he never led the army, as so many expected him to do (although he sometimes hinted he might[46]), he controlled it from his inauguration until Appomattox. He ran the War Department, appointed all generals and colonels, and personally conducted the government's relations with the army. He never permitted his secretary of war to act too independently, or indeed with any authority over the operations of the army. Whoever did was removed or forced to resign.

Davis ignored suggestions by officers and congressmen that he name a general in chief to run the war. because he wanted to run it. He was willing to conduct the war without help, never understanding that, in addition to expertise and assistance, a winning general in chief could symbolize success for the president and boost his prestige. A general in chief is also an easy lightning rod for criticism from Congress, the press, and the public when campaigns go awry, deflecting it from the president.

Davis also disregarded suggestions by army officers and cabinet members that two or three large armies battle the Federals and instead divided the army into six different geographic departments, sending troops wherever people in those areas requested, which stretched his forces thin and made if difficult to reinforce armies that were hundreds of miles apart. These proved to be fatal mistakes when Sherman advanced on Atlanta in 1864 and during the last days of the conflict.

Determined to let no one interfere with the conduct of the war, President Davis ran into immediate trouble with his generals. Unwilling to listen to veteran commanders, Davis plunged ahead to select generals based almost solely on favoritism. From the start, he distanced himself from capable military leaders who were not his personal friends or former West Point or Mexican War companions.

He reached back in time to name generals from among his West Point classmates. While that list included Robert E. Lee, Joe Johnston, and Albert Sidney Johnston, it also named Leonidas Polk, who had never enjoyed army life and was a minister when the war began. He put generals' bars on friends from the Mexican War, such as sickly, seventy-one-year-old David Twiggs; John Floyd, who had succeeded him as secretary of war; on officers he knew from his own days as secretary of war, including Sam Cooper, William Hardee, George Thomas, and Earl Van Dorn; and political appointees, such as former Governor Henry Wise of Virginia.

Davis made certain that every single colleague from his old regiment in the Mexican War, the First Mississippi Rifles, despite fourteen years' intervening inactivity was made a colonel in the Confederate Army. Davis had named Hardee superintendent of West Point when he was secretary of war, and Hardee had immediately instituted a summer training camp named for Jefferson Davis. Whenever Hardee heard that Davis was sick, he would take a train to Washington, D.C., to visit him. There, while Davis reclined, barely able to see or talk, Hardee would read him novels long into the night. Hardee became one of President Davis's first appointments to general.[47]

No one made much of his appointments at first. Who knew more about the military than the hero of Buena Vista? Later, however, as his favorites faltered, a torrent of controversy came down around the president.

Much of the controversy which plagued and considerably weakened the Confederate Army was initiated by Jefferson Davis himself. He would accept no criticism of his campaign plans from generals, and no one was permitted to question his appointments or promotions, even when he was wrong. That is exactly what happened in July 1861, right after Bull Run, when Joe Johnston legitimately questioned why he was only the fourth-ranking general in the army, even though he had been one of the first appointed. In honoring an army promotion rule, Davis had made a mistake, but he would never admit it. Instead, he questioned Johnston's loyalty, and the dispute over rank tore apart their initial friendship.[48] "[Your letter's] arguments and statements [are] utterly one-sided, and its insinuations as unfounded as they are unbecoming," Davis snapped.[49] He told friends he considered Johnston "petulant."

The feud lasted much of the war and made the other generals reluctant to criticize anything Davis did. It was quickly followed by an all-out war between Davis and Beauregard. The flamboyant Beauregard, the very popular hero of Fort Sumter, first drew Davis's anger by complaining to some of his opponents in Congress that his men were being woefully undersupplied by General Lucius Northrop, the head of the Commissary Department and a longtime personal friend of the president. Then Beauregard wrote a report about Bull Run in which he took all credit for the victory, downplaying any role played by Davis, and ending by accusing the president of preventing him from chasing McDowell's army to Washington and winning the war.

Davis was livid. Not only was the report inaccurate and unfair, but he did not receive it from Beauregard; he read it in a newspaper. Davis berated Beauregard immediately, calling him a liar and accusing him of "an attempt to exalt yourself at my expense."[50]

A shaken Beauregard backed off from his accusations at once. Later, when Beauregard took sick leave without Davis's approval, the President relieved him of command, refusing to reinstate him for months, despite a petition signed by over half the members of Congress. Davis made constant fun of Beauregard in letters and conversation, noting that Mississippi's troops spent much of their time "retreating under Beauregard."[51]

Indeed, no one in Richmond cared for Beauregard. Mallory called him a "self sufficient, vain army idiot"[52] and Mary Chesnut said he was "puffed up with vanity."[53] The feud between the president and Beauregard escalated, as Davis frequently skewered him by saying that "there are those who can only walk a log when it is near to the ground."[54] The feud continued through their entire lives, and on several occasions help that Beauregard might have rendered the army was ignored because of it.[55]

On October 1, 1861, the president visited his two Virginia generals at Fairfax Court House to plan strategy. The two generals had a rather intriguing idea. The Union Army was in disarray, trying to rebuild itself, and concentrated around Washington. Why not take an army of sixty thousand men and attack Maryland to threaten Washington or, better yet, strike deep into the heart of the United States and seize Pittsburgh, Pennsylvania, which would frighten everybody in the Union?

Davis was startled. First, he told them, their army only had forty thousand men. Second, the South hadn't the railroad capability to move men that far. Third, he was determined to fight a defensive war, making the Union armies come to him, rather than an offensive one. He told them to forget big attacks and, instead, to stage small raids throughout Virginia. They disagreed loudly with Davis, wondering what was the point of a forty thousand man army which had just defeated a huge Union force, if it was only going to stage tiny raids? The three men argued on for hours, until both the strikes into the North and the raids in Virginia were scrapped and the army just sat. Davis, on leaving them, was convinced that Joe Johnston and Beauregard were too angry, too bullheaded, and too obstinate to make good generals. They could not know much about running an army if they disagreed with him.

The president had made scant efforts to work with the governors of the seceded states. He quickly became mired in political quicksand regarding generals he sent to their states. Sterling Price was at odds with other generals in Missouri, so Davis decided to send Henry Heth to work with him, but the governor of Missouri refused to accept Heth, who then refused to go, because he was not a Missourian.

Davis needed weeks to find generals for his forces in Tennessee because the governor of Tennessee insisted that all three areas of the state—east, west, and central—needed generals; he suggested a few who had political connections. Davis told the governor sarcastically that he would put military men at the head of his armies, not "pathfinders and holiday soldiers."[56] Meanwhile, little was happening in Virginia because the state's regiments, to be raised by the legislature, were unavailable for two long months during which the members of the legislature bickered among themselves.[57] Davis put his old friend David Twiggs in charge of the defenses of New Orleans, but civic leaders there objected to him and Davis was forced to replace him with the untested Mansfield Lovell, who would soon be overwhelmed by events.

The only truly outstanding appointments Davis made, he was certain, were generalships for Robert E. Lee and Albert Sidney Johnston. Colonel Robert E. Lee was fifty-four when the war began. He was the perfect soldier, graduating with honors from West Point, where in four years he did not incur a single demerit. He had spent his entire life in the army and had received numerous decorations for valor during the Mexican War, where he was overshadowed only by Winfield Scott and Zachary Taylor. Lee had served as superintendent at West Point, where he was an innovative administrator. In 1859, after years of service with the army in the west, he was brought back to Washington, where he led the army unit that captured abolitionist John Brown at Harper's Ferry in 1859.

Lee, who opposed slavery all of his life, was one of the best commanders in the United States Army. Just before Virginia seceded he had been offered command of the entire Union Army by Winfield Scott. After an evening pacing the floor of his home, he turned the offer down with great reluctance. Lee, though he considered secession open rebellion and treason, could not bring himself to fight against his fellow Virginians. Thereupon Colonel Lee resigned from the U.S. Army and was named head of all forces in Virginia.

He did not know Jefferson Davis well—they knew each other casually from the Mexican War—and made the mistake of refusing to travel to Montgomery to meet with the president while the seat of government was still there. Yet Davis, who usually considered such an action worthy of a lifelong grudge, did not seem to mind. He finally met Lee in late May 1861 and was impressed with his military savvy and personal integrity. Davis then sent Lee on a series of raids in West Virginia and next assigned him to head up coastal defenses in Georgia, where Lee chafed. The president, convinced that Robert E. Lee was extraordinary, would eventually bring him to Richmond as his personal aide. The partnership of the two men would profoundly change the course of the war and, for a while, the fate of the South.

Frustrated by bad generals and defeats, Davis once threatened to join the army himself. He said, "If I could take one wing of the army and Lee the other, I think we could between us wrest a victory from those people."[58]

His other outstanding appointment was General Albert Sidney Johnston, another West Point and Mexican War acquaintance, and Davis's hero. His fondest hope had been that Johnston, a star in the U.S. Army, would quit and join the Confederacy. Davis was overjoyed when Johnston did and soon put him in charge of the western forces, certain that Johnston would be the greatest single general in the war. He told his critics that if Johnston was not a general, the South had no generals.

Davis's careful orchestration of appointments in the military had no parallel elsewhere in the executive branch. Davis did appoint friends to jobs and sometimes even found positions for people who barged into his office. He made no effort, though, to control patronage of government jobs, ranging from the hundreds he commanded in Richmond to Confederate government positions in the various states, cities, and towns, right down to post-office jobs, so valuable as political plums because those jobholders controlled the mailing and distribution of political flyers, literature, and newspapers.

Davis did not believe he needed to waste his time on patronage: he was president in a one-party system, after all. He would never stand for reelection, so the absence of an opposition party meant that the executive branch of his government did not have to be a political stronghold. Nor did he need the help of governors and congressmen for reelection, since he served a single, six-year term. Finally, he disdained any efforts to build a strong governmental machine to help them win election so they could support him and his government.

PRESIDENT Davis was under enormous pressure to raise money to fight the war and run the country. The newly created Confederacy had no gold reserves and no currency of its own. Davis and Treasury Secretary Christopher Memminger had to create a whole new system of financing, capable of raising some $200 million a year to pay for the struggle. Instead of the most obvious method, high taxes and heavy borrowing from banks at home and abroad, Davis and Memminger elected to ask for low taxes. They ordered Southerners to pay any outstanding debts owed to Northern governmental entities to the new Confederate government. Monies owed banks or businesses there had to be paid to the Confederate government. Davis ordered the printing of great amounts of brand-new Confederate money which would be used to pay bills.

The taxes realized under the Davis plan represented just two percent of the budget. The transferred debt, which Davis predicted would bring in $200 million, wound up at just $12 million. The huge amount of currency in circulation began an inflation which by the end of 1861 hovered at 35 percent, and would grow catastrophically in the next few years.[59] The money Davis did decide to borrow—he did not want to borrow much—by means of promissory notes and a loan from Europe was far too little to cover the enormous costs of the war. He quickly found, too, that the newly formed government had no reliable system for collecting taxes. The agrarian Southerners, who had paid low taxes before the war, were opposed to them, and he had to deal with state governments that were reluctant to turn over the tax monies they collected to the national government. The result was a tax system, opposed by many newspapers,[60] which produced an extremely small percentage of tax revenue for the governments.[61]

Davis's disregard for the cabinet or executive departments was evident throughout the summer and fall of 1861 as he engineered diplomatic missions to England and France to gain foreign recognition of the Confederacy,[62] rarely seeking advice from his State Department. If Europe recognized the seceded states as a new nation, and not just a collection of rebels, as the North insisted, it would mean billions in foreign aid, shipping which would force the North to lift its blockade, and perhaps the threat of war with England or France, which would force the Union to end the war and allow the new Confederacy to live in peace.[63]

Davis slowly came to blame England for the South's inability to win. He said, "Not only have the governments [England and France] which entered into these arrangements [with the United States] yielded to the prohibition against commerce with us which has been dictated by the United States in defiance of the law of nations, but this concession of their neutral rights to our detriment has on more than one occasion been claimed in intercourse with our enemies as an evidence of friendly feeling towards them."[64]

A general lack of understanding of British and French politics, and a reluctance by Davis to learn much about them, prevented him from choosing the right men or using the proper approach to bring the two European powers into the war. England had abolished slavery in the British Isles and in all of its far-flung colonies in the 1830s after a century-long campaign by religious organizations and civic leaders.[65] Now, a generation later, Parliament found it very difficult to support a new country whose secession was based almost entirely on slavery; members of the Houses of Commons and Lords immediately balked.[66]

To induce England to recognize the Confederacy and join the war on the Southern side, Davis and his advisers decided on a policy of economic strangulation. The embargo was supposed to be a volunteer movement by wealthy planters, not officially opposed by Davis, to withhold all cotton from England until the British recognized the Confederacy. Southern political leaders believed that Britain's textile industry relied on Southern cotton; the lack of it not only meant no clothing, but thousands of unemployed workers.[67] The cotton embargo was vigorously opposed by some in the Confederate Congress, particularly Vice President Stephens, who suggested just the opposite. He advocated sending all of the South's cotton to England, millions of bales of it, for storage in British warehouses until prices rose and it could all be sold in England at huge profits. The money thus realized, projected at over $800 million, would pay for the war. Some planters went further, suggesting holding back cotton from all foreign ports to drive up the price.[68]

Davis managed to convince the national government, the individual states, and the cotton planters that the embargo idea would work.[69] He was armed with newspaper clippings from cotton trade journals that predicted four million unemployed workers in England if cotton was withheld[70] and with letters from British merchants who agreed with him. One English editor wrote, "The government will be compelled to sink policy...or submit to a revolution."[71]

The idea of recognition and financial support from France and above all England took hold early in the Southern psyche. Southern newspapers carried speeches of pro-Southern Parliament members every week, and their pages were flooded with stories about prospective support from the British. The *Richmond Examiner* even had a weekly column on England's possible recognition.[72] Southern newspapers reprinted as many pro-South columns from British newspapers as they could find.[73] Other editors wrote numerous columns suggesting that the British were still angry over the loss of their colonies in the American Revolution and of subsequent trade to businesses in the United States and would welcome the collapse of the old federal government and rise of the Confederacy.[74] They all ran stories of rumors brought by travelers to Southern ports that Parliament was about to support the South.[75] Southern newspapers were filled with well-reasoned letters from Southerners explaining why British support was logical.[76] For more than two years, most people in the government and the public firmly believed that the British would eventually intervene and save them.

This belief persisted despite early speeches from members of the British cabinet and of Parliament opposing recognition of the Confederacy, as well as strident editorials by leading London newspapers against it.[77] These Englishmen were opposed to slavery, worried about the war threatened by the United States if Britain recognized Jeff Davis's government, and believed they could suffer strikes and somehow survive without Southern cotton for some time.

Davis's work in the British scheme was unsuccessful from the start. He knew that Parliament's biggest objection to the Confederacy was slavery, yet he sent a mission to England headed by William Yancey, the internationally famous proslavery firebrand. He knew that France was bogged down in military operations in Mexico, yet he cavalierly demanded it abandon them to fight for the South. Davis then undermined missions to both countries by recalling all of his diplomats after just six months, a sign he had no faith in them or in the nations with whom they dealt. He also failed badly, thanks to Yancey and his aides, in efforts to win over the British press. The press in England, highly critical of the government at times, might have been more supportive of the South if minimal efforts had been made to work with editors and reporters to explain the Southern cause, but few such pains were taken.[78]

By the end of 1861, the South had experienced more failures than successes. The South did win decisively at Wilson's Creek, Missouri, in August, and Stonewall Jackson and his men blew up a dam near Harper's Ferry in November. There were many more failures, however: the Federals easily captured Hilton Head Island, South Carolina, in early November, and took Biloxi, Mississippi. Two ships attempting to run the Union blockade, carrying needed supplies, were caught as the blockade, sneered at by Davis and others in the spring, began to become effective. Pro-Union Virginians in the western part of the state held a convention and declared their area a separate state, West Virginia, and planned to join the Union.

The few military setbacks did not annoy President Davis as he prepared for his formal inauguration, however. He had Robert E. Lee at his side in the eastern theater, and in the west he had his hero, the unbeatable General Albert Sidney Johnston, who was getting ready to drive Union forces commanded by an unknown young colonel, U. S. Grant, into the Ohio River.

The nonmilitary news was not good, either. Efforts to improve the South's primitive and limited railroad system, vital for the transportation of supplies and troops, made no headway despite an urgent plea by the president in his yearly message in November.[79] The Davis administration's financial scheme of issuing currency resulted in the worst inflation in the history of the United States, with the cost of dry goods up nearly 100 percent.[80] The cabinet was dominated by bickering, and there were governmental military leaks throughout Richmond. On December 31, the last day of the year, Davis complained that Northern newspapers seemed to know more about the position and strengths of the Confederate army than he did.[81]

Davis never blamed all the South's woes completely on himself. There was no reason to do so. He had worked hard for months not only to build and arm a new army, but to strengthen a brand-new economy, to create hundreds of new positions in a new government, and to bolster sagging morale. It had been a daunting challenge and Davis had achieved a certain success. Many of the South's troubles could not have been solved by the president. He had no control over battlefield outcomes. He could not make British politicians do what he wanted. He sincerely believed withholding cotton from England was a sound policy whose goal, England's participation in the war, may have been worth the risk. He could not hold down inflation from his office in Richmond; only the free market economy could do that. There were many forces working against the Confederacy in its first days, and the president, despite his troubles getting along with people, was not entirely to blame for any of them.

President Davis was certain that nothing could destroy the will of the people to fight. In speech after speech he declared that determination was more important than anything else. He told Congress in 1861, "Liberty is always won where there exists the unconquerable will to be free, and we have reason to know the strength that is given by a conscious sense, not only of the magnitude, but the righteousness of our Cause."[82]

On February 22, 1862, President Davis rode in a carriage with his wife to an outdoor park in Richmond to be sworn in as the Confederacy's first president in symbolic proximity to a statue of George Washington. He then delivered an inaugural address before what should have been an upbeat rally. Instead, mirroring larger events that morning, the skies opened early to deluge Richmond with heavy downpours of rain all day. Davis, an umbrella held over him, again pale and sickly, read his address in his usual wooden manner, looking out over a small crowd of bedraggled, inattentive people, also under umbrellas and all eager to go home. Once again, he told the crowd that "Never has a people evinced a more determined spirit than that now animating men, women, and children in every part of our country....It was, perhaps, the ordinance of Providence that we were to be taught the value of our liberties by the price we pay for them...."[83]

The dark and rain of inauguration day was an omen of the coming year. The somber mood as the rain poured down in the park that day would be nothing, however, compared to the mood that would result from the news of three important battles fought in Tennessee—horrible news.

12

THE LINCOLNS AT HOME

IT WAS A CHILLY EVENING in early March. The White House was ablaze with gas lamps which gave the huge building a soft glow. From the sidewalks of Pennsylvania Avenue the White House was gorgeous, looking like a brightly lit postcard, its illuminated windows dotted with the distant figures of Supreme Court justices, senators, congressmen, and the most important people in the nation, all gathered for Mary Lincoln's first formal reception. Men in their finest suits, with diamond pins and expensive watches, talked in small circles; the women, in their finest hoopskirts, vying for attention in the fashion parade, moved about the crowded rooms.

Expensive carriages were backed up on the semicircular driveway, unable to move for the crush of people. There were so many guests trying to get in through the front doors that no one could move, and the crowd was backed up on the portico. Dozens managed to open windows and, holding hats and clinging to purses, climbed in through them, to the alarm of the servants. It was the 1861 postinaugural reception, a coming-out party of sorts for the Lincolns. The president, not a social lion, looked forward to it only because his wife Mary was determined to make it a showcase.

Washington's high society had scoffed when the Lincolns arrived in town. Abe was dismissed as an awkward, ungainly, homely looking prairie lawyer whose sole skill was telling hilarious stories. Mary was sniped at as a coarse western woman, born and raised in the hills of Kentucky and married to a railsplitter with calluses on his hands and dirt under his fingernails. Tonight, with the White House as pretty as any Arabian palace in a fairy tale, Mary Lincoln would show everybody. She had spent weeks preparing the reception and attending to every tiny detail to make certain everything would go right.

From a logistic point of view everything went wrong. The evening started and ended in chaos. Mary fumed and fretted upstairs in her living quarters. Her seamstress, Elizabeth Keckley, a free black woman, was late. The seamstress, who wanted employment in the White House, had worked so hard preparing the first lady's gown for the evening that she lost track of time. She was just racing up the backstairs at the White House as Mary paced around the bedroom. The first lady had no gown; she would have to find something in her closet and improvise some alterations so that it would be special, but she wasn't succeeding. She snapped at the president that he should make his grand entrance to the reception by himself; she was not going. She told him to find some other woman and walk in with her. Lincoln rolled his eyes as he always did when his wife flew into a rage. He sat down on a sofa, his long legs dangling out into the middle of the room, and waited.

Mrs. Keckley finally arrived, apologizing profusely while Mary scolded her for being so late on one of the most important nights of her life. The first lady's anger subsided quickly when she put on the lovely, bright rose-colored dress, which fit her perfectly. Mary wore a necklace and earrings and let Mrs. Keckley put red roses in her hair. Everyone thought she looked beautiful. The president's eyes widened as he stood and took her hand. "Mother, you look charming in that dress," he said.

The Lincolns were about to leave their living quarters and go downstairs to greet the crowd when Mary realized she had left her lace handkerchief on the dressing table. The Lincolns and their servants turned the room upside down, searching without success, when Mary took a moment to look at her rambunctious eight-year-old son Tad, who was laughing. Tad then raced to where he had hidden the handkerchief and gave it to his mother. As always, Mary was angry at him and, as always, the president found Tad's little trick highly amusing.[1]

The party itself was a great success. Washington's high society and government circles had an opportunity to meet the president and the first lady, and the Lincolns seemed pleasant. Hayseed did not drip from the president, and the first lady did not slop hogs or reek of sawdust. She was, her friends felt, quite elegant in her new dress. "No queen accustomed to the usages of royalty all her life could have comported herself with more calmness and dignity than did the wife of the President," said Mrs. Keckley, who was hired that night and remained Mrs. Lincoln's seamstress and confidante as long as she lived in the executive mansion.[2]

The evening ended as it had began, however, in pandemonium. Everyone left at the same time, and it quickly became apparent that there were far too few people working in the coatcheck rooms. The first wave of people trying to retrieve their coats had to wait long periods of time while the second wave of partygoers pressed up against them. Women's hoop skirts were bent and crushed, flower corsages were torn from dresses, men's watch fobs were knocked to the ground and hats and coats passed from workers to the guests were dropped, trampled on, and lost. More than eighty percent of the guests lost a hat or coat that night, and they all blamed Mary Lincoln.[3]

Mary Lincoln could never do anything right in Washington. It seemed the harder she tried, the more she did wrong. The sniping from Washingtonians was relentless. It began the day she arrived at Willard's Hotel with her husband, and the women of official Washington snubbed her, and it continued until she left the White House years later, dressed in black.

The first lady was seen as a traitor by everyone. Washington was a Southern not a Northern town and was bordered by the slave states of Maryland and Virginia. Southerners who remained there after the Southern legislators fled when their states seceded saw Mary Lincoln as a traitor because she was from a prominent Kentucky family, and had betrayed Southern slaveholding tradition and married a radical Northern abolitionist. Northerners saw Mary as traitor too. To them, the wife of the Union's president was a genuine Southerner from Kentucky. Later on, her brothers would fight in the Confederate Army. She continued to consort with cousins and sisters-in-law from the far-flung Todd family of Kentucky. Lincoln, never fond of the Todds, joked that "one 'd' is good enough for God, but not for the Todds."[4]

Mary Lincoln wanted to be a very different first lady. She saw being first lady, just as her husband saw the presidency, as an extension of her own personality. Prior to her arrival, all first ladies, except for Dolley Madison, a distant cousin of Mary's, had kept out of the public spotlight. Not Mary Lincoln. She hosted balls, dinner parties, and receptions. She had military bands give regular concerts at the White House. She had soirees at the White House for important politicians, legislators, writers, and businessmen. She tried to be a fashion plate, wearing the latest gowns designed in New York and

Philadelphia. She began a massive campaign to redecorate the run-down White House, launched a drive to restore its disheveled gardens, and turned the roof of the executive mansion into a large playground for her children.

Everything she did landed her in trouble. The women of Washington found her crude and appalling. She had not only stepped out of women's domestic sphere and into the men's by her undue influence over her husband but had practically become a political aide, meddling in everything.

She was roundly faulted for her taste in clothes. Her critics were astounded that in an era of subdued colors she not only wore brightly colored dresses in public, but adored dresses with daring, low-cut necklines. These annoyed the president as well. Her fashion tastes were not only criticized by the women of Washington, but by their men, too. "She was vain...wore her dresses shorter at the top and longer at the train than even fashions demanded," said Alex McClure, a Lincoln Pennsylvania political operative.[5] William Howard Russell, a British correspondent, said she was "the most preposterous looking female I ever saw...a damned old Irish washerwoman," and a legislator, gazing at the first lady's low-cut dress and array of roses in her hair, told his wife that Mary had her "bosom on display and a flower pot on her head."[6]

Washingtonians were very critical of her wild shopping sprees in New York, where the press would report every expensive purchase and make up others. Mary and friends went to New York eleven times to shop in 1861 alone. There they visited the most expensive stores, including the block-long Alexander Stewart's Department Store (which novelist Henry James called "fatal to feminine nerves"), where she routinely spent $2,000 or more in a single visit. She allowed Stewart and others to host luncheons and dinner parties for her and, impressed with their friendship, returned to spend even more money in their establishments.

The first lady also made the mistake of accepting expensive clothes, jewelry, and furniture which she assumed were gifts, only to be billed large amounts later. She took outright gifts as well, including diamonds from a man who then lobbied her to have him named a naval agent. She did. She purchased just about anything she wanted, carefully hiding the costs from her husband. By 1865, according to her seamstress Keckley, who kept track of the first lady's inventory, Mary Lincoln owed more than $70,000. She was such an obsessive shopper, and so oblivious to bills, that when she wrote one letter to a department store begging them to give her more time to pay her bills she ended it by ordering a $1,000 black camel's hair shawl.[7]

The first lady hosted receptions for government officials and Washingtonians twice a month throughout 1861. Her expensive dinner parties not only landed her in financial trouble, but caused political tangles that took her husband weeks to straighten out. One example was her insistence on breaking tradition and having the president, and not the secretary of state, host the new administration's first dinner party for the diplomatic corps. She did this because she hated William Seward. She called Seward a manipulator and a hypocrite and tried to bar him from the cabinet.[8] An additional reason for her animus was her belief that she should be appointed to the cabinet, which her husband refused to do. Showing Seward up at the dinner was a way to get back at him.[9]

There was trouble the morning after the party when the wives of the diplomats, who hadn't been invited, discovered that Mary and her gossipy cousin Lizzie Grimsley had been the only two women at the festivities. So they began a campaign to undermine Mary in the diplomatic community. Meanwhile, federal accountants complained profusely to the president that the party had cost $900, or more than three times the cost of similar parties.[10] That did not deter Mrs. Lincoln. A few months later she threw another expensive soiree for Prince Napoleon, nephew of Napoleon III, the ruler of France, on which Mary spent an enormous amount of money. She later seethed when the prince told his friends in Europe that William Seward looked like a farmer and Abraham Lincoln reminded him of a bootmaker.[11]

The first lady's extravagant parties were routinely criticized in the Democratic newspapers; the Republican papers, while not critical, poked fun at their ostentation. One referred to them as royal gatherings of the "Republican Court of America."[12] Southern newspapers often reprinted Northern articles about the parties to show their readers that Lincoln was trying to be a king while the Confederates had a government of the common people.[13]

Mary Lincoln's biggest financial problem was the debt she had run up trying to refurbish the White House. The president's mansion was run down and a general eyesore to the people of Washington. The wallpaper was peeling, rugs were worn out, the furniture was old and sometimes decrepit, the gardens were overgrown with weeds, and nothing had been painted in years. Mary decided that as an active first lady her very first project would be the total restoration of the White House as a home for her husband and the people. She plunged into this new endeavor with her usual fervor and total disregard for cost. Her congressional allowance for refurbishing the building was $20,000 for four years. Mary went through that sum in nine months, managing to spend $7,000 over and above it.

This time, because the money came out of appropriations and creditors demanded to be paid, the president found out about it. Lincoln was enraged. He went through the bills one by one, increasingly incredulous. Two items infuriated him: the $10,000 restoration of the entire East Room and a $2,500 carpet. "What carpet could possibly be worth $2,500?" he snapped at one of his secretaries.

The president was angrier at his wife than at any time in his life, especially when she and her friends tried to make it look like the cost overruns were the fault of architects and interior decorators. He told an aide, "It would stink in the nostrils of the American people to have it said that the President of the United States had approved a bill overrunning an appropriation of $20,000 for flub dubs for this damned old house, when the soldiers cannot have blankets."[14]

At about the same time, Lincoln learned that Mary was scrambling to keep other cost overruns from him and was dishonestly charging certain overruns to other accounts. She tried to bill the $900 diplomatic dinner bill to the White House gardening account, coercing the gardener to approve it, and reportedly covered subsequent bills with phantom appropriations through the gardener's office. She attempted to cover up the White House refurbishment overruns, helped by people in the administration, by burying the bills in still other accounts.[15]

There were rumors that she had asked government workers to pay her bills while keeping them secret from her husband. At one point Mary became hysterical and arranged a yard sale to raise money to pay the bills, offering old furniture from the White House at cut-rate prices to passersby. After making little money at that, she began, together with the gardener, trying to sell manure from the White House stables at inflated prices, which made her a target of derision in social circles and in the press.[16] The president, exasperated, offered to pay all the bills out of his own pocket, but was persuaded to let accountants cover Mary's tracks until the costs could be sorted out, to avoid a public scandal. She feared that public knowledge of her debts and extravagant spending might be used as a campaign issue against her husband in 1864. Later, after he was reelected, Lincoln joked to friends that now he had a guaranteed income for four more years and could use it to pay off his wife's debts.

Mary's travels presented Lincoln with yet another problem. She and Lizzie Grimsley and other companions thought nothing of taking short vacations to spas in Long Branch, New Jersey, and vacation jaunts to New York and Philadelphia, all covered extensively in the press. The president once again came under harsh criticism by the press and the people for his wife's extravagances in the middle of a war. Soldiers wrote home that they had no weapons, shoes, or food—and yet the newspapers were filled with stories of the first lady hosting parties at fancy resorts.

Mary Lincoln was criticized by the press even more than her husband. The journalistic sniping was so bad that at the end of summer, 1861, a friendly editor wrote that "If Mrs. Lincoln...were a condemned convict on the way to execution, she could not be treated more indecently than she is by a portion of the New York press....No lady of the White House has ever been so maltreated by the press."[17]

THE Lincoln White House was the youngest in history: Lincoln was fifty-one, the first lady only forty-two, son Willie just ten, and Tad only eight. The president's eldest son, Robert, eighteen, was at Harvard College, becoming ever more distant from his father. He grew up during the years that his father was deeply immersed in politics, first in the state legislature and then in various campaigns for the Senate and the presidency. In those days Lincoln was rarely home.

The two had very dissimilar personalities. Robert was quiet and subdued and found it difficult to get along with different kinds of people, unlike his gregarious father. Their relations chilled when Lincoln was elected and became even busier. "Any great intimacies between us became impossible. I scarcely even had ten minutes quiet talk with him during his Presidency," said his eldest son years later.[18]

Since he was the first son, Robert provided the first childrearing experience for his parents, who were told by friends and relatives that harsh discipline was the only way to raise a child. Robert was frequently reprimanded or punished and many of his requests were denied. The stern discipline turned him against his parents. Finding that such discipline did not really work, the Lincolns abandoned it entirely, raising their other children without many rules at all. Robert and his brothers were thus very different.

Robert Lincoln waged a three-year-battle with his parents to get into the army. The president, grief-stricken by so many deaths in the war, absolutely forbade his son to join the army and put himself at risk. He and Mary had already lost one child, Edward, in 1850, when he was three years old, and did not want to lose another. Their eldest son was just as adamant about going to war. He argued that his friends looked upon him as a coward protected by his father while the sons of every other American father were either enlisting or being drafted. Finally, unable to hold out any longer, the president worked out an agreeable compromise. He had General Grant name Robert as one of his aides, which put him in the army yet kept him in Grant's tents, safely out of the line of fire.

Willie and Tad moved into the White House while their older brother was at college. They lived there under minimal control from their parents, particularly the president, who gave them the freedom to do practically anything they wanted. Friends and associates complained that the president never reprimanded his children for their antics, which annoyed many, but the president did not care. His attitude was simple: Let the boys have a good time.[19]

The president and first lady went to extraordinary lengths to turn the executive mansion into the nation's largest playhouse. The attic of the building was renovated into a huge play area for the boys, where they would have their adventures and produce little plays for their family and neighborhood children. The White House roof became a vast open-air playground where, in good weather, the Lincoln offspring and their neighborhood friends, Bud and Holly Taft, children of a local judge, staged circuses and built a Union Army fort of their own, designed to defend the White House against the Confederate Army. The fort had a large log for a cannon and some old, unworkable rifles the president managed to sneak out of an arsenal for them. The playground was also renovated to serve as a U.S. navy ship, often at war with the ships of just about every nation on earth.[20]

The Lincolns gave Willie and Todd the run of everything: the White House, the grounds, and Washington itself. The boys were seated with guests at most state dinners and allowed to attend parties, often racing back and forth between irate guests. They wandered through Washington, too, sending the president into a panic one day when they disappeared for over four hours, hopelessly lost in the underground tunnels beneath the Capitol, which they had been exploring.

The president never minded their sudden arrivals in the middle of cabinet meetings. He sometimes conducted these while the boys played army in the hallway outside. Tad would even interrupt important cabinet meetings, sitting down on the floor and leaning against his father's chair while the meeting continued. Lincoln stopped them once after they clanged pots and pans they stole from the kitchen to make artillery sound effects so loud and authentic that some members of the cabinet jumped up from their seats when they heard the noise.

Since Willie and Todd were permitted to use the White House as their personal clubhouse, it was common to find them making sleds and riding through hallways on them or sliding down the three stories of banisters. They often rigged up boxes with wheels and had their pets pull them through the hallways, sometimes during official functions. The boys and their friends, the Tafts, formed their own military company, "Mr. Lincoln's Zouaves," with their own uniforms, and played soldier on the White House lawn. When it rained, they pretended to shoot up the newly redecorated East Room fighting their battles indoors.

One of their inventions was a doll dressed as a soldier whom they named "Captain Jack." He was constantly in trouble, and the boys often had him shot for desertion, then dug up the White House lawn to bury him, angering the gardener. He told Julia Taft, the Taft boys' teenage sister, who said they should all get a pardon for Jack from the president so he could never be shot or buried again. They burst in on a meeting and delighted the president with their request. While the business of the country waited, the president held a full court martial for the doll, found him guilty and then immediately pardoned him.[21]

The president entrusted his boys with jobs few presidents would give key aides. If there were not enough servants working to man all the doors of the White House for official nighttime functions, Willie was drafted as the White House doorman by the president, who bragged that he was better than the paid doormen. He thought nothing of handing his children important papers to carry to some office in the building for him and did not mind if they were left in the kitchen. He gave his son Robert his only copy of the inaugural address on the train from Springfield to Washington, and the boy promptly lost it in one of the cars. Lincoln and others frantically searched the entire train until they found it.[22]

The president would even stop cabinet meetings to see his children. Mrs. Lincoln complained that she never saw him, because he usually worked from 7 A.M. until 10 or 11 P.M., but the children could be with him whenever they wanted. Tad and his father had learned a special code at the telegraph office of the War Department, and used it in a series of secret knocks to enter each other's rooms. Tad frequently interrupted meetings in Lincoln's office with the secret knocks, to the delight of the president, who loved to see his son and reveled in the little intrigue.[23] Tad thought nothing of slipping into meetings and listening in.[24] The boys often begged the president to hoist them on to his shoulders and carry them around the White House because, at his height, they could touch all the ceilings with their outstretched hands. White House staffers often told important people waiting for the president's morning appointment that he would be delayed: they had just seen him on the floor of his bedroom wrestling with his sons. Adults who saw the president pinned to the floor by his boys would be urged by one of his sons to sit on the president's stomach.[25]

Lincoln spared no expense with his boys. He bought them ponies which were stabled in the White House barn. A dog, Jip, became the president's own pet and sat in his lap and ate off his dish at lunch. Lincoln bought his sons candy, toys, and even goats, which became the president's favorite pets. Mary had no love for the goats, especially after her gardener informed her that all the strawberries grown for a particularly important state dinner had been devoured by one of them. One of the hardest letters Lincoln ever had to write was to inform the boys, away with Mary, that one of the goats had disappeared.[26] In the utilitarian White House, the goats were also used for the children's transportation, hooked up to sleds.[27]

Lincoln spent as much time as he could with his boys. The Lincolns declined to put them in a local school and had tutors school them in the White House. Both parents dutifully checked homework and made suggestions. One of Lincoln's favorite pastimes was to gather the children, his own and the Tafts, positioning some on his knee, and read fairy tales and books to them.

He took the boys everywhere. Willie and Tad loved to visit Army camps with their father because he would let them ride on horses in the formal review of the troops he always conducted. The president would ride past a regiment stiff and solid, offering a salute or two and acting very formal. A moment later his sons would ride past, shouting, yelling, and waving to the men. These visits would sometimes last five days; to the boys it was like going on a vacation. They would get the men to show them how to fire cannons and rifles and how to put up and tear down tents. The boys got so carried away after returning from one trip that Tad went over to the Capitol and ordered a half dozen real rifles and ammunition sent to the White House for him and his friends. Fortunately, someone intercepted the shipment.

Willie Lincoln was the president's favorite son. The boy was a carbon copy of the president. He was brilliant, publishing poetry at eleven, and well read and possessed the same keen, analytical mind as his father. He had a marvelous, outgoing personality and told wonderful stories. All who met him fell in love with him. He was one of the most popular boys in Springfield. A natural leader, he led youngsters in parades which followed the adult parades for his father when he ran for president. At the end of a parade, Willie would stand on a platform or barrel and give his own speech thanking his nine-year-old supporters, delivered with amazing similarity to his father's speeches. Whenever Willie walked out of a room, the president would lovingly watch him go, keeping his eyes on his son's back for long moments until he disappeared down the hallway or across a lawn. Mary loved him far more than any of her other children and often told friends that he was the perfect child, well behaved, intelligent, attentive, and kind.[28]

Tad was a hurricane Lincoln never tried to rein in, and his love for the free-spirited boy grew as the war continued. Tad Lincoln probably suffered from attention deficit disorder and a variety of learning disabilities. He had a serious speech impediment, partially caused by a cleft palate, which resulted in garbled talk. At times, a crude metal brace was put in his mouth to help his speech, but it did no good. He could not learn to read or write, despite a series of tutors. He was quick tempered and frequently burst into tears. He insisted on always winning whatever games were played and hoarded all prizes from contests. He threw tantrums, constantly interrupted conversations, and veered from one topic to another for no reason. He often locked himself in rooms, never thought of the consequences of what he said or did, and demanded attention from his parents and everybody around him. The president and first lady, aware in Tad's early years that something was clearly the matter with him, at first tried their best to help him but finally gave up and simply accepted him the way he was, loving him the best they could. "He is a peculiar child," the president told a photographer whom Tad had locked out of a room.[29]

He had always been an independent child. Tad delighted residents and visitors to Springfield after the 1860 election by standing in his front yard and, at the top of his lungs, singing the campaign theme song, "Old Abe Lincoln Came Out of the Wilderness." In Washington, he was thrilled to learn how the White House bell system worked. Bells were rung with a velvet chain in a certain series to indicate meetings, meals, visitors, and events. Tad would often wait until dozens of important government officials were in different rooms of the White House and then hit the bell code for emergency, sending people into a panic.[30] The boy would accompany the president to a speech, sometimes waving an American flag as his father spoke. On one occasion, he appalled a crowd by sneaking up behind the president and waving a Confederate flag he had somehow obtained. The president, who had turned around to see what the anger was about, merely laughed.

Tad spent much time with the soldiers guarding the White House. He would march up and down with the captain inspecting the cavalry at the White House, mimicking his stride and haughty looks. Once the captain, as always, was criticizing the men for their appearance, and finished by saying that "you men look like—." at which Tad chimed in with "Hell!" Another time, after learning what different whistle blasts meant, he stole a corporal's whistle, ran to the second floor of the White House, and for half an hour blew different codes on the whistle, laughing as the soldiers mounted their horses, got down, and mounted up again.[31]

Tad did not like Secretary of War Edwin Stanton, whom he considered a blustering old man, and one day, as Stanton was leaving the White House, he took a garden hose and sprayed him with it. He ran off as the president, laughing, told a guard to catch him. Tad then turned the hose on the guard, drenching him, but the guard managed to wrestle the boy to the ground. The angry Stanton demanded some kind of action by the president. Lincoln, still laughing at the sodden secretary of war, suggested they make the guard a colonel for being brave enough to wrestle Tad.[32] At last even the crusty Stanton was won over by the boy, and later in the war the secretary had the army make Tad a complete uniform, cut to scale. In an official ceremony in the White House, Stanton commissioned Tad an honorary lieutenant, as his father beamed.[33]

The laughter ended in February of 1862. Tad and Willie, who may have consumed tainted water from the Potomac River, fell violently ill the night the Lincolns hosted the most lavish ball of his presidency. Both parents kept up appearances at the ball, but each raced upstairs several times to check on the boys, who were burning up with fever and racked with pain. Tad survived, but after two weeks of torment, twelve-year-old Willie, the love of the president's life, died, on Thursday, February 20.

The president was distraught. "It is hard…hard…" he murmured. When his son slipped away, he burst into tears. "He was too good for this earth…we loved him so," the president muttered sadly to a nurse as he left his son.[34] He took little time off from his duties; instead, he tried to immerse himself in work to chase away his grief. Every Thursday, for more than a year, he stopped all official business and, in long sad steps, walked to Willie's room and locked himself inside for an hour, crying and grieving. Lincoln carried a copy of Shakespeare's *King John* with him and would read the lament of Constance for her dead son and weep. "I never saw a man so bowed down in grief," said Mrs. Keckley.[35] Almost a year to the day after Willie died, there was a fire in the White House stables. A manic Lincoln raced into the barn, desperate to save Willie's pony, and nearly perished himself.

Willie's death threw Mary into a deep depression. She was inconsolable. She wept for hours every day for three long weeks and was bedridden and unable to leave her room. She did not attend Willie's wake and funeral in the White House, nor did she accompany her husband to the cemetery in Georgetown where he was temporarily laid to rest. Mary began to suffer physically from her deep sobbing bouts. She developed a hacking cough and bad eyesight, felt weak, and her body shook. She never again entered the guest room in which her son died or the room in which his body was embalmed. She sent all his toys to Springfield. Lincoln would hold her hand and tell her that they could take care of Willie's toys when they went back to Springfield after his second term. She wore black and mourned, publicly and privately, for more than a year.[36] Mary told her friends that if she didn't have to cheer up the depressed president, she would never bother to smile again.[37] Mary Lincoln never got over Willie's passing. It stirred up all her anger and insecurities. Her health declined, her wild temper flashed constantly, and she began to act strangely.

ABRAHAM Lincoln loved his troubled and despondent wife just as much in the early 1860s as when he first met her in the 1840s. For all that, she meddled in his business, caused him constant problems with her endless shopping and overspending, frightened him with her bill padding and fiscal chicanery, routinely snubbed important people, upset his staff (they called her the "hellcat"), and frequently annoyed him with her temper tantrums. Mary became worse after Willie's death. She talked of Willie constantly. After she began having visions of her dead son coming to her in her room at night, she summoned mediums to the White House, where she and the president tried to communicate with Willie in the next world.[38]

The first lady developed schizophrenic tendencies, appearing calm and friendly one moment and flying into a blind rage the next. She complained of chronic headaches which, as 1862 continued, became worse and caused her distemper. An autopsy after her death purportedly revealed a small brain tumor whose pressure might have been the cause of her headaches.[39] She snapped at Lincoln constantly. "In one of her wayward and impulsive moods, she was apt to say and do things that wounded him deeply," said Mrs. Keckley.[40] White House aide Stoddard never understood her mood swings. He said, "[Difficult] to understand why a lady who could be one day so kindly, so considerate, so generous, so thoughtful and hopeful, could, upon another day appear so unreasonable, so irritable, so despondent...."[41]

Her wildest rages were due to fits of jealousy. Mary loved her husband for the same reasons that everyone else who knew him loved him. She was terrified that another woman would steal him away. She clung to him in public, never straying far from him at receptions and scolding him whenever she caught him in conversation with another woman. She criticized him for talking to women so much at one reception that he turned and asked her whether, since all the men in the room were with women, she expected him to stand alone in the corner all night, talking to no one.[42]

She was extremely upset when she heard that, on a dare, a woman had run up to her husband on one of his army camp visits and kissed him on the cheek.[43] She carried on a long social feud with the vivacious Kate Chase, daughter of Salmon Chase, who found it easy to host parties when Mary found it so hard. Chase had toyed with the idea of running against Lincoln in 1864, and when Mary saw his name on the list for the annual cabinet dinner, along with Kate and her husband, William Sprague, the new senator from Rhode Island, she crossed them off. Nicolay, who had made up the list, went to the president, who told him to "put back Ohio and Rhode Island." Mary and the president fell into a heated argument over it, and then Mary ran off to cross Nicolay off the list, which triggered yet another series of arguments.[44] She refused to attend Kate's wedding and forbade her husband to go, clearly something he had to do. Workers said that her screaming could be heard from the far ends of the White House. When the president returned after the wedding he was locked out of the bedroom.[45] She ended the long tradition of the president choosing a woman from the guests to help him lead the promenade at receptions; she led the promenade. She once walked into Lincoln's office as a distraught, but attractive, woman was on her knees, her hands clutching the president's coat, begging Lincoln for something. Mary jumped to conclusions, shouted, "Out, baggage!" and chased the woman into the hall, where she ordered a servant to put her out on the street.[46]

Her most torrid scene came toward the end of the war, in March 1865, when she arrived at an army parade review to find her husband riding, by sheer chance, next to General William Ord's attractive wife. Mary got out of her carriage, berated the president in front of everybody and snapped at Mrs. Ord. Later, unable to control herself, she flew into a rage at General Grant and his wife over the Ord incident. People who were there said that Lincoln bore her outbursts with "pain and sadness."[47] Julia Grant became convinced that Mary Lincoln was mentally ill.

Lincoln turned down most of her suggestions on political appointments and completely disagreed with her assessments of certain people, but he valued her judgments on public affairs of any kind, knowing she shared his feel for the pulse of the people. The president always complimented Mary on how beautiful she looked, even when she did not; never made fun of the wild flower arrangements in her hair, which the press lampooned; showed her off proudly at parties; and blithely dismissed the terrible things she said to him when she was in one of her moods.

He missed her desperately when she was away, sending her a telegram every day, sometimes twice a day.[48] In chilly weather, he always reminded her to wear a coat or shawl, which he would tenderly put on her shoulders, and would send her telegrams on the weather in Washington if she was traveling great distances to come home. Whenever Mary indicated that she wanted to return home, he would rush for an aide to arrange immediate train transportation for her.[49] At one White House party a man remarked that Mary looked nice in her gown. The president, admiring her, said in a rare moment that "my wife is as handsome as when she was a girl and I a poor nobody then, fell in love with her and once more have never fallen out."[50]

The Lincolns cleared their calendar so that each Sunday afternoon they could take long carriage rides in and around Washington. They went to the theater as often as they could. The president enjoyed the stage far more than his wife and particularly liked to go to Ford's Theater, just a few blocks from the White House. They hosted receptions twice a week in 1861 and early 1862. These were reduced sharply after Willie died. The couple spent much time together at the Soldier's Home, a large house on the outskirts of Washington which served as the summer White House.

Throughout the war, Mary's gloom increased, and Lincoln feared she was going mad. Her moods became worse after she hit her head on a rock when thrown from a carriage in a bad accident in the summer of 1863. The loosened bolts in the carriage led White House staffers to suspect sabotage.[51] Her personal misery increased as the war began to claim her half-brothers from Kentucky, who had ridden off with such gusto to fight for the South. Mary's brother Sam was killed at Shiloh, her brother Alex at Baton Rouge, her brother-in-law John Helm fell at Chickamauga, and her brother David was badly wounded at Vicksburg.[52]

Few had sympathy for Mary over the deaths of her insurgent relatives. Their presence in the war, and that of her other brothers, only increased the venom in Washington for her, especially after her sister Emilie, married to a Confederate officer, began to visit the White House. Complaints about visiting rebels escalated when Mary's sister Martha White arrived, and exploded when the press wrote that Martha had smuggled several trunks of medicine for rebel troops out of Washington and made it through Union lines unchecked because she was the president's sister-in-law.[53] There were whispers that Mary Lincoln had helped her sister smuggle the medicine and that her sisters were obtaining secret documents from Mary and bringing them South.

The whispers and rumors that the first lady was an enemy spy became so great in 1863 that the Committee on the Conduct of the War (established early in the war to curb presidential powers) met in secret to discuss them. The members had just seated themselves when a clerk rushed into the room, a startled look on his face, and nodded toward the door. He did not have any time to speak because, seconds later, in a slow stride, the president of the United States entered. The senators were speechless. President Lincoln stood at the end of the long table, facing them, looking unendurably sad, and, hat in hand, said, "I, Abraham Lincoln, president of the United States, appear of my own volition before this Committee of the Senate to say that I, of my own knowledge, know that it is untrue that any of my family hold treasonable communication with the enemy." He stopped, turned, and walked out of the room. The senators, mesmerized, left the chamber, and the matter of Mrs. Lincoln's alleged treason was never discussed again.[54]

Mary worked on her image. She accompanied her husband on visits to nearby army camps, traveled to local hospitals to talk to soldiers, and helped with the care of the wounded. She joined the "Contraband Relief Association" and raised money to aid blacks freed by her husband's Emancipation Proclamation. The first lady traveled to Northern cities to appear with abolitionist leaders in fund drives for the relief of struggling black families. She worked hard to spend time with senators and congressmen, particularly the influential Charles Sumner, to help her husband's political agenda.[55]

Above all, she loved her husband, despite all the troubles in their marriage and the long hours he spent away from her trying to run the country and end the terrible war. Mary listened attentively as he explained his political problems, often waiting up until 11 P.M. or midnight, when he finished the day. She grieved with him when he grieved for Willie. She understood when he exploded in wrath about his bungling generals. She tried to cheer him up when he fell into his own long and melancholy depressions. She listened to his stories of dreadful nightmares which caused him to wake up panting and sweating, nightmares about his own death, the death of Willie and, later in the war, the death of Tad.[56]

She looked forward to a quiet second term. The end of the war would mean that her husband would not be up until midnight worrying about the army, that assassins would not be waiting for him, newspapers not be scolding him, troops not be camped in her living room. His second term would be a blissful time for the two of them and little Tad, a time to reunite, patch up their differences, and resume life as a close-knit family.

Her husband talked of going back to Springfield after his second term, but Mary wanted him to move to cosmopolitan Chicago, with its cultural and commercial life. There, on the shore of Lake Michigan, he could return to his law practice if he wanted, swap stories with his reporter friends, and tell his tall tales to his political cronies. Lincoln would only be fifty-nine at the end of his second term and Mary would only be fifty. They could grow old together in Chicago.

13

THE DAVISES AT HOME

THE LITTLE GIRL had held the bouquet of flowers tightly in her small hands for over an hour as the crowd of well-wishers lining the street grew into the thousands. Nearly every resident of Richmond was outside awaiting the arrival of Confederate president Jefferson Davis to take up residence in their city, now the capital of the Confederacy on June 1, 1861.[1] As Davis and his pregnant wife rode through the city streets in an expensive carriage with a satin interior and pulled by four magnificent horses they were pelted with so many bouquets that the floor of the carriage looked like a sea of flowers.[2] The carriage came up the street toward the waiting little girl. She arched her arm and threw the bouquet at Jefferson Davis as hard as she could. It fell several feet short.

Davis, his good eye roving from left to right, saw her face turn grim when the flowers landed on the street. The president told the driver to stop. He climbed down from the carriage, picked up the bouquet, then gave it to Varina and waved at the little girl. A thunderous shout erupted from the crowd.[3]

Jefferson Davis's arrival in Richmond with his wife and children was followed by celebration after celebration. He was cheered by workers building defensive breastworks outside the city Saturday morning. He, his wife, and family were serenaded by a crowd of over three thousand people at their temporary home, the Spotswood Hotel, on Saturday night. That first week was filled with receptions and parties, and at each Jeff Davis, usually a wooden speaker, managed to offer genuinely moving words ("Every proud heart beats high with indignation at the thought that the foot of the invader has been set upon the soil of old Virginia...").[4]

Richmond loved him. "Never were a people more enraptured with their chief magistrate than ours are with President Davis," wrote a local editor.[5]

The Davises left the hotel in July, when the Confederate government bought Louis Crenshaw's lavish gray, three-story, twenty-room mansion at 12th and Clay Streets. The gray mansion overlooked the James River. It sat on several acres of finely manicured lawns and included a separate building for the kitchen and a large stable to house Varina's carriage and Davis's horses.

The mansion had an ordinary front porch, but its rear porch, the length of the building, boasted a stately three-story-high portico held up by four large double columns. This veranda overlooked large carefully cultivated gardens, where the family spent much of its leisure time. The impressive home was quickly dubbed the "Confederate White House."

Guests entered a small lobby area decorated by life-sized "comedy" and "tragedy" sculptures and then proceeded through double doors into two large parlors where the president and first lady entertained. Men were later led by Davis into a nearby sitting room where they were offered the black cigars the president favored and talked of war and politics. It was in the small, cozy sitting room that Varina first met Robert E. Lee, who apologized profusely for walking on her brand-new white carpet with his muddy boots. To the south of the parlors was an enormous dining room with an eight-foot-high, gold-framed mirror hung over a fireplace that looked down on the fourteen-foot-long rosewood table. The table served as a place for frequent early morning and late night cabinet meetings. Ceilings in the Southern White House were fourteen feet high, and all the rooms had ceiling-to-floor windows which let in substantial amounts of sunlight. The walls had handcrafted moldings, the drapes were custom made, and a wonderful circular staircase in the middle of the building connected all the floors.

President Davis worked in a rather opulent office on the second floor of the White House. A tiny anteroom was used as an office by his two secretaries, Burton Harrison and William Preston Johnston. A large wooden desk was the centerpiece of the office. There was a small round table near the window where Davis and Robert E. Lee laid out maps and planned military strategy. Visitors sat on a pair of luxurious wooden chairs or on a long green couch that faced Davis's desk. When he was sick, he would recline on the couch and servants would read books to him.

Davis and his wife slept together in a large bed covered with mosquito netting in a room adjacent to his office. Varina often fell asleep by herself while her husband, an insomniac, stayed up until one or two o'clock in the morning reading. The children's bedroom, the largest room in the mansion, stood at the opposite end of the hall. It was spacious enough for several beds and cribs. Like all the rooms in the mansion, it was lit by gas lamps and warmed by a fireplace. The third floor contained five small bedchambers.

Like the White House in Washington, the Confederate White House was home to a young family. Although Davis was fifty-three, his wife was only thirty-four when the couple moved in. They brought three small children: Jeff, four, Margaret, six, and Joe, two. Varina would give birth to two more children there, Billy, in December 1861, and Varina, nicknamed Winnie, in June 1864. Children raced through the building playing games, knocking things over as they went. Young Jeff and Maggie quickly made friends with other children who arrived, ready to play, at all hours of the day. Maggie and her friends played with dolls and dressed up as grown women. Jeff and his friends, including Walter Ezekial and Billy Grant, played soldier and watched the soldiers in town march in front of their home.[6] The boys spent hours gathering fist-sized-rocks, which they piled up and planned to throw at the Yankees if they ever made it to Richmond.[7] The boys also spent countless hours carefully walking on top of the rail that surrounded the home on two sides and overlooked a fifteen-foot drop to a brick walkway. Little Joey, like Jeff, loved to walk on top of the railings, to his parents' horror.

The Davises insisted on a tutor, Gussie Daniel, for their children, although they could have attended a nearby private school. Each day Jeff and Maggie lugged their schoolbooks downstairs to the sitting room, where classes were held.[8] After school the children took pony rides on horses from the stable and played with friends.

Maggie was a demure, attentive little girl of whom her parents were very proud. She was a good student, engaged adults in pleasant and mature conversation, curtsied to guests, dressed nicely, read aloud when asked, went to receptions with her mother, and neatly arranged her part of the large children's bedroom. She fancied herself a budding actress and appeared in little plays with the children of friends at weekend gatherings in front of the adults, including the president, who never missed one.[9] "She is gentle, loving and considerate...warmhearted. She and I are good friends," said Varina of the girl, six years old when the Davises moved to Richmond.[10]

Young Jeff was a terror. He arrived in Richmond with a bigger explosion than his father, Lee, and the entire Confederate armies combined. The boy threw a temper tantrum his very first day in Richmond, throwing away his brand-new hat after an argument with his mother.[11] He quickly decided to make the Spotswood Hotel his personal playground and, alone or with new-found friends, raced up and down its halls, hid in its nooks and crannies, raided the kitchen, and in general terrorized the staff. Within days, his foul language was the talk of the town. The four-year-old boy was criticized for his frequent cursing, and his father was criticized for letting him get away with it.[12]

The president scolded his son constantly about his language, but it never did much good. Two years later, when Jeff was seven, Mrs. Davis was entertaining a group of genteel, upper-crust women in the back parlor of the White House when Jeff ran through the room. He stepped on an exposed carpet tack and howled in pain. Mrs. Davis held her breath, hoping her son would not burst out with one of his usual rude expressions, and was amazed that he did not. The young boy opened his mouth, saw the women, thought better about what he was about to say, sat down on the floor and rubbed his foot. A thankful Varina asked him if his foot hurt.

"Christ! Yes!" blurted the boy as the faces in the room turned deep crimson.[13]

Young Jeff also helped form his own gang. The White House was part of an exclusive neighborhood of expensive homes on a hill which overlooked "Butchertown," the working-class district of Richmond. Young boys in Butchertown had their own gang, the Butchercats, which often wound up in disputes and sometimes fistfights with other juvenile gangs in the city. Determined to prevent the boys from the bottom of the hill from intruding on his neighborhood, young Jeff and his friends formed the Hillcats, which often fought the Butchercats. Some of the children were hurt in the fights and, at the urging of neighbors who insisted he use his influence, President Davis went to the police to have the gangs eliminated. The chief of police shrugged and told him they had tried to do that for years without success, and did not anticipate any in the future.

Frustrated, the president then boldly walked into the lair of the Butchercats themselves to bring peace to the streets of the neighborhood. The local toughs, who feared no gang in Virginia, certainly did not fear the president of a country. They listened to his plea, nodded, agreed to cooperate, and then ignored him. The disputes and fights went on throughout the war.

Varina was an outgoing woman who at first made friends easily. The women introduced to her at small receptions arranged to welcome Varina liked her. "She is as witty as he is wise....She is awfully clever," said Mary Chesnut, the wife of James Chesnut, a military aide to Davis and a wealthy Charleston, South Carolina businessman, who became Varina's closest friend.[14]

Mrs. Davis was friendly to the neighbors' children, whom she had in the house constantly for snacks, and to black children in the area. The Davises made Jim Limber, son of an abusive black father, part of their extended family, and he and young Jeff became close friends. They fed and clothed any children of freedmen or slave children who looked neglected.[15]

Much of Varina's time was spent supervising her staff of servants, a mix of slaves from Brierfield, local slaves borrowed from other families, black freedmen, and a few white servants. The staff ranged in size from about ten to fifteen servants. Many of the slaves who worked in the Confederate White House looked for opportunities to escape, and three did, bolting toward Union lines when the enemy armies were close enough. The staff got along with the president but often suffered from the first lady's sharp tongue. They all loved the children, though. One maid, Betsy, who had decided to escape, went to the White House early one morning, lit the fireplace in the children's room while they slept so they would be warm, pulled the covers up to their necks, neatly piled up their toys, and then fled to freedom.

The president's relationship with his children was remarkable. A cold, aloof, obstinate, and difficult man to most, he was warm and generous to his children and spent as much time with them as he possibly could. It was not unusual for visitors to the White House, particularly in the morning, to find the president of the Confederacy in the children's nursery, lying on his back wrestling with Jeff or Joe, or both at once, and laughing as he risked injury to his bad eye. The president often gave his children pony rides on the small horses he kept in the stable and, when they were old enough, taught them to ride. Toward the end of the war he repeatedly told the story of how Jeff Jr., then eight, tried to talk him into letting him ride with him "to fight Yankees."[16] Davis spent days searching Richmond and the towns around it for fine horses he could buy for them.[17]

Davis always saw the White House as the family home and not a presidential mansion. He usually brought his children with him to official state receptions. When they came to parties to which they were not invited, he sent them away, but not without a smile and a brief conversation. One of his favorite tricks was to steal candy from trays at official White House functions, making the heist when no one was looking, then stuff his pockets with his booty and take it upstairs to the children. Whenever Varina and the children were away, he would drop into downtown shops, buy as much candy as he could, and mail it to Jeff, Joe, and Maggie.[18]

The sounds of the Davis children romping through the White House were lost amid all the other noises emanating from the building at the corner of 12th and Clay. The Confederate White House quickly became a small hotel housing anywhere from ten to fifteen full-time residents, plus ten or more slaves and servants. The president and his wife had up to four children living with them there at any one time. Varina's mother was a semiresident, spending months out of each year at the mansion. Her teenaged sister, Maggie, said to be a more severe critic and worse gossip than Varina, if that was possible, moved in soon after the government arrived in Richmond, and she stayed, managing to annoy at least half the people she met. A frequent longterm guest was Eliza Davis, the wife of Jefferson's brother Joe. Varina despised her and frequently accused her of meddling in her business. Davis's two secretaries, Harrison and Johnston, also lived in the house, sleeping in the bedchambers on the third floor. Mary Jane Brodhead and Helen Keary, Jeff's nieces also visited and stayed for months.

Visitors, who would stay from one night to several weeks, added to the din. His mother-in-law and sister-in-law gave the president endless advice on everything from Yankees to childrearing, and castigated him for his black cigars. Visitors complained to him that liquor in the North was better than in the South. His secretaries told him the children made too much noise, and the children complained about each other. Eliza Davis constantly criticized Varina and Varina criticized Eliza. Announced and unannounced visitors arrived all day long, from irate congressmen to ministers to old friends from Mississippi to job seekers. Despite secretaries, an office, and an enormous staff and servants, all such visitors somehow found the president, interrupting his breakfast and dinner, asking for jobs or favors.[19] Friends said Davis insisted on an official office in the Customs Building just to get out of his house.

Jefferson Davis was comfortable in the White House and quickly established a familiar routine there. He rose around nine every morning, sometimes later, depending on what hour of the early morning he finally fell asleep. He left for the downtown office around ten and returned around 4:30 P.M. He would play with his children and then, before dinner, have servants saddle up one of his six horses. He would ride through the city streets and into the countryside, even when the Yankee army was nearby. Davis had loved horses since his army days so many years before, and once told his daughter that his fantasy was to spend the rest of his life as a cavalry officer, riding horses all day.[20] People who saw him astride one of his gorgeous horses claimed he was the finest horseman in the country.

He dined with his family, where the conversation ranged from life in the home, the children's schooling, city life, the war, politics, events in Europe, literature, and, without fail, denunciations of Northern politicians by Varina. Toward the end of the war she regularly denounced William Seward, a prewar friend of her husband.

After dinner, President Davis sometimes went to his office to do paperwork, but usually spent more time with the children or sat in the sitting room having a cigar or talking to his wife. He spent long hours reading newspapers, particularly the Richmond papers, and books. He enjoyed reading both books serialized in newspapers and complete books. His favorites were books on politics and history, the poetry of Byron, architecture and, appropriately for all of his personal and political troubles, the Book of Job. He amassed several hundred books in his library during his four years in Richmond. If he was feeling joyful, he would entertain his family and guests by singing, usually finishing with his favorite, "Annie Laurie." Guests said he was pretty good.

The middle hours of the night were a lonesome time for the president, who usually could not fall asleep until morning. He looked forward to the arrival of any late-night visitors to keep him company. One night, in terrible pain from another eye infection, he was pleasantly surprised when an old friend he had not seen in ten years, Edwin DeLeon, arrived from Europe. Davis lit up a cigar for DeLeon, fixed him a drink, sat back, and listened to all the news from the political, military, and social worlds across the Atlantic. They talked of the old days, the war, and their families, until they were finally halted at 2:30 A.M. by Varina, who shouted down the stairs that it was time for the president to come to bed.[21]

Davis hosted numerous receptions at the White House after he took office, at which he entertained generals, colonels, and local and political figures. The receptions, supervised by Varina, were weekly affairs. The president and Varina also held intimate breakfasts with friends. Varina also hosted afternoon musicales, to which she invited amateur musicians and singers from Richmond to perform for an audience made up of government workers, neighbors, and army officers. James and Mary Chesnut were usually in attendance.[22]

At these gatherings guests would engage Davis in discussions about the war and the future of the new country once the war was over. One striking scene involved Hetty Cary, the daughter of a prominent Virginian, who arrived dressed as a slave, with her hands bound by rope. She asked Davis to untie the rope, which symbolized, she said, the shackles that held the South down. He did, with a wide smile, to applause from the crowd, led by the loud clapping of his wife.

JEFFERSON Davis and his wife were deeply in love in the spring of 1861. Varina had given up her longing for total independence within her marriage long before, and become a loving and supportive spouse. She had learned how to influence her husband and his friends at dinner parties and social gatherings. She was a brilliant woman and enchanting conversationalist. Extremely well read, she devoured newspapers and knew much about the key issues of the day. She could jump from an explanation of the French monetary system to the problems of the Army of Northern Virginia to an analysis of the Quaker religion.[23] She held her own, whether talking with a neighbor or a cabinet secretary or Robert E. Lee, who admired her. Guests at her parties looked forward to talking to her. She was able to help her husband by generating admiration and respect from people who could not get along with the president himself.

Varina exercised great influence over her husband through their conversations about the war and politics at breakfast, lunch, and dinner. She was a source of great support to him. She not only discussed government and politics with him, but carefully read all the letters he received and went over all those he planned to mail. She helped him with his speeches and with proposed bills.[24] When he was sick, she often met with cabinet secretaries or army colonels at the White House and interviewed them, relaying what they said to her husband.[25] A delighted Varina also wrote letters to the daughter of minister to France James Slidell which included secret codes for the State Department.[26]

Most of all, she was a politically sensitive and extremely knowledgeable sounding board for her husband, a woman who understood that a statesman needed someone to understand his concerns and listen to him, but that he also needed a loving wife who empathized with him when no one else would. Varina listened to all of her husband's thousands of complaints about his generals, the cabinet, and the Congress, and always nodded knowingly in agreement. Friends saw them as a good political team; enemies, such as *Richmond Examiner* editor Edwin Pollard, said she totally controlled the president.

Varina did not think her husband was a good politician, but she did believe he was trying his best as a president and statesman and was a strong, if lonely, champion of the cause of Southern independence. "All I can say is that my husband will never cry for quarter and that all we can hope for is that the spirit of the people may enable him to defend the women and children of our unhappy land."[27]

She was so knowledgeable about government and politics that, just as in Montgomery, men quickly surrounded her at parties to listen to her views.[28] She often attracted as much attention as the president and visiting generals. She not only had a grasp of current affairs, but could analyze events and interpret them as well. She was adept at gauging how Northerners would react to whatever Southerners did, a political weather vane. Varina probably knew more about government, and had more effect on the president, than any American first lady before Eleanor Roosevelt.

She also defended her husband against charges that he was a despot or dictator, telling friends that extraordinary measures were necessary in extraordinary times. "A strict construction of our constitution is incompatible in the successful prosecution of a war," she said.[29]

Varina quickly became fed up with the belligerent Confederate Congress. Whenever a congressman arrived at the White House to meet the president, or to attend a party, she would take him into a room far from guests and scold him for his opposition to her husband.[30] She also made it a point to keep the wives of offending congressmen out of her social circles and to snub them publicly whenever she could.

Much of her time was spent caring for her husband when he was ill, which was frequently. She stayed up as late as she could when he was sleepless from neuralgia or insomnia, reading novels to him until he or she fell asleep. She worked closely with Dr. Garnett, his physician, in helping her husband get through his periods of sickness and made sure he followed all of the doctor's instructions when he was not there. She mixed the prescribed medicines for him, washed his infected left eye whenever necessary, shooed the children away, kept the stress of the job to a minimum, in short, did everything she could for him when he was bedridden. It may have been Varina's endless attention that prevented Davis's death on the several occasions when he fell desperately ill.

Even though her husband was devoted to her, Varina was insanely jealous. She never took her eyes off her husband at parties, where, as the president, he was constantly engaged in conversation with women. Her judgment of certain aides and generals was based on the beauty of their wives. If the wives were plain, she liked their husbands. If they were beautiful, she did not care for their husbands and suggested to the president that they were not as talented as he believed.

Varina worried about her husband's contacts with other women when he was alone in Richmond in the summer of 1862 and when he traveled throughout the South to confer with the generals and lift popular morale. President Davis was often feted with parties and parades in the towns and asked to deliver speeches. Women at receptions and rallies would come up to him and, upon introduction, lean up and kiss him on the cheek. Davis's physician let the women's attentions slip in a casual one-liner in a letter to Varina. Mrs. Davis was furious. The storm at the White House did not die down until her husband repeatedly denied any interest in other women and assured her that he did not kiss them back and that he certainly did not enjoy their attention. He was supported by Garnett and Henry Wise, the former governor of Virginia, an eyewitness, who had to write a long letter to Varina to calm her down.[31]

The initial reaction to the arrival of Mrs. Davis was good. Everyone was impressed that, as the telegraphs and riders with dispatches brought reports of the battle on the night of Bull Run, she went from room to room in the Spotswood Hotel, and then from home to home in the city, to console women whose husbands had been killed or wounded in the fighting.[32] She visited hospitals and comforted the wounded.[33] She led drives to raise money and clothes for the soldiers. Word spread quickly whenever she gave money to indigent people. Varina's finest hour, some said, was the day she forged a pardon to prevent the execution of a man whose wife had come to the White House begging for help.[34] Men and women approved of her superb parties. One friend said that "she moves about as in triumph."[35]

As time passed, however, there was little love for Varina in Richmond. Jefferson Davis was increasingly blamed for the inability to win the war, and

Varina defended him, saying her husband was a "willing victim going to his funeral pyre."[36] The women of Richmond began to find fault with everything she did, and Mary Chesnut complained that all the civilians hated her.[37] They went to her parties, but agreed that there was really no place in Richmond society for her because she was a "coarse, western woman."[38] The local newspaper, the *Richmond Examiner,* even poked fun at her weight, which had increased through childbirths over the years, writing that she was "portly and middle aged."[39]

Varina soon could do nothing right. They criticized her for walking along Franklin Street, one of the prettiest thoroughfares in the city, on Sunday afternoon, along with hundreds of other women in a Richmond tradition, complaining that she should not be spending money on new dresses when the boys on the front lines had no shoes.[40] They whispered malignantly whenever she rode through town in her new and expensive carriage, driven by two, beautiful bay horses, charging that she should not be living so royally while General Lee and his men had so little to eat.[41] They criticized her for not throwing parties to give the Confederate White House some needed elegance and stature. Then, if she did host a party, she was criticized for wasting government money. Women sniped at Varina and her sister for buying fine gowns in New Orleans.[42] In the spring of 1864, when she was pregnant with her last child, Winnie, she was roundly castigated by the local women for the scandal she caused by hosting parties while pregnant.[43] Her response to these criticisms was to simply spend more time walking on Franklin Street, drive through town in her carriage more often, and throw more parties.

The women of Richmond grumbled that her Mississippi clothes, particularly her flat hats, were oafish and out of style, that her relatives were fashion disasters, and that none of them knew anything about high culture. One story that quickly made the rounds concerned soldiers' underwear. A seamstress sadly told a group of women that mistakes in sewing resulted in hundreds of soldiers' undershorts with two right legs. The women frowned, but Varina thought it was hilarious and laughed loudly. She was accused of slapping one of her slaves, hoarding her husband's salary, having private feasts while the citizens rationed food,[44] arguing with tutors, shouting at stable boys, berating her driver, and even harboring Union spies, all of which were no more than rumors.[45]

"How I wish I were the wife of a dry goods clerk," she told friend Mary

Chesnut[46] and complained to friend Mrs. H. L. Clay that "scandal is rife here."[47]

Varina's complete crucifixion in Richmond society came in May of 1862, when one of three Confederate White House slaves who ran off during the war, William Jackson, gave an interview to the *New York Tribune* telling the world how Varina constantly criticized the women of Richmond behind their backs. The escaped slave, who had often worked as Varina's driver, said the first lady not only told almost everyone she saw how plain and slow-witted she found the women of Richmond society, but considered 90 percent of them Union sympathizers and traitors.[48]

Varina's sharp tongue was no revelation to anyone who knew her. The first lady was very defensive of her husband and did not hesitate to lambaste anyone who criticized him. She made no secret of her loathing for certain people either, frequently dissecting locals in front of guests at the dinner table or at parties, often to her husband's distress.[49] Her tongue frequently landed her in trouble and brought gentle rebukes from the president, as when she visited North Carolina and, in just a few days, let the people of Raleigh know how depressed she was about the lack of progress in the war. Her husband quietly told her never to tell people that anyone in the first family had doubts about eventual victory. "We must measure our words with a caution proportionate to the value others place on them," he said to her.[50]

William Trescott, an assistant secretary of state, said she was "the vulgarest woman I know,"[51] and T. C. DeLeon, a friend, called her "sharp tongued...dangerous."[52]

Her problems were not helped any by her cavalier sister Maggie or her cousin Jane Howell, who breezed into church one summer Sunday, attired in their most expensive dresses, to find Mrs. Robert E. Lee sitting in *their* pew, whereupon they had a stunned usher boot her out. Mrs. Lee, looking worn and weary, got up and left the pew with great dignity, as the entire congregation began hissing at the two girls, who ignored everybody and sat down.[53]

Varina's response to any opposition to her, her family, or the president was sharp. She and her husband dramatically cut back the number of parties at the White House and shunned families who shunned them. She began to fire back at women who criticized her and within months was involved in numerous spats, particularly with the wives of men in politics or the army.

She became embroiled in a torrid feud with Charlotte Wigfall, the wife of Congressman Louis Wigfall, one of President Davis's earliest supporters. The feud grew in intensity; as it did, the congressman turned against the president, denouncing him day after day in speeches in the House of Representatives that were so vile that local newspapers refused to report them.[54] Neither Varina nor her friend Mary Chesnut cared for Secretary of State Robert Toombs or his pretentious wife, and when they all moved to Richmond, sparks flew between the women. Mrs. Toombs's hatred of Jefferson and Varina was so deep that when word swept Richmond that Jefferson Davis was dying, Mrs. Toombs laughed at the news and said the Davises were making it up. The president's arguments with General Joe Johnston over his official rank in the army brought about a heated exchange between Varina and Lydia Johnston that not only ended what had been a good friendship but began a lifelong quarrel, one which was so deep and lasted so long that in her later years Mrs. Johnston said she feared "Varina's ghost" would haunt her in eternity.[55]

Sometimes her feuds directly affected the conduct of the war. A. C. Myers had performed well as quartermaster general and was up for promotion. He probably would have received it, but Varina heard that his wife, who did not like her, had told friends that Varina's height and weight made her look like "an old squaw." The president turned down the promotion.[56] He reputedly turned down promotion for another man whose wife made fun of Varina's weight.

President Davis always defended Varina and never sided against her, even when she was wrong. Her enemies were his enemies. His feelings about his wife were so strong that when persons who had shunned or insulted her tried to apologize, he would turn away from them. His protectiveness of her increased dramatically after October 1862, when she and Joe Johnston's wife Lydia were nearly killed when their carriage ran off a road and crashed down an embankment. Mrs. Johnston suffered a broken arm and Varina was badly shaken.

The president longed for Varina whenever he was away from her, even when he went to his office at the old U.S. Customs House. He missed her desperately whenever he was at the front or traveling, or she was not in Richmond, and wrote her longing and loving letters. "I thought of you as though you were with me yesterday and the fire of the enemy's artillery did not prevent me from remembering that you were in the same hours praying for me and making sacramental communion with our Redeemer. Farewell, dear wife, may every consolation attend you and your happiness be reflected back on your devoted husband," he wrote in a letter to her during the Seven Pines battle outside Richmond in 1862.[57]

On another occasion, unable to bear her absence, he wrote tenderly: "Good night, dear wife. May every consolation be yours until it shall be our fortune to again be united. Ever affectionately remembered when waking, sleep brings you to me in such reality that it would be happier to sleep on."[58]

The deep love Jefferson Davis had for his wife and children was underlined when, fearful for their safety as McClellan's army threatened Richmond in May of 1862, he sent them to Raleigh, North Carolina, for their safety. He was savaged by Richmond locals for this act, though many of them also sent their families away. Davis did not care. "My health, my life, my property I can give to the cause of my country. The heroism that would lay my wife and children on any sacrificial altar is not mine," he said.[59]

The arrival of Varina and her children in Raleigh was bumpy. Little Billy, just six months old, fell ill as soon as they arrived, and the president, 120 miles away, was inconsolable about his baby. Many infants died in the Southern states in the summertime from malaria, and even though Raleigh was an elevated city, he feared the worst. "The vision of my angel baby Billy in exhaustion haunts me," he wrote his wife.[60]

As the child's condition became worse, Davis talked to doctors in Richmond. He suggested to Varina that the baby might have consumed tainted milk and that she should try another type of milk and hire an extra nurse.[61] That did not help, and Davis then suggested that she have more local doctors look at him, believing the child might have come down with some rare type of disease known only in that area of North Carolina. When that investigation did not avail, the president sent his personal physician down to Raleigh to help, risking his own health without him.[62] The baby was finally diagnosed with carbuncles and soon recovered. Davis put complete faith in Varina's love of the infant and her motherly powers. "May God preserve you and sustain you in the midst of the sea of troubles which surround us," he wrote her.[63]

The summer of 1862 was one of military anguish for Davis because the Union Army was encamped on the York Peninsula, but there was personal anguish, too. He had been separated from his wife for months in the past, particularly on trips to Washington, but he had never been separated from the children for such a long time. He missed them dearly.

Late one night, the White House quiet, he walked down to the nursery where the children slept to kiss them each good night and suddenly realized they were not there. "I go into the nursery as a bird may got to the nest...." he wrote Varina, expressing his loneliness for them.[64] He thought about his children constantly, seeing visions of them in empty rooms and on city streets. One day, walking home from his office, he passed a little boy who had rolled up his pants legs so he could frolic in a large puddle of water left from a late afternoon shower. "He looked something like Jeff," the president wrote to his wife. He told the boy he should not play in the water because he might get the chills. The boy, smiling as Jeff often smiled, dismissed the advice and told the president he planned to keep right on playing in the water. The president, certain he had seen his son in the boy, chuckled and walked on.[65]

He finished every letter to Varina that summer with deep affection for his children. He would write, "Kiss my dear children, tell them how much father loves them, how constantly he longs to see them and prays that they may be good and happy."[66]

Through that long and dangerous summer, he thought of Varina constantly, talking of her every day, counting the days until McClellan's army could be driven off so that his wife could return. He wrote Varina long, passionate daily letters that underscored his affection for her. In one he told her that "our house is dreary at night and there is no loving sounds to greet me in the morning."[67]

The family was reunited at the end of that summer, with little Billy recovered. Young Jeff returned to the Hillcats, Maggie went back to her tutors, Varina resumed hosting parties and withstanding criticism from local women. As a family, the Davises grew stronger than ever through the end of 1862 and during 1863 and 1864. The whole family was in excellent spirits in the spring of 1864. Lee's army had Virginia protected and was prepared to fight U. S. Grant to a standstill if he invaded the state. Jubal Early's army still held the Shenandoah Valley. Abraham Lincoln's popularity was still low in the North, and his almost certain defeat in the November elections might bring an end to the war. The Union army attempt to kidnap or kill Jefferson Davis in February had failed badly.

In good spirits, Varina, seven months pregnant with her final child, Winnie, left the White House shortly before noon on April 30, 1864, to take her husband lunch in his downtown office. Shortly after she left, Joe, then five years old, began to walk on top of the porch railing which surrounded the mansion, which was off limits because of the long drop underneath it. He made it to the southwest corner, taking small and careful steps, as if he were on a tightrope, and then, for some unknown reason, lost his footing and fell. The boy tumbled through the air, landed on his head and shoulders on the brick walkway below, broke his neck, and died within an hour.

Jefferson Davis and his wife grieved deeply over the loss of their second child. The president had loved little Joe, playing with him whenever he could and teaching him to ride ponies. He had not worried about the boy, who was never sick, and his death shocked Davis. Varina, who had always referred to Joe as "the greatest joy of my life," was grief-stricken for months.[68]

The funeral of Joe Davis was one of the most somber in Richmond history. Thousands of mourners took part in the procession from the White House to St. Paul's Church and then on to Hollywood Cemetery. A large contingent of neighborhood children, numbering over one hundred, each carrying a single green bough,[69] including the Hillcats and the Butchercats, was part of it. Everyone felt the president's loss. A woman who sat behind him in St. Paul's the following Sunday said that he seemed, dressed all in black and hunched over in grief, the saddest man she had ever seen.[70]

The tragedy of the little boy's death was followed by months of anguish in the Davis home. Grant's army pressed Lee and his men north of Richmond in a series of fierce and bloody engagements. Richmonders feared the Federals would break through and take the city, thereby ending the war. While the armies clashed in desperate battles, families throughout the South continued to complain of starvation and extortion; supplies dwindled, and thousands continued to die. It was a brutal time. Later, just after the war ended, President Davis would sum everything up in a heart-tugging love letter to his wife which compared their present grief to better days long ago. "This is not the fate to which I invited [you] when the fortunes were rose colored to us both, but I know you will bear it even better than myself."[71]

The gloom that enveloped the president, first lady, and the others in the White House lifted when Winnie was born in June. The Davises, who had become more religious since the start of the war, saw her birth as a gift from God. She could never replace Joe in the household, but the cheerful little baby brought great joy to her parents, and, as time went by, the girl who would grow up to be revered as "the daughter of the Confederacy" helped push back the dark days of Joe's death.

Christmas 1864 was the baby's first, and it was memorable. The first lady, determined to rebuild her image in Richmond, worked hard to lead a city-wide toy drive. She organized a committee to collect old toys and toys children made themselves, which were then distributed to the poor of the capital. Her own children ransacked the White House to find their old toys and cheerfully gave them away. On Christmas Day the entire Davis family gathered for prayers in the White House, exchanged small gifts, and shared a joyful and rewarding holiday together. Christmas 1864 was a good one.

Christmas, 1865, would not be.

PART V

A TIME OF HOPE
AND DESPERATION

14

ABRAHAM LINCOLN AT WAR: 1862

IF NINETEENTH-CENTURY NOVELISTS ever needed to imagine a perfect general, it was George McClellan, the boy-wonder of the United States Army. The diminutive, five foot four inch, wafer-thin, blue-eyed McClellan was nicknamed Little Mac by his men, who adored him. Handsome, sophisticated, charming, McClellan—the soldier's soldier, the officer's officer—graduated second in his class at West Point and served in the Mexican War. The army and then secretary of war, Jefferson Davis, thought so much of his potential that he was sent as an observer to the Crimean War. He quickly rose to captain but, like so many others, quit the army, which was inactive in the peacetime 1850s. His rise in civilian life was spectacular, too, exceeding even his meteoric army career. By 1860 the thirty-four-year-old McClellan was president of the Illinois Central Railroad, one of the country's largest, and earning the impressive salary of $10,000 a year.[1]

The Civil War called him back to the army. He was in such demand when he announced his intention to return that the governors of two states sought his services for their troops.[2] Here was a soldier, tried and true, a West Pointer, army to the core. He was no mayor turned colonel, no governor become general. McClellan knew everything there was to know about the army. He also knew how to play the Washington political game and was a master of public relations. There was no one who could compare to

McClellan—dressed in his best parade uniform, buttons polished, hat cocked just right—astride his horse, prancing in front of cheering troops.

Following several minor victories in western Virginia, McClellan was named commander of the Army of the Potomac after McDowell was relieved following Bull Run. In October 1861 Lincoln appointed him general in chief of the entire Union Army. Told what a difficult task lay in front of him, he confidently told everyone: "I can do it all." The army loved him, generals battled for his attention, the press adored him, his troops idolized him, the House and Senate applauded his every appearance, and the people were wild for him. Yet Abraham Lincoln wrung his hands over him.

McClellan reorganized the army, trained it, staged parade after parade, and wrote out campaign plan after campaign plan, but he would not fight. Lincoln pressed him for months to go on the offensive and attack the Confederates in Virginia, but he would not. The army, he said, was not ready. "I will advance and force the rebels to a battle on a field of my own selection. A long time must yet elapse before I can do this," he said.[3] McClellan's army was never ready.

Lincoln and Cameron, and, later Stanton, had worked tirelessly to increase the size of McClellan's army to 108,000 men, the largest in U.S. history, yet the general would not move. The president pleaded with McClellan to attack. "Once more, let me tell you, it is indispensable to you that you strike a blow...*you must act.*"[4]

Lincoln, exceedingly frustrated with McClellan, finally exploded when he learned that McClellan had spent an enormous amount of money building pontoon bridges to be used in crossing the Potomac but, when finished, the bridges turned out to be too wide. "Why in tarnation...couldn't the Gen[eral]. have known whether a boat would go through that lock, before he spent a million of dollars getting them there? I am no engineer; but it seems to me that if I wished to know whether a boat would go through a...lock, common sense would teach me to go and measure it."[5]

The more Lincoln pleaded with him to attack, the more McClellan's dislike for the president grew. McClellan had voted against Lincoln for president in 1860 and, as an Illinois resident, for senator in 1858. He bragged to friends that he had once ordered engineers to force the breakdown of an Illinois Central train carrying Lincoln supporters to the polls in the senatorial election.[6] McClellan wrote that Lincoln was an "idiot"[7] and told his wife, over the course of several months, that the President was "a well meaning baboon,"[8] a "coward,"[9] a "gorilla,"[10] and "not a gentleman."[11] His disdain for Lincoln reached a crescendo on the evening of November 13, 1861, when he was visited by Lincoln, Seward, and John Hay. McClellan had his porter tell them he was too tired to see them, could not be bothered, and had the president of the United States shown the door.

His contempt for the cabinet was just as strong. He called Secretary of State Seward a "meddling, incompetent little puppy,"[12] Secretary of the Navy Welles "weaker...than an old woman,"[13] and Bates "an old fool."[14] He said after one cabinet meeting at which he had been feted, as he always was in the early days of the war, that he was "bored and annoyed" and that the cabinet members were "the greatest geese I have ever met."[15]

Lincoln's reaction was the same as always. He held his temper and told friends that he did not mind the insults, that he would work with McClellan in any way he could to win the war, and that, if McClellan wanted, the president would even hold his horse.

Even as pressure was growing in the country for McClellan to move, there was sharp criticism of the War Department and Secretary Cameron. He was accused of buying shabby uniforms and shoes, paying six times what he should have for guns, agreeing to outrageous railroad shipping overcharges, paying $25 a ton for supplies worth just $8 a ton, purchasing broken-down wagons, buying $500,000 worth of hay which, on arrival, turned out to be rotted prairie grass,[16] awarding huge contracts without competitive bidding, and paying finder's fees to middlemen, some of whom were congressmen.[17] People had warned Lincoln that Cameron was corrupt, and now the evidence was mounting. Lincoln was doubly frustrated by the charges because he had named Cameron to the cabinet in return for the Pennsylvanian's support at the Republican convention. Congress decided that an investigation of both McClellan and Cameron was needed and created a permanent committee to oversee the conflict, the Committee on the Conduct of the War, comprising three Republicans and two Democrats. The committee served as a vigilant watchdog of Lincoln and the executive branch throughout the war. It was a formal and powerful political committee that the president had to answer to and to which he had to explain policy. He was able to cajole and manipulate its members reasonably well, as he always did, but it served the two-party system as a means to curb the executive.

Lincoln, who did not think McClellan was any of Congress's business, had to suddenly go on the defensive to protect the administration in the

Cameron affair, as newspapers called for the war secretary's head. Many agreed with one editor's charge: "The country has had enough of Simon Cameron."[18] The confrontation ended quietly when the president ousted Cameron and sent him off to Russia as ambassador. Wags joked that with Cameron on his way, the Russian tsar should lock up his silverware. Even then the gentle Lincoln could not be harsh with Cameron. He withdrew the dismissal papers and had friends talk Cameron into resigning gracefully, so Lincoln could praise him on his departure to Moscow.[19] To let Cameron down easily, Lincoln had Seward write the letter of appointment to Moscow for him[20] and arranged for Chase to hand Cameron the letter containing his cabinet dismissal. He also arranged for both Chase and Seward to be with him on the night Cameron was fired.[21] Instead of condemning Cameron after his departure, Lincoln went out of his way to praise him even after the House had censured Cameron.[22] Lincoln said that he and the cabinet were just as responsible for the operations of the war as the secretary, actions he the president certainly did not have to take.[23]

Once Cameron was out and a new War Department head named, the cabinet settled down, after nearly a year of turmoil. Except for the departure of Postmaster General Montgomery Blair and Treasury boss Chase in 1864 for political reasons, the cabinet that met with the president from January 1862 through the end of Lincoln's first term didn't change.

The man who replaced Cameron as secretary of war was Edwin Stanton, fifty-seven. The short, burly, rough-looking, tough-talking, bearded Stanton had been President Buchanan's attorney general. He was a lifelong Democrat who routinely denounced Lincoln in private letters and a friend of General McClellan. Moreover, he was a lawyer who, when asked to work with Lincoln in Chicago in the 1850s, had snubbed him in court and been highly critical of the way Lincoln worked and the way he looked. Lincoln, who never held grudges and who all his life worked for the greater good as hard as he could with those who did not like him, thought Stanton a good choice because he had the respect of everybody. That included Seward, who no one believed would agree to a second powerful personality who would have Lincoln's ear.[24] Stanton was a hard worker and good administrator. He was known as efficient and direct, qualities Cameron lacked. He had a reputation for honesty, too, which was needed in a successor to Cameron. Lincoln was also determined to have as much of a coalition government as possible, and having a well-known Democrat like Stanton in a key job helped.[25]

Stanton was at first reluctant to take the post. It meant a cut in pay—from over $50,000 a year in his law practice, twice what the president made, to just $8,000—and his wife was strongly opposed. Stanton's friends and business associates persuaded him to take the job by appealing to his patriotism.[26]

In the years they would work together, and become close personal friends, Lincoln never once mentioned Stanton's frequent verbal abuse of him, or his criticism, in the prewar years. He did not worry about Stanton's powerful personality, just as he did not worry about Seward's. The president told a friend that Stanton was like a minister he once knew who was so energetic that to stop him from leaping about the pulpit parishioners had to put bricks in his pockets. "We may be obliged to serve Stanton the same way," the president said.[27]

Stanton, who took office in January, 1862, was a brusque, no-nonsense lawyer who wasted no time on corrupt contractors, suppliers, or businessmen trying to make excessive profits from the war. The new secretary of war, at his office from early in the morning until late at night, liked to work standing up at his desk, like a captain of a ship in a storm, and his staff was just as driven. He told Lincoln he wanted nothing but professionals running the War Department, and Lincoln let him have his way, eager to have the department run itself. Stanton brought in hardworking administrators, promoted others from within, and encouraged capable holdovers, like the dynamic quartermaster general, Montgomery Meigs.

With Stanton on board, the Lincoln war cabinet was set. Historians later claimed that despite infighting it was perhaps the most effective cabinet in the history of the United States. It contained the two most radical Republicans in the land, Seward and Chase, who both harbored hopes of being president one day; a Democrat, Stanton; several moderate Republicans; some former Democrats; and, in effect, the entire Blair family. Lincoln had no fear of being intimidated or overshadowed by strong personalities because he knew he was stronger than any of them. He took no chances, though. While urging the individual secretaries to be firm with Congress and keep control of their employees, he deliberately kept loose rein over his cabinet in the early days of the war—so sensitive was he to warnings that two or three of them might form a coalition and undermine him. That proved a mistake.

After the raucous days of Fort Sumter, during which the cabinet met nearly every day, Lincoln reduced the frequency of his cabinet meetings considerably. For a while, they met once a week, then formal meetings became even rarer. In another effort to build good relations between the two, Lincoln put Seward in charge of the cabinet, assuring him that he had his complete confidence. He let him schedule the meetings, which irritated all the other secretaries, and had Seward sit at his right at every session. The other members started calling Seward "the prime minister." The president let Seward bring his aides to meetings and set the day's agenda. He knew that cabinet meetings twice a week had been standard in the government for generations, yet he did not balk when Seward decided to cut them out and meet whenever the secretary of state thought necessary.[28] "[He] yielded almost everything to Seward," Welles complained.[29]

When given an inch, Seward, of course, took six miles. He held meetings between himself, the president, and only one or two other cabinet members at a time—barring the others—but sat in on all other cabinet meetings or meetings between other cabinet members and Lincoln.[30] When he was unable to attend a meeting, whether full or partial, he infuriated the cabinet by sending his son, Fred, in his place.[31] Seward went to the White House almost every day in the spring and summer of 1861, and often spent most of the day there huddled with Lincoln or one of his aides or holding a meeting of some kind.

When he was not at the White House, charming anyone who dropped in, Seward could be seen racing about the halls of the War Department, arriving unannounced at some undersecretary's office to demand a meeting[32] or going through someone's file cabinet, all to the chagrin of Cameron, who complained to no effect to the president.[33] Seward insisted on knowing what was going on in all the departments but divulged nothing of his own work, keeping major diplomatic operations secret from the cabinet.[34]

Lincoln was delighted with the way his relationship with Seward was turning out. Seward and he had got off to an edgy start when Seward tried to usurp many of Lincoln's powers, then botched the Fort Sumter negotiations. He could have been fired for either transgression, but Lincoln was convinced that if he could turn Seward into his ally, he would have a marvelously gifted secretary of state.

He also needed Seward. He could not lose the support of the radical wing of the Republican Party, of which Seward was the champion. He could not afford to lose the politically powerful northeastern and mid-Atlantic Republican bloc of votes in the House and Senate which Seward controlled. Lincoln also needed the big-city Republican newspapers, such as the *New York Times,* and the *Albany Evening Journal,* which Seward had in his hip pocket. He dared not cut his own Republican supporters off from the seemingly unlimited campaign war chest of Seward and Thurlow Weed if he was going to keep the party under control after the 1862 elections, expand its base in 1864, and get himself re-elected. So, as he often did, Lincoln decided to make his most dangerous enemy his good friend.

The two men became close. Lincoln genuinely liked Seward, and the secretary of state grew to like him, as so many enemies did. They shared a fine sense of humor and enjoyed each other's company. Most of all, they shared a love of politics. They were political warhorses. They had been in politics nearly seventy years, and they had hundreds of humorous stories about politics in their home states that they shared. Each was a fine storyteller. They were so close that it was not unusual for Lincoln, when he heard a good joke, to walk through the dark streets of Washington to Seward's home to tell it to him.

Lincoln's reliance on Seward was rewarded immediately by the early decision of England not to recognize the Confederacy as a legitimate government and by the *Trent* affair. Two Confederate statesman, John Slidell and James Mason, were on their way to London aboard the *Trent,* a British ship, to plead with England to enter the civil war on the Southern side, when a U.S. warship, without Lincoln's knowledge, stopped the ship, seized its crew, and imprisoned the two Southerners. England claimed a violation of international law. Lincoln, thrilled with both a diplomatic and public relations coup, did not want to give up the two Confederates, but he could not risk war with England, either. He decided to sit back and let Seward deal with the crisis, intervening only to soften the wording of some of Seward's cables. Finally, after months of haggling and brilliant diplomacy by Seward, and despite the great reluctance of the president, the United States released the two men.[35]

The *Trent* settlement was the latest in a long series of diplomatic efforts by Seward to keep France and England out of the war. The secretary, along with the personable and superbly gifted ambassador to Great Britain, Charles Francis Adams, began his campaign to keep England neutral as soon as he was sworn in and sent Lincoln his note suggesting a war with England. He threatened war with Great Britain again when Queen Victoria issued her Neutrality Act, in which she refused to recognize that the new Confederacy was a belligerent and was free to trade with England, which Lincoln and Seward saw as a step to Confederate support. Seward told the French ambassador that "the Emperor could commit no graver error than to mix himself in our affairs." Seward was always tough in his messages to French and British diplomats and lawmakers, always threatening that recognition or aid to the Confederate states would lead to war.[36]

Lincoln laid down policy and helped Seward write his directives to Adams, but it was Seward who bullied England. Adams's instructions from Seward as to his relations with the British were blunt. "No one of these proceedings [discussions with Southern diplomats] will *pass unnoticed,*" he told Adams to tell the prime minister, and later, getting tough, had Adams tell him that "When this act of intervention [Southern recognition] is distinctly performed, we, from that hour, shall cease to be friends and become once more, as we have twice before been forced to be, enemies of Great Britain."[37]

Seward was so threatening, and fired off hundreds of sharply worded notes,[38] that British politicians who did not really believe that the United States wanted a war with England thought they might wind up in one anyway because Seward was so adamant. Lord Palmerston, the prime minister, called Seward a "blustering, ignorant man" who might start a war for no good reason.[39] Many leading British diplomats, uncertain of Seward's real intentions after relentless intimidation, always hedged on entering the war on the Southern side; it was that hesitancy that helped the Union.[40] Lincoln realized, too, that while he was an unknown commodity from the frontier, Seward was America's most famous politician. His fame and influence were key factors in his ability to frighten the British.[41] His efforts paid off, particularly in the late summer of 1862, after the British government came as close as it would to recognizing the Confederacy following McClellan's defeat at the hands of Lee in Virginia. A barrage of threatening letters from Seward and careful diplomacy by Adams persuaded the British to defer a decision into the fall.

Lincoln's attitude at the early cabinet meetings was overly casual. He often read the secretaries sections of humorous novels or what he considered funny magazine articles and regaled them with his own stories. His secretaries would sit stiff and formal, but Lincoln pushed his chair back and put his feet up on top of the long cabinet table. The president would often walk into the room only to announce that he did not feel like a meeting that day and send everyone home. Sometimes he didn't go at all, and had his secretary, Hay, ask the cabinet to hold its own meeting.

The cabinet was initially torn by anger and jealousies among its members. Lincoln was quite right when he said, just before his inauguration, that the cabinet members would eat up each other, not him. Nobody liked the charismatic Seward, whom they saw as a hopeless self-promoter and socialite. "Too much the politician for me," said Chase. "An evil genius," added the *Chicago Tribune*.[42] The cabinet fumed when Seward laughed long and hard at Lincoln's stories in what they felt was a stratagem to ingratiate himself with the president. They did not like Seward's inevitable social success at any party he attended, his fancy carriages, custom-made suits, incredible ability to get his name in newspapers, or his unprecedented personal military adviser.[43] His vanity irked them all, especially when the artist Francis B. Carpenter finished the official painting of the signing of the Emancipation Proclamation and Seward, not Lincoln, was at the center of it.[44]

"[Seward] had a craving desire that the world should consider him the great and controlling mind...of the nation," said Navy Secretary Welles,[45] while Bates saw Seward as a nineteenth-century Machiavelli. "He always shuffles around a knotty point by some trick," he said.[46]

Chase thought Gideon Welles was boring and mentally slow. Welles later skewered Chase in his memoirs, criticizing his overly serious manner[47] and making fun of his many efforts to get the War Department to let him plan military campaigns.[48] All of them, including Lincoln, made fun of Welles's gargantuan beard: They called him "Father Neptune." They all thought Simon Cameron a thief and his successor, Stanton, socially unacceptable and too close to Lincoln. "The government should not be carried on in the War Department," Welles wailed in 1863.[49] They were annoyed when Stanton, who missed half the meetings,[50] would pull Lincoln into a far corner of the room and whisper to him.[51] Interior Secretary Caleb Smith, the other cabinet secretaries felt, was nothing more than another Lincoln political toady. Montgomery Blair, most agreed, was a lightweight. Charles Francis Adams called them "a motley mixture."[52] Frank Blair was even harsher, calling the whole bunch of them "poltroons" and "apes."[53]

By the end of 1861, the cabinet began to balk at Lincoln's relationship to it. Chase, Welles, Bates, and the others complained to Lincoln that the government was never as strong as it could be because the cabinet did not meet regularly and Lincoln did not consult its members.[54] They argued that too much power had been given to Seward and suggested that if the cabinet secretaries met with each other at least once a week, it would make it easier for them to run their departments with more efficiency and less overlapping.

Among themselves the cabinet members saw Lincoln's style as highly ineffective. He made no effort to rein in the rambunctious Seward, let Stanton miss many critical meetings, and seemed to take a contemptuous view of the cabinet by his casual demeanor. This was the cabinet of the United States, they told each other, not one of Lincoln's general stores back in Sangamon County. Above all, several members of the cabinet, like many other people, began to see Lincoln as weak, exactly the kind of ineffectual, unfocused leader they had feared when he emerged out of nowhere as his party's nominee. "He lacks will and purpose and, I greatly fear, he has not the power to command," said Bates at the end of 1861, summing up the feelings of many.[55]

Lincoln listened closely, and instituted necessary changes to make the cabinet more influential in the government in the course of 1862. Despite Seward's objections, the president began regularly scheduled meetings of the cabinet which he attended at least once, and often twice, a week. He curbed Seward's influence in departments other than State. The forceful Stanton made sure Seward stayed out of the War Department, which was the chief concern. Lincoln took steps to cut down the hours Seward spent with him in the White House or elsewhere.

The cabinet's great strength was the freedom Lincoln gave each department and its secretary. The president knew he had competent men, no matter how much they groused about each other, and that their handpicked aides, particularly in State and War Departments, were experienced professionals. He provided policy, guidance, and support, and made all the key decisions, but Lincoln let the cabinet officers run their departments alone, without his intervention, delegating enormous authority to them as their departments exploded in size. In return, despite their bickering and jealousies, the cabinet officers worked hard for Lincoln and the Union. From the autumn of 1862 on, the secretaries got along well with the president.

He permitted them considerable lattitude in important undertakings. With some restrictions, he let Seward spend the entire war working to keep England and France out of American affairs. He allowed Stanton free reign in building the Union army into the largest, best trained, and best equipped in the country's history and, in cooperation with him, permitted Stanton and his top military men to run the army. By the middle of the war, the total U.S. military forces sometimes numbered a million men, and they were stretched out over fifteen-hundred miles of territory. The logistics of running them were daunting. The War Department had to muster thousands of men into the service each week, feed and clothe them, transport them to their destinations, supply them with weapons and training, and pay them a monthly salary.

The War Department under Quartermaster General Montgomery Meigs purchased or built thousands of supply wagons, gun caissons, railroad bridges, pontoon crossings, field hospitals, and even camp churches. The War Department had to provide over three hundred thousand horses and keep them healthy; serve over three thousand tons of food each day; and produce millions of shoes. The department had to find lawyers or law students in the ranks to serve as judge advocates, or army prosecutors, recruit doctors and chaplains, and arrange for newspaper delivery, bands, sutlers to sell goods, and burial for the dead. By mid-1862, Stanton, Meigs, and their men did that as smoothly and efficiently as any country ever had.[56]

Lincoln's intervention in the development of the navy was minimal. Gideon Welles took over a puny navy with few ships and skeleton crews, then was ordered to win a war at sea, blockade nearly twenty-five hundred miles of coastline, chase blockade runners, and transport armies up and down the coasts and on rivers. Left alone to do so, Welles created one of the largest and most efficient navies of the nineteenth century. Under his guidance, the navy provided seventy-five ships carrying twelve thousand men for the capture of Hilton Head Island off South Carolina, and sixteen ships to carry seventy-five hundred men for the capture of Roanoke Island, North Carolina. It blockaded most of the ports of North Carolina, put five hundred ships to sea for the national blockade, and captured or sank fifteen hundred blockade runners. In the first years of the war, the U.S. Navy cut Southern shipping by over one-third, causing enough supply shortages to create runaway inflation in the South, a major cause of the Confederacy's eventual downfall.[57]

Financially, Lincoln let Salmon Chase, working with bankers, develop new systems of specie finance and government borrowing and use an innovative sale of bonds to permit the U.S. to pay the $1 million a day the war cost. He left it up to Chase to devise a system to collect the new taxes imposed to help cover the war's expense.[58]

In giving them the freedom to make decisions and run their departments, Lincoln was blunt in admitting that he had never been a general, a diplomat, an admiral, or a banker. He bowed to their expertise and put the responsibility in their hands. He gave an example of his attitude toward the cabinet the day he approved some controversial financial recommendations by Salmon Chase. "You understand these things. I do not," he said.[59]

Lincoln used his cabinet wisely. He went to them with his problems, whether it was the timing of the Emancipation Proclamation, his deteriorating relations with General McClellan, the firing on Fort Sumter, the *Trent* affair, the possibility of war with England, the naming of key administrators, the nation's financial problems, or key legislative bills. The president may have given Seward considerable latitude in cabinet meetings, but he often ignored his advice on important issues. Lincoln went into meetings with an open mind and often changed his position, as with the Fort Sumter decision and the *Trent* affair.

Cabinet meetings also gave Lincoln time and space to vent his rage about bad news on the military or domestic fronts. The secretaries often calmed him down and restored the critical inner balance which had made him so successful. Lincoln had, over the first two years of his administration, become close friends with Seward and Stanton, and was able to maintain good relationships with all the other cabinet members—even asking the aloof and difficult Chase to handle his family banking problems for him—strengthening personal ties between them. The members of his cabinet slowly came to see Lincoln as a strong and creative leader who constantly took them into his confidence. They worked increasingly well with him to save the Union they all loved so dearly. Just as he had done so successfully in Illinois politics, he managed in Washington to get everyone, friend and foe, to help him accomplish things that served them all.

His cabinet running smoothly for the first time since the war began,[60] Lincoln returned to his pleading with McClellan to fight in Virginia, where Union victories might end the war. The early months of 1862 were good for the Union armies, particularly those in the west. An unknown young general named Ulysses Grant captured both Fort Henry and Fort Donelson, then, facing defeat, won a great but costly victory at Shiloh. Union armies in Missouri had won several battles against Confederate forces in that border state, which had so many Southern sympathizers, securing it for the United States. The Federals won at Pea Ridge, Arkansas; seized Memphis; and captured the wealthiest city in the South, New Orleans. They had occupied huge areas of land and controlled nearly one thousand miles of critical riverways. In the east, amphibious forces under Admiral Samuel du Pont captured Hilton Head Island, and others took Roanoke, North Carolina.

There was little personal joy in these victories for Lincoln, whose son Willie, twelve, died that February of typhoid fever. The loss of their second son sent Abraham and Mary Lincoln into deep depressions. The president tried to plunge himself into work to fight off his despair, but Mary sank into a depression from which she never really emerged. Some noted, too, that the loss of his son during the war, even though he had not been in the army, made Lincoln truly understand the horror of the war between Americans.

Away from the battlefields, Lincoln enjoyed great success with his legislative packages in Congress. Working closely with both Republicans and Democrats, he pushed through several important pieces of legislation which would have great effect during the war and influence generations after the war ended: (1) the Homestead Act opened up hundreds of thousands of acres of land to settlers in the west; (2) the Internal Revenue Act allowed the federal government to increase tax revenues to pay for the cost of the war; (3) the National Banking Act created a national currency and a network of national banks across the Union, and transferred power over money from the states to the federal government; (4) new tariffs were authorized to protect American businesses; (5) land grant colleges, which would be crucial to higher education in the future, were approved; (6) a series of bills was passed to encourage development of railroad and telegraph line construction; and (7) Lincoln, who grew up on a farm, got Congress to approve the creation of a Department of Agriculture. Pushing through this complex package of nonwar bills was easy for Lincoln, who had a Republican majority in both houses and majorities on all the important House and Senate committees, including Ways and Means.[61]

None of this would matter if the Union lost the war, however, and the Federals, after early successes, suffered severe setbacks in 1862. Stonewall Jackson defeated federal forces several times in Virginia's Shenandoah Valley. The Confederates successfully raided Kentucky and Ohio. General John Pope was defeated at Second Bull Run. Federal forces besieging Vicksburg, Mississippi, were bogged down, and rebels defeated a Union army at Corinth, Mississippi. On top of all that, the Confederate ironclad *Merrimack* was terrorizing the U.S. Navy, causing havoc in coastal waters by sinking ships as if they were defenseless.

The Federals needed some big victories, for political as well as military purposes. The losses in the east, particularly Second Bull Run, in Washington's back yard, shocked Northerners. Congressmen and federal workers in Washington were appalled by the long trains of ambulances, full of badly wounded soldiers, coming back to the city from Manassas. The elections of 1862 were just a few months away, and people were losing faith in Lincoln and the Republicans, who couldn't seem to win the war. The Republican Party had been swept into office in 1860 and now, just two years later, it faced the possibility of being swept right out again. The Democrats, leaderless since Stephen Douglas's death in June 1861, had regrouped and begun well-financed campaigns to recapture Senate and congressional seats, governorships, and state legislatures.

Lincoln was fed up with McClellan and wanted to fire him in the summer 1862, as did most of the cabinet.[62] By then, however, McClellan had become the darling of the Democratic Party, particularly in New York and New Jersey, two key states. The president feared the dismissal of McClellan would be seen as the act of a bumbling president taking out his frustrations on a heroic general whom, McClellan would charge, he never gave enough men to win the war. That would be just the ammunition the Democrats needed to cut into Republican majorities at federal, state, and local levels.

The president was frustrated with all of his generals. How could the United States so completely overwhelm the Confederacy in every criterion, from men to artillery to ships, and still be unable to win? Whenever possible, particularly when among politicians, he turned his fabled wit on his generals. He once read a dispatch that the rebels had just captured a brigadier general along with some horses and mules. Lincoln commented, "I didn't care so much for the brigadier general; I can always make them. But horse and mules cost money." On another occasion he said the only reason he was promoting a man to general was because his wife was forcing Lincoln to do it. One politician asked him how he rated the abilities of Democratic generals versus Republicans. "It is comparing failures," the President smiled.[63]

One of the least reported incidents of the war underscored Lincoln's belief that it did not take a military genius to win a battle. He and Chase visited Fort Monroe, a U.S. facility on the Potomac, on May 4, 1862, and Lincoln suggested that forces there should seize Norfolk, Virginia. General John Wool admonished the president; the military had considered that strategy and decided the city was too well fortified. Lincoln and Chase then insisted on scouting the area around the city that night. After sailing down the river on the *Miami,* they landed just outside the Confederate fortifications. Lincoln, smiling broadly, strolled up and down the narrow beach there as if he were going for a Sunday walk with his children. He not only ordered an attack on Norfolk the next day, but, in a show of disdain for the army, asked Chase, an armchair general, to lead the attack. Union forces, with the well-dressed secretary of the treasury in charge, landed the next morning and captured Norfolk. The success of "General" Chase and his men confirmed the president's belief that the generals did not know all that much more about warfare than did well-informed civilians.[64]

Lincoln's pressure on McClellan finally worked. After refusing to fight at Manassas, Lincoln's idea, McClellan sailed the army to the southeastern Virginia peninsula to advance on Richmond. Lincoln opposed the idea of taking a city instead of finding the Confederate Army and whipping it but, as he always did with his generals at first, went along with the idea. McClellan halted repeatedly before Richmond, pleading for more troops, and being denied by the president.[65] The general continued to stall for time, crediting erroneous reports on the size of the army in front of him.[66]

McClellan also refused to accept any politically connected officers, notably Brigadier General Charles S. Hamilton. Lincoln tried to impress upon McClellan, and all of his generals, that he needed politically influential men in the army to please the leaders of the Democratic and Republican parties and senators and congressmen, that the war was as much about politics as tactics and that he, the president, needed to keep the two-party system in balance in order to wage war successfully. He also warned McClellan to stop writing nasty letters to senators whose support Lincoln needed.[67] He told McClellan that a delegation representing twenty-three senators and eighty-four representatives had just urged him to have Hamilton, who had been relieved by McClellan, restored to command.

He tried to impress upon General McClellan the connections between the army, the war, the congress, national politics, and the White House. "When you relieved General Hamilton...you lost the confidence of at least one of your best friends in the Senate. And here let me say...that Senators and Representatives speak of me in their places as they please, without question..."[68] Still, McClellan refused.[69]

Exasperated by everything about McClellan, but most of all by his reluctance to go on the offensive, Lincoln begged his commander to stage an assault against Richmond. McClellan refused. The argument was settled when Robert E. Lee's Army of Northern Virginia attacked McClellan and drove him out of the area.

McClellan would accept no blame, and turned a venomous pen on Lincoln. "The government has not sustained this army," he wrote. Lincoln never saw the complete telegram. McClellan's final lines were scathing. He snapped, "If I save this army now, I tell you plainly that I owe no thanks to you," and then finished by telling the President that "you have done your best to sacrifice this army."[70] His words were so harsh that the young telegraph operator at the War Department, who had become friendly with the president, who visited the office regularly for war news, cut them out of the telegram for fear of hurting Lincoln's feelings.[71] Lincoln continued to back McClellan, hoping to convince him to fight harder somewhere else. Lincoln had not been so kind to anyone, dismissing John C. Frémont after one bad campaign and Irvin McDowell after one bad day.

The president thought his perseverance had paid off months later. On September 17, 1862, McClellan's entire army of seventy-five thousand men attacked Lee's army, which was trying to invade the North, at Antietam Creek, in Sharpsburg, Maryland. In one of the bloodiest one-day battles in U.S. history, the two sides suffered a total of twenty-six thousand men killed, wounded, or missing. The Federals pushed the rebels back into Virginia. Tactically, Antietam was a draw, but Lincoln called it a victory and used it to issue the Emancipation Proclamation, which freed all slaves in states in rebellion.

Lincoln's happiness was quickly muted when he learned that McClellan had had twenty-four thousand fresh troops whom he did not send into the battle, despite pleas by other generals to use them, and refused, despite Lincoln's exhortations, to chase Lee farther into Virginia in hopes of crushing him once and for all. Years later, Longstreet said that the twenty-four thousand reserves, if sent in, would have been enough to completely crush Lee's army and probably end the war.[72] Angry, but still unwilling to get rid of the popular general, Lincoln visited McClellan at his camp in Maryland for nearly a week, pressuring him daily to invade Virginia again and receiving yet more assurances from the commander that he would carry on an aggressive campaign.

One day Lincoln walked to the top of a hill near McClellan's city-size camp with an old friend and asked him to describe the sight below. "It is the Army of the Potomac," said the friend. "No," the president said, his voice dripping with sarcasm, "it is McClellan's bodyguard."[73]

A few weeks later, punctuated by dozens of letters complaining, as always, that the War Department did not give him enough supplies, McClellan moved into Virginia, but after five weeks of inactivity he announced that his men were too tired for another vigorous campaign.[74] Lincoln's eternal patience with

McClellan ended in late October 1862, when the general wired him that his horses were too fatigued for any attack. Lincoln wired back: "Will you pardon me for asking what the horses of your army have done since the battle of Antietam that fatigue anything?"[75]

With great reluctance, Lincoln, telling Frank Blair the general "had the slows," finally fired McClellan on November 7, 1861, and replaced him with Ambrose Burnside.[76] The perfect general was sent home to Trenton, New Jersey.[77]

Lincoln was demoralized. He had to let McClellan go because McClellan would never win the war. The soldiers were furious over McClellan's firing, and so were the newspapers. Although he did not know it then, Lincoln's decision to fire McClellan, together with the battle of Antietam, finally convinced England that it should stay out of the war. The president brooded for weeks, his old depression grabbing hold of him once more. One day a group of women trying to find ways to comfort the soldiers in the field called on him and asked for a word of encouragement about the war effort. "I have no word of encouragement to give," he said.[78]

Toward the end of September the president, irritated by the Southern sympathizers he saw everywhere he looked, once again suspended the writ of habeas corpus. Once more federal agents and army officials began jailing suspected traitors across the country, particularly in Maryland. These new suspects joined the more than two hundred jailed the previous year. The men in charge of the hunts, at first Seward and then Stanton, told army commanders to spread a wide net to snare Confederates, spies, and sympathizers. Lincoln insisted on the arrests despite a U.S. Supreme Court ruling, *Ex Parte Merryman,* that they were unconstitutional. He was convinced that his majority in Congress would back him up, and it did, approving the arrests in March, 1863.[79]

Although Congress later supported him, the president had badly misjudged both the long-term reaction to the Emancipation Proclamation and, far more damaging, another round of arrests after suspension of the habeas corpus writ. This time the federal government began a massive shutdown of newspapers overly critical of the administration, in a shameful abuse of freedom of the press. It began in July 1862, when Charles Fulton, editor of the *Baltimore American,* was put in prison because Lincoln thought a story he planned to publish contained too many details about the Union Army.

There were twelve different suspensions of papers in Baltimore alone, and by the end of the war eight papers there had been shut down permanently, and two more had gone out of business after their editors were imprisoned. Anti-Lincoln papers began to shut down quickly. The *New York Daily News* had to suspend publication when the local postmaster refused to mail it, and detectives confiscated copies its owner tried to ship via trains. James McMaster, editor of the New York *Freeman's Journal* was jailed for treason and held in prison for eleven weeks. James Wall, editor of the Trenton, N.J., *True American,* was jailed for a week. Charles Fuller was convicted of treason and fined for writing that Lincoln was a "mad, revolutonary fanatic."

A New York grand jury selected five newspapers for presentments and a New Jersey grand jury singled out five more. Daniel Flanagan, editor of the Mason, Ohio, *Democrat,* was sentenced to six months in prison for opposing the draft. There was even an effort, never carried out, to imprison several New York editors for merely having criticized Lincoln in private conversations. Another New York grand jury went so far as to draw up a list of 154 newspapers critical of the government and considered dangerous. Dozens of newspapers were shuttered in the fall of 1862, and again in 1863 and 1864, in an effort to mute criticism, but the suspensions themselves sparked criticism. Finally, in perhaps his most ill-advised political move, the president ordered the army to arrest members of the Maryland legislature on charges of disloyalty.[80]

The excitement and romance of the war long since buried in thousands of coffins, the public was disgusted with the new wave of arrests, which were relentlessly criticized even in loyal newspapers. Lincoln's former law partner, John Stuart, refused to debate Leonard Swett, another friend of the president, in their Illinois congressional race because he was afraid Lincoln would have him arrested. The suspensions of the writ and the arrests which followed were a huge political miscalculation by the normally shrewd president.

Lincoln, certain that the Emancipation Proclamation would be a political gold mine for his party, did little politicking for congressional and state Republicans in the elections of 1862. He felt that the party was stronger than ever and that his appeal to the working man in his message to Congress in late 1861 had won over many blue-collar workers. He was wrong.

The criticism of the new wave of civil rights suspensions, coupled with opposition from many quarters to the Emancipation Proclamation, and the growing unpopularity of the war, combined to hurt the Republicans badly in the 1862 elections. The Republicans won 61.7 percent of the vote in the

Midwestern states in 1860, but the percentage there dropped to just 41.9 in 1862. In New England and the Northeastern states, the Republican party plunged from a commanding 75 percent of the vote to just 58 percent.[81] Six states which the Republicans carried in the 1860 elections—New York, Pennsylvania, Ohio, Indiana, Illinois, and New Jersey—swung over to the Democrats; New York even elected a Democratic governor, Horatio Seymour. Powerful Republican congressmen such as New York's Roscoe Conkling, Ohio's John Bingham, and Speaker of the House Galusha Grow all lost. The Democrats even carried Sangamon County, Lincoln's home county, defeating his longtime friend and political adviser Leonard Swett.[82]

The Republicans managed to retain control of the House of Representatives and the Senate, but the elections enabled the formerly moribund Democratic Party to rebound and once again give the United States a strong two-party system. Lincoln could no longer depend on an overwhelmingly Republican House and Senate to do what he wanted. He would have to bring more Democrats into the government, work more closely with Democratic politicians to pass legislation, and work even harder with his fellow Republicans to rebuild the party for the 1863 elections. He believed the Emancipation Proclamation was a plus, not a minus, politically, and that the arrests under the habeas corpus writ suspension were necessary. The president did not feel those were the reasons the Republicans had lost so many races; they had lost because the Lincoln administration could not end the war. Now, in 1863, the government had to win the war. Otherwise the Republicans would fare worse in the next elections, in which key statehouses and state legislatures would be at stake, and possibly lose their House and Senate majorities in 1864. As the head of his now embattled party, he had to lead the Republicans to victory—and he had to end the war to do it.

On November 26, the president traveled to Acquia Creek to discuss the plans of his new top general, Ambrose Burnside, to invade Virginia and win the war. Burnside, determined to show off his expertise, devised an attack on Fredericksburg, Virginia. He told Lincoln that the forces defending the city were thin. If he could get there right away and cross the Rappahannock River before anyone noticed, he could take Fredericksburg and then head directly south to capture Richmond. Lincoln, by the winter of 1862 an accomplished strategist, was highly skeptical. He approved the plan with one overriding condition—the general had to move fast. The army would be doomed if it lost the element of surprise.[83]

Burnside was an impressive-looking man, with his stylish and well-tended mutton chops ("sideburns" was coined from his name to describe them) and his nicely fitted dark blue uniform. The men seemed to like him, especially since the general, himself a voracious eater, took great pains to improve the commissary. He had served in the army during the Mexican War and later, as a civilian in the firearms business, gained notoriety when he invented a new breech-loading rifle, in 1856.

But Burnside was a hopeless bungler. He fancied himself a great cardplayer and played with great enthusiasm—but always lost. On the day he was supposed to be married, his fiancée told the minister about to tie the knot that she could not go through with it and rushed out of the church.[84] Now, in front of Fredericksburg, Burnside was about to bungle again.

Like so many of Burnside's operations, the plan was ill conceived. The pontoon bridges needed to cross the river were over a week late in arriving. Instead of sending orders via telegraph, along wires hanging right over their heads, Burnside's aides sent them by mail. Burnside's chaotic orders resulted in all eighty thousand Union troops colliding together on the far side of the river from Fredericksburg, then sitting there for days under the eyes of Confederate sentinels. The delay gave Lee plenty of time to move his army to the city and reinforce it. Burnside at last crossed the river, only to order a shortsighted charge up a hill, Marye's Heights, where thousands of Stonewall Jackson's men were posted behind a near-impregnable stone wall. Jackson told Lee that "a chicken could not cross that field and live." The Federals charged up the hill again and again with remarkable bravery, only to be mowed down by rifle and artillery fire and driven back over the river in one of the Union's most humiliating defeats.[85]

Lincoln learned of the rout, but he also learned of the courage of the men at Fredericksburg. He was deeply moved. He wrote a striking open letter to the troops, which was published in many newspapers. The president's letter was read to the Union army, then posted and hung in the cold, wet December air on boards and poles for all to read:

> Although you were not successful, the attempt was not an error, nor the failure other than an accident. The courage with which you, in an open field, maintained the contest against an entrenched foe, and the consummate skill and success with which you crossed and recrossed the river, in face of the enemy, show that you possess all the qualities of a great army, which will yet give victory to the cause of the country

and of popular government. Consoling with the mourners for the dead, and sympathizing with the severely wounded, I congratulate you that the number of both is so comparatively small. I tender to you, officers and soldiers, the thanks of the nation.[86]

Soldiers reading it, some sick, some wounded, some demoralized, found new hope in their struggle. Their commanders may have been bunglers, but the commander in chief was not.

The president knew he had brave men, but he did not have good generals. As the end of the year approached, the lack of leadership was destroying morale in the army and in the nation. The catastrophe at Fredericksburg was the worst example. Desertions soared, and by the end of January 1863 over eighty-five thousand men had fled.[87] So many deserted each week that Lincoln had to sadly sign orders to post hundreds of soldiers in Washington to catch them. General Joseph Hooker told the *New York Times* that the army was "played out" and needed a dictator.

General Carl Schurz, a close Lincoln political ally, said that the army was "melting away." General Oliver Howard felt the entire army was now uninterested in fighting anymore. Incompetent lower-level army administrators wrecked food supply operations, while thousands of soldiers lay sick from scurvy. The generals reported that only one out of every three soldiers in the Army of the Potomac was fit to fight.[88] The press and public castigated Lincoln and his cabinet, holding them responsible for the defeat. Public respect for Lincoln was lower than at any time in his presidency. As if all that were not enough, on the very last day of 1862 the ironclad *Monitor*, in which Lincoln had placed so much hope, sank at sea.

Aides said he was more demoralized about the war than at any time since it started. Friends said that he no longer joked and the twinkle that lit up his eyes had disappeared. Physically, Lincoln looked worn out and tired for the first time in his life. Even so he had no time to recover from the disaster at Fredericksburg. Just three days later, he found himself thrust into the middle of the worst cabinet crisis of his administration.

Radical Republicans, joined by Democrats, had decided to have Seward removed from the cabinet. They blamed him for much of the nation's woe, (much of their information had come from Salmon Chase). They formed a caucus and tried first to get the Senate to censure the secretary of state. The effort failed by just three votes. Then they met with Lincoln, who managed to deflect their heated criticisms by using an old lawyer's trick; he made them sit and listen for an hour while he read dispatches to McClellan which showed that he and the cabinet had backed the general for months and never abandoned him, as the radicals claimed.

The next day Lincoln called an emergency meeting of the cabinet and demanded to know from each man if he felt that Lincoln had not cooperated with him. He did it skillfully and sternly in order to confront Chase, knowing that if Chase said Lincoln did not cooperate it would prove that he was not only the leak, but disloyal to the president. If Chase said Lincoln had cooperated it would show that he had lied to the caucus of senators. Unable to squirm, Chase merely blustered when confronted and the effort to oust Seward died.[89]

The cabinet furor over, Lincoln decided to fire Burnside and find yet another commander. He could not bring himself simply to boot the fumbling Burnside out of the army, as he should have, but, instead, reassigned him to another command so the general would not have his pride hurt.[90]

Burnside was a bungler right to the very end of his tenure as head of the Army of the Potomac. Summoned to the White House to be fired, the general did something that perfectly symbolized the army leadership—he missed his train.[91]

15

ABRAHAM LINCOLN: EMANCIPATION

ABRAHAM LINCOLN WATCHED disinterestedly as the members of his cabinet discussed the movement of John Pope's army at their weekly cabinet meeting on July 22, 1862. He was uncertain how to begin what would become one of the most important meetings in American history. He did what he always did when uncertain; the president went to his seemingly endless reservoir of humor. He stopped the discussions and told the men he had just read an amusing passage from a recent book by humorist Artemus Ward. Staring intently at the pages of the book, he read it to them and they chuckled.

Now that he had relaxed them, he looked directly at each and told them that he had made up his mind to do something by executive order and wanted to read them a statement. They would discuss it, but no one was going to change his mind. Regardless of their view, the statement he had written *would* be law. Then Abraham Lincoln picked up the papers, held them casually in his huge hands and read the cabinet the Emancipation Proclamation.

There was immediate turmoil. Montgomery Blair said freeing the slaves would severely endanger the Republican Party in several Northern states. Chase, one of the country's leading abolitionists, offered only reluctant support, fearful that freeing the slaves might cause tremors on Wall Street. Seward, who had discussed the idea briefly with the president a week before, was against issuing it soon, insisting that unless it was coupled with a military victory it would appear the act of a desperate man.

Prior to his cabinet meeting, Lincoln made an ironic mistake. He caught it as he sat in his office in the White House and looked over his first draft of the Emancipation Proclamation one last time before he took it to the meeting. Toward the end of his first draft he wrote that Southern states in rebellion had to voluntarily accept the "adoption" of slavery. He reached for a pen and scratched out "adoption," the mistake, and scrawled on top of it the word he was supposed to have written but had not: "abolishment."[1]

The abolishment of slavery, ordered by the Emancipation Proclamation, was something Abraham Lincoln had yearned for all his life. Yet, year after year, it always seemed out of his grasp or the grasp of any other politician, or any political party, or the country itself. Now, on July 22, 1862, extraordinary circumstances and events had made it possible for Lincoln to scratch out "adoption" and write in "abolishment," pick up the papers, rise from his desk, and walk down the hall to read to his war-weary cabinet a message that would, he hoped, give new spark to his troops in the field, new hope to the people of the Union and, somehow, end the war and transform his country.

The emancipation of the slaves was not a new idea for Lincoln. He tried to get a bill into Congress in 1848, during his lone term in the House of Representatives, to free the slaves in the District of Columbia. As early as 1852, he advocated the freeing of the slaves and the deportation of all four million slaves back to Africa, where they could establish a colony of their own.[2] In October 1854 he again advocated freedom for slaves with owners compensated for their loss.[3] He argued that slavery was wrong in every campaign he participated in, whether a candidate or a supporter. He led the Midwestern opposition to the Kansas-Nebraska Act in an effort to forbid slavery in the new territories.

Lincoln could never publicly promise that if he became president he would abolish slavery. A statement like that, in the climate of the late 1850s, would have ruined his career. He, and others, had to continue their unwilling acceptance of slavery where it existed, hoping that events would bring the issue to a boil once and for all. The war, which droned on through the hot summer of 1862 without resolution, did that. It gave Lincoln a new landscape on which to undermine the institution of slavery.

The president did not believe that either the public or the army was totally committed to the war. The people, he felt, still believed the war could be won overnight, but were tired of it and might, if given the opportunity, let the South go its own way. Morale in the army was at an all-time low because defeats and desertion rates were high. If he could change the reasons for fighting the war to include freedom for the slaves and a broadened sense of democracy for all, as well as the preservation of the Union, it would lift the spirits of the soldiers and the citizens alike. He strongly believed that some sort of an emancipation edict would prevent England and France from recognizing and supporting the Confederacy, which could be fatal. His ministers to England, Austria, and Spain confirmed his view.[4] There was also the very real chance that thousands of blacks would fight for the Union army, where they might be needed to replace the troops who were disappearing or make up needed regiments in the future if the war continued.[5]

Most of all, though, Abraham Lincoln saw the chance not only to emancipate the slaves, but to free the entire American populace from slavery, which had poisoned it for two hundred years,[6] and renew the American revolutionary leaders' sense of equality for all men, the sense that all men, white or black, rich or poor, were entitled to the same chances in life.[7]

Lincoln had made his way through life as a man of opportunity, constantly maintaining his visibility and building political connections so that as events changed he might take advantage of new possibilities. He sensed such a possibility regarding slavery in the spring of 1862, and began to move carefully toward the emancipation of the slaves, taking advantage of events or the moves of other men to build a framework for freeing the slaves. Rarely more than a dream for Abraham Lincoln, emancipation had now become a goal.

He was certain that he could free the slaves, but he needed five conditions: (1) the clamor for emancipation from others so that he could position himself as a man driven to free the slaves by political tides and public opinion, not by his own volition; (2) emancipation had to be a last step because other plans had failed; (3) a way in which to free the slaves without driving the border states, with their slaves, into the arms of the Confederacy; (4) pressure from newspapers demanding emancipation; and (5) timing. He could never free the slaves while the Union was losing the war, because it would look like a desperate act.

Lincoln waited for some opportunities and created others. His first step was a bill he sent to Congress in March 1862 which would free the slaves via a simple compensation plan. The United States would pay each slaveowner $400 per slave—market value—in compensation for the manumission of their slaves. In return, the slaveowners would end the war and end slavery. It was not a new idea. Henry Clay had advocated it a generation before, but it grew in urgency as the war continued. The president felt it had merit for everyone. The slaves would gain freedom and their owners could use the money—for large plantation owners, a fortune—to reorganize their plantations and employ paid labor to continue their profitable businesses. Importantly, the elimination of slavery, Lincoln felt, would end the war.

The president sold his plan as hard as he could. He promised critics that it would be cheaper to compensate every single slave owner in the Southern states than continue the war. He told Henry Raymond, editor of the *New York Times,* that the compensation was cheap. Lincoln explained that the cost of one morning of the war could pay for the emancipation and compensation of all the slaves in Delaware and that the cost of the war for eighty-seven days would pay for the release of all the slaves in Delaware, Maryland, the District of Columbia, Kentucky, and Missouri.[8]

Lincoln produced a cost effectiveness chart for Senator James McDougall which showed that freedom through compensation for the 432,622 slaves in four border states plus the District of Columbia would cost $173,048,800 and that the cost of the war for eighty-seven days was $174 million. "Do you doubt that [it]...would shorten the war more than eighty seven days and thus be an actual savings of expense?" he argued. McDougall disagreed.[9] If the plan had worked, Lincoln would have freed the slaves and saved $2.2 billion dollars, over $256 billion in current money, in what the war, which continued three more years, eventually cost.

He lobbied hard with Republican congressmen and senators, but the bill went nowhere. Even members of his own party thought the idea was too bold to work. Abolitionists fumed that the buying off of the slaves did not underscore the moral wrong of slavery and reminded slaves, and Northerners, that slaves were nothing more than property to be bought and sold. The bill may have failed, but the strategy succeeded. All the publicity about the freeing of the slaves set in motion the idea that the slaves should be free; the government just needed a better plan. It also worked for Lincoln because it eliminated one scenario—compensation—and opened the door to another—emancipation.

Lincoln did not have to wait long for others to clamor for emancipation. General David Hunter took it upon himself to declare martial law and free all the slaves in Florida, Georgia, and South Carolina in May 1862, following the occupation of Hilton Head Island, in South Carolina. Lincoln immediately overruled him, reminding him that a general could not emancipate slaves—only the government could.[10] Earlier, in August 1861, another general, the flamboyant John C. Frémont, the Republican candidate for president in 1856, had done the same thing, issuing an order which would free slaves in areas occupied by the Union army. He also infuriated Southerners by threatening to shoot any captured Confederate soldiers. Lincoln reprimanded Frémont and pubicly rescinded his order,[11] but while he fumed publicly, he was not unhappy with Frémont or Hunter. Their efforts to free the slaves, which received enormous publicity, were applauded in the Northern press. This helped create the heated public climate for emancipation which Lincoln needed.

There had been pressure from members of his cabinet to free the slaves since the beginning of his administration. William Seward was the leading abolitionist in America. Salmon Chase, who had started the Free-Soil party in Ohio as a fiery abolitionist, begged Lincoln to let Hunter's emancipation order stand. Simon Cameron had urged Lincoln to free the slaves by presidential order as early as December 1861. Influential Massachusetts Senator Charles Sumner went to the White House the day news of the bombardment of Fort Sumter was received and asked Lincoln to free the slaves, explaining very carefully that the attack on the fort gave the president the chance to use his war powers to do anything he wanted, emancipation included.[12] Friend William Sprague, a Rhode Island senator, urged him to free the slaves so that they could enlist in the army.[13] Lincoln's cabinet was ahead of him on emancipation, and in the summer of 1862 their public and private views, which everyone in Washington knew, gave him needed political support for it.

The president proposed numerous bills to Congress, and signed orders in spring and summer of 1862 which were building blocks toward emancipation. He asked Congress to recognize the newly created black republics of Haiti and Liberia, and rumors flew that this was yet another effort to free slaves and deport them to African colonies. Congress changed military rules to prohibit officers or soldiers from returning any fugitive slaves they encountered to their owners. One bill forbade officers to appear at any court proceedings, or initiate them, when asked by slaveowners. Another bill freed all slaves in the new territories. An act allied the United States with England in a new effort to curb the African slave trade. Still another promised education to newly freed black children and permitted blacks to serve as postmasters. The army was encouraged to hire New England schoolteachers and send them to occupied slave states to set up schools for emancipated slave children.

Finally, the Second Confiscation Act, passed in July 1862, ruled that any runaway slave captured by the Union army in a slave state was free. Another regulation declared any former slaves who made it to an army camp to be free. Lincoln let his generals know that any resourceful views they had on the thousands of runaways arriving at army camps each day were fine with him. The generals routinely classified any arriving slave and his family as "contraband," or goods confiscated from the enemy, and gave them their freedom. All of these bills and rulings, carefully crafted by the president, were stepping stones to the Emancipation Proclamation.

Lincoln had been under pressure to free the slaves from religious groups for a long time. In June 1862 a delegation of Quakers visited the White House and urged emancipation. After a reception on a warm summer day, its leader told the president that the Constitution could not free the slaves, but he could. Freed slaves would mean the end of the war. "The abolition of slavery is indispensable to your success," he said and then asked all to pray for Lincoln.

Lincoln, seeing an opportunity to move toward freeing the slaves while cloaking the act in a religious mantle, acknowledged that he felt he needed "Divine assistance" and that perhaps he was "an instrument in God's hands."[14] As late as September 21, the day before the proclamation was officially announced, a group from the Reformed Presbyterian Church of Washington, D.C., urged freedom for the slaves, telling the president that "God's wrath cannot be appeased."[15]

By late summer of 1862 he had come under withering fire from the Northern press, which was advocating freedom for all the slaves and pressuring Lincoln to do something about it. By August, he had submitted the first draft of the Emancipation Proclamation to the cabinet, but it was kept secret until it could be announced. His mind made up, Lincoln continued his campaign to prepare the public for it in a series of careful steps. One area he knew was important was the press. Lincoln told friends he never read newspapers because they only told him what he knew already, but he did— carefully. He waited patiently, going through editorial after editorial, until he finally found an attack he wanted to respond to in order to continue his gradual move toward emancipation. It came from the Horace Greeley in the *New York Tribune* on August 19.

In what became one of American journalism's most famous editorials, Greeley first wrote an eye-catching headline: "The Prayer of Twenty Millions." Under it, he declared that Lincoln was "strangely and disastrously remiss" in not freeing the slaves and that the president was a prisoner of bad advice from the border states which protected slavery. Arguing that his newspaper reached a total of twenty million people, Greeley demanded an answer.[16]

Lincoln, who almost never responded to newspaper editorials, knew any response at all would be read carefully. In one of his best letters, he wrote: "My paramount objective in this struggle is to save the Union, and is not either to save or to destroy slavery. If I could save the Union without freeing any slave, I would do it, and if I could save it by freeing all of the slaves, I would do it; and if I could save it by freeing some and leaving others alone, I would also do that."

It was a wonderfully direct and yet elusive answer from the president. It satisfied everybody. Readers in the border states saw it as protection for their slaves while abolitionists saw it as freedom for all slaves. Everyone saw it as the response of a man who did not have any plan to free the slaves but wished he did. The letter was hailed throughout the North.[17]

Five days before Greeley's editorial, Lincoln took another step toward preparing the public for emancipation when he invited a large group of influential black leaders, led by Frederick Douglass, to the White House for a reception. The men, uncertain why they were summoned, were incredulous as Lincoln once again outlined a plan to either buy freedom for slaves or get the government to order it, but only if the slaves—all four million of them— left the country and resettled somewhere else, hopefully in Central America or Africa. That would guarantee their freedom, remove them from the South, where they could not flourish as free men, and prevent blacks from taking white jobs in the North. His attitude was extremely cheerful and confident. Douglass and his friends were appalled. They had no intention of cooperating in sending slaves anywhere outside the United States. They simply wanted Lincoln to free the slaves and let them live in the United States.

Lincoln feigned anger that Frederick Douglass and his colleagues would not go along with his plan. Around that same time, he also encouraged longtime political friend Cassius Clay, of Kentucky, to float the idea of freeing all the slaves and sending them to Florida to establish an all black state there.[18] Lincoln said he was interested in a proposal by Senator Pomeroy to found an all-black colony in Central America and a proposal by a Frenchman who took a lease on a small island near Haiti, A'Vache, to build a colony for America's slaves.[19] He supported an idea to start huge timber industries in Haiti, run by deported slaves, that might sell wood to the army at one-third market value.[20]

Douglass and other black leaders and the country's most influential abolitionists all balked at these ideas. Their opposition was exactly what he predicted and needed. He never really wanted the slaves to leave the country, but talked up his colonization idea to let others kill it. This longtime favorite Lincoln plan joined his other plan, compensation for freed slaves, in the drawer of discarded ideas. Now, in mid-August, he had shrewdly allowed many others to narrow his options to what he really wanted to do in the first place—simply free those in bondage.

The real barrier to emancipation was the border states of Kentucky, Maryland, and Missouri, slave states which had remained loyal to the Union. Lincoln could not free all the slaves against the wishes of leaders in those states without driving them out of the Union and jeopardizing the war itself. He summoned the leaders of the border states to the White House on July 12, 1862, and in a long meeting reminded them that he knew their opposition to the compensation plan to free slaves had killed it and that "the war would essentially be ended" if they had endorsed it. He was pleased that they had rejected offers to join the Confederacy, that they had remained loyal to the Union, and that volunteers from their states had fought for the Union. He was not pleased, however, that they still condoned slavery and told them that as long as they did, they would be pressured by the South to fight with the Confederacy. If they eliminated slavery, the South would leave them alone and then the war could be won. "We all know what the lever of their power is [slavery]. Break that lever before their faces," he said.

Lincoln used several arguments with the men, who sat stonefaced. Finally, he told them that when the Union won the war, victory would bring the end of slavery, and they knew it. Their slaveowners would lose their slaves without compensation. Why not agree to a gradual emancipation plan now, free some of their slaves, and end the war with prosperity for slaveowners? Pleading with them to go along with some version of the plan he was drawing up, he said that "our common country is in great peril, demanding the loftiest views and boldest action to relieve it."[21]

The border state congressmen would not go along, though, and the effort died stillborn. Lincoln, however, had let the political leaders of the Union slave states know that he was still toying with some kind of emancipation project. Lincoln had also learned he could never free the slaves in those borders states, particularly Kentucky, without risking their loss to the Confederacy. "I think to lose Kentucky is nearly the same as to lose the whole game," the president wrote Orville Browning. "Kentucky gone, we cannot hold Missouri, nor, as I think, Maryland. These all against us, and the job on our hands is too large for us."[22] He reminded Browning that as soon as Frémont issued his proclamation in 1861, a company of Union volunteers from Kentucky dropped their rifles and disbanded.

One goal of emancipation he did not discuss with the border state congressmen was the idea that freedmen and liberated slaves would join the Union army and fight against the Confederates, both for revenge and for a chance to liberate slaves. It was not until nearly a year after he had issued the Emancipation Proclamation that Lincoln said it might have spurred black enlistment, but, in fact, that idea was one of the major reasons he wanted to free the slaves from the very beginning.

He knew by the early summer of 1862, through Frederick Douglass and others, that freed blacks were willing to join the army and fight. No one wanted them. Politicians and army commanders alike viewed freed blacks and slaves as childlike fools, who were also lazy and shiftless. They would never make decent soldiers. Lincoln did not agree. He knew that freed black slaves had enjoyed great success as soldiers in Haiti. A friend had hand-copied a letter sent to the *New York Post* which paraphrased a memoir of French General Amphile de la Croix, who led French and emancipated slave troops in a war in Haiti. De la Croix said that the freed slaves were not at all disorganized, childlike, or lazy, as many Northerners believed, but fought as tough and disciplined soldiers. "The history of Haiti shows that blacks will fight with enthusiasm wherever they are led by whites or by men of their own color," the general said.[23]

Lincoln expressed an interest in recruiting black troops as early as July 22, 1862, the day he first told his cabinet of the Emancipation Proclamation, when he issued to generals in occupied Southern states and border states guidelines on the recruitment of blacks (all were eligible on a volunteer basis except those who belonged to border state slaveowners who objected to the idea).[24] The enlistment of black soldiers was also discussed after Lincoln read his cabinet the first draft of the proclamation on July 22.

The proclamation itself underwent several small changes in the autumn of 1862. In its final form, in which it went into effect January 1, 1863, it ordered freedom for slaves in states in rebellion—*not* slaves in any of the border states—thereby keeping the border states in the Union. The proclamation also incorporated previous acts of Congress and presidential orders: army commanders were to free any slaves in areas they occupied in rebellious states; they were not to help slaveowners track runaway slaves; and if any runaway slaves arrived at their camps, they were to free them.

Lincoln had made up his mind to issue the proclamation months before he informed his cabinet. The president then assumed a pose familiar to those who knew him well from his days as a politician in Illinois. Having explored every single opinion possible on emancipation, he suddenly had no opinion on emancipation. He responded to any questions about it with indifference. He feigned ignorance of public opinion in border states, told visitors he knew nothing about black soldiers, thought the press made too much of what he wrote in letters to editors, and, above all, told anyone who came in contact with him at the White House that he had no plans to free the slaves. This stance frustrated everyone. Massachusetts Senator Sumner wrote his friend John Bright in early August 1862 that Lincoln refused even to discuss emancipation, telling him that a word about it would cause his troops in Kentucky to desert.[25]

Lincoln had played this game well all his life; it worked just as well in the White House as it did in the Illinois statehouse. He managed to keep the entire Congress, press, and public in the dark as he took dozens of critical steps toward his goal.

Montgomery Blair and others continually warned the President that there was no strong sentiment in the North for freeing the slaves, that doing so might endanger the Republican Party in the upcoming fall elections, that a weakened party meant a weakened White House.[26] Lincoln could only deal from political strength to free the slaves, and he needed a significant military victory to boost public morale enough to permit him to free the slaves despite some Northern opposition. That came at Antietam, where McClellan's army forced Lee's army out of Maryland. The battle itself was a draw, and Lincoln rebuked McClellan for keeping twenty-four thousand troops in reserve and refusing to chase Lee into Virginia. But he had a precious piece of paper from McClellan with four sentences which were all he needed to free the slaves: "[Cavalary General Alfred] Pleasanton is driving the enemy across the river. Our victory was complete. The enemy is driven back into Virginia. Maryland and Pennsylvania are now safe.—Geo. B. McClellan, Maj. Gen'l."

Now armed with a "great" victory, Lincoln issued the Emancipation Proclamation on September 22, 1862. Two days later, it had been published in nearly every newspaper in America. The afternoon it was issued, Seward sent an official circular to all U.S. diplomatic and consular officers to explain emancipation to them. Thereupon they immediately explained it to the leaders of the countries where they were stationed.

The proclamation was greeted with jubilation by the abolitionists and received warmly by most Northerners. Rallies were held and bonfires lit in celebration. Lincoln was pleased by its initial reception in the North. Unexpectedly, a crowd of several hundred people gathered on the front lawn of the White House and called for Lincoln the night the proclamation was issued, cheering lustily for the president when he appeared. Telling the people that he hoped he had not made a mistake, he said it was now time for Northerners to band together to fight slavery. He quickly turned to the war to tell the crowd that he had difficulties as commander in chief, but they were nowhere near the difficulties of the soldiers fighting for the Union "[They] are endeavoring to purchase with their blood and their lives the future happiness and prosperity of this country," he said.[27]

When Lincoln finished, the crowd marched down Pennsylvania Avenue to the home of Treasury Secretary Salmon Chase, and called him out for a speech. Then it moved on to the home of Attorney General Edward Bates. The crowd grew larger as it moved, and cheered louder at the home of each statesman it stopped at, forming its own parade of support for the proclamation.

Religious groups hailed it, many sending Lincoln petitions that ranged from twenty[28] to over five hundred signatures.[29] "We hail the proclamation as a step in the direction of national repentance and truth with God that it may be crowned with happy results," wrote the head of the First United Presbyterian Synod of the West.[30]

Republicans applauded it. "God bless you! All good men upon this earth will glorify you and all the angels in heaven will hold [a] jubilee!" wrote several state legislators from Pennsylvania.[31] The Minnesota state legislature issued a proclamation hailing it, with almost all of its members signing, and praising Lincoln. "This act of devotion to country increases our confidence in the ability and integrity of the President," it read.[32]

The army supported the edict; General McClellan ordered it read to all of his troops when they were assembled for parade. Some cheered lustily, and some ignored it.[33]

"The people are jubilant," wrote one Boston man.[34] "Slavery has received a death blow," wrote a New Yorker.[35] "Thank God that he put it in your heart to issue it," wrote J. M. McKim, head of an antislavery group in Philadelphia.[36] One music composer, George Fawcett, of Muscatine, Iowa, was so overjoyed that he wrote a piece about the proclamation, *The Emancipation March.*[37]

Lincoln was encouraged by letters of support from some Southerners. One New Yorker who spent most of his life as a professor at the University of North Carolina told him that a war defined as a crusade against slavery, and not the Southern people, could bring about a North-South reunion when the fighting stopped,[38] and a Virginia man told him that the end of slavery could mean the end of the fighting. "Slavery is not only the cause of the war, but its strength," he said.[39] A man from the border state of Missouri told the president that "It is the noblest [proclamation] yet of the age on this continent and I trust that God may uphold you and keep you in his safe keeping."[40]

There was considerable opposition to the proclamation, though, and it was strong, widespread, and, in places, surly. Most Southerners, of course, denounced it, as Lincoln expected. Jefferson Davis belittled, it and other Southern leaders saw it as a sign of weakness: Lincoln, unable to win the war, had turned to emancipation as a last ditch to drum up Northern support. Southerners were so angry about it that General Benjamin Butler, commander of Union troops in Louisiana, told Lincoln that if the proclamation stood, the state would not reenter the Union for years.[41] Immediately after its release, dozens of secessionists in Kentucky began petition drives to get their candidates on ballots for the November elections in an effort to take their state out of the Union.[42]

But there was fierce opposition in the North, too, much stronger than Lincoln had envisioned. Many newspapers hailed it, such as Horace Greeley's *New York Tribune* ("God bless Abraham Lincoln!"), the *New York Independent* ("God bless you for a good deed..."), and the *Chicago Tribune* ("the grandest proclamation issued by man"). Others opposed it, even the abolitionist *Liberator,*[43] whose editor said it did not free *all* the slaves. Abolitionist leader Gerrit Smith complained that it only offered limited freedom.[44] Other opponents included the *New York World,*[45] which claimed Lincoln had become a radical, and the *New York Evening Express,* which described it as an act of revolution.[46] Many of the leading newspapers in New Jersey, whose corporations had much prewar business with Southern states, opposed it. Even newspapers in Illinois, the president's home state, were against it. "White Men Will Not Be Demoralized by Niggers" read one headline, while another shouted that "Illinois Will Not Be Made a Free Negro Asylum."[47] A Maryland newspaper told its readers that the proclamation would backfire on Lincoln because it would push Kentucky out of the Union[48] and into the Confederacy. Another said it was worthless because the government could not enforce it.

Some believed that by ignoring Congress and issuing the proclamation himself, Lincoln had taken the road to dictatorship. "It is the exercise of despotic power," wrote the editor of the *Indiana State Sentinel*, who added that freed slaves would murder thousands of whites in the Southern states.[49] The editor of New York City's *Evening Express* agreed, calling the president "an abolition military despot" and argued that he had no constitutional power to free the slaves. He also thought what Lincoln did was predictable. "The President has at last done what the New England abolitionists have so long been boring him to do," he said, and added, as did many Northern papers, that freed black slaves would threaten white jobs.[50]

Lincoln received heated letters from Northerners arguing that they had backed a war to preserve the Union, not to free the slaves. The war had changed into a war, a woman told him, "for the subjugation of the South and the destruction of their social system"; she wrote that Lincoln was no longer president of the United States but "head of the abolition faction, warring for the destruction of slavery."[51]

The proclamation had no direct effect on the slaves in the Confederate states, except where the Union army occupied areas of those states and could abolish it, as it did in parts of Louisiana and South Carolina. It had no effect on the lives of slaves in the border states, which it did not cover. Even where it was well received, the edict hurt Lincoln politically because opposition to it in the North was greater than he had anticipated. The combination of the proclamation and the habeas corpus controversy which followed shortly afterward caused Republicans across the North to suffer heavy losses in the elections of 1862, which cost them thirty-four congressional seats (including nine in Lincoln's native Illinois) and control of statehouses in Illinois, Indiana, and New Jersey.[52] States which the Republicans had carried in the 1860 elections—New York, Pennsylvania, Ohio, Indiana, Illinois, and New Jersey—swung over to the Democrats, and New York even elected a Democratic governor. Powerful Republican congressmen such as New York's Roscoe Conkling, and Ohio's John Bingham, and Speaker of the House Galusha Grow were defeated. The Democrats even carried Sangamon County, Illinois, Lincoln's home county, defeating the president's close friend Leonard

Swett.[53] The Republicans managed to keep control of the House of Representatives and the Senate, but the elections enabled the moribund Democratic Party to rebound and once again give the country a strong two-party system.

Lincoln, of course, did not blame the party's crushing reverses on the proclamation—he blamed them on the war—but he knew that freedom for four million slaves had a price far higher than the billions in compensation he had originally proposed. He had risked his party as well as his own popularity in the 1862 elections, and lost.

There were gains. Although the Republicans surrendered many House seats, they increased their representation in New England, the heart of the abolitionist movement, where thousands of new troops would be recruited in 1863 and 1864. The Emancipation Proclamation, combined with the strategic victory at Antietam, seemed to cement the resolve of leaders in Europe to stay completely out of the American war. Lincoln's hope that freedmen and former slaves would fight for the United States would be realized in the spring and summer of 1863 as blacks began enlisting in huge numbers: Over 180,000 would eventually serve in the army. Their presence rejuvenated an increasingly lethargic army. It also gave soldiers in that army, and the public, a new and important reason to fight. The Civil War was no longer a war to preserve the Union, but a war to preserve democracy, a war to rebuild America into a country where all men were equal, a war not only to end slavery, but, as Lincoln would say later at Gettysburg, a war that would bring a new birth of freedom.

The biggest gain of all, in Lincoln's view, was that America was no longer a slave nation. He had given freedom to its four million blacks. They might not be free until their states were occupied, or until the war was over, but ultimately they would obtain their freedom. Lincoln would no longer have to walk past slave markets in the nation's capital, and families would no longer be torn apart and sold off in New Orleans. The overseer's lash would never cut the skin of a black man's back again. The Emancipation Proclamation might have cost congressional seats and popularity in a single fleeting autumn, but it would change America forever.

16

JEFFERSON DAVIS AT WAR: 1862

Jefferson Davis reeled from one military defeat to another from the time of his rain-drenched inauguration to Sunday evening, April 6, 1862. Reports he received early that morning, after he returned from worship at St. Paul's Church, indicated that General Grant's forces had recovered from the first day of a bloody battle near Shiloh church, in Tennessee, and had driven the Confederates from the field, claiming a major victory and inflicting some of the heaviest losses of the war. Davis fretted all day, nervously pacing back and forth on the oversized back porch of the Confederate White House as his children played in the gardens. Varina was at his side, for the reports also carried a heart-sickening rumor that his best friend, his hero, his first general, Albert Sidney Johnston, had been killed there.

The president spent the entire day pushing the reports out of his mind, certain the invincible Johnston, in whom he had such hopes, must be alive. As twilight fell, an official report from Beauregard arrived and confirmed the worst. Johnston was wounded and, not realizing the extent of the wound and being unwisely separated from his surgeon, continued to lead his troops. He fell in an isolated area of the field, and bled to death. Davis was staggered. He broke down and wept shamelessly. "The cause could have spared a whole state better than that great soldier," he told the people trying to comfort him.[1]

The death of Albert Sidney Johnston was only the worst thing that happened to him in the spring of 1862. The year had started off badly and rapidly grown worse. A Confederate force led by General George Crittenden was defeated January 19 at Mill Springs, Kentucky, on the Cumberland River, by Federals led by Union general George Thomas, forcing the first break in the western line of defenses critical to Davis's overall border strategy. Two key forts on the Cumberland, Fort Henry and Fort Donelson, fell to Union troops . commanded by Grant in early February. His demand for the "unconditional surrender" of Donelson won him his nickname of "Unconditional Surrender" Grant. On February 25, Nashville, Tennessee, fell, and Pea Ridge, Arkansas, on March 6. The Federals had dealt a severe blow to the Confederate west, securing the Cumberland and Ohio Rivers, keeping Kentucky in the Union, and opening the door to Tennessee.

Events were just as gloomy in the east. Federals under Ambrose Burnside took Roanoke Island, North Carolina, in an amphibious assault, on February 8, and New Bern, North Carolina, on March 14. The *Merrimack*, the South's ironclad, which had wreaked havoc on the Federal fleet when first launched, was stopped by the North's ironclad, the *Monitor*, on March 9. Fort Pulaski, in Georgia, was captured on April 11 and, in a major setback to the Confederacy, the Crescent City, New Orleans, one of the South's largest and wealthiest, was under attack and would be taken by the U.S. Navy in weeks. Varina's sisters, Maggie and Jane, were in New Orleans as the Federals approached and managed to escape in a pig boat.[2] Joe Johnston's army, which was supposed to hold northern Virginia and intimidate the Yankees whenever it could, was forced to abandon its fortifications at Centreville and retreat.

Lincoln now had large armies in Tennessee, Arkansas, Louisiana, and Mississippi. He had three more armies in Virginia, all within ninety miles of Richmond. His navy was quickly becoming the world's largest, and its blockade of Southern ports was starting to create supply shortages.

There were personal losses for the Davises as well. That spring the Federals invaded Mississippi and overran both Brierfield and Hurricane, and burned Hurricane to the ground. A local Confederate commander set fire to most of the cotton bales stored at Brierfield before the Union troops could commandeer them, and his brother Joseph, who escaped, hid all of Jefferson's books in a nearby warehouse, but the home itself was now occupied by soldiers. Davis's possessions were destroyed or stolen, including the gold-headed cane President Pierce had given him, and his furniture was ripped by bayonets. A private painted on the wall of a porch "This is the house that Jeff built."[3] Davis's beloved Brierfield would soon fall into hopeless disrepair and become unrecognizable. Davis was proud that twenty-three of his slaves took plantation rifles and fired on the Yankees for a few minutes before they surrendered.[4] He wrote Varina that when the war ended he wanted to find and help his former slaves, some of whom returned and worked there as paid laborers.[5] The Davises no longer had a home in Mississippi.[6]

Morale slumped throughout the South as one defeat followed another. Families from Richmond to Montgomery held funerals for their fallen soldiers, who were coming home in coffins in ever growing numbers. Congressmen fumed that Davis's military strategy was not working, the press howled that the army should attack Washington, businessmen declared that England's immediate support was a necessity, and housewives complained of inflation. Newspapers throughout the Confederacy reported that the people suffered from both apprehension and depression and that they were losing faith in the Cause.[7] Many verged on panic, fearing Union troops might smash into the Southern states at any moment, bringing death and destruction.[8] Everybody blamed President Davis.

Jefferson Davis worked hard to be fair in his decisions to disperse armies throughout the Confederacy. He put in long hours in his office in efforts to move armies so that they could protect Southern cities and states threatened in any way by Union forces. Yet no matter how hard he worked to be even-handed in troop movements, he was criticized. He was criticized by editors and politicians for continuing to insist that soldiers from one state fight in another, and not for their home towns. He was accused of losing New Orleans by local politicians following his transfer of local troops out of the city.[9] The people of Texas were furious when he ordered Texans to fight elsewhere. "Texas can defend herself better than the Confederate government can defend her," snapped editor Robert Rhett in a *Charleston Mercury* editorial dripping with sarcasm.[10] The Texans' counterparts in Missouri accused Davis of being "mortally intent on killing the Cause of the Confederate states" there.[11] He was upbraided for requesting too few troops and charged with scuttling the navy before it was born.[12]

Some editors even criticized Davis's idol, Albert Sidney Johnston, calling him a "mechanical and unimaginative warrior" and thus, naturally, a favorite of President Davis. Furthermore they blamed Davis for the misguided orders which resulted in Johnston's evacuation of Bowling Green, Kentucky, in February of 1862, six weeks before his death.[13]

The most influential Southern newspapers pounced on the president. They pressed him to abandon his system of military departments and to send troops where they were needed instead of confining them to geographic areas.[14] They urged him to fire his entire cabinet (the editor of the *Richmond Examiner* said, "This country does not contain many great men, but it certainly [has more] than the present cabinet contains").[15] He was pressured to form a whole new government and to find "active and energetic men."[16] The *Charleston Mercury* said his war policy was "unwise and most disastrous and his conduct of the war weak and incompetent."[17] The British press said he was losing the war.[18] The newspapers blamed him for riding around town on expensive horses while the people starved[19] and even for shutting down the bars in Richmond.[20]

The biggest criticism was that Jefferson Davis had become a dictator. The people had not elected him and he had become a civilian and military tyrant, sending unpopular bills to Congress, vetoing bills the people wanted, and single-handedly running the army.[21] It was a charge that weakened him in the spring of 1862 and undermined the rest of his term.

"We rightfully live under despotism.... Jefferson Davis is our master," charged editor Rhett in Charleston, and added that congressmen and government officials who supported him were traitors. "The political parasites and pimps around him in substance say: Down with discussion! Down with the Press! Down with the people! Hurrah for Jefferson Davis!"[22]

Citizens wrote vicious letters to newspaper editors denouncing his dictatorial attitude. "Will making him omnipotent inspire the people with more enthusiasm or him with more wisdom?" asked one.[23] Many accused him of becoming a king and exceeding the powers of all the American presidents put together and felt he should "give up the notion of being a Washington, Jackson and Calhoun combined, and find his proper level."[24]

Anyone who worked with him or under him was charged with being part of a government which encouraged him to reign as a despot. Congress, which never overrode a veto, was seen as part of the conspiracy.[25] His wife, always more of a realist that Davis, told him frankly after a trip to Augusta, Georgia, in the summer of 1862 that residents there assured her that if Federal troops captured any cities in Georgia, the state would return to the Union and the war would be over.[26]

The president weakened a bit and grudgingly said he had made some mistakes that permitted the Union gains that spring, but like most men who cannot admit they are wrong, Davis had excuses, blaming his generals, his troops, and suppliers.[27] He wrote an Alabama man, "I acknowledge the error of my attempt to defend all the frontier, seaboard and inland, but will say in justification that if we had received the arms and munitions which we had good reason to expect, that attempt would have been successful."[28] Davis told others that if desertions were not so high he could win the war "in a few weeks,"[29] and that he could have won battles the Confederacy had lost if his orders had been followed.[30]

He could never bring himself to admit mistakes and change direction. He was an authoritarian who saw any critic, whether a congressman or a Richmond housewife complaining about the prices of bread, as trying to thwart his policies and undermine the government.[31] He saw all critics who attacked power—his own—as weak because they had no power themselves. In his mind, they were attacking him out of jealousy and could not be trusted.[32]

"Recent disasters have depressed the weak and are depriving us of the aid of the wavering. Traitors show the tendencies heretofore concealed and the selfish grow clamorous for...personal interests," he said of citizens who were profiteering from the war.[33]

He saw all critics as enemies. "The effect of such assaults, so far as they succeed in destroying the confidence of the people in their...government, must be to diminish our chances of triumph over the enemy," said Davis,[34] who could not understand criticism in war.[35]

Davis found it difficult to rally the people in the face of the losses. An appointed leader in a one-party system, he had no public mandate. As a selected, not elected, leader, he derived no power from the people. He had not taken the reins of government backed by a full slate of elected officials. Beyond advocating secession, he had no platform. His cabinet was cobbled together to promote regional harmony, not to promote specific policies with public approval. His administration, named during a period of just a few weeks, was never perceived by the Congress or the people as a government by popular choice deserving their support. Davis also felt he was above politics— he had been all of his life—and would not stoop to build a political machine as president.[36] When events went badly, President Davis had no political party apparatus to help him in Richmond and no operatives in the states, counties, cities, and villages to rally support.[37]

Davis was no revolutionary leader, either. Men who start revolutions to overthrow governments are usually charismatic leaders who combine forceful public oratory with fiercely loyal associations with other political leaders in the rebellion. They are viewed as the personification of the rebellion itself, and middle-level and lower-level politicians within the revolution, and all of the people, see themselves in him and attach themselves to him. Because the people believe in such a leader, all mistakes are forgiven. Few bonded to the serious, long-winded, and uninspiring Jefferson Davis, and nobody believed in him.

The people dared not blame their hard-fighting soldiers, or their generals, for defeat, so they blamed the president. Davis believed that if he succeeded, the South succeeded, forgetting that if he failed, the South failed. He failed to understand that a people does not judge a leader by what happens to him, but by what happens to them.

THE Confederate Congress met in a large ornate chamber on the southern side of the Virginia statehouse. It was a single-party legislative body. Some of its members said they were still Whigs, others still Democrats, and some even called themselves Unionists, but they were in reality the representatives of the secession party. They ran for office in open elections against each other, without the support of parties. Two to five men would run for each seat in a district carved out of their state and represent its residents in Richmond. Several states held conventions to pick their congressmen. Although many had held public office in the past, some were elected simply because they were well known. There was no political opposition to challenge them on policy. Most of the senators and representatives viewed their goals as the preservation of the new country—economically and diplomatically—and the upkeep of the armies. The overwhelming majority of members, in Congresses elected in 1861 and 1863, supported the general program of the Davis government. Of the 106 members of the first House, eighty-two were pro-Davis. The figure dropped to sixty-five in the second Congress. About sixty percent of the senators supported Davis.[38]

The Congress was jolted by angry debates over several of Davis's unpopular proposals, however, and even though they were passed, the arguments helped fan dissent throughout the country as well as undermine the administration. Congress passed hundreds of bills, from tax bills to treaties to local appointments, yet never got around to establishing a Supreme Court, leaving the country without a judicial branch to curb the executive.

It was also a Congress filled with flamboyant characters. Their antics were chronicled in the pages of dozens of major Southern newspapers and relayed from dinner parties in Richmond to riverboat poker games in New Orleans. A weak, sometimes comical and always raucous group, it never earned the real respect of the people. That lack of trust hampered the government from its first days.

Some Congressmen could not wait to be seated to make headlines. John Tyler, the aging former U.S. president, who lived in Virginia, ran against William McFarland for a House seat. McFarland, a banker, was accused of threatening to foreclose home and farm loans on anyone who voted for Tyler. Archibald Arrington and Josiah Turner caused a riot in their election debate in North Carolina, and it had to be halted by police. John J. McRae gave speeches in army camps. Toombs, who quit as secretary of state in July to join the army, decided to get back into politics and ran for one of the two Senate seats from Georgia. He was outraged that he was the *second* senator chosen and that it took five ballots. He refused the seat. At least he made it out of the statehouse alive. W. A. Lake did not. He became involved in a heated campaign debate with his opponent, Henry Chambers, who challenged him to a duel with rifles and killed him.[39]

Others made headlines after they were seated. Senator Henry Foote got into a fistfight with the commissary general during a committee hearing.[40] Benjamin Hill hit William Yancey in the head with an inkwell after Yancey challenged him to a duel.[41] One man became so upset about the low pay of congressmen, $2,760 a year, that in order to save money on laundry he wore the same clothes all week, inducing others to keep a discreet distance. A lady of the evening horsewhipped Senator George Vest. An angry clerk killed his boss just outside the statehouse.[42] Some of their wives created stirs, too, such as Mrs. Louis Wigfall, who demanded that the president, Congress, or *somebody* promote her son to colonel. Many argued long and then, after hours, drank hard: local newspapers complained that numerous congressmen arrived in the statehouse hung over. "Pardon me, but is the majority always drunk?" wrote Senator R. M. T. Hunter of Virginia.[43]

Competent legislators were exasperated with Congress. "I would rather plough and feed hogs than legislate for the Confederacy," lamented Representative Josiah Turner.[44] So were military leaders. General Lee complained to his son that the legislature kept holding up promotions and supplies and asked,

"What has Congress done to meet the exigency, I may say extremity, in which we are placed?"[45] Vice President Stephens called them "children in politics and statesmanship."[46]

While the South's one-party system did not provide for an opposition, an anti-Davis faction formed within months of the first session of Congress, led by Davis's own vice president, Alexander Stephens, something which would never happen in a two-party system. The men in the anti-Davis faction hated the president and did all they could to undermine him. Fifty-nine of them signed a petition protesting Davis's removal of Beauregard as commander of the Army of Tennessee, but Davis ignored them. His opponents fumed. L. M. Keitt, who left Congress in disgust and went into the army, said that "to be a patriot you must hate Davis."[47]

The problem with faction government, rather than two-party government, is that faction government requires no policies. A party in a two-party system wins seats and maintains popularity not by chronic complaints but by offering hundreds of bills suggesting new policies and programs for the government. Its success is determined by its ability to pass these bills, nearly always working in conjunction with members of the minority party. Faction government only results in bickering and pettiness because the only policy is that of the government.

The Confederate Congress quickly descended into political dissension and squabbling. Critics charged that the petty feuds between Davis and Congress prevented important legislation from being passed and argued that in time of crisis a stronger Congress was needed.

"Our public bodies did not seem to realize the fact that they were called together in an emergency requiring the most prompt and vigorous action," wrote an editor at the *Richmond Daily Examiner*.[48] The *Richmond Dispatch* claimed that the legislators worked themselves senseless with little result and passed "bills of no particular interest."[49] A soldier stationed in Richmond put it more bluntly. "Too much talk and too little action," he said.[50]

The collapse of the Congress started with the introduction of President Davis's Conscription Bill in the spring of 1862, which called for the drafting of all Southern men between the ages of eighteen and thirty-five. The bill, however, permitted draftees to buy their way out by paying $200 or more to substitutes who would take their place and granted exemptions to many public officials and to men who owned more than twenty slaves. Opposition to the bill was heated, but Davis insisted on its passage because the Southern armies were outmanned two to one in troops and desertion rates had started to climb.[51] He needed soldiers.

"It was absolutely indispensable; that numerous regiments of twelve months' men were on the eve of being disbanded," he said, and added that there were no new recruits[52] and that if regimental ranks were not filled the South would face "the most disastrous results."[53]

Many congressmen and people in the South felt that a draft—the first in American history—was an intrusion on state and individual rights, for which, they argued, the Civil War was fought in the first place. It was also a draft for the lower classes only, and its introduction began the sneering slogan that the conflict was "a rich man's war and a poor man's fight." Any national government—Jeff Davis's government—that would force young boys into the army in such an unfair system was tyrannical.[54]

Even though the conscription bill passed, many of the men who voted for it used the bill to once again castigate Davis, charging that his incompetent management of the army made the bill necessary. "[It was] caused by the imbecility of the government," said Rep. Thomas Cobb of Georgia.[55]

The notion of a tyrannical government was greatly advanced by Davis's bill to suspend the writ of habeas corpus in February 1862, something Lincoln did without asking Congress as soon as the war began. Davis rammed through Congress three different suspension acts, in February 1862, October 1863, and February 1864, which made many wary that he was trampling on individual rights, and even worse, doing so in secret legislative sessions, which infuriated his opponents.

Davis was adamant about the need to jail troublemakers without trials. "Organized bands of deserters will patrol the country, burning, plundering and robbing indiscriminately," he said, adding that the country should not "be put in peril...for the sake of conforming to technicalities of the law."[56]

Southerners were dismayed by Davis's suspension of the writ, which resulted in the jailing of hundreds of Southerners by army commanders on shaky charges of sedition and disloyalty. How could the South, which had universally denounced Lincoln's suspension of the writ, for many a symbol of his growing dictatorship,[57] suspend individual freedom itself? Newspaper editors denounced Davis and Congress for what they called outright tyranny. "A despot is a despot," thundered Robert Rhett. "The voice of all history, through the vista of ages, proclaims that once surrendered by a people, it [freedom] is gone forever."[58]

Many Virginia and South Carolina editors were bitter that the president, knowing the writ suspension would be controversial, had ordered Congress to meet for weeks in secret sessions in order to dodge criticism by state and local leaders and the press.[59] It was, Southerners charged throughout the Confederacy, another move by Davis to rule as a tyrant, scheming behind closed doors and using the army to do his bidding. As soon as the bill was passed, the president declared martial law in Norfolk and Portsmouth, Virginia, and he placed Richmond and Petersburg under military rule.[60]

It was impossible for the faction which despised Davis to impeach him because they were always a distinct minority, and most did not like Vice President Alexander Stephens either. Sometimes Congress fought back. It put so much pressure on Davis, out of unhappiness with Secretary of War Judah Benjamin, that Davis was forced to fire him, but he then made Benjamin his secretary of state. The Confederate Congress passed a bill to create a general in chief, like the Union army's, and give him control of the army, answering to the president. Davis vetoed this in the same disdainful fashion he vetoed thirty-eight other bills, for he controlled Congress with an iron fist. (Davis was to veto more bills than all the U.S. presidents from Washington to Lincoln combined.)

Davis was often denounced as a liar by congressmen, some of whom also periodically warned that he was a tyrant. His statements about Congress and its members were routinely attacked by representatives in the statehouse. Several congressmen were always of the belief he was their demon, not their savior, even though they knew that without a two-party Congress he could not be toppled.[61] The most vitriolic of these attacks, so defamatory they were not reported in the papers, were made by Davis's old archenemy Henry Foote, whom he once beat up. Despite many efforts by friends, Davis refused to reach any reconciliation.[62] To Davis, an enemy was always an enemy.

It was the attacks by Foote and Alexander Stephens that helped convince the public that although Davis could secure passage of his legislation, he could only do so in a fashion which angered legislators. He was often chided by congressmen for his disdain for conciliation and his reluctance to build coalitions.

Vice President Alexander Stephens was a diminutive, sickly man who had originally opposed secession. As presiding officer of the Senate, he led the attacks on Davis, particularly over his policies on cotton, conscription, and habeas corpus, a role Vice President Hannibal Hamlin, or any U.S. vice president, would never assume. Day after day, whether in speeches in Congress, in the Georgia legislature, or in letters or interviews published in newspapers, Stephens blasted the president's policies, striving to create a government with distinctly separate branches of government and to prevent the president from declaring martial law and instituting military rule. "Constitutional guarantees are above the power of Congress or any officer of the government," Stephens argued,[63] and in a strident set of resolutions to the Georgia legislature said that "the [conscription] act is a dangerous assault on the constitutional power of the courts and upon the liberty of the people."[64]

The vice president disagreed with Davis, but he also felt powerless in the new government. He was, after all, the number-two man in the government, represented the powerful interests of Georgia, and had had strong support for president. Yet Davis ignored him. Stephens was consulted only once or twice after the government moved to Richmond,[65] and he must have resented it. By 1864, he privately called the president "weak, vacillating, timid, petulant, peevish, obstinate" and compared him to "my poor, blind and deaf dog."[66] Of the cabinet and government, Stephens told congressmen that the Confederacy was strong, but that it needed "brains to manage" it.[67] Davis had once again turned a prospective ally into an enemy.

Stephens's attacks were not sporadic. He was just as opposed to Davis and his policies in 1864 as in 1861 and 1862.[68] "He [Davis] is a weak, timid, sly, unprincipled arch aspirant, after absolute power...a sly, hypocritical, aspiring knave," Stephens's brother Linton snapped when asked to describe Davis, and the vice president, while never saying that publicly, probably agreed.[69] The sideshow of the country's vice president battling the president throughout the war was divisive. Southerners trying to win a war felt they were being led by men at each other's throats constantly.

Nor did Davis make any effort to work with Congress. "He regards any question put to him by Congress as a presumptuous interference in matters which do not concern them," said a reporter observing Davis's bills and how they were enacted.[70] He did not socialize with congressmen, hold intimate breakfasts with congressional leaders, go out of his way to land them some patronage, help their friends, laud them in the press, or urge legislation which would help their districts and make them look good—all ways in which he might have won their support. He was always aloof to them, as he was with everyone; congressmen who met Davis were annoyed that he would not look up at them but peered at his desk or a clock. "Few men could be more chillingly, freezingly cold," said Secretary of the Navy Stephen Mallory of Davis's meetings with congressmen.[71]

The president and his Congress soon found themselves in the middle of a vicious game of states' rights. State legislatures, often backed by the press, demanded the right to be the sole arbiters of taxation. Furthermore, they did not believe Congress had the right to draft the citizens of any state, suspend personal liberties, or establish a national bank.[72] State leaders wondered why they continued to fight the war. Was Jefferson Davis not simply waging a war to rid them of one tyrannical national government to replace it with another?

Debate in Richmond over the political issues which had divided the state and national governments and the president and Congress quickly ceased one spring day in 1862. On May 31, hard-riding couriers brought to the Confederate White House the news which everyone had dreaded: the Army of the Potomac had invaded the Virginia peninsula at Yorktown and was on its way to Richmond.

ALL day long, Jefferson Davis, who had sent his wife and family to North Carolina for safety, listened to the sounds of distant cannon and gunfire through his office window. By late afternoon he could take the suspense no more. He carefully loaded two pistols and shoved them into the waistband of his coat. He walked through the front doors of the Customs House at a brisk pace, out under the stone portico, mounted one of his horses and, with his aides, rode to the battlefield, near Fair Oaks, five miles away. Davis rode back and forth so often during that week that the army gave him his own passport to show sentries so he would not constantly be slowed down with checks by soldiers who had no idea who he was.[73]

Joe Johnston and Robert E. Lee had engaged the enemy in one of the many battles of what became known as the Peninsular Campaign. Davis, pistols ready, rode back and forth through the Confederate camps, cheered by the men. He met with Lee and Johnston and others as segments of McClellan's huge, cumbersome army of over one hundred thousand men inched forward. The president wound up in the thick of the fighting, just as he had wished, with shells exploding all around him. Seeing an opening at one side of the field, and unable to find a commander, he regrouped troops and ordered an attack. A few minutes later, with Lee, he raced to the rear as enemy shells hit nearby, blowing up artillery batteries, killing and maiming men, and sending shell fragments flying through the air, some raining down on Lee and the president as they galloped toward safety. Later, he told his wife he was at the front, but he did not describe the real nature of the danger.[74]

As he reached the rear, Davis came upon his foe, Joe Johnston, lying on a stretcher. Johnston had been hit by a bullet in the shoulder and by shell fragments in the chest. Forgetting all the animosity between them, Davis rode over to Johnston, took his outstretched hand, and offered as much comfort as he could, even asking Johnston if he wanted to recover at the White House.[75]

With Johnston wounded, the president turned to Lee, his trusted aide, and within days put him in charge of the army. Davis visited Lee on the lines every day, but he fell ill again in June and was confined to his bed for two weeks.[76] Lee acted as he always did, boldly. He regrouped his forces and, certain that McClellan would tarry, as he always did, attacked with ferocity a few weeks later in the Seven Days battles, pounding McClellan's much larger army with everything he had. The president was with him every day, riding about at the rear of the battlefield, holding meetings and rallying the troops, which the men enjoyed.[77] He even slept on the battlefield with the enlisted men. Twice he was almost killed, once when a house was destroyed moments after he left it and again when, as he tried to organize stragglers, a shell burst in a tree next to him. The day after the striking series of Southern victories, Davis rode around the countryside trying to buy whiskey to help his soldiers celebrate.[78]

Lee drove McClellan off the peninsula, and a few weeks later, Stonewall Jackson defeated the Federals in a series of battles in the Shenandoah Valley, securing a geographic highway for the rebels to move northeast and southwest, striking the Union forces when and where they pleased. In late August, even though outnumbered 75,000 to 48,000, Lee's army, merging with Jackson and Longstreet, defeated Pope and the Federals in a second battle at Bull Run.

Davis, in Richmond, marveled at the sensational turn of events. Just a few months before it had seemed that McClellan would march into Richmond and end the war. Now, thanks to Lee, the Confederates had not only saved the capital, but secured the entire state, driven the Union army out of Virginia, and thrown the Lincoln administration into disarray. In July, John Hunt Morgan made four successful raids into Kentucky and Tennessee. Nathan Bedford Forrest captured Murfreesboro, Tennessee. The Confederate ironclad *Arkansas* held off a fleet of thirty-seven Federal ships near Vicksburg. Davis was now convinced that even though his army was just half the size of Lincoln's, his stewardship of the war and Lee's battlefield brilliance would bring victory.

Davis's confidence in Lee was total. The perfect general for the president, the Virginian completely understood every effective concept of battle; in many ways he adhered to the textbook formulations of warfare. He fought in classic European style, moving his men on interior lines to meet the enemy and moving quickly, much too fast for the enemy to encircle him. Lee wanted to seize cities and towns in the Northern states, just as Davis did, certain that enough cities under Southern control would bring the North to the bargaining table.

Lee was a bold commander, taking chances and running risks, always cognizant that as the underdog, the leader of smaller armies, he had to be wildly innovative to be successful. He would attack when most generals would not, and pressure the enemy at as many points on a battlefield as he could. His losses were high, but no one seemed to mind. He would never hesitate to divide his forces in two, as he did in several key battles, and his daring paid off handsomely. He was never reluctant to ride as close to the fighting as possible, and in many battles was near enough to be shot at and killed. He *was* the commander in the eyes of his men, who would fight for him as hard as humanly possible and follow him anywhere. No other general had the love and respect of his men that Lee did.

The president said of Lee after the war, "with an eye fixed on the welfare of his country, he never faltered to follow the line of duty to the end. His was the heart that braved every difficulty; his was the mind that wrought victory out of defeat."[79]

President Davis and Lee's remarkably close relationship was due to Lee, not Davis. Lee quickly sized up Jefferson Davis, seeing all of his faults clearly. Others, put off by Davis, soon developed difficult relationships with him, but Lee decided the best way to get along with Davis, and to win the war, was to work with him, not against him. Stonewall Jackson, who, like others, feuded with Davis, said that Lee was the only person he knew who fully understood Davis. Lee also understood that to retain influence over the army he had to share power with the president. He did so throughout the war, never pushing to make a distinction between himself as field commander and the commander-in-chief.[80]

Other generals complained to Lee as soon as the war began that Davis had the annoying habit of sending numerous letters and telegrams to his generals, forcing them to respond. Most of his letters were unnecessary, and his questions were vague. The officers considered dealing with them a waste of time, needless work to fill time for an unhappy president. Lee quickly understood that Davis was a man who needed close contact with his generals, right or wrong, and Lee adapted to Davis's style. Throughout the war, the two men wrote or telegraphed each other every single day, sometimes twice a day.[81] They became such close friends that when Lee's fabled horse, Traveler, seemed sick, Davis offered to give Lee one of his favorite horses as a gift.[82]

Lee repeatedly humbled himself in front of Davis, always deferring to the president. The first day he was given command, he cleverly took Davis aside and asked him what he would do if he were the commander. The president, flattered, told him. General Lee nodded and then did what he wanted to do anyway, but acted on some of the president's suggestions so that Davis knew he was contributing. This constant deference to the president, very diplomatically handled by Lee, enabled him to gain Davis's complete support and confidence. For his part, Lee never wavered in his support of Davis, standing by him to the end of the war and in Davis's postwar troubles as well. "Few people could have done better than Mr. Davis [as president]," he told all. The president bickered with every other general in the army, but he never, never argued with Lee. He gave Lee a near free rein to run his army.[83]

Lee was a constant visitor at the Confederate White House, day or night, and one of the few people permitted to meet with the president when he was sick. Lee was the only general permitted to walk into Davis's office or cabinet meetings unannounced.[84]

"He possessed my unqualified confidence, both as soldier and patriot," Davis said.[85] "Lee rises with the occasion...and seems to be equal to its inception."[86]

His faith in Lee unshakable, he then let Lee talk him into a full-scale invasion of the North.[87] Lee knew that Davis was opposed to offensive strikes into the North, and had turned down thrusts by Joe Johnston in October 1861 and Stonewall Jackson in the summer of 1862,[88] but he believed the South had the momentum and that McClellan's army could not beat him. Davis believed, too, in Lee's ridiculous scheme to hand out pamphlets throughout Maryland when he invaded, certain that tens of thousands of residents, when they saw Lee, would take up arms and join the fight.[89]

Lee's invasion went as far as Antietam Creek, Maryland, some sixty miles from Washington. McClellan, who by a stroke of luck had learned of Lee's route, caught him with a larger force and cornered him. Lee managed to escape total destruction because General A. P. Hill, clad in his fire engine red battle shirt, was able to arrive with reinforcements at a crucial hour and because McClellan foolishly held twenty-four thousand men in reserve. Beaten, the Army of Northern Virginia limped back across the Potomac, without pursuit by McClellan.

The defeat did not annoy Davis, who saw the battle as a standoff, which in tactical terms it was, and assumed Lee would recover and return to the field stronger than ever, which he would. What Davis did not know was that the Federals' defeat of Lee at Antietam had changed the course of the war forever. The purported victory, chancy as it was, gave Lincoln the opportunity he needed to introduce the Emancipation Proclamation. It also ended forever any chance of England entering the war. On the morning of the battle, British Foreign Secretary Lord John Russell and Prime Minister Palmerston agreed that if the Union army lost one more major battle, or if the Confederate army was able to invade the North and capture a city, the British government would step into the middle of the conflict, demand a ceasefire, and mediate a peace which would result in two countries. Antietam ended any real British interest in the war.[90]

Confederate troops in the west, a department which gave Davis ceaseless trouble, were unsuccessful in a number of battles in the fall of 1862. Then, in December, the Rebels won a stunning victory at Fredericksburg, Virginia, a victory they never should have had. Union commander Ambrose Burnside believed he could surprise the thin forces defending the city, seize it, and march straight to Richmond. He might have, too, but he botched the entire campaign by taking ten extra days to begin crossing the Rappahannock at Fredericksburg, not only giving Lee time to get there with reinforcements, but allowing him to prepare a murderous artillery barrage which decimated the Federals and drove them back across the river. The Confederates had once again driven the Yankees out of the heart of Virginia. Lee, with Stonewall Jackson, won another major victory. During the last week of 1862, Confederate General Pemberton defeated Sherman at Chickasaw Bayou, in Mississippi, and early reports were that Braxton Bragg had beaten Rosecrans in Kentucky. Jefferson Davis, on a tour of army camps in Tennessee and other states through much of December, arrived back in Richmond a few days after the end of the year. The people of Richmond, who had maligned him for so long, turned out in large crowds to give him a hero's welcome.

The night after Davis arrived at the White House, a large group of well-wishers with a band serenaded him and urged him to give an impromptu speech. The president, smiling and full of confidence from the war news, delivered perhaps the best and most amiable speech of his life, a speech filled with personal passion and goodwill. That night he lost his stiffness, too, and talked in a melodious, lilting, loving voice that no one had heard him use before. Calling the Union troops the "offscourings of the earth," he told the crowd the armies were getting stronger as the war continued, but that recent victories showed that it would not continue long. Joking that Union troops would, indeed, reach Richmond, but as prisoners, he told the people that the South was "invincible" and that the Confederate army was now winning every battle.

Thanking them for such a warm turnout, he promised to spend more time with them and forget former grievances. Then he grinned and walked into the White House, where a small fire was heating up the sitting room. There one of his aides, who had listened to the speech, complimented him on it and told him it was the single finest talk he had ever given. Davis smiled at him and felt the warmth of the fire on his hands. That night he knew that the Confederacy would win the war.[91]

17

ABRAHAM LINCOLN AT WAR: 1863

PRESIDENT LINCOLN ROSE UP from the chair in his White House office, paced the room, stared at the war map on his wall and then left to walk down the hall. He was back in a minute, sat down, frowned, and then got up again, walked to the window, and stared out. He asked everyone who came into the office if they had news from Chancellorsville. None did. He sent messengers back and forth to the telegraph room at the War Department across the street, but still, as the agonizing afternoon wore on, there was nothing but silence from the Virginia forests where the Army of the Potomac clashed head on in terrible and bloody encounter with the Army of Northern Virginia.[1] Lincoln, rubbing his huge hands together, the lines on his face deeper than ever as he shifted from one foot to another, was very upset. "I believe I feel trouble in the air before it comes," he once told his secretary, and today he felt it.[2] "Hooker is licked...Hooker is licked," he muttered to himself as newspaper reporter Noah Brooks moved about the room with him. "He was anxious and harassed beyond any power of description," Brooks said.[3]

The president prowled the halls of the White House all afternoon and finally, shortly after 3 P.M., came back to his office, his face ashen and his body trembling slightly. He handed a telegram to Brooks. He said, "Read it—news from the army." Brooks stopped reading after a few lines, when it was evident that Hooker's army had been routed by Robert E. Lee in one of the greatest defeats of the war, and had barely managed to escape to safety across the Rappahannock River.

Brooks looked up at the president, whom he said was "dispirited and ghostlike." He had never seen a man so shaken. Lincoln turned slightly, clasped his hands behind his back as he always did when under stress, and paced back and forth, inconsolable. "My God! My God!" he muttered. "What will the country say! What will the country say!"⁴

Hooker's army had been on its way deep into Virginia, to take Richmond and end the war. Now it had been chased back over the river, giving Lee free rein to campaign where he wanted. The Army of the Potomac had gone into the battle outnumbering the rebels more than two to one. Hooker's enormous forces had swelled to over 133,000 men, including the largest cavalry units in history and supply trains that stretched miles. But they had been crushed by the brilliant maneuvering of Lee, who daringly split his army in half, sneaked twenty thousand men through a thick forest for a surprise attack, and at one point surrounded the Union soldiers on three sides.⁵ It was not only a catastrophic defeat for the North, but a huge morale boost for the South.⁶

The political fallout from Chancellorsville was immediate. "All is lost! All is lost!" wailed Republican senator Charles Sumner, when he heard the news at the Navy Department.⁷ A Democrat in New York said Lincoln was a donkey in a china shop and that the people had to get him out "or he will smash the crockery." In Missouri, Republicans ordered Lincoln to get rid of all of his abolitionist generals.⁸ Politicians in New Jersey renewed their efforts to have the state secede from the Union.

The press was extremely harsh on Hooker and Lincoln. "Once again the Army of the Potomac, controlled by an imbecile department and led by an incompetent general, has been marched to fruitless slaughter," complained the *New York World*. "Once again tempting fate, the President gave this thrice shattered army to the care of an adventurous soldier...whose chief merit was his proclaimed knowledge of his own incompetence."⁹

The president, again assaulted on all sides, said that although many thought it was a "misfortune" that he had been elected, he *was* the president and intended to perform his duty "according to his best understanding, if he had to die for it."¹⁰

THE defeat at Chancellorsville could not have happened at a worse time. Union efforts to beat Lee and seize Richmond in 1863 ended with Hooker's defeat. Attempts to capture Charleston by sea failed miserably after a fruitless naval bombardment of Fort Sumter. Grant's army was bogged down around Vicksburg. General Nathaniel Banks's move out of New Orleans toward Vicksburg had come to nothing. General William Rosecrans, ordered to capture Chattanooga, sat and waited, endlessly complaining that he should outrank Grant, as Confederate forces there grew.

The winter of 1863 was one of the most demoralizing in Lincoln's life. His generals were under constant attack, even the good ones. Sherman was criticized for his blunders at Chickasaw Bluffs. Grant was castigated for his drinking problems. The editor of the *Cincinnati Commercial* called him "a poor drunken imbecile."[11] Even religious controversy arose when Grant banned salesmen from his camp, calling them "Jew peddlers." Lincoln rescinded the order and rebuked Grant, reminding him that many Jews were fighting in his army.[12] The garrulous Ben Butler, the politician-turned-general from Massachusetts, earned so many enemies in New Orleans by implying that the city's rebel women were all whores that he had to be transferred.

Lincoln was reprimanded daily in the press for not winning the war. "President Lincoln has shown himself utterly destitute of the statesmanlike tact required for dealing with a great people in revolt," said the *Hunterdon* (N.J.) *Democrat.*[13] He was accused of driving the country to bankruptcy with his National Banking Act. "There is no subject so fitted to inspire anxiety as the national bankruptcy and repudiation which loom up in colossal proportions if the House bill shall pass the Senate and become law," said the editor of the *New York World.*[14]

Opposition to the president grew throughout the North with the formation of a half dozen secret societies with names such as the Knights of the Golden Circle, Sons of Liberty, Circle of Hosts, the Union Relief Society, and Order of American Knights, with reported memberships of over one million men.[15] The new draft law, passed in March, met with a considerable opposition. Textile manufacturers throughout the Northeast told the president that Northern speculators were secretly making fortunes buying the embargoed Southern cotton and selling it to them at outrageous prices, and worse, that some of the speculators were Union army officers.

Visitors traveled in and out of Washington, a bustling wartime town of over two hundred thousand people now filled with bars and houses of prostitution. They reported that Lincoln had lost much of his political support. Wrote author Richard Dana, "The most striking thing is the absence of personal loyalty to the President. It does not exist. He has no admirers, no enthusiastic supporters."[16] Samuel Morse, inventor of the telegraph, and now a peace Democrat, turned on him and called him "a President without brains."[17] The editor of an Ohio newspaper, familiar with the Lincoln's seances with mediums, described him as "a victim of spiritualism."[18]

A peace movement had sprung up, and was particularly strong in Lincoln's own Midwest. Farmers there said they were going bankrupt. Because the South controlled the Mississippi River, their normal trade route, they were forced to pay much higher prices to ship produce on railroads and canals. They claimed the high tariffs may have helped eastern manufacturers, but hurt western consumers. Many were staunchly opposed to the emancipation of the slaves, fearful that they would head for their states and take jobs away from whites. The Democratic majority in the Illinois legislature, Lincoln's backyard, demanded that the president withdraw the proclamation and seek an immediate peace conference with Jefferson Davis. Members of the Indiana state legislature refused to meet to appropriate money to the pro-Union government: Lincoln had to loan the state $250,000 in War Department funds to keep it solvent. The president, calling the trouble in the Midwest a "fire in the rear," was so worried about a general fracture there that he authorized Illinois's governor to put troops on alert and to seize the statehouse if the uproar continued much longer.

The peace movement gained ground everywhere, not just in the west. Legislators in New Jersey introduced bills to authorize the state to circumvent the federal government and, on its own, seek peace with the Confederacy. There was also dissension in New York, where Seward had lost his grip. The new Democratic governor, Horatio Seymour, announced that he would oppose any federal efforts to implement the upcoming draft, which he said was a violation of Americans' "most sacred rights,"[19] and that he would oppose "all Lincoln assumptions of power."[20]

A Peace Party, started in 1862, grew in size throughout 1863. It had considerable influence through its leader Fernando Wood, the mayor of New York City, who visited Lincoln frequently at the White House to push for a negotiated peace.[21] There were even whispers of meetings at which the impeachment of the president was discussed.

Lincoln was routinely called an incompetent fool by members of his own party. Washington insiders told their friends back home that besides his wife and Seward he did not have a friend in the world. One said he would not be surprised if the despondent president killed himself.[22]

The biggest unhappiness with the president remained his continued suspensions of the habeas corpus writ and the jailing of administration critics on questionable charges. The vendetta against his critics, carried out by the army, intensified as the winter of 1863 wore on. The army rounded up and arrested two thousand deserters in Illinois. A minister in St. Louis who baptized a baby with the name of a Confederate general was arrested and his church closed. Dozens of newspaper editors were imprisoned for anti-Lincoln editorials, and others were fined, while dozens of newspapers were shut down entirely. The newspaper crusade finally ended when Burnside tried to close down the influential *Chicago Times* and Illinois legislators, many of them Lincoln's friends, protested. Lincoln backed off.

The most controversial imprisonment involved Congressman Clement Vallandigham, who sternly rebuked Lincoln and the administration in a speech in the House in January 1863. He repeated his attacks in May, blasting the president as a tyrant and calling him "King Lincoln." He was then arrested, tried by a military tribunal, convicted, and imprisoned. A storm of protest ensued, with editors, legislators, and even one of Lincoln's closest friends, Supreme Court justice David Davis, telling the president he had gone too far, that a congressman should not be jailed for exercising freedom of speech and should certainly not be tried by the army. The president came under so much pressure, even within his own cabinet, that he ordered Vallandigham released two weeks later and had the army deliver him to the Confederacy as punishment. The congressman quickly made his way to Canada and returned to Ohio several months later.[23]

Lincoln never budged from his belief that as president in wartime he could jail whomever he wanted and close offensive newspapers. "The benefit of habeas corpus may be suspended when in cases of rebellion or invasion the public safety may require it. [The president] holds the power and bears the responsibility of making [decisions]," he told Ohio legislators in 1863.[24] A year later, he aroused even more controversy when he had the army arrest and imprison Lamden Milligan, a Midwest protest leader.[25]

Lincoln insisted that the public must trust him, and, in one of his colorful stories, told one group that he and the government were like a man on a high wire. It is better for people to say nothing and trust that he'll make it across than yell and scream at him, with a hundred different pieces of advice, that might make him fall. "They [government] are doing the very best they can. Don't badger them. Keep silence and we'll get you safe across."[26]

The president had always been a very funny man, and through his first year in office amused everyone who met him. He told those who criticized his humor during a war that mirth was the only thing that permitted him to keep his senses.[27] He stopped telling his funny stories by the spring of 1863, however, and gloom fell over the White House that winter as his old melancholy gripped him again. The poet Walt Whitman, who frequently saw him ride through town, said that he had "a deep, latent sadness."[28] Others said that he no longer slept well at night, walked much more slowly, and smiled less often. The lines on his face seemed deeper, his head tilted downward more often, his body slumped in chairs most of the time. He was sad, angry, frustrated, and unnerved that he had to fight a war on two fronts. "The enemy behind us is more dangerous to the country than the enemy before us," he sighed to a friend.[29]

THE country seemed to come apart after the rout at Chancellorsville, but not the president. Oddly, like the Army of the Potomac, Lincoln seemed energized after the disaster. The president saw it as a turning point, a wake-up call to the army, the people, and himself, to make changes to win the war and reunite the Republic. The president was a new man, White House aides said, and he plunged into the reorganization of the army. Lincoln never stuck with bad generals. He had fired McClellan, McDowell, Pope, and Burnside; he had transferred Banks and Butler. He would soon demote Henry Halleck, his general in chief, in an effort both to streamline operations and to let generals know that when orders arrived they were from the commander in chief, not Henry Halleck. Next, he fired Hooker as head of the Army of the Potomac and transferred him, even as Hooker was on his way to meet Robert E. Lee's Army of Northern Virginia somewhere in Pennsylvania. In his place, he appointed General George Meade, whom he did not know, hopeful that new leadership would produce victory. The president, a civilian all his life, did not know any of his generals, had no obligations to them, and thus could promote and fire them at will—which he did.

Lincoln then turned to his plan to recruit black troops, an option he had created for himself by signing the Emancipation Proclamation. Black leader Frederick Douglass and others had assured him that thousands of blacks would enlist in the army to defend their freedom and to fight for the liberation of those still in bondage. In the spring of 1863, Lincoln began extensive efforts to recruit regiments of black freedmen and newly freed Southern slaves. By late summer, his efforts paid off handsomely. Black troops would not only distinguish themselves in the attack on Fort Wagner, outside Charleston, but fight bravely in Florida, Mississippi, and other theaters, earning praise from whites and pride for blacks. Eventually, over one hundred eighty thousand African-Americans would fight for the Union army—nearly thirty thousand would die—and at times they represented up to fifteen percent of the army. Their presence not only made up for deserters, but spurred in 1864 enlistments of men who no longer minded fighting for blacks who were fighting for themselves. The fighting record of blacks in the army seemed to symbolize a fight for free labor and free men everywhere in the North.[30]

The president would try any stratagem to win a battle or end the war. He never saw himself tied to a concrete plan. Once, after another army defeat, Nicolay wrote his wife that the president shrugged and said, "Well, we'll have to try something else." In the spring of 1863 he invited a wild array of inventors to the White House to showcase gadgets he considered trying for the army. Most were eccentric: hand grenades disguised as White House paperweights, cannons made of brass, and swords so heavy even the muscular Lincoln could barely lift them. He even spent long hours listening to an inventor explain how he could predict when it would rain. He told the president on April 24 that his invention assured him it was certain that it would not rain again in Washington until May 1. The following day it poured. The president told him not to return.[31] There was nevertheless merit to what critics called his childish experiments—one of the inventions he tried out was the repeating rifle, which soon became operational and was a great help to Union forces.

Those forces soon collided with the Army of Northern Virginia at Gettysburg. Lincoln, as always anxious for battlefield news, spent most of his time each day at the telegraph office of the War Department. Close to midnight, July 4, a telegraph came to the War Department, addressed to Secretary Welles, from a newspaper reporter informing him that Meade's army had badly defeated Lee at Gettysburg.[32] The president, who had been lounging in the office all night, his body leaning back in a chair and his long legs draped over the top of a desk, was jubilant. He was so ecstatic that he took the unprecedented step of sending a congratulatory telegram to the Army of the Potomac and then sending copies of it to every major newspaper in the North, where the message was widely read.

[The news] is such as to cover that army with the highest honor, to promise a great success to the cause of the Union and to claim the condolence of all for the many gallant fallen; and that for this, [the president] especially desires that on this day He, whose will, not ours, should ever be done, be everywhere remembered and reverenced with profoundest gratitude.[33]

Three days later, Lincoln was in his office, staring at a map, with pins placed in different areas to designate armies, when Welles burst in to tell him that Vicksburg had finally fallen. The Mississippi was open, and thirty thousand men, Pemberton's entire army, had surrendered. Lincoln's face brightened and, a man there said, his entire body sagged with physical relief. He flung his arm around Welles. "I cannot, in words, tell you my joy over this result...it is great Mr. Welles. It is great!"[34]

Lincoln's enthusiasm was soon muted. The overly cautious Meade had not pursued Lee, as Lincoln hoped. Meade thus missed an opportunity to destroy Lee's army, and end the war, when the Confederate Army of Northern Virginia found itself trapped on the north bank of the Potomac while flood waters made it impossible to cross. The rebels sat there, unmolested, for days while Meade did nothing, and finally crossed over to safety. Lincoln was irate. In a hastily written note he told Meade that "[Lee] was within your easy grasp and to have closed upon him would, in connection with our other late successes, have ended the war. Your golden opportunity is gone and I am distressed immeasurably because of it." Then, as he often did, he slid the letter into a cubbyhole near his desk and never sent it, telling Stanton to send a much less severe telegram.

Privately, Lincoln fumed that the Army of the Potomac had missed a second chance (the first being Antietam) to crush Lee and win the war. The rebels were just sitting there, stranded, and Meade did not attack, he told his son Robert. "If I had gone up there, I could have whipped them myself!"[35]

He did send a letter to Grant, expressing his deepest apologies for not having fully believed in the general's plan to take Vicksburg. Lincoln wrote numerous letters of apologies to people when he believed he was wrong. "I write this now as a grateful acknowledgment for the almost inestimable service you have done the country....I never had any faith...that the Yazoo Pass expedition, and the like could succeed. When you got below [Vicksburg] and took Port Gibson, Grand Gulf and vicinity, I thought you should go down the river and join Gen. Banks; and when you turned Northward east of the Big Black, I feared it was a mistake. I now wish to make the personal acknowledgment that you were right, and I was wrong."[36]

Cabinet members and many government workers had, finally, by the summer of 1863, come to see that their civilian president was a better general than his generals. He had been right to constantly change the leadership of the Army of the Potomac, right to attack armies and not cities, and right to back Grant, without any interference, in his long siege of Vicksburg. "His own convictions and conclusions are infinitely superior to General Halleck's," said Navy Secretary Welles.[37]

THE victory at Gettysburg, despite its high casualties, resulted in driving of Lee out of the North for the second, and final, time. The capture of Vicksburg was not only militarily important—it once again opened the river for transportation of troops and supplies—but a public relations coup, signifying that the Union could beat the rebels in the west as well as the east.

The victories were not just a turning point for the army, but for the president. He was almost giddy about them. Lincoln even wrote a poem, "Gen. Lee's Invasion of the North," which ended with Lee "skedaddled back again." Unfortunately, the good news from the army was followed by bad news in New York. There riots over the proposed military draft, with its proviso that men could buy their way out of it by hiring a substitute, erupted, resulting in one hundred deaths. Democratic newspapers complained that the draft gave the president "complete and unlimited power...over the purse and sword of the nation."[38] Unhappy, but eager to end the controversy, the president carefully decided not to appoint a commission to investigate the riot, which would result in more press coverage and yet another feud with Governor Seymour. He postponed the call-up and amended portions of the draft to end most resistance to it.

Once the draft disruptions settled down, Lincoln went back to the business of directing the army's campaigns, increasing supplies, drafting legislation, supervising the new national currency—the "greenbacks"—and running the government, all with renewed self-confidence. "The Tycoon is in fine whack!" said secretary John Hay.[39]

Lincoln also plunged into the pardoning of men convicted of desertion and other crimes. Desertion rates climbed in 1863 and 1864, and in any one week over eighty thousand men were missing. In 1863 about twenty-four percent of the men in most regiments had deserted.[40] Although most deserters left because they had no more interest in fighting, many did not understand army rules, and others departed to care for sick relatives at home. Some even misunderstood the duration of their enlistment.

Deserters were supposed to be shot, but the president, opposed to shooting anyone, commuted most death sentences: Out of a total of two hundred thousand deserters over four years, just 276 were executed. Lincoln listened to the pleas from fathers, mothers, wives, sisters, and brothers of the men scheduled to be executed and wrote pardons for most of them. One man had deserted to go home to win his girlfriend back from another suitor, who had captured her affections while he was in the army. He was arrested and scheduled to be shot. Lincoln quickly pardoned him, telling the deserter: "When I was young I probably would have done the same fool thing myself." He pardoned just about any soldier whose parents pleaded his case and always, no matter what the circumstances, pardoned boys under the age of eighteen who had lied about their age to get into the army.

Lincoln looked for reasons to pardon soldiers. He told one woman that he was pardoning her brother just because, unlike most petitioners, she did not arrive with a politician. His eyes brightened when he heard that a man who deserted with no grounds for pardon had once been wounded in battle. Lincoln signed the pardon with enthusiasm, telling those present that the Bible said anyone who had shed blood was entitled to the remission of their sins. Another man was guilty of blatant cowardice: he had run from battle and even hid behind a tree. Lincoln pardoned him when he heard he ran and told listeners that this was a "leg case," that "his body was brave, but his legs were cowards and it was the legs that carried him away."

The president pardoned one man because his son Tad heard a tearful story from the man's wife in the hallway at the White House and insisted he do so. He pardoned soldiers at breakfast, lunch, and dinner. He pardoned them late at night. He once woke up in the middle of the night, worried that the wording of his pardon was not clear, walked over to the telegraph office at the War Department and sent a second, clearer pardon. He insisted on going over the complete court martial transcripts of most men scheduled to be shot, and sometimes spent as much as six hours a day just reviewing clemency requests.

He pardoned rebels, too. Lieutenant Samuel Davis's case was clear-cut. The twenty-four-year-old Confederate, a distant relative of Jefferson Davis, was captured as a spy, carrying papers. International and national law mandated the death sentence. Lincoln pardoned him the night before he was scheduled to be hanged, telling the army that international law is always murky. He pardoned a member of the ruthless Mosby's Rangers regiment after a tearful story from the man's wife. He pardoned dozens of men in Missouri prisons scheduled to die with a single order.

Generals wrung their hands at Lincoln's clemency. They told him that the army needed discipline, but there could be none when most deserters were pardoned. Lincoln shrugged. They had their job to do, and he had his. Stanton became so upset with him at one point, and scolded him so severely over his acts of clemency, that Lincoln promised not to sign any more pardons. A few days later he was at it again, pardoning dozens of soldiers scheduled to be shot via telegram—so that he didn't have to sign anything.[41]

PRESIDENT Lincoln looked over the lists of job seekers carefully in the early days of his administration, alert to the names of local politicians and, just as important, newspaper reporters and editors. Hundreds of journalists, many reminding him of their positive coverage of his presidential campaign, sought government positions. Whenever Lincoln spotted a name he recognized, or the name of a newspaper whose coverage was favorable, he put the man on a separate list and tried to find him a government job. He gave journalists some plum assignments, too, such as minister to Switzerland and minister to Italy. That built good feelings between the president and journalists and their papers.[42]

Patronage for reporters was just one of many efforts by Lincoln to build a bridge to the press, just as he had done in Illinois. Lincoln anticipated criticism because newspapers of that era were owned or controlled by the political parties, so that any president would be criticized by papers of the opposing party. But Lincoln also believed that the papers should support the government in wartime. That most of the Democratic papers and some of the Republican papers did not angered him. He felt the shutdowns and jailings were an effective warning to all.

Many newspapers supported the government, such as the *Newark* (N.J.) *Advertiser,* a typical pro-Lincoln paper. Its editor wrote after Lincoln's year-end message to Congress in 1862: "[It] manifests great confidence that his plan would shorten the war, lessen our expenses, save blood and precious lives and restore the national authority and prosperity...."[43]

Lincoln had always tried to think the way newspapermen did. He talked to reporters and editors as often as he could in Illinois and whenever he traveled, always trying to see things as they did in order to gain their support for his policies and himself. He surrounded himself with newspapermen when he took office. He wanted at least one editor in his cabinet, and chose Gideon Welles, former editor of the *Hartford Courant,* as his secretary of the navy. He named John Nicolay, a reporter from Chicago, as his personal secretary so that he could get a journalistic perspective on virtually everything he did.

Lincoln's greatest concern when he took office was that a Washington newspaper would turn on him. He needed the support not only of Congress and the cabinet, but of all the thousands of government workers who lived in Washington—and the goodwill of the tens of thousands of army troops stationed there during the war. If just one Washington newspaper were to be critical of the president—a local paper these people read every day— government employees might be tainted by reading it. Fortunately, all the Washington newspapers were supportive of the Union. Lincoln took no chances, however, bringing John Forney, a Philadelphia editor and former Democrat, to Washington to start a new paper, the *Chronicle.* A paper loyal to Lincoln and the government and boasting a thirty thousand plus circulation, the *Chronicle* built considerable goodwill in the capital for the president.[44] Its funding was a mystery.

He had provided a press car on his train when he made his journey from Springfield to Washington to be inaugurated. Now he encouraged editors to write him with their advice on how to run the government, and hundreds did. He always managed to get copies of speeches to reporters. He would talk to reporters in the White House to complete their stories (always on an off-the-record, background basis) and let them visit him in his office to discuss the war. He offered all the help he could to the Associated Press, whose stories went over the wires to every paper in the country and whose support was crucial. He gave his final draft of the Gettysburg Address to an AP reporter because he knew that way it would reach the most people. The president often went around his generals to supply passes to army encampments for reporters and editors. He frequently invited important editors to White House functions and solicited their advice. In that era editors were deeply involved in politics and had great influence with other political figures. Since many served as state Republican and Democratic chairmen, Lincoln in courting them was helping his own political interests as well as his press relations.

Lincoln read as many newspapers as he could and made certain he read the *Chronicle, National Republican,* and *Evening Star,* all Washington papers, every day. His secretaries put together news and editorial summaries from a dozen major Northern papers each morning and he devoured them. Each morning after breakfast he would ask a White House worker to walk across the street to buy him a newspaper. If he could not find anyone for the errand, Lincoln walked over himself.[45] He grilled job seekers and his hundreds of morning visitors about what was in newspapers they had read that morning. He read every Southern newspaper he could obtain and learned much about the battle of Vicksburg by reading the Richmond papers.[46]

Wary of press reaction to his newspaper shutdowns, he was careful to maintain friendships with editors of important papers, particularly Horace Greeley, the editor of the influential *New York Tribune.* The *Tribune* was not only one of the largest papers in New York City, where Lincoln needed the support of politicians and the financial markets, but had a national edition, sent by rail all over the nation, which gave it a total readership of over a million. Lincoln corresponded with the impetuous and unpredictable Greeley, asking for his advice and frequently inviting him to the White House. Against his better judgment, he even let Greeley go to Canada in 1864 to conduct a useless peace conference with Southern intermediaries.[47] The president wooed Henry Raymond, the editor of the *New York Times* and Seward's man, just as ardently. At one point in 1864 he brought him to the White House for a long discussion of how Raymond would end the war, and proposing that Raymond himself go to Jefferson Davis with the peace plan (that did not happen).

Lincoln always worried about the press. He let many reporters into army camps to write about battles, but he denied passes to those who gave away army plans. He ordered the generals to censor any stories sent to newspapers over telegraph wires in order to prevent the spreading of information about troop movements. The president always wondered about the veracity of stories published in papers. He had read scores of Southern newspapers full of fabricated accounts, ranging from the great Southern victory at Gettysburg to the deaths of half his cabinet members. He himself was burned badly by a story about his visit to Antietam. A report appeared in hundreds of newspapers, attributed to the *Essex Statesman,* that Lincoln had interrupted a solemn tour of the burial grounds there by asking army musicians to play harmonicas and sing frivolous songs. The story was a complete fabrication and, after an investigation, it was learned the *Essex Statesman* did not exist.[48]

Lincoln's problems with the press seemed minimal in the fall of 1863, as the army and navy continued to triumph. The navy, under Welles, further tightened the blockade the Southern ports, depriving the Confederacy of supplies of medicine and weapons. The Union army suffered defeats, as at Chickamauga, Georgia, but it won more battles than it lost. Lincoln's avid recruitment of black soldiers paid off handsomely that summer and fall, as black regiments distinguished themselves in battles throughout the country. General Rosecrans, despite his disputes over rank, managed to hold Tennessee and Kentucky for the Union. Crafty Confederate guerrilla leader John Hunt Morgan was finally captured July 26, 1863, near Lisbon, Ohio.

Lincoln's confidence in Stanton, whom he left alone in the running of the War Department, succeeded, too. When it seemed that the Union might lose Chattanooga because of insufficient forces, Stanton engineered a near miracle by managing to transfer thousands of troops from Virginia to that city in just seven days by railroad cars, insuring victory. Lincoln smiled, too, when he learned that in the middle of July, in an incident which had no relation to the war, the *Wyoming,* under David McDougal, had fired on and sunk several Japanese ships, and destroyed a number of shore batteries, as the ship broke through a blockade outside of Yokohama, imposed in a trade dispute, giving the United States its first victory over Japan.

The victories in the fall, and at Gettysburg and Vicksburg, had helpful international repercussions. Seward and Charles Francis Adams, with Lincoln's prodding, pushed the British government to pressure British shipyards not to complete work on two Confederate ironclads. The British, now optimistic that the Union would win the war, ordered the work stopped and the ships seized. Everything seemed to be going right for the president.

Success came at an opportune time, too, because critical gubernatorial and legislative elections were being held in most Northern states in early October. Everyone looked to them as a barometer of the public feeling on the war and the president. Most crucial were the elections in New York and Ohio. New York was important because Horatio Seymour had become a Lincoln foe, and the summer draft riots there had alienated thousands of voters. Ohio was even more important because the controversial Clement Vallandigham had been nominated by the Democrats to run for governor, with substantial backing, in an effort to win the statehouse and to embarrass the president.

This time, unlike 1862, Lincoln worked with local Republican Party bosses to win the elections. He met with as many people from the party as he could, all from different states, to gain a consensus on policy.[49] The president and his operatives merged Republicans and War Democrats (members of the Democratic Party who strongly supported the Republican administration's handling of the war) into a "Union" ticket, which replaced the "Republican" column on the ballot, in an effort at broad-based conciliation to defeat the Democrats. The president also permitted General Burnside to declare martial law in Kentucky and jail several Democratic candidates. He worked with Stanton to allow Pennsylvania soldiers to go home to vote and authorized a two-week vacation for all federal government workers from Pennsylvania, so they could return to cast their ballots, certain that large percentages of soldiers and workers would vote Republican. He urged all the friends he had in Ohio to work for the Union candidate, John Brough, and asked Stanton to send Ohio troops home to vote. Lincoln not only supported campaigning by Treasury Secretary Chase, a former Ohio governor, to help Brough, but asked the Republican governors of Illinois and Indiana to stump for the Ohio candidate as well.

The president had his hand in every single state election, making shrewd and sometimes brilliant political decisions. He persuaded Senator William Sprague, former Democratic governor of Rhode Island, to campaign for his Union ticket, headed by a radical Republican, and the Unionists captured the Rhode Island state house. Unable to come up with a strong Republican or Union slate in Kentucky, Lincoln cobbled together what he called a "Union Democratic" ticket, with radical Republicans and War Democrats running together; it captured five congressional seats. In California, Lincoln supported a Union ticket which had Democrats running for governor and lieutenant governor and Republicans running for all other offices. It won.

The radical Republicans, far more intent on harsh measures toward the South and more freedom for former or newly emancipated slaves, were enemies, too. In some states the president backed Union tickets to defeated radicals in his own party. In Maine Lincoln and his campaign aides put together a Union ticket to defeat Governor Abner Coburn. Perhaps the political coup de grace was his decision to have Stanton talk New Hampshire's popular Colonel William Harriman into leaving the army to run for governor as a Union man against both a Peace Democrat and a Republican in order to draw enough votes away from the Democrat, holding him below 50 percent of the vote and forcing the election into the state legislature, where the Republican won.[50]

Lincoln had worried over the elections. The Republicans had suffered large losses in the 1862 elections. If that trend continued, it could mean the loss of the House, Senate, and White House in 1864 and a negotiated settlement to end the war and establish the Confederacy as an independent nation. If the voters responded well to the victories at Gettysburg and Vicksburg and elsewhere, as he hoped, it would not only boost the Republicans, but bolster the prestige of the president and give him far more power and freedom to prosecute the war.

"I'm more nervous about these than my own in 1860," he told Welles the day before the elections. He had no reason to worry. The people not only voted as he predicted, but gave the Union ticket landslide victories in many states. Union tickets swept to victory in nearly seventy percent of the legislative districts in New York State, delivering a damaging blow to Seymour. Republican Andrew Curtin was reelected governor of Pennsylvania. The Union coalition was victorious in most legislative races in Indiana and Iowa.[51] Lincoln was gratified that over ninety percent of the absentee soldier vote went to the Union ticket, and thrilled that his old nemesis Vallandigham was trounced in Ohio, buried under a hundred thousand vote avalanche (Lincoln's candidate captured sixty-one percent of the vote in Ohio).[52]

"The President is in good spirits and greatly relieved," said Welles the day after the returns came in.[53]

LINCOLN's decision in 1860 to install his party rivals for the presidency in his cabinet was a master stroke. Though Republican congressmen, senators, and state officials opposed him, the cabinet stood with the president. Its members publicly supported everything he did and showed a tremendous solidarity, which strengthened the presidency. Lincoln also had great support from Vice President Hannibal Hamlin, who never criticized the president and maneuvered his bills through Congress. Hamlin urged Lincoln to introduce the Emancipation Proclamation, and vigorously championed it. He later urged the president to recruit black troops, bringing his own son and some of his friends to the White House to volunteer to lead black regiments. When Lincoln was floundering politically in the winter of 1863, radical Republican leaders offered Hamlin the presidential nomination in 1864; he angrily turned them down and told them to support the president. The White House never had to worry about the loyalty of the vice president.

Nor did Lincoln have to worry about the economy. Industry was booming throughout the Northern states. Europe experienced bad harvests in 1861, 1862, and 1863, but harvests in the United States set records. American farmers were able to export millions of bushels of wheat and corn to Europe, reaping considerable profits. Between 1850 and 1860, railroads in northern states exploded in size, increasing their total track from 9,000 miles to 30,000 miles as their investment in new track, equipment, and labor grew to nearly $1 billion by 1861, and over $750 million of it in the previous ten years and realized huge profits throughout the war. The Erie Canal, completed in 1825, did record business. Steamship lines, especially those which leased vessels to the navy, made enormous profits. The iron industry was at full employment, with forges and rolling mills running at capacity. The shortage of cotton, due to the Southern cotton embargo, meant a record demand for woolen goods, and the wool and textile industries prospered.[54]

One of the major reasons for the surge in the Northern economy was the war itself. The army purchased 7,892 cannons, 11,787 artillery carriages, four million revolvers, one billion bullets, one billion percussion caps, fourteen million cannon primer and fuses, two million rounds of artillery ammunition, twelve million artillery projectiles, twenty-six million pounds of gunpowder, ninety million pounds of lead, and over two million uniforms. Every shipyard in the North was fully employed from 1861 to 1865 in building new vessels for the navy.[55]

The departure of men for the army also brought previously unemployed women into the workforce. At times, nearly thirty-three per cent of all Northern workers in any industry were women. There was an eighty percent inflation rate by 1865, but full employment and rising wages—despite some small strikes—more than made up for that. The northern half of the country was more economically prosperous than at any time in history.[56]

The confident Lincoln plunged back into legislative politics right after the elections, trying to build upon the congressional coalition he forged in the spring of 1861. The Republican Party had complete control of the House and Senate, and the president had no trouble with the passage of any bills connected to the war or the eradication of slavery, the party's signature issues.[57] He often ran into roadblocks with other bills, however, because of the overall composition of Congress.

Ordinarily, a president deals with Republicans and Democrats, but Lincoln had to work with four distinct groups. His own party was divided into the radical Republicans, who were hardliners on emancipation and a harsh reconstruction, and moderate Republicans, who also backed antislavery measures, but preferred a softer reconstruction and leaned toward conciliatory policies toward the South to end the war early. The radicals represented about sixty percent of the Republicans. The Democrats were also divided, half War Democrats, supportive of most of the president's policies, and Peace Democrats, who favored an early end to the war by any means. Although the Democrats stuck together on most measures, the Republicans often disagreed among themselves, and Lincoln had to gingerly woo the four different groups to pass his bills and maintain support for his war policies.

He was able to do so because he was a shrewd politician. He had worked successfully with different factions in the Illinois legislature. He was working with an argumentative Congress, but a professional one. While there were many brand-new faces because of the Republican sweeps in the 1856, 1858, and 1860 elections, nearly seventy percent of the legislators, although not national figures, had spent years working in state legislatures. They all knew the rules and they all understood the game.[58]

Lincoln politicked hard. He befriended Seward, who knew everybody, as soon as he arrived in Washington. Through Seward the president became close to Senator Charles Sumner of Massachusetts, head of the Foreign Relations Committee, and Sumner kept the Senate and House in line for Lincoln in his critical dealings with England throughout the war. The president invited dozens of senators and congressmen to the White House for parties, receptions, and afternoon talks. He lobbied them alone or in groups, always trying to persuade them that what was good for the country was good for them. He never balked at "emergency" visits by large delegations of congressmen upset about one thing or another and, while often doing little or nothing about their specific complaints, made each feel that he was genuinely interested in his concerns. He socialized with them, too, often taking Sumner to plays and enjoying music concerts with others. Lincoln constantly cajoled one legislator to convince another to change his vote. He made certain that their sons were given army commissions or put in government jobs. He consulted with them on federal patronage in their states.

Lincoln was almost always able to put together a coalition of radical and moderate Republicans to pass a bill. If that did not work, he forged the moderate Republicans and War Democrats together; if even that didn't work, he would mix elements of radical and moderate Republicans and War Democrats. His renaming the Republicans the "Union Party" in the 1863 elections meant that he would support and fund Democrats running on the coalition Union ticket, earning the loyalty of all those elected. To win Lincoln's bipartisan backing, the Democrats often refused to nominate antiwar candidates.[59] Lincoln's coalitions with loyal Democrats helped him pass dozens of pieces of important legislation, including the National Banking Act, which created a string of federal banks and shifted banking responsibility from the states to Washington; the Legal Tender Act, which created permanent government bill money ("greenbacks"); the Morrill Act to permit states to use federal land for colleges; a bill to construct a transcontinental railroad; numerous tariff bills to maintain high prices on imports to protect American industry; and bills to promote telegraph, road, and bridge construction, and river and harbor improvements. These bills together not only helped boost the Northern economy and open the door to western expansion, but dramatically changed the role of the federal government, giving it considerably more power and influence.[60]

When all else failed, the president resorted to simple "horse trading," promising congressmen whatever they wanted in exchange for their votes on something he wanted. Three votes short of passage of a bill to bring Nevada into the Union, he had Richard Dana call in the three recalcitrant congressmen and to offer them anything they wanted, including comfortable government jobs, in exchange for their votes. Nevada became a state a week later.[61]

The president, who had spent so much time alone in the winter of 1863, became more social after the elections. He hosted more receptions, traveled about town more, attended the theater more often. One of his most enjoyable nights was attending *The Marble Heart,* starring John Wilkes Booth.[62]

THE president had agreed to speak at the dedication of the national cemetery at Gettysburg on November 19, 1863. His secretaries enjoyed the train ride up from Washington with "the tycoon." Lincoln was engrossed in his stories most of the way, smiled at the hundreds of people he saw, greeted the conductors, and graciously accepted a bouquet of flowers from a little girl. Everyone he met seemed genuinely glad to see him, and he was warmly welcomed at Gettysburg when his train chugged into the small station shortly after 5 P.M. Nothing made him happier than a telegram from Stanton handed to him by a man at the station, which informed him that his son Tad was feeling much better. The president almost canceled the trip that morning when his wife, hysterical, insisted he remain home in case Tad, too sick for breakfast, became violently ill.

Lincoln had finished writing half of his address at the White House, spending considerable time on it. The dedication ceremony was the perfect time to redefine the struggle for the people. Northerners' view of the president, the elections showed, was considerably better since the victories at Vicksburg and Gettysburg. Lincoln was now dealing from a position of strength, not weakness. The reflective Thanksgiving and Christmas seasons were on their way, followed by the winter hiatus in the war. Gettysburg was the time and place not only to remind the American people what the war was about, but why it had to be fought to a conclusion in order not only to restore the old nation, but to bring about a new one.

The president, looking very awkward on his horse, a black mourning band for his son Willie still around his stovepipe hat, rode to the cemetery with the other dignitaries, and then sat through a two-hour oration by Edward Everett. As he rose to speak, a photographer tried to set up his equipment for a photo. "Four score and seven years ago..." he began, and launched into his two-minute speech as thousands listened, expecting another long address.

The carefully crafted speech was designed to celebrate the Union army's victory over Lee and the Army of Northern Virginia in July and to prepare the way for ultimate victory, but it was also constructed to let the country know that the war had evolved into more than a conflict to restore the Union. Lincoln reminded the crowd that the nation was older than the Union, that it was born with the signing of the Declaration of Independence in 1776, when the Founders promised that every man had an even chance. He never used the words "Union" or "Confederacy," but used the word "nation" five times to remind people that, as he had insisted for nearly three years, this was a struggle for America, not for the North or the South.

"Our fathers," Lincoln continued, "brought forth upon this continent a new nation, conceived in liberty, and dedicated to the proposition that all men are created equal." The Emancipation Proclamation and the appearance of tens of thousands of blacks in Union uniforms, engineered by the president, had expanded the goals of the war to include the elimination of slavery and the equality of all men (a complete democracy). The presence of hundreds of thousands of free white men fighting for the Union alongside those black soldiers recalled and underscored the Republican slogan of the 1850s—"Free Labor, Free Soil, Free Men"—and supported Lincoln's contention at Gettysburg that the war had taken several new turns. It was now a war for racial equality, a war for free labor, a war for free market economy, and a war for a reunited, indivisible country in which all men, north and south, black and white, were equal. The United States could no longer be a nation of Northern and Southern political factions, but a nation "under God" with a government "of the people, by the people, for the people."[63]

The war, Lincoln told anyone considering a peace settlement, was not going to end in a stalemate. The president would not let it end until the Union had been restored, the slaves permanently made free, and the country given a "new birth of freedom."[64]

The tentative applause from the crowd made Lincoln believe the speech had failed,[65] and so did the initial reaction of newspaper editors, who buried it in the interior pages of their daily publications and gave most of their attention to Everett. The two minute, 272-word speech was so powerful and moving, however, that by the end of the week hundreds of northern newspapers were printing it in its entirety on their main news pages and editorial writers were praising it. Many of the newspapers received their copies of the address from the Associated Press, the national wire service. The wire service had the speech because Lincoln made certain of it: he hand-delivered a copy to one of their men at Gettysburg. In his address, Lincoln was speaking to the people, the politicians, and the newspaper editors, asking them to remember his words in everything they did. Gradually, over the following weeks, most Northerners grasped the meaning of the speech, applauded its beauty and eloquence, and, for the moment, agreed to fight on.

The speech at Gettysburg was one of Lincoln's rare public speeches. The president, perhaps the best public speaker in the United States, with the possible exception of Seward, was reluctant to make public appearances or deliver speeches, even though he had been very successful in speaking in the past. He turned down numerous requests to speak and had his annual messages to Congress read for him. While he wanted to adhere to the presidential tradition of avoiding public speeches, he had other reasons as well. Any public speech, no matter how good, would bring down the wrath of Lincoln's Democratic newspaper critics—half the editors in the country— and begin new controversies. Any public speech might be misunderstood and misinterpreted. The president might slip in a public address and, given his military knowledge, inadvertently tip off military plans to the South. He also knew the dangers of overexposure, and so spoke infrequently and issued rare statements in order to maximize the impact of what he did say.

This tactic worked. Lincoln's very few letters to his troops, such as his eloquent thanks for their sacrifices in the Fredericksburg disaster, were printed in newspapers across the North. His response to Horace Greeley's editorial on the war, in which he said he would do anything to end the war, was not only read by Greeley's readers, but reprinted and read by millions of others. His oft-quoted note to Mrs. Lydia Bixby, the Massachusetts mother who was said to have lost lost five sons in the war, was also extensively reprinted. It was a fine example of Lincoln's ability to be brief and yet touching. "I feel how weak and fruitless must be any words of mine which should attempt to beguile you from the grief of a loss so overwhelming. But I cannot refrain from tendering to you the consolation that may be found in the thanks of the Republic they died to save...the solemn pride that must be yours, to have laid so costly a sacrifice upon the altar of freedom."[66]

He was invited to his hometown, Springfield, in September 1863 to deliver an address, but could not go. Instead, he asked a friend to read, out loud and "very slowly," a speech he wanted delivered. It was another masterpiece. The president defended all of his policies and then, in a region by region summary, discussed the valor of soldiers in the army and applauded the support of the people. "Thanks to all," he said. "For the great Republic—for the principle it lives by, and keeps alive—for man's vast future—thanks to all."[67] Most Northern newspapers carried the speech verbatim, and the Republicans printed several hundred thousand copies. Nearly every Northerner read it in some form.

In his first inaugural address Lincoln had pleaded for the Union with great eloquence, asking everyone to remember the "mystic chords of memory" which held Americans together. In his message to Congress in 1862, he told the people in rich prose that "We cannot escape history....We shall nobly save or meanly lose, the last, best hope of earth. Other means may succeed; this could not fail. The way is plain, peaceful, generous, just—a way which, if followed, the world will forever applaud and God must forever bless."[68] And at Gettysburg he had clearly and precisely defined the struggle and the search for a "new birth of freedom."

President Lincoln, in all his public speeches and published letters, managed to clearly explain exactly what the war was about, what people were fighting and dying for. By explaining it to the populace, he enabled them to explain it to themselves. By believing in his goals so strongly himself, he made it possible for them to believe in them, too.

Writing in his diary on New Year's Eve, 1863, Gideon Welles was prophetic as to the coming impact of the events of the previous turbulent year. "The President has well maintained his position and under trying circumstances acquitted himself in a manner that will be better appreciated in the future than now."[69]

18

"ASSASSINATE DAVIS"

GENERAL AUGUST WILLICH was thin and weak. His new uniform did not fit him well and his face looked drawn and tired. Everyone who noticed him as he strode through the corridors of the White House on his way to meet President Lincoln on the morning of May 8, 1863, looked more than once. He looked like a man at death's door. Willich had been one of thirteen thousand Union prisoners of war incarcerated in dreary, badly run camps and jails in Richmond, including Libby Prison and Belle Isle, where hundreds of them had died. Willich had been freed in an exchange of prisoners in early May. Yet he was not in the White House to tell Lincoln about his captivity, but what he had seen and learned in the capital of the Confederacy.

The fifty-four-year-old general, sitting ramrod stiff despite his pain, told Lincoln, who slumped casually in his office chair, that while he had been imprisoned he was startled to see Union cavalry led by General George Stoneman, sent southward to stir up trouble in the Richmond area while the battle of Chancellorsville was being fought, just outside the city limits. Stoneman's men, Willich told the President, had come within two miles of the heart of the Confederate capital and been seen by dozens of prisoners of war before being chased by small Confederate forces.[1]

Lincoln, shifting his body in the wooden chair, listened carefully to the general's story. He knew all about Willich and had enormous respect for him. The general was the son of a veteran of the Napoleonic wars in Europe. A former officer in the Prussian army, Willich had fled Europe after taking part in the unsuccessful revolution of 1848. Arriving in America, he worked as a land surveyor and then newspaper reporter before joining the Union Army. Willich had moved swiftly up the ranks to general by virtue of a steady string of victories.[2] He was a capable general and when he said Stoneman and his men were so close that prisoners could see them, Lincoln believed him.

Willich explained the dreadful conditions in the Richmond prisons at length. He then reported to Lincoln on the spare forces defending Richmond. Willich said a well-planned cavalry raid on the Confederate capital could destroy buildings and capture prisoners at will. As Willich talked, Lincoln's face began to brighten. As usual, the president's mind was moving on several different levels at once. Why not, he thought suddenly, as he registered Willich's experienced analysis of the defenses of Richmond, send a small unit of swift cavalry raiders into downtown Richmond to kidnap Jefferson Davis and other Confederate leaders?

General Willich was not alone in his plea for a surprise attack on Richmond. Another paroled Union general gave an interview to a reporter from the *Philadelphia Evening Bulletin,* published the same day Willich saw the president, and told him that cavalry could have "bagged the whole administration, and set Union prisoners free."[3]

Numerous prisoners returned from Richmond describing the vile conditions there to reporters, prodding dozens of newspapers to urge some kind of attack on the Southern capital to free the prisoners.[4] It was reported that over forty Federals a day were dying in Richmond army hospitals.[5] Other prisoners, reports said, simply starved in the prisons, some of them little more than converted warehouses, and would be found dead in the morning by their cellmates. Word of the Confederacy's atrocious treatment of prisoners spread throughout the army and, via the press, to the Northern cities. Northerners became extremely upset about the misery in the prison camps. (Meanwhile, Southerners complained accurately that Northern prisons, such as that at Elmira, were just as pathetic.) The camps at Richmond offered easy targets for critics, in the army, the government, and the public, because they were in the rebel capital, and only ninety miles from Washington, D.C.

Lincoln, of course, was appalled by the reports. General Neal Dow brought him a letter addressed to him, smuggled out of a Richmond prison, which described in harrowing detail how men were dying daily. Now, for the first time he knew that the prisoners in Richmond were not as heavily guarded as everyone had thought. Willich told him that a quick cavalry raid might free thousands of prisoners, after which a simple rescue operation might get most of them out of Richmond and, moving them at night along well-known escape routes, through Confederate and Union lines to Washington, where safety and, for those in need, large and sanitary hospitals awaited them.

But it was Jefferson Davis whom Lincoln was after. Capturing the president of the Confederacy seemed simple, Lincoln thought, as he finished with Willich that morning. If the defenses were so weak, a cavalry squadron could race into Richmond by night, open up the prisons, and perhaps set any military building they found on fire. Richmond was a comparatively small city. The raiders could take advantage of the chaos, rush Davis's mansion near the James River, and capture him. President Lincoln was so obsessed with the idea that he wrote Hooker that same afternoon, telling him about Willich. "He says there was not a sound pair of legs in Richmond, and that our men, had they known it, could have safely gone in and burnt everything & brought us Jeff. Davis."[6]

Lincoln was open to any and all ideas on how to end the war. He had had Seward talk to peace commissioners before Sumter. He had listened to peace overtures from Northerners and Southerners. He had offered to buy all the South's slaves to end the war. The idea of kidnapping Jefferson Davis as yet another means to end the conflict appealed to Abraham Lincoln. The capture of the enemy's president would be an enormous political and psychological blow. Davis could be bartered for a ceasefire. He could be tried for war crimes in the hopes that the South would sue for peace. His capture would be a symbol that the South was collapsing. How could any Southern city hope to hold out if its very capital had been raided and burned? How could the Confederate armies protect their states and citizens if they could not even protect the president?

There was a larger reason why Lincoln was eager to capture Davis, however. Jeff Davis had become his own secretary of war in addition to being commander in chief. He had his fingers in every piece of the South's military pie. He controlled all its campaigns, approved all its attacks, coordinated all the retreats, and directed all the armies in all the regions of the Confederacy. He made every promotion. He also controlled all the military's finances. He was so involved in running the army, had usurped so much power, that his removal would throw the war effort into chaos. The South's best generals, such as Lee, could fight on with some success without him, but the others would flounder. Davis had refused to name Lee or anyone else general of the army—he himself was the unofficial general of the army. There was no one to pick up the reins if Davis was taken. The Confederate armies might well collapse, and the war would end.

What must have struck Lincoln about the idea was how simple and how cheap it could be. He did not need the Army of the Potomac, its one hundred thousand men, miles of costly supply trains, and wagonloads of generals. He didn't need a spring offensive, nor millions of dollars. All he needed to snatch Jefferson Davis was a few hundred good men, a little surprise, and a bit of luck.

There was ample precedent for capturing civilians. Union armies in the west, particularly in Missouri, where allegiances were divided, often captured civilians who were thought to be Southern sympathizers, frequently in retribution for the capture of Northern sympathizers. Union commanders routinely ordered the arrest of noncombatants, often indiscriminately. General Stephen Hurlbut ordered home guards in Hannibal, Missouri, to kidnap five prominent secessionists in the area, he didn't care who, in retribution for the capture of a Union officer.[7]

The idea stuck in Lincoln's mind, but he was unable to do anything about it for months. The Confederate secret service picked up rumors of two Union attempts to attack the Richmond prisons and release prisoners in the winter of 1863. After alerting the public, Jefferson Davis quickly increased and solidified the defenses around the Southern capital. By January of 1864, however, spies were routinely reporting that the defenses around Richmond were again weak, due to high levels of Confederate desertions. At the same time, spies reported ominous rumors that the Confederates, again fearful of a raid on their capital, were planning to take all thirteen thousand prisoners out of the city and put them in a hastily designed and newly built prison in Andersonville, Georgia. Union generals told Lincoln that no prison could hold that many men; they predicted that thousands of northern POWs would die at Andersonville.

In mid-January, General Isaac Wistar, hearing of the reports on the weak defenses and the plans to move the POWs, suggested to his superior, General Ben Butler, that a cavalry raid might not only set the prisoners free, but also give troops a chance to burn Richmond to the ground, which would be a grave psychological blow to the South. Butler accepted the idea and sent it up the chain of command. Eventually the suggestion reached first Stanton, then Lincoln.

The president jumped at the idea. After eight months, there was another opportunity to kidnap Jefferson Davis. The same elements were in place—weak defenses, solid intelligence, and surprise—and this time there was also a real chance to stop thirteen thousand Union soldiers, many already quite sick, from being moved to Andersonville.

Butler was summoned to Washington on January 19, where he explained his plan to Secretary of War Stanton and General Henry Halleck. The next morning he had a long meeting with President Lincoln at which the plan was discussed again, although the president's aides told the press it was a routine meeting about prisoner exchange. Lincoln must have approved Butler's plan to kidnap Davis, for mysterious things began to happen. Suddenly, Baker's Rangers, an elite cavalry force retained exclusively at Washington for the protection of the capital, and under the direct command of the president, were ordered to ride with Wistar. Suddenly, for no apparent reason, General John Sedgwick received orders to begin decoy demonstrations against Lee's army in Virginia, in order to draw Lee's men away from a route between Washington and Richmond. Simultaneously, Horace Greeley, who took great pride in scooping all the other New York newspapers on military stories, received an exclusive letter from his friend and Republican politician James White, who reported Wistar was going to sneak in to Richmond, burn the city, rescue the POWs, and try to capture Jeff Davis. Greeley hid the letter in his desk drawer.[8]

Wistar and his men began their ride toward Richmond on Saturday night, February 6. Wistar was carrying direct and explicit orders from Butler to capture Davis. Butler had given Wistar three goals: He was to free the prisoners; destroy public buildings, arsenals, the Tredegar Ironworks, and railroads; and "capture some of the leaders of the rebellion....If any of the more prominent can be brought off, I believe a blow will be given to the rebellion from which it will never recover."[9] White's note to Greeley had been more specific. He said Butler told him the target of the raid was Jeff Davis.

Wistar had no doubts about the importance of his mission. He was taking men right into the capital city of the Confederacy on a raid not only to free as many prisoners as he could, but to torch the town and kidnap the president of a country. He hoped for little resistance and total surprise, but was so fearful of heavy casualities that he even ordered an additional twenty stretchers for all the men he expected to be killed and wounded in the battle ahead.[10]

Wistar and his men did not get very far. The bridge over which they planned to cross the Chickahominy River was heavily defended by Confederates, and scouts found no nearby areas suitable for fording by cavalry. Wistar, with no practical options, and fearing now that the city was even better defended than the river, engaged in a minor skirmish, then turned around and went home, his mission a complete failure.[11]

The raid received extensive publicity in Virginia, where Richmond newspapers had solid information on its objectives. A reporter wrote that intelligence delivered to the Confederate army had predicted a raid aimed at freeing prisoners, burning buildings, and seizing officials. The only difference between the reports and the actual orders was the newspapers' claim that the key goal was not to kidnap Davis, but to murder him. One headline read: "Discovery of an Alleged Plot to Liberate the Prisoners and Assassinate the President."[12]

The failure of the raid—and the rather accurate information about it published in Richmond newspapers—enraged Ben Butler, who was certain that the Confederate secret service had received its information, and leaked it to the press, from somewhere within the Union Army. Butler believed that Southern agents had been tipped off by a certain prisoner pardoned by Lincoln, who, Butler was certain, had heard of the raid before bribing a guard and fleeing to Virginia, where he alerted the government. Butler was also angry that Union spies had provided such bad information. The Union secret service was never as accurate as it might have been; its agents felt it was underfunded. Cash for it was dispersed so haphazardly that in September 1862 a congressman told Lincoln the entire secret service fund was penniless and needed a hundred thousand dollars in emergency cash.[13]

The failure of the raid disappointed Lincoln, but did not dim his interest in kidnapping Jefferson Davis; it only whetted it. The war had dragged on for three years and the people were sick of it. The South was not on the verge of defeat in the winter of 1864, as he had hoped. The Confederacy was weak, it was underfinanced, its supplies were low, the naval blockade was tightening a noose around the Southern economy, and desertions were high, yet it still had armies in the field, and they still won battles. Lincoln feared that the war would simply grind on, the Union winning one day and the South the next, without conclusion. He worried also about the upcoming 1864 elections. Not only was his own reelection in jeopardy if the war continued through the elections, but his entire party could suffer defeat. The Republicans had experienced dozens of losses in Senate and congressional races in the off-year elections of 1862; in 1862 and 1863 the party had lost key governor's races in states such as New Jersey and New York. A continuing war might mean the loss of the House or the Senate to the Democrats and, with it, the evaporation of all the strength the Republicans had gained in their ten years of existence. He needed an impressive move of some kind, and the capture of Jeff Davis was it. President Lincoln hoped that Wistar's raid would not be his only chance.

Lincoln did not have to wait long for another. On February 13, General H. Judson Kilpatrick, at twenty-eight one of the war's youngest generals (he was nicknamed "Kill Patrick" for his aggressive battle tactics), arrived at the White House for a secret meeting with President Lincoln. Kilpatrick was one of the boy wonders of the Union army, a West Point graduate who had risen in the ranks from lieutenant to general in just two years. He had fought bravely at a number of places, including Gettysburg, and was renowned for his courage.[14] That morning, going behind the backs of his superiors, including Meade, whom he thought would veto it, he brought Lincoln the most daring plan of all.

The final version, organized by either Kilpatrick or Lincoln or both (there were no written records, and aides later told the press that Lincoln only wanted Kilpatrick to distribute amnesty proclamations in the Richmond area), called for a two-pronged nighttime attack on the Confederate capital. Kilpatrick and his force of thirty-five hundred men would strike from the Northwest and a force of five hundred cavalry led by Colonel Ulric Dahlgren, son of Admiral John Dahlgren, would attack from the southeast. Kilpatrick's action was diversionary, to draw out Richmond's defending troops while Dahlgren raced into town, freed prisoners, set fire to military installations, and kidnapped Jefferson Davis. Kilpatrick's men would meet Dahlgren's in the center of the city. They would also have some four to five thousand freed Union prisoners to fight with them. Kilpatrick assured Lincoln that there was no chance that the men would be trapped in the city or would be overwhelmed because, in addition to their numbers, all his men were highly trained, the veterans of dozens of raids and fights, and were armed with the new, seven-shot repeating rifles, which were particularly suited to cavalry work. This time Lincoln gave Kilpatrick and Dahlgren the men they needed, and army intelligence people who, in touch with Southern spies, reported that they knew nothing of the raid.

The president had great confidence in Kilpatrick. He knew little about Dahlgren, but everyone in the army saw him as a future general. He had already served on the staffs of Sigel, Burnside, Hooker, and Meade. The president did know the twenty-one-year-old soldier was tough. The tall, poised, handsome Dahlgren, now sporting a slight growth of beard, had lost a leg shortly after Gettysburg, but fought on, now riding his horse with an artificial limb. Besides, as the son of one of the world's better-known admirals, and a man who was a close friend of the president, military blood ran in his veins.

Lincoln needed a success. He had spent the previous few weeks as the target of sharp darts tossed by newspaper editors from Maine to Michigan over his ill-fated efforts to seize parts of Florida in order to get that state back into the Union. What had started out as a simple political mission had turned into a debacle, and the president was still suffering from it. He had sent his secretary, John Hay, to Florida to offer captured Confederates and civilians an amnesty if they would sign loyalty oaths. That, it was planned, would then lead to Lincoln's recognition of Florida as a repentant state which could be readmitted to the Union. It was part of a scheme to get states to renounce their allegiance to the Confederacy and rejoin the Union, but it also aimed at gaining Lincoln an additional three electoral votes in the 1864 election.

A Union general had decided he should accompany Hay and seize as much of Florida as he could, compelling the Floridians to accept the amnesty and showing the South that the Union army could move in and out of any state it pleased, even a state as far south as Florida. Union forces bungled the campaign, however, and were badly defeated by Confederate militia peppered with home guard troops in their fifties and sixties at Olustee. The Federals suffered 1,861 casualties and limped home.

Hay's initial success at getting amnesty signatures ended as soon as Florida civilians heard of the Union defeat. Hay and the army sailed home empty-handed. The press howled that Lincoln had lost nearly two thousand men on an unneeded military mission to win a paltry three votes in the electoral college, once again, many said, sacrificing the lives of young men for his political ambitions. Lincoln was particularly stung by charges that he had traded blood for votes.[15] He needed some kind of significant victory to mute the Florida debacle and saw the capture of Davis, which he knew would snare huge headlines, as all the more urgent. The entire venture was pleasing to Lincoln. He had just celebrated his fifty-fifth birthday the day before, and he was in high spirits. This raid looked like a fine present.[16]

It was not to be. Richmond's defenders were ready: apparently they knew all about it in advance. The great "secret raid" was a secret to no one. Kilpatrick later said that on his return from Washington, he found that many

Union soldiers already knew about the raid.[17] Secretary of the Navy Gideon Welles, who was never consulted about the attack, learned all the details through the White House rumor mill soon after it was first broached.[18] On the night the raid took place, a reporter for the *New York Herald* had the entire story; and the paper held back its publication so the raiders would not be in jeopardy. The *Herald* even had a headline printed and ready to go which read: "The Union Prisoners to Be Released and the Rebel Capital Sacked."[19] George Meade not only knew about it, but realized that the purpose of the raid was political. So dangerous did he deem it that, in a very unusual step, he let Kilpatrick know that he, Meade, wanted nothing to do with it if the raid did not succeed and anyone was captured, reminding Kilpatrick that this was a private arrangement the young cavalry general had with Stanton and the president: Meade's hands were clean.[20]

The raiders left at midnight and reached Ely's Ford at dawn, splashing through the quiet waters of the Rapidan easily, then moved fifteen miles, unimpeded, to Spotsylvania, where Dahlgren split off with his five hundred men and rode toward Richmond. Kilpatrick, his plan proceeding well, stopped at Beaver Dam Station, where he tore up railroad track to prevent Lee's men from going to Richmond by rail if they learned of the raid. Riding hard the next day, February 29, his horses' hooves kicking up dust storms in the Virginia morning, Kilpatrick's men made it to the banks of the South Anna River by dusk. He roused his men at 1 A.M., March 1, and then, despite a bitter, icy rain, the raiders rode all night and into morning to reach the outskirts of Richmond.

There Kilpatrick was startled by an enemy attack. Pulling his men up, he moved into a defensive position as enemy artillery dropped shells all around him and rifle rounds cut the air. The attack was so relentless and the shelling so precise that he assumed that Lee had discovered his plans and rushed regulars back to Richmond to augment the home guard. Certain now that the element of surprise was gone and that the city was well defended, Kilpatrick skirmished briefly, then rode back toward Washington, sure Dahlgren had done the same. What Kilpatrick did not know was that the withering fire that scared him away was not from the regular army but a ragtag collection of old men, schoolboys, office clerks, and other remnants of an inexperienced and probably frightened home guard.[21]

Dahlgren's men reached the James River near Belle Isle prison. They fared no better than Kilpatrick. They arrived at Jude's Crossing, led by a freed slave named Martin Robertson, who promised them they could ford the James there. Two days of rain had caused the river to swell, however, and it was not fordable anywhere. Thinking he had been betrayed by the slave, Dahlgren ordered him hanged on the spot. Angry now, and fearing that his where-abouts were known, he moved south cautiously and soon encountered gunfire. Hearing artillery in the distance, Dahlgren assumed that Kilpatrick, too, had encountered heavy opposition and would retreat. Dahlgren was quickly beset on all sides by Confederates, however, and, at a local courthouse, was surrounded and killed.[22] His body was then mutilated. His valuables were stolen, his sword and revolver snatched, and his ring removed—after the finger it was on was cut off. One rebel even stole Dahlgren's wooden leg as a souvenir.[23] What happened next rocked North and South.

A thirteen-year-old boy at the scene of the fight, William Littlepage, ran to Dahlgren's body after the soldiers had ransacked it and found a packet of two sets of folded-up papers and a notebook, which he turned over to local home guard commander Edward Halback. The contents of the papers shocked Halback. The first, in Dahlgren's handwriting, was an address to his men telling them that the purpose of the raid was not only to free prisoners but to "destroy and burn the hateful city," and "do not allow the Rebel leader Davis and his traitorous crew to escape." The second set was a list of instructions for the different officers taking part in the raid, including guides, scouts, and signal corps men. The final instructions provided that "the men must keep together and well in hand, and once in the city it must be destroyed and *Jeff Davis and cabinet killed.*" The third and final written document on Dahlgren's body was a notebook, with entries in pencil, and there Halback found a note that *"Jeff Davis and Cabinet must be killed on the spot."*[24]

Halback turned over the papers to Lt. Edward Pollard, who had them sent to Ninth Virginia Cavalry commander Colonel Richard Beale. The papers then reached Fitzhugh Lee in Richmond, who, realizing their explosive nature, had them to sent to Jefferson Davis. They were circulated around the War Department and by late afternoon a decision was made to let the press see them. As expected, the Richmond press complained bitterly that the Lincoln administration had reached a new low in planning the assassination of the Confederate president and his cabinet, blaming it directly on Lincoln.[25]

An editor at the *Richmond Sentinel* wrote, "Dahlgren's infamy did not begin or die with him. He was but the willing instrument for execution of an atrocity which his superiors had carefully approved and sanctioned. Truly there is no depth of dishonor and villainy to which Lincoln and his agents are not capable of descending."[26]

The United States Army and federal government immediately charged that Dahlgren's address to his troops and the other documents were forgeries, and that the only purpose of the raid had been to distribute amnesty proclamations. Officers throughout the chain of command denied any plans to kill Davis or his cabinet members. Meade, who had been afraid something exactly like this might happen, absolved himself of any complicity in the raid and ordered Kilpatrick to submit a report on the raid, putting him on the spot because he had gone around Meade to Lincoln to get approval.

Kilpatrick could place no blame on Dahlgren, now a martyr to the Union cause, and was not about to admit that he had any intention of killing Davis. He conducted a careful investigation, interviewing many of Dahlgren's men, who told him young Dahlgren had read them his little speech, with the orders, but had never said a word about kidnapping or murdering Jeff Davis or his cabinet. Satisfied, Kilpatrick quickly pronounced the papers forgeries. Meade, naturally, backed him up. Throughout the month of March, Meade vehemently denied that the raid had been undertaken to capture or kill any Confederate leader.

The Confederate government was not about to let go of this bombshell. They distributed copies of local newspapers which had published the Dahlgren papers throughout the South and in Europe as well, along with sets of photographs they had made of the papers to prove their authenticity. The effect was very damaging. It not only raised eyebrows throughout the South, but was used in yet another effort to convince England's leaders to back the South in the war.

In a shrewd move, a set of photographs was sent to Meade by Robert E. Lee, from one commander to another, demanding an explanation of this breach of the rules of war. Meade had to cover up all over again, denying that the raid was intended to kill Davis and charging once more that the photographed papers were forgeries. Meade's official response to Lee was odd, however. He did not respond just as a soldier, but as the official representative of the government of the United States, an unusual move. General Meade, who did not want responsibility for the raid, was now suddenly speaking for Lincoln and Stanton. "Neither the United States Government, myself nor General Kilpatrick authorized, sanctioned or approved the burning of the city of Richmond and the killing of Mr. Davis and cabinet," he wrote Lee. He then sent off the set of photographs and correspondence from Lee to Stanton, laying the controversy at his door. Stanton put them in a drawer and refused to make any public comment on the matter. Meanwhile, a curtain of silence fell over the White House. Lincoln, who had surely authorized the raid, never uttered a word about it except to send condolences to Admiral Dahlgren. Lincoln's secretaries and official biographers, Hay and Nicolay, maintained all their lives that Lincoln had never talked to Kilpatrick about kidnapping anyone and that the only purpose of the raid had been to distribute amnesty flyers.

Privately, Meade began to believe that the papers were authentic and that Lincoln had used Kilpatrick and Dahlgren to carry out at least an attempted kidnapping, if not an assassination. He wrote his wife that "Kilpatrick's reputation, and collateral evidence in my possession, rather go against this [forgery] theory."[27] Meade always wondered whose orders Dahlgren did carry.

Army officials apparently worked hard to discredit the Dahlgren papers. Someone finally sent Admiral Dahlgren copies of the photographs to see if he could find anything in them which might lead him to agree that they were forged. The admiral was startled to notice immediately what hundreds of others had missed—his son's signature on the damning papers was spelled wrong! It was a fraud!

Now the U.S. army had what it considered proof that the papers were forged. The Confederates, put on the spot, contended that ink letters on the reverse side of the paper had leaked through and turned up on the photographs, making an accurate signature look misspelled. Northerners, of course, discredited that explanation. The furor over the papers and the planned assassination of Jefferson Davis continued for months, despite Lincoln and Stanton's silence on the issue.

The raid had lasting consequences. The Southern press was convinced that no regiment or its commander would dream of murdering the president of another country without authorization from the White House and that Dahlgren's papers showed he had that authorization from Lincoln. The affair had changed the rules of war, and the Southern press sought revenge. "Let Lincoln and Kilpatrick remember that they have bidden their subordinates give no quarter to the Confederate chiefs. Perhaps even a Scotch cap and a military cloak will not prevent a just and stern vengeance from overtaking

This late 1850s photograph shows Lincoln as a successful lawyer whose legal career supported his passion—politics. (Photo courtesy of the Lincoln Museum, Fort Wayne, Indiana)

This unusual picture of Lincoln, his hair a mess as always, was taken in February, 1857, a year after he returned to politics and joined the brand-new Republican Party. (Photo courtesy of the Lincoln Museum, Fort Wayne, Indiana)

(*Below*) His 1858 debates with Stephen Douglas in the Illinois U.S. Senate race gave Lincoln his first real national visibility and convinced him that he could be elected president. (Photo courtesy of the Lincoln Museum, Fort Wayne, Indiana)

Lincoln and his wife Mary, seen here when she was first lady, had a tempestuous but loving marriage. Once, at a White House reception, Lincoln blurted out that he had loved her since the day he met her. (Photo courtesy of the Lincoln Museum, Fort Wayne, Indiana)

(*Below*) The Lincoln family lived in this large, wood-frame home in Springfield. The original home was the front section. The wing at the rear was added as the family grew in size. (Photo courtesy of the Lincoln Museum, Fort Wayne, Indiana)

"Honest Old Abe" was one of several songs used by the Republicans in the 1860 election. The party stressed honesty in the campaign, capitalizing on various corruption scandals in the Democratic administration of James Buchanan. (Photo courtesy of the Lincoln Museum, Fort Wayne, Indiana)

This print of a presidential reception shows how far the six-foot-four president had to bend over to greet most people. (Photo courtesy of the Lincoln Museum, Fort Wayne, Indiana)

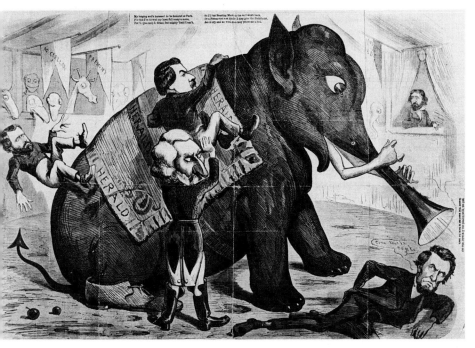

Lincoln was lambasted by cartoonists in hundreds of newspapers and magazines throughout most of his Presidency. In this 1864 cartoon, Lincoln has been booted off the Republican elephant as McClellan, his opponent in the 1864 election, tries to climb on with assistance from George Washington, while General Grant slides off the back. (Photo courtesy of the Lincoln Museum, Fort Wayne, Indiana)

(*Right*) Lincoln spent much of his time reading to his son, Tad, who appeared to be learning disabled and could barely read. (Photo courtesy of the Lincoln Museum, Fort Wayne, Indiana)

(*Opposite*) This lithograph, based on a Francis Carpenter painting, showed the Lincoln family at the White House in 1861. Willie is sitting in the middle, legs crossed, while Tad listens to the president read, and the eldest boy, Robert, watches in the background. (Photo courtesy of the Lincoln Museum, Fort Wayne, Indiana)

This lithograph of the issuance of the Emancipation Proclamation was one of the most widely distributed during and after the war. (Photo courtesy of the Lincoln Museum, Fort Wayne, Indiana)

Lincoln meets with General George McClellan during a five-day visit to the Army of the Potomac following the battle of Antietam. He fired the slow moving McClellan a few weeks later. (Photo courtesy of the Lincoln Museum, Fort Wayne, Indiana)

Lincoln's long parade of commanders for the Union Army finally ended when he appointed Ulysses S. Grant. (Photo courtesy of the Lincoln Museum, Fort Wayne, Indiana)

An artist invented this meeting between Lincoln and his generals. The president, seated, talks to (left to right) General David Hunter, Admiral David Farragut, William Sherman, George Thomas, U. S. Grant, and Phillip Sheridan. (Photo courtesy of the Lincoln Museum, Fort Wayne, Indiana)

Lincoln died the morning after he was shot by John Wilkes Booth at Ford's Theater. Here he is surrounded by cabinet members, army officers, his son Robert, and his wife Mary, seen weeping. Secretary of War Edwin Stanton, when the President slipped away, told the others that "now he belongs to the ages." (Photo courtesy of the Lincoln Museum, Fort Wayne, Indiana)

One of the first postassassination lithographs published, this popular reproduction of the president captured Lincoln's vulnerability. (Photo courtesy of the Lincoln Museum, Fort Wayne, Indiana) them [a veiled reference to Lincoln's disguise on his 1861 preinaugural arrival in Washington to avoid assassins]," wrote the one newspaper editor.[28]

Another believed that all of Dahlgren's men now held prisoners of war should be hanged and that the government should "insist on the most scrupulous carrying out of retaliation for murders, robberies, and other outrages, with the most punctual exactitude."[29]

Confederate officials felt the same way. Judah Benjamin and other cabinet members, all potential targets of Dahlgren and his soldiers, fumed over and debated the issue day and night in Richmond, outraged that Lincoln would abandon the battlefield and try to win the war with assassins. Several advocated executing all, or some, of Dahlgren's captured men. Lee stepped in and ended the effort, sure that executions by the South would only lead to executions of Confederate prisoners by the North. President Davis, too, was livid about the assassination attempt. He knew of Butler's attempt to kidnap him and now, just six weeks later, here was another. This time he was certain the Federals had planned to kill him. He feared they would try until they succeeded. In his public message on fasting a week later, Jeff Davis called the Dahlgren raid "a nefarious scheme to burn and plunder" the city and to kill "the chosen servants of the people."[30] Secretary of War Seddons was even angrier, writing: "That such horrors should have been deliberately planned and ordered by the authorities of any people professing to be civilized and Christian, must inflict an indelible stigma of hypocrisy and infamy."[31]

The people living in Jeff Davis's White House that week were outraged. Their anger was summed up best by the president's mother-in-law, Mrs. William Howell. "The vile wretch [Dahlgren] was shot as he deserved!"[32]

Shortly afterward, Davis and other Confederate officials decided that they, too, could play by this new set of rules introduced by Lincoln. They began to plan a complicated and daring game of their own—a game which, when out of hand, grew deadly.

[*The Confederates went to great lengths to protect and preserve the Dahlgren papers as proof that Lincoln had tried to have Davis killed. The originals were packed in boxes and placed on Davis's escape train when Richmond fell in April, 1865. They were removed in Charlotte, North Carolina, and stored in a warehouse with instructions to have them turned over to federal authorities for safekeeping when the war ended. In May 1865 the Dahlgren papers were taken to Washington,*

D.C., with thousands of other Confederate documents as part of the Confederate archives. Seven months after the assassination of President Lincoln, Secretary of War Stanton ordered Dr. Francis Lieber, in charge of the Confederate archives, to send all of the Dahlgren papers to him. The papers reached his office in late November 1865. They were never seen again.]

19

THE PLOT TO KIDNAP
ABRAHAM LINCOLN

Confederate General James Chesnut Jr. sat down at his desk, looked over his daily secret messages on February 8, 1865, and scrambled them via the complicated, secret Confederate cipher code. Something was very odd. The old secret code, COMPLETE VICTORY, which had been in place since Sherman invaded Georgia and the Confederates tried to fight back, was gone. In its place was a bizarre new code: COME RETRIBUTION.

It was a signal that, as it shot across the South, confirmed what many had suspected for nearly a year—the Confederate government was going to seek revenge on Abraham Lincoln for the attempted murders of Jefferson Davis and his cabinet in March 1864. The Confederacy had just as many powerful reasons to kidnap or kill Abraham Lincoln as Lincoln did to capture or kill Jefferson Davis, and now, finally, it appeared to many that Jeff Davis, who had so long vetoed any plan to seize or harm Lincoln, had changed his mind. The government, via the army, secret service, and a long string of spies and friendly citizens, was going to capture Abraham Lincoln and win the war.[1]

The attempt on Davis, to kidnap or to kill, may have been the final incentive Confederate leaders needed to avenge themselves on the White House. Yet Southerners had many more reasons to hate Lincoln. They believed he had started the war. He had permitted Union armies to pillage and burn their way through Southern states. He was trying to starve women and children with the naval blockade. His prisons were deplorable. His freeing of the slaves would destroy their social systems and their economy. Worst of all, he was responsible for the deaths of over a quarter million Southern soldiers.

Southerners hated Lincoln for these alleged crimes, but so did many Northerners. One editor of a Democratic newspaper came right out and advocated the murder of the president. "And if he is elected...for another four years, we trust some bold hand will pierce his heart with dagger point for the public good," he wrote.[2]

The kidnapping or killing of President Lincoln had been in the works since before the 1860 election. The plot to kill him at a Baltimore train station, which had forced Lincoln to disguise himself and slip into Washington in the middle of the night, to the later derision and scorn of the press, was just one in a series of plots—most of them real—to assassinate him.

The inability of the Confederacy to win the war spurred a whole new series of plots during Lincoln's presidency. The final plot, the one set in motion after the attempt on Davis, the COME RETRIBUTION plot, was merely the latest.

On April 18, 1861, Jean Davenport, a well-known actress married to a Union colonel, went to the White House to see Lincoln, who was sleeping, and instead talked to John Hay. She told him she had just met a Virginian who was in town to buy a saddle and he had told her that he and several other men, including a man whose name sounded like "Ficklin," planned to murder Lincoln. Two months later, Camille DeKalb went to Confederate Secretary of War Walker and proposed blowing up the U.S. Capitol when Congress reconvened there to hear Lincoln give his first congressional message. The plan, for which DeKalb wanted a million dollars, would not only kill Lincoln, but the entire U.S. Congress as well, destroying the Union political system. Walker held a second meeting with him, with Judah Benjamin present, but nothing happened.

The most serious proposal to kidnap Lincoln came in the summer of 1862 from Major Joseph Taylor of Kentucky, a cousin of Jeff Davis's first wife. Taylor, a bold soldier, donned civilian clothes, took a train to Washington, buying a ticket like any passenger, and arrived in the capital undetected. Encouraged by his success, he proceeded to spend several days reconnoitering the city to discover the best place to seize the president and the best escape route out of town. The egomaniacal Taylor, who was well known in Kentucky, grew brassier. He used some political connections to get invited to a reception at the

White House, where he was introduced to Lincoln himself and spent the rest of the night scouting the mansion for his plan. Taylor passed the next weeks following Lincoln whenever the president left the White House or appeared at an official function, trying to devise a foolproof scheme to kidnap him.

Convinced he could spirit Lincoln away, Taylor went to Richmond to see Jefferson Davis, who listened intently for a long time. The more he listened the more he became convinced that Taylor's plan could not work, because he had no way to truss up Lincoln immediately. Davis knew that Abraham Lincoln, who had gained early fame as a champion wrestler and was said in his youth to be the strongest man in Illinois, would never let himself be taken without a fight. The Confederate president feared that one of the kidnappers would kill Lincoln in the struggle, and then the entire Union would turn on the Confederacy in a murderous rage. Davis rejected the idea.

Other plans were organized and eliminated. A major on Lee's staff wrote his wife in the summer of 1863 that there were some in the Army of Northern Virginia who had a plot to kidnap Lincoln. Private Robert Stanton, of the Fifth Texas Infantry, wrote Secretary of War Seddon a few days later that he, too, had put together a foolproof plan to kidnap Lincoln. Seddon told him that the government had no interest and that "the laws of war and morality, as well as Christian principles...forbid the use of such means." A few weeks later, Sergeant Henry Durham, Sixty-Third Georgia Infantry, wrote Jeff Davis and asked him to put Durham at the head of a five hundred man unit entrusted with the kidnapping of Lincoln. Davis never answered his letter. Colonel Bradley Johnson told his superior, General Wade Hampton, that he wanted to lead two hundred cavalrymen in a raid on the Soldiers' Home, which Lincoln often visited to get away from the White House, kidnap the president and, in a very complicated plan, bring him back to Virginia. Hampton told him to proceed with the planning, but Johnson was later transferred, and he dropped the idea.

One man almost killed Lincoln on a quiet summer night in 1864. Lincoln was riding alone from the White House to the Soldiers' Home, as he often did despite repeated warnings from his bodyguard, Ward Lamon. Within five hundred yards of the Home, he was fired at by an unknown sniper, the bullet ripped through the president's stovepipe hat. Lincoln then spurred his mount and, coattails flapping in the evening breeze, raced to the protection of the Soldiers' Home. Lincoln, as always, laughed off the attempt. He joked that the bullet ruined a perfectly good hat, but he never rode alone again.[3]

All these would-be kidnappers and assassins felt their task would be rather easy for several reasons: (1) Lincoln never took any of the varied kidnap or assassination plots seriously. (2) Lincoln was an easy target. He often rode about Washington all by himself, or with one of his sons, frequently walked through city streets alone, and went to plays and receptions in town alone or with his wife—with no guards. (3) Although the capture of Lincoln would be known within the hour, there were enough roads out of Washington and across Maryland, particularly through the Chesapeake area, that the commandos would have a better than average chance of getting out of the city safely.

Lincoln's carefree attitude annoyed Lamon, who kept track of all rumors of plots to kill his friend. Lincoln dismissed word of plots to harm him, telling those trying to warn him that they were fantasizing. He even joked that since his vice president, Hannibal Hamlin, was more hated in the South than Lincoln, Hamlin was his life insurance. He blithely ignored even minimal safety precautions. He walked back and forth on foot to the War Department near the White House almost every night, despite Mary's warnings.

Whenever Lincoln rode in boats, he tried to sit on the lower deck, where he was an easy target, and had to be ushered to the upper deck. He would go horseback riding on his own whenever he felt like it, ignoring security precautions. Lamon once ordered a small detail of cavalrymen to ride with Lincoln as he went for a carriage ride with Mary, but the president dismissed them all on the spot, joking that since they were green recruits he was in more danger of being shot accidentally by one of them than he was of being killed by Confederates.[4] One real fear among his few security agents was that Lincoln's extraordinary height made him any easy target: The six foot four president usually towered over crowds by a foot.[5]

One night Ward Lamon learned that the president had decided to once again ignore protection and go to Grover's Theater to see an opera with Senator Charles Sumner and a foreign diplomat—with no guard. Lamon fired off a hot note to his boss which stressed Lincoln's danger: "You are in danger. Neither Sumner nor the diplomat could defend himself from an assault from any able-bodied woman in this city."[6]

The kidnapping of Lincoln would have had just as far-reaching consequences—political, psychological, and military—as the abduction or murder of Jeff Davis. Lincoln had become one of the United States' most powerful presidents, gathering all of the reins of government in his hands. He may have earned high marks from public officials for his ability to delegate power to cabinet figures such as Seward, Bates, and Stanton, but everyone knew that he ran the country—they didn't. Under his leadership, the federal government had grown in size and was foreshadowing the huge, sprawling bureaucracy to come. This bureaucracy was not only run by Lincoln, but it was filled, every step of the way, from local post offices to cabinet posts, by men appointed by Lincoln through political patronage. The allegiance of every one of these appointed federal workers was to Lincoln and to Lincoln alone. His kidnapping would send the United States government spiraling.

Militarily, the elimination of Lincoln was even more important. Jeff Davis may have stuck his fingers into every nook and cranny of the Confederate military, but Abraham Lincoln had established himself as a smooth and effective commander in chief of the U.S. armed forces. He had put together a large army quickly and efficiently, expanded the navy, and, in a short period, prodded manufacturers to produce record numbers of rifles, cannon, and shot. He oversaw all campaigns. He controlled all promotions and signed all pardons. He determined who would lead the army and, if they displeased him, fired them immediately.

The capture of Lincoln might, at long last, show England that the Confederacy had not only not gone away but had rebounded and was stronger than anyone in Parliament suspected. They could prove that by seizing Lincoln. The Confederates might achieve the release of their prisoners of war from horrid Union prisons by kidnapping and holding Lincoln hostage. The Union leader could be traded for peace. Jefferson Davis would be happy to return Lincoln to Washington, D.C., in exchange for a cessation of hostilities and the recognition of the Confederacy as a separate nation.

None of this was discussed at any length in high circles of the Confederate government until after the second attempt at kidnapping, or murdering, Davis and other administrators in March 1864. It was only then that Davis and others genuinely feared that the Federals might capture them, or kill them, that they decided it would be better to grab Lincoln before he grabbed them. They then began devising an elaborate scheme involving hundreds of soldiers, spies, civilians—and an actor named John Wilkes Booth—to kidnap the president of the United States.

THE Union knew that the Confederacy had some sort of secret service, but it never realized its scope, and did not know that it was directly under the supervision of President Davis. He created a secret service in the War

Department, via the signal corps, when the conflict began. Davis was very familiar with the operations of the signal corps from his days as secretary of war under Franklin Pierce. He knew that he could use all of its far-flung communication outlets, its wire operators and telegraphers, to operate as an undercover network to gather and disseminate information and that its operatives could be used with great effect to work as spies. Davis also authorized a second, less effective secret service unit within the State Department, nominally under the direction of the secretary of state but really under his own. On paper, Mosby's Rangers was a secret service group, but in reality the guerrillas were a military unit.

Both secret services were marginally effective in running the South's military telegraph lines. Both put out disinformation to suspected Union spies in the Virginia area. Both had spies working in Washington, D.C., and in northern cities. Both passed on false rumors to prisoners of war who were being exchanged. Confederate agents were made "prisoners" for short periods of time so they could be exchanged and sent north as legitimate parolees—and function as agents. This was Jeff Davis's idea, and he supervised the operation himself. Still, until March of 1864, both services were low key, low level, and infrequently utilized.

Within weeks after the second attempt to kidnap, or kill, President Davis, secret legislation was introduced in the Confederate Congress to combine the two secret service units into one, for clandestine purposes. Beginning in March 1864 the previously neglected secret service became a beehive of frenetic undercover activity and a hub for hundreds of agents, officers, soldiers, and sympathetic civilians, North and South, in a top-secret clandestine operation. Unusual things began to happen:

• Lt. Lewis Blackford, an outstanding young Confederate engineer and before the war one of the country's best mapmakers, was transferred out of his North Carolina regiment and brought to Richmond, where he began to draw detailed maps of Stafford, Prince William, and Fauquier counties in northern Virginia, adjacent to Washington, D.C.

• General Wade Hampton wrote Lee that a large number of men from his previously quite healthy Ninth Virginia Cavalry were all going away on disability leave at the same time and had to be replaced. All of the "sick" men turned up a few days later as a large security force guarding Chaffin's Farm, an empty site outside Richmond which had no military value.

• In an unprecedented order, the secretary of war, with Davis's approval, ordered the Treasury Department to give the Richmond paymaster $250,000 to distribute to large numbers of army officers and soldiers who were about to be furloughed in Richmond, but could not stay in the city and needed the money right away.

• Several secret service agents were sent by Davis to Montreal, Canada, where they took rooms on long-term leases at the luxurious St. Lawrence Hall Hotel. Their expenses were paid by the Confederacy from a secret one million dollar fund in a London bank. The man in charge of the group was George Sanders, a former drinking companion of French novelist Victor Hugo, who as early as 1854 had advocated the assassination of unpopular political leaders and developed a theory that any political leader who acted as a tyrant, in the judgment of the people, should be murdered.

• The secret service leased a small home on the Potomac River, Boyd's Hole, where signal corps operatives could observe movements on the Potomac for several miles. The home was just across the river from Maryland towns which were very sympathetic to the Confederate cause.

• Secret service agents, under Davis's direction, met with numerous pro-Confederate civilians throughout the northern Virginia, Washington, D.C., and southeastern Maryland area, including Dr. Samuel Mudd and John Surratt, who might be available to help in a major clandestine operation.

The operation was the kidnapping of Abraham Lincoln.

Jefferson Davis, of course, never kept notes on plans to abduct the president of the United States. No one did. Researchers, particularly William Tidwell, James Hall and David Gaddy (*Come Retribution,* University Press of Mississippi, 1988), and William Hanchett, have put together considerable evidence that Davis organized the plot, approved all its activities and, right down to the fall of the Confederacy, was convinced it could be carried out.

The plot was probably organized between early March and early April of 1864,[7] when Davis sent to Canada a "peace commission" comprising Senator Jacob Thompson of Mississippi, former U.S. Senator C. C. Clay of Alabama, law professor J. P. Holcombe of Virginia, purchasing agent Beverley Tucker, Dr. Luke Blackburn, and Sanders. They set up headquarters in Montreal at the luxurious, five-story high, city block–long St. Lawrence Hotel—it advertised itself as "a household word to travelers"—which had some of the best restaurants in Canada, a telegraph office for communications with

Richmond, and a one hundred-foot long, heavily populated bar which specialized in mint juleps for all the Southerners who lived there. The hotel also maintained a store which sold dozens of Northern and Southern newspapers. The team took out ads in Richmond papers that sent messages to the government via coded phrases in the ads.[8]

Professedly, the peace commission was in Canada to attempt to influence, via Canada's neutrality and its geographic proximity to the Union, the upcoming 1864 presidential and congressional elections. They told anyone they met that their job was to work with Copperheads and Peace Democrats in the Union to defeat Lincoln and Republican candidates, but their real job was to serve as an organizing group for paramilitary activities and clandestine work. The hotel, dubbed the "Little Confederacy," quickly became a meeting place for agitators who took advantage of Canada's neutrality to plot and plan various activities in an effort, overtly and covertly, to overthrow the government of the United States.[9]

Davis was satisfied that by the spring of 1864 the plans to kidnap Lincoln were organized and moving along well, but he thought a direct attack on the White House by an army unit was an even better idea. He authorized Lee to order General Jubal Early, a bearded, forty-seven-year-old bachelor and former lawyer, to join with General John Breckinridge, former U.S. vice-president, to launch a surprise assault on Washington, D.C., in July. Union intelligence, always weak, never picked up the movement of Early's eight-thousand infantry and four thousand cavalry. They crossed the Potomac quietly and moved on to the Monocacy River, where they lost 1,500 men, killed and wounded, in a fierce battle.[10]

Undaunted, Early and his men trudged on toward Washington, reaching the outskirts of the capital at Silver Spring, Maryland, on July 11. The defenses of the town, and at nearby Fort Stevens, had been reinforced overnight as Lincoln ordered every available man in Washington to go to the fort as quickly as possible. Even soldiers on leave, walking around town, were rounded up by cavalry and ordered to Fort Stevens.[11] Lee might have attacked, but Early delayed a full day. The next morning, July 12, he engaged federals for several hours in skirmishing around Fort Stevens, but finally withdrew and returned to Virginia.[12]

Ironically, Lincoln himself raced out to Fort Stevens on the morning of July 12, along with his wife and hundreds of local residents, many of whom took the trolley, to get a firsthand look at what he expected to be a great battle, much to the chagrin of Ward Lamon and others on his tiny security team. Lincoln climbed up to the top of the fort's walls and, at his full six foot four height, soon became a target for Confederate sharpshooters.

One young soldier, Oliver Wendell Holmes, watched as two or three bullets hit the walls near Lincoln and another killed an army surgeon five feet away from him, and finally shouted loudly, "Get down, you damned fool!" The president, startled by the shout rather than the bullets, ducked down behind the wall. There, leaning against the wall, a small boyish grin on his face, his long legs tucked up in front of his chest, sat the man all these governments, regiments, and international kidnappers were after.[13]

Early's debacle, and the irony of Lincoln rushing out to greet the men intent on capturing him, angered Confederate leaders and made them firmer than ever in their desire to kidnap the American president.

The Canadian base was the hub of numerous activities, including the operation to kidnap Lincoln, but most failed. Operatives there planned to sink a number of ships on the Great Lakes, but were unable to sink any. Another plan was for a group of commandos to travel from Canada and liberate all the Southern prisoners of war held in a prison at Elmira, New York. That never went past the planning stages. The only marginal success the Canada group had, besides the Lincoln scheme, was a well-organized raid on St. Alban's, a small town in Vermont. Raiders shot up the town, robbed three banks of $200,000, and then tried to burn it down—all to show Northerners that the Confederates were still strong and could strike anywhere at any time. The raid backfired, however, when the fires were quickly extinguished. Canadian authorities captured fourteen of them and confiscated $90,000. Instead of a show of strength for the Stars and Bars, the raid had the impact of a bad bank robbery.

It was at Montreal's St. Lawrence Hall hotel that Confederate agents first met actor John Wilkes Booth in July, 1864. Booth, who was recruited sometime earlier in the summer in New York or Washington, made up an elaborate cover story that he needed to go to Montreal to ship theatrical costumes from a theater there back to New York. Since Booth was a well-known performer who worked in theaters all over America, including those in Montreal, a trip to the St. Lawrence was not at all unusual. The fact that it took the actor ten days to do what could have been done in a single morning stirred no suspicion.

In Montreal, Booth and the others began planning the abduction of

Lincoln. A few months later, the actor visited Washington, D.C., and met with John Surratt, a Confederate spy, and others to finalize plans to seize the president outside the Old Soldiers' Home and take him to Virginia.[14]

Davis apparently monitored the Canadian group carefully and was pleased at its progress, and its mission to snatch Lincoln, but he also wanted an operative close to home. He chose Thomas Conrad. Conrad was a perfect agent. Who would suspect a minister?

Conrad was, in 1864, the quiet and unassuming chaplain of the Third Virginia Cavalry. He had trained to be a minister at Dickinson College and worked as a lay preacher at Georgetown Institute, where he angered locals by ordering the school band to play "Dixie" at graduation exercises.

Conrad moved to Richmond and joined the army. His superiors decided he would make an excellent spy and assigned him to J. E. B. Stuart's cavalry, where he was employed for missions into Maryland to gather information. As a cover, Conrad became a very religious chaplain for the Third Virginia Cavalry. In August 1864, after the decision to abduct Lincoln was made final, Davis transferred Conrad to army intelligence. In September the president sent him to Washington, D.C., on a dangerous mission, not only to scout the grounds of the White House and several public buildings in the capital— which might be good places to abduct President Lincoln—but to follow the president on a daily basis so kidnappers would know his routine.[15]

In September, Booth and others concluded their plans to capture Lincoln and spirit him out of Washington. They spent time in Washington, Maryland, and Virginia mapping their escape route. The plan was to grab Lincoln, tie him up, gag him, and hold him in the back of a closed carriage. He would be driven out of Washington into Maryland and then down the eastern shore of the Potomac to a dock where he would be put on a boat and taken across the river to Boyd's Hole, where Confederates had laid mines in the Potomac to blow up any ships pursuing the Booth party. Once in Virginia, Lincoln would be put in another carriage and, under heavy guard, driven over a designated safe route, far from Union troops, to a well-appointed house or farm which would serve as his jail.[16] This elaborate plan, involving so many people and so much Confederate money, clearly had to have been approved at the very top of the Confederate government—by Jefferson Davis.

Discussions became intense in October 1864 when Booth returned to Montreal to meet with the peace commission at the St. Lawrence, this time under the cover of readings of Tennyson and Shakespeare at a local theater, where he was booked for two weeks. He performed by night and plotted by day. One afternoon, shooting billiards in the St. Lawrence's ornately appointed billiard room, he slipped when discussing the American presidential election a month away and told a man that "Abe's contract was near up and whether re-elected or not, he would get his goose cooked."[17]

Lincoln, as always, scoffed at any kidnap talk, but Ward Lamon, his devoted friend and bodyguard, did not. Lamon listened to all the rumors and tracked down as much information as he could. In the autumn of 1864, he was certain that there was a very real plot to either capture or kill Lincoln, but evidently did not know who was behind the idea.

It is not known whether Lamon discussed the plot with Lincoln—he probably did—but he demanded a meeting with Edward Wright, a former aide to General George McClellan, the Democratic candidate for president in 1864. Certain he could end all plots by laying each at McClellan's door, he heatedly told Wright that he was there on instructions from Lincoln and that they both knew there was a plot to harm Lincoln which had been hatched by close McClellan supporters in an effort to seize the government if McClellan lost. Lamon told Wright that the planning had to stop, or there would be drastic legal consequences. Wright was startled since neither McClellan or anyone close to him had anything to do with a scheme, but the message was clear—Lamon knew of a plot.[18]

No one in the South was surprised when Lincoln was reelected president in November 1864. Sherman's capture of Atlanta, along with Sheridan's victory in the Shenandoah Valley, turned public opinion in the North and Lincoln was able to beat McClellan handily. His reelection hastened plans to kidnap him. Lincoln was no longer the minority president he had been when he first took office; now he had a mandate from the people to prosecute the war. All indications from the White House were that he was now determined to win the war as quickly as possible, probably in the spring of 1865, when Grant could conclude his siege of Petersburg and then move on Richmond itself.

Confederate secret service operatives speeded up their activities. A group of them set fire to twenty-two hotels in New York City on November 25, hoping that the flames would leap to other buildings and set the entire city on fire. Just a week after the election, John Wilkes Booth began buying guns and knives for his attempt on Lincoln. In the winter of 1864–65 Confederate forces secured Ashland, a resort fifteen miles north of Richmond, which had a hotel and a series of cottages, where they planned to hold Lincoln after his abduction. General John Mosby was sent on a raid of Williamsburg, Virginia, on February 10, 1865, for no apparent reason, except to gauge how many Federals were in the areas north and east of Richmond, and near the Potomac, the route Lincoln's captors planned to take.[19]

The spiderweb plot also involved efforts to capture other high-ranking officials in the U.S. government, not just Lincoln. Vice President Andrew Johnson was another target. In December 1864 a small group of Confederates attempted to kidnap him during his visit to Louisville, Kentucky. They discovered that no one would have stopped them when they climbed a staircase and walked down a corridor right to Johnson's hotel room door. They had a closed carriage waiting in an alley and a well-organized escape plan. They were armed. They had surprise on their side. But Johnson, for some unknown reason, had decided to leave town six hours early and checked out just before the kidnappers knocked on his hotel room door.[20]

The band of kidnappers put together by John Wilkes Booth, aided by information from both Conrad and Stringfellow, tracked Lincoln all over Washington. At first they wanted to grab him in his box during a performance of a play at Ford's Theater, haul him out of his chair and down to the stage, then handcuff him and push him out a back door into a carriage which would take him out of town and into Virginia. They were dissuaded when they realized that Ford's was often full of Union soldiers who went to the popular theater for entertainment.[21]

They concocted a new plan when on March 17 an actor friend tipped off Booth that the Washington Theater company of *Still Waters Run Deep*, led by actor E. L. Davenport, was going to stage a performance for a group of wounded soldiers at Campbell Hospital, just outside Washington. The actor, who knew nothing of Booth's intentions, told Booth that he understood that the president would be there. This was perfect for Booth and his men. The president would have to travel on the Seventh Street Road through a sparsely settled neighborhood to the hospital, which sat in a heavily wooded area. There were several places where the conspirators could hide and then pounce on Lincoln when his carriage bumped down the road. They did not even need their own carriage to seize the president; they could steal his.

One of the conspirators, David Herold, loaded Booth's buggy with arms, including shotguns, knives, and a sword, and drove to Surrat's Tavern, south of the Navy Yard bridge. There he deposited them so the soon-to-be-fleeing kidnappers could pick them up on their way to Maryland and their waiting boat, which would take them across the Potomac to Boyd's Hole and then on to Ashland, Lincoln's prison. The others rode out of town to meet Booth at a tavern along the Seventh Street Road. They were nervous. After all of their meticulous planning, this seemed too easy.

Shortly after 2 P.M., right on schedule, a single, closed carriage came down the road, unprotected, as Lincoln's carriage always was, and the men sensed their moment of immortality had arrived. The conspirators, sucking in their breath, spurred their horses gently and rode up to the carriage and peered in, expecting to see the familiar face of Abraham Lincoln, but it was not the president.[22] It was someone else. Lincoln was attending a flag-raising ceremony that day. Booth and his men had their chance and it vanished.

They would try again.[23]

PART VI

MORTAL CONFLICT
WITHOUT END

20

JEFFERSON DAVIS AT WAR: 1863

PRESIDENT DAVIS LEANED BACK in the chair of his office across from the statehouse and listened carefully. The president's various illnesses flared up on February 5, after a month of stress from military problems. He had been sick ever since, completely bedridden for the first month and unable to get much work done. A thief had sneaked into his stables the night before, April 1, 1863, and stolen one of his favorite horses. It had been a bad morning, and now he heard a buzzing noise of some kind and sensed more trouble on its way.

In moments, he learned that the women of Richmond, disgusted with short supplies of food, soaring inflation, and high prices, were rioting in the streets after failing to gain help from the governor of Virginia. The women were so emaciated their frail bodies reminded some of skeletons. Many had husbands, fathers, and sons in the army. Others worked for the war effort in the nearby Tredegar Ironworks.[1] Hundreds of the unruly women had broken into stores on Cary Street, some armed with knives, and looted them for food. Davis rushed out of the Customs House and walked briskly toward the noise, leaving aides well behind and moving through the streets of the city and down the hill to Cary Street as quickly as he could.

It was an ugly scene. Governor John Letcher, who met the women earlier, had been unable to quell the disturbance. The military mayor of Richmond, Joseph Mayo, had given them five minutes to disperse before he ordered the police to fire on them. No one noticed the president rushing through the streets, perhaps because he was walking so quickly, his heart pounding as he sensed terrible trouble. In just a moment he made his way through the crowd and leaped to the top of a parked horse-drawn wagon, where he waved his arms and yelled as loudly as he could to get the attention of the crowd.

The president of the Confederacy scolded the women for their illegal actions and noted that many had jewelry and clothing, not just bread. Davis warned them that farmers would not send any food to Richmond, or any other cities, if they knew it would be stolen. The women fell quiet, some still angry, some remorseful, but did not disperse. The president then threw all the coins he had in his pockets into the crowd, but the women still did not move. Angered, he ordered the police to load their weapons and prepare to fire. Then he took out his watch and resumed Mayor Mayo's count. "We do not desire to shoot anyone, but this lawlessness must stop," he said in a curt, clipped tone and glowered at them.[2] Slowly, in a sour mood, the women began to drift away and the crisis was over.[3]

The Richmond bread riot of April 2, 1863, was just the latest crisis for Davis in the spring of 1863. Women in Salisbury, North Carolina, had rioted two weeks earlier, finally forcing stores there to cut prices and sell food at the same prices they sold it to the army. Both riots came soon after the president's proclamation declaring March 27, 1863, a day of fasting and prayer. His own war clerk joked that it was "fasting in the middle of famine." Another riot occurred in Mobile, Alabama, in September, with looters screaming "bread or blood!" The riots were symptomatic of the food shortages throughout the Confederacy, and even in the army.

Throughout 1863 Davis admonished the women of Richmond and the Southern states for their violent activities following unsuccessful efforts to obtain food. Yet he listened to their bitter complaints about extortion and soaring prices.

The shortage of food and supplies was compounded by the tens of thousands of refugees streaming into the cities of the Confederacy from areas occupied by Union armies or from towns or cities partially destroyed by the war, such as Fredericksburg. These people had to be fed, too, and sheltered, and they put an enormous strain on the urban centers where they relocated.

Food shortages were so great in the army that on March 26 Congress passed the Impressment Act,[4] which authorized the army to seize whatever food it needed and pay farmers the market rate, which was fixed by government price schedules. The law was quickly mangled. Prices in Virginia were more than triple the amounts paid in Tennessee, so Tennessee farmers demanded what Virginians were being paid. Some goods were priced correctly, but some far too low. By the end of the year farmers were complaining that the government was only paying twenty percent of market value for food. Some officers, their men starving, simply seized what supplies they needed and gave farmers receipts. All payment was made in Confederate dollars, worth very little, and payment was so sporadic that by the end of the war farmers were holding over $500 million in unpaid receipts.[5] In retaliation, incensed farmers withheld their goods, or did not grow food, and the shortages became even worse. Local officials were outraged. "If God almighty had yet in store another plague worse than all others which he intended to have let loose on the Egyptians in case Pharaoh still hardened in his heart, I am sure it must have been a regiment or so of half armed, half disciplined Confederate cavalry."[6]

Another critical problem for the government was the virtual price exploitation within the Confederacy for vital items such as corn and salt, necessary for farmers. Citizens would hoard food to drive up prices. Very little salt was produced in the primitive Confederate salt mines. (Most salt had been imported from Northern states prior to the conflict.) What was taken out of the ground was rarely delivered due to atrocious rail transportation. The result was not only high prices—the price of salt went from $2 a pound to $60 a pound by 1863—but a vicious army of speculators. President Davis, powerless to stop price gouging by 1863, called price exploitation a "gigantic evil" and newspapers referred to speculators as "contemptible wretches."[7]

The food and salt shortage was one of the many failures of Davis's homefront policies. Perhaps his biggest failure was the economy, crippled by runaway inflation. Davis paid little attention to the thirty-five percent rate of inflation at the end of 1861, but by the early weeks of 1863 inflation had become a monster. Banks were paying just $1 in gold for $10 in Confederate notes.[8] A Richmond resident claimed that flour which sold at $7 in 1861 cost $28 in 1863. Meat went from ten cents a pound to $1, bacon twenty cents to $1.25 a pound and the price of tea leaped from $1.25 to $15. One woman said the monthly family food bill in 1863 was $68, compared to $6.65 at the start of the war.[9] Because of the shortages of supplies, the South had to import food, coffee, and other staples via blockade runners, and these supplies dwindled throughout 1863 as the blockade tightened.[10] Women bitterly denounced storeowners who could get food and staples and then charged ten times market value for them.

The initial war tax brought in little revenue: The states' attempts to collect it collapsed rather quickly. The Davis government, so reluctant to borrow money from European banks, wound up short of capital each year of the war. The South had only $27 million in loans to fight a four-year war. To raise money, Davis and Treasury Secretary Memminger continually printed new money, causing runaway inflation.

The cotton embargo against England, which wiped out at least $400 million in potential revenue, perhaps as much as $800 million, failed badly. To be sure, holding back cotton hurt England. There was a great shortage of cotton for manufacture and tens of thousands of jobs were lost, but British workers put up with their hardships because of their antislavery views. At one raucous rally, a young British textile industry worker whose wages were slashed in half because of the cotton crisis stood up and told the crowd that he would rather face financial ruin than help a country with slavery.[11] Davis had completely misjudged the depth of the British hatred of slavery. The cotton embargo did not induce England to enter the war or even to recognize the South, either. British politicians would not risk trouble over the slavery issue because, as they quickly found out, the American Civil War never became a heated issue with the British public.[12]

Cotton planters, stuck with millions of bales and no market, began to secretly sell some of it to third party intermediaries from Northern corporations in order to prevent bankruptcy. The practice became so widespread that President Davis, while condemning it, admitted that it might be acceptable as a last resort for destitute farmers.[13] Finally, on April 10, 1863, recognizing the plan had failed, Davis ordered cotton farmers to plant corn instead so that the troops could be fed.

What food could be grown in the South rarely made it to the army or civilians because of the South's primitive and limited railroads. There were no railroad links between some states; in others, the gauge of tracks for one railroad did not match those of another. Planters refused to provide slaves to build the much needed railroad lines. Southern ironworks could not produce enough iron rails for track. The owners of the South's railroads did little to cooperate with the government, and Davis refused to take over the railroads, which Congress had authorized.[14]

These failures led to sagging morale and a growing disenchantment with the war throughout the South. Rebel soldiers, many without socks or shoes, began to write home that they saw no purpose in a continued fight, while women complained that their children were starving, and businessmen were bitter that the war had ruined trade.

The war began to go badly again in 1863. Reports of Bragg's late December 1862 victories in Kentucky proved erroneous. Braxton Bragg, a longtime friend of the president, did not defeat the Federals. His campaign failed, and he had to retreat out of the state. In the east, the Union navy had been bombarding Fort Sumter since the beginning of the year. Twelve hundred shells had pounded the fort since then, and Davis worried that if Sumter fell, Charleston might go with it. The siege of Vicksburg continued Grant's army seemed to be dug in for a fight to the death. Confederate desertions continued to climb.

There were some bright spots on the military map which hung in Davis's office. On January 21, 1863, Confederates at Sabine Pass, Texas, manning a small fort with just a few guns, managed to sink two large Federal gunboats and capture seventy men, forcing General Nathaniel Banks to withdraw. The mercurial victory was hyped for months in the Southern press and took on legendary status to help keep morale high for a while.

Then there was Chancellorsville. Lee and the Army of Northern Virginia, outnumbered more than two to one, scored an impressive victory over the Army of the Potomac and its new commander, Joe Hooker. It was a classic Lee battle. He went on the offensive early and, in a dangerous gamble, split his army in two, sending Stonewall Jackson on a long, circuitous trek west so that he and his men could emerge from a thick forest to smash through the Federal lines. Lee then pressured the Federals along three different angles, forcing them to retreat across the Rappahannock in disgrace. Lee suffered twelve thousand casualties, Hooker seventeen thousand, but the victory boosted morale throughout the Confederacy.

Chancellorsville made Lee, the taciturn, somber, commander, glow with confidence. He had met the ever-growing, 133,000-man Army of the Potomac head on and crushed it. He had once again proved that a small, well-trained, innovative army, with daring commanders, could defeat a much larger force. His feelings were bolstered by uplifting stories in Southern papers and demoralized stories in the Northern press about Chancellorsville. The ecstasy of Lee and Davis was tempered by gloom quickly, however, when Stonewall Jackson was accidentally shot by his own men in the battle, and died. The loss of Lee's "right arm" would turn out to be catastrophic for the army.

Jefferson Davis was never better as head of state than he was at Stonewall Jackson's funeral. The president met the train carrying the general's body, along with five thousand grieving residents, when it arrived at the Richmond train station at 5 P.M. on May 11. The next day, Davis led the mourners who walked past the glass-enclosed coffin, lying in state in the statehouse rotunda. Pale and weak, he rode in his carriage at the head of a funeral cortege observers said probably included every adult living in Richmond and the surrounding area.[15] The president was further debilitated by Jackson's death. He told friends after the funeral, "Too devoted to the cause he served to have any personal motives, he shared the toils, privations and dangers of his troops....He was the complement to Lee....His place was never filled."[16]

He told Lee that the loss was "a national calamity"[17] and that night, unable to pay any attention to a man talking to him, said, "You must excuse me. I am still staggering from a dreadful blow. I cannot think."[18]

Now was the time, Lee told Davis and his cabinet, in what was one of his few politically induced ideas, for another surprise invasion of the North, an attack right into the heart of Pennsylvania that would not only result in another beating for Hooker's army, but a propaganda coup. Lee first broached the idea of a Northern invasion in April, but nothing was done about it because Davis fell ill and was bedridden for a week.[19] The stress of Stonewall Jackson's death in May made the president sick again, and he spent several more weeks in bed.[20] The sight of a large, fast-moving rebel army sweeping across Pennsylvania would terrify the entire population of the North. The pressure on Lincoln to go to the negotiating table afterward would be overwhelming. Lee was so cocky after Chancellorsville he told Davis that he, Lee, would send couriers to Washington to invite Lincoln to a peace conference on his way to Pennsylvania.

Davis, of course, loved the idea, as he did anything Robert E. Lee proposed. The president was mesmerized by Lee. Here was a chance, the Confederate president thought, to end the war immediately. He took the rather unusual step of presenting the plan to the cabinet, whom he never consulted on war matters. They loved it, too. Davis's cabinet was as enchanted with Lee as was the president.

In approving the invasion, they ignored two other very substantive competing proposals. One was a cry for help from Vicksburg, where commanders believed that twenty to thirty thousand men from Lee's army shipped there as reinforcements might enable them to break the siege and beat the bulldog Grant, thereby saving the Mississippi River water transportation route and stopping the man who was emerging as the Union's toughest general. The other was a plea from Longstreet, Beauregard, and D. H. Hill to send twenty thousand of Lee's men to General Bragg, so that he could succeed in his plan to take both Cincinnati and Louisville, which might regain Kentucky, a key border state, open up the Ohio River, and shake up all of Ohio, home of U.S. Secretary of the Treasury Salmon Chase.

Lee was insistent. Hooker would have to come after Lee if he invaded Pennsylvania, and then Lee would beat him. The annihilation of his army would mean that Lincoln would have to recall other armies back to Maryland to protect Washington, where Lee would defeat them. The invasion itself would frighten the entire North, he told everyone, and it would sue for peace. There was a final reason, with which he dared not go public, for the invasion scheme. Lee and Davis knew that desertions were much higher,[21] and supplies much lower, than they admitted; that rations were down to a quarter pound of meat per man per day;[22] and that the Army of Northern Virginia, and the other Confederate armies, could not keep fighting much longer. Lee hinted to Davis that the war might not last beyond 1863 and that if a daring strike were not made now, the South would lose.[23]

His plan approved, Lee began to move right away, crossing the Potomac on June 25. He was forced to advance cautiously because his eyes and ears, J. E. B. Stuart and his cavalry, were off scouting somewhere in Pennsylvania, well out of reach. Lee edged forward blindly, nervous without Stuart and the accurate information he relied upon him to provide. The Army of Northern Virginia, swollen to more than seventy five thousand men,[24] trudged into Pennsylvania—still no Stuart—and stumbled into the tiny little town of Gettysburg, where they accidentally collided with the Army of the Potomac, now commanded not by Hooker, but by George Meade.[25]

The strain of waiting for the news from both Lee and Vicksburg was too much for President Davis. His neuralgia flared up again from the stress. This bout may have been the worst attack of his life. He fell ill in the last few days of June, and on July 2 collapsed and was put to bed, where he remained for over a week. Davis was so ill he could talk to no one, and nobody saw him except his wife. Even the secretary of war and clerks from the War

Department were kept away.[26] The wait for news of Gettysburg and Vicksburg seemed interminable, made more nerve-wracking by wild, unsubstantiated reports from dispatchers that Lee had beaten Meade badly, capturing forty thousand prisoners.[27] A terrible, somber pall fell over the White House as Jefferson Davis lay upstairs, growing weaker and weaker. One of the clerks in the War Department told friends that Davis could never resume office. "[His] health is apparently gone and it may be doubtful whether he will ever be quite well again."[28] Rumors flew that it was entirely possible that Lee's army might be defeated, the garrison at Vicksburg fall, and the president die on the same day.

THE defeat of Lee at Gettysburg on July 3, the loss of Vicksburg on the Fourth of July, followed by the loss of Port Hudson, Louisiana, on July 8, and letters from western governors who assumed the Confederacy would now abandon them,[29] destroyed Davis's morale. He was certain Lee was going to end the war. "Had their [Union] army been...defeated," he wrote years later, "it would have ended the war."[30] He told Mississippi's Governor Pettus that the loss of the river town in their home state was "a painful disappointment,"[31] and General Kirby Smith that it was "a disaster" and that "we are now in the darkest hour of our political existence."[32]

All, however, was not lost. Thanks to the hesitancy of Meade, Lee and his army managed to cross the Potomac and avoid destruction.[33] General Lee reported that his army was in "good condition" despite the savage fight in Pennsylvania.[34] There was also news from the North which buoyed Davis. At the same time Northerners should have been celebrating the fall of Vicksburg and the battle at Gettysburg, they were instead rioting in numerous cities, particularly New York, over Lincoln's draft. Many Northerners were fed up with the war, no matter who controlled Vicksburg.

Davis falsely believed there was still hope from England, too. Several New York newspapers, including the *New York Herald,* shaken by the draft riots there, assumed the British Parliament had decided to intervene in the American war and ask for a peace agreement which would result in an independent Confederacy. Actually, Antietam decided England's stand. In the summer of 1863 British officials not only had no intentions of recognizing the Confederacy and intervening in the war, but halted all construction of Confederate vessels in their shipyards.[35]

Davis felt better about the ultimate outcome of the conflict, even though army desertions now hovered near fifty percent and supplies for the troops were low. Lee told him the Army of Northern Virginia would not move again until the men had shoes.[36] Stung by criticism from the press and from certain congressmen, Lee offered his resignation after Gettysburg. He was turned down. "There is nothing which I have found to require a greater effort of patience than to bear the criticism of the ignorant," said Davis, who knew something about critics, to the general.[37] While Lee was planning new attacks, Confederate troops under scored a victory at Chickamauga, in Georgia. Joe Johnston's army in the west was still strong. Davis's old friend Braxton Bragg was regrouping.

Davis had made some critical mistakes in 1863, which he refused to admit, in both planning campaigns and choosing generals. He had learned nothing from the controversial promotion of his nephew, Joe Davis, from an aide to general in the fall of 1862, or from the criticism he had absorbed at the beginning of the war, when he named so many old army comrades generals. The average age of Confederate generals was fifty-seven making them Davis's contemporaries, compared to just forty-four in the Union army.

President Davis's support of Lee's invasion of the North in July 1863, while on the surface sensible, came at a high cost. Vicksburg fell because there were no reinforcements for the beleaguered city. Grant had surrounded it and his guns pounded it until most of the city's women and children were forced to live in caves. The Confederates were forced to surrender, and surrender on the Fourth of July, the day U. S. Grant said he would have dinner in the best restaurant in Vicksburg. Lee had been certain his invasion of Pennsylvania would force the Union to pull troops away from Vicksburg and other areas to reinforce the Army of the Potomac, but no troops were withdrawn, leaving Vicksburg vulnerable.

Lee's troops were not the only ones Davis refused to send to Vicksburg. His latest secretary of war, George Randolph, had infuriated the president in a paperwork mixup by ordering eleven thousand troops to Vicksburg from Arkansas without the president's permission. Davis immediately counter-manded the order, not because he did not approve of sending help, but solely because he would not let Randolph get away with what he saw as a personal insult to the president.

As the war dragged on, Davis began to spend more time running the War Department and less time on the economy and problems on the homefront. The war consumed him. The president sincerely believed that those serving under him, particularly in the War Department, simply did not have the enthusiasm or capacity for work that he did. Davis took it upon himself, day after day, to do the work of twenty men and women. He did so because he felt he could do it with more skill than anyone else and because, as desertions rose and the spirit of the people sagged, he had come to believe, by the summer of 1863, that government workers no longer had their hearts in the war or their work.

Davis spent hours each day doing nothing but sending out letters and orders to generals. He wrote Lee at least once a day and sent long, repetitive letters filled with excruciating detail to his other generals. Some of his letters were more than fourteen pages long. He wasted countless hours writing dispatches over tiny amounts of supplies, inconsequential promotions, and petty disputes among officers. His greatest fault in the conduct of the war, however, was his never-ending support of bad generals who were personal friends.

Davis's most notorious sponsorship of a bad general was of Braxton Bragg. The general was a depressed, sickly man with large, bushy eyebrows, a thin frame, and a light gray beard who walked slightly stooped over. He was not an aggressive commander, avoiding battles where he could and, when engaged, fighting tentatively.[38] Bragg was brutally criticized for high casualties under his leadership. While riding one day, he asked a man he spotted at the side of a road dressed in butternut and not a uniform, if he was in Bragg's army. The man, not recognizing him, told him that Bragg had no army, that all his men had been killed in his battles.[39] Bragg once asked his own commanders what they thought of him: They replied honestly that he was not fit for command. [40]

The low point of Bragg's command came in an invasion of Kentucky in 1862, when he failed to link up with Kirby Smith's army, bungled his own attack, and defied his orders. He was forced to withdraw from the entire state. That prompted Davis to launch an investigation which stung Bragg. The general's own aides, who by army tradition must support their commander, shredded him in their meeting with Davis, urging the president to dismiss Bragg. Davis refused. Bragg was his friend and Bragg would stay. General Longstreet hinted later that perhaps Bragg didn't have to be effective, that his friendship with Davis would always save him.[41] Davis not only supported Bragg, but believed that people criticized Bragg to belittle the president. He told Bragg, "You have the misfortune of being regarded as my personal friend and are pursued therefore with malignant censure by men regardless of truth. Revolutions develop the high qualities of the good and the great, but they cannot change the nature of the vicious and the selfish."[42]

Davis made ill-considered decisions, based on personal favoritism, which left large cities open to attack. Earlier, in 1862, Davis had left New Orleans vulnerable when he transferred all its regiments to Tennessee, confident that it was impossible for the U.S. Navy to sail up the Mississippi, past Confederate forts, and take the Crescent City, the financial capital of the South and its second largest urban center. He had to remove his handpicked commander and good friend David Twiggs because New Orleans officials complained that the seventy-one-year-old Twiggs was a doddering old man who was unreliable and incapable of command. Davis replaced him with Mansfield Lovell, another friend, who had never risen above the rank of captain in the U.S. Army but whom the president promptly made a general. Lovell wrote Davis as soon as he arrived that the defenses of the city, now that the army was gone, were deplorable, and that he had only a few unreliable gunboats and some three thousand untrained local militia. He told Davis he would even have to borrow rifles from farmers in the area. "I find great confusion, irresolution, and want of system in everything," he complained.[43] Davis ignored him. New Orleans fell the following spring, and many blamed the president.[44]

Vicksburg may have fallen because Davis insisted on backing another untested general, John Pemberton. Pemberton was a native Philadelphian who had become a Southerner when he married a Virginia woman. As a "transplanted Yankee" he was not welcome in Vicksburg. Pemberton had joined the Confederate army when the war broke out, become an artillery specialist, and wound up in Charleston in 1863. Although he had no leadership experience, Davis sent him to Vicksburg to command all Confederate forces there. Irascible, crusty, whining, aloof, and disdainful, Pemberton soon annoyed everyone in Vicksburg, soldier and civilian.

Pemberton's assessment of the situation in Vicksburg was shortsighted. He was so certain that Grant had failed and was leaving the area that he sent his cavalry to Bragg and, shortly afterward, hosted a gala ball in the city to celebrate its safety. In the middle of a lively dance, the sound of the band's music drifting out over the Mississippi, the atmosphere was shattered by explosions and flashes of light. Grant was back. He had crossed the Mississippi south of Vicksburg and approached the city from that direction, foraging for supplies as he went. One planter, seated on a mule, found Grant and complained that Grant's men had taken everything he had. Grant, non-plussed, stared at him and said that they could not have been his men, because "if they were my men, you wouldn't have that mule."[45]

Pemberton miscalculated the size of Grant's army and just about its every move, ignored the long siege trenches Grant was digging closer and closer to the city, and paid little attention to pleas from his men for food and water, until he received a letter assuring him that the soldiers were at the point of mutiny.[46] Unable to get help from Joe Johnston, who could not break through Grant's ring, and having sent many of his men to Bragg, Pemberton was forced to surrender. Instead of chastising him for losing a key city, Davis sympathized with Pemberton and told him he was a victim of "malign" critics.[47]

One of Davis's worst generals, whom he strongly backed, was Earl Van Dorn, an old companion from Mississippi. Davis had taken care of Van Dorn throughout his army life. One of the worst students in West Point history, Van Dorn never made it beyond lieutenant, but as soon as Jefferson Davis became secretary of war he promoted his friend Van Dorn to captain. The high-living, finely dressed Van Dorn, who fancied himself a ladies' man, lost Corinth, Mississippi, and suffered one of the highest casualty rates, twenty percent, of the war. A sergeant at Corinth said Van Dorn was constantly drunk and another general, T. H. Holmes, said the battle was lost because of Van Dorn's "mismanagement and stupidity."[48] Van Dorn was murdered by the jealous husband of one of his girlfriends in 1863.

Leonidas Polk was an old crony of Davis's from West Point, but resigned from the army just three months after graduation, without receiving a commission, and became a minister, rising in the ranks of his church to bishop of Louisiana by the beginning of the war. Davis made Bishop Polk a general, jumping him over hundreds of far better qualified men. Within months of that he put him in charge of a western department and expanded Polk's influence throughout much of the west. Polk, a wretched general, ordered his troops into Kentucky, violating the state's neutrality and causing a political firestorm. Instead of firing Polk, Davis defended him.[49]

Davis also squandered good generals because of personal feuds. The most important of these was P. G. T. Beauregard, the hero of Fort Sumter, who broke with Davis when he objected to his rank and to the decision not to attack Washington, D.C., after Bull Run. Beauregard began firing off letters to Congressman Lewis Wigfall, one of Davis's biggest congressional enemies.

"Jefferson Davis should be hanged," he wrote him.[50] Beauregard's letters earned Davis's eternal wrath.[51] Throughout the war, Davis consistently overlooked Beauregard, a good general, and other capable generals. In return, Beauregard, out of spite, delayed moving his men on many occasions when he was ordered to do so by Davis.

Joe Johnston, with Lee one of the two finest generals the South had, always found himself feuding with Davis, right down to the day he was relieved at Atlanta, and was never sure of his support by the president and the War Department. Johnston complained throughout the war that the president was constantly undermining him and interfering with his plans. Even when he did agree with Johnston, the president told him so in insulting letters. When Johnston wrote he was unsure of Davis's orders, the president shot back that "language cannot be plainer than this."[52] Davis blamed him for anything that went wrong in his department and, when Vicksburg fell, unfairly said of Johnston that "he wouldn't fight."

Davis practically accused Johnston of cowardice many times. "Not once during the [Vicksburg] campaign did he act on the maxim of attacking the foe," Davis said, and accused him of being afraid to fight in Georgia. "The enemy commenced advancing in May and General Johnston began retreating."[53]

The feud with Johnston, too, exemplified the president's inability to accept any criticism or get through any conversation or exchange of letters without feeling he was being victimized and had to somehow fight back. Davis was aware of it and yet could not change his attitude. "I wish I would learn just to let people alone who snap at me, in forbearance and charity to turn away as well from the cats as the snakes," he wrote Varina.[54]

Davis's relationship with Johnston was also an example of his tendency to hold a grudge for years. He became so obsessed with his hatred of the general that after the war he would not attend veteran reunions if he knew Johnston would be there. Those grudges against Johnston and dozens of other generals severely curbed his effectiveness as commander in chief.

But the worst example of the calamitous results of Davis's support of incompetent longtime friends was General Lucius Northrop, the man responsible for the procurement and distribution of food for the entire Confederate army. Generals started to complain about Northrop immediately after the first battle of Bull Run, in 1861, when Joe Johnston wrote several congressmen that the only reason the army had not attacked Washington was because, thanks to Northrop's ineptness, it was woefully supplied and could not advance. Others began to complain, too, charging that the men were starving, and Northrop quickly became "the most cussed and vilified man in the Confederacy."[55] He was so inept that Beauregard suggested he be booted out of the army and sent to China.

Northrop was a hopeless bungler. He had accidentally shot himself in the knee in 1839. He left large supplies of meat in Manassas, where it rotted. He once lost two entire herds of cattle he was supposed to send Lee. He illegally traded cotton for meat with intermediaries from the North after Davis vetoed the idea. When supplies were so low the rations were cut back to a quarter pound of beef per man per day, General Lee asked Northrop to issue a national plea for more food. Northrop turned him down. Lee also suggested trading sugar, which the commissary had in abundance and rarely used, for bacon for the troops, but Northrop again turned him down, telling Robert E. Lee, brusquely, to mind his own business.

Like so many others in the army, Northrop kept his job throughout the war because of his friendship with Jefferson Davis. The two met in the army in the 1830s and remained friends for thirty years. Davis first helped out Northrop when he tried to keep his commission in the army after agreeing to give it up so he could go to medical school. The army turned him down, but Davis, then a U.S. senator, went right to President Polk and not only got Northrop reinstated, but promoted. Davis made him head of commissary as soon as the war began, and defended Northrop throughout the conflict and until the end of his life. "Much credit is due for his well directed efforts to provide both for immediate and prospective wants," he said.[56]

Northrop was despised by everybody else. He was frequently charged with corruption, malfeasance, and, at the very least, an inability to provide enough food for the fighting men. Northern prisoners of war bitterly accused him of keeping meat out of prison camps in an effort to kill them. Prisoners of war and Confederate soldiers alike complained that the food they did get tasted awful. The president stuck with Northrop until the last days of the war, when he finally relieved him. A few months after the war, Northrop spent several months in a federal prison before charges against him were dropped. He complained bitterly about the bad food.[57]

Southerners wrote long and harsh letters to the president complaining about generals like Bragg, T. H. Holmes, and Pemberton. A chaplain in the First Missouri Cavalry told Davis that "in the matter of selecting generals...

there is universal dissatisfaction. This dissatisfaction is now about to culminate in utter ruin to our cause." He urged Davis to fire Pemberton, who he said was a "traitor," and to replace Holmes with Sterling Price. He warned Davis that if he did not start appointing talented generals, the blame for Vicksburg and all other losses would be pinned on him.[58]

Some generals quit and went away; some quit and stirred up trouble. Milledge Bonham, of South Carolina, left the army after a dispute with Davis. He was then elected to Congress, where he was a key player in the anti-Davis faction. W. H. T. Walker resigned after a much publicized feud with the president, involving the quarrelsome Georgia delegation, which, using Walker's resignation, solidified its opposition to Davis in Congress.

Davis also faced daily opposition from several of the South's leading newspapers. Most Southern newspapers supported the government, and any criticism of Davis was usually mild. They also grossly misled their readers about the fighting, constantly trying to make the Southern armies look good, as Northern papers did with Union forces. They would print rumor after rumor about nonexistent Southern victories, for example, the early stories which appeared in dozens of newspapers about Lee's smashing victory over Meade at Gettysburg. Several major papers criticized Davis for not attacking Washington after Bull Run in 1861. At least one in each state lamented that one of its own favorite sons was not president. The Georgia papers clamored for Howell Cobb, which annoyed Varina.[59] Yet for the most part their barbs were infrequent.

The most constant critics, however, were probably the four most important papers in the South: the *Richmond Whig,* the *Richmond Examiner,* the *Charleston Mercury,* and the *Raleigh Standard.* While the *Whig* was critical, the *Examiner,* run first by John Daniel and later by Edward Pollard, was relentless. The other two Richmond papers, the *Enquirer* and *Dispatch*, were progovernment. The hostile papers hurt Davis considerably, because their daily attacks on almost everything he did were read by everyone in government who had power and the support Davis needed: the cabinet, the executive departments, and Congress, in addition to influential visitors from other states.[60]

President Davis was exasperated by the local papers and the few critical of him in other states. He fumed that there was a war going on and that Southern newspapers should at least be loyal to the South's hard-fighting army and its government. The Washington newspapers were strong supporters of

Abraham Lincoln, yet Richmond's papers helped neither the Southern president nor his government. Davis believed throughout the war that the local press was harsh and unfair.

As the war wore on, the *Examiner's* attacks grew savage. Edward Pollard, its editor, attacked almost all of Davis's economic policies, appointments, and military campaigns and routinely criticized the cabinet. His disdain for Davis and his policies and appointments carried well beyond the normal boundaries of criticism, even for the often vicious nineteenth-century press. When Davis named Bragg a military aide in Richmond, after he had failed so badly as a field commander, the *Examiner* told its readers that in the Mexican War General Taylor had been reportedly critical of Bragg and had yelled at him, in reference to cannonfire, "a little more grape, Captain Bragg." The *Examiner* parodied the line and wrote of Bragg as an advisor, "a little more *brains*, Captain Bragg."[61] As early as 1862, when all of Richmond approved of the president's regular visits to church, the *Examiner* accused him of praying too much and said he was wasting time on rosary beads, hoping for some miracle, when he could be winning the war.[62] In 1864, after a runaway slave set fire to the Confederate White House during a party and all escaped without harm, all of Richmond gasped when the *Examiner* wrote that he should have torched the building late at night, when the Davises were asleep and could not get out.[63]

Robert Rhett, the owner of the *Charleston Mercury,* whom Davis originally wanted to make secretary of state, split with the Davis administration early and became a heated critic, savaging the president and his cabinet every day in front-page editorials. Rhett said that Secretary of the Navy Mallory was not ill after the fall of New Orleans, but that "he keeps to bed because he loves it, and because he finds the seclusion of the sheets very comfortable."[64] Rhett belittled everything about Davis, even his health, telling readers that "when another battle is won...we won't have to wait half a year for Jeff Davis to recover his health."[65] The *Mercury* was important because South Carolina had been the first state to secede and was the moral leader of the entire secession movement. Charleston was one of the wealthiest cities in the South and home to men who became influential congressmen.

The *Raleigh Weekly Standard* was important because it had wide readership in North Carolina. A key state, North Carolina supplied many troops. Its independent governor, Zebulon Vance, was also critical of Davis's policies. The *Standard* routinely criticized Davis and often advocated a negotiated peace to end the war. The combination of an obstinate governor and an angry newspaper hurt. Davis said that William Holden, the paper's editor, was guilty of treason for his articles against the administration.[66] The men in the army saw the *Standard* as so pro-Union that when a regiment of Georgia troops was marching through Raleigh in September 1863 they shot up the building with rifles.[67]

There were other anti-Davis papers, such as the *Chattanooga Rebel,* whose criticism of Braxton Bragg was so strong that the general tried, unsuccessfully, to get its editor fired; the *Macon* (Ga.) *Telegraph,* the *Columbus* (S.C.) *Sun,* the *Augusta* (Ga.) *Chronicle & Sentinel,* and the *Savannah Republican,* but none had the influence of the *Examiner, Mercury,* and *Standard.*

Friends urged Davis simply to shut down newspapers like the *Examiner,* which he might have done when Richmond was under martial law, but he refused (he later called Pollard a "malignant"). Davis was no champion of a free press, but he did not want to curb newspapers.

Cabinet members understood that in a two-party system each party owned hundreds of newspapers, but in a one-party system that influence was lost. They urged the president to start his own newspaper or convince one of the existing pro-Confederate dailies in Richmond, such as the *Enquirer* or *Dispatch,* to become more of a forum for the president and the government.[68] (Davis and his brother were certainly wealthy enough to buy one of their own.) He refused.

All his cabinet members, themselves irate at the constant criticism,[69] then tried to get the president to have more contact with the press, particularly the Richmond editors, including the men at the *Examiner,* and perhaps even include editors in discussions on policy to make them feel important, so they would sheathe their editorial knives. Davis did bend a bit, and held one or two informal meetings with reporters from friendly papers in 1863, just after Gettysburg,[70] but he never met editors who were critical of him, such as the *Examiner*'s Pollard. John Daniel, Pollard's flamboyant predecessor and one of the best-dressed men in Richmond, had attended several receptions for Davis—his presence shocked the president's friends—but there is no record they talked politics or journalism.[71]

Clerks in the War Department, with Davis's approval, wrote press releases about army victories and carried them to the offices of the friendly papers in the capital. They were usually printed word for word. Nevertheless, Davis made no effort to befriend or communicate with William Pritchard, the head of a news agency in Richmond, whose reporters wrote stories which were telegraphed to dozens of large Confederate state newspapers. He similarly neglected the heads of the Press Association of the Confederate States, formed in 1863, which did the same thing.[72]

Davis never did a thing to improve his relations with the press at any level. He had always held newspapers in contempt, and his views were only strengthened when some editors criticized him and his administration after he took office. Davis paid no attention to the views of editors and told generals not to pay attention to the press either, that any criticism that came their way was unwarranted.[73]

"The indulgence of evil passion against myself injures not the individual only but the cause also of which I am a zealous though feeble representative," he said of the attacks on him in the press.[74]

His refusal to establish any kind of relations with the Richmond editors, or to correspond with editors around the Confederacy, ruined whatever chance he had to win support in the press. His terrible relations with the *Examiner*, which might have been better if he had tried to cultivate its headstrong editors, were particularly harmful because the government was in Richmond. When people in his government see a president shredded in a hometown newspaper every day, they begin to feel that he *is* wrong, and even if he is right, the poor public perception makes him weak and ineffective in his dealings with those in the government.

While Davis ignored editors and reporters, he never antagonized them. In fact, when editors complained that they could not publish their newspapers if they were drafted, he rewrote the Conscription Act to exempt them. He had no use for their newspapers, though, and promptly vetoed a bill approved by Congress granting free distribution of newspapers to the troops.[75] Nevertheless, Davis never contemplated censoring or shutting down any critical newspapers in the South, even after the Union began to close newspapers, for a time, with regularity.[76] Outside Richmond and Charleston, the Southern press had little power by the middle of 1864. Many editors had enlisted in the army, and their papers had gone out of business. Newspapers in occupied states were either shut down or taken over by the Union army. There were over eight hundred Southern newspapers in 1861, but only 123 in 1865.[77]

He was also a firm believer in freedom of the press. Editors and reporters never lavished their praise on Davis, but he refused to follow the advice of many in the cabinet and the army to close hostile newspapers. He knew that critical newspapers undermined his ability to govern, especially the local papers in Richmond, but he believed strongly in the right of newspapers to publish without government censorship. Their barbs stung him repeatedly, but he never once considered retaliating.

Davis had his supporters throughout the war. They responded to his numerous critics that he was not only doing his best to win the war and to solve the problems of the economy, but was governing as a humanitarian interested in preserving individual liberties, while running the army as an enlightened commander, not a merciless field marshal.

His backers used his policy on deserters as an example. Thousands of soldiers had deserted the Confederate army. They all knew the penalty was death by firing squad. Indeed, hundreds of deserters in Northern armies had been shot. Jefferson Davis never authorized a single execution for desertion. As a former army officer, he knew that most desertions had extenuating circumstances. His benevolent attitude was not only accepted, but applauded by his generals. Furthermore, while Northern generals and officials conveniently looked the other way when minors (under eighteen) enlisted in the army, Jefferson Davis forbade the enlistment of minors until the war was almost over.

Despite his humanitarian feelings about the army, freedom of the press, and the families of the South, Davis and his staff governed with little imagination. Davis had enormous powers as president, largely because he had a guaranteed six-year term and ruled over a Congress that had to support most of what he did because it was fighting a revolution, yet he never broke new ground.

The war gave Jefferson Davis opportunities to implement policies that would bring about sweeping economic, social, and cultural progress, yet he did nothing. Southerners had always paid light taxes, and he could not tax them to pay for the war. His foreign policy showed no knowledge of British politics, though he continued to believe England would enter the war. He was incapable of changing his belligerent personality in an office in which reasonably amiable relationships with people were part of the job. The presidency did not transform Davis, and Davis did not transform the presidency.

The calamitous year of 1863 ended with a rather gloomy message from the president to Congress in which he warned the people that they had to continue to sacrifice for the Cause, and that the army had to fight longer and harder to win the war. But the war's tide had turned at Gettysburg and Vicksburg and in a thousand smaller places where the well-oiled Union war machine grew stronger and stronger under brilliant and innovative leadership. The Congress and the people of Richmond listened to what Jefferson Davis said, too, about the vile Yankees, because they had an ominous feeling that in 1864 they would not be fighting them in Pennsylvania and Mississippi, but in their own backyard.

21

JEFFERSON DAVIS: EMANCIPATION

JEFF DAVIS HAD BEEN A HERO to slaveholders in Mississippi and throughout the old South all his life. He had been one of the old South's largest slaveholders, owning as many as 107. In Congress and in the Senate he had fought every bill to curb slavery in the South or in the territories with all his strength. He firmly believed that slaves were property and that if their owners chose to use that property to work plantations, there was nothing wrong with it. His entire fortune, and much of of his brother's wealth, was built on slavery.

Davis was more than just a typical slaveholder, though—he was a benevolent owner. He was often criticized for becoming very friendly with his slaves, such as James Pemberton, probably the closest friend he ever had, and treating them just as he would treat white people: bringing in doctors and dentists for them, building them a hospital, letting them run the slave quarters with their own courts and system of justice. Other owners rebuked him for stopping and tipping his hat to blacks he met on the street in Washington.

They were critical, but they all knew that their best defense against Northern charges about slavery was Jeff Davis. He was very good to his slaves, and they were quite satisfied with their lives on his plantation, his friends said, proving that slaveowners could treat their slaves well and that there was nothing wrong with the system. Jefferson Davis gave up his career as a U.S. senator for slavery, and put his entire fortune in jeopardy to defend it. Now, on

369

November 7, 1864, Jefferson Davis did the unthinkable. In his annual message to Congress he shook the foundation of the entire Confederacy; like Abraham Lincoln before him, he raised the possibility of the emancipation of the South's slaves.

By the start of the cold winter of 1864, the Confederate army had begun to lose its will to fight. It had been driven out of the North twice and had lost New Orleans and Vicksburg. The army had failed to prevent Sherman from taking Atlanta and starting his march through Georgia to the sea. The army had been driven out of the Shenandoah Valley, where it had prospered for years. Desertion rates were high. Food and supplies for the troops were low. The draft had taken just about every able-bodied man left, even youngsters under eighteen, who sneaked into the ranks, and old men over sixty, who fought to keep the Federals out of Richmond the previous winter. Nearly two hundred fifty thousand soldiers had died. The army needed fresh, new troops—and the only men left were the slaves.

The Southern states held nearly four million African Americans in bondage. Approximately seven hundred thousand of them were men between the ages of eighteen and sixty. Davis believed that if just half of them could be persuaded to fight, the infusion of so many soldiers could turn the tide of the war. In return, the president of the Confederacy would give any slave who had fought his freedom at the end of the war and, in a shrewd move designed to placate Southerners who feared free blacks living among them, help the freed soldier-slaves settle new Confederate colonies in the far west after the war was won.

The idea of emancipation for slaves who fought in the army did not originate with Davis, and it was not new. Emancipation had first been proposed two years earlier, in 1862, by Louisiana Congressman Duncan Kenner. The astute Kenner told Davis that freeing the slaves was certain to bring England and France into the war on the side of the Confederacy, while as long as the South held its slaves those nations would never support Davis.

Emancipation was discussed again in late 1863 by a Southern commander, General Patrick Cleburne, who, with thirteen other officers, signed a petition calling for the government to draft slaves and grant them freedom as an incentive to fight.[1] Cleburne, like several other leaders, realized that the Confederate army had become a shadow of its self, its glory days behind it. It could not continue in the field against always growing and well-supplied federal armies without new troops, particularly troops that would fight harder than anyone because victory meant freedom—the greatest incentive of all.[2]

Davis dismissed Cleburne's petition when he heard of it, but the idea stuck in his mind. Cleburne's view of a slave army was far more realistic than that of possibly any other of Davis's commanders, because Cleburne was a transplanted Irishman who moved to Arkansas as an adult. None of the South's centuries' old slavery traditions were his. He could speak plainly while others, planters or the friends of planters, could not. Cleburne was also one of Davis's most trusted commanders.

Cleburne was a tough soldier who knew what he was talking about when it came to analyzing men. He had formed his own regiment, the Yell Rifles, before Arkansas seceded, and with it he captured a federal arsenal in Little Rock. He became a general in 1862 and fought at Shiloh, Richmond, Perryville, Stones River, and Chickamauga. He was wounded but returned to the service immediately. Cleburne succeeded Hardee as commander in the Atlanta campaign, and was cited by the Confederate Congress for bravery when he saved Bragg's artillery and wagons at Ringold Gap. Soldiers and the press nicknamed him the "Stonewall Jackson of the West."[3] If Cleburne said the army needed help, the army needed help.[4]

Cleburne received no support from the army. Its leaders assumed slaves would not fight well and, naturally, were reluctant to give firearms to slaves who might then turn them on their former masters. Yet there were others who pressured Davis to draft slaves in return for freedom. In September, 1864, a friend told him that if freedom was the carrot, he could draft all the slaves he needed.[5] Several, out of earshot of War Department personnel, pointed out that at Fort Wagner, Olustee, and other places, freed blacks and runaway slaves fighting in black regiments for the Union had distinguished themselves as brave soldiers.[6] Several congressmen had discussed bills to permit slaves to serve in the army as combat soldiers during 1864, but they got nowhere. In October 1864 the governors of North Carolina, South Carolina, Georgia, Alabama, Mississippi, and Virginia met in Augusta, Georgia, in a general states' meeting on the progress of the war. Prodded by Governor William Smith of Virginia, who succeeded Letcher in 1864, they urged Davis to expand the role of slaves impressed into the army far beyond their serving as laborers, although they did not recommend arming them.[7]

Even though commanders were against utilizing slave soldiers, none complained to Davis about the slaves who worked for the army. Local commanders were borrowing slaves from area planters for menial work as early as October 1861.[8] The Impressment Act of 1863 authorized the borrowing of slaves by any commander in the South.[9] A February 1864 bill proposed by Davis and passed by Congress permitted the army to use local slave labor to build defenses for camps over short periods of time. The slaves, loaned to the army by planters, worked hard. Other slaves were used to do menial work in warehouses, depots, and hospitals. Virginia, under Governor John Letcher, did the same thing in 1863, freeing slaves from plantation chores for employment by the Army of Northern Virginia,[10] for which they worked building roads and as teamsters.[11] These slaves had no offers of freedom, however, and after a period of several weeks were returned to their owners.

The idea of complete freedom for slave soldiers was a landmark reversal in thinking for any Southern leader, especially the president. Was not slavery the reason the war was being fought? Why continue the war if the slaves would be free? What kind of a country would the Confederacy be with freed slaves living among the whites?

Davis was careful in his speech to Congress, which did not proclaim emancipation but rather let the people know that if conditions in the army continued to deteriorate, he was prepared to enroll slaves in its ranks. He did break new ground, however, in his view of the slaves and his view of the old South. He began the message with a startling opening, telling Congress that the slaves were not property, as the South had viewed them for two hundred years, but people. He had to define them as people in order to use freedom as an incentive. Property needs no incentive; people do. He knew he was on dangerous ground. Defining slaves as people eliminated the property argument which planters had used for so long and opened up the door to human rights for people of any color.

Davis quickly let the congressmen know that the owners of any slaves who joined the army would be immediately compensated at their full market value so the slaveholders would profit by it. Carefully outlining his plan, he explained that he would recruit no more than forty thousand slave soldiers at first and that the total would never exceed more than twenty-five percent of the total adult male slave population, so that plantations would not be shorthanded. The president added that two hundred years of efforts by planters to Christianize slaves had turned them into people who, when free, would not cause trouble, fending off generations of charges, some made by

Davis himself, that free black men would rape and pillage the white South.[12]

Jefferson Davis never really wanted to free the slaves, but the war forced him to consider it. He believed until the very end that the Confederacy could win the war, but the evidence in front of him in the winter of 1864–1865 indicated that the South was facing defeat. The army needed new soldiers, and there were none. Possibly the only way to keep the army in the field was through slave regiments. He had come to believe that the Confederacy as a nation was far more important than slavery as an institution. The nation could not survive unless the slaves joined the army, and the slaves would not join the army unless they were freed. Thus, the salvation of the Confederacy could only be assured by freeing the slaves to fight in the army.

Jeff Davis had told Varina in a moment of uncertainty on the eve of the war that in several years events would bring the slaves freedom. He would do anything to save his country, and if freeing the slaves would preserve the Confederacy, he would follow Lincoln's policy as published in his letter to Greeley, when he said he would do anything to preserve the Union. Davis told the Congress and his friends in Richmond, particularly those opposed to the idea, that if the South lost the war, Lincoln would free the slaves anyway. Wasn't it better to free them now and have them fight to save the Confederacy? Finally, he told friends that loyalty to the slavery system risked victory in the war itself. "If the Confederacy falls, there should be written on its tombstone, 'Died of a theory.'"[13]

The first reaction to Davis's speech was negative. "The suggestion of the employment of negroes as soldiers finds little favor except with that portion who represent imaginary constituencies," wrote Robert Kean, head of the Bureau of War,[14] who added that he was against a postwar society in which blacks were free.

Howell Cobb, a longtime Davis foe, said the idea betrayed the whole notion of Southern rights. "The day you make soldiers of them [slaves] is the beginning of the end of the revolution. If the slaves will make good soldiers our whole theory of slavery is wrong."[15]

Southern newspapers were shocked. Many agreed with the stand of the *Richmond Dispatch,* that to free the slaves would be doing exactly what the abolitionists had campaigned for during the past one hundred years.[16] Besides, the newspapers argued, if the government were going to free the slaves and the war had been fought to keep slavery, what was the point of the war?

Slowly, however, support grew for emancipation.[17] Governor Smith of

Virginia again supported the idea. He was joined by Governor Henry Allen of Louisiana. A few congressmen supported the concept at first, a distinct minority, but over the next few weeks their ranks increased.

Davis remembered Duncan Kenner's recommendation on emancipation's benefits in European political circles and sent him to England in January, 1865 to update officials on Davis's emancipation bill. Kenner, a Louisianan who lost his slaves when the Union army occupied his state, asked British cabinet ministers to call for a sixty-day ceasefire in the American Civil War and for the opening up of the U.S. blockade to allow the entry of European shipping.[18] But by that time neither nation was willing to become involved in the American conflict, and officials in England told Kenner bluntly that as far as they were concerned, the war was over.[19]

THE emancipation of the slaves to fight in the weakened Confederate army was perhaps the only political campaign that Jeff Davis conducted well in his entire presidency. Unpopular himself, he knew he had to marshal the support of politicians highly regarded by Congress and the public and, most of all, he needed the support of Robert E. Lee. His friend was a longtime opponent of slavery[20] and now, finally, was in a position where he desperately needed every soldier he could get. Davis was certain that Lee would support him because Lee kept sending reports about the declining strength and sagging morale of the army.

Confederate soldiers, too, complained bitterly about the conditions in the army. Over one hundred men were deserting each day.[21] "There are a good many of us who believe this shooting match has been carried on long enough. A government that has run out of rations can't expect to do much more fighting," wrote one soldier from Maryland in the winter of 1864–65.[22]

Lee's support would prove critical. He was not only the most beloved man in the country, Lee *was* the army. Davis needed the army behind the plan and Lee gave him the army. General Lee personally courted congressmen and senators to swing their support behind Davis and the bill. He talked to Richmond newspaper editors about it and, whenever he could, conferred with influential private citizens with strong political ties to certain congressmen and senators.

Davis, who had such trouble getting along with people, made a Herculean effort to court men he had disdained throughout the war: among them governors, senators, congressmen, and state legislators. He also used members of his cabinet, such as Judah Benjamin, to work on legislators who loathed the president and to build support for the proposal with the Richmond press, whose editors had, at best, shaky relations with the President.[23] To every one, Davis's message was the same as Lee's: get the slaves into the Confederate army and not the Union's.[24]

Lee worked alongside Davis in pushing for the legislation, writing several congressmen of his need for black troops.[25] "[Slaves] are not only expedient but necessary...the enemy will certainly use them against us if he can get possession of them," he told anyone who would listen, assuring them the slaves would make efficient soldiers[26] if only emancipation had to be assured.[27] Davis also ordered an informal survey to be taken in the army itself in order to gauge the reaction of officers and men to the idea of black troops fighting under them or next to them, and was pleased at the positive reception.[28]

Davis took his emancipation campaign to the public, too. For symbolic reasons he decided to give his major speech at the African Church, in Richmond, where he was joined by Judah Benjamin, where Benjamin delivered, reporters said, one of his best wartime orations. The noontime speech had been heavily advertised throughout the city and county, but Davis was surprised at the huge turnout of more than ten thousand people. Rivers of people flowed through the aisles, and the throng overflowed outside, surrounding the church. Windows were thrown open so the crowds could hear the president. Hundreds of people unable to get seats jammed in the choir loft, which seemed so overloaded with humanity that it might tumble down on those below.

The president was the first speaker at the rally. He waited in the small church lobby until he was introduced. Davis was sick again, his eye clouded over and his thin frame racked with pain. He was uncertain of the reaction he would get, even though he had had his aides spread the word of Lee's support of the black troops. When he stepped forward as his name was called, his head shot up and applause broke like a thunderclap around him. Everyone was on his or her feet. Men threw their hats in the air and kicked the benches in front of them. Women stomped their feet against the old wooden floor. Children yelled as loud as they could. The president moved slowly down the main aisle, a smile slowly spreading across his face. As he walked forward, he reached out to shake hands, the roar of approval drowning out anything that was said to him. The applause did not stop as he took his place behind the lectern. The moment was perhaps the highlight of his time in office.

Jefferson Davis, inspired by the crowd and by the presence of Varina, delivered the speech of his life, castigating the North and Abraham Lincoln and calling for Southerners to do all they could to help the army. Referring to veiled peace feelers that had surfaced in the newspapers, Davis told the crowd he would stand with the Confederacy, that he would "live and die with it," to a new burst of applause.

Davis began with great emotion,[29] telling the crowd that Sherman's march through Georgia would be his last. He said the time had come to take desperate steps. He outlined his plans for black troops, saying that "we are reduced to choosing whether the Negroes shall fight for us or against us."[30] Davis quickly danced around the 240-year-old notion of the slave as property and explained to a rather shocked audience that slaves were people. "The slave, however, bears another relation to our state...that of a person," he said, opening the door for his argument, which was that property could not defend a plantation, but people could. "In this respect [fighting for the South] the relation of a person predominates so far as to render it doubtful whether the private right of property can consistently and beneficially be continued."

He went on to carefully propose that the states and Congress consider emancipation for slaves who joined the army. "The policy of engaging to liberate the Negro on his discharge after service faithfully rendered seems to me preferable to that of granting immediate manumission or that of retaining him in servitude." He finished by looking up at the choir loft and, raising his voice toward all Southerners, told the people, "Let us unite our hands and our hearts; lock our shields together, and fight on." A tidal wave of noise roared down on him and the building shook from the sound.[31]

Despite efforts by Davis, Benjamin, and others, there was so much opposition to the bill—led by the ever growing anti-Davis faction—that it was not voted on until March 13, 1865, and then only after Davis asked Lee to help him woo congressmen.[32] But it was too late.[33] The emancipation bill barely passed Congress and went down to defeat in the Senate by one vote—from Virginia. Thereafter it floundered until the Virginia legislature ordered its senators to change their votes and approve it. Even at the last moment, slaveholders tried to scuttle it by insisting that although slaves could serve in the army, and at the same pay as whites, they could only gain freedom if emancipation came from their owners and not Jefferson Davis. Davis got around that a week after passage, adding that owners had to provide manumission papers when a slave *joined* the army, not when he *left* it.

No longer able to defer help for their boys in the field, the Virginia state legislature, on its own, passed emergency legislation that authorized emancipation for any slave who joined the Army of Northern Virginia.[34] The Virginia lawmakers were spurred on by Lee, who told them that "the services of these men are now *necessary* to enable us to oppose the enemy."[35] The law directed him to begin recruiting as many able-bodied slaves as he could. Within days, Lee had men combing plantations in the middle counties of Virginia in search of slaves to join the army.[36] Jeff Davis, fed up with the Congress, had urged Lee to cooperate with his own state legislators and to recruit troops under their jurisdiction as quickly as possible, not to wait for the dawdling congressmen.[37] Davis told Virginia's newly elected governor William Smith to work quickly to enlist those blacks most likely to run away to join the Union army in order to increase black recruits for the Confederate army, while holding down the number of black troops in the Union army.[38]

Several dozen slaves did join the army, and were scheduled to be emancipated, but they did not arrive in Richmond for training until the beginning of April. They never saw action, but they were freed. With the fall of Richmond and its occupation by the Union army they were automatically free under the Emancipation Proclamation—of Abraham Lincoln.

22

ABRAHAM LINCOLN AT WAR: 1864–1865

Most of the important people gathered for the president's weekly reception arrived in elegant carriages under the White House portico with great fanfare on March 8, 1864. The men were dressed in their best suits, the women in splendid gowns. Ornate watch fobs dangled from the men's vests, and expensive jewelry sparkled around the women's necks. They joined the large throng inside the executive mansion, where a low din of animated conversation drowned out the tinkling of glasses. There was excitement at seeing the president, clearly visible, thanks to his height, wherever he moved in the room, but there was added anticipation tonight: General Grant was rumored to be in town to take command of all Union armies. Partygoers kept one eye on the festivities and the president, and another on the windows. They expected to see Grant, a national hero, arrive at the head of a large, noisy parade or in the biggest carriage of a long carriage caravan or, at the very least, surrounded by dozens of immaculately dressed cavalry troops, perhaps with a band leading them.

Shortly after 8 P.M. the doorman noticed a very ordinary-looking, short, bearded man in a military uniform, a cigar sticking from the side of his mouth, walk quietly up the driveway, accompanied by two other soldiers. General Grant had arrived in Washington.

"Why, here is General Grant!" the president said, walking across the room to meet him. "Well, this is a great pleasure!" The president took Grant's hand, shook it warmly, and the two men talked for a few moments in a friendly way. Lincoln then led Grant into the East Room, where everyone turned to see him. The two greeted Seward, and the secretary of state began to introduce Grant, but the crowd surged around them, threatening to crush them. Seward, noticing a nearby couch, helped to hoist the general up on it, where he could be seen by everyone, and Grant waved to the crowd as the president looked on, beaming. Grant was not able to get down from the couch for over an hour, as well-wishers pressed around him to welcome him to Washington.[1]

The president was pleased at the crowd's enthusiasm for the hero of Vicksburg. Even Mary Lincoln liked Grant. The president had found his latest, and he hoped his last, general in chief, the man who, he prayed, would take the Army of the Potomac into Virginia, crush the rebels once and for all, and win the bloody war that had tormented him and the American people for so long.

Grant met with Lincoln later that night. He completely understood who was the commander in chief. He had already promised Lincoln he would not run for president against him in 1864[2] and now, at the late-night, post-party meeting, Grant agreed that at his formal appointment the next day he would tell the cabinet exactly what the president told him to say.[3] In subsequent meetings Grant would abandon his own plans for the Army of the Potomac and other armies, which involved sending small forces into the South to cut off railroads while leaving Washington unprotected, in deference to the president's wishes. The general recognized, too, that by the spring of 1864 the civilian president had become a very good general.[4]

Lincoln's strategy for winning the war was the same as always—defeat Lee. He had been frustrated by all the earlier leaders of the Army of the Potomac; they had wanted to capture cities, not Lee and his men. Hooker, especially, had exasperated him. Lincoln told Hooker in 1863 that "Lee's army, and not Richmond, is your true objective point. If he comes towards the Upper Potomac, follow on his flank, and on the inside track, shortening your lines, whilst he lengthens his. Fight him when the opportunity offers. If he stays where he is, fret him, fret him."[5]

Lincoln was able to make Grant commit the Army of the Potomac to another invasion of Virginia with Lee's army its target. He liked Grant. Whenever cabinet members or congressmen would criticize him, Lincoln would tell them, "Grant fights!" He liked his aggressive attitude, his handling of his men, his candor, his casual manner, and his businesslike approach to the war. One of the things he liked most about Grant was that he did not flood Lincoln's office with pointless or self-serving telegrams and letters, as most generals did. He appreciated Grant's protection and care for the freed slaves who poured into Union camps after the Emancipation Proclamation, especially Grant's sensitive decision to put them all under the care of an army chaplain and not a commander.[6]

Grant admired Lincoln. He fully understood, like Lincoln, that the war had a political as well as a military purpose. He was able to see beyond his cannons, to grasp how each battle and campaign fit into the overall political effort to end the war. Lincoln carefully explained to him that Lee had to be trapped not only to beat him, but to prevent any more wild invasions of the North, which panicked the public and hurt support for the war. Washington had to be protected at all costs. The loss of the capital to the Confederates, even though the government might escape, would be a disaster. Grant took politicians Lincoln had made generals and put them where they would earn the most honor and do the least harm. He took on Robert Lincoln as his personal aide so he could join the army, yet stay out of the line of fire.

It was politics that consumed Lincoln in the winter of 1864, as Grant prepared his army for an attack on Virginia in the spring. The president still needed to complete his reconstruction package, which had lingered in the Congress for weeks. Reconstruction, efforts to bring occupied and future Southern states back into the Union while at the same time guaranteeing freedom to slaves and securing work for them, was one of Lincoln's grand economic and political schemes.

As soon as New Orleans fell to federal forces in 1862, Lincoln worked around Congress, using his position as commander in chief, to have the army, under Butler and then Banks, begin the reconstruction of occupied areas of Louisiana, naming a military governor, establishing new legislatures, procuring paid labor jobs for slaves (often at the old plantations for their former masters), and severing all ties between the state and the Confederacy. Under constant pressure from the president, Banks conducted elections among eleven thousand white male voters and managed to get his man elected governor.

The president hoped to use the Louisiana success as a model. His formal Reconstruction Plan, announced in his message to Congress at the end of 1863, called for restoration of all rights and properties to Southerners who took a loyalty oath to the Union, freedom for all slaves, amnesty for all Confederate soldiers, and new state governments to be elected when ten percent of the voting population of any state agreed to rejoin the Union. He carefully left Congress options on the implementation of reconstruction,[7] telling Congress it could determine whether to readmit former congressmen and senators from rebellious states.[8]

Lincoln's plan was overturned by radical Republicans, who insisted that fifty percent of the residents of Southern states had to approve reentry to the Union; that Southerners had to free their slaves legally, a step past Lincoln's inferred freedom; and that Congress, and not the president, had complete control over reconstruction. The bill was introduced by Henry Winter Davis of Maryland, who had an ulterior motive for getting back at the president and the Blair family, his longtime nemesis, over issues in Maryland. The bill was cosponsored by Ohio senator, and fiery abolitionist leader, Ben Wade. Both houses approved the bill, thereby forcing Lincoln into a corner. The people wanted reconstruction. The logical step beyond emancipation was citizenship for the slaves, a goal of many Northerners. Signing the bill would please many, but it would give Congress, and not Lincoln, control of reconstruction. The reentry of the Southern states, when the war ended, would be difficult and contentious. The president was afraid reconstruction would fail badly if the different factions of Congress fought over it, particularly if the radicals emerged victorious, because they favored treating the seceded states like conquered provinces.

Lincoln then did what he always did—he gave himself time. Throughout his career, he put different sides in disputes at a distance with small steps which gave him more time to maneuver. With time on his side, he could juggle people and proposals on his terms, not theirs. Time also gave him an opportunity to improvise and develop a variety of attacks on any one object.[9] As time passed, his friends' support would grow and his enemies' ardor would cool. With time, he would able to work out agreeable solutions. Seeking time again, Lincoln told Congress that reconstruction was too important to be decided so hastily. He refused to sign the Wade-Davis bill, convinced that Congress would see that, with more time, a better plan could be worked out. Meanwhile, lacking in legal authority, Congress could do nothing on reconstruction, while the president worked as hard as he could to continue it on his terms as commander in chief.

It was not reconstruction that kept Lincoln up nights in the spring of

1864. The Army of the Potomac, Grant at its head, his top button undone and his boots dirty, plunged into a Virginia forest called the Wilderness on May 1, to unexpectedly encounter Lee's army there. More than two thousand Federals died in fierce hand-to-hand combat or perished in hundreds of forest fires ignited by the hail of bullets and exploding cannonballs in the dry trees and underbrush. Both sides battled ferociously amid the smoke, fires, and explosions, and Grant's men stumbled out of the forest badly beaten, with 17,666 casualties. But the general, unlike all his predecessors, did not fall back and turn north and run for home—he moved south. He sought another encounter with Lee, whose army was almost half as large as Grant's. And the soldiers in the Army of the Potomac cheered.

That encounter came soon enough. A week later, Lee's army clashed with Grant's in terrible fighting at Spotsylvania. This time the Union army suffered 11,000 more casualties in the effort to drive the Confederates from their trenches. Again, two weeks later, at Cold Harbor, Grant's men viciously attacked the Army of Northern Virginia. Wave after wave of soldiers assaulted the Southern lines, only to be cut down again and again. Frustrated, Grant ordered a final charge on June 3. Federals swept across a wide, open field and were annihilated by fire from a semicircle of Southern lines. It was butchery unsurpassed in any previous war. In just eight minutes, more than 7,000 men were killed or wounded.

Under Grant, the Union's brand-new commander, the army had suffered over fifty thousand casualties, or forty-one percent of the whole, in a single month of fighting. Northerners were stunned by the human devastation, and newspapers and politicians labeled Grant the "butcher" and called for his replacement. Lincoln was demoralized. Grant was doing exactly what the president told him; the result was catastrophic. The entire country was turning against the president and Grant.

Lincoln slept little, and servants at the White House sometimes caught him wandering the halls at night, his head buried in his hands. "Why do we suffer reverses after reverses?" he asked Schuyler Colfax, the new speaker of the House. "Could we have avoided this terrible, bloody war!... Is it ever to end!" Later, he told an Indiana congressman, "Doesn't it strike you as queer that I, who couldn't cut the head off of a chicken, and who was sick at the sight of blood, should be cast into the middle of a great war, with blood flowing all about me?"[10]

The president's melancholy gripped him often. For comfort he had become very religious, reading the Bible every day and quoting scriptures in many conversations in an effort to convince people that God's hand was at work in the war. "We hoped for a happy termination of this terrible war long before this; but God knows best and has ruled otherwise...we must work earnestly in the best light he gives us....Surely, He intends some great good to follow this mighty convulsion, which no mortal could make and no mortal could stay," he told a Quaker leader.[11]

Lincoln believed in Grant, however. He would stick with him no matter what happened. That confidence was never higher than on the night of May 6, after the debacle in the Wilderness, when a reporter just back from the battle delivered a personal message from Grant to Lincoln. Lincoln, glum, stared at the young writer and expected terrible news. "General Grant said to tell you...that there would be no turning back." Lincoln grabbed the young man, flung his arm around him, leaned down and kissed his head.[12]

Wherever he went that spring, the president urged everyone to pray for Grant and the brave men of the Army of the Potomac, whose morale was higher than ever despite their tragic losses.[13] On the very day that Grant's tragic last charge at Cold Harbor was repulsed, Lincoln told New Yorkers organizing a political rally that "My previous high estimate of General Grant has been maintained and heightened by what has occurred in the remarkable campaign he is now conducting....He and his brave soldiers are now in the midst of their great trial and I trust that at your meeting you will so shape your good words that they may turn to men and guns moving to his and their support."[14]

Grant moved down to Petersburg, south of Richmond, and laid siege to the city, now defended by Lee and his army. The Union commander was constantly thwarted and, throughout a hot and miserable summer, made no progress. Sherman's army, attempting to slash its way into Georgia in an effort to take Atlanta, became continually tangled in small fights with the Confederate army of Joe Johnston, and was making no headway. A planned attack on Mobile Bay, Alabama, fizzled.

Lincoln had always refused to remove Grant or to countermand his plans. He would stick with this man until the end, whatever it might be. He told Grant on April 30, as he was about to invade Virginia, that he had his complete support. "I wish to express my entire satisfaction with what you have done up to this time. The particulars of your plans I neither know or seek to know. You are vigilant and self reliant.....If there is anything wanting which is within my power to give, do not fail to let me know....May God sustain you."[15] Later, after the terrible losses in the Wilderness, Spotsylvania, and Cold Harbor, he again supported him. "I begin to see it," the president said of Grant's overall plans in June. "You will succeed. God bless you all!"[16]

Criticism of Lincoln, curbed after the victories at Vicksburg and Gettysburg and during the 1863 elections, grew again. The president kept calling up more troops, and thousands of soldiers kept coming home in coffins. More than three hundred thousand Northerners had been killed by the summer of 1864. It seemed like every town in America had lost some loved ones and welcomed home others with a limb missing. The war went on, without much prospect for an end to it, and peace movements flourished once again. Lincoln, so hopeful about peace in 1863, was despondent.

Several factions within his own party talked about denying him re-nomination. Salmon Chase authorized a group to mail "secret" circulars which promoted Chase for president and finally, embarrassed by them, pulled out of the race. Horace Greeley and others abandoned Lincoln and named a committee to search for a successor. Women in Washington pressed Julia Grant to get her husband to run against Lincoln, but at each suggestion she emphatically told them the general would *never* try to unseat the president.[17] Thurlow Weed, who had worked so hard for Lincoln's election in 1860, privately told friends the president had no chance of reelection. There was so much anger with Lincoln's inability to end the war that a Republican splinter group held its own convention in Cleveland and nominated John C. Frémont as a third-party candidate. Fremont never forgave Lincoln for overruling his proclamation freeing the slaves.

Using all of his political skills, Lincoln steered a safe and clear course toward a second term. On June 7, he was nominated for president by the Republican convention in Baltimore. Once again he made a bold political move, dropping Republican loyalist Hannibal Hamlin as vice president and working behind the scenes—in the open balloting for the second spot on the ticket—to get the convention to back Andrew Johnson, the provisional governor of Tennessee and a lifelong Southerner and Democrat. Lincoln was seeking a unity ticket which would not only appeal to radicals and conservatives in both parties, but to create a genial atmosphere for the return of the seceded states when the war ended and, with a War Democrat at his side, better relations with Congress and an easier path for reconstruction.

The selection of Johnson was one of Lincoln's most adroit moves. He never expressed displeasure with Hamlin and did not mention Johnson to anyone, even his closest aides, but in the spring of 1864 two Lincoln confidants secretly took trains to Knoxville to investigate Johnson. The governor's loyalty to the Union was unquestioned. He not only supported Lincoln's policies and understood the importance of the border states, but in the summer of 1863 had been the target of Confederate sharpshooters, who opened fire on him and his aides as they rode through the Cumberland Gap.[18] He had above average administrative abilities and his rumored drinking, they found, was no worse than that of most. The president then worked behind the scenes to get delegates to support Johnson.[19]

Lincoln told a visitor he was· "thrilled" that Johnson was nominated on the night the vote on the vice presidency was taken.[20] He was even more pleased a few days later when Johnson gave a rousing speech that not only supported everything president Lincoln was doing, but tied the Republicans and Democrats into another Union ticket, telling the cheering delegates that "there are but two parties now: one for the country and one against it!"[21]

Still, the inability of the military to end the war—and the raid on Washington by General Jubal Early in June—dogged Lincoln throughout the summer. He became convinced that not only would the South hold out, but that his failure to end the conflict would mean his defeat, and the defeat of hundreds of Republicans in the November elections. His Democratic opponent was General George McClellan, still popular among the people and, Democratic strategists believed, among the troops. The Democrats hammered out a peace platform at their convention which heralded a negotiated end to the war as soon as the party took office. In a confused series of messages, McClellan supported the platform but finally denied that if elected he would negotiate a settlement. John C. Frémont, even though he had the support of only a few Republicans following the rump convention, might cut into Lincoln's Republican support just enough to hand McClellan the White House.

The president's strategy to end the war, with a three-pronged offensive in Virginia, Georgia, and Alabama, produced no results. His plans to capture Jefferson Davis had failed. Now, in the summer of 1864, with so many dead and maimed soldiers, he decided to improvise, as he always had, to "try something else," a new wrinkle in presidential power. Lincoln made up his mind to send emissaries on a top-secret mission to Richmond to extend an extraordinary proposal to Jefferson Davis.

Lincoln authorized a peace mission by editor Horace Greeley to Niagara Falls. There Greeley was to meet with Confederates who, he assumed, had the power to make an agreement to end the war. The president never had any hope of the mission's success, and saw in it a chance to feed Greeley's soaring ego and make him look bad. He did not appreciate the New York editor's lecturing him, telling him that "I fear you do not realize how intently the people desire...peace,"[22] and was still miffed at Greeley for suggesting he abandon the war in the summer of 1863, and for rallying Republicans against him in the spring of 1864. Lincoln sent him to Niagara Falls and let him trumpet a mission which would never work. "Oh, I just thought I'd let him crack that nut himself," the president said off-handedly when asked about his motives.[23] No one in the cabinet had much faith in the unpredictable editor any longer. "Nothing can be done with him," lamented Welles.[24]

Lincoln also considered a peace mission offer by Henry Raymond, editor of the *New York Times,* who wanted to see Jefferson Davis to work out an end to the war. He had his entire cabinet meet with Raymond to show him how important they felt he was, even though the mission never took place.[25] Raymond never left Washington, because, just a month before, Lincoln had dispatched two men deep into the heart of the Confederacy on the one peace mission he was hopeful might end the awful war.

J. C. Gilmore, a journalist, visited Lincoln at the White House in the summer of 1863, invited, as so many journalists and public figures were, so that the president could sound them out on public opinion. Gilmore had another reason for the visit. The reporter told Lincoln that a friend of his, a minister named James Jaquess, a Union army chaplain, wanted to act as a secret intermediary between North and South to arrange a peace. Lincoln, his mind working on several levels at once, talked with Gilmore while the possibilities of a peace mission led by Chaplain Jaquess raced through his mind.

He casually told Gilmore that if *someone* could arrange peace, he would authorize a general amnesty to all Southern troops and officers and compensate slaveowners for their losses. "The blacks must be free. Slavery is the bone we have been fighting over. It must be got out of the way, to give us permanent peace; and if we have to fight this war till the South is subjugated, then I think we shall be justified in freeing the slaves without compensation."

Then, as he often did, Lincoln contradicted himself and said the Southerners would never let their slaves go, even for compensation, and would not end the war. Then he crisscrossed back to Jaquess. "Here is a man who got it into his head that God has laid this work upon him...the impulse is overpowering."

Nothing came of the meeting, but Gilmore returned ten months later, in the summer of 1864, to push the idea again. This time Lincoln, desperate to end the war, urged Chaplain Jaquess to go and to take Gilmore with him because the writer was far more politically savvy than the minister. Gilmore reminded the president, too, that if the mission failed it would show the country that it was Davis, not Lincoln, who would not end the war.

President Lincoln warned Gilmore that he could imply that he was carrying Lincoln's offer, but that Lincoln would never acknowledge it. Lincoln could write or sign nothing, and if Gilmore did not make it to Richmond and was killed or imprisoned, the president could not even acknowledge that he knew him. Gilmore agreed.

Lincoln called in Salmon Chase so that he could have an adviser and a witness to history. "Well, now that we have arranged the preliminaries, Mr. Chase, what terms shall we offer the rebels. Draw your chair up to the table, Mr. Gilmore, and take down what Mr. Chase says," said the president.

Chase looked sternly at the president. "You had better name them, Mr. Lincoln," he said. "I will make any suggestions that may seem necessary."

Lincoln told Davis that the Confederate government and its army had to be dissolved, slavery had to be abolished everywhere, the seceded states had to return to the Union, and all Southerners, army officers, and elected officials had to recognize the fully restored United States. In return, Lincoln would grant total amnesty to all Confederate officers and soldiers, all public officials and federal officials, including Davis and the members of his cabinet, and Lincoln would pay five hundred million dollars (approximately eighty billion dollars in contemporary currency) to slaveholders to compensate them for their losses.[26]

Gilmore and Jaquess, with passes through lines from General Grant himself, met with Jefferson Davis, but the Confederate president, hopeful he could win the war, turned down the proposals.

On August 23, Union forces seemed stagnant everywhere. Praise for McClellan appeared in hundreds of Democratic papers and some Republican papers. Lincoln's own 1860 campaign managers were turning against him. "He cannot win," said Thurlow Weed. "He is failure," said Orville Browning. Henry Raymond told him "all is lost," and Leonard Swett told him to do whatever the South wanted. His peace missions failing, and the antiwar movement growing, a downhearted Lincoln wrote a letter to his cabinet, to be unsealed in November, in which he acknowledged he would not be reelected and urged them to support President McClellan.[27]

SHERMAN, Grant, and Admiral David Farragut, who understood Lincoln's political problems, pressed the enemy as hard as they could throughout late summer, 1864. They finally broke through fiercely defended Confederate lines. In late August, news came that earlier that month Farragut, who snatched some naval lore for himself when he lashed himself to the mast during an attack and told his men, when warned torpedoes would be fired at their ship, "Damn the torpedoes, full speed ahead!" had captured Mobile Bay. On September 1, amid a barrage of mortars, John Bell Hood's Confederate army evacuated Atlanta; the Federals under Sherman marched in the following morning, seizing perhaps the most important city in the South.[28] On September 4, crafty Confederate guerrilla leader John Hunt Morgan, a legendary hero throughout the South, was killed in a Union army ambush. Just two weeks later, armies led by Phil Sheridan, in a series of battles, drove the Confederates out of Virginia's Shenandoah Valley forever.

Northerners celebrated the fall of Atlanta as if it were the end of the war. Church bells rang in a hundred cities. Union armies throughout the country fired cannon salutes. president Lincoln issued a proclamation calling for a day of thanksgiving.[29] Secretary of State Seward, vacationing in his home town of Auburn, N.Y., walked throughout the small village when he heard the news, gleefully telling everyone he met that Atlanta had fallen.[30] Horace Greeley, who had sulked over the summer about his failed peace mission and tried to unseat the president, lent the Lincoln campaign enormous support just after Sheridan's series of victories in the Shenandoah, telling all that from now on, the *Tribune,* America's most influential newspaper, "would fly the banner of Abraham Lincoln for president."[31] In a slim, three-week period, the tide of the war turned completely around, the Union army was on the move, newspaper criticism of the war diminished considerably, and the vicious attacks on Lincoln stopped.

"Success...was a political necessity," Sherman later said of his campaign in Georgia. "Atlanta...made the election of Mr. Lincoln certain."[32]

The president, now with an even chance at reelection, plotted a careful political strategy to win the White House again. He approached moderate Republican Senator Zachariah Chandler of Michigan to serve as intermediary between the president and two of his harshest radical critics, Wade and Davis, in order to win their endorsement and, with it, that of the whole radical wing of the party. He had others see John Frémont in an effort to get him to drop out of the race, giving Lincoln all of the Republican vote. Frémont's price and the price for the Wade-Davis coalition was the same—Lincoln had to dismiss Montgomery Blair. The postmaster general had been a thorn in the radicals' side since 1861. He had denounced the abolitionists, pushed hard for the colonization of blacks, and berated the radicals for their reconstruction proposals. Lincoln liked him, but on September 23 Blair graciously exited.

Shortly afterward, the radicals fell in line behind the president, Frémont dropped out of the race, and the Thurlow Weed machine worked, as it had in 1860, to elect Abraham Lincoln. The president's spirits were higher than they had been in three years. "Jordan has been a hard road to travel," he told one visitor, "but I feel now that, notwithstanding the enemies I have made and the faults I have committed, I'll be dumped on the right side of that stream."[33]

Salmon Chase left the cabinet in late summer, at Lincoln's request. He hungered for the job of chief justice of the United States after Taney died on October 12, 1864. Friends pestered Lincoln to name Chase but the president refused, waiting for some signal from Chase. The former secretary of the treasury, a political warhorse himself, got the message quickly and for a solid month campaigned for Lincoln throughout Ohio, with no promises from the president.

Lincoln let it be known that there might be an ambassadorship for James Gordon Bennett, the feisty anti-Lincoln editor of the *New York Herald;* a week later the newspaper's avid criticism of the president seemed to cool, and General McClellan was called "a failure."[34] Prominent politicians in several states who were reluctant to support the party's congressional candidates and the national ticket in their areas, were called to the White House to be told bluntly that the president needed and expected their support. Union generals were asked to furlough troops (Lincoln knew he had strong support among soldiers) so they could return home to vote in the elections.[35] He lobbied behind the scenes to procure the necessary votes in the Maryland legislature to pass its new constitution, which outlawed slavery, in October.[36]

Union troops were ordered to New York by Stanton to guard polling places on election day to prevent fraud.[37] Quaker ministers reminded the nation's churches how strongly the president had supported their drives for emancipation, and had given them patronage approval. Hundreds of clergymen not only endorsed him, but from their pulpits demanded their congregations vote for the president. One Methodist bishop told his flock to "march to the ballot box, an army of Christ, with the banners of the Cross, and deposit a million votes."[38]

Lincoln did not campaign, as he did not in 1860, but spent as many as four or five hours each day at the White House working with campaign leaders. In one last move to obtain every single available vote, Lincoln told each of his cabinet members to return to their home districts and vote.[39] Of course, no one did this with more fanfare, stage management, and publicity than Seward, in his latest effort to befriend Lincoln and garner yet more publicity for himself.

Lincoln believed that he would be reelected, but others did not. Some suggested that he declare martial law and suspend the elections until the war was over. He refused. "We can not have free government without elections; and if the rebellion could force us to forego, or postpone a national election, it might fairly claim to have already conquered and ruined us," he said.[40]

President Lincoln was reelected on November 8 with 2,330,552 votes (55 percent) to George McClellan's 1,835,985. He won 212 electoral votes to just 21 for his Democratic opponent, capturing all but the states of New Jersey, Delaware, and Kentucky. He won eighty-three percent of soldier ballots (state laws prevented the votes of about one hundred thousand additional soldiers).[41] It was not just a sweeping victory for the president, but for the Republicans. They won the governor's mansion and a majority in twenty-one of twenty-four Union state legislatures, and a surprising seventy-five percent of all congressional seats.[42] The Republican machine in New York, driven hard by Lincoln, Seward, and Weed, took particular delight in defeating Horatio Seymour, who had been such an irritant to Lincoln, as governor and replacing him with Reuben Fenton. The people had not only given the president and his party support and confidence, but a mandate to fight on to win the war. "The victory is worth more to the country than a battle won," wired Grant.[43]

"It [the election] shows...how *sound* and how *strong* we still are. It shows that, even among candidates of the same party, he who is most devoted to the Union, and most opposed to treason, can receive most of the people's vote," Lincoln told a large group of people who paraded to the White House after the election, carrying torches and banners, to congratulate him.[44]

Lincoln's reelection did not weaken the resolve of the Confederates to fight on. Neither did Sherman's march to the sea. The Union general burned down several cities and towns, including Atlanta; set fire to farms and plantations; and did everything he could to crush the will of the Southern people to press on with the war. After civic leaders surrendered Savannah to prevent its destruction, Sherman gave it to Lincoln as a Christmas gift. The general then turned north and captured additional towns, including Colum- bia, South Carolina, much of which burned to the ground in a fire caused by his troops. He then headed toward Richmond, while Grant's armies pounded nearby Petersburg, Virginia, with cannon day after day, week after week, month after month. Still, the South would not quit.

Lincoln now worried that die-hard Southern leaders and zealous generals might escape and begin a guerrilla war which might last for years and make reconciliation impossible. He sent Francis Blair Sr. on one final peace mission to end the war, choosing the elder statesman because he had been friendly with the Davises before the war and was a favorite of Mrs. Davis.

Once again, Lincoln wrote nothing and signed nothing, but let Blair tell Davis he was speaking officially as a private citizen but unofficially on Lincoln's behalf.[45] Blair strongly endorsed Lincoln's latest plan, which was even more extraordinary than the one he had sent via Gilmore. Now President Lincoln would not only grant amnesty to all soldiers and public officials, and pay five hundred million dollars in compensation for freeing the slaves, but suggested to Davis that the United States wanted to declare war on Mexico, where the French were trying to establish a presence, and send a joint army to fight there. The army, the largest on earth, would include all of the current armies of the Union and the Confederacy and would have Grant, Sherman, Sheridan, Lee, Longstreet, Johnston, and others as its top generals. The army would be led by General in Chief Jefferson Davis. This also meant, clearly, that war hero status from the Mexican venture could elevate Jefferson Davis to become the seventeenth president of the United States.

The president may also have worried about more rumors of plots against his life. He had frightened Grant by telling about a dream he had most nights, that he was riding a ship through a fog to an unknown shore, and in the middle of the election campaign surprised a crowd by telling them about the things he wanted to do as president, not if he was reelected, but "that if I shall live."[46] Metropolitan police now guarded the White House day and night, and one stood outside Lincoln's door as he slept. Lamon, his friend and bodyguard, would not let him go to Ford's Theater, or any of his favorite theaters, without armed guards. Stanton was terrified that someone would shoot the president.

Blair crossed both sets of lines and arrived unnoticed in Richmond, where he stayed, unregistered, at the Spotswood Hotel. He saw President Davis the night of his arrival. Davis shook his hand warmly and told him he was glad to see him, and Varina hugged him.[47] Lincoln knew the prospect of a new Mexican venture would appeal to the soldier in Davis. The Southern leader thrilled Blair by telling him he would agree to a secret meeting; he would send Alexander Stephens and two other men, all well known for their opposition to the continuation of the war, to a peace conference.

The secret meeting between Lincoln and the three Confederate commissioners took place on board the steamboat *River Queen* on the Potomac on February 3, 1865. Lincoln was tense all day. He was very careful about everything he did and said, to maintain a veil of secrecy over the conference, as rumors flew that some kind of meeting was being held to end the war. He was asked bluntly by a congressman if there was a conference going on in the city. Craftily, Lincoln answered no, because, in fact, it was being held on the river. When he finally received word that the three commissioners were on their way to the boat, he quickly put his hat on, summoned his aides and, looking very serious, headed for a river launch.

The conference, for which Lincoln had such high hopes, never made any progress. Davis had instructed his men to insist that all language in any agreement had to stipulate that there were two countries—not one, as insisted on by Lincoln. The Union president insisted that the Confederate armies surrender, lay down their arms, and go home. The Southerners said they could not do that unless there was a cease-fire first, then a negotiated settlement. Lincoln insisted that slavery had to be legally abolished, and told them the recently passed Thirteenth Amendment, to do exactly that, had just been sent to the States for ratification, which shocked them. They argued over reconstruction, slave compensation, and other items for three hours. The Southerners threatened to walk out, at which Lincoln, angered, reminded them that they were insurrectionists, telling one commissioner that he knew for a fact there were hundreds of trees on his plantation and that he could be hanged from any one of them. Tempers flared. The conference broke up with nothing accomplished.[48]

President Lincoln hurried back to the White House to continue his lobbying for passage of the Thirteenth Amendment, which promised complete freedom for African Americans held in bondage anywhere, before he was sworn in for his second term on March 4. On March 5, he would have lopsided majorities in the House to pass the constitutional amendment, but passage then would be meaningless, nothing more than the culmination of radical Republican rule. He wanted to show the country, North and South, that a bipartisan Congress—with its large Democratic membership—wanted to end slavery. The president had little doubt that each of the individual states would ratify the amendment.

The president, working with Seward, targeted a dozen or so Democratic congressmen whose terms were ending, whom they thought might vote for the Thirteenth Amendment. The Lincoln administration promised the men jobs and an assortment of other favors. On January 31, after several days of political horsetrading, which the president was so good at, most of the "lame ducks" switched their votes, and the Thirteenth Amendment was passed by just three votes. Congressmen erupted into wild applause and many hugged each other, some crying, at the historic moment. The galleries, packed, burst into spontaneous applause when the final tally was announced. Outside, cannons fired off one-hundred-gun salutes throughout the city.[49]

IT had rained hard in Washington for days. The streets of the capital, usually dusty, were turned to mud. Sheets of rain pounded storefronts and the porches of residential homes. Horses pulling carriages plodded through deep puddles, splashing water on the expensive gowns of women on their way to Lincoln's second inaugural. Everyone was certain that the war would soon be over, that it was just a matter of time, and there was a growing sense of jubilation in the city. The hotels were so crowded that many guests slept on cots in the halls. Residents crammed their homes with relatives visiting from all over the country to listen to the president's speech. Police estimated over thirty thousand people gathered in front of the capital, beginning at 10 A.M., for the noontime swearing in by newly installed Chief Justice Salmon Chase. The irony of abolitionist Chase replacing Taney, who wrote the Dred Scott decision, was lost on no one.

Inside, Lincoln was edgy as he watched Andrew Johnson sworn in as vice president. Johnson was clearly drunk and an embarrassment to everyone. Lincoln told marshals to whisk his vice president through the crowds to make certain he did not talk to anyone. The vice presidential swearing in over, the procession moved outside.

The tall figure of the president could be seen emerging from the capitol over the heads of the dozens of other dignitaries. As soon as he came into view a throaty, thunderous roar poured forth from the crowd. It was a loud, prolonged ovation for the coming end of the awful war and for the man who had taken them through it. Hundreds of American flags decorated the wooden platform on which Lincoln would be sworn in, and more dotted the crowd. Bands played patriotic tunes.

Lincoln, now fifty-six, was tired. He complained to his wife that he had lost too much weight and often felt weak. He told friends that his hands and feet often felt cold and that he had blood circulation problems. The lines on his face had become very deep. As winter now dwindled away, his face had no color and looked gray and ashen. Today, however, as the cheers of the crowd engulfed him and he stepped forward to deliver his second inaugural address, the sun emerging just as he started to speak, Abraham Lincoln felt satisfied.

He knew that the war was almost over and that he had held the United States of America together, resisting large and powerful groups of people, influential public officials, and hundreds of newspaper editors who tried to talk him into peace settlements which would have left the country divided. The price for Union had been dreadful, over six hundred thousand soldiers dead on both sides and another half million maimed and wounded, but his people, under his leadership, had paid it. He had not only freed the slaves in 1863, but, a month before the inauguration, worked to pass a constitutional amendment to guarantee their freedom. Through his work, he had changed the racial makeup of his country forever. By his appointments of men such as David Davis and Salmon Chase, he had changed the Supreme Court from a conservative, state's rights, proslavery institution to a nationalistic, antislavery court which would, in the years ahead, approve a series of laws and amendments giving blacks voting and property rights and making them full American citizens.

The Homestead Act, lost in the news of the war, had opened up hundreds of thousands of acres of land for homesteaders and, in the next generation, would mean the full development of the west. Under Lincoln, helped by his politicking, the states of Kansas, West Virginia, and Nevada had joined the Union. The new greenbacks he had authorized became the country's first paper currency, ending one hundred years of gold and silver currency. His support of Chase's idea of dozens of linked national banks helped give the nation economic security.

The bill to charter a transcontinental railroad presaged the connecting of the Atlantic and Pacific oceans by rail; its completion in 1869 would foster dramatic growth in the far west and the founding of hundreds of brand-new cities and towns along rail routes. The creation of a Department of Agricultures facilitated the growth of farms, particularly in the Midwest, for the next hundred years.

Lincoln's draft act, although unpopular, did give the federal government the power, later, to fight world wars. On the international front, his tough policies toward England kept that nation out of the Civil War and earned a healthy respect for America.

Lincoln functioned as the hands-on leader of the Republican Party, turning it into a huge and powerful political organization. By 1864 it controlled the House, the Senate, the White House, twenty-one of twenty-four Northern state legislatures, and the majority of the governors' mansions. He understood the chasm between the radicals and conservatives and carefully brokered deals with both, as well as with the Democrats, whose support was critical to winning the war.

He turned pre–Civil War America on its head. The country was now moving toward industrialization and away from total reliance on farming; a country of free laborers, not slave laborers; a nation of continental size, expanding rapidly to the West Coast and doubling its size. The federal government, under Lincoln, had grown: there were new cabinet posts, a huge army and navy, and an enormous, multilevel bureaucracy, based in Washington, which had seized power from the states and would keep it. Only days after Abraham Lincoln was born, Thomas Jefferson left the White House; he had presided over a tiny federal government which relied on the states to run the country. Now, three weeks after Lincoln's fifty-sixth birthday, he had changed that. A huge and powerful federal government was running the country.

Lincoln had dramatically expanded the powers of the presidency. Prior to his election, presidents did little beyond propose a few bills, send annual messages to Congress, and administer the government, unless forced to act in crisis or to expand, such as James Polk in the Mexican War, Andrew Jackson in the bank crisis, or Jefferson with the Louisiana Purchase. Lincoln changed all that. He was a bold innovator who, through the force of his personality and his charm, changed the way the president operates. He truly made the presidency an independent force. He bypassed Congress to call up emergency troops; ignored the courts to suspend the writ of habeas corpus; forced a draft; tried to reach secret peace agreements with the Confederates on his own;

directed the growth of the army and navy without any guidance or approval from Congress; served as an active and aggressive commander in chief; hired and fired important generals; and through his eloquent speeches, letters, and messages—and in his use of the media to make them public—made unprecedented and direct connections between the president and the people. He framed his speeches in beautiful, yet very clear language that enabled the public to see and share his vision.

Lincoln was the first president to understand the dramatic growth of the power of the press. He worked with the Republican-controlled newspapers to get elected. He cooperated with their editors, despite the shutdown of some papers and the censorship of battlefield stories, to present his policies to their readers. He lobbied and cajoled reporters and editors, stroking the important ones with letters, lunches, and invitations to the White House. He even gave some a hand in peace negotiations. He admitted reporters to the White House, answered their questions, and tried through charm and perseverance to win them to his side. He was the first president to read summaries of daily stories and, through his daily meetings with dozens of job seekers, to learn everything he could about the news of the day. He accommodated the press with special cars on his trains, designated places on platforms where he spoke, and always made certain that reporters had copies of his speeches.

Lincoln grew in office. He relied on the framework of the presidency at first, but later expanded it, constantly trying new methods, some brilliant and some dubious, to win the war, and he used the powers of the presidency to forge dozens of intricate political alliances. Flexible himself, Lincoln saw the presidency as elastic, expanding at times and contracting tightly at others. He fully explored the president's powers to persuade and cajole, to threaten and to reward. He used his own personality to bring the president and the people closer together and worked hard within the Republican Party to get the party to support the president so the president could support the party. He had grown from a slavery-hating lawyer who was a pretty good politician to a magnanimous national leader who was a brilliant politician.

Abraham Lincoln had not merely led his country, he had transformed it.

On March 4, 1865, president Lincoln looked out over the crowd gathered for his second inaugural and began to speak. It was one of the shortest inaugural addresses in American history, just 703 words, and took Lincoln only six minutes to deliver. He began by reminding his audience that the North did not seek and did not start the war, but had had to fight it once it came. He quoted scripture in several places to assure the crowds in front of him, and the millions who would read his remarks within hours, that the Union would press the war to its final conclusion. There was no peace agreement at the Hampton Roads, Virginia, conference; there would be none elsewhere.

Lincoln was very careful in his speech to talk to the nation about the *nation,* just as he had at Gettysburg, in a public step to bring about reconciliation through peaceful reconstruction. He very carefully referred to the enemy as "the insurgents," and not the Southern states or the Confederacy, to permit the forgiveness and absorption of the people of the seceded states without tying them to the leadership of their government or armies. He reminded all that Northerners and Southerners "read the same Bible, and pray to the same God."

As the clouds started to drift away above him and the sun shone bright in the noontime sky directly over Washington, Abraham Lincoln finished with a heartfelt plea for reunion and forgiveness: "With malice toward none, and with charity for all, with firmness in the right, as God gives us to see the right, let us strive on to finish the work we are in; to bind up the nation's wounds; to care for him who shall have borne the battle, and for his widow, and his orphan—to do all which may achieve and cherish a just, and a lasting peace, among ourselves, and with all nations."[50]

As a long explosion of applause erupted from the crowd, he turned and took the oath of office from Chief Justice Chase. As he finished, he said loudly and firmly, "So help me God!" and another loud roar greeted him as, in the distance, dozens of cannons were fired in celebration, hundreds of American flags waved, and bands began to play as loudly as their instruments would allow.[51]

23

JEFFERSON DAVIS AT WAR: 1864–1865

UNITED STATES PRESIDENTS traditionally flung open the doors of the White House on New Year's Day to permit anyone, regardless of position or wealth, to visit and meet the president and first lady. Davis copied the popular custom and opened the Confederate White House to everyone on January first each year. New Year's Day, 1864, was a festive one. Varina had all the gas lamps in the mansion turned on, trays of food were everywhere, glasses clinked together throughout the day in hundreds of small toasts, the Davises' young children, dressed impeccably, romped through the gathering, and the president thoroughly enjoyed himself.

The house was jammed with cabinet members and politicians, but the long lines of people waiting to meet the Davises also included merchants, soldiers, neighbors, and ordinary citizens. They all agreed the Davises had thrown a good party, but they worried about the president. He had aged considerably since his election three years earlier. He was thinner than ever, his cheeks sallow and his complexion very pale. His hair had turned from black laced with gray to nearly all white. Davis, only fifty-six, looked like a very old man.

Davis did his best to get along with everyone, even some of his enemies in Congress. His aides were aghast to see him smiling and sipping wine in a circle of men which included bitter foes. He moved about the two parlors,

398

made into one reception room by opening the sliding doors, and the dining and sitting rooms, where cigar smoke drifted in the air, shaking hands and exchanging pleasantries. Davis shook so many hands, he later told a friend, that his arm was stiff for three days. He wasn't complaining—he was bragging. The president had such a fine time that he surprised everyone by inviting a delegation of congressmen to his home the following evening for a cordial discussion of the war and the government.[1]

The euphoria did not last. Davis, believing that he was trying harder than ever to cooperate with people, came under critical fire from all over the South the very next day. The *Lynchburg Virginian* said that Davis should resign and General Lee should be named dictator. The *Raleigh Progress* said the troops were starving and it was time to sue for peace and end the war.[2] Editors from every state denounced Davis's latest conscription bill, which would permit exemptions for only one editor or reporter at each paper and put the rest in the army. It was later modified to exempt more journalists.[3] Davis learned from aides that there were so few men in the commissary general's department that he was now sending all his clerks into the field and the Richmond office was run by old men, the handicapped, and women.[4] On February 4, Rep. Augustus Wright of Georgia introduced several peace resolutions in an effort to circumvent the president and end the war.[5]

President Davis often felt that he was surrounded by critics and that they undermined his ability to win the war. He had generals who argued against his military campaign plans, newspaper editors who lashed him repeatedly in the pages of their publications, and state legislators who believed they were more important than the country's president. Many legislators accused Davis of trying to become a dictator, yet they seemed to act to undermine whatever powers the president had, floating peace resolutions and constantly feuding with men in the government. Davis, in Richmond and running a vast war machine, could not stop them.

Among his problems were constant feuds with two of the Confederacy's strongest and most important governors, Joe Brown of Georgia and Zebulon Vance of North Carolina. The rest of the governors of the Southern states supported the president, but these two were constant thorns in his side. Maintaining good relations with them was important because Georgia had been the most vocal of all the states when secession took place and had powerful political figures in Brown, who was governor; Alexander Stephens, who became vice president; Howell Cobb, who became a general; and Robert

Toombs, who became secretary of state and then a general. North Carolina was important because it joined the Confederacy reluctantly; and Davis feared that if it dropped out, other states would follow. It was home to the Heroes of America, a secret Southern organization dedicated to ending the war and restoring the Union, and thousands of deserters, whom the locals hid. Raleigh was also the home of the vehemently antiwar *Raleigh Standard,* edited by William Holden, who urged an immediate end to the conflict.

Joe Brown had sparred with Davis for years, but he and Vance both exploded over the draft and habeas corpus acts of February 1864.[6] Sixteen of the nineteen congressmen from these two states voted against conscription. Vance wrote Davis sharp and critical letters, charging that the government had no right to draft North Carolina's men. Under the principle of state's rights, only North Carolina could do that. Instead of ignoring him or writing him diplomatic rejoinders, Davis, as always, not only sent scathing letters to Vance, but told him they should end all correspondence, and wound up a step short of calling Vance a traitor after Vance said North Carolina might leave the Confederacy. He rebuked Vance: "No true citizen, no man who has our cause at heart can desire [peace negotiations]....Such course would receive the condemnation of those true patriots who have given their blood and their treasure to maintain freedom."[7]

Soon after that, Vance again fought with Davis over North Carolina's state-owned blockade-running ships. Vance, a patriot to the cause if not its leader, had a fleet of ships that regularly ran the blockades, bringing much-needed supplies to his state. The national government insisted that fifty percent of all space on any of his ships be reserved for Confederate government supplies. Vance balked. Another heated battle between the two leaders ensued.[8] In 1863, they battled after rowdy Confederate troops threatened to harm North Carolinians, including Vance, and the governor nearly withdrew all North Carolina troops from the Confederate army.[9] In early 1864, when antiwar zealots threatened to disrupt North Carolina politics, Davis told Vance to put down the movement. The president insinuated that he did not believe the governor would, and that if he did not, the governor would be as guilty of treason as the peace movement leaders. Davis further accused him of harboring traitors.[10] He wrote Vance, "I warned you of the error of warming traitors into active life by ill timed deferences or timid concession, instead of meeting their insidious attempts to deceive the people. Your needless defence of [the traitors] takes me by surprise."[11]

Davis pounced on Vance later, telling him that he did little as governor to root out traitors. "The promoters of the unfounded discontent now prevalent in your state would be put down without the use of physical force if you would abandon a policy of conciliation," he said.[12] And, yet again, in February 1864, Davis accused Vance of attacking him, charging that he made "unjust reflections on my official conduct."[13]

His battles with North Carolina were not limited to its governor. Earlier, president Davis had called in the North Carolina Senate and House delegations to read them a letter which accused them all, and their friends back home, of being traitors to the Cause. They argued that they were not, that they were patriots, and resented the implication. Davis shot back, in one of his usual outbursts, that everyone had to be loyal to the national government and to him. Senator Reade accused Davis of wanting to be a dictator, and Davis lashed out at him verbally.[14] Still later, in September of 1864, Vance set up his own factories to produce uniforms for North Carolina troops and Davis tried to shut them down, precipitating yet another feud between the two that was never resolved.[15] The battles between Davis and Vance became so heated that in February 1864 Secretary of War Seddon said that if a pro-Vance North Carolina judge did not change his mind and support the draft, he would have him arrested.[16]

The president's relations with Joe Brown, the crusty, cantankerous, yet popular, four-term governor of Georgia, who spoke with a heavy nasal accent, were even worse. Davis had hoped to get rid of Brown in the 1863 elections. The president refused to lower himself to any politicking, but assumed Brown would not run, as had been rumored. Who should come to Brown's aid, convincing him to run and campaigning for him, but Alexander Stephens. His support won the election for Brown and turned Davis against both of them. Their latest feud started when Brown objected to the conscription act and sent Davis a hot letter. The president, eager to make Brown look bad rather than patch up their differences, sent the letter to dozens of newspapers, which published it.[17] The feud escalated from there. Brown fought the law as hard as he could and then, the battle lost, fought the habeas corpus law and the confiscation of food from Georgians for the army.

"Hardship, privation, sacrifices must be suffered for the sacred cause...and I am sure that the people of Georgia will prove themselves in other respects as they have on the field of battle," Davis haughtily wrote Brown when the governor complained that the army was taking the people's food.[18] Brown had Stephens's full support in both confrontations. In 1864, Brown threatened to pull his state's troops out of the army and bring them home to fight Sherman as he marched across Georgia. Next, he and Stephens announced plans to have Georgia secede from the Confederacy. Then the two tried to end the war themselves, introducing peace resolutions into the state legislature. They were written by Stephens's brother Linton.

The peace resolutions irritated Davis, who, with no party to support him had no leverage to keep people like Brown and Vance in line. The governors were undermining his power and authority and playing on the fears of Southerners, particularly people in Georgia, who were afraid of what Sherman might do next. What Sherman did do next, with Lincoln's approval, was invite Joe Brown and Alexander Stephens to a meeting in which he planned to congratulate them on their peace resolutions and strike a peace agreement with the state of Georgia. At this point, both Brown and Stephens realized they had made a complete mess of everything and refused to meet with Sherman.

Jefferson Davis felt betrayed and trapped. His own vice president had considered a peace accord with Sherman's army, Georgia had threatened to pull its troops off the field, North Carolina seemed to feel it was its own nation, and newspapers criticized just about everything he did. Instead of rallying around the president to show the world solidarity, as they should have, hundreds of influential generals, legislators, and journalists had abandoned him. He increasingly believed he was governing a huge nation all by himself.

In 1864 the defensive Davis began to lash out at everyone. In several speeches he accused the Southern people of not supporting the cause. "While brigade after brigade of our brave soldiers who have endured the trials of the camp and battlefield are testing their patriotism...discontent, disaffection, and disloyalty are manifested among those who, through the sacrifices of others, have enjoyed quiet and safety at home," he told one crowd. "Public meetings have been held, in some of which a treasonable design is masked by a pretense of devotion to state sovereignty."[19]

He savaged the British for staying out of the fight. His secretary wrote in a letter for him, "[A] neutrality most cunningly audaciously fawningly and insolently sought and urged, begged and demanded by one belligerent, and repudiated by the other, must be seen by all impartial men to be a mere pretext for aiding the cause of the one at the expense of the other and...treacherous, malignant hostility."[20]

Davis also had enormous problems with state legislatures and county governing bodies. These lower-tier legislative groups were the ones actually responsible for collecting the taxes the national government needed and for drafting and dispatching soldiers. They were the ones who had to step in as mediators in disputes between the national government and the farmers whose food was being confiscated or supplies seized by the army. These men, even more so than the governors, were extremely local in their focus and were champions of state's rights. Most did not have much experience in finances or military matters, and their inability to understand fiscal policies or the machinations of a national army call-up hurt the Confederate cause. Of all the speakers of Southern state legislatures, only two had traveled outside their state before the war, seventy-five percent had never traveled outside their county and all had businesses or law firms in their states. Anyone who did gain experience in tax or supply matters was unable to use it because almost all of the speakers of legislatures served just a year or less before going into the army.

The rocky relationship between the national government and the state legislatures was not due merely to matters of enlistment and the draft. The strength of the state legislatures before the war had been a strong two-party system in which one party attempted to achieve and hold power by means of programs that they could persuade some members of the opposition and most of the public to support. Several state legislators and speakers said that the one-party system during the war eliminated the pressure of a second party necessary to make the one legislature effective, while factions caused endless debates and little legislation.

There was also a chasm between the ideas of President Davis and state legislators. As the war dragged on, the government and the president seized increasing power through the draft, the impressment of food, and the suspension of habeas corpus writs. Local legislators slowly began to feel that the new Confederate government was just as opposed to state's rights as the old federal government from which they seceded. The local legislatures fought back, arguing with the president, sidetracking national legislative mandates, and deliberately taking their time collecting taxes and drafting soldiers. Little effort was made at state and local levels to introduce any innovative legislation to help local areas supply the army with food or clothing. Tax collection became disorganized. The local secession governments, adrift without a competitive two-party system, achieved little.[21]

The feeling that Jefferson Davis was ignoring local and state's rights grew from the first conscription act in 1862 through the end of the war, even though the North drafted its citizens and had high taxes as well. Resistance to the draft increased dramatically when Alexander Stephens, the vice president, jumped into the battle against it, arguing that the national government did not have the power to draft soldiers, only the power to ask governors to provide soldiers. The split in national leadership on this issue, which would never happen in a two-party system, stunned Southerners and increased their belief that Davis had no right to make demands of them.[22] Residents, newspaper editors, merchants, and public officials all came to believe that their rights were being trampled by Davis so that he could grab more power. Consequently, like some of the troublesome governors, many state legislatures rebelled against the national government, further weakening the Davis administration.[23]

President Davis, though he had been a long-term U.S. senator and congressman from Mississippi, had spent most of his time in Washington, not his home state. He never understood why local officials there, and in other Southern states, saw politics and government as local, and any efforts by the national Confederate government to influence them as offensive. As a man who never involved himself in lower-level state and county politics, he simply did not understand that grassroots politicians do not need connections to the national government to get elected.[24] He never understood that the real goal of these local politicians was not really a Confederate States of America, but states of their own that they ran for their very localized constituents. They were happy to help the national government in the early days of the Davis administration, when state and county legislators assumed the war would be over in a few months. As it dragged on, however, they saw Davis and his government as much their enemy as Lincoln and his government.

The South's brand-new political system, devised to give Southern states the freedom to govern themselves and to maintain a slave economy, had become a system in which many thought the man at the top of the pyramid, the president, had too much power. The man at the top, however, thought that while the system gave him the power to influence others near the top, it gave him no power to control those in the middle or at the bottom. The bottom of the system sagged badly, like the rotted timbers of a barn about to fall.

State and local governments also reflected popular views against intervention by a large national government, Northern or Southern, in people's lives.

Southerners had chafed at efforts by the U.S. government to curb slavery in the 1850s, because they saw slavery as a local, and very personal, issue. They lived in states which were almost entirely dependent on agriculture, with few cities of more than thirty thousand people, and they saw no need for a monolithic national government to rule over them. That feeling did not change with the war. Although there was a Confederacy, there were no real Confederates, and no new culture to undergird a brand new-country.[25] The Davis administration had to fight these views as hard as it had to fight Grant's armies—often with the same result.

The shortages became dramatic in 1864, as the three-year-old federal blockade of Southern ports tightened like a vice, as more and more ships joined the growing Union navy. Both sides now estimated that over one-third of all foodstuffs, clothing, and medicine bound for Southern ports were confiscated by Union ships. Merchants selling these items on the crude black market were charging higher and higher prices (seven-dollar boots were selling for one hundred dollars). Southerners saw such extortion not only as economically crippling, but as a gross violation of Christian principles and a symbol of cultural and religious collapse. Extortion also destroyed Southern unity, pitting Southerner against Southerner.[26] It especially ranged women against the extortionists, and worse, producers and retailers, not only resulting in women looting bakeries, but committing armed robbery (twenty-eight women in Georgia, armed with guns and knives, held up wagons delivering clothes from a factory).[27]

Inflation of produce prices had soared to nearly one thousand percent since the early days of the war. Confederate money was worth just five cents on a dollar. High casualty rates, the now substitute-free draft, and the continuing war meant that many of the able-bodied men needed to run farms were dead, maimed, or simply gone. By early 1864, the Southern people had been put through so many deprivations—two hundred thousand deaths, famine, burned-out farms, inflation—that the great will to win they exhibited in the spring of 1861 had died. They simply had no more spirit left.[28]

The war caused extended anxiety among women at home, creating ulcers, nervous conditions, sleeplessness, and malnourishment. The war was badly straining many women's nerves; hysterical crying fits were frequent. Some even had to be committed to insane asylums; doctors said the horrors of the war on the homefront had put them there.[29] Women, struggling with their children to run the farms, could not do the work of the slaves, many of whom had escaped. It was now a common sight to see a formerly wealthy woman, whose slaves had fled as the Union army approached, spending the entire day on her knees, her small children beside her, trying to grow corn just to survive.[30]

The shortages on the homefront, hastened by the failed economic policies of the Davis government, had a dramatic effect on the army. The Southern women who were fed up with the war complained frequently to their husbands. They told their husbands to leave the army and come home to save their families. Let Jefferson Davis fight the war himself. "I think you have done your share," said one woman to her husband in the army.[31] "The people is all turning to Union here since the Yankees got Vicksburg. I want you to come home as soon as you can as soon as you git this letter," said another.[32]

Thousands of soldiers, reading letters like that one day after day, laid down their rifles and went home to their farms and families. This was particularly common among those who had no slaves and for whom the Cause was more state's rights and honor than it had ever been the slave system. Their departure caused regimental desertion rates in the spring of 1864 to run routinely at over fifty percent. The deserters all blamed the president. Wrote one Virginia private: "They are whipping us...at every point. I hope they would make peace so that we that is alive yet would get home...but I suppose Jeff Davis and Lee don't care if all is killed."[33]

Davis was alarmed and hurt by the staggering desertion rates. "Can they hear the wail of their suffering countrywomen and children and not come [back]. If there is one who will stay away at this hour, he is unworthy the name Georgian," he said in a Georgia speech denouncing deserters. "To the young ladies, I would say when choosing between an empty sleeve and the man who had remained at home and grown rich, always take the empty sleeve."[34]

Davis exhorted all able-bodied men to join the army and fight. He spoke several times on the matter in 1864, working hard not only as president, but as a morale booster, constantly exhorting Southern men to fight and imploring their wives and families to support them. "The time for action is now at hand. There is but one duty for every southern man. It is to go to the front," he said in Montgomery.[35] In Columbia, a few weeks later, he made another plea. "There is but one means by which you can hope to gain independence and an honorable peace and that is by uniting with harmony, energy and determination in fighting those great battles."[36]

"Every man able to bear arms must go to the front, and all others must devote themselves to the cause at home," he said. "We are fighting for our existence..."[37]

News from the battlefields and the political front remained bleak throughout the winter and early spring of 1864 for Jefferson Davis. On January 8, the Union, firmly in control of New Orleans and Louisiana, began reconstruction there, and army officials worked with local residents to patch together a new legislature. Just a week later, a pro-Union government was installed in occupied Arkansas; a week after that Tennessee set up a provisional Union government, with Andrew Johnson as governor. Sherman, with twenty thousand men, marched into Mississippi, Davis's home state, in February, and captured Meridian and several small towns, tearing up miles of railroad track. Later, in the first week of May, Sherman began his campaign to capture Atlanta. The South lost one of its greatest heroes on May 4, when J. E. B. Stuart was shot and killed in a battle at Yellow Tavern, in Virginia. Davis rushed to his side and was one of the last people to speak to him, gently holding the colorful cavalry leader's hand as he slipped away.

The only major victory the Confederacy had that spring was the capture of Fort Pillow, in Tennessee, by General Nathan Bedford Forrest. Nearly half the defenders of Fort Pillow, he knew, were black troops. The victory turned into a public relations debacle when Forrest's men reportedly massacred Union soldiers, opening fire on surrendering troops. They targeted the blacks, chasing them down like dogs and killing 261.[38] Davis refused to acknowledge the massacre.[39]

DAVIS made about a dozen speeches outside Richmond during the war, beginning with a few short ones when he visited Tennessee to see Braxton Bragg in December of 1862. The president delivered small talks to people he met in walking trips in and around Jackson after his forceful speech to the legislature there in 1862.[40] He gave a few more speeches to townspeople in several states in 1863 during visits to his generals. In 1864 Davis traveled through cities in Georgia to speak to the people and to cheer up the troops following the loss of Atlanta; he also gave talks in South Carolina and at the statehouse in Montgomery, Alabama.[41]

Davis's speeches defended the administration and himself, attacked the Yankees, thanked the people for their support, and predicted an early end to the war in victory for the Confederacy. Some of these addresses, like his talk to the Mississippi legislature, were quite eloquent; others, usually impromptu talks to small groups of people, were disorganized but well meant. Davis could always deliver ringing, patriotic lines that perked up crowds. He told one group, in a standard exhortation, that if they doubted the success of the Cause, "let them go to those places where brave men are standing in front of the fore, and there receive the assurance that we shall have final success and that every man who does not live to see his country free will see a freeman's grave."[42]

Despite all his hundreds of thousands of words and many hours of speaking, however, Jefferson Davis was never able to articulate clearly what the South was fighting for. He could never define the kind of independent country his people sought or how it would differ from the country they once had. Never able to explain convincingly to his people a bloody and heartsickening war that was taking the lives of hundreds of thousands of Southern men, he could not get the people to explain it to themselves.

President Davis didn't have to explain anything to the rich—they knew the war was over slavery. He had great difficulty explaining it to the middle class, and the poor, because they had no slaves and needed an inspirational vision in order to fight on as things went badly. Davis gave them none. The support of the firebrands is not enough for a revolution to succeed: It must have the support of the broad-based middle class, the backbone of the economy and the culture.[43] President Davis's failure to define, simply and eloquently, what the war was about to the middle class, as its will to fight crumbled, contributed mightily to his inability to win it.

Davis's belief that the army could hold off the Yankees forever, and thus win the war, collapsed in the summer of 1864. Mobile Bay, Alabama, had seemed impregnable. It had more than adequate defenses, militia in reserve, and even an ironclad to patrol the waters. Yet it fell in late August to the forces of David Farragut. It was a devastating blow to the Davis government because Mobile Bay was the last open blockade runners' port east of Texas.[44] Its capture ended the South's ability to import anything.

All eyes then turned to Atlanta, under siege for weeks by Sherman's men.

Atlanta was critical to the South because it was a large inland city and rail center. It was also a gateway to Georgia. Sherman could march right across the state if he captured Atlanta. Davis had worked on the defense of Atlanta for months with General Joe Johnston, who began to tangle with Sherman's men in early summer, far from the city, and then slowly retreated toward it.

Davis, and everyone else, wanted Johnston to take a stand and fight, yet he kept pulling back. Richmond workers snickered that Joe Johnston was the best retreater in America. Davis bluntly asked him whether or not he planned to hold Atlanta and Johnston gave him an evasive answer.[45] Finally, on July 17, the president fired the popular Johnston and replaced him with John Bell Hood. Davis knew that firing Johnston would create controversy. To protect himself he took the rare step of asking his cabinet for approval, which they gave.[46]

Davis always claimed that in dismissing Johnston he only did what the people wanted. "Popular disappointment [in him] was extreme," he said. "The possible fall of the 'gate city,' with its important railroad communications, vast stores, factories for the manufacture of all sorts of military supplies... was now contemplated for the first time at its full value and produced intense anxiety far and wide... if the Army of Tennessee was found to be unable to hold positions of great strength like those at Dalton and Kenesaw... I could not reasonably hope that it would be more successful in the plains below Atlanta."[47]

Atlanta fell on September 1, 1864, and the shock of its collapse spread quickly through the South.[48] For perhaps the first time, Southerners felt that the barbarians not only were at the gate, but had knocked it down and were pouring through. Sherman later evicted all the residents and burned much of the city to the ground in a successful attempt to show Southerners that the Union army could strike and destroy them everywhere. One month later, Phil Sheridan defeated the Confederates in a series of battles in the Shenandoah Valley, booting out Early's army and reclaiming the valley for the Federals in another great victory. Sheridan's men destroyed over two thousand farms and seventy mills, seized seven thousand cattle and sheep and set fire to so many barns and wheat fields that a reporter said that there was a line of smoke that ran the entire length of the valley.[49]

The fall of Atlanta, the capture of Mobile Bay, and the collapse of Early's army in the Shenandoah reignited the old debates about Davis's policy of geographic departments for his armies and the absence of a general in chief. The president had come under fire consistently throughout the war for maintaining small armies in different parts of the South, instead of deploying men to areas where more men were needed to fight Grant and other federal generals.

Atlanta, the critics said, was the perfect example of what can happen with a shortsighted, departmentalized strategy. The Confederacy lost one of its most important cities because Joe Johnston, and then John Bell Hood, did not have enough men. Sherman's total strength on the day Atlanta fell was about 85,000 men. Hood's total strength was just 42,000 (37,000 of his own men and 5,000 from the Georgia militia). Hood fought valiantly, but, Davis's critics said, he was outnumbered two to one and never had a chance. Why couldn't some of Beauregard's men go to Atlanta? Lee had Grant tied down in the siege of Petersburg when Atlanta fell. Why couldn't Davis send 20,000 of Lee's men to Atlanta? Newspapers, congressmen and civic leaders loudly denounced the fall of Atlanta as a perfect example of Davis's inept strategy. Given the duration of the total Atlanta campaign, over six weeks, the president had had time to transfer thousands of men, critics said, but did nothing. Johnston's style of constantly retreating seemed like cowardice, and not strategy, to Southerners, who demanded that their armies fight.[50]

Rhett, in the *Charleston Mercury,* pinned all of the blame for Atlanta on Davis. "General Hood's egregious failures, it appears to us, have proved, beyond question, that what was wanted by our army at Atlanta was not a *change of generals,* but *reinforcements.*"[51]

Governor Brown was outraged that Davis refused to reinforce Johnston and Hood. Brown had begged Davis for reinforcements in early July, and warned him "if your mistake should result in the loss of Atlanta and the occupation of other strong points in this State by the enemy, the blow may be fatal to our cause."[52]

Davis had assured Brown in June that Johnston had enough men and that he had misjudged the size of Sherman's army. "The disparity of forces between the opposing armies...is less than reported," he said, and told the governor that "I do not see how I can change the disposition of our forces so as to help General Johnston more effectively."[53]

Brown wrote back that his information on the strengths of the armies was wrong, that Johnston needed help right away, and that the whole country expected the president to send it.[54] Davis angrily turned on Brown. "Your dicta cannot control the disposition of troops in different parts of the Confederate States. Most men in your position would not assume to decide on the value of the service to be rendered by troops in distant positions. I will be glad also to know the sources of your information as to what the whole country expects," he snapped.[55]

Many senators and congressmen were Joe Johnston supporters. They claimed Davis had fired Johnston because of their longstanding feud and charged that if Davis had kept him in command somehow Johnston would have saved Atlanta. Hood, many said, was worse than Johnston. "Hood had a fine career before him until Davis undertook to make of him what the good Lord had not," bellowed the cantankerous Wigfall in the halls of Congress.[56]

The soldiers were stunned by the dismissal of Johnston. Five pickets in Johnston's army threw down their rifles, walked out of camp, and were never seen again. Colonels reported that there was real concern for mutiny among the troops.[57] Private citizens, too, familiar with the spats between the president and Johnston, were critical of Johnston's removal and blamed the fall of Atlanta on Davis.[58] Not a single state governor or influential state legislator in Georgia or in any other Southern state came to the president's defense. In what may have been one of the lowest moments of the war for Jefferson Davis, no one stepped forward to offer advice, consolation, or simple friendship.

The loss of Atlanta, Mobile Bay, and the Shenandoah Valley, plus the ever-growing size of the Union army, cast a pall of gloom over everyone working at the War Department in Richmond. "There is...the deepest uneasiness among the military authorities, from the weakness of our army and the recruiting of the enemy's," said Robert Kean, head of the Bureau of War, the administrative office of the War Department,[59] who had been trying to change the departmental system, warning of its shortcomings for more than a year and receiveing no help from the president.[60] He concluded that the army was weakening and had no more men to draft. "We are exhausted," he said.[61]

Davis's stranglehold on the one-party Congress began to unravel after the summer and fall losses. The Senate faction against him, strengthened in the 1863 elections, managed to gather enough votes to finally override one of his vetoes of a bill to name more naval officers and to give Congress some say in the selections. The override died in the House. Both houses finally mustered enough strength to override a later veto, when the president tried to kill a bill to permit free distribution of newspapers in army camps. Next, both houses passed a bill to create a general in chief, against Davis's wishes, but he coopted them by giving the job to Lee anyway.

The Senate and House factions against Davis worked feverishly in November and December to kill his bill to enlist slaves in the army, tying it up for months as the army fought on, overwhelmed by the enemy.[62] In the fall of 1864, Representative Foote accused the latest secretary of war, James Seddon, of profiteering by selling his wheat at inflated prices.[63] Seddon, exasperated over the trumped-up charges, resigned. Later, a group of senators forced Davis to reinstall Johnston as head of the Army of Tennessee. Then, in the worst blow of all, President Davis learned in January that the Virginia delegation was ready to call for the resignation of the entire cabinet and introduce a no-confidence vote against him.

As always, Davis saw the proposed bills as personal attacks. He was unable to get the Virginians to table them through friendly persuasion. Instead, he screamed at them in a particularly strident outburst, telling the Virginians that the cabinet members had to do what he told them to do and that Congress had no right to interfere with the president and his work.[64]

Inwardly, Davis fumed at the opposition in Congress, which he believed was holding up efforts to win the war. His brother Joseph, knowing how badly the president took criticism, tried to console him, telling him, "I hope the badgering of Congress does not bother you. Much of it I am convinced is from personal resentment."[65]

The answer to his problems at this point, Davis hoped, was the elimination of Abraham Lincoln, one way or another. His mission to Canada, with its agents in New York and Washington, had been working on a plan to capture the American president since the spring. Now, in the fall, Davis wanted that same team to engineer Lincoln's defeat at the polls, but that would be difficult after the combined Union victories of Mobile Bay, Atlanta, and the Shenandoah Valley. Lincoln, so weak in summer, was strong in the fall.

Once again, Davis's lack of practical political experience was evident. He genuinely believed that the purchase of key Northern newspapers by his Canadian team—he authorized funds for their mission, including monies for electioneering[66]—could dramatically influence the vote in certain states. He was also convinced of the truth of rumors of a five hundred thousand man secret organization in the northwest that would vote against the president and work secretly to disrupt the Republican campaign and to make the army look bad.[67] He firmly believed, as well, that Northerners were so fed up with the war they would turn Lincoln out of office.

The only way the Confederate government could have worked effectively to defeat Lincoln would have been to secretly contribute enormous sums of money, and provide manpower, to aid McClellan's campaign. Yet the Confederate government had little money by the fall of 1864, and certainly could not have used Confederate money. Second, McClellan, a good patriot if not a good general, would never have consorted with Confederates because it was treasonous and, if the association were ever learned, would have likely brought about his impeachment if he did win. Besides, Davis told a dumbfounded Alex Stephens in one of their rare friendly conversations, he had no real desire to disrupt the Northern elections, because he did not believe a head of state should interfere in the political life of a foreign country.[68] Stephens later published a letter in which he charged that Davis's inaction guaranteed Lincoln's reelection.[69]

Lincoln's victory at the polls in November 1864, the strain of the war, and constant battles with Congress (the newspapers routinely avoided publishing what congressmen said in public about the president because they considered it too vile to print) made Davis sick again and in early December he was bedridden again, unable to work for nearly two weeks.[70] Rumors swept through the capital anew that he was dying because, just as he fell ill, vice president Alexander Stephens arrived, unscheduled, in Richmond. Many people there, particularly those who hated Davis, were certain Stephens would take over after the president's funeral.[71]

Throughout his dozens of lengthy illnesses in office, Davis never discussed resigning because he was incapacitated and unable to run the country. His long periods of bedridden confinement clearly show that he could not govern then, particularly in times of crisis. Davis's ego and his belief that only he could run the government prevented him from leaving office. His personal physician, Garnett, never advised him to quit. Since there was no opposition party in Congress to pressure him out of office for legitimate health reasons, he remained president. He also clung to office to prevent Alexander Stephens from becoming president. The vice president was not a true secessionist and had been an enemy of Davis from the start of the war. Had Stephens become president, he would probably have led the South in a movement to rejoin the Union, something Davis feared. The president knew, too, that in the one-party system dominated by the secessionists, no faction would try to oust him for medical reasons because they would then wind up with Stephens.

DESPITE the burning of Atlanta and Columbia, the fall of Savannah, starvation at home, extortionists in the marketplace, and no overseas help, Jefferson Davis continued to believe the South could win the war, despite assurances from his most trusted commander, Robert E. Lee, that the army was falling apart. "We have no troops disposable to meet movements of the enemy, or strike when opportunity presents...our ranks are constantly diminishing by battle and disease and few recruits are received; the consequences are inevitable," Lee wrote in September of '64, but Davis ignored him.[73]

By January of 1865, the South had lost two hundred and fifty thousand soldiers, or one of every four adult white men within its borders, one of the highest death-to-population ratios in world history. Another two hundred thousand or more had lost arms and legs or suffered injuries which would incapacitate them for the rest of their lives. President Davis had rejected two generous offers to end the war, lost total casualties of a half million men and, by refusing to surrender, permitted the North to begin a reconstruction program which would, in later years, debilitate the South and, after Southern white backlash, prevent any genuine mix of the black and white races for a hundred years.

"The disaster [must be blamed on]...Mr. Davis himself," Stephens said later. "He proved deficient in developing and directing the resources of the country, in finances and diplomacy, as well as in military affairs...In ability...he is not above a third rate man."[74]

At last, the Petersburg line collapsed. On April 1, Grant's army smashed Pickett's army at Five Forks, near Petersburg, and poured through the countryside around the city. Lee's army, worn out from defending Petersburg, depleted by desertions, low on supplies, and exhausted, retreated west. Lee hoped that he could get his diminished army, down to less than fifty thousand men (compared to Grant's force of over one hundred and twelve thousand men), to a railroad, and then travel south to hook up with Joe Johnston's army in the Carolinas. Lee's troops were hounded by Sheridan's cavalry, though, and forced toward Appomattox, with Union forces snapping at their heels.

On April 2, a Sunday morning, Lee sent a soldier galloping to Richmond on horseback with a note. He entered the front door of St. Paul's Episcopal Church quietly since church was in session. Its walls contained gorgeous stained glass windows that encircled the congregation seated on long, low-slung wooden benches below.[75] All eyes turned from the minister to the soldier, who gave the note to a sexton, who moved up the aisle, his eyes on President Davis's back. He reached the pew and handed the president the note, which told him that Grant had smashed through the lines at Petersburg, that Lee was on the run, and that Davis had to evacuate Richmond immediately. Davis rose quietly, eyes downcast, face pale, and walked out of the church.[76]

Late that night, vowing never to surrender, the president of the

Confederacy, several cabinet members, and a group of aides boarded a train for Danville, a small city in central Virginia, where they planned to form a traveling government and continue fighting the war. They were fortunate to get out of town. The news of Lee's defeat swept through the city within hours. Guards had to hold back surging throngs of frustrated people at the train station, all trying to board the last trains. Thousands of Richmond residents, belongings flung in bags or sacks, jammed the bridges and roads out of the Confederate capital, desperate to flee. Guards at the jails ran away and let their prisoners escape.

Soldiers poured huge kegs of beer and liquor into the streets to prevent drunkenness. Residents frantically tried to scoop it up in containers as it ran through dirty gutters. Looters broke into shops to steal whatever they wanted, then ran down the sidestreets with their arms piled high with jackets, clothes, and boots, strands of jewelry hanging out of their pockets. Government workers shredded important papers. Men and women leaned against buildings and wept openly. Children dodged oncoming carriages racing for the bridges. Cotton, tobacco, and other supplies were set on fire by the army to keep them out of the hands of Union troops expected momentarily,[77] but the flames were soon out of control. As the flames reached them, local arsenals blew up with loud roars. Confederate gunboats in the James River exploded, lighting up the night sky.[78]

Jefferson Davis sat next to a window, ramrod straight as always, as his train rumbled down the tracks and out of Richmond. He looked through the glass at his city, in chaos and on fire, panic everywhere, as the train picked up speed and disappeared into the night.

PART VII

THE LAST YEARS

24

ABRAHAM LINCOLN:
FINAL DAYS

PRESIDENT LINCOLN STARED out the window of his office at the Potomac, his hands clasped together behind his back, fretting, as always, about the never-ending war. He was full of optimism on April 4, when Richmond fell. He visited the city, looted and half burned down by its own citizens when the Confederate army and the government fled. Lincoln felt a sense of great self-confidence as he sat in Jefferson Davis's chair in the Confederate White House,[1] and was cheered as "Father Abraham" by hundreds of freed black slaves there. He hosted a reception at which he was assured by his generals that the fall of the rebel capital meant the end of the war.[2]

It did not. Now, on April 9, Lee was on the run through Virginia, and the Union army was chasing him. If Lee escaped, and Jefferson Davis avoided capture, the South could carry on a guerrilla war for years, and the United States would remain fractured. Finally, late at night, a messenger from the War Department rushed into the White House with the news Lincoln had prayed for—Grant had trapped Lee near Appomattox, Lee had surrendered his army. Joe Johnston's army was still at large in North Carolina, pursued by Sherman, but Lee's surrender truly ended the war. The president left the office, and, with fast steps and long strides, raced through the White House to his wife's bedroom, where he woke her and told her the news.

Residents of Washington who were sleeping the next morning were awakened shortly after dawn by a number of loud explosions which soon turned into continuous reports. Cannons were firing all over the city, in the surrounding counties, and up and down the Potomac River. Five hundred cannons blasted away for hours, sending a veil of light smoke drifting toward the skies. People, frantic, burst out of their homes to learn the news—the war was over. Young newsboys ran through streets and alleys, holding their morning newspapers up and shouting "Surrender of General Lee! Surrender of General Lee!"[3] All morning, loud bells rang throughout the city. Men fired weapons into the air, children laughed and hugged each other. People ran through the streets brandishing unfurled American flags, while the Stars and Stripes seemed to appear out of nowhere to adorn porches and windows.[4] Women broke down and wept. "All are jubilant," wrote Gideon Welles.[5]

"Our struggle is over," wrote Horace Greeley in the *New York Tribune,* "The new birth of the nation is accomplished."[6]

Thousands of celebrants poured into the streets and formed an ad hoc parade that wandered down the middle of avenues, serenading workers at various government buildings. The crowd, which police estimated at over three thousand, added people as it went, growing larger and larger. By the time it turned toward the White House, several wagons with American flags flying from them had joined the sea of people. Musicians found their way to the parade, a band quickly formed, and the group marched down Pennsylvania Avenue singing "Rally Round the Flag."[7] The jubilant people surged across the lawns of the White House, crowding the portico, the carriageways, and the grass. They pressed hard against each other, shouting and singing songs as the band played. They yelled, "Where is the President? The President! Mr. Lincoln!" The mass of people were so happy they chuckled when Tad Lincoln waved a Confederate flag out of a second story window. Finally, unable to ignore the pleas for an appearance, Lincoln emerged onto the second-floor porch of the north portico to greet them. Smiling broadly, the deep lines on his face melting away for a few moments, he gave a short speech and then, to the delight of the crowd, asked the band to play one of his favorite songs, *Dixie.*[8]

PRESIDENT Lincoln was intent on going to Ford's Theater on April 14, Good Friday, to see Laura Keene in *Our American Cousin.* He just had been through one of the busiest weeks of his life: sending off countless wires to Grant and Sherman, working with the generals to stabilize Richmond, writing army leaders in Louisiana to push ahead with reconstruction, delivering a controversial speech in which he promised the vote to freed slaves. John Wilkes Booth, who had been at both Lincoln inaugurals, was at that speech, too, and told a friend that Lincoln now wanted "nigger citizenship" and "ought to be killed."[9] Lincoln was also spending long hours on foreign affairs since Seward, badly injured in an April 5 carriage accident, was bedridden. He wanted to relax, get away from the White House, and catch another play at Ford's, his favorite theater.

Mary Lincoln was reluctant to go, but she knew that a comedy would make her husband happy. He had been unusually despondent lately. He told her about a bizarre dream he had in which he walked through the White House and saw a man lying in a coffin at a wake. Someone in the dream then told him the slain man was the president, that he had been assassinated. That afternoon, he told a very uneasy cabinet about his recurring dream that he was in a boat adrift in a mist and heading toward some unknown and distant shore.[10]

Mary Lincoln heard from the president's aides that instead of celebrating the fall of Richmond on the riverboat ride back from that city, he read the death scenes from *Macbeth*. Lincoln was told of yet another plot to murder him on the boat and had to move to a different deck in case someone tried to shoot him. While in Richmond, his guards thought they saw a Confederate soldier aim a rifle at him out of a second-story window. That very afternoon, he received a letter from General James Van Alen chastising him for walking about in Richmond and begging him not to make any public appearances for some time in order to avoid assassination.[11]

Several people begged Lincoln not to go to the theater that night. He had originally asked Grant and his wife to join him, but Julia Grant refused to spend any time with Mrs. Lincoln, who she thought was mentally ill, and the general begged off. His appearance at the play with the president had been announced in the papers, though, and Ward Lamon told the president that the chance to kill both the president and Grant would be too enticing for a prospective assailant. Lamon urged the president not to tempt fate and to stay home. Stanton, who had become very morbid toward the end of the war, turned down the president's offer to join him when Grant declined; he told Lincoln to skip the play and stay within the safe confines of the White House.[12] Invitations were then extended by Lincoln to Illinois governor

Richard Oglesby and General Isham Haynie, who visited him that afternoon, but they declined. He was also turned down by Thomas Eckert, one of Stanton's aides.

Just before he left for the theater, Lincoln went to the War Department with one of his bodyguards, William Crook, to see if there was news of Johnston's surrender to Sherman. He walked across the White House lawn, which was starting to turn green as the spring approached, and shocked him. "I believe there are men who would take my life and I have no doubt they will do it," said Lincoln in an abrupt change in conversation.

Crook assured him that since the war was over there was no reason to believe anyone would try to kill him, and that he was guarded at all times. "You are mistaken, Mr. President," he said. Lincoln took leave of Crook when they returned to the White House. "Well, goodbye, Crook," he said, and walked off. Crook stared after him. Whenever the president had left him before, he always said goodnight.[13]

The Lincolns were late for the play at Ford's Theater. The president had finally talked Major Henry Rathbone and his girlfriend, Clara Harris, into accompanying them, and they arrived in the middle of the drama. The band struck up "Hail to the Chief" as soon as the president was seen taking his seat in the presidential box, eleven feet above the stage. Lincoln smiled at the crowd of over sixteen hundred people, as everyone in the audience stood and cheered him. It was one of the longest ovations he had ever received, even longer than the cheering at his second inaugural; those at the theater estimated it lasted nearly five minutes. He nodded his thanks to the crowd, and Mary beamed.[14]

Just before the presidential party arrived, actor John Wilkes Booth was seen walking into the theater once again. The actor, a familiar figure at Ford's and other city theaters, had been at the theater since late morning, opening his mail and chatting with dozens of actors and crew members. He had had a beer with two actors in late afternoon at a bar across the street from Ford's and had been in and out of the theater all day.

He was putting the finishing touches on the final version of the year-long plan to capture Abraham Lincoln, which, with the fall of Richmond and escape of the Confederate government, had collapsed. Booth and his crew now believed that Lincoln and others had to die for their sins. They hoped also that their deaths might still throw the Union into chaos and somehow, some way, enable Joe Johnston's army, still fighting in North Carolina despite Lee's surrender, to win the war.

Booth and his conspirators coordinated their plans in the early evening. George Atzerodt was to murder Vice President Andrew Johnson, who was staying at Kirkwood House, a local boarding home. Lewis Paine and David Herold were to murder William Seward, bedridden at his house, and Booth was to kill president Lincoln—all at precisely 10:15 P.M.[15]

The plot started to unravel when Azterodt arrived at Johnson's boarding house and lost his nerve after consuming several drinks at its bar. He rode off into the night. Herold and Paine arrived at Seward's home and gained entry by telling a servant that they had an important message from Seward's doctor. Paine followed the servant to Seward's room, but the secretary's son Fred, suspicious, stopped him and told him he would take the message and deliver it to his father. Paine pulled out a gun and fired it at Fred Seward, but it did not discharge. He then smashed Seward over the head with the gun, fracturing his skull as the force of the blow covered him with blood. Paine rushed into the secretary of state's bedroom and began to stab Seward in the face, nearly severing his jaw, blood gushing from the wounds,[16] until his other son, Augustus, and a nurse-soldier pulled him off. Both were stabbed in the scuffle before Paine fled the room, raced downstairs, discovered Herold had left, and rode off, leaving five people wounded, three seriously. None died.[17] "It was a night of horrors," Welles wrote later.[18]

Just past 10 P.M., John Wilkes Booth strode up to the doorkeeper of Ford's Theater, John Buckingham, whom he knew well, smiled at him, and jokingly asked if he needed a ticket, eliciting a grin from the doorkeeper. Booth, humming a tune, then casually walked up the stairs to the dress circle, the level of the presidential box, prepared to shoot whoever got in his way. He was surprised to find the security guard, John Parker, was missing. Parker, who had replaced an earlier guard fired by Mary Lincoln for laziness,[19] was several yards away, watching the play from a theater seat. The only man protecting the president was his valet, Charles Forbes, who was standing unobtrusively near the door.

Booth was seen by a number of people as he walked behind the seats. Many had seen him on the stage and knew who he was. Others, noticing his good looks and expensive suit, did not think him suspicious. An army captain and his brother, a doctor, sitting just a few rows from the back of the theater, stared at him for several minutes as he lounged against a wall and then entered the presidential box. The two then turned to continue watching the play.[20] Forbes, who probably recognized the actor, let him in to see the president when Booth convinced him he had an urgent message for him and showed him some business cards.

Booth, carrying a small derringer in his pocket, immediately closed off the doorway behind him, forcing a piece of wood between the door and a hole he had carved into the interior wall of the passageway earlier. He moved quickly down the narrow hall, bent over, looked through a small hole he had drilled in the door at the box itself, and saw that the president was right in front of him, slightly bent over, his head resting on his right hand. Booth opened the door at 10:13 P.M., stared at Lincoln, aimed the gun at the left side of his head and, from a distance of about two feet, fired.[21] Lincoln noiselessly raised his hands toward his head, then dropped them into his lap and slumped forward.[22]

Major Rathbone leaped from his seat at the sound of the shot and turned, but before he could do anything Booth pulled out a seven and a quarter inch-long hunting knife and stabbed him in the arm, dragging the sharp blade down to his elbow, sending blood spurting all over his blue uniform.[23] The actor then jumped down to the stage. Catching the spur of his boot on the bunting which covered the front of the box, he landed badly, spraining his ankle. "*Sic semper tyrannis!* [Thus always to tyrants] The South is avenged!" he shouted and then ran off the stage as several people began to yell, "That's John Booth!"[24]

Patrons in the audience did not know what had happened until they heard Mary Lincoln's bloodcurdling scream: "They have shot the president! They have shot the president!"[25]

Chaos filled the theater. Men in uniform scrambled through the crowd toward the president's box but couldn't get through. Actors poured on to the stage and looked up at the box, where dozens of people had surrounded the president. Hundreds of people in the theater charged the stage, some leaping on orchestra chairs and breaking them, others knocking over musicians' stands. No one was certain if the shooting was still going on, or if there were gunmen still in the theater. Laura Keene, the star of the show, pushed her way to the middle of the crowd on stage and at the top of her lungs shouted "Order! Order!" but there was none.[26]

Charles Leale, a twenty-three-year-old U.S. Army doctor who had been a physician for just six weeks, pushed his way into the presidential box and bent over the president, examining his chest and back for stab wounds, not realizing he had been shot. Minutes went by before he discovered the bullet wound in the back of Lincoln's head. Leale closed his eyes, certain the wound was fatal. With the help of two other, older doctors, he ordered men to carry the limp body of the president to any nearby house, afraid a carriage ride to the White House would kill him immediately. They took him to the home of William Petersen, a merchant-tailor, where he had to be laid on a bed diagonally because his body was too long to lay straight.

Hundreds of people left the theater to follow the men carrying the president. They were startled at the thick trail of blood on the pavement. The theatergoers, too upset to go home, milled about in the street, joined by hundreds of others who had heard about the assassination of the president and Seward. The crowd grew in size and flowed down neighboring streets. Armed soldiers and police had to cordon off the entrance to the home.[27]

Edwin Stanton was about to go to sleep when men arrived at his house to tell him that both Lincoln, fifty-six, and Seward, sixty-four, had been murdered. Visibly agitated, the burly secretary dressed quickly and left for Seward's house, despite his wife's insistence that there might be a plot to kill everyone of importance and that he could be murdered. Stanton checked on Seward, was told he would probably die, and then raced by carriage to the Petersen House. With the secretary of state nearly dead, the president dying, and the vice president, possibly a target, asleep at his boarding house, Stanton took it upon himself to lead the government from a small room down the hallway from where the president lay. Like his wife, Stanton suspected a massive conspiracy.

Stanton sent armed guards to get Andrew Johnson at the boarding house and bring him, under tight security, to the Petersen house. Other guards were told to bring as many members of the cabinet as they could find to the home for protection.[28] Stanton sent orders to General Grant to return to Washington from New Jersey, where he had gone with his wife, and told him to travel under heavy protection. Julia Grant began to cry when she heard the news.[29] Stanton then launched an immediate investigation into the attacks, ordered the closing of all roads and bridges into and out of the city, commanded the army to search for the killers, ordered provost marshals in all Northern seaports to stop everyone boarding ships, and dictated the official story of the attack on the president, which was sent out over the wires to the press.[30]

The president slipped away slowly, never regaining consciousness. The most important people in the government, from cabinet members to White House workers, were in and out of his room from midnight on. Abraham

Lincoln died at 7:22 in the morning. His wife cradled his head in her arms, kissed him hundreds of times, and addressed him in sweet, endearing words. His son Robert, who had arrived in the night, broke down and sobbed uncontrollably, as did Senator Charles Sumner. Stanton, who had scorned this man in the 1850s, deriding his intelligence, his politics, and even his ill-fitting clothes, but had come to love him very deeply in the 1860s, said solemnly, as the president died, "Now he belongs to the ages."

25

JEFFERSON DAVIS:
FINAL DAYS

A SINGLE LOUD GUNSHOT split the early morning air around the campsite near Irwinville, Georgia, where Jefferson Davis, his wife, and some aides were sleeping on their way to the Mississippi region to continue the fight against the Union, even though Richmond had fallen and all of the Southern armies had surrendered. Davis and some cabinet members had tried to administer the country from Danville, Virginia, then Greensboro and then Charlotte, always on the run. Now, a month later, the president, his wife, and a few aides were all that was left of the Confederacy, an entire administration that could fit around a single campfire.

The shot awakened Davis, who slept with his head resting on a rolled-up blanket, in his clothes in case he had to flee quickly. Still sleepy, he greeted his freed black coachman, James Jones, who told him the camp was under attack by a company of Yankee soldiers. Davis, rubbing his eyes, could see the blue-uniformed cavalrymen through the thick woods.

He turned and went into a tent to tell Varina the Union soldiers were coming. She urged him to flee, to save himself, but he delayed, afraid she might be hurt. She walked out of the tent with him and, when they saw soldiers walking around the horses and wagons, told him to walk casually the other way, toward a thick swamp which might provide safety. Davis reached for his coat, but by mistake picked up his wife's waterproof cloak and put it on.[1] Varina threw her shawl over his head and shoulders as a disguise and he began to walk, but his spurs gave him away. Corporal George Munger stopped him, and when Davis defiantly flung off the shawl, Munger recognized him and aimed a rifle at his chest, ordering him to surrender. Davis said something and moved his body in such a way that Varina feared he would try to charge the man on horseback and be shot. She ran to her husband and grabbed him from behind. Fearful that a wrong move now might result in harm to Varina, he gave up.[2]

The war was finally over. The president and his small party, all that remained of the government, were captured on May 9, 1865.

President Davis had been determined to carry on the fight for years more. After the fall of Richmond on April 3, he and members of the cabinet found themselves on the run, an administration without a country. Davis, defiant to the end, told people that "the Cause is not yet dead" and that he would "remain with the last organized band upholding the flag."[3] Speaking to a small crowd in Danville, he said that even though Lee was on the run, Grant in his shadow, the war was far from over and that he would never give up: "Animated by that confidence in your spirit and fortitude which never yet failed me, I announce to you, fellow countrymen, that it is my purpose to maintain your cause with my whole heart and soul....I will never consent to abandon to the enemy one foot of soil of any of the states of the Confederacy....Let us not despond, my countrymen, but meet the foe with fresh defiance, with unconquered and unconquerable hearts."[4]

His cabinet members and generals had finally urged him to surrender and Joe Johnston said it would be "a human crime" to continue, but Davis would not listen. The majority of the cabinet members then fled, most making it out of the country to safety, but Davis decided to travel back to Mississippi, where he would fight on as a guerrilla general. His wife and family, with other families, had left Richmond days before the government fell and the president fled. Varina and the children fled to Charlotte, and then headed west, through Georgia, as Joe Johnston's army surrendered to Sherman in North Carolina. Davis met up with them there.

The rebel president was taken to Savannah, where he met Alexander Stephens, also a prisoner. They were taken to Fort Monroe, outside Washington. Stephens was separated from Davis there and incarcerated in Fort Warren, in Massachusetts, where he remained for five months.

Varina and the children said their goodbyes, expecting Davis to be freed within weeks. Although he did not know it until years later, Davis was nearly assassinated on the steamship *Clyde*, which took him to Washington. The *Clyde* was guarded by another ship, the USS *Tuscarora*, whose crew held a mock trial of Davis for the murder of Lincoln, found him guilty, and sentenced him to be killed by a crew member who was a superior marksman. The seaman had Davis in his sights on the other boat and was about to pull the trigger when Davis's daughter, Winnie, jumped into his lap, ruining the shot.[5]

Davis was treated like a common criminal when he was imprisoned on May 22. The jailer, General Nelson Miles, ordered Davis put in a small, damp cell and shackled with leg irons. His shackling in irons enraged Americans, Northerners as well as Southerners, and so many complained to the War Department that Edwin Stanton ordered Miles to remove the leg irons after five days.

Northerners had no objections to his imprisonment, however, and, except for the shackling, were not unhappy with the poor conditions of his jail. Many thought it was just what he deserved. Bragged one editor: "Jefferson Davis...was duly but quietly and effectively committed to that living tomb prepared within the impregnable walls of Fortress Monroe....He is buried alive."[6]

President Davis had to drink his water from a dirty wooden bucket, was given standard prison rations, allowed little exercise, awakened every fifteen minutes for cell inspection, and prevented from getting much sleep by a lamp which was kept lit in his cell all night. He was forbidden to speak to anyone. Dr. John Craven, who examined him regularly, reported that he was becoming very ill. His neuralgia flared up again, he had lost considerable weight, and he was constantly feverish. In August 1865 his neuralgia was so bad that his entire face, neck, and upper back were covered with infectious sores, and he developed carbuncles on his legs.[7] As Davis began to fall apart physically, his emotional well-being was further undermined when news of his capture disguised as a woman became public. Thousands of newspapers carried the stories, and Davis became a national joke, as cartoonists depicted him fleeing through the woods in a bonnet and hoop skirt.

He learned later that his children, living in a hotel with his wife in Savannah, were taunted mercilessly by other youngsters, who often sang long choruses of the John Brown song, which Northerners had changed to a Jeff Davis song, "Let's Hang Jeff Davis From a Sour Apple Tree." Some boys even taught two-year-old Willie how to sing the song, which mortified Varina. Jeff Jr. often wound up in fights over his father with other boys and one day was tied up and nearly whipped by two adult women. The children were told by young and old in Savannah that their father was not only a traitor, but a thief who stole eight million dollars from the Confederate treasury.[8]

Davis did not know that he was lucky to be alive. Reports had surfaced in the press that the orders for Lincoln's murder had come from Richmond, ostensibly from President Davis, and editors and citizens wanted him tried and hanged, just as other of the conspirators had been hanged. As late as summer, 1866, when President Johnson barnstormed through the country, people shouted, "Hang Jeff Davis!"[9] Davis was held for conspiracy in the murder of Lincoln and the attack on Seward, but, with no evidence linking him to the killings, the only charges filed against him were for treason. Davis was stunned when he received the news that Booth had gone beyond his very explicit kidnap orders and killed Lincoln. He had assumed that the entire plot had collapsed when Richmond fell. Davis felt terrible that Lincoln was dead, and he knew that his successor, Johnson, was not strong enough to restrain radical Republicans from forcing a harsh reconstruction on the South.[10]

The federal government did not know what to do with Davis. Many who were eager for reconciliation wished he had made it to England, as had Judah Benjamin and others. The army continued to hold him for a year, without charges ever being formally filed or a trial date set, and during that time he became very ill from stress-induced neuralgia. Davis became despondent, often sitting in the chair in his cell all day, saying nothing. He knew from letters that as he sat defenseless in jail, former officials and generals of the Confederacy, in order to absolve themselves of any guilt, blamed him for the war, for the Union dead, for his refusals to negotiate a peace agreement, and, in stories in the Southern press, for the mismanagement that had caused defeat.

Throughout that first year, Varina, nearly destitute, kept up a vigorous letter-writing campaign to government officials on behalf of her husband. She wrote a series of letters to Quartermaster General Montgomery Meigs which finally convinced him to let her visit her husband in prison.[11] Next, she began a feverish campaign to convince government officials that her husband should be either pardoned or released and that a year in prison was enough punishment. She wrote to everyone in an official capacity she could think of, including Secretary of War Stanton, and influential people who might help unofficially, such as old family friend Francis Blair Sr. Her letters were dignified, but were written in a pleading, loving narrative which could only come from a wife who wanted her husband back for herself and her small children.

Her July 1866 letter to Reverdy Johnson, a friend of Andrew Johnson and Stanton, was typical. After asking for Davis's release or pardon, she then recounted his deteriorating health and begged for his transfer to a healthier prison. Varina wrote touchingly: "When I look at the husband of my youth, now beatified by such holy resignation, slowly dying away from his little ones to whom I could offer no higher example, or better guide, I feel it is a bitter cup and doubt if my Father wills that we should drink it."[12]

She also kept up a steady correspondence with Dr. Craven, the prisoner physician who cared for her husband, begging him to keep her husband healthy. "I dread paralysis for him; his nerves have been so highly strung for years without relief. If you can, and perhaps you may, prevail upon the authorities to let him sleep without a light. He is too feeble to escape," she wrote five months after he was imprisoned.[13] In a letter to Horace Greeley she said, "[F]or thirteen months I have prayed and tried to cheerfully grope through the mist to find the end, and now it seems no nearer. I see my husband patiently, uncomplainingly fading away and cannot help him...."[14] She wrote Dr. Craven in June, 1865, in a panic when she read in several newspapers that her husband's health had turned for the worse. "Is he dying?" she asked."[15]

President Davis's prison letters to his wife, although censored, showed his continuing love for her and his growing faith in God. "As none could share my suffering, and as those who loved me were powerless to diminish it, I greatly preferred that they should not know of it. Separated from my friends of this world, my Heavenly Father has drawn nearer to me. His goodness and my unworthiness are more sensibly felt but this does not press me back, for the atoning Mediator is the way and His hand upholds me," he wrote in late 1865.[16]

President Davis never publicly discussed his imprisonment. In his memoirs he merely wrote that "bitter tears have been shed by the gentle, and stern reproaches have been made by the magnanimous on account of the needless torture to which I was subjected."[17]

After a year, president Johnson replaced Miles with a new jailer, Colonel H. S. Burton, who was sympathetic to Davis. Burton moved him to a better, drier cell, authorized daily exercise, permitted him to send letters to whomever he wanted, allowed Varina to visit her husband and, eventually, to live at the fort with him.

The government began to come under enormous pressure from the public to either free Davis or bring him to trial. His supporters charged that no civilian could be held in a military prison if arrested on civil charges and that Davis was being denied his constitutional right to a speedy trial. Only four other rebels had been jailed at the end of the war. Henry Wirz, commandant at Andersonville prison, where thousands died, was hanged. Vice President Stephens and cabinet secretaries George Trenholm and Charles Memminger were released within the year. No field generals were imprisoned.

Davis's continued incarceration was deemed so unfair that his growing army of supporters included some of his former enemies, such as Horace Greeley and abolitionist Gerrit Smith, who contributed to his legal defense fund. The letters to President Johnson from Smith, a strident hater of slavery and of anyone who ever owned slaves, were particularly effective. He told the president, "I deem his very long confinement in prison without a trial an insult to the South, a very deep injustice to himself and a no less deep dishonor to the government and the country."[18]

The movement to free Davis gained support from the publication of a graphic and scathing book about his life in jail, *The Prison Life of Jefferson Davis,* written by Dr. Craven and writer Charles Halpine, which described in detail the shabby conditions under which the president of the Confederacy was held and told how badly his health had deteriorated.

President Johnson decided to free Davis and end the controversy by offering him a pardon, if he applied for it. The former Confederate president, haughty as always, refused the offer and demanded a trial where he would prove himself innocent of all charges. His refusal of the pardon angered his wife and supporters, but they continued to work to free the obstinate prisoner, and finally, a year later, in a negotiated settlement, the government turned him over to civilian courts in Virginia, with Robert E. Lee as his character witness, which freed him on bail. Jefferson Davis never stood trial. Dates were continually set and then postponed. Finally, in December 1868, Chief Justice Chase threw out the indictment against Davis and President Johnson issued a general amnesty two weeks later, which resulted in Davis's pardon.

Jefferson Davis moved to Montreal, Canada, after he was bailed out of jail in 1867, eager to be out of the United States. He was penniless, but former

Confederate friends in Montreal helped him out. He lived there for several years. Davis tried to find work in England, where he hoped former Confederate officials could help him, but there were no jobs for the head of a failed rebellion. He finally landed a job as head of Carolina Life Insurance, in Memphis, which was owned by former Tennessee governor Isham Harris, at a salary of close to twenty thousand dollars a year, and returned to America. Varina fell ill in England, her nerves shot from the trauma of the last few years, and stayed behind for a year, trying to recover, while her husband went to Memphis.

The insurance company failed within two years, and Davis resigned. He was once again out of work. He thought of reviving Brierfield as a working farm, with paid black labor, but learned that his brother Joseph had given it to his daughter, who had sold it to freed slaves. Davis broke with his family over that. He sued Joseph's daughter, Lise Mitchell, and his former slaves living there in an effort to get Brierfield back. He won, but did not regain control until 1881. The plantation, with its fields run down and the cotton market depressed, was practically worthless. Davis was broke again and out of work, and his wife was sick. In 1870, his brother Joseph, eighty-six, and his beloved commander, Robert E. Lee, died. "He was my friend, and in that word is included all that I could say of any man," he said of Lee.[19]

Tragedy struck closer a year later, when he lost his third son, Willie, twelve, to diphtheria. His sister Lucinda Stamps died in 1872. Davis was crushed. "I have had more than the ordinary allotment of disappointment and sorrow," he said, and told friends, "May God spare you such sorrow as ours."[20]

THE end of Reconstruction in the southern states in 1876 seemed to change life for Davis, who had not been able to find permanent work in either the United States or England. His daughter Maggie married J. Addison Hayes, of South Carolina, whom Davis liked. His health improved. Friends in Mississippi who had shunned him since the end of the war renewed their friendships. He was able to pay many of his bills when individuals and groups gave him money in appreciation of his work in the war.

Davis steered clear of politics. He turned down an offer to return to the U.S. Senate in the late 1870s, an offer which must have tempted him, because he feared his reentry into public life would open all the old wounds in the South. He had nothing to do with federal or state politics, suggesting no bills, and did not participate in the activities of any political party.

He did agree to write his memoirs. He was eager to refute many of the charges leveled against him in other books and magazine articles by former generals, North and South, and eager, too, to make some money. In his memoirs, Davis felt he could not only change opinions Americans had formed about him, but make them understand that he had been right all along about the need for slavery, Southern political power, state's rights, and secession. He would show them, every one of them, in chapter and verse, that he had been right and they all wrong.

In the end, the autobiography, written with journalist W. T. Walthall, was two long, boring volumes filled with copies of hundreds of letters and notes and chapters of slow-moving narrative that tried to tie secession to the American Revolution. He revealed nothing of the intimate conversations between him and his generals, and he provided little analysis of why the war was lost. The book's price was high, and it was published in the middle of a long wave of Civil War memoirs.

Writing the book created enormous personal problems for Davis. While in England he had told friends in Mississippi that he wanted to return to his home state to write his memoirs. A friend of Varina's, the secessionist firebrand Sarah Dorsey, invited him to stay in a cottage at her plantation at Beauvoir, near Biloxi, Mississippi, with his servant and son Jeff Jr. Varina would remain in England for her health.

The relationship between Sarah and Davis changed quickly. She soon took over the job of his secretary, handling manuscript work and taking dictation. Sarah liked the project and, friends said, she liked Jefferson Davis even more. Over the next few months, Davis began to mention her help in glowing detail in letters to Varina, who became jealous. Newspaper and magazine stories which appeared in the British press made it seem that Mrs. Dorsey was not just Davis's secretary, but his coauthor. Varina seethed. She finally exploded when she read a story in which her husband spoke warmly of Mrs. Dorsey and said that he was feeling well because Mrs. Dorsey had nursed him back to health.

Varina returned to America in 1877, after a separation of over a year, but moved in with Maggie in Memphis, not with her husband. She told him that she had no intentions of moving into Sarah Dorsey's house. She referred to Beauvoir as "Mr. Davis' earthly paradise" and called him the "gentle hermit in the dale."

Davis, still deeply in love with Varina, and not Sarah Dorsey, begged her to move to Beauvoir. She finally did so in the summer of 1878, to discover that Sarah's relationship with her husband had been blown out of proportion by gossips and the press. Mrs. Dorsey, reestablishing her long friendship with Varina, quickly drifted away from Davis, and Varina plunged into the work of the memoir. Their time together at Beauvoir also restored their marriage. He loved being with her and she enjoyed him as always, and delighted whenever he would sing "Annie Laurie" for her.

The Davises, stalked by personal tragedy all their lives, lost Jeff Jr., twenty-one, their fourth son, to yellow fever in 1878. Both became ill from the stress of his death. Davis's neuralgia flared again, and Varina was bedridden for weeks, cared for lovingly by Sarah Dorsey. The autobiography, when completed, was another disappointment for Davis. It did not sell well, received bad reviews, and only stirred up old feuds with political foes.

The end of Reconstruction brought a great feeling of redemption to Jefferson Davis, however. He had lived long enough for the history of his country to shift and a new era of reunion to begin. The year 1881 was the twentieth anniversary of the start of the war. It began a decade-long series of commemorative parades, rallies, dinners, lunches, and celebrations. Citizens of both sides began to celebrate Memorial Day, created to honor all American dead, but especially the slain soldiers of both sides in the Civil War.[21] The mourning of all Americans, North and South, for president James Garfield when he was murdered in 1881 contributed to that reunion.[22] Various armies, brigades, and regiments formed associations to honor the North and the South. The Daughters of the Confederacy was created to honor the men and women of the conflict, and it became a forceful public relations group for Southern memory.

Articles favorable to the Confederate cause began to appear in numerous national magazines as journalists, a generation removed, offered a more conciliatory view of the war. Novels and short stories which featured warm relations between slaveowners and slaves in the prewar South became popular.[23] Railroads, so inefficient in the prewar South, now flourished, funded by Northern investment. Northern financiers backed new Southern ventures, and hundreds of Northern investors bought controlling interests in Southern mills.[24]

Northern carpetbaggers, scorned by former Confederates, helped some-what to get ruined plantations back in business, utilizing freed slaves as sharecroppers. Northerners helped in crisis, too. They raised millions of dollars and sent hundreds of doctors and nurses south when the yellow fever that claimed Jefferson Davis's son and hundreds of others swept through Mississippi and Louisiana in 1878. Southerners were surprised and appreciative. "The noble generosity of the northern people in this day of our extreme affliction has been felt with deep gratitude," Davis wrote a friend.[25] Now, a generation after Shiloh, Chancellorsville, and Gettysburg, Americans on both sides began to forgive and forget.

In his seventies, Davis was invited to hundreds of fairs, rallies, parades, barbecues, and memorials. He had been the martyr of the South during his imprisonment, and now, twenty years later, he had become its symbol of undying hope. The Cause lived because he lived. He was greeted at an agricultural fair in Houston Texas in 1875 as if he were a head of state, and was the subject of a warm reception when he visited his birthplace in Kentucky a few months later.[26] In 1878 he received a thunderous ovation when he spoke at a meeting of the Association of the Army of Tennessee. Officials at Bowdoin College, in Maine, who had infuriated the North by awarding him an honorary degree in 1861, wrote to tell him they still had the degree and were proud of their decision twenty years before. His appearance at a commemorative event at the Shiloh battlefield brought such a long ovation that he was asked to give a speech. He was greeted with fireworks and a parade when he visited Montgomery, Alabama, in 1886, to help lay the cornerstone for a monument to Confederate soldiers. He was welcomed warmly in New Orleans in 1887 at the unveiling of a statue to General Albert Sidney Johnston, his good friend who had been slain early in the war. Davis's arrival a few weeks later in Savannah, Georgia, for another commemorative was so boisterous that his ride to a hotel turned into a parade. His daughter Winnie, born during the war, became "the daughter of the Confederacy" in those years. Magazine and newspaper illustrators, North and South, began to portray Lee as a hero soon after the war, but by the late 1870s they had turned their attention, finally, to Davis. Although he never achieved the stature of Lee, he was presented to the public as a dignified old man, an elder statesman, erasing the infamy of the 1865 drawings of him in his prison cell, to give him a new image by the late 1880s.[27]

Davis was at last seen as a great man throughout the South, a man who lost almost everything, economically and politically, for the Confederacy, who had, more than anyone except Lee, represented the Confederate hopes. "He still stands for the Confederacy. He was covered with it...his destiny was as broad as his country," said Arthur Marks at a typical speech about Davis at a reunion in Tennessee.[28]

Davis, nearing his eightieth birthday, remained too tied to the war to ever become a reunion figurehead. He continued to champion state's rights and the Confederacy in most of his speeches. "Is it a lost cause now? Never...a thousand times, no! Truth crushed to earth will rise again...can never die!" he told crowds.[29] All the same, particularly after long addresses, he often asked his audience to strive for reunion with the rest of the country. Davis told one crowd in Mississippi City, "To you, self sacrificing, self denying defenders of imperishable truths and inalienable rights, I look for the performance of whatever man can do for the welfare and happiness of his country."[30]

Former soldiers wrote Davis frequently, thanking him for his wartime efforts and peacetime work to honor the war dead.[31] Many men and women wrote him that they were refuting published stories in newspapers critical of him.[32] Others mailed him copies of newspaper articles and speeches that were favorable to him.[33] Hundreds of Southerners named their children after him.[34]

In his last years, Davis mellowed considerably. He had a vast correspondence with people, North and South, greeted frequent visitors at his home, traveled to many states for celebrations, and offered his political views on the issues of the day. He even invited reporters to his home when they wanted to do stories about him, not only sitting through interviews but walking through his fruit groves to pick oranges for them.[35]

At eighty-one, Jefferson Davis fell ill with acute bronchitis in late November 1889 after a riverboat trip and never recovered. He died shortly after midnight on December 6. The family wished a small, private funeral service, but all plans for that had to be canceled when public officials and police realized how many Southerners were planning to descend on New Orleans to pay their final respects to President Davis. At official insistence, Varina finally decided to let her husband's body lie in state in New Orleans City Hall, to hold the funeral in that city, and to inter her husband temporarily in a local cemetery.

The turnout was unprecedented. Police estimated that over one hundred fifty thousand people viewed Davis's bier in the council chamber at city hall during the three days he lay in state, including a contingent of former slaves who had worked for him at Brierfield twenty years before. Dozens of trains brought mourners from all over the South. Most of the main streets of New Orleans had to be closed for the funeral cortège because the crowds were so large. The procession began precisely at noon, December 11. At that moment dozens of cannons in New Orleans boomed a memorial salute. All across the old Confederacy, in Richmond, San Antonio, Vicksburg, Charleston, Atlanta, Chattanooga, anywhere the Stars and Bars had flown, cannons fired and church bells tolled.

The funeral processions included fourteen former Confederate generals and their families; the governors of several states; justices of the United States Supreme Court; seven bands; Thomas Drayton, eighty one, a classmate of Davis's at West Point in 1828; nearly ten thousand Confederate army veterans; thirty old men who had fought with Davis in the Mexican War; and a contingent of Union veterans who lived in New Orleans and wanted to pay their respects. So many people jammed the streets that hundreds of extra police had to work, many on horseback, to keep control. The procession itself was so long that it took over and hour and a half to pass through the streets and head to Metarie cemetery.[36]

Jefferson Davis was applauded in death in the North as strongly as he had been vilified during the war. Charles Dana, Lincoln's assistant secretary of war, said of him in the *New York Sun* that he was a dignified man who "bore defeat and humiliation in the high Roman fashion." The *New York World* said that "he sacrificed all for the cause he cherished and he alone of all the South has borne the cross of martyrdom. He was a man of commanding ability, spotless integrity and controlling conscience....He was proud, sensitive and honorable...." The *New York Times* looked to the future as well as the past and wrote that "Jefferson Davis will live longer in history and better than will those who have ever spoken against him."[37]

Several governors begged Varina to reinter her husband in their states. Mississippi claimed him because he lived there all of his adult life. Kentucky wanted him because that state was his birthplace. Georgia wanted him, too. The strongest claims came from Virginia, whose governor reminded Varina that many of America's greatest men were buried there: George Washington, Thomas Jefferson, James Madison, Robert E. Lee, Stonewall Jackson, James Monroe, John Tyler, and J. E. B. Stuart. The Davises had loved their four years in Richmond, too, and their little boy was interred there. Varina agreed, and in late May 1893, after another impressive ceremony, the president of the Confederacy was laid to rest forever in the capital of the Confederacy.

AFTERWORD

THE DEATH OF HER HUSBAND crushed Mary Lincoln. She was so overwrought with grief that it took her five weeks to pack her belongings and leave the White House. Unable to bear residing in either Washington or Springfield, with all their memories of her husband and dead children, she moved to Chicago and lived in a residential hotel with Tad, then fourteen. Robert moved to a nearby apartment and became a lawyer. Mary Lincoln mourned the president's death the rest of her life, wearing black for years.

Her final days were lonely and turbulent. The political enemies she had made during the war caught up with her as a widow. Although Congress awarded her $22,000, her husband's presidential salary for the rest of 1865, it refused to award her a pension. She asked for a $5,000 annual pension because, she argued, the widows of generals and officers killed in the Civil War received pensions and her husband was commander in chief of the Union army. Congress refused. She eventually received a pension of $3,000 a year in 1869, when General Grant became president and urged Congress to approve it.

Mrs. Lincoln did not like hotel life and was certain that after public officials raised enough money to purchase and award Grant three different homes, plus a library, she would have a home donated, too. She was unpopular, however, and friends could not raise money for her.

Mary was badly wounded emotionally in 1867 when Lincoln's old law partner, William Herndon, whom she had never liked, went on a speaking tour and made public the story of Anne Rutledge, Lincoln's first love, whom the president had never mentioned to Mary. The story was then published by Herndon and picked up by most of the nation's newspapers. Shortly afterward, her trusted domestic, Elizabeth Keckley, published a tell-all memoir in which she painted an unflattering portrait of Mary and told readers how critical Mary had been in private of the politicians and women of Washington.

Desperate to raise money, Mary sold some of the letters she had written to friends to a newspaper, and even many of her clothes. The public was outraged that the president's widow would do such a thing. Deluged by negative publicity, Mary Lincoln plunged into grief once again when Tad, eighteen, died in the summer of 1871 after a long bout of pleurisy, leaving only one of her four children, Robert, alive.

Tad's death made Mary, high-strung under normal circumstances, begin to exhibit unusual behavior. She became obsessed with the idea that she would die in a fire and that the entire city of Chicago, which had suffered extensive damage in an 1871 fire, would burn to the ground. She complained to doctors that she had uncontrollable headaches that made her unable to sleep and that she was depressed all of the time. She told one doctor that people were trying to kill her by pouring poison into her coffee when she was not looking. She told Robert that someone had stolen her purse when no one had. On another occasion, she fled her rooms after an argument with her son and took the elevator to the hotel lobby, dressed in her nightgown. When her son tried gently to direct her back to her room, she shouted that he was trying to kill her.

Robert, unnerved by his mother's behavior, went to court and persuaded a judge to remand her to an insane asylum in 1875. Around that time Robert also became the holder of all his mother's stocks and bonds. Mrs. Lincoln, not insane but suffering from an endless series of emotional setbacks, was released after just four months following a letter-writing campaign by friends. Mary Lincoln was so bitter toward Robert that on several occasions she told friends she wanted to shoot him.

Mrs. Lincoln, aging, alone, and with nowhere to go, finally traveled back to Springfield and moved in with her sister and her husband, Ninian Edwards, who had introduced her to Abraham Lincoln thirty-five years before. She remained there, except for a lengthy trip to Europe, until her death in 1882. She and Robert patched up their differences in 1881 when he visited Springfield with his family to see her. On July 24, 1882, Mary Lincoln was buried in Oak Ridge Cemetery, Springfield, next to her children and her husband, the sixteenth president of the United States.

Harvard-educated Robert Lincoln gained quick success as an attorney in Chicago and in 1881 was named secretary of war by James Garfield, a post he held until 1884. He later served for several years as ambassador to England. Ironically, he was standing on a railroad platform with Garfield in Washington when Charles Guiteau shot the president. Just two days before, Garfield had insisted Robert tell him the story of his father's murder. Twenty years later, Robert would be nearby when president William McKinley was assassinated by Leon Czolgosz in Buffalo, New York.

Robert Lincoln was traumatized for years by his father's assassination. He did not remember an ironic incident tied to it until 1909, forty-five years later. He told a friend then that in 1864, a year before the assassination, he was standing on the platform of a train station in Jersey City, New Jersey, waiting to purchase a ticket, when someone accidentally shoved him toward a moving train. Robert Lincoln lost his balance and fell between the moving car and the side of the platform, certain he would be crushed to death. Just as the wheels of the train were about to run over him, a man reached down with his hand, grabbed his coat collar, and yanked him to safety. The man who saved his life was Edwin Booth, John Wilkes Booth's older brother.

Robert Lincoln was mentioned several times in the 1880s and 1890s as a presidential candidate, but there was never any serious effort to nominate him. He never ran for public office and resumed his lucrative law practice in 1885. Lincoln became a lawyer for the Pullman Railroad Company and, in 1897, its president. He died in 1926.

In 1868, Robert Lincoln married Mary Harlan, the daughter of a U.S. senator. Robert and Mary Lincoln had two daughters—Mamie, born in 1869, and Jessie, born in 1875—and a son, Abraham II ("Jack"), born in 1873. They were the only grandchildren of Abraham Lincoln. None was interested in politics. Mamie married Charles Isham in 1891. Their only child, Lincoln Isham, died in 1971 without male heirs. Jessie married Warren Beckwith in 1897 and had two children, Robert Lincoln Beckwith, born in 1904, and Mary Lincoln ("Peggy") Beckwith, born in 1898. Peggy died in 1975. She made headlines in 1963 when, interviewed as a Lincoln descendant during the civil rights movement, she snapped that she was against President Kennedy's efforts to integrate the South. When Robert L. Beckwith, the last descendant, died in 1985, leaving no male heirs, his death ended the family line of Abraham Lincoln.

OVER the years, members of the Lincoln family cooperated in the establishment of an historic site at President Lincoln's longtime home at 413 South Eighth St., Springfield, Illinois. It is open year round, and visitors can take tours free of charge. The National Park Service built a monument to Lincoln in Lincoln City, Indiana, on the site of the farm where young Lincoln lived as a boy for fourteen years and where his mother, Nancy Hanks Lincoln, is buried. The site includes a large monument to the president and, nearby, a re-creation of a small farm designed to look like the one where Lincoln lived. A third Lincoln home site is the re-created village of New Salem, twenty miles northwest of Springfield, where Lincoln worked as postmaster and met Anne Rutledge.

THE last years of Varina Davis were quite different from those of Mary Lincoln. Mrs. Davis had spent her entire postwar life working, first to free her husband from a federal prison and then to refurbish his public image. She was sixty-two when he died and, despite periodic illnesses in the 1870s and 1880s, was in generally good health. An active woman, she had no plans to pass the years sitting on the porch of the now empty Beauvoir. She met a writer and, with his assistance, wrote her memoirs. The sixteen-hundred-page book did not earn good reviews, since it was little more than a lengthy defense of her husband's wartime policies. It shed scant light on her relationship with her husband or on his stormy relationships with political figures and generals.

The first lady of the Confederacy shocked the South when she moved to New York City in 1892 and took up residence in a Manhattan hotel. She told friends that her daughter Winnie, now a budding writer, needed to live in New York in order to be close to publishers, who were eager to produce the works of the famous "Daughter of the Confederacy." The Davises, mother and daughter, had little money and would depend on Winnie's writing for income. Many suspected Varina no longer wanted to live in the South without her husband.

Mrs. Davis was overly protective of Winnie. In 1889, Winnie fell in love with Fred Wilkinson, of New York, and the engagement announcement caused an uproar below the Mason-Dixon line. Wilkinson was not only a Yankee, but the grandson of the Rev. Samuel May, one of the leading abolitionists of the prewar era. Varina put pressure on Winnie to break off the engagement. Winnie refused. Varina, rebuffed, then decided to respect her daughter's decision and support her against the attacks, but the damage was done. Within a few months, the engagement collapsed anyway. Winnie, twenty-seven when she moved to New York with her mother, never married. She became very ill from malarial gastritis on a cross-country train trip in 1898 and died soon afterward at age thirty-three.

Varina settled into an agreeable lifestyle in New York. The city was home to thousands of ex-Confederates who absorbed her into their social circle. She went to the theater and opera often and was invited to many parties. She wrote dozens of lengthy articles for New York City newspapers. New Yorkers were genuinely happy to have her. Varina's real contribution, however, was her sincere efforts to bring North and South back together. She met Julia Grant at West Point in 1893 when Mrs. Grant, to the surprise of her friends, walked to Varina's room and introduced herself. Mrs. Davis graciously thanked her for coming and they talked all night on the hotel veranda. The women became friends, and several years later Mrs. Davis appeared arm in arm with Mrs. Grant at the dedication of Grant's Tomb in New York, in what the press called a symbolic gesture of North-South reconciliation. In 1901, Varina was asked to write a newspaper article about Grant. Varina, who had never met him, wrote a laudatory article about her husband's nemesis, ending it with a heartfelt plea for North and South to reunite. The article by the widow of the Confederate president, reprinted in many papers, impressed all Americans, North and South, and was said by many to be one of the major causes of the reunion between the two sections of the country that took place as the nineteenth century ended, along with heroic participation by soldiers from both Northern and Southern states in the Spanish–American War.

Varina's last child, Maggie, married a banker, Addison Hayes, whom Jefferson Davis had liked. Hayes had so much respect for Davis that after he died his son-in-law had his name legally changed to Addison Hayes-Davis to honor the Confederate president. Hayes-Davis and Maggie moved to Colorado Springs, Colorado, because of his failing health. They had several children and grandchildren and, over the years, dozens of descendants. Every other year, all of the Hayes-Davis family gathers at Beauvoir for a family reunion to honor the memory of Jefferson Davis.

Varina died of pneumonia in 1906 at the age of eighty. New Yorkers and other Northerners who had come to admire her grieved. Her body was taken from a funeral home to a ferry to Jersey City, New Jersey, for the trip to

Richmond, where she would be buried with her husband. The mayor of New York sent a large escort of mounted police to accompany the catafalque with the coffin through the streets. General Frederick Grant, president Grant's son, ordered federal troops to lead the procession, the first time in U.S. history federal troops escorted a funeral procession for a woman. A large contingent of United Confederate Veterans, in uniform, marched with her as an honor guard. A military band volunteered to lead the funeral procession, repeatedly playing "Dixie" as the procession moved through city streets and thousands stopped to watch. The coffin, appropriately, was draped with a large Confederate flag.

On October 19, 1906, Varina Davis was buried in Richmond's Hollywood Cemetery with her children and her husband, the president of the Confederate States of America.

SEVERAL of Jefferson Davis homes are open to the public: Rosemont, in Woodville, Mississippi, the Davis family plantation where Jefferson Davis spent his boyhood, has been restored. Visitors can tour the home and walk through the family cemetery, where five generations of Davises are buried. Beauvoir, on the Mississippi River near New Orleans, where Davis spent his last years and where he wrote his memoirs, is also open to the public. The Confederate White House, in Richmond, where the Davises spent the war years, was restored in 1896, with Varina Davis's assistance, and opened to the public as a museum. Sharing the site, overlooking the James River, is the Museum of the Confederacy. Brierfield, the plantation Jefferson Davis built and lived on until the outbreak of the war, is under water, victim of a Mississippi River reclamation project.

SOURCE NOTES

Note to Reader: To facilitate easy citation reference, several sources often noted will be abbreviated. They are:

AL   Albert Beveridge, *Abraham Lincoln,* 2 vols. (Boston: Houghton-Mifflin Co., 1928).

ALP   Abraham Lincoln Papers, Firestone Library Collection, Princeton University.

CTG   Gerry Van der Heuvel, *Crowns of Thorns and Glory* (New York: E. P. Dutton, 1988).

CW   Bell Wiley, *Confederate Women* (Westport: Greenwood Press, 1975).

CWAL   Roy Basler, ed. *The Collected Works of Abraham Lincoln,* 8 vol. (New Brunswick: Rutgers University Press, 1953–55).

CWD   Mark Boatner, *The Civil War Dictionary* (New York: Vintage, 1991).

CWPGM   George McClellan, *The Civil War Papers of George McClellan* (New York: Ticknor and Fields, 1989).

DGW   Howard Beale, Jr., *The Diary of Gideon Welles,* 2 vols. (New York: W. W. Norton & Co., 1960).

FLS   Ishbel Ross, *The First Lady of the South* (New York: Harper & Bros., 1958).

ICG   Robert Kean, *Inside the Confederate Government* (Westport: Greenwood Press, 1973).

IWAL   Michael Burlingame, *The Inner World of Abraham Lincoln* (Chicago: University of Illinois Press, 1994).

JDMH   William C. Davis, *Jefferson Davis: The Man and His Hour* (New York: Harper Collins, 1991).

JDHC   Patrick, Rembert, *Jefferson Davis and His Cabinet* (Baton Rouge: Louisiana State University Press, 1961).

JDTH   Hudson Strode, *Jefferson Davis, Tragic Hero* (New York: Harcourt, Brace and World, 1964).

LBHE   Mark Neely, *The Last Best Hope of Earth* (Cambridge, Mass.: Harvard University Press, 1993).

LDCW   Roman Heleniak and Lawrence Stewart, eds., *Leadership During the Civil War* (Shippensburg, Pa: White Mane Publishing Co., 1992).

LFS   Richard Current, *Lincoln and the First Shot* (Philadelphia: J. B. Lippincott & Co., 1953).

MCCWD   C. Vann Woodward, ed., *Mary Chesnut's Civil War Diary* (New Haven: Yale University Press, 1981).

Memoir   Varina Howell Davis, *Jefferson Davis: Ex-President of the Confederate States of America: A Memoir,* 2 vols. (New York: Belford Publishing, 1890).

PJD   Linda Crist, ed., *Papers of Jefferson Davis* (Baton Rouge: Louisiana State University Press, 1983).

PPMP   Richard Neustadt, *Presidential Power and the Modern President* (New York: Free Press, 1990).

RAF   *Jefferson Davis, The Rise and Fall of the Confederate Government,* 2 vol. (New York, 1881).

RML   Dawn Simmons, *A Rose for Mrs. Lincoln* (Boston: Beacon Press, 1970).

Rowland   Dunbar Rowland, *Jefferson Davis, Constitutionalist: His Letters, Papers and Speeches,* 10 vol. (Jackson, Mississippi, 1923).

RWCD   J. B. Jones, *A Rebel War Clerk's Diary at the Confederate States' Capital,* 2 vols. (Philadelphia: J. B. Lippincott, 1866).

SLT   Benjamin Thomas and Harold Hyman, *Stanton: The Life and Times of Lincoln's Secretary of War* (New York: Alfred A. Knopf, 1962).

SOS   Roy Meredith, *Storm Over Sumter* (New York: Simon & Schuster, 1957).

TCW   Shelby Foote, *The Civil War,* 3 vols. (New York: Random House, 1986).

TRFS   Bruce and William Catton, *Two Roads to Fort Sumter* (New York: McGraw-Hill, 1963).

VH   Eron Rowland, *Varina Howell: Wife of Jefferson Davis* (New York: MacMillan, 1931).

·

Introduction: November 1860

1. Roy Basler, ed., *The Collected Works of Abraham Lincoln* (hereafter cited as *CWAL*), 2: 461–462.

2. Dunbar Rowland, *Jefferson Davis, Constitutionalist: His Letters, Papers and Speeches* (hereafter cited as *Rowland*), 2: 72–81.

3. Ibid., 4: 60–90.

4. Davis to Rhett, November 10, 1860, Linda Crist, ed., *Papers of Jefferson Davis* (hereafter cited as *PJD*), 6: 368–371.

5. Ibid., 6: 368–371.

6. Ibid., 6: 371–372.

7. Donald Reynolds, *Editors Make War,* pp. 150–165.

Chapter 1. The Gentleman From Brierfield Plantation

1. Jefferson Davis to Susannah Davis, August 2, 1824, William C. Davis, *Jefferson Davis: The Man and His Hour* (hereafter cited as *JDMH*), p. 16.

2. *PJD,* 1: lxvii.

3. *New York Herald,* August 11, 1895.

4. *PJD,* 1: lxviii, lxiii.

5. Ibid., 1: lxxvi.

6. *JDMH,* p. 15.

7. *PJD,* 1: lxxvii.

8. Varina Howell Davis, *Jefferson Davis: Ex-President of the Confederate States of America: A Memoir* (hereafter cited as *Memoir*), 1: 27–29.

9. Jefferson Davis to Joseph Davis, January 12, 1825, *PJD,* 1: 17.

10. Hudson Strode, *Private Letters of Jefferson Davis,* p. 48.

11. Jefferson Davis notes to Varina Davis, *Memoir,* 1: 138–142.

12. Jefferson Davis to Sarah Taylor, December 16, 1834, Hudson Strode, *Private Letters of Jefferson Davis,* p. 11.

13. Hudson Strode, *Jefferson Davis: 1808–1861,* p. 104.

14. *PJD,* 1: 414.

15. *JDMH,* p. 84.

16. *Belford's Magazine,* January, 1890.

17. *PJD,* 4: 364.

18. Joseph Ingraham, *The Southwest, by a Yankee,* 1: 115–116.

19. Clement Eaton, *A History of the Old South*, pp. 270, 273.

20. *Memoir,* 1: 576.

21. Ibid., 1: 176–177.

22. *Sewanee Review,* 16 (1908), p. 412.

23. *PJD,* 6: 137.

24. Ibid., 6: 129.

25. Jefferson Davis to William Howell, April 18, 1859, *PJD,* 6: 246.

26. Jefferson Davis to Howell, April 24, 1859, *PJD,* 6: 247.

27. Jefferson Davis to Joseph Davis, August 30, 1857, *PJD,* 6: 137.

28. Ibid., 6: 130.

29. *Sewanee Review* 16 (1908), p. 408.

30. Letter from Ulrich Phillips collection at Yale University Library, in Linda Kerber and Jane DeHart, eds., *Women's America: Refocusing the Past,* p. 101.

31. Ibid., pp. 104–117.

32. Bruce and William Catton, *Two Roads to Fort Sumter* (hereafter cited as *TRFS*), p. 61.

33. Joseph Davis to Jefferson Davis, July 23, 1840, *PJD,* 1: 464–65.

34. Jefferson Davis to W. Allen, July 24, 1840, Rowland, 1: 4–5.

35. Ishbel Ross, *The First Lady of the South* (hereafter cited as *FLS*), p. 4.

36. Ibid., p. 4.

37. Jefferson Davis to Varina Howell, March 8, 1844, Strode, *Private Letters,* p. 18.

38. *PJD,* 2: 705.

39. *Memoir,* 1: 206.

40. *Vicksburg Sentinel,* November 6, 1843.

41. Ibid., June 24, 1844.

42. *Macon Jeffersonian,* August 2, 1844.

43. Speech to the Mississippi Democratic State Convention, January 3, 1844, when he was selected as a presidential elector, Rowland, 1: 7.

44. Ibid., 1: 9.

45. *PJD,* 2: 336.

46. See *JDMH.*

47. Frederick Blodi, ed., *Herpes Simplex Infections of the Eye,* pp. 4–11.

48. JDMH, p. 174–75.

49. Varina Howell to Mrs. William Howell, January 30, 1846, Museum of the Confederacy Library.

50. Speech in the House of Representatives, December 19, 1845, Rowland, 1: 23–24.

51. Speech in the House of Representatives, February 6, 1846, Rowland, 1: 34.

52. *Vicksburg Sentinel,* July 21, 1846.

53. *PJD,* 3: 140.

54. Joseph Chance, *Jefferson Davis's Mexican War Regiment,* pp. 78–103.

55. *Memoir,* 1: 332

56. *PJD,* 3: 142.

57. *Lafayette* (La.), *Statesman,* June 26, 1850.

58. JDMH, pp. 171–172

Chapter 2. A Humble Man

1. Abraham Lincoln to Mary Speed, September 27, 1841, *CWAL,* 1: 259–261.

2. Mark Neely, *The Last Best Hope of Earth* (hereafter *LBHE*), pp. 3–4.

3. Mrs. Thomas Lincoln statement to William Herndon, September 8, 1865, Herndon-Weik Papers, Library of Congress.

4. Biography in *Congressional Globe,* April 1847.

5. *TRFS,* p. 36.

6. Frances Carpenter, *Six Months in the White House With Abraham Lincoln,* pp. 96–97.

7. David Donald, *Lincoln* pp. 34–35.

8. Carl Sandburg, *Abraham Lincoln: The Prairie Years and the War Years,* p. 49.

9. Donald, p. 33.

10. Robert L. Wilson to Herndon, February 10, 1866, Herndon-Weik Papers, Library of Congress.

11. Edgar Lee Masters, *Lincoln the Man,* pp. 31–32.

12. Benjamin Thomas, *Lincoln's New Salem,* p. 95.

13. Ibid., p. 47.

14. Donald, p. 40.

15. "Communication to the people of Sangamon County," a letter Lincoln published in the *Sangamon Journal* on March 9, 1832, in *CWAL,* 1: 8–9.

16. *LBHE,* p. 7.

17. Michael Burlingame, *The Inner World of Abraham Lincoln* (hereafter cited as *IWAL*),

p. 238.

18. Ibid., p. 238.

19. William Herndon, "Analysis of the Character of Abraham Lincoln," *Abraham Lincoln Quarterly* (December, 1941), pp. 410–411.

20. *CWAL,* 1: 509–510.

21. Sandburg, pp. 61–66.

22. Ibid., pp. 79–80.

23. Ibid., p. 84.

24. Donald, pp. 56–57.

25. Ibid., pp. 66–67.

26. Coleman Smoot to Herndon, May 7, 1866, Herndon-Weik Papers, Library of Congress.

27. From a description of Lincoln by lawyer Henry Whitney, Albert Beveridge, *Abraham Lincoln* (hereafter cited as *AL*), 1: 503–504.

28. William Herndon letter to Isaac Arnold, Herndon-Weik Papers, Library of Congress.

29. Sandburg, p. 98.

30. *LBHE,* p. 32.

31. Sandburg, pp. 132–138.

32. Donald, p. 198.

33. Ibid., p. 108.

34. Emanuel Hertz, ed., *The Hidden Lincoln: From the Letters and Papers to William Herndon,* p. 141.

35. *CWAL,* 4: 55.

36. *LBHE,* p. 26.

37. John Nicolay and John Hay, *Abraham Lincoln: A History,* 1: 111–112.

38. Abraham Lincoln to Rev. J. M. Peck, May 21, 1848, ALP.

39. Abraham Lincoln speech, House of Representatives, July 27, 1848, ALP.

40. Thomas, p. 88.

41. *CWAL,* 2: 22.

42. Abraham Lincoln to James Smith, February 22, 1849, ALP.

43. J. T. P. Stapp to Lincoln, May 30, 1849, ALP.

44. S. Chace to Lincoln, March 4, 1849, ALP.

45. Allen Francis to Lincoln, June 12, 1849, ALP.

46. William Henderson to Lincoln, June 11, 1849, ALP.

47. Lincoln to John Clayton, March 10, 1849, ALP.

Chapter 3. Jefferson Davis:
War Hero and Rising Political Star

1. Varina Davis to Mrs. William Howell, November 12, 1847, *FLS,* pp. 35–36.

2. Joel Williamson, *A Rage for Order,* p. 227.

3. Speech in the Senate, February 13 and 14, 1850, Rowland, 1: 286.

4. Speech in the Senate, January 29, 1850, *PJD,* 4: 66.

5. Davis speech at Holly Springs, Mississippi, October 25, 1849, *PJD,* 4: 47–51.

6. Zachary Taylor to Davis, August 16, 1847, Papers of Zachary Taylor, Library of Congress.

7. Jefferson Davis speech in the Senate, February 13 and 14, 1850, Rowland, 1: 266.

8. Jefferson Davis speech in the Senate, March 14, 1850, *PJD,* 4: 89.

9. Jefferson Davis speech in the Senate, May 15, 1850, *PJD,* 4: 103.

10. Jefferson Davis speech in the Senate, February 13 and 14, Rowland, 1: 265.

11. Robert Barnwell to Davis, October 20, 1851, *PJD,* 4: 227.

12. Jefferson Davis speech in Boston, Oct. 11, 1858, Rowland, 3: 323.

13. *Jackson Mississippian,* January 3, 1851.

14. *PJD,* 3: 314–315.

15. Jefferson Davis to Horatio Harris, April 17, 1851, *PJD,* 4: 179.

16. *JDMH,* p. 180.

17. Speech in Fayette, Mississippi, July 11, 1851, *Natchez Free Trader,* July 16, 1851.

18. Jefferson Davis to David Yulee, July 18, 1851, *PJD,* 4: 218.

19. Strode, *Jefferson Davis: 1808–1861,* p. 44.

20. Jefferson Davis speech in the Senate, February 13 and 14, 1850, Rowland, 1: 266.

21. *RAF,* 1: 78.

22. Jefferson Davis speech in the Senate, February 13 and 14, 1850, Rowland, 1: 284.

23. Jefferson Davis speech to the Mississippi legislature, November 16, 1858, Rowland,

1: 357.
24. Joel Williamson, *A Rage for Order*, p. 11.
25. W. J. Cash, *The Mind of the South*, p. 66–67.
26. Ibid., p. 182.
27. Rowland, 2: 72–81.
28. *JDMH*, p. 213.
29. Jefferson Davis letter to William Brown, May 7, 1853, *RAF*, pp. 20–21.
30. *RAF*, 1: 20.
31. *FLS*, p. 64.
32. Jefferson Davis to Sam Cartwright, September 23, 1851, *PJD*, 4: 225.
33. *FLS*, pp. 64–68.
34. Franklin Pierce to Jefferson Davis, December 7, 1852, *PJD*, 4: 307–308.
35. Mrs. Roger Pryor, *Reminiscences of Peace and War*, p. 81.
36. Varina Davis to Jefferson Davis, January 24, 1849, Museum of the Confederacy Library.
37. Varina Davis to Jefferson Davis, January 24, 1849, Museum of the Confederacy Library.
38. Varina Davis to Jefferson Davis, April 18, 1859, in Bell I. Wiley, *Confederate Women* (hereafter cited as *CW*), p. 94.
39. Jefferson Davis to William Howell, April 24, 1859, *PJD*, 6: 247.
40. Varina to Jefferson Davis, April 10, 1859, Musem of the Confederacy Library.
41. Jefferson Davis to Scott, September 7, 1855, Rowland, 2: 491.
42. Jefferson Davis to Lewis Cass, *PJD*, 5: 97n.
43. *FLS*, p. 84.
44. *Jackson (Miss.) Observer and State Gazette*, June 9, 1858.
45. Jefferson Davis to Franklin Pierce, April 1, 1858, in Strode, *Jefferson Davis: 1808–1861*, p. 304.
46. Jefferson Davis speech to troops at the Belfast encampment, August 1858, in Rowland, 3: 288–289.
47. Jefferson Davis speech at Portland, Maine, August 1858, Rowland, 3: 288.
48. Jefferson Davis speech at state fair in Augusta, Maine, September 29, 1858, Row-land, 3: 310.
49. *CWAL*, 3: 295.
50. *PJD*, 6: 227–229.
51. Strode, *Jefferson Davis: 1808–1861*, p. 305.
52. Rowland, 4: 61–88.
53. Strode, *Jefferson Davis: 1808–1861*, p. 342.

Chapter 4. Abe Lincoln: Master Politician

1. *Albion (Ill.) Weekly Courier*, June 5, 1856.
2. Elwell Crissey, *Lincoln's Lost Speech* (New York: Hawthorn, 1969), p. 239.
3. Crissey, p. 178.
4. Abraham Lincoln's speech at Bloomington, Illinois, May 29, 1856, *CWAL*, 2: 341.
5. William Herndon, *Herndon's Lincoln*, 2: 384.
6. Crissey, *Lincoln's Lost Speech*, p. 240.
7. James McPherson, *The Battle Cry of Freedom*, pp. 123–130.
8. Abraham Lincoln to Owen Lovejoy, August 11, 1855, *CWAL*, 2: 316.
9. *AL*, 2: 679.
10. Fragment of a speech in Galena, Illinois, July 23, 1856, *CWAL*, 2: 3.
11. Abraham Lincoln speech, October 16, 1854, in Peoria, Illinois, *CWAL*, 2: 247–283.
12. *CWAL*, 2: 242.
13. Abe Jonas to Abraham Lincoln, September 16, 1854, ALP.
14. Richard Wilson, October 20, 1854, ALP.
15. Abraham Lincoln notes, November 27, 1854, ALP.
16. *CWAL*, 2: 222.
17. *CWAL*, 3: 440.
18. Abraham Lincoln to Stephen Douglas in Lincoln-Douglas debates, *AL*, 2: 683.
19. Abraham Lincoln speech, September 18, 1858, *CWAL*, pp. 145–201.
20. Abraham Lincoln in the Lincoln-Douglas debates, *AL*, 2: 683.
21. Ibid., 2: 649–650.
22. William Herndon, "Analysis of the Character of Abraham Lincoln," *Abraham Lincoln Quarterly* (December, 1941), pp. 410–411.
23. Ward Lamon to Abraham Lincoln,

August 17, 1860, ALP.

24. Lincoln always had his hands full with the quixotic Wentworth and in the 1860 campaign had to ask him to stop hopelessly pro-abolitionist editorials, which threatened to paint Lincoln as a radical.

25. Ward Lamon to Abraham Lincoln, November 21, 1854, ALP.

26. Elihu Washburne to Abraham Lincoln, November 14, 1854, ALP.

27. Henry Grove to Abraham Lincoln, November 18, 1854, ALP.

28. Julian Sturtevant to Abraham Lincoln, September 27, 1856, *CWAL,* 2: 378–379.

29. Abraham Lincoln to Theodore Canisius, May 17, 1859, ALP.

30. *CWAL,* 2: 348.

31. *Boston Daily Advertiser,* September 12, 1848.

32. Abraham Lincoln to Thomas Marshall, April 23, 1858, *CWAL,* 2: 443.

33. *AL,* 2: 571–572.

34. Abraham Lincoln speech at the Republican Convention, June 16, 1858, *CWAL,* 2: 461.

35. Donald, p. 209.

36. Fehrenbacher, Don, *Prelude to Greatness: Abraham Lincoln in the 1850s,* p. 145.

37. Abraham Lincoln to Samuel Galloway, March 24, 1860, ALP.

38. Abraham Lincoln speech at Cooper Union, February 27, 1860, in Donald, *Lincoln,* p. 239.

39. *Ohio State Journal,* September, 1859.

40. McPherson, *The Battle Cry of Freedom,* p. 198.

41. Abraham Lincoln to Charles Wilson, June 1, 1858, *CWAL,* 2: 456–57.

42. Anne Rose, *Victorian America and the Civil War,* p. 208.

43. Thomas Pitkin, "Western Republicans and the Tariff in 1860," *Mississippi Valley Historical Review,* December 1940, p. 407.

44. Erwin Bradley, *Simon Cameron: Lincoln's Secretary of War,* pp. 150–156.

45. Abraham Lincoln to David Davis, May 17, 1860, *CWAL,* 4: 50.

46. Frances Morehouse, *The Life of Jesse*

Fell, p. 61. Fell was in charge of printing the tickets and told the story to his family. It was not made public until 1909.

47. *CWAL,* 3: 423.

48. Ibid., 3: 424.

49. Ibid., 3: 422.

50. Ibid., 4: 22.

51. Ibid., 3: 406.

52. Ibid., 3: 423.

Chapter 5. Jefferson Davis: Secession

1. Ralph Wooster, *The Secession Conventions of the South,* pp. 18–25. An engrossing study in which Wooster analyzes secession tendencies on a state by state basis.

2. *Charleston Mercury,* December 21, 1860.

3. Charles Cauthen, *South Carolina Goes to War: 1860–1865,* p. 70–71.

4. Rowland, 4: 553.

5. Ulrich Phillips, *The Course of the South to Secession,* p. 66.

6. Joseph Hodgson, *The Cradle of the Confederacy,* p. 455.

7. *TRFS, p.* 247.

8. E. Merton Coulter, ed., *A History of the South,* 7: 1–10.

9. *Thomas R. R. Cobb: The Making of a Southern Nationalist,* p. 199.

10. See Ralph Wooster, *The Secession Conventions of the South.*

11. John Pendleton Kennedy, *The Border States: Their Power and Duty in the Present Disordered Condition of the Country,* pamphlet, p. 5.

12. *RAF,* 1: 83.

13. *TRFS,* p. 250.

14. *RAF,* 1: 47–48.

15. Ibid., pp. 53–54.

16. Ibid., pp. 75–76.

17. James Stirling, *Letters From the Slave States,* p. 59.

18. Jefferson Davis speech in Congress, January 10, 1861, *RAF,* 1: 3–4.

19. James Buchanan, fourth annual message to Congress, December 3, 1860, *Congressional Globe,* II, Appendix, 1–7.

20. James Buchanan, *Mr. Buchanan's Administration on the Eve of the Rebellion,* p. 132.

21. Herschel Johnson to Belmont, Nov. 27, 1860, printed in the *Daily Missouri Democrat,* December 12, 1860, in Dwight Dumond, *The Secession Movement: 1860–1861,* p. 151.

22. Thomas Cobb speech, *Congressional Globe,* 36 Cong. I, 59.

23. Jefferson Davis, *RAF,* 1: 63–64.

24. C. C. Clay to Davis, *RAF,* p. 206.

25. Dumond, p. 166.

26. Pugh, Remarks in the Senate, December 20, 1860, in *Congressional Globe,* 36 Cong., 2d Sess., II, Appendix, 33.

27. *JDMH,* p. 290.

28. *Richmond Whig,* December 16, 1860.

29. *Sugar Planter,* November 24, 1860.

30. *Memphis Daily Appeal,* November 29, 1860.

31. Donald Reynolds, *Editors Make War,* pp. 150–153.

32. Clement Eaton, *A History of the Southern Confederacy,* p. 25.

33. *RAF,* 1: 226.

34. Rowland, 4: 561.

35. William John Grayson, *James Louis Petigru: A Biographical Sketch,* pp. 146–47.

36. *RAF,* 1: 228–229.

37. Mark Boatner III, ed., *The Civil War Dictionary* (hereafter cited as *CWD*), p. 729.

38. Joel Williamson, *A Rage for Order,* pp. 11–13.

39. Coulter, *A History of the South,* p. 10.

40. W. J. Cash, *The Mind of the South,* pp. 73–78.

41. Jefferson Davis speech at Aberdeen, Mississippi, May 26, 1851, Rowland, 2: 74–75.

42. Ibid., 2: 75–82.

43. See James DeBow, *The Interest in Slavery of the Non-Slaveholder.*

44. Hammond to F. A. Allen, February 2, 1861, Hammond Papers.

45. Steven Channing, *Crisis of Fear,* note, p. 256. The idea cropped up several times in letters to editors of Southern newspapers. There is no record of planters giving slaves to others, however.

46. Ritchie Devon Watson Jr., *Yeoman Versus Cavalier,* pp. 118–120.

47. Wooster, p. 149.

48. *Central Georgian,* March 6, 1861.

49. C. Vann Woodward, ed., *Mary Chesnut's Civil War Diary* (hereafer cited as *MCCWD*), p. 11.

50. Jefferson Davis to Pierce, January 20, 1861, *PJD,* 7: 17–18.

51. Strode, *Jefferson Davis: 1808–1861,* p. 388.

52. Strode, p. 396.

53. Jefferson Davis's speech of retirement in the Senate, January 21, 1861, Rowland, 5: 40–45.

54. *RAF,* pp. 221–226.

55. Jefferson Davis's Farewell, January 21, 1860, *PJD,* 7: 18–23.

56. *Memoir,* 1: 696–98.

Chapter 6. Lincoln: Secession

1. Note of Henry Sanford, November 9, 1860, *CWAL,* 4: 138.

2. Abraham Lincoln to Paschall, November 16, 1860, *CWAL,* 4: 139.

3. Abraham Lincoln to Weed, December 17, 1860, *CWAL,* 4: 154.

4. Abraham Lincoln to Stephens, December 22, 1860, *CWAL,* 4: 160.

5. Abraham Lincoln to Hale, January 11, 1861, *CWAL,* 4: 172.

6. *New York Herald,* January 28, 1861.

7. Abraham Lincoln to Seward, February 1, 1861, *CWAL,* 4: 183.

8. Abraham Lincoln to William Kellogg, December 11, 1860, *CWAL,* 4: 150.

9. Abraham Lincoln to Elihu Washburne, Dec. 13, 1860, *CWAL,* 4: 151.

10. William Seward to Abraham Lincoln, December 29, 1860, *CWAL,* 4: 170.

11. *Cincinnati Commercial,* November 1861, in Donald Reynolds, *Editors Make War,* pp. 139–160. Several major Northern papers supported the idea of a Southern Confederacy.

12. *Daily Illinois State Journal,* December 20, 1860.

13. Charles Coleman, *Abraham Lincoln and Coles County, Illinois,* pp. 198–199.

14. Donald, *Lincoln,* p. 271.

15. William Herndon interview with Mrs.

Sarah Lincoln, September 9, 1865, Herndon-Weik Collection, Library of Congress.

Chapter 7. Jefferson Davis Takes Office

1. *JDMH,* pp. 300–303.
2. *Natchez Courier,* February 14, 1861.
3. *Vicksburg Weekly Whig,* February 13, 1861.
4. *New Orleans Delta,* February 14, 1861.
5. Jefferson Davis speech in Atlanta, Georgia, February 16, 1861, *PJD,* 7: 43–44.
6. Jefferson Davis to Varina Davis, February 14, 1861, *PJD,* 7: 40–41.
7. *JDMH,* p. 306.
8. *Natchez Courier,* February 19, 1861.
9. E. Merton Coulter, *The Civil War and Readjustment in Kentucky,* p. 118.
10. Frank Moore, ed., *Rebellion Record: A Diary of American Events, Documents, Illustrative Incidents, Poetry, Etc.,* 3: 258.
11. *Kentucky Statesman,* July 20, 1860.
12. Burton Hendrick, *Statesmen of the Lost Cause,* p. 79.
13. Richard Johnston and William Browne, *The Life of Alexander Stephens,* pp. 389–392.
14. Alexander Stephens to brother Linton Stephens, February 23, 1861, Alexander Stephens Papers, Southern Historical Collection, University of North Carolina, Chapel Hill.
15. Emory Thomas, *The Confederate Nation: 1861–1865,* p. 59.
16. Hamilton Eckenrode, *Jefferson Davis: President of the South,* p. 111.
17. *Richmond Whig,* February 9, 1861.
18. *RAF,* 1: 240.
19. *RAF,* 1: 241.
20. Jefferson Davis to Alexander Clayton, January 30, 1861, *PJD,* 7: 27–28.
21. *Richmond Dispatch,* February 13, 1861.
22. Jefferson Davis inaugural speech, February 18, 1861, copy *PJD,* 7: 49.
23. Jefferson Davis inaugural Speech, February 18, 1861, *RAF,* 1: 235.
24. Jefferson Davis to Varina Davis, Rowland, 5: 53–54.
25. J. B. Jones, *A Rebel War Clerk's Diary at the Confederate States Capital* (hereafter cited as *RWCD*), pp. 38–39.

26. Rembert Patrick, *Jefferson Davis and His Cabinet,* pp. 104–120.
27. Clement Eaton, *Jefferson Davis,* p. 130.
28. William Russell, *My Diary North and South,* p. 173.
29. James Coulter, *A History of the South,* p. 21.
30. Jefferson Davis to Francis Pickens, February 20, 1861, *PJD,* 7: 55.
31. *JDMH,* p. 316.
32. *JDMH,* p. 314.
33. Hudson Strode, *Jefferson Davis: Confederate President,* pp. 14–15.
34. *JDHC,* p. 321.
35. Burton Hendricks, *Statesmen of the Lost Cause,* p. 90.
36. *Natchez Courier,* February 20, 1861.
37. *Charleston Courier,* May 29, 1861.
38. Hudson Strode, *Jefferson Davis: 1808–1861,* p. 21.
39. *JDHC,* pp. 319–322.
40. *JDMH,* p. 314.
41. William Russell, *My Diary North and South,* p. 66.
42. *MCCWD,* p. 79.
43. James Rabin, "Alexander Stephens and Jefferson Davis," *American Historical Review* 57, January 1953, p. 291.
44. Coulter, p. 32.
45. Hendricks, p. 93.
46. James Rabin, "Alexander Stephens and Jefferson Davis," *American Historical Review* 57, p. 296.
47. Strode, pp. 24–25.
48. Dean Simonton, "Presidential Style: Personality, Biography and Performance," *Journal of Personality and Social Psychology* 55, No. 6, 1988.
49. Jefferson Davis to Johnston, July 10, 1861, *PJD,* 7: 231.
50. Varina Davis, *Memoirs,* 1: 12.

Chapter 8. Lincoln Takes Office

1. Donald, *Lincoln,* pp. 277–279.
2. John Wilson to Abraham Lincoln, November 28, 1860, ALP.
3. *New York Tribune,* February 25, 1861.
4. Richard Neustadt, *Presidential Power and*

the Modern Presidents (hereafter cited as PPMP), pp. 29–49.

5. See James Barber, Presidential Character.

6. New York Tribune, February 25, 1861.

7. Lyman Trumbull to Lincoln, December 2, 1860, ALP.

8. Leonard Swett to Abraham Lincoln, November 30, 1860, ALP.

9. John Sanderson to Leonard Swett, November 23, 1860, ALP.

10. Art Nocholson (of Little Rock, Arkansas) to Abraham Lincoln, November 30, 1860, ALP.

11. Dwight Janis to Abraham Lincoln, November 25, 1860, ALP.

12. Francis Blackburn to Abraham Lincoln, November 24, 1860, ALP.

13. J. P. Moorhead to Abraham Lincoln, November 23, 1860, ALP.

14. W. A. Swanberg, First Blood, p. 196

15. John Nicolay and John Hay, John Nicolay, 3: 371.

16. Donald, Lincoln, p. 282.

17. Margaret Leech, Reveille in Washington, pp. 42–45.

18. Shelby Foote, The Civil War (hereafter cited as TCW), 1: 38–39.

19. New York Tribune, March 5, 1861.

20. New York Times, March 5, 1861.

21. E. B. Long and Barbara Long, The Civil War: Day by Day, p. 45.

22. New York Tribune, February 15, 1861.

23. LBHE, p. 63.

24. National Intelligencer, March 5, 1861.

25. New York Times, March 5, 1861.

26. New York Times, March 5, 1861.

27. CWAL, 4: 262–271.

28. New York Times, March 5, 1861.

29. St. Louis Tribune, March 6, 1861.

Chapter 9. Fort Sumter: War

1. Catton, Two Roads to Fort Sumter, p. 256.

2. W. A. Swanberg, First Blood, pp. 232–234.

3. Clement Eaton, Jefferson Davis, p. 136.

4. RAF, p. 271.

5. Richard Wheeler, A Rising Thunder, p. 69.

6. Richard Current, Lincoln and the First Shot (hereafter cited as LFS), pp. 52–53.

7. Seward was urged to hold meetings with powerful Virginia politicians, even in secret. Thomas Fitman to Seward, April 1, 1886, Seward Papers, Firestone Library, Princeton University.

8. LFS, pp. 52–53.

9. W. A. Swanberg, pp. 236–237.

10. Roy Meredith, Storm Over Sumter (hereafter cited as SOS), p. 132.

11. Justice Campbell to Jefferson Davis, April 2, 1861, PJD, pp. 88–89.

12. Swanberg, pp. 230–231.

13. RAF, 1: 269.

14. Campbell to Jefferson Davis, April 3, 1861, PJD, 7: 88–89.

15. Hudson Strode, Jefferson Davis: Confederate President, p. 9.

16. JDMH, p. 304.

17. Jefferson Davis to Perkins, February 20, 1861, PJD, 7: 55.

18. Rowland, 5: 56–58.

19. LFS, p. 140.

20. LFS, p. 143.

21. Jefferson Davis to Bragg, April 3, 1861, PJD, 7: 85–86.

22. PJD, 7: 141

23. LFS, p. 129.

24. Texas Governor Edward Clark to Jefferson Davis, April 4, 1861, PJD, 7: 91.

25. PJD, 7: 148.

26. Strode, p. 14.

27. McPherson, The Battle Cry of Freedom, p. 269.

28. New York Times, April 3, 1861.

29. Boston Journal, April 6, 1861.

30. Boston Daily Evening Traveler, March 30, 1861.

31. Lafayette (Indiana) Daily Courier, March 12, 1861.

32. New York Herald, quoted in the Charleston Courier, March 18, 1861.

33. LFS, p. 121.

34. Notes re: Justice Campbell April 3 letter to Jefferson Davis, PJD, 7: 90.

35. Carl Schurz to Abraham Lincoln, April 5, 1861, ALP.

36. Peter Deyo to Seward, April 3, 1861. Seward Papers.

37. Richard Wheeler, *A Rising Thunder,* pp. 69–71.

38. *LFS,* 134.

39. He received several in March. One from Joehan Gallaher to Seward, on April 1, 1861, also warned that coercion might force war. Seward Papers.

40. John Breckinridge to Seward, March 19, 1861. Seward Papers.

41. *SOS,* pp. 134–136.

42. Ibid., p. 136.

43. Abner Doubleday to Mary Doubleday, March 29, 1861, ALP.

44. *SOS,* pp. 138–139.

45. *LFS,* p. 113.

46. Ibid., pp. 119–120.

47. Gideon Welles, *Lincoln and Seward,* pp. 57–58

48. *LFS,* pp. 78–79.

49. Welles to Abraham Lincoln, March 29, 1861, ALP.

50. Bates to Abraham Lincoln, March 29, 1861, ALP.

51. Seward to Abraham Lincoln, March 29, 1861, ALP.

52. *SOS,* p. 137.

53. Scott to Abraham Lincoln, March 30, 1861, ALP.

54. McPherson, p. 272.

55. Browning to Abraham Lincoln, February 17, 1861, ALP.

56. Strode, pp. 32–33.

57. Abraham Lincoln to Seward, April 1, 1861, ALP.

58. *LFS,* p. 145.

59. *JDMH,* p. 522.

60. Ibid., p. 35.

61. Donald, *Lincoln,* p. 290.

62. Strode, pp. 32–33.

63. John Botts, *The Great Rebellion,* pp. 275–277.

64. Lincoln note, April 6, 1861, ALP.

65. Thomas Schott, *Alexander H. Stephens of Georgia: A Biography,* p. 334.

66. *LFS,* p. 121.

67. Ibid., p. 275.

68. *RAF,* 1: 292.

69. *TCW,* 1: 48–54.

Chapter 10. Abraham Lincoln at War: 1861

1. Robert Johansen, *Stephen Douglas,* pp. 858–860.

2. Helen Nicolay, *Lincoln's Secretary: A Biography of John Nicolay,* p. 101.

3. *Washington Daily Morning Chronicle,* October 26, 1864.

4. George Milton, *The Eve of Conflict: Stephen A. Douglas and the Needless War,* p. 563.

5. Ibid., p. 563.

6. Damon Wells, *Stephen Douglas: The Last Years, 1857–1861,* p. 281.

7. T. Harry Williams, *Lincoln and His Generals,* p. 5.

8. James McPherson, *The Battle Cry of Freedom,* p. 328.

9. Abraham Lincoln to Ohio Governor William Dennison, October 7, 1861, *CWAL,* 4: 550.

10. Oliver Dyer to Lincoln, May 12, 1861, ALP.

11. Martin Sheffer, *Presidential Power: Case Studies in the Use of the Opinion of the Attorney General,* pp. 1–29.

12. Edwin Corwin, *The Presidency: Office and Powers, 1787–84,* p. 264.

13. Richard Current, "Lincoln, the War and the Constitution," in Roman Heleniak and Lawrence Hewitt, eds., *Leadership During the Civil War,* p. 3.

14. *Baltimore Sun,* May 31, 1861.

15. Roman Heleniak and Lawrence Hewitt, eds., *Leadership During the Civil War* (hereafter cited as *LDCW*), pp. 6–7.

16. *LBH,* pp. 136–137.

17. Donald, *Lincoln,* p. 303.

18. Corwin, p. 265.

19. Preston King to Abraham Lincoln, May 2, 1861, ALP.

20. Wells, p. 272.

21. Clinton Rossiter, *The Supreme Court and the Commander-in-Chief,* p. 25.

22. Address to Congress, July 4, 1861, *CWAL,* 5: 421–444.

23. *CWAL,* 4: 341–342.

24. See Rossiter, *The American Presidency.*

25. Fred Greenstein, "Lasswell's Concept of Democratic Character," *Journal of Politics,* (30), 1968, p. 701.

26. Thomas Bailey, *Presidential Greatness,* p. 293.

27. Abraham Lincoln to Reverdy Johnson, April 24, 1861, *CWAL,* 4: 342–343.

28. Scott to Abraham Lincoln, April 8, 1861, ALP.

29. Scott to Abraham Lincoln, April 4, 1861, ALP.

30. James Wells to Abraham Lincoln, April 11, 1861, ALP.

31. William Sprague to Abraham Lincoln, April 11, 1861, ALP.

32. Schurz to Abraham Lincoln, April 4, 1861, ALP.

33. James Stockton to Abraham Lincoln, April 8, 1861, ALP.

34. Charles Stone to William Seward, April 5, 1861, ALP.

35. E. L. Corvant, 14th N.J. Volunteers, to Abraham Lincoln, May 7, 1862, ALP.

36. *The Weekly Press* (California), May 2, 1861.

37. Anonymous letter to Abraham Lincoln, April 4, 1861, ALP.

38. Letter of March 3, 1861, with attached petition with 120 names of state legislators, congressmen, state governors, and U.S. senators, ALP.

39. James Wilson to Abraham Lincoln, March 31, 1861, ALP.

40. D. R. Minton to Abraham Lincoln, March 1, 1861, ALP.

41. Robert Duell to Abraham Lincoln, March 30, 1861, ALP.

42. *LBHE,* pp. 167–168.

43. John Hickman to John Bingham, copy to Abraham Lincoln, April 1, 1861, ALP.

44. William Dennison to Abraham Lincoln, April 1, 1861, ALP.

45. James Wilson to Abraham Lincoln, March 31, 1861, ALP.

46. Abraham Lincoln to Salmon Chase, May 10, 1861, *CWAL,* 4: 363.

47. Abraham Lincoln to William Pickering, October 7, 1861, *CWAL,* 4: 550.

48. Abraham Lincoln to Chase, July 18, 1861, *CWAL,* 4: 452.

49. Abraham Lincoln to William Thomas, May 8, 1861, *CWAL,* 4: 362.

50. Abraham Lincoln to Edward Bates, October 4, 1861, *CWAL,* 4: 548.

51. David Davis to Abraham Lincoln, July 26, 1861, ALP.

52. Abraham Lincoln to Seward, March 30, 1861, *CWAL,* 4: 302–303.

53. Abraham Lincoln to Caleb Smith, October 14, 1861, *CWAL,* 4: 554.

54. Abraham Lincoln to Jesse Dubois, March 30, 1861, *CWAL,* 4: 302.

55. Abraham Lincoln to John Stuart, March 30, 1861, *CWAL,* 4: 303.

56. Abraham Lincoln note, April 5, 1861, ALP.

57. Donald, pp. 392–393.

58. Scott to Abraham Lincoln, May 1, 1861, ALP.

59. Abraham Lincoln to Scott, November 1, 1861, ALP.

60. Proclamation, May 3, 1861, *CWAL,* 4: 353–354.

61. Helen Nicolay, *John Nicolay: A Biography of Lincoln's Secretary,* p. 101.

62. Donald, p. 307.

63. *New York Times,* July 27, 1861.

64. A Lt. Curtis sent the dispatches from 11:20 A.M. to 5:30 P.M., ALP.

65. *Charleston Daily Courier,* July 3, 1861.

66. Nicolay, pp. 109–110.

67. Theodore Runyon to J. B. Fry, July 26, 1861, ALP.

68. G. Davidson to Seward, August 12, 1861, ALP.

69. W. C. Coles to Abraham Lincoln, July 23, 1861, ALP.

70. Edwin Morgan to Abraham Lincoln, July 23, 1861, ALP.

71. Andrew Curtin to Abraham Lincoln, August 12, 1861, ALP.

72. Oliver Morton to Abraham Lincoln, July 23, 1861, ALP.

73. C. A. Stetson to Abraham Lincoln, July

22, 1861, ALP.

74. Notes, July 27, 1861, ALP.

75. T. Harry Williams, "The Military Leadership of North and South," David Donald, ed., *Why the North Won the Civil War*, pp. 43–47.

76. Abraham Lincoln to Hooker, April 11, 1863, ALP.

77. T. Harry Williams, *Lincoln and His Generals*, p. 7.

78. Abraham Lincoln to Cameron, August 7, 1861, *CWAL*, 4: 475.

79. Abraham Lincoln to Cameron, June 17, 1861, ALP.

80. Abraham Lincoln to John McClernand, August 7, 1861, ALP.

81. Abraham Lincoln to Cameron, November 14, 1861, ALP.

82. Abraham Lincoln to David Hunter, October 24, 1861, *CWAL*, 5: 1.

83. Abraham Lincoln to McClellan, December 1, 1861, *CWAL*, 5: 34.

84. Memorandum, October 1, 1861, *CWAL*, 4: 544–45.

85. Abraham Lincoln to General David Hunter and Admiral Samuel DuPont over a dispute, April 14, 1863, ALP.

86. Neely, *LBHE*, p. 162.

87. Abraham Lincoln to McClernand, November 10, 1861, *CWAL*, 5: 20.

Chapter 11. Jefferson Davis at War: 1861

1. *TCW*, p. 72.

2. *JDMH*, p. 351.

3. *RAF*, 1: 350–352.

4. *Richmond Dispatch*, July 23, 1861.

5. *CWD*, p. 101.

6. Jefferson Davis memo, October 30, 1861, *PJD*, 7: 385.

7. *Richmond Whig*, May 2, 1861.

8. Jefferson Davis Richmond speech, July 23, 1861, *PJD*, 7: 261.

9. Jefferson Davis speech in Richmond, June 1, 1861, *PJD*, 7: 184.

10. *Richmond Dispatch*, December 7, 1889.

11. *Richmond Enquirer*, May 30, 1861.

12. Charles Girard, *A Visit to the Confederate States of America.*

13. Jefferson Davis message to Congress, July 20, 1861, Rowland, 5: 111–118.

14. *Charleston Courier*, September 24, 1861.

15. Bell Wiley, *Confederate Women*, p. 468.

16. *Richmond Examiner*, August 7, 1861.

17. *Richmond Examiner*, November 15, 1861.

18. *RAF*, 1: 442.

19. Varina Davis to Mrs. William Howell, *PJD*, 2: 329–332.

20. Harris Riley Jr., *Journal of Mississippi History*, vol. 14, November, 1987, p. 267.

21. Ibid., p. 268.

22. William Howell to wife, September 10, 1862, Museum of the Confederacy Library.

23. *New York Tribune*, May 24, 1862.

24. Riley, pp. 268–280.

25. *Richmond Dispatch*, June 7, 1905.

26. Alexander Stephens to Linton Stephens, June 3, 1864, Emory University Library Manuscript Collections.

27. Jefferson Davis to J. Johnston, September 14, 1861, *PJD*, 7: 340.

28. *JDMH*, p. 354.

29. *RWCD*, 1: 49.

30. *JDHC*, p. 113.

31. *RWCD*, 1: 64.

32. *JDHC*, pp. 116–117.

33. *Richmond Examiner*, December 12, 1863.

34. *North Carolina Standard*, March 5, 1862.

35. *JDHC*, p. 67.

36. Ibid., p. 71.

37. *Richmond Examiner*, February 22, 1862.

38. *CW*, p. 24.

39. *PJD*, 8: 57n.

40. Robert Kean, *Inside the Confederate Government* (hereafter cited as *ICG*), p. 27.

41. William Davis, "John C. Breckinridge and the Confederate Defeat," Roman Heleniak and Lawrence Hewitt, *Leadership During the Civil War*, p. 140.

42. *CW*, pp. 20–21.

43. Grady McWhiney, "Jefferson Davis and Confederate Military Leadership," *LDCW*, p. 19.

44. Ibid., p. 30.

45. *PPMP*, pp. 30–33.

46. *LDCW*, p. 17.

47. Nathaniel Hughes Jr., *General William*

J. Hardee pp. 59–61.

48. Craig Symonds, *Joseph E. Johnston: A Civil War Biography,* pp. 126–129.

49. Jefferson Davis to J. Johnston, September 14, 1861, *PJD,* 7: 340.

50. Jefferson Davis to Beauregard, October 30, 1861, *RAF,* 1: 367.

51. Jefferson Davis to Varina Davis, June 3, 1862, Rowland, 5: 266.

52. *MCCWD,* p. 130.

53. Ibid., p. 129.

54. Jefferson Davis to Varina Davis, June 13, 1862, Museum of the Confederacy Library.

55. *JDMH,* p. 359.

56. Jefferson Davis to Rep. W. P. Harris, December 13, 1861, Rowland, 5: 179.

57. *ICG,* p. 22.

58. *PJD,* 8: viii.

59. James McPherson, *The Battle Cry of Freedom,* pp. 436–438.

60. *Richmond Examiner,* August 16, 1861.

61. *RAF,* 2: 494–495.

62. *Vicksburg Whig,* February 16, 1861 on Davis's first official message concerning England.

63. *Vicksburg Whig,* May 23, 1861.

64. Jefferson Davis message to Congress, December 7, 1863, Rowland, 5: 99.

65. David Brion Davis, *The Problem of Slavery in the Age of Revolution: 1770–1823,* pp. 453–455.

66. *Richmond Dispatch,* February 8, 1861.

67. *Richmond Examiner,* November 19, 1861.

68. *Charleston Courier,* September 24, 1861.

69. Lewis Cruger to Davis, July 30, 1878, Rowland, 8: 243–245.

70. *Cotton Supply Reporter,* editorial reprinted in *Richmond Dispatch,* February 9, 1861.

71. *Richmond Examiner,* May 28, 1861.

72. *Richmond Examiner,* January 31, 1862.

73. *London Herald,* May 2, 1861.

74. *Richmond Dispatch,* June 1, 1862.

75. *Richmond Examiner,* February 4, 1862.

76. *Richmond Examiner,* October 4, 1861.

77. *London Times,* January 31, 1862.

78. *Richmond Whig,* May 23, 1861.

79. *Richmond Examiner,* November 20, 1861.

80. *RCWD,* p. 54.

81. Ibid., p. 62.

82. Davis's message to Congress, November 18, 1861, *PJD,* 7: 419.

83. Davis Inaugural Address, February 22, 1862, Rowland, 5: 201.

Chapter 12. The Lincolns at Home

1. Gerry Van der Heuvel, *Crowns of Thorns and Glory* (hereafter cited as *CTG*), pp. 87–90.

2. Elizabeth Keckley, *Behind the Scenes: Thirty Years a Slave, and Four Years in the White House,* p. 89.

3. *CTG,* pp. 89–90.

4. Dawn Simmons, *A Rose for Mrs. Lincoln* (hereafter cited as *RML*), p. 84.

5. Ibid., p. 84.

6. Ibid., p. 84.

7. Jean Baker, *Mary Todd Lincoln: A Biography,* p. 194.

8. *IWAL,* p. 284.

9. Ibid., p. 202

10. Ibid., p. 199.

11. Ibid., p. 200.

12. *New York Herald,* February 12, 1862.

13. *Richmond Examiner,* February 13, 1862.

14. *RTM,* p. 117.

15. *IWAL,* p. 301.

16. Baker, p. 190.

17. *Chicago Daily Tribune,* August, 1861, Patricia Bell, "…Mary Todd Lincoln," *Civil War Times Illustrated,* November, 1968, p. 9.

18. Robert Lincoln to J. G. Holland, June 6, 1865, in Rufus Wilson, ed., *Intimate Memories of Lincoln,* p. 499.

19. Ruth Randall, *Lincoln's Sons,* p. 94.

20. *CTG,* pp. 191–192.

21. Randall, pp. 113–114.

22. *IWAL,* p. 64.

23. Sandburg, *Abraham Lincoln: The Prairie Years and the War Years,* 2: 331.

24. Wayne Whipple, *Tad Lincoln: A True Story,* p. 20.

25. *RML,* p. 94.

26. Abraham Lincoln to Mary Todd Lincoln, August 8, 1863, *CWAL,* 6: 371–372.

27. *RML,* p. 95.

28. Baker, p. 210.
29. *RML*, p. 97.
30. Randall, p. 98.
31. Sandburg, 2: 331.
32. Whipple, pp. 24–25.
33. Ibid., p. 36.
34. Randall, p. 130.
35. Keckley, p. 103.
36. Baker, pp. 230–233.
37. *RML*, p. 131.
38. *CTG*, p. 129.
39. Patricia Bell, "Mary Todd Lincoln," *Civil War Times Illustrated*, p. 7.
40. Keckley, p. 146.
41. William Stoddard, *Lincoln's Third Secretary: The Memoirs of William O. Stoddard*, p. 62.
42. *IWAL*, p. 286.
43. *CTG*, p. 135.
44. Ibid., p. 132–133.
45. *IWAL*, p. 287.
46. Schuyler Hamilton, *New York Tribune*, March 24, 1889.
47. Baker, p. 239.
48. Abraham Lincoln to Mary Todd Lincoln, June 11, 1863, *CWAL*, 6: 260.
49. *CWAL*, 6: 472.
50. J. G. Randall, *Lincoln the President*, 1: 70.
51. *CTG*, p. 135.
52. Ibid., p. 131.
53. Ibid., p. 140.
54. Sandburg, 2: 314–315.
55. *CTG*, p. 132.
56. Abraham Lincoln to Mary Todd Lincoln, June 9, 1863, *CWAL*, 6: 256.

Chapter 13. The Davises at Home

1. Eron Rowland, *Varina Howell: Wife of Jefferson Davis* (hereafter cited as *VH*), p. 44.
2. Varina Davis to Mrs. Margaret Howell, June, 1861, Museum of the Confederacy Library.
3. *Philadelphia Weekly Times*, April 15, 1882.
4. *Richmond Dispatch*, June 3, 1861.
5. *Richmond Daily Enquirer*, May 31, 1861.
6. Notes from Walter Ezekial, in scrapbooks, 1865, Museum of the Confederacy Library.
7. Notes from W. E. Grant, in scrapbooks, 1903, Museum of the Confederacy Library.
8. *FLS*, p. 134.
9. Ibid., p. 173.
10. *CTG*, p. 106.
11. Ibid., p. 107.
12. *Richmond Evening Journal*, October 17, 1906.
13. T. C. DeLeon, *Belles, Beaus and Brains of the '60s*, p. 66.
14. *MCCWD*, p. 56.
15. Ibid., p. 568.
16. *FLS*, p. 201.
17. Jefferson Davis to Varina Davis, June 3, 1862, Museum of the Confederacy Library.
18. Jefferson Davis to Varina Davis, June 19, 1862, Museum of the Confederacy Library.
19. John Reagan, *Memoirs*, p. 163.
20. Article by Winnie Davis, *New York Herald*, August 11, 1895.
21. T. C. DeLeon, *Thirty Years of My Life on Three Continents*, p. 324.
22. *VH*, p. 187.
23. Margarett Howell notes, circa 1870, Museum of the Confederacy Library.
24. *VH*, p. 319.
25. *CTG*, p. 113.
26. Ibid., p. 165.
27. Varina Davis to John Preston, April 1, 1865, Museum of the Confederacy Library.
28. *VH*, p. 207.
29. Ibid., p. 207.
30. *CW*, p. 106.
31. Henry Wise to Varina Davis, November 14, 1863, Museum of the Confederacy Library.
32. *FLS*, p. 124.
33. *CTG*, p. 164.
34. Ibid., p. 164.
35. *CW*, p. 99.
36. *CTG*, p. 150.
37. *MCCWD*, p. 578.
38. Joan Cashin, "Varina Davis," in Catherine Clinton, C. J. Barker-Benfield, *Portraits of American Women*, pp. 268–269.
39. *MCCWD*, p. 127.
40. Tom Conolly, diary, March 12, 1865,

Museum of the Confederacy Library.

41. Cashin, p. 142.

42. *CTG*, p. 103.

43. See *FLS* for background.

44. Ibid., p. 169.

45. *VH*, p. 310.

46. *MCCWD*, p. 330.

47. *CW*, p. 100.

48. *New York Tribune*, May 24, 1862.

49. Conolly, March 13, 1865.

50. Jefferson Davis to Varina Davis, May 11, 1862, Museum of the Confederacy Library.

51. William Trescott letter, unpublished version, July 23, 1861 entry, Museum of the Confederacy Library.

52. *CW*, p. 110.

53. *FLS*, 157.

54. Alvy King, *Louis Wigfall: Southern Fire Eater*, p. 134; Ross, p. 206.

55. *FLS*, p. 211.

56. Ibid., p. 100.

57. Jefferson Davis to Varina Davis, June 2, 1862, Museum of the Confederacy Library.

58. Jefferson Davis to Varina Davis, May 11, 1862. Museum of the Confederacy Library.

59. Jefferson Davis to Varina Davis, June 13, 1862, Museum of the Confederacy Library.

60. Jefferson Davis to Varina Davis, June 19, 1862, Museum of the Confederacy Library.

61. Jefferson Davis to Varina Davis, June 11, 1862, Museum of the Confederacy Library.

62. Jefferson Davis to Varina Davis, June 13, 1862, Museum of the Confederacy Library.

63. Jefferson Davis to Varina Davis, June 25, 1862, Museum of the Confederacy Library.

64. Jefferson Davis to Varina Davis, June 3, 1862, Museum of the Confederacy Library.

65. Jefferson Davis to Varina Davis, June 13, 1862, Museum of the Confederacy Library.

66. Jefferson Davis to Varina Davis, June 11, 1862, Museum of the Confederacy Library.

67. Jefferson Davis to Varina Davis, June 3, 1862, Museum of the Confederacy Library.

68. *Memoirs*, 2: 496.

69. Ibid., 2: 496.

70. *Harper's Weekly*, June 4, 1864.

71. Jefferson Davis to Varina Davis, April 23, 1865, Museum of the Confederacy Library.

Chapter 14. Abraham Lincoln at War: 1862

1. Bruce Catton, *Bruce Catton's Civil War*, p. 34.

2. Ibid., pp. 34–35.

3. McClellan to Mary McClellan, October 11, 1861, *The Civil War Papers of George McClellan* (hereafter cited as *CWPGM*), p. 106.

4. Abraham Lincoln to McClellan, April 9, 1862, *CWAL*, 5: 184–185.

5. John Nicolay Diary, February 27, 1862, Nicolay MSS, Library of Congress.

6. Stephen Sears, *George McClellan: The Young Napoleon*, p. 59.

7. Sears, p. 85.

8. Ibid., p. 85.

9. George McClellan to Mary McClellan, October 31, 1861, *CWPGM*, p. 114.

10. George McClellan to Mary McClellan, November 17, 1861, *CWPGM*, p. 135.

11. Sears, *George McClellan: The Young Napoleon*, p. 59.

12. George McClellan to Mary McClellan, October 11, 1861, *CWPGM*, p. 106.

13. George McClellan to Mary McClellan, October 11, 1861, *CWPGM*, p. 107

14. George McClellan to Mary McClellan, October 30, 1861, *CWPGM*, p. 114.

15. George McClellan to Mary McClellan, October 11, 1861, *CWPGM*, p. 106.

16. *Richmond Examiner*, November 20, 1861.

17. James McPherson, *The Battle Cry of Freedom*, p. 324.

18. *Evening Transcript*, August 1, 1861.

19. David Donald, *Lincoln*, p. 326.

20. Erwin Bradley, *Simon Cameron: Lincoln's Secretary of War*, p. 216.

21. Ibid., p. 207.

22. Ibid., p. 200.

23. Ibid., p. 216.

24. Howard Beale, ed., *The Diary of Gideon Welles* (hereafter cited as *DGW*).

25. Ibid., 1:58.

26. Benjamin Thomas and Harold Hyman, *Stanton: The Life and Times of Lincoln's Secretary of War* (hereafter cited as *SLT*), p. 137.

27. Ibid., p. 151.

28. *DGW,* 1: 242–244.

29. Ibid., 1: 525.

30. Ibid., 1: 390.

31. Ibid., 1: 319.

32. Ibid., 1: 242.

33. Ibid., 1: 243.

34. Ibid., 1: 391.

35. Donald, 321–323.

36. Norman Graebner, "Northern Diplomacy and European Neutrality," in David Donald, ed., *Why the North Won the Civil War,* pp. 58–81.

37. William Seward to Charles F. Adams, May 21, 1861, *CWAL,* 4: 376–380.

38. Glyndon Van Deusen, *William Henry Seward,* p. 349.

39. Ibid., p. 294.

40. Burton Hendrick, *Lincoln's War Cabinet,* p. 210.

41. Ibid., p. 210.

42. Donald, p. 401.

43. Ibid., p. 60.

44. Hendrick, p. 363.

45. *DGW,* 1: 36–39.

46. Hendrick, p. 188.

47. *DGW,* 1: 522.

48. Ibid., 1: 130.

49. Ibid., 1: 351.

50. Ibid., 1: 320.

51. Ibid., 1: 546.

52. Van Deusen, p. 274.

53. David Donald, ed., *Inside Lincoln's Cabinet,* pp. 11–13.

54. *DGW,* 1: 526.

55. Donald, p. 328.

56. McPherson, *The Battle Cry of Freedom,* pp. 323–325.

57. Ibid., p. 371.

58. Donald, pp. 40–41.

59. Ibid., p. 24

60. *DGW,* 1: 124–127.

61. David Brady, *Critical Elections and Congressional Policy Making,* pp. 40–44.

62. *CWAL,* 5: 486n.

63. T. Harry Williams, *Lincoln and His Generals,* p. 13.

64. Donald, p. 351.

65. Meigs to McClellan on behalf of Abraham Lincoln, May 17, 1862, *CWAL,* 5: 220.

66. McClellan to Abraham Lincoln, July 12, 1862.

67. Abraham Lincoln to McClellan, May 9, 1862, *CWAL,* 5: 208–209.

68. Abraham Lincoln to McClellan, May 9, 1862, *CWAL,* 5: 208.

69. Abraham Lincoln to McClellan, May 21, 1862, *CWAL,* 5: 227.

70. McClellan to Abraham Lincoln, Stanton, June 28, 1861, *CWAL,* 5: 290–291.

71. Donald, p. 358.

72. Catton, *Bruce Catton's Civil War,* p. 578.

73. Williams, p. 173.

74. Sears, *George McClellan,* pp. 330–331.

75. Abraham Lincoln to McClellan, October 24, 1862, *CWAL,* 5: 474.

76. Williams, p. 177.

77. Halleck to McClellan, November 5, 1862, *CWAL,* 5: 485.

78. *CWAL, 5: 178.*

79. *LDCW,* pp. 8–9.

80. Robert Harper, *Lincoln and the Press,* pp. 113–129.

81. Brady, p. 28.

82. Donald, p. 382.

83. Abraham Lincoln to Burnside, *CWAL,* 5: 511.

84. Catton, p. 232.

85. Williams, p. 199.

86. "Congratulations to the Army of the Potomac," Abraham Lincoln to the troops, December 22, 1862, *CWAL,* 6: 13.

87. Boatner, *Civil War Dictionary,* p. 858.

88. Catton, p. 279–280.

89. Donald, p. 404.

90. William Marvel, *Burnside,* p. 215.

91. Ibid., p. 216.

Chapter 15. Abraham Lincoln: Emancipation

1. First draft, Emancipation Proclamation, July 22, 1862, ALP.

2. Lincoln speech in Springfield, Illinois, July 6, 1852, *CWAL,* 2: 132.

3. Lincoln speech in Peoria, Illinois, October 16, 1854, *CWAL,* 2: 260.

4. Carl Sandburg, *Abraham Lincoln: The*

Prairie Years and the War Years: 1861–1864,
2: 202.

5. Ibid., 2: 194–5

6. Henry Jaffa, "The Emancipation Proclamation," Robert Goldwin, ed., *One Hundred Years of Emancipation,* p. 23.

7. William Gienapp, "Abraham Lincoln and Presidential Leadership," in James McPherson, ed., *We Cannot Escape History,* p. 79.

8. Abraham Lincoln to Henry Raymond, March 9, 1862, *CWAL,* 5: 152–153.

9. Abraham Lincoln to James McDougall, March 14, 1862, *CWAL,* 5: 152–153.

10. Proclamation revoking General Hunter's order, May 19, 1862, *CWAL,* 5: 222–224.

11. Abraham Lincoln to Frémont, September 2, 1861, *CWAL,* 4: 506–507.

12. David Donald, *Lincoln,* p. 363.

13. William Sprague to Abraham Lincoln, September 26, 1862, ALP.

14. *CWAL,* 5: 278–279.

15. Reformed Presbyterian Church statement, September 21, 1862, ALP.

16. *New York Tribune,* August 19, 1862.

17. Abraham Lincoln to Greeley, August 22, 1862, *CWAL,* 5: 388–389

18. Cassius Clay to Eli Thayer, September 29, 1862, ALP.

19. "Colonization of the Negroes," *Philadelphia Press,* September 26, 1862.

20. Jacob Van Vleet to Abraham Lincoln, October 4, 1862, ALP.

21. Abraham Lincoln memo, July 12, 1862, ALP.

22. Abraham Lincoln to Browning, September 22, 1862, *CWAL,* 4: 532–33.

23. Copy to Abraham Lincoln of letter to *New York Post,* ALP.

24. Abraham Lincoln memo, July 22, 1862, *CWAL,* 5: 338.

25. Sandburg, p. 198.

26. *CWAL,* 5: 337n.

27. Abraham Lincoln's reply to crowd, September 24, 1862, *CWAL,* 5: 438–439.

28. Alexander Hamilton to Lincoln, containing de la Croix memoir, July 21, 1862, ALP.

29. Tremont St. M. E. Church of Boston petition, September 24, 1862, ALP.

30. U.S. Christian Citizens petition, September, 1862, ALP.

31. First United Presbyterian Synod of the West petition, September 30, 1862, ALP.

32. H. Catlin, and J. F. Downing to Abraham Lincoln, September 23, 1862, ALP.

33. Minnesota legislative proclamation, September 29, 1862, ALP.

34. McClellan to Abraham Lincoln, October 7, 1862, ALP.

35. James Stone to Abraham Lincoln, September 23, 1862, ALP.

36. A. Spier to Abraham Lincoln, September 24, 1862, ALP.

37. J. M. McKim to Abraham Lincoln, September 27, 1862, ALP.

38. Abraham Lincoln to Fawcett, a letter of thanks, January 26, 1863, *CWAL* 6: 78.

39. B. Hedrick to Abraham Lincoln, September 23, 1862, ALP.

40. John Allison to Abraham Lincoln, September 23, 1862, ALP.

41. B. Brown to Abraham Lincoln, September 27, 1862, ALP.

42. General Ben Butler to Abraham Lincoln, notes, *CWAL,* 5: 343.

43. Anonymous to Abraham Lincoln, October 1, 1862, ALP.

44. Donald, p. 380.

45. Gerrit Smith, *Peterboro Gazette,* October 6, 1862.

46. *New York World,* September 24, 1862.

47. *New York Evening Express,* September 24, 1862.

48. Bruce Tap, "Race, Rhetoric and Emancipation: The Election of 1862 in Illinois," *Civil War History,* June, 1993, p. 120.

49. *Indiana State Sentinel,* January 1, 1863.

50. *New York Evening Express,* September 23, 1862.

51. Newspaper clip, January 2, 1863, ALP.

52. Anna Carroll to Abraham Lincoln, July 14, 1862, ALP.

53. Tap, p. 102.

54. Donald, pp. 382–83.

Chapter 16. Jefferson Davis at War: 1862

1. William Preston Johnston to Rosa Johnston, May 3, 1862, Mason Barret Collection.

2. *CTG,* p. 155.

3. Hudson Strode, *Jefferson Davis: Confederate President,* p. 287.

4. *Charleston Courier,* November 3, 1863.

5. *Chicago Tribune,* June 2, 1885.

6. *CTG,* p. 157.

7. *Richmond Examiner,* October 4, 1862.

8. *Richmond Examiner,* November 11, 1862.

9. Governor Thomas Moore to Davis, September 7, 1861, *PJD,* 7: 331.

10. *Charleston Mercury,* March 5, 1862.

11. Ibid.

12. *Charleston Mercury,* March 6, 1862.

13. *Richmond Examiner,* February 20, 1862.

14. *Charleston Mercury,* April 14, 1864.

15. *Richmond Examiner,* February 22, 1862.

16. *Richmond Examiner,* February 24, 1862.

17. *Charleston Mercury,* April 4, 1862.

18. *London Post,* July 23, 1861.

19. Edward Pollard, *The Life of Jefferson Davis,* pp. 358–360.

20. *Charleston Mercury,* March 6, 1862.

21. *Charleston Mercury,* October 6, 1864.

22. *Charleston Mercury,* April 5, 1862.

23. *Charleston Mercury,* August 7, 1863.

24. *Charleston Mercury,* March 4, 1862.

25. *Charleston Mercury,* May 22, 1862.

26. Varina Davis to Jefferson Davis, June, 1862, Museum of the Confederacy Library.

27. James Barber, *Presidential Character,* pp. 12–13.

28. Mark Grimsley, "His Nation's Commander in Chief," *Civil War Times Illustrated,* July/August, 1991, p. 51.

29. Jefferson Davis to Varina Davis, July 11, 1862, Museum of the Confederacy Library.

30. Jefferson Davis to Varina Davis, July 11, 1862, Museum of the Confederacy Library.

31. R. C. Tucker, "The Georges' Wilson Re-examined," *American Political Science Review* (71), 1977, pp. 606–618.

32. Fred Greenstein, Introduction, *Journal of Social Issues,* July, 1968, pp. 10–20.

33. Jefferson Davis to J. Johnston, February 28, 1862, Rowland, 5: 209.

34. Jefferson Davis to Judge W. M. Brooks, March 13, 1862, Rowland, 5: 218.

35. Dean Simonton, "Presidential Style: Personality, Biography and Performance," *Journal of Personality and Social Psychology* 55 (June, 1988), p. 931.

36. *PPMP,* p. 139.

37. *PPMP,* p. 73.

38. Wilfred Yearns, *The Confederate Congress* p. 58.

39. Ibid., pp. 44–45.

40. George Skoch, "The Man Who Fed the South," *Civil War Times Illustrated,* November, 1983, pp. 40–44.

41. Strode, p. 369.

42. David Donald, *Why the North Won the Civil War,* p. 114.

43. Clement Eaton, *Jefferson Davis,* p. 213.

44. Ibid., pp. 212–213.

45. Strode, p. 370.

46. James Rabin, "Alexander Stephens and Jefferson Davis," *American Historical Review* 57 (January 1953), p. 303.

47. *CW,* p. 84.

48. *Richmond Examiner,* February 14, 1861.

49. *Richmond Dispatch,* January 22, 1864.

50. F. G. Fontaine, *Army Letters of F. G. Fontaine,* p. 103.

51. Eaton, p. 148.

52. Jefferson Davis to Florida Governor John Milton, September 1, 1863, Rowland, 6: 20.

53. Jefferson Davis to Georgia Governor Joseph Brown, May 29, 1862, Rowland, 5: 262.

54. Ibid., 5: 142.

55. *JDMH,* p. 453.

56. Jefferson Davis message to Congress, February 3, 1864, Rowland, 6: 164–169.

57. *Richmond Whig,* June 1, 1861.

58. *Charleston Mercury,* April 18, 1863.

59. *Richmond Dispatch,* January 2, 1864.

60. *CW,* p. 55.

61. *Charleston Mercury,* March 25, 1862.

62. *Richmond Examiner,* February 21, 1862.

63. *Richmond Examiner,* October 3, 1862.

64. Richard Johnston and William Browne, *Life of Alexander Stephens,* The resolutions

were written jointly with brother Linton, p. 457.

65. Johnston and Browne, p. 426.

66. Rabin, p. 310.

67. Ibid., p. 304.

68. *Charleston Mercury,* October 18, 1864.

69. Stephens to his brother Linton, June 3, 1864, Emory University Library.

70. *Charleston Mercury,* March 7, 1862.

71. Eaton, p. 214.

72. *Richmond Examiner,* October 10, 1862.

73. Davis passport, Museum of the Confederacy Library.

74. Jefferson Davis to Varina Davis, May 16, 1862, Museum of the Confederacy Library.

75. Jefferson Davis to Varina Davis, June 2, 1862, Museum of the Confederacy Library.

76. Steven Woodworth, *Davis and Lee at War,* p. 153.

77. *MCCWD,* p. 208.

78. *JDMH,* pp. 430–433.

79. Jefferson Davis remarks at the organization of the Lee Monument Association, in 1870, Rowland, 7: 282.

80. Burke Davis, *The Gray Fox: Robert E. Lee and the Civil War,* p. 65.

81. Woodworth, *Davis and Lee at War,* p. 154.

82. Ibid., p. 154.

83. *RWCD,* p. 74.

84. *FLS,* p. 194.

85. *RAF,* p. 340.

86. Jefferson Davis to Varina Davis, May 31, 1862, Rowland, 5: 264.

87. John McKenzie, *Uncertain Glory: Lee's Generalship Re-examined,* p. 200.

88. Byron Farwell, *Stonewall,* p. 205.

89. Eaton, p. 159.

90. Belle Sideman and Lillian Freedman, eds., *Europe Looks at the Civil War,* p. 149.

91. *JDMH,* pp. 489–490.

Chapter 17. Abraham Lincoln at War: 1863

1. *DGW,* 1: 293.

2. Helen Nicolay, *John Nicolay: A Biography of Lincoln's Secretary,* p. 102.

3. Carl Sandburg, *Abraham Lincoln: The Prairie Years and the War Years,* 2: 278–279.

4. Ibid., p. 279.

5. *CWD,* pp. 139–140.

6. McPherson, *The Battle Cry of Freedom,* pp. 644–645.

7. *DGW,* 1: 293.

8. David Donald, *Lincoln,* p. 437.

9. *New York World,* May 8, 1863.

10. *Chicago Tribune,* June 11, 1863.

11. Murat Halstead to Salmon Chase, April 1, 1863, ALP.

12. *CWAL,* 6: 71.

13. *Hunterdon Democrat,* December 13, 1863.

14. *New York World,* January 29, 1863.

15. Sandburg, 2: 297.

16. Ibid., 2: 312–313.

17. Ibid., 2: 293.

18. *Burlington* (Ohio) Argus, May 23, 1863.

19. Stewart Mitchell, *Horatio Seymour of New York,* p. 293.

20. *New York World,* January 3, 1863.

21. Helen Nicolay, pp. 182–183.

22. Donald, p. 423.

23. *LDCW,* p. 10.

24. *CWAL,* 6: 300–306.

25. *LDCW,* p. 10.

26. Sandburg, 2: 304.

27. J. G. Randall, *Mr. Lincoln,* p. 227.

28. Sandburg, p. 338.

29. Ibid., p. 290.

30. See Eric Foner, *Free Soil, Free Labor, Free Men* for a more extensive summary analysis.

31. Abraham Lincoln memo on Francis Capen's weather forecasts, *CWAL,* 6: 190–1.

32. *DGW,* 1: 357

33. *New York Times,* July 5, 1863.

34. *DGW,* 1: 364.

35. Helen Nicolay, p. 171.

36. *CWAL,* 6: 326.

37. *DGW,* 1: 364.

38. *Hunterdon Democrat,* March 11, 1863.

39. John Hay Diary and Papers, Library of Congress, p. 76.

40. *CWD,* pp. 358–359.

41. Sandburg, 3: 635–658.

42. Robert Harper, *Lincoln and the Press,* pp. 76–77.

43. *Newark* (New Jersey) *Advertiser,* December 2, 1862.

44. Harper, p. 180.

45. Randall, *Mr. Lincoln,* p. 220.

46. Ibid., p. 97.

47. Harlan Horner, *Lincoln and Greeley,* pp. 320–360.

48. Harper, p. 307.

49. Polsby, *The Consequences of Party Reform,* p. 107.

50. Christopher Dell, *Lincoln and the War Democrats,* pp. 230–240.

51. Long, *The Civil War Day by Day,* p. 421.

52. James McPherson, p. 688.

53. *DGW,* 1: 470.

54. George Smith and Charles Judah, eds., *Life in the North During the Civil War,* pp. 192–211.

55. Annual Report of the War Department to President Andrew Johnson, November 14, 1866, Andrew Johnson Papers, University of Tennessee.

56. McPherson, p. 449.

57. Edward Carmines and James Stimson, *Issue Evolution: Race and the Transformation of American Politics,* pp. 12–13.

58. Allen Bogue, *The Earnest Men: Republicans of the Civil War Senate,* p. 56.

59. Sundquist, p. 102.

60. David Brady, *Critical Elections and Congressional Policy Making,* pp. 142–144.

61. Sandburg, III, p. 505.

62. Longs, p. 432.

63. Abraham Lincoln's final copy of the Gettysburg Address, *CWAL,* 7: 22–23.

64. *New York Times,* November 20, 1863.

65. Abraham Lincoln to Edward Everett, November 20, 1863, *CWAL,* 7: 24.

66. Abraham Lincoln to Lydia Bixby, November 21, 1864, *CWAL,* 8: 116–117.

67. Abraham Lincoln to James Conkling, August 26, 1863, *CWAL,* 6: 406–410.

68. 1862 message to Congress, December 2, 1862, *CWAL,* 5: 537.

69. *DGW,* 1: 500.

Chapter 18. "Assassinate Davis"

1. Joseph George Jr., "Black Flag Warfare: Lincoln and the Raids Against Richmond and Jefferson Davis," *Pennsylvania Magazine of History and Biography* (July 1991), pp. 291–318.

2. *CWD,* p. 929.

3. *Philadelphia Evening Bulletin,* May 8, 1863.

4. *New York Herald,* November 8, 1863.

5. William Hesseltine, *Civil War Prisoners: A Study in War Psychology,* p. 118.

6. *CWAL,* 6: 202–203.

7. Hurlburt to the Hannibal home guard, August 1, 1861, ALP.

8. George, p. 303.

9. Butler to Wistar, February 5, 1864, in Ben Butler, *Autobiography and Personal Reminiscences of Major General Benjamin F. Butler,* 3: 373–374.

10. Wistar to Butler, February 3, 1864, *Butler,* 3: 368.

11. Butler to Stanton, February 8, 1864, *The War of the Rebellion: A Compilation of the Official Records of the Union and Confederate Army,* series I, vol. 32, pp. 143–144.

12. George, p. 301.

13. U.S. Rep. James Hamilton to Lincoln, September 26, 1862, ALP.

14. *CWD,* p. 459.

15. *TCW,* 2: 903–906.

16. Ibid., 2: 909–915.

17. Kilpatrick to E. B. Parsons, February 16, 1864, in *The War of the Rebellion: A Compilation of the Official Records of the Union and Confederate Army,* series I, vol. 33, pp. 172–173.

18. *DGW,* 1: 538.

19. George, p. 313.

20. A. A. Humphries (Meade's chief of staff) to Kilpatrick, February 27, 1864, Meade Papers, 3: 54–55.

21. *TCW,* 3: 912–915.

22. *CWD,* p. 218.

23. Bruce Catton, *Bruce Catton's Civil War,* p. 470.

24. James Hall, "The Dahlgren Papers: A Yankee Plot to Kill President Davis," *The Civil War Times* (November, 1983), p. 35.

25. *Richmond Dispatch,* March 2–5, 1864.

26. *Richmond Sentinel,* March 7, 1864.

27. Hall, p. 37.

28. Ibid.

29. John Daniel, *The Richmond Examiner During the War,* pp. 176–177.

30. *New York Daily News,* March 17, 1864, p. 1.

31. *The War of the Rebellion: A Compilation of the Official Records of the Union and Confederate Army,* series IV, vol. 3, p. 326.

32. Mrs. William Howell to her son Jeffrey, March 4, 1864, Museum of the Confederacy Library.

Chapter 19. The Plot to Kidnap Abraham Lincoln

1. William Tidwell, James Hall, and David Gaddy, *Come Retribution,* p. 346. Much of the information on the plot to capture Lincoln in this and other works is from the Tidwell, Hall, and Gaddy research.

2. *Lacrosse* (Wisconsin) *Democrat,* August 20, 1864, in Tidwell et al., p. 234.

3. All of these stories were chronicled in Tidwell et al., pp. 234–237.

4. Gene Smith, *American Gothic,* p. 110.

5. William Hanchett, "The Happiest Day of His Life," *Civil War Times Illustrated* (November/December, 1995), p. 79.

6. Ward Lamon, *Recollections of Abraham Lincoln,* pp. 260–270.

7. Tidwell et al., p. 304.

8. Adam Mayers, "Montreal's Posh Rebel Rendezvous," *Civil War Times Illustrated* (January/February, 1993), pp. 44–46.

9. Ibid., p. 248.

10. Walt Albro, "The Forgotten Battle for the Capital," *Civil War Times Illustrated* (January/February, 1993), p. 60.

11. Edmund Halsey Papers, Rockaway (New Jersey) Library.

12. Mark Boatner III, ed., *The Civil War Dictionary,* p. 255–257

13. Albro, p. 61.

14. Smith, p. 110–113.

15. Tidwell et al., p. 334.

16. Ibid., p. 320.

17. Mayers, p. 74. The anecdote was printed in the *Hamilton Times* and, later, in the *New York Times* one month after Lincoln's assassination.

18. Tidwell et al., p. 333.

19. Ibid., pp. 350–370.

20. Eli Evans, *Judah Benjamin: The Jewish Confederate,* p. 273.

21. Smith, p. 121.

22. Ibid., p. 122.

23. Tidwell et al., p. 414.

Chapter 20. Jefferson Davis at War: 1863

1. James McPherson, *The Battle Cry of Freedom,* p. 617.

2. *Memoir,* 2: 374.

3. *JDMH,* p. 498.

4. Wilfred Yearns, *The Confederate Congress,* p. 118.

5. McPherson, p. 616.

6. Paul Escott, *After Secession: Jefferson Davis and the Failure of Southern Nationalism* p. 111.

7. McPherson, p. 441.

8. *RWCD,* p. 243.

9. Stephen Channing, *Confederate Ordeal* p. 84.

10. Clement Eaton, *Jefferson Davis,* pp. 203–204.

11. Philip Foner, *British Labor and the American Civil War,* p. 112.

12. Donald Jordan and Edwin Pratt, *Europe and the American Civil War,* p. 137.

13. McPherson, p. 622.

14. Eaton, p. 200.

15. *RWCD,* p. 207.

16. *RAF,* 2: 365.

17. Jefferson Davis to Lee, May 11, 1863, *The War of the Rebellion: A Compilation of the Official Records of the Union and Confederate Army,* series 25, vol. 1, p. 791.

18. *Memoirs,* pp. 382–383.

19. *RWCD,* p. 190.

20. Jefferson Davis to Governor Joseph Brown, May 20, 1863, Rowland, 5: 490.

21. Zebulon Vance, Governor of North Carolina, to Jefferson Davis, May 13, 1863, Rowland, 5: 485–487.

22. *RWCD*, p. 246.
23. Stephen Woodworth, *Davis and Lee at War*, p. 243.
24. *CWD*, p. 339.
25. *TCW*, 2: 468.
26. Ibid., 2: 246.
27. *RWCD*, p. 237.
28. Ibid., p. 237.
29. Jefferson Davis to Arkansas Senator R. W. Johnson, July 14, 1863, Rowland, 5: 548–550.
30. *RAF*, 2: 448.
31. Jefferson Davis to J. J. Pettus, July 11, 1863, Rowland, 5: 542.
32. Jefferson Davis to Kirby Smith, July 14, 1863, Rowland, 5: 552.
33. Lee to Jefferson Davis, July 7, 1863, Rowland, 5: 536.
34. Lee to Jefferson Davis, July 10, 1863, Rowland, 5: 539.
35. *RWCD*, p. 249.
36. Lee to Jefferson Davis, July 12, 1863, Rowland, 5: 567.
37. *Memoir*, 2: 397.
38. Eaton, pp. 161–162.
39. *TCW*, 2: 170.
40. Ibid., p. 171.
41. Jeffrey Wert, *General James Longstreet*, p. 306.
42. Jefferson Davis to Bragg, August 5, 1862, Rowland, 5: 312.
43. M. Lovell to Davis, October 18, 1861, *PJD*, 7: 362.
44. *Charleston Mercury*, May 5, 1862.
45. Bruce Catton, *Grant Moves South*, p. 438.
46. *Official Records of the Union and Confederate Navies in the War of the Rebellion*, series I, vol. 25, p. 118.
47. Jefferson Davis to Joe Johnston, July 15, 1863, Rowland, 5: 556.
48. Robert Hartje, *Earl Van Dorn*, p. 103.
49. William Davis, *Jefferson Davis: The Man and His Hour*, pp. 376–377.
50. *MCCWD*, p. 498.
51. T. Harry Williams, *P. G. T. Beauregard: Napoleon in Gray*, p. 105.
52. Jefferson Davis to Johnston, July 15,

1863, Rowland, 5: 556.
53. Jefferson Davis to J. Phelan, March 1, 1865, Rowland, 6: 491–503.
54. Jefferson Davis to Varina Davis, May 11, 1862, Museum of the Confederacy Library.
55. *MCCWD*, p. 124.
56. *RAF*, 2: 315.
57. George Skoch, "The Man Who Fed the South," *Civil War Times Illustrated* (November, 1983), pp. 40–44.
58. B. T. Kavanaugh to Davis, August 13, 1863, Rowland, 5: 590–591.
59. *MCCWD*, p. 141.
60. *JDHC*, p. 42.
61. *MCCWD*, p. 596.
62. *Richmond Examiner*, May 19, 1862.
63. *Richmond Examiner*, January 21, 1864.
64. *Charleston Mercury*, May 7, 1862,
65. *JDMH*, p. 439.
66. Jefferson Davis to Z. B. Vance, January 8, 1864. Rowland, 6: 143–146.
67. Wert, p. 305.
68. Eaton, p. 235.
69. *ICG*, p. 103.
70. *RWCD*, p. 242.
71. *MCCWD*, p. 155.
72. Hodding Carter, *Their Words Were Bullets: The Southern Press in War, Peace and Reconstruction*, pp. 32–33.
73. Jefferson Davis to Pemberton, August 9, 1863. Rowland, 5: 587–588.
74. Jefferson Davis to Mrs. Howell Cobb, March 30, 1865, Rowland, 6: 524.
75. Davis to the Senate, April 30, 1863, Rowland, 5: 478.
76. Hudson Strode, *Jefferson Davis: Confederate President*, p. 159.
77. Ibid., p. 22.

Chapter 21. Jefferson Davis: Emancipation

1. Mark Grimsley, "The Will to Win and Denying Reality," *Civil War Times Illustrated* (July/August, 1991), pp. 66–67.
2. Howell and Elizabeth Purdue, *Patrick Cleburne: Confederate General*, pp. 268–278.
3. *CWD*, p. 158.
4. Clement Eaton, *Jefferson Davis*, pp. 258–259.

5. *JDMH*, p. 597.

6. Joseph Glatthaar, "Black Glory," in Gabor Boritt, ed., *Why the Confederacy Lost,* pp. 160–161.

7. W. Buck Young, ed., *The Confederate Governors,* p. 229.

8. *Richmond Examiner,* October 3, 1861.

9. *Vicksburg Daily Whig,* April 2, 1863.

10. Young, p. 223.

11. Douglas Freeman, *R. E. Lee,* 3: 544.

12. *RAE,* 2: 515–518.

13. Ibid., 2: 518.

14. *ICG,* p. 177.

15. Mark Grimsley, "A Reason to Loathe Davis," *Civil War Times Illustrated* (July/August, 1991), pp. 68–69.

16. *Richmond Dispatch,* November 9, 1864.

17. *JDMH,* p. 598.

18. Eli Evans, *Judah Benjamin: The Jewish Confederate,* p. 263.

19. Ibid., p. 263.

20. R. E. Lee Jr., *My Father: General Lee,* pp. 232–33.

21. Burke Davis, *Gray Fox: Robert E. Lee and the Civil War,* p. 347.

22. Douglas Southall Freeman, *R. E. Lee,* 3: 542.

23. Evans, p. 287.

24. Jefferson Davis to John Forsyth, February 21, 1865, Rowland, 6: 482.

25. Davis, p. 353.

26. Lee to Virginia State Senator Andrew Hunter, January 11, 1865, Evans, p. 279.

27. Henry White, *Robert E. Lee and the Southern Confederacy,* p. 14.

28. *The War of the Rebellion: A Compilation of the Official Records of the Union and Confederate Army,* series I, vol. 51, part 2, p. 1063.

29. *RWCD,* 2: 415.

30. Rowland, 6: 482, 513, 526.

31. Evans, p. 282.

32. Jefferson Davis to Lee, March 13, 1865, Rowland, 6: 513.

33. E. B. and Barbara Long, *The Civil War: Day by Day* (Garden City, N.Y.: Doubleday, 1971), p. 651.

34. *The War of the Rebellion: A Compilation of the Official Records of the Union and Con-*

federate Army, series I, vol. 46, part 3, p. 1339.

35. Freeman, 3: 544.

36. Jefferson Davis to Lee, April 1, 1865 (Davis's letter book), Rowland, 6: 526.

37. Jefferson Davis to Lee, March 30, 1865, Rowland, 6: 524.

38. Jefferson Davis to Smith, March 25, 1865, Rowland, 6: 522.

Chapter 22. Abraham Lincoln at War: 1864–1865

1. William McFeely, *Grant,* pp. 154–155.

2. Ibid., p. 162.

3. John Nicolay and John Hay, *Abraham Lincoln: A History,* 8: 340–341.

4. *LFS,* pp. 158–159.

5. *LFS,* p. 152.

6. John Eaton to Grant, July 23, 1863, in John Simon, ed., *The Papers of U. S. Grant,* 8: 343. Eaton met with Lincoln and conveyed the president's esteem of Grant to the general.

7. Message to Congress, December 8, 1863, *CWAL,* 7: 36–53.

8. Proclamation of Amnesty and Reconstruction, December 8, 1863, *CWAL,* 7: 53–55.

9. Richard Overy, *Why the Allies Won,* pp. 245–281. Overy examined leadership qualities in Joseph Stalin, Winston Churchill, and Franklin Roosevelt and concluded their best features were all similar to Lincoln's.

10. Louis Warren, *Lincoln's Youth: Indiana Years, Seven to Twenty-one,* p. 225.

11. Abraham Lincoln to Mrs. Eliza Gurney, *CWAL,* 7: 535.

12. *SLT,* p. 300.

13. *TRFS,* pp. 486–489.

14. Abraham Lincoln to Frederick Conkling, June 3, 1864, *CWAL,* 7: 374–375.

15. Abraham Lincoln to Grant, April 30, 1864, *CWAL,* 7: 324.

16. Abraham Lincoln to Grant, June 15, 1864, *CWAL,* 7: 393.

17. McFeely, p. 164.

18. *New York Tribune,* June 23, 1861.

19. Lately Thomas, *The First President Johnson,* pp. 268–270.

20. S. Newton Pettis to A. Johnson, June 10, 1864, Leroy Graf and Ralph Haskins, *The*

Papers of Andrew Johnson, 6: 722.

21. Graf and Haskins, 6: 723–727.

22. Greeley to Lincoln, July 7, 1864, *CWAL,* 7: 435.

23. Ida Tarbell, *The Life of Abraham Lincoln: Drawn From Original Sources and Containing Many Speeches,* 2: 198.

24. *DGW,* 1: 111–112.

25. Notes of meeting between Raymond, Lincoln, and the cabinet, August 24, 1864, *CWAL,* 7: 517–518.

26. Edmund Kirke, "An Untold Story," *Atlantic Magazine,* April, 1887, pp. 435–448.

27. Abraham Lincoln memo, *CWAL,* 7: 514–515.

28. James Merrill, *W. T. Sherman,* p. 262.

29. *TCW,* 3: 552.

30. Van Deusen, *William Henry Seward,* p. 387.

31. *TCW,* 3: 558.

32. William T. Sherman, *Memoirs,* pp. 109–110.

33. *TCW,* 3: 558.

34. Harper, *Lincoln and the Press,* p. 320.

35. Abraham Lincoln to W. T. Sherman, September 19, 1864, *CWAL,* 8: 11–12.

36. Abraham Lincoln to Henry Hoffman, October 10, 1864, *CWAL,* 8: 41.

37. *SLT,* p. 332.

38. David Donald, *Lincoln,* p. 542.

39. *SLT,* pp. 332–333.

40. Abraham Lincoln speech at the White House, November 10, 1864, *CWAL,* 8: 100–101.

41. Longs, *The Civil War Day by Day,* p. 594.

42. James McPherson, *The Battle Cry of Freedom,* p. 805.

43. Carl Sandburg, *Abraham Lincoln: The Prairie Years and the War Years,* 3: 689.

44. Abraham Lincoln speech, November 10, 1864, *CWAL,* 8: 100–101.

45. *CWAL,* 8: 188–189.

46. Abraham Lincoln speech to a crowd gathered at the White House, October 19, 1864, *CWAL,* 8: 52–53.

47. *JDTH,* pp. 135–137.

48. Ibid., pp. 136–141.

49. James Randall and Richard Current, *Lincoln the President: Last Full Measure,* pp. 307–313.

50. Second Inaugural Address, March 4, 1864, *CWAL,* 8: 332–333.

51. *National Intelligencer,* March 5, 1864.

Chapter 23. Jefferson Davis at War: 1864–1865

1. *JDMH,* pp. 534–535.

2. *RWCD,* p. 322.

3. Ibid., p. 330.

4. Ibid., p. 331.

5. Ibid., p. 333.

6. *CW,* p. 69.

7. *JDTH,* p. 6.

8. Clement Eaton, p. 228.

9. Vance to Jefferson Davis, September 11, 1863, Rowland, 6: 30–31.

10. Jefferson Davis to Vance, January 8, 1864, Rowland, 6: 143–146.

11. Ibid., 6: 143–146.

12. *JDTH,* p. 7.

13. Jefferson Davis to Vance, February 29, 1864, Rowland, 6: 193–7.

14. Ibid., 6: 193–197.

15. *RWCD,* p. 424.

16. *ICG,* p. 438.

17. *JDMH,* p. 535.

18. Jefferson Davis to Brown, May 24, 1864, Rowland, 6: 260–261.

19. *JDTH,* p. 8.

20. Ibid., p. 27.

21. Cornelius Cotter, James Gibson, John Bibby, and Robert Huckshorn, *Party Organizations in American Politics,* p. 7.

22. Rudolph Von Abele, *Alexander Stephens,* p. 212.

23. Jon Wakelyn, "The Speakers of the State Legislatures' Failure as Confederate Leaders," *LDCW,* pp. 153–167.

24. Cotter, p. 76.

25. Drew Faust, *The Creation of Confederate Nationalism,* p. 7.

26. Ibid., p. 23.

27. *Edgefield (S. C.) Advertiser,* May 6, 1863, in Faust, p. 52.

28. James McPherson, "American Victory, American Defeat," Gabor Boritt, ed., *Why the*

Confederacy Lost, p. 34.

29. Drew Faust, *Mothers of Invention,* pp. 235–242.

30. Joseph Halsey Papers, University of Virginia Library.

31. Faust, p. 241.

32. *CW,* p. 65.

33. Ibid., p. 65.

34. Jefferson Davis speech in Macon, Georgia, September 29, 1864, Rowland, 6: 341–344.

35. Jefferson Davis speech in Montgomery, Alabama, October 3, 1864, Rowland, 6: 345–347.

36. Jefferson Davis speech in Columbia, South Carolina, October 6, 1865, Rowland, 6: 349–356.

37. *JDTH,* p. 96.

38. *CWD,* pp. 295–296.

39. *RAF,* 2: 546.

40. Hudson Strode, *Jefferson Davis: Confederate President,* p. 351.

41. *FLS,* p. 204.

42. *TCW,* 3: 609.

43. Henry Lindgren, *Leadership Authority and Power Sharing,* p. 54.

44. *TCW,* 3: 492–510.

45. *RAF,* 2: 561.

46. Eaton, p. 254.

47. *RAF,* 2: 556–557.

48. *Richmond Dispatch,* September 5, 1864.

49. Foote, 3: 563.

50. Gary Gallagher, "'Upon Their Success Hang Momentous Interests': Generals," in Boritt, *Why the Confederacy Lost,* pp. 106–107.

51. *Charleston Mercury,* September 6, 1864.

52. Rowland, 6: 280.

53. Jefferson Davis to Brown, June 29, 1864, Rowland, 6: 278–279.

54. Brown to Jefferson Davis, July 5, 1864, Rowland 6: 280.

55. Jefferson Davis to Brown, July 5, 1864, Rowland 6: 280–281.

56. Alvy King, *Louis Wigfall: Southern Fire Eater,* p. 209.

57. Craig Symonds, *Joseph E. Johnston: A Civil War Biogrpahy,* pp. 330–331.

58. *FLS,* p. 204.

59. *ICG,* p. 174.

60. Ibid., p. 80.

61. Ibid., p. 80

62. King, pp. 200–204.

63. Rembert Patrick, *Jefferson Davis and His Cabinet,* p. 68.

64. Jefferson Davis to Seddon, February 1, 1865, Rowland, 6: 459.

65. Joseph Davis to Jefferson Davis, March 19, 1865, Davis Papers, Transylvania, in William Davis, *Jefferson Davis: The Man and His Hour,* p. 583.

66. Jefferson Davis to R. M. T. Hunter, April 14, 1864, Rowland, 6: 226–227.

67. J. W. Tucker to Davis, March 12, 1864, Rowland 6: 204–206.

68. Jared Rabin, "Alexander Stephens and Jefferson Davis," *American Historical Review* 57 (January, 1953), p. 314.

69. *Augusta* (Ga.) *Constitutionalist,* November 16, 1864.

70. *FLS,* p. 206.

71. Myrta Avary, *Recollections of Alexander H. Stephens,* pp. 51–52.

72. A. Stephens to L. Stephens, December 3, 1864, in Richard Johnston and William Browne, *The Life of Alexander Stephens,* p. 475.

73. Lee to Jefferson Davis, September 2, 1864, Rowland, 6: 327–329.

74. Stephens prison diary, July 13, 1865, Rabin, p. 314.

75. *RAF,* 2: 667.

76. *JDTH,* p. 168.

77. *RAF,* 2: 666.

78. *CWD,* pp. 663–664.

Chapter 24. Abraham Lincoln: Final Days

1. *New York Herald,* April 7, 1865.

2. *National Intelligencer,* April 8, 1865.

3. *National Intelligencer,* April 11, 1865.

4. James McPherson, *The Battle Cry of Freedom,* p. 851.

5. *DGW,* 2: 278.

6. *New York Tribune,* April 10, 1865.

7. *National Intelligencer,* April 11, 1865.

8. *New York Herald,* April 10, 1865.

9. Gene Smith, *American Gothic,* p. 132.

10. Longs, *The Civil War Day by Day,*

p. 675.

11. James Van Alen to Lincoln and Lincoln reply, April 14, 1865, *CWAL,* 8: 413.

12. *SLT,* p. 395.

13. Gene Smith, *American Gothic,* p. 143.

14. *National Intelligencer,* April 15, 1865.

15. William Tidwell, James Hall, David Gaddy, *Come Retribution,* pp. 436–437.

16. Van Deusen, *William Henry Seward,* p. 414.

17. Ibid., p. 414.

18. David Donald, *Inside Lincoln's Cabinet,* p. 267.

19. Smith, p. 146.

20. Captain Oliver Gatch, quoted in Tom Good, ed., *We Saw Lincoln Shot,* pp. 125–126.

21. Carl Sandburg, *Abraham Lincoln: The Prairie Years and the War Years,* 3: 864–866.

22. *New York Herald,* April 15, 1865.

23. Rathbone quoted in Good, pp. 41–48.

24. *National Intelligencer,* April 15, 1865.

25. Jim Bishop, *The Day Lincoln Was Shot,* pp. 206–211.

26. Jason Knox, W. H. Roberts and Spencer Bronson, quoted in Good, pp. 40, 57, 155.

27. *New York Herald,* April 15, 1865.

28. *National Intelligencer,* April 15, 1865.

29. William McFeely, *Grant,* p. 224.

30. *SLT,* pp. 396–399.

Chapter 25. Jefferson Davis: Final Days

1. Jefferson Davis to Crafts Wright, October 13, 1877, Rowland, 8: 35–36.

2. *RAF,* 2: 701–703.

3. *Lynchburg Daily Virginian,* August 31, 1866.

4. *JDTH,* p. 177.

5. *JDMH,* p. 643.

6. *JDTH,* pp. 231–232.

7. Ibid., p. 259.

8. Varina Davis to Dr. John Craven, October 10, 1865, Rowland, 7: 44–48.

9. Eric Foner, *Reconstruction: America's Unfinished Business,* (New York: Harper and Row, 1988), p. 265.

10. *RAF,* p. 683.

11. Varina Davis to Montgomery Meigs,

June 3, 1865, Museum of the Confederacy Library.

12. Varina Davis to Dr. John Craven, October 10, 1865, Rowland, 7: 44–48.

13. Ibid.

14. Varina Davis to Horace Greeley, September 2, 1866, Rowland, 7: 75–76.

15. *JDTH,* p. 245.

16. Jefferson Davis to Varina Davis, October 11, 1865, Rowland, 7: 49–52.

17. *RAF,* 2: 705.

18. Gerrit Smith to President Johnson, August 24, 1866, Rowland, 7: 73–74.

19. Rowland, 7: 284.

20. *Memoir,* 2: 814–815.

21. Paul Buck, *The Road to Reunion,* pp. 116–121.

22. Ibid., p. 141.

23. Ibid., p. 201.

24. Ibid., pp. 140–146.

25. Jefferson Davis to J. C. Derby, October 6, 1878, Rowland, 8: 283

26. *JDTH,* p. 101, 109.

27. Mark Neely Jr., Harold Holzer, and Gabor Boritt, *The Confederate Image: Prints of the Lost Cause,* pp. 169–188.

28. Museum of the Confederacy Library.

29. *Frank Leslie's Illustrated Weekly,* May 8, 1886.

30. Speech at Mississippi City, July 10, 1878, Rowland, 8: 227–237.

31. J. B. Fay to Davis, January 13, 1889, Rowland, 10: 95–96.

32. Thomas Munford to Davis, May 22, 1889, and E. W. Carmack to Davis, May 25, 1889, Rowland, 10: 113–116.

33. J. W. Godwin to Jefferson Davis, June 22, 1889, Rowland, 10: 124.

34. W. J. Pearce to Jefferson Davis, March 4, 1889, Rowland, 10: 99.

35. *JDTH,* p. 467.

36. Ibid., pp. 512–523.

37. Ibid., pp. 526–527.

SELECT BIBLIOGRAPHY

Avary, Myrta. *Recollections of Alexander Stephens.* New York: Da Capo Press, 1971.

Bailey, Thomas. *Presidential Greatness.* New York: Appleton, Century Crofts Co., 1966.

Baker, Jean. *Mary Todd Lincoln: A Biography.* New York: W. W. Norton, 1987.

Barber, James. *Presidential Character.* Englewood Cliffs, N.J.: Prentice-Hall, 1972.

Basler, Roy, ed. *The Collected Works of Abraham Lincoln.* 8 vols. New Brunswick: Rutgers University Press, 1953–1955.

Beale, Howard, Jr., *The Diary of Gideon Welles.* 2 vols. New York: W. W. Norton, 1960.

Bell, Patricia. "Mary Todd Lincoln." *Civil War Times Illustrated* (November, 1968).

Beveridge, Albert. *Abraham Lincoln.* 2 vols. Boston: Houghton-Mifflin Co., 1928.

Bishop, Jim. *The Day Lincoln Was Shot.* New York: Harper Brothers, 1955.

Blodi, Frederick. *Herpes Simplex Infections of the Eye.* New York: Churchill Livingstone Co., 1984.

Boatner, Mark, III, ed. *The Civil War Dictionary.* New York: Vintage, 1991.

Bogue, Allen. *Earnest Men: Republicans of the Civil War Senate.* Ithaca: Cornell University Press, 1981.

Boritt, Gabor, ed. *Why the Confederacy Lost.* New York: Oxford University Press, 1992.

Botts, John. *The Great Rebellion.* New York, 1866.

Bradley, Erwin. *Simon Cameron: Lincoln's Secretary of War.* Philadelphia: University of Pennsylvania Press, 1966.

Brady, David. *Critical Elections and Congressional Policy Making.* Stanford: Stanford University Press, 1988.

Buchanan, James. *Mr. Buchanan's Administration on the Eve of the Rebellion.* Salem, N.H.: Ayer Co., 1865.

Buck, Paul. *The Road to Reunion.* Boston: Little, Brown Co., 1937.

Burlingame, Michael. *The Inner World of Abraham Lincoln.* Chicago: University of Illinois Press, 1994.

Butler, Ben. *Autobiography and Personal Reminiscences of Major General Benjamin F. Butler.* 3 vols. Boston, 1892.

Carmines, Edward, and James Stimson. *Issue Evolution: Race and the Transformation of America.* Princeton: Princeton University Press, 1989.

Carpenter, Frances. *Six Months in the White House With Abraham Lincoln.* New York: Hurd & Houghton, 1866.

Carter, Hodding. *Their Words Were Bullets: The Southern Press in War, Peace and Reconstruction.* Athens: University of Georgia Press, 1969.

Cash, W. J. *The Mind of the South.* New York: Alfred A. Knopf, 1941.

Catton, Bruce, and William. *Two Roads to Fort Sumter.* New York: McGraw-Hill, 1963.

————. *Bruce Catton's Civil War.* New York: Fairfax Press, 1984.

————. *Grant Moves South.* Boston: Houghton-Mifflin, 1960.

Cauthen, Charles. *South Carolina Goes to War, 1860–1865.* Chapel Hill: University of North Carolina Press, 1942.

Chance, Joseph. *Jefferson Davis's Mexican War Regiment.* Jackson: University Press of Mississippi, 1991.

Channing, Steven. *Confederate Ordeal.* Alexandria, Va.: Time-Life Books, 1984.

————. *Crisis of Fear.* New York: Simon & Schuster, 1970.

Clinton, Catherine, and C. J. Barker-Benfield. *Portraits of American Women.* New York: St. Martin's Press, 1991.

Coleman, Charles. *Abraham Lincoln and Coles County, Illinois.* New Brunswick: Scarecrow Press, 1955.

Corwin, Edwin. *The Presidency: Office and Powers, 1787–1984.* New York: New York University Press, 1984.

Cotter, Cornelius, James Gibson, John Bibby, and Robert Huckshorn. *Party Organization in American Politics.* Pittsburgh: University of Pittsburgh Press, 1984.

Coulter, E. Merton. *The Civil War and Readjustment in Kentucky.* Gloucester: Peter Smith, 1966.

————, ed. *A History of the South.* Baton Rouge: Louisiana State University Press, 1950.

Crissey, Elwell. *Lincoln's Lost Speech.* New York: Hawthorn, 1969.

Crist, Linda. *Papers of Jefferson Davis.* 10 vols. Baton Rouge: Louisiana State University Press, 1983.

Current, Richard. *Lincoln and the First Shot.* Philadelphia: J. B. Lippincott & Co., 1953.

Daniel, John. *The Richmond Examiner During the War.* New York: Frederick Daniel, 1868.

Davis, Burke. *The Gray Fox: Robert E. Lee and the Civil War.* New York: Rinehart and Co., 1956.

Davis, David Brion. *The Problems of Slavery in the Age of Revolution: 1770–1823.* Ithaca: Cornell University Press, 1975.

Davis, Jefferson. *The Rise and Fall of the Confederate Government.* 2 vols. New York: Yoselof Publishing, 1958 edition.

Davis, Varina Howell. *Jefferson Davis: Ex-President of the Confederate States of America: A Memoir.* 2 vols. New York: Belford Publishing, 1890.

Davis, William C. *Jefferson Davis: The Man and His Hour.* New York: HarperCollins, 1991.

DeBow, James. *The Interest in Slavery of the Non-Slaveholder.* Charleston: Evans & Cogswell, 1860.

DeLeon, T. C. *Belles, Beaus and Brains of the '60s.* New York: [n.p.], 1907.

————. *Thirty Years of My Life on Three Continents.* London: Ward and Downey Publishers, 1890.

Dell, Christopher. *Lincoln and the War Democrats.* Cranbury, N.J.: Associated University Presses, 1975.

Donald, David. *Lincoln.* New York: Simon & Schuster, 1995.

————, ed. *Why the North Won the Civil War.* New York: Simon & Schuster, 1960.

Dumond, Dwight. *The Secessionist Movement, 1860–61.* New York: Negro University Press, 1968.

Dyer, John. *The Gallant Hood.* New York: Bobbs-Merrill, 1950.

Eaton, Clement, *A History of the Old South.* New York: Macmillan, 1975.

————. *A History of the Southern Confederacy.* New York: Macmillan, 1954.

————. *Jefferson Davis.* New York: Free Press, 1977.

Eckenrode, Hamilton. *Jefferson Davis: President of the South.* Freeport, N.Y.: Books for Libraries, 1923.

Escott, Paul. *After Secession: Jefferson Davis and the Failure of Southern Nationalism.* Baton Rouge: Louisiana State University Press, 1978.

Evans, Eli. *Judah Benjamin: The Jewish Confederate.* New York: Free Press, 1988.

Farwell, Byron. *Stonewall.* New York: W. W. Norton, 1992.

Faust, Drew. *Mothers of Invention.* Chapel Hill: University of North Carolina Press, 1996.

————. *The Creation of Confederate Nationalism.* Baton Rouge: Louisiana State University Press, 1988.

Fehrenbacher, Don. *Prelude to Greatness: Abraham Lincoln in the 1850s.* Stanford: Stanford University Press, 1962.

Foner, Eric. *Free Soil, Free Labor, Free Men.* New York: Oxford University Press, 1970.

————. *Reconstruction: America's Unfinished Revolution.* New York: Harper and Row, 1988.

Foner, Philip. *British Labor and the American Civil War.* New York: Holmes and Meier Publishers, 1981.

Fontaine, F. G. *Army Letters of F. G. Fontaine.* Columbia, S.C.: War Record Publishing, 1897.

Foote, Shelby. *The Civil War.* 3 vols. New York: Random House, 1986.

Freeman, Douglas. *R. E. Lee.* 4 vols. New York: Charles Scribner's Sons, 1935.

George, Joseph, Jr. "Black Flag Warfare: Lincoln and the Raids Against Richmond and Jefferson Davis." *Pennsylvania Magazine of History and Biography* (July, 1991).

Girard, Charles. *A Visit to the Confederate States of America.* Tuscaloosa, Ala.: Confederate Publishing Company, 1962.

Goldwin, Robert. *One Hundred Years of Emancipation.* Chicago: Rand McNally Co., 1964.

Good, Tom, ed. *We Saw Lincoln Shot.* Jackson: University Press of Mississippi, 1995.

Graf, Leroy and Ralph Haskins. *The Papers of Andrew Johnson.* 13 vols. Knoxville: University of Tennessee Press, 1983.

Grayson, John. *James Louis Petigru: A Biographical Sketch.* New York, 1866.

Greenstein, Fred. "Introduction." *Journal of Social Issues* (July, 1968).

————. "Lasswell's Concept of Democratic Character." *Journal of Politics,* no. 30 (1968).

Grimsley, Mark. "A Reason to Loathe Davis." *Civil War Times Illustrated* (July/August, 1991).

————. "His Nation's Commander in Chief." *Civil War Times Illustrated* (August, 1991).

————. "The Will to Win and Denying Reality." *Civil War Times Illustrated* (July/August, 1991).

Hall, James. "The Dahlgren Papers: A Yankee Plot to Kill President Davis." *Civil War Times Illustrated* (November, 1983).

Halsey, Joseph. Papers, in folders. University of Virginia; Charlottesville, Virginia.

Hammond, James. Papers, on microfilm. University of South Carolina, Columbia, South Carolina.

Harper, Robert. *Lincoln and the Press.* New York: McGraw-Hill Co., 1951.

Hartje, Robert. *Earl Van Dorn.* Nashville: Vanderbilt University Press, 1967.

Hay, John. Papers, on microfilm. Library of Congress, Washington, D.C.

Heleniak, Roman and Lawrence Hewitt, eds. *Leadership During the Civil War.* Shippensburg, Pa.: White Mane Publishing Co., 1992.

Hendrick, Burton. *Lincoln's War Cabinet.* Boston: Little, Brown Co., 1946.

————. *Statesmen of the Lost Cause.* New York: Literary Guild of America, 1939.

Herndon, Billy. *Herndon's Life of Lincoln.* 3 vols. Cleveland: World Publishers, 1930.

Herndon, William. "Analysis of the Character of Abraham Lincoln." *Abraham Lincoln Quarterly* (December, 1941).

————. Papers, on microfilm. Library of Congress, Washington, D.C.

474 SELECT BIBLIOGRAPHY

Hertz, Emanuel, ed. *The Hidden Lincoln: From the Letters and Papers of William Herndon*. New York: Viking Press, 1938.

Hesseltine, William. *Civil War Prisoners: A Study in War Psychology*. New York: F. Ungar Co., 1964.

Hodgson, Joseph. *The Cradle of the Confederacy*. Mobile, Ala.: Mobile Register Printing Office, 1876.

Horner, Harlan. *Lincoln and Greeley*. Champagne, Ill.: University of Illinois Press, 1953.

Hughes, Nathaniel Jr. *General William J. Hardee*. Baton Rouge: Louisiana State University Press, 1965.

Ingraham, Joseph. *The Southwest, by a Yankee*. New York, 1835.

Johansen, Robert. *Stephen Douglas*. New York: Oxford University Press, 1973.

Johnston, Richard, and William Browne. *The Life of Alexander Stephens*. Freeport, N.Y.: Books for Libraries, 1878.

Jones, J. B. *A Rebel War Clerk's Diary at the Confederate States Capital*. New York: [n.p.] 1953.

Jordan, Donald and Edwin Pratt. *Europe and the American Civil War*. Boston: Houghton-Mifflin, 1931.

Kean, Robert. *Inside the Confederate Government*. Westport: Greenwood Press, 1973.

Keckley, Elizabeth. *Behind the Scenes: Thirty Years a Slave and Four Years in the White House*. New York: G. W. Carleton and Co., 1868.

Kennedy, John Pendleton. *The Border States: Their Power and Duty in the Present Disordered Condition of the Country*. Philadelphia: J. B. Lippincott & Co., 1861.

Kerber, Linda, and Jane DeHart, eds. *Women's America: Refocusing the Past*. New York: Oxford University Press, 1991.

King, Alvy. *Louis Wigfall: Southern Fire Eater*. Baton Rouge: Louisiana State University Press, 1970.

Kirke, Edmund. "An Untold Story." *Atlantic Magazine* (April, 1887).

Lamon, Ward. *Recollections of Abraham Lincoln*. Cambridge: Cambridge University Press, 1895.

Lee, R. E. Jr. *My Father: Robert E. Lee*. Garden City, N.Y.: Doubleday, 1900.

Leech, Margaret. *Reveille in Washington*. New York: Harper Brothers, 1941.

Lincoln, Abraham. Papers, on microfilm. Princeton University, Princeton, New Jersey/Illinois State Historical Library, Springfield, Illinois.

Lindgren, Henry. *Leadership Authority and Power Sharing*. Malabar, Fla.: Kreiger Publishing, 1982.

Long, E. B., and Barbara Long. *The Civil War: Day by Day*. Garden City, N.Y.: Doubleday, 1971.

McClellan, George. *The Civil War Papers of George McClellan*. New York: Ticknor and Fields, 1989.

McFeely, William. *Grant*. New York: W. W. Norton Company, 1981.

McKenzie, John. *Uncertain Glory: Lee's Generalship Re-Examined*. New York: Hippocreme Books, 1997.

McPherson, James. *The Battle Cry of Freedom*. New York: Oxford University Press, 1988.

———, ed. *We Cannot Escape History*. Chicago: University of Illinois Press, 1965.

Marvel, William. *Burnside*. Chapel Hill: University of North Carolina Press, 1991.

Masters, Edgar Lee. *Lincoln the Man*. New York: Dodd, Mead, 1931.

Meade, George. Papers, on microfilm. Historical Society of Pennsylvania, Philadelphia, Pennsylvania.

Mearns, David, ed. *The Abraham Lincoln Papers*.

Meredith, Roy. *Storm Over Sumter*. New York: Simon & Schuster, 1957.

Merrill, James. *W. T. Sherman*. New York: Rand, McNally Co., 1971.

Milton, George. *The Eve of Conflict: Stephen A. Douglas and the Needless War.* Boston: Houghton-Mifflin, 1934.

Mitchell, Stewart. *Horatio Seymour of New York.* Cambridge: Harvard University Press, 1938.

Moore, Frank, ed. *Rebellion Record: A Diary of American Events, Documents, Illustrative Incidents, Poetry, Etc.* New York: G. P. Putnam's Sons, 1861.

Moore, Thomas. Papers, on microfilm. Louisiana State University, Baton Rouge, Louisiana/ Emory University Library, Atlanta, Georgia.

Morehouse, Frances. *The Life of Jesse Fell.* Chicago: [n.p.], 1910.

Murray, Robert, and Tim Blessing. *Greatness in the White House.* State College, Pa.: Pennsylvania State University Press, 1994.

Museum of the Confederacy Library. Papers, in folders. Richmond, Virginia.

Neely, Mark, Jr., Harold Hozer, and Gabor Boritt. *The Confederate Image: Prints of the Lost Cause.* Chapel Hill: University of North Carolina Press, 1987.

————. *The Last Best Hope of Earth.* Cambridge: Harvard University Press, 1993.

Neustadt, Richard. *Presidential Power and the Modern Presidents.* New York: Free Press, 1990.

Nicolay, Helen. *John Nicolay: A Biography of Lincoln's Secretary.* New York; Longman, Green & Co., 1949.

Nicolay, John. Papers, on microfilm. Library of Congress, Washington, D.C.

————, and John Hay. *Abraham Lincoln: A History.* 10 vols. New York: Century Co., 1890.

Niven, John. *Samuel P. Chase.* New York: Oxford University Press, 1995.

Overy, Richard. *Why the Allies Won.* New York: W. W. Norton, 1995.

Patrick, Rembert. *Jefferson Davis and His Cabinet.* Baton Rouge: Louisiana State University Press, 1961.

Perdue, Howell, and Elizabeth Perdue. *Patrick Cleburne: Confederate General.* Hillsboro, Texas: Hill Junior College Press, 1973.

Phillips, Ulrich. *The Course of the South to Secession.* Gloucester: Peter Smith, 1958.

Pitkin, Thomas. "Western Republicans and the Tariff in 1860." *Mississippi Valley Historical Review* (December 1940).

Pollard, Edward. *The Life of Jefferson Davis.* Philadelphia: Philadelphia National Publishing Company, 1869.

Polsby, Nelson. *The Consequences of Party Reform.* New York: Oxford University Press, 1983.

Pryor, Mrs. Roger. *Reminiscences of Peace and War.* New York: Macmillan, 1904.

Rabin, James. "Alexander Stephens and Jefferson Davis." *American Historical Review,* no. 57 (January, 1953).

Randall, J. G. *Lincoln the President.* 4 vols. New York: Dodd, Mead & Co., 1945-1955.

————. *Mr. Lincoln.* New York: Dodd, Mead & Co., 1957.

Randall, Ruth. *Lincoln's Sons.* Boston: Little, Brown Co., 1955.

Reagan, John. *Memoirs.* New York: Neale Publishing, 1906.

Reynolds, Donald. *Editors Make War.* Nashville: Vanderbilt University Press, 1966.

Riley, Harris, Jr. *Journal of Mississippi History,* no. 14 (November, 1987).

Rister, Carl. *Robert E. Lee in Texas.* Norman: University of Oklahoma Press, 1946.

Rose, Anne. *Victorian America and the Civil War.* Cambridge: Cambridge University Press, 1992.

Ross, Ishbel. *The First Lady of the South.* New York: Harper Brothers, 1958.

————. *The President's Wife: Mary Todd Lincoln.* New York: Putnam, 1973.

Rossiter, Clinton. *The Supreme Court and the Commander-in-Chief.* Ithaca, N.Y.: Cornell University Press, 1976.

Rowland, Dunbar. *Jefferson Davis, Constitutionalist: His Letters, Papers and Speeches.* 10 vols. Jackson: Mississippi Department of Archives and History, 1923.

Rowland, Eron. *Varina Howell: Wife of Jefferson Davis.* New York: Macmillan, 1931.

Russell, William. *My Diary North and South.* New York: [n.p.], 1863.

Sandburg, Carl. *Abraham Lincoln: The Prairie Years and the War Years.* 3 vols. New York: Harcourt Brace, 1926.

Schott, Thomas. *Alexander Stephens of Georgia: A Biography.* Baton Rouge: Louisiana State University Press, 1988.

Sears, Stephen. *George McClellan: The Young Napoleon.* New York: Ticknor and Fields, 1988.

Seward, William. Papers, on microfilm. Princeton University, Princeton, New Jersey.

Sheffer, Martin. *Presidential Power: Case Studies in the Use of the Opinion of the Attorney General.* New York: University Press of America, 1991.

Sherman, William. *Memoirs.* Bloomington: University of Indiana Press, 1957.

Stephens, Alexander. Papers, on microfilm. Emory University Library, Atlanta, Georgia.

Sideman, Belle, and Lillian Freedman, eds. *Europe Looks at the Civil War.* New York: Collier Books, 1960.

Simmons, Dawn. *A Rose for Mrs. Lincoln.* Boston: Beacon Press, 1970.

Simon, John. *The Papers of U. S. Grant.* 10 vols. Carbondale, Ill.: University of Southern Illinois Press, 1979.

Simonton, Dean. "Presidential Style: Personality, Biography and Performance." *Journal of Personality and Social Psychology,* no. 55 (June, 1988).

Skoch, George. "The Man Who Fed the South." *Civil War Times Illustrated* (November, 1983).

Smith, Gene. *American Gothic.* New York: Simon & Schuster, 1992.

Smith, George, and Charles Judah, eds. *Life in the North During the Civil War.* Albuquerque, N.M.: University of New Mexico Press, 1966.

Stoddard, William. *Lincoln's Third Secretary: Memoirs of William O. Stoddard.* New York: Exposition Press, 1955.

Stirling, James. *Letters From the Slave States.* New York: Negro Universities Press, 1969.

Strode, Hudson. *Jefferson Davis: 1808–1861.* New York: Harcourt, Brace, 1955–1964.

———. *Jefferson Davis: Confederate President.* New York: Harcourt, Brace, 1955–1964.

———. *Jefferson Davis: Tragic Hero.* New York: Harcourt, Brace and World, 1964.

———. *Private Letters of Jefferson Davis.* New York: Harcourt, Brace and World, 1966.

Swanberg, W. H. *First Blood.* New York: Charles Scribner's Sons, 1957.

Symonds, Craig. *Joseph E. Johnston: A Civil War Biography.* New York: W. W. Norton, 1992.

Tarbell, Ida. *The Life of Abraham Lincoln: Drawn From Original Sources and Containing Many Speeches,* 4 vols. New York: Lincoln Historical Society, 1924.

Taylor, Zachary. Papers, on microfilm. Library of Congress, Washington, D.C./University of North Carolina, Chapel Hill, North Carolina.

Thomas, Benjamin and Harold Hyman. *Stanton: The Life and Times of Lincoln's Secretary of War.* New York: Alfred Knopf, 1962.

Thomas, Benjamin. *Lincoln's New Salem.* Springfield: Abraham Lincoln Association, 1934.

Thomas, Emory. *The Confederate Nation, 1861–1865.* New York: Harper & Row, 1979.

Thomas, Lately, *The First President Johnson.* New York: William Morrow Co., 1968.

Tidwell, William, James Hall, and David Gaddy. *Come Retribution.* Jackson: University Press of Mississippi, 1988.

Tucker, R. C. "The Georges' Wilson Re-examined." *American Political Science Review,* no. 71 (1977).

Van Der Heuvel, Gerry. *Crowns of Thorns and Glory.* New York: E. P. Dutton, 1988.

Van Deusen, Glyndon. *William Henry Seward.* New York: Oxford University Press, 1967.

Von Abele, Rudolph. *Alexander Stephens.* New York: Alfred Knopf, 1946.

Warren, Louis. *Lincoln's Youth: Indiana Years, Seven to Twenty One.* New York: Appleton, Century, Crofts Co., 1959.

Watson, Ritchie Jr. *Yeoman Versus Cavalier.* Baton Rouge: Louisiana University Press, 1993.

Welles, Gideon. *Lincoln and Seward.* New York: [n.p.], 1874.

Wells, Damon. *Stephen Douglas: The Last Years, 1857–1861.* Austin: University of Texas Press, 1971.

Wert, Jeffrey. *General James Longstreet.* New York: Simon & Schuster, 1993.

Wheeler, Richard. *A Rising Thunder.* New York: HarperCollins, 1994.

Whipple, Wayne. *Tad Lincoln: A True Story.* New York: George Sully & Co., 1926.

White, Henry. *Robert E. Lee and the Southern Confederacy.* New York: G. P. Putnam's Sons, 1897.

Wiley, Bell I. *Confederate Women.* Westport: Greenwood Press, 1975.

Williams, T. Harry. *Lincoln and His Generals.* New York: Alfred Knopf, 1952.

—————. *P. G. T. Beauregard: Napoleon in Gray.* Baton Rouge: Louisiana State University Press, 1954.

Williamson, Joel. *A Rage for Order.* New York: Oxford University Press, 1986.

Wilson, Rufus, ed. *Intimate Memories of Lincoln.* Elmira, N.Y.: Primavera Press, 1945.

Woodward, C. Vann. ed. *Mary Chesnut's Civil War Diary.* New Haven: Yale University Press, 1981.

Woodworth, Stephen. *Davis and Lee at War.* Manhattan: University of Kansas Press, 1995.

Wooster, Ralph. *The Secession Conventions of the South.* Princeton: Princeton University Press, 1962.

Yearns, Wilfred. *The Confederate Congress.* Athens: University of Georgia Press, 1960.

Young, Buck, Jr. *The Confederate Governors.* Athens: University of Georgia Press, 1985.

Newspapers

The following is an alphabetical list of the newspapers and the years of their editions used as sources.

Albion (Ill.) *Weekly Courier,* 1856
Atlanta (Ga.) *Constitution,* 1864
Baltimore Sun, 1861
Belford's Magazine, 1890
Boston Daily Advertiser, 1848
Boston Daily Evening Traveler, 1861
Boston Journal, 1861
Burlington (Ohio) *Argus,* 1863
Central Georgian, 1861
Charleston Courier, 1861–63
Charleston Mercury, 1860–64
Chicago Tribune, 1863, 1895
Cincinnati Commercial, 1861
Daily Illinois State Journal, 1860
Daily Missouri Democrat, 1860
Edgefield (S.C.) *Advertiser,* 1863
Frank Leslie's Illustrated Weekly, 1886
Hunterdon (N.J.) *Democrat,* 1863

Indiana State Sentinel, 1863
Jackson (Miss.) *Observer and State Gazette,* 1858
Jackson Mississippian, 1851
Kentucky Statesman, 1860
Lafayette (Ind.) *Daily Courier,* 1861
Lafayette (La.) *Daily Statesman,* 1850
London Herald, 1861
London Post, 1861
London Times, 1862
Lynchburg Daily Virginian, 1866
Macon Jeffersonian, 1844
Memphis Daily Appeal, 1860
Natchez Courier, 1861
Natchez Free Leader, 1851
National Intelligencer, 1861–65
New Orleans Delta, 1861
New York Daily News, 1864

New York Evening Express, 1862
New York Evening Transcript, 1861
New York Herald, 1861–62, 1895
New York Post, 1861
New York Times, 1861–63
New York Tribune, 1861–65, 1889
New York World, 1862–63
Newark (N.J.) *Advertiser,* 1862
North Carolina Standard, 1862
Ohio State Journal, 1859
Peterboro (N.H.) *Gazette,* 1862
Philadelphia Evening Bulletin, 1863
Philadelphia Press, 1861

Philadelphia Weekly Times, 1882
Richmond Dispatch, 1861–65, 1889, 1905
Richmond Enquirer, 1861
Richmond Evening Journal, 1906
Richmond Examiner, 1861–65
Richmond Whig, 1860–61
Sangamon Journal, 1832
St. Louis Tribune, 1861
Sugar Planter, (La.), 1860
Vicksburg Sentinel, 1844, 1848
Vicksburg Whig, 1861–63
Washington Daily Morning Chronicle, 1864
Weekly Press (Calif.), 1861

INDEX